AA *Motorist's*

ATLAS OF
BRITAIN

Reprinted March 1993
Reprinted November 1992
15th edition September 1992
14th edition September 1991
13th edition September 1990
12th edition October 1989
11th edition October 1988
10th edition October 1987
9th edition October 1986
Reprinted March 1987
8th edition October 1985
7th edition October 1984
Reprinted May 1985
6th edition March 1984
5th edition January 1983
4th edition October 1981
3rd edition January 1981
2nd edition January 1980
1st edition April 1979

Produced by the Publishing Division of The Automobile Association

Mapping produced by the Cartographic Department of The Automobile
Association. This atlas has been compiled and produced from the Automaps
database utilising electronic and computer technology.

Published by The Automobile Association, Fanum House, Basingstoke,
Hampshire RG21 2EA.
ISBN 0 7495 0601 6

Printed by Graficromo S A, Spain

The Contents of this atlas are believed correct at the time of printing,
although the publishers cannot accept any responsibility for errors or
omissions, or for changes in the details given. They would welcome
information to help keep this atlas up to date; please write to the
Cartographic Editor, Publishing Division, The Automobile Association,
Fanum House, Basingstoke, Hampshire RG21 2EA.

A CIP catalogue record for this book is available from the British Library.

Information on National Parks provided by the Countryside Commission for
England & Wales.

Information on National Scenic Areas - Scotland provided by the Countryside Commission
for Scotland.

Information on Forest Parks provided by the Forestry Commission.

The RSPB sites shown are a selection chosen by the Royal Society for the
Protection of Birds.

Picnic sites are those inspected by the AA and are located on or near
A and B roads.

National Trust properties shown are those open to the public as indicated in the
handbooks of the National Trusts of England, Wales and Northern Ireland, and Scotland.

Contents

Using this atlas

ROUTE PLANNING
Pages 10 – 15 contain specially designed route-planning maps. These clearly show the basic road network – motorways, primary routes and most A-roads – and enable you to plan your long-distance journey both quickly and easily.

Motorway

A road

Primary routes

THE ATLAS
Clear and easy-to-read mapping helps you plan more detailed journeys, and provides a whole host of information for the motorist. All motorways, primary routes, A-roads, B-roads and unclassified roads are shown. The atlas also identifies those roads outside urban areas which are under construction. Additional features include rivers, lakes and reservoirs, railway-lines, places to visit, picnic sites and tourist information centres. To assist you in estimating the length of your journey distances (in miles) are shown between blue marker symbols.

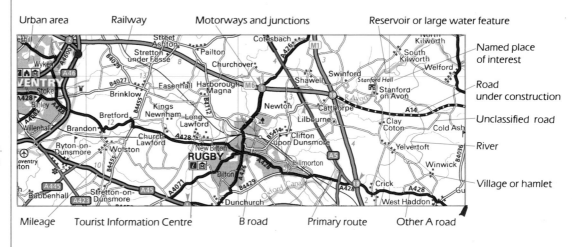

Urban area   Railway   Motorways and junctions   Reservoir or large water feature

Named place of interest

Road under construction

Unclassified road

River

Village or hamlet

Mileage   Tourist Information Centre   B road   Primary route   Other A road

FERRY AND RAIL ROUTES
Coastal stretches of mapping provide basic offshore information including ferry routes within Great Britain and to the Continent, to assist you with planning an overseas journey. Throughout the atlas, railway lines, stations and level crossings are marked in order to assist with general navigation or with rail travel requirements.

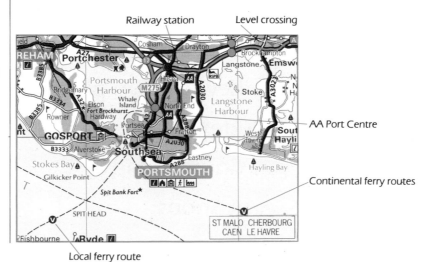

Railway station   Level crossing

AA Port Centre

Continental ferry routes

Local ferry route

TOURISM AND LEISURE

Red pictorial symbols and red type highlight numerous places of interest, catering for every taste. Red symbols within yellow boxes show tourist attractions within towns. These can be used to plan days out, or to choose where to visit on holiday. In order to avoid disappointment, you should always remember to check opening times before you set out.

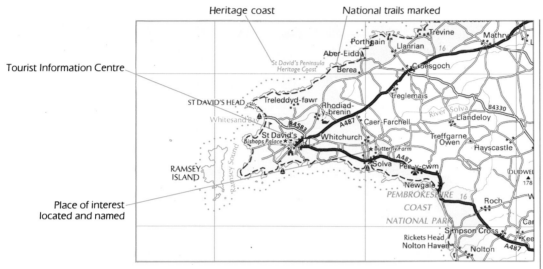

Heritage coast

National trails marked

Tourist Information Centre

Place of interest located and named

TOWN PLANS

Up-to-date, town plans show AA recommended roads and other practical information such as one way streets, car parks and restricted roads, making navigation much easier.

Town parking facilities

AA recommended throughroutes clearly identified

Major buildings and places of Interest highlighted and named

Pedestrian areas located

One way streets shown

Churches located

LONDON

Easy-to-read, fully-indexed street maps of Inner London, provide a simple guide to finding your way around the city.

AA recommended routes for easier navigation

One way systems clearly shown

Underground railway stations located and named

Major places of tourist interest shown

Open spaces and parks highlighted

Garage parking identified

Journey planning

Call AA Roadwatch or listen to local radio to avoid delays on your journey

Delays and hold-ups

Motorways are — despite ever increasing traffic — the quickest means of getting from A to B. Nevertheless, a hold-up on a motorway can easily delay you for hours. There are several ways of gleaning information on the stretches of motorway to avoid; by phone, radio and newspaper.

AA Roadwatch

If you need as much information as possible about your journey before you set out, you can call AA Roadwatch. Updated every 15 minutes, this service provides details of major roadworks and weather conditions for the whole country, and can be used as part of your basic journey-planning. AA Roadwatch also supplies information on current road - works to many daily newspapers.

Radio

Frequent radio bulletins are issued by both the BBC and by independent local radio stations on road and weather conditions, likely hold-ups, etc — and these can be of great assistance. By tuning into the local radio stations as you pass through the area, you can avoid delays and prepare to make changes to your route. However, local radio does not yet cover the entire country; consult the regional route-planning pages for radio frequencies. (Some local radio stations also offer flight information from and to nearby airports.)

Always plan your route carefully — doing so will save you time in the long run

How to get there

Special route-planning maps on pages 10 – 15 enable you to plan a basic route, while referring to the main pages of the atlas allows you to arrange a more detailed route. It is probably a good idea to make a note of the road numbers, towns and general directions, since this should mean you will not need to consult the atlas on the journey.

Road classification

London is the hub for the spokes of roads numbered A1 to A6, Edinburgh the hub for the A7, A8 and A9. Beginning with the A1, running north from London, the roads radiate clockwise from the capital; the A2 runs roughly east, the A3 south-west, and so forth. This system has made the numbering of other roads very simple; generally, the lower the subsequent number, the closer the road's starting point to London (or Edinburgh). Motorways roughly approximate to this plan as well.

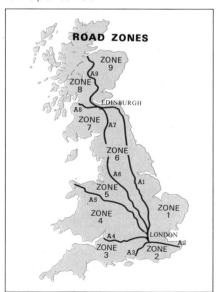

Are you fit to drive? Food, tiredness, drink and medicines all affect your driving.

Fit to drive?

Many accidents are caused by one or more of the drivers involved being unfit to drive when the accident occurred. The most obvious reason for such accidents is alcohol; even the smallest quantity can affect driving performance. The only safe advice is; if you drive, don't drink — and if you drink, don't drive. However, alcohol is just one of a number of factors that can make someone unfit to drive.

Tiredness

Some people become tired sooner than others, but the following are guidelines which you should aim to keep: for every three hours on the road, take 20 minutes' rest; if possible, share the driving ; limit yourself to a maximum of eight hours behind the wheel in any day; and try to avoid driving when you are usually asleep or resting. Also, you should avoid driving after hard exercise, a large meal and, of course, after consuming alcohol. Other factors which can contribute to tiredness are temperature inside the car and medication; a stuffy atmosphere — and some drugs, even those bought over the counter — can induce drowsiness. If you are on medication, check with your doctor whether you should be driving at all. One final point; not driving during peak hours keeps delays to a minimum, reduces frustration and minimises journey time.

Driving abroad

A further cause of accidents is unfamiliarity with driving regulations in foreign countries. Always ensure you know the specific legal requirements and road signs *before* you set out — and make sure your car conforms to such requirements. If you take an overnight ferry crossing, remember that you will probably be tired the next morning; do not set yourself too long a drive after arriving on the Continent. When you begin driving again after taking a break, be especially careful to drive on the correct side of the road.

Carry out regular checks to make sure that you and your car arrive safely.

Daily checks

Before you start every journey, you should always ensure that:

✓ you check the dashboard warning lights both before and after starting the engine

✓ there are no unusual noises once the engine is running

✓ all the lights are both clean and working

✓ the windscreen and all other windows are clean

✓ you have sufficient petrol for your journey

Weekly checks

Every week — or before you set out on a long journey — you should also ensure that:

✓ the engine oil level is correct, looking for any obvious signs of leakage

✓ the coolant level is correct, checking the anti-freeze before the onset of winter

✓ the battery connections and terminals are clean and free from corrosion

✓ the brake (and clutch, if hydraulic) fluid is correct

✓ the tyres (including the spare) are properly inflated and not damaged in any way

✓ the tyres are changed if the tread falls below 2mm

✓ the fan belt is not worn or damaged and that the tension is correct

✓ the windscreen wipers are clean and that the screen wash reservoir is topped up with a mixture of water, non-smear and freezing inhibitor additive

Where exactly are you going? You can find on the map any place listed in the index of this atlas by using the National Grid, explained in simple terms below.

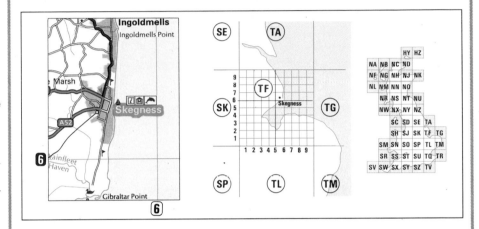

Finding your place

One of the unique features of AA mapping is the use of the National Grid system.

The National Grid

The National Grid covers Britain with an imaginary network of squares, using blue horizontal lines called northings and vertical lines called eastings. On the atlas pages these lines are numbered along the bottom and the left hand side.

The Index

Each entry in the index is followed by a page number, two letters denoting an area on the map and a 4-figure grid reference. You will not need to use the two letters for simple navigation, but they come in useful if you want to use your map in relation to the rest of the country and other map series.

Quick reference

For quick reference, the four figures of the grid reference in the index are arranged so that the 1st and 3rd are in bolder type than the 2nd and 4th. The 1st figure shows which number along the bottom to locate, and the 3rd figure, which number up the left hand side. These will indicate the square in which you will find the place name.

Pinpoint accuracy

However, to pinpoint a place more accurately, you use the 2nd and 4th numbers also. The 2nd will tell you how many imaginary tenths along the bottom line to go from the first number, and the 4th will tell you how many tenths up the line to go from the 3rd number.

Where these two lines intersect, you will locate your place, e.g. Skegness 77TF5663. Skegness is located on page 77, within grid square 56 in National Grid square TF. Its exact location is 5663.

Remember

If you find you get the numbers confused, it might help if you can imagine entering a house, walking in the door and along a corridor first, and then going up the stairs, then you will remember how to get them in the correct order.

Motorways

M1 LONDON - LEEDS

Northbound	Junction	Southbound
No exit. Access only from northbound lane of A1	2	No access. Only exit is to southbound lane of A1
No exit . Access only from northbound lane of A41	4	No access. Only exit is to southbound lane of A41
No exit . Access only from M25	6A	No access. Exit only to M25
No exit . Access only from M10	7	No access. Exit only to M10
No access. Exit only to M45	17	No exit. Access only from M45
No access. Exit only to M6	19	No exit. Access only from M6
No access. Exit only to A616	35A	No access. Access only from A616
No exit. Access only	44	No access. Exit only
No access. Exit only	45	No access. Access only
No restriction	46	No access. Exit only
Full interchange between M1, M621 & A653 using gyratory system	47	Access only by slip road from A653 Dewsbury Road gyratory

M2 ROCHESTER - FAVERSHAM

Westbound	Junction	Eastbound
Only exit is to A2 westbound	1	Access only from A2 eastbound

M3 SUNBURY - SOUTHAMPTON

South-westbound	Junction	North-eastbound
No access. Exit only to A303	8	No exit. Access only from A303
Only exit is to A33 southbound	10	Access is from A33 northbound
No access from A335 to eastbound lane of M27	13	No restriction
The only exit is to M27 & A33	14	The only access is from M27 & A33

M4 LONDON - SOUTH WALES

Westbound	Junction	Eastbound
Access only from A4 westbound	1	Only exit is to A4 eastbound
Access/exit available to/from westbound lane of A4 only	2	Access/exit available to/from eastbound lane of A4 only
No access. Exit only to A48(M)	29	No exit. Access only from A48(M)
No access from A48	38	No restriction
No exit. Access only from A48	39	No exit or access
No exit. Access only from A48	41	No access. Exit only to A48
No access. Exit only to A48	46	No exit. Access only from A48

M5 BIRMINGHAM - EXETER

Southbound	Junction	Northbound
No access. Exit only to A4019	10	No exit. Access only from A4019
No exit. Access only from A38	12	No access. Exit only to A38
No exit. The only access is from the westbound lane of A30	29	No access. The only exit is to eastbound lane of A30

M6 RUGBY - CARLISLE

Northbound	Junction	Southbound
Access is from M1 northbound	M1	Only exit is to M1 southbound
No exit to northbound lane of M42. No access from M42 southbound	4	No exit to M42. No access from southbound lane of M42
No exit. Access only from southbound spur of M42	4A	No access. Exit only to M42
No access. Exit only to A452	5	No exit. Access only from A452
No access. Exit only to M54	10A	No exit. Access only from M54
No direct access to eastbound lane of M56 (use A50 junction)	20	No direct access from westbound lane of M56 (use A50 junction)
No exit. Access only from A58	24	No access. Exit only to A58
No access. Exit only to A49	25	No exit. Access only from A49
No exit. Access only from M61	30	No access. Exit only to M61

M8 EDINBURGH-GLASGOW-BISHOPTON

Westbound	Junction	Eastbound
No access from southbound lane of M73 or from A8 & A89 eastbound	8	No exit to northbound lane of M73 or to A8 & A89 westbound
No exit. Access only	9	No access. Exit only
The only access is from M80	13	The only exit is to M80
No exit. Access only	14	No access. Exit only
No access. Exit only to A804	16	No exit. Access only from A804
The only exit is to A82	17	The only exit is to A82
No access. Exit only to Charing Cross	18	No access. Exit only to Charing Cross
No access from Argyle Street A814	19	No exit to Argyle Street A814
No exit. Access only	20	No exit. Access only
No exit. Access only	21	No access. Exit only
No access. Exit only to M77	22	No exit. Access only from M77
No access. Exit only to B768	23	No exit. Access only from B768
The only exit/access is to/from Clyde Tunnel A739	25	The only exit/access is to/from Clyde Tunnel A739

M9 EDINBURGH - DUNBLANE

North-westbound	Junction	South-eastbound
No access. Exit only to A8000 spur	1	No access only from A8000
No exit. Access only from B8046	2	No access. Exit only to B8046
No exit. Access only to A803	3	No access. Exit only from A803
No exit. Access from A904 & A905	6	No access. Exit only to A905
No access. Exit only to M876	8	No access. Access only from M876

M10 ST ALBANS BYPASS

Northbound	Junction	Southbound
The only exit is to M1 northbound		Only access is from M1 s'thbound

M11 LONDON - CAMBRIDGE

Northbound	Junction	Southbound
The only access is from A406	4	The only exit is to A406
No access. Exit only to A1168	5	No access. Access only from A1168
No access. Exit only to A11 spur	9	No exit. Access only from M11 spur
No access. Exit only to A1303	13	No exit. Access only from A1303
No exit to A1307 or A45 westbound. No access from A45 eastbound	14	No entry from A1307 or A45 eastbound

M20 SWANLEY - FOLKESTONE

South-eastbound	Junction	North-westbound
No access. Exit only to A20	2	No exit. Access from A20 & A227
No exit. Access only from M26	3	No access. Exit only to M26

M23 HOOLEY - CRAWLEY

Northbound	Junction	Southbound
The only exit is to A23 northbound	7	Only access is from A23 s'bound

M25 LONDON ORBITAL MOTORWAY

Clockwise	Junction	Anti-clockwise
Exit only to A225 & A296. No access (use slip road via Jct 2)	1B	Access only from A225 & A296. No exit (use slip road via Junction 2)
No exit to M26	5	No access from M26
No restriction	9 (south)	No exit or access
No exit or access	9 (north)	No restriction
No access. Exit only to A41 spur	19	No exit. Access only from A41 spur
The only exit is to northbound lane of M1. The only access is from southbound lane of M1	21	The only exit is to northbound lane of M1. The only access is from southbound lane of M1
No link from M1 to A405	21A	No link from A405 to M1
Access only from A13 & A1306. No exit (use slip road via Junction 30)	31	Exit only to A13 & A1306. No access (use slip road via Jct 30)

M26 SEVENOAKS - WROTHAM

Eastbound	Junction	Westbound
The only access is from the anti-clockwise (eastbound) lane of M25	M25 Jct 5	The only exit is to the clockwise (westbound) lane of M25.
The only exit is to the south-eastbound lane of M20	M20 Jct 3	The only access is from the north-westbound lane of M20

M27 CADNAM - PORTSMOUTH

Eastbound	Junction	Westbound
The only exit is to northbound lane of M3. No access from northbound lane of A33	4	The only exit is to northbound lane of M3. No access from A335 or northbound lane of A33
No access. Access only from A32	10	No access. Exit only to A32
No access from A27 spur	12 (west)	No exit to A27 spur
The only exit is to A27 eastbound	12 (east)	Access is from A27 Westbound

M40 LONDON - BIRMINGHAM

North-westbound	Junction	South-eastbound
No access. Exit only to A40	3	No exit. Access only from A40
No access. Exit only to A329	7	No exit. Access only from A329
No access. Exit only to A452	13	No exit. Access only from A452
No exit. Access only from A452	14	No access. Exit only to A452
No exit. Access only from A3400	16	No access. Exit only to A3400

M42 BROMSGROVE - MEASHAM

North-eastbound	Junction	South-westbound
No exit. Access only from A38	1	No access. Exit only to A38
No access. The only exit is to M6	7/7A	No exit. The only access is from northbound lane of M6
No exit. Access only from southbound lane of M6	8	Exit only to northbound lane of M6. Access is from M6 southbound

M45 DUNCHURCH SPUR

Eastbound	Junction	Westbound
The only exit is to M1 southbound	M1	Access is from M1 northbound
No access from A45 east of Dunchurch. Exit only	With A45	No exit to A45 east of Dunchurch. Access only

M53 WALLASEY - CHESTER

Southbound	Junction	Northbound
The only exit is to eastbound lane of M56. The only access is from westbound lane of M56	11	The only exit is to eastbound lane off M56. The only access is from westbound lane of M56

M54 TELFORD MOTORWAY

Westbound	Junction	Eastbound
Access is from M6 northbound	M6	The only exit is to M6 southbound

M56 NORTH CHESHIRE MOTORWAY

Westbound	Junction	Eastbound
The only access is from the westbound lane of M63 or southbound lane of A34	1	The only exit is to the eastbound lane of M63 or northbound lane of A34
No access. Exit only to A560	2	No exit. Access only from A560
No exit. Access only from A5103	3	No access. Exit only to A5103
No access. Exit only	4	No exit. Access only
Access via slip road from A556	7	*No restriction*
No exit to southbound lane of M6 (possible via A50 interchange)	9	No access from northbound lane of M6 (possible via A50 interchange)
No access. Exit only to M53	15	No exit. Access only from M53

M57 LIVERPOOL OUTER RING ROAD

Northbound	Junction	Southbound
No exit. Access only from A526	3	No access. Exit only to A526
No exit (use Jct 4). Access only from westbound lane of A580	5	No access (use Jct 4). Exit only to eastbound lane of A580

M58 LIVERPOOL - WIGAN

Eastbound	Junction	Westbound
No exit. Access only	1	No access. Exit only

M61 GREATER MANCHESTER - PRESTON

North-westbound	Junction	South-eastbound
The only access is from M62	1	The only exit is to M62
No exit. The only access is via spur from westbound lane of A580	2	The only exit is via spur to eastbound lane of A580
No access. Exit only to A666 spur	3	*No restriction*
No access. Exit only to A6 spur	9	No exit. Access only from A6 spur
The only exit is to M6 northbound	M6	Access only from M6 southbound

M62 LIVERPOOL - HULL

Eastbound	Junction	Westbound
The only access is from M61 & spur from eastbound lane of A580. The only exit is to M61	14	The only access is from M61. The only exit is to M61 and spur to westbound lane of A580
No exit. Access only from A666	15	No access. Exit only to A666
No access. Exit only to A640	23	No access. Exit only from A640

M63 MANCHESTER OUTER RING ROAD

Southeast/Eastbound	Junction	West/North-westbound
No exit (use slip road via Jct 6). Access only from A56	7	No access (use slip road via Jct 6). Exit only to A56
No access from or exit to northbound lane of A5103	9	No access from or exit to southbound lane of A5103
No exit to M56 or northbound lane of A34. No access from southbound lane of A34	10	No exit to northbound lane of A34. No access from M56 or southbound lane of A34
No access. Exit only to A560 spur	11	No exit. Access only from A560
No access. Exit only to A560	13	No exit. Access only from A560
No exit or access	14	*No restriction*
No restriction	15	No access from A560 & A6017

M65 CALDER VALLEY MOTORWAY

North-eastbound	Junction	South-westbound
No access. Exit only to A679	9	No exit. Access only from A679
No exit. Access only	11	No access. Exit only

M66 GREATER MANCHESTER

Southbound	Junction	Northbound
Access is from A56 southbound	With A56	Only exit is to A56 northbound
No exit. Access only from A56	1	No access. Exit only to A56

M67 HYDE BYPASS

Eastbound	Junction	Westbound
No access. Exit only to A6017	1	No exit. Access only from A6017
No exit. Access only from A57	2	No access. Exit only to A57

M69 COVENTRY - LEICESTER

Northbound	Junction	Southbound
No exit. Access only from A5070	2	No access. Exit only to A5070

M73 HAMILTON BYPASS - MOLLINSBURN

Northbound	Junction	Southbound
No access to or from A89. No access from eastbound lane of M8	2	No access to or from A89. No exit to westbound lane of M8
The only exit is to north-eastbound lane of A80	3	The only access is from the south-westbound lane of A80

M74 GLASGOW - GRETNA

Southbound	Junction	Northbound
The only access is from A74	A74/A721	Only exit is to A74 westbound
No access. Exit only to A72	7	No exit. Access only from A72
No access. Exit only to B7078	9	No exit or access
No exit. Access only from B7078	10	*No restriction*
No access. Exit only to B7078	11	No exit. Access only from B7078
No exit. Access only from A70	12	No access. Exit only to A70

M77 DUMBRECK SPUR, GLASGOW

Southbound	Junction	Northbound
Access is from M8 westbound	M8	Only exit is to M8 eastbound

M80 BONNYBRIDGE - STIRLING

Northbound	Junction	Southbound
No access. Exit only to M876	5	No exit. Access only from M876

M80 STEPPS BYPASS

North-eastbound	Junction	South-westbound
No access. Exit only	Hornshill	No exit. Access only

M85 PERTH EASTERN BYPASS

Southbound	Junction	Northbound
No exit to A912	M90	No access from A912

M90 FORTH ROAD BRIDGE - PERTH

Northbound	Junction	Southbound
No exit. Access only from A91	7	No exit. Access only to A91
No access. Exit only to A91	8	No exit. Access only from A91
No access from A912. No exit to southbound lane of A912	10	No exit to A912. No access from northbound lane of A912

M180 THORNE - BRIGG

Eastbound	Junction	Westbound
No access. Exit only to A18 & A614	1	No exit. Access from A18 & A164

M606 BRADFORD SPUR

Northbound	Junction	Southbound
No access. Exit only	Merrydale Road	*No restriction*

M621 LEEDS - GLIDERSOME

South-westbound	Junction	North-eastbound
No restriction	M1	Access to M1 via gyratory system
No access. Exit only	A621	No exit. Access only

M876 BONNYBRIDGE - KINCARDINE BRIDGE

North-eastbound	Junction	South-westbound
Access is from M80 northbound	M80	The only exit is to M80 southbound
No access. Exit only to A9 & A88	2	No exit. Access from A9 & A88
No exit to north-westbound lane of M9	M9: Jct 8	No access from south-eastbound lane of M9

A1(M) SOUTH MIMMS - BALDOCK

Northbound	Junction	Southbound
No restriction	2	No exit. Access only from A1001
No restriction	3	No access. Exit to A414 & A1001
No exit. Access only from B197	5	No access or exit

A1(M) SCOTCH CORNER - TYNESIDE

Northbound	Junction	Southbound
No access. Exit only to A66(M)	A66(M)	No access. Access only from A66(M)
Only exits are to A194(M) & A1	A194(M)	Only access is from A194(M) & A1

A3(M) HORNDEAN - HAVANT

Southbound	Junction	Northbound
The only access at Horndean is from southbound lane of A3	A3	The only exit at Horndean is to northbound lane of A3
No exit. Access only	Purbrook Way	No access. Exit only

A38(M) ASTON EXPRESSWAY, BIRMINGHAM

Northbound	Junction	Southbound
No exit. Access only	Victoria Rd	No access. Exit only

A40(M) WESTWAY, LONDON

Eastbound	Junction	Westbound
No access. Exit only to Westbourne Terrace	Paddington	No exit. Access only from Gloucester Terrace
The only exit is onto the Marylebone Flyover	Marylebone Flyover	The only access is via the Marylebone Flyover

A48(M) CARDIFF SPUR

Westbound	Junction	Eastbound
Only access is from M4 westbound	M4	The only exit is to M4 eastbound
Only exit is to A48 westbound	29A(A48)	Only access is from A48 eastbound

A57(M) MANCUNIAN WAY, MANCHESTER

Eastbound	Junction	Westbound
No access (use Cambridge Street)	A5103	No exit (use Cambridge Street)
No exit (use A5103 junction)	Cambridge St	No access (use A5103 jct)
No access. The only exit is to southbound lane of Brook St.	A34	No exit. Access only from Brook Street, A34

A58(M) A64(M) LEEDS INNER RING ROAD

Eastbound	Junction	Westbound
No restriction	Westgate	No access. Exit only
No direct access from northbound lane of A660	A660	No direct access from northbound lane of A660
No access form Clay Pit Lane, A58	A58	No exit to Clay Pit Lane, A58
No exit to North Street	North St	Access available via New Briggate
No exit to A61	Eastgate	No access from A61

A66(M) DARLINGTON SPUR

North-eastbound	Junction	South-westbound
Access is from A1(M) northbound	A1(M)	Only exit is to A1(M) southbound

A102(M) BLACKWALL TUNNEL APPROACH ROADS

Northbound	Junction	Southbound
No exit to Blackwall Lane A2203	A2203	*No restriction*
No restriction	Hackney	Access only. No exit to Wick Rd
The only exit is to the eastbound lane of Eastway, A106	Eastway	The only access is from the westbound lane of Eastway, A106

A167(M) NEWCASTLE CENTRAL MOTORWAY

Northbound	Junction	Southbound
No exit. Access only	Camden St	No exit or access

A194(M) TYNESIDE

Southbound	Junction	Northbound
Only exit is to A1(M) southbound	A1(M)	Access only from A1(M) n'bound

Routeplanner

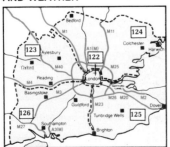
The Motorist's Atlas of Britain combines superb mapping with accurate and practical route-finding information which is designed to help you complete a journey as quickly and easily as possible.

Planning your route
The route planning maps on the following pages are an invaluable guide when deciding on a *general route.*

These maps show the principal routes throughout the country and you can use them to plan a *basic route.*

Look for the name of your destination in the index section at the back of the book. The entry is followed by an atlas page number and a National Grid reference.

Turn to the atlas page indicated and use the grid reference to pinpoint the place (see page 7 for an explanation of how to use the reference).

When you have located it, find the nearest place to it shown on the route planning maps.

In the same way, by locating the nearest place to your start point, you can plot the route between the two.

A more detailed route can be worked out from studying the main atlas.

Remember to take a note of road numbers and directions, then you will not need to stop to use the atlas while on the journey.

Traffic Information
Frequent bulletins on road conditions, local hold ups, the weather etc are issued both by national and local radio stations, and also the AA Roadwatch telephone service, these can be of great assistance to the driver.

Local and regional radio frequencies and AA Roadwatch telephone numbers are shown on the pages of the Route Planning Maps. The names of radio stations are in **bold type** and are followed by the FM frequency (MHz), then the MW frequency (KHz) eg **RADIO SCOTLAND** 92.5-94.7 810. In some cases stations do not broadcast on medium wave (MW).

BBC
Radio Scotland
92.5-94.7 810 North West
Scotland 97.7-99.3 810

INDEPENDENT
Central FM
Stirling 96.7
Moray Firth Radio
Inverness 97.4 1107
Northsound Radio
Aberdeen 96.9 1035
Radio Clyde
Glasgow 102.5 1152
Radio Forth
Edinburgh 97.3 1548
Bathgate 97.6
Radio Tay
Dundee 102.8 1161 Perth 96.4
1548

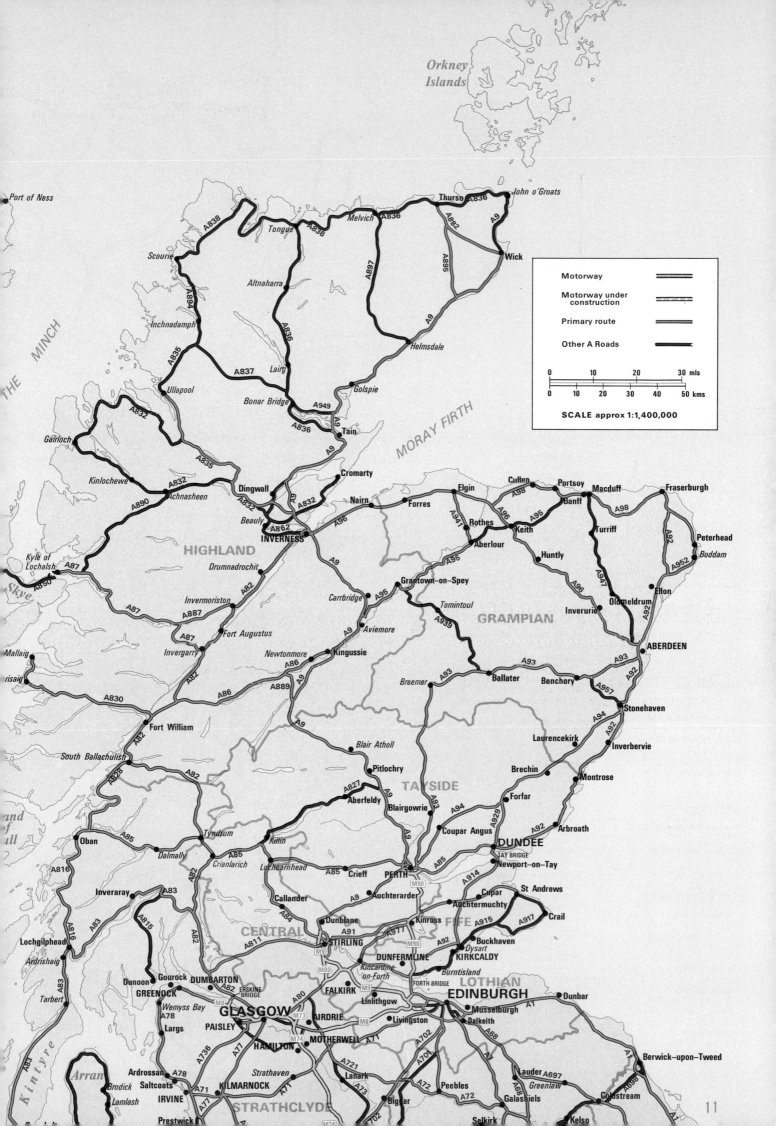

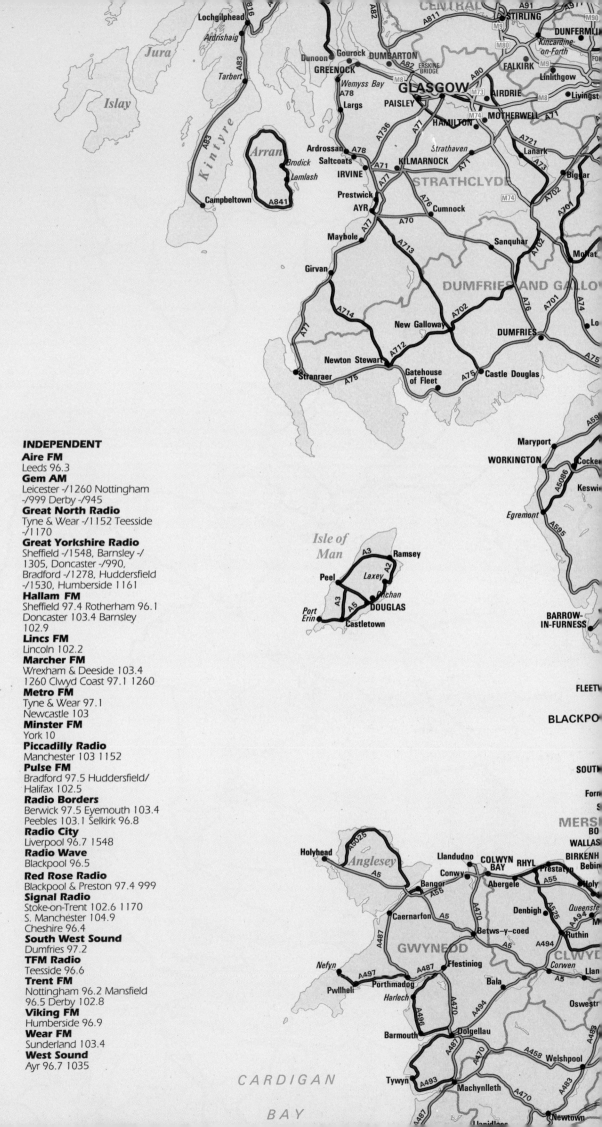

BBC

Greater Manchester Radio
95.1 1458

Radio Cleveland
95.0 Whitby 95.8

Radio Cumbria
North Cumbria 95.6 756
Whitehaven 95.6 1458

Radio Cumbria (Furness)
South Cumbria 96.1 837
Kendal 95.2 837
Windermere 104.2 837

Radio Derby
104.5 1116 Derby 94.2 1116
Bakewell & Matlock 95.3

Radio Humberside
95.9 1485

Radio Lancashire
95.5 855 Lancaster 104.5 1557
South Lancashire 103.9 855

Radio Leeds
92.4 774 Leeds 103.9 Ilkley/
Otley 95.3 774

Radio Lincolnshire
94.9 1368

Radio Merseyside
95.8 1485

Radio Newcastle
NE Northumberland 96.0 1458
Newcastle 104.4 1458
Durham 95.4 1458

Radio Nottingham
103.8 Central Notts. 95.5

Radio Sheffield
104.1 1035 Sheffield 88.6 1035

Radio Shropshire
96.0 Ludlow 95.0
Shrewsbury 96.0

Radio Stoke
94.6 1503

Radio Wales
882/340 Radio Cymru
(Welsh Language Service)
92.5–94.5

Radio York
103.7 666 Scarborough 95.5
1260 Central N. Yorks 104.3
666

INDEPENDENT

Aire FM
Leeds 96.3

Gem AM
Leicester -/1260 Nottingham
-/999 Derby -/945

Great North Radio
Tyne & Wear -/1152 Teesside
-/1170

Great Yorkshire Radio
Sheffield -/1548, Barnsley -/
1305, Doncaster -/990,
Bradford -/1278, Huddersfield
-/1530, Humberside 1161

Hallam FM
Sheffield 97.4 Rotherham 96.1
Doncaster 103.4 Barnsley
102.9

Lincs FM
Lincoln 102.2

Marcher FM
Wrexham & Deeside 103.4
1260 Clwyd Coast 97.1 1260

Metro FM
Tyne & Wear 97.1
Newcastle 103

Minster FM
York 10

Piccadilly Radio
Manchester 103 1152

Pulse FM
Bradford 97.5 Huddersfield/
Halifax 102.5

Radio Borders
Berwick 97.5 Eyemouth 103.4
Peebles 103.1 Selkirk 96.8

Radio City
Liverpool 96.7 1548

Radio Wave
Blackpool 96.5

Red Rose Radio
Blackpool & Preston 97.4 999

Signal Radio
Stoke-on-Trent 102.6 1170
S. Manchester 104.9
Cheshire 96.4

South West Sound
Dumfries 97.2

TFM Radio
Teesside 96.6

Trent FM
Nottingham 96.2 Mansfield
96.5 Derby 102.8

Viking FM
Humberside 96.9

Wear FM
Sunderland 103.4

West Sound
Ayr 96.7 1035

12

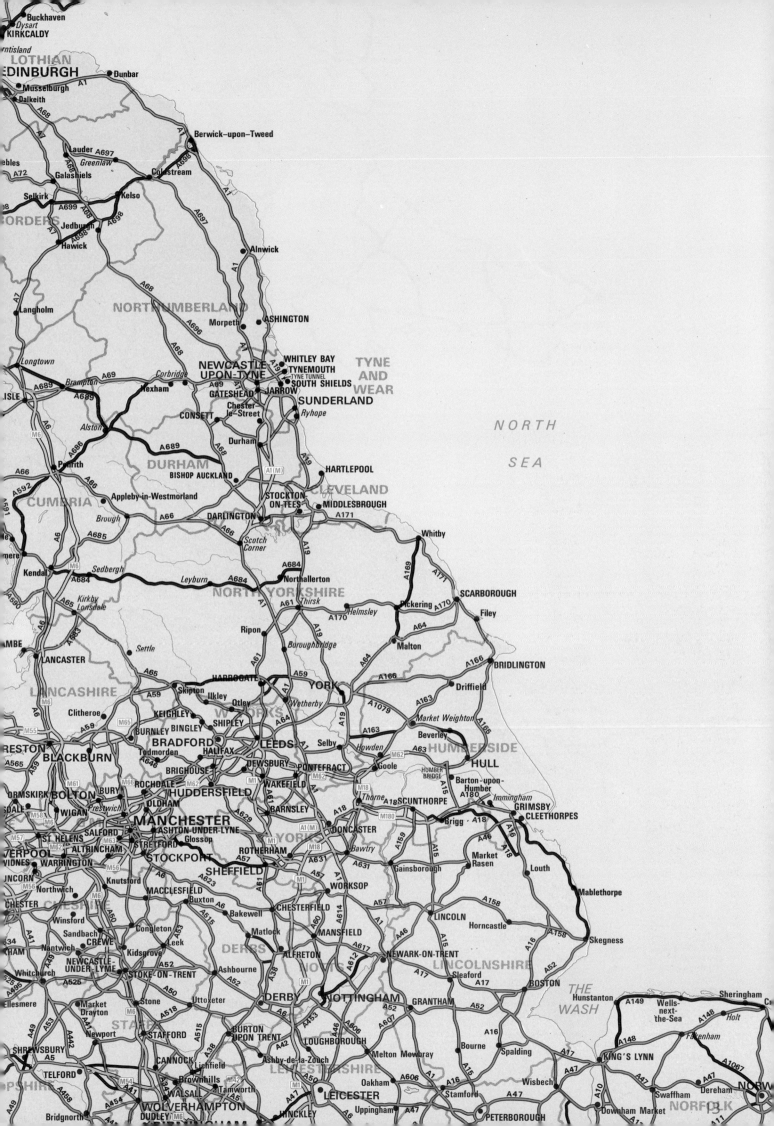

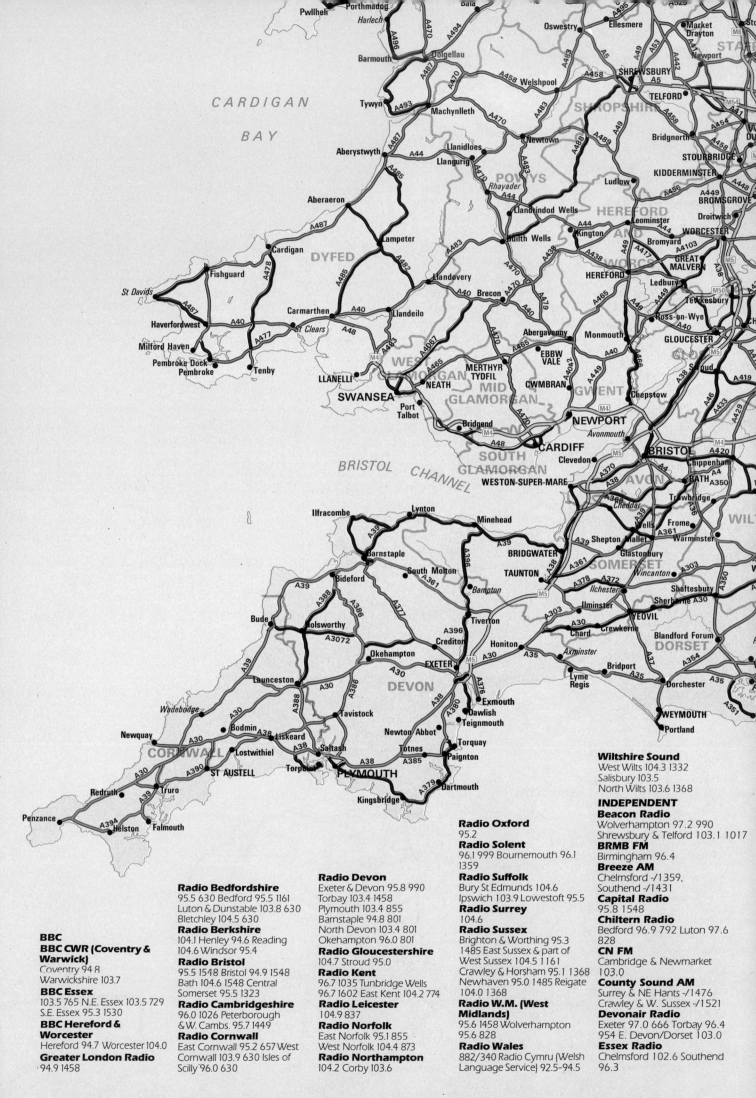

Radio Bedfordshire
95.5 630 Bedford 95.5 1161
Luton & Dunstable 103.8 630
Bletchley 104.5 630
Radio Berkshire
104.1 Henley 94.6 Reading
104.6 Windsor 95.4
Radio Bristol
95.5 1548 Bristol 94.9 1548
Bath 104.6 1548 Central
Somerset 95.5 1323
Radio Cambridgeshire
96.0 1026 Peterborough
& W. Cambs. 95.7 1449
Radio Cornwall
East Cornwall 95.2 657 West
Cornwall 103.9 630 Isles of
Scilly 96.0 630

Radio Devon
Exeter & Devon 95.8 990
Torbay 103.4 1458
Plymouth 103.4 855
Barnstaple 94.8 801
North Devon 103.4 801
Okehampton 96.0 801
Radio Gloucestershire
104.7 Stroud 95.0
Radio Kent
96.7 1035 Tunbridge Wells
96.7 1602 East Kent 104.2 774
Radio Leicester
104.9 837
Radio Norfolk
East Norfolk 95.1 855
West Norfolk 104.4 873
Radio Northampton
104.2 Corby 103.6

Radio Oxford
95.2
Radio Solent
96.1 999 Bournemouth 96.1
1359
Radio Suffolk
Bury St Edmunds 104.6
Ipswich 103.9 Lowestoft 95.5
Radio Surrey
104.6
Radio Sussex
Brighton & Worthing 95.3
1485 East Sussex & part of
West Sussex 104.5 1161
Crawley & Horsham 95.1 1368
Newhaven 95.0 1485 Reigate
104.0 1368
Radio W.M. (West Midlands)
95.6 1458 Wolverhampton
95.6 828
Radio Wales
882/340 Radio Cymru (Welsh
Language Service) 92.5–94.5

BBC
BBC CWR (Coventry & Warwick)
Coventry 94.8
Warwickshire 103.7
BBC Essex
103.5 765 N.E. Essex 103.5 729
S.E. Essex 95.3 1530
BBC Hereford & Worcester
Hereford 94.7 Worcester 104.0
Greater London Radio
94.9 1458

Wiltshire Sound
West Wilts 104.3 1332
Salisbury 103.5
North Wilts 103.6 1368

INDEPENDENT
Beacon Radio
Wolverhampton 97.2 990
Shrewsbury & Telford 103.1 1017
BRMB FM
Birmingham 96.4
Breeze AM
Chelmsford -/1359,
Southend -/1431
Capital Radio
95.8 1548
Chiltern Radio
Bedford 96.9 792 Luton 97.6
828
CN FM
Cambridge & Newmarket
103.0
County Sound AM
Surrey & NE Hants -/1476
Crawley & W. Sussex -/1521
Devonair Radio
Exeter 97.0 666 Torbay 96.4
954 E. Devon/Dorset 103.0
Essex Radio
Chelmsford 102.6 Southend
96.3

14

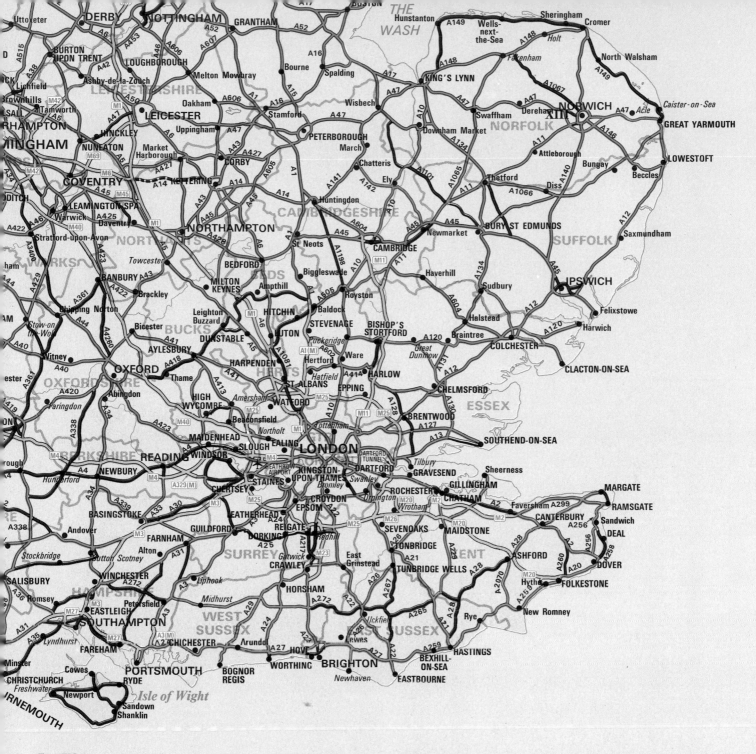

Fox FM
Oxford 102.6 Banbury 97.4
GWR (East)
Swindon 97.2 1161
West Wilts 102.2
Marlborough 96.5 936
GWR (West)
Avon & N Somerset 96.3
1260 Bath 103.0 1260
Hereward Radio
Peterborough 102.7 133.2
Horizon Radio
Milton Keynes 103.3
Invicta FM
Kent 103.1 1242 Canterbury
102.8 603 Thanet 95.9 603
Dover/Folkestone 97.0 603
Ashford 96.1 603
Kings Lynn FM
96.7
LBC
London 97.3
Lantern Radio
N. Devon 96.2
Leicester Sound
Leicester 103.2
London Talkback Radio
-/1152
Magic AM
Leeds -/828

Melody Radio
London 104.9
Mellow AM
NE Essex -/1557
Mercia FM
Coventry 97.0 Leamington
Spa 102.9
Northants Radio
96.6 1557
Ocean Sound
Southampton 103.2
Winchester 96.7 Portsmouth,
Chichester 97.5
Orchard FM
Yeovil 97.1 Taunton 102.6
Pirate FM
E. Cornwall 102.2
W. Cornwall 102.8
Plymouth Sound
Plymouth 97.0
Radio 210
Thames Valley 97.0 1431
Basingstoke, Andover 102.9
1431
Radio Broadland
Gt Yarmouth & Norwich 102.4
1152

Radio Mercury
Crawley/Reigate 102.7
Guildford 96.4
Horsham 97.5
Radio Orwell
Ipswich 97.1 1170
Radio Tavistock
96.6
Radio Wyvern
Hereford 97.6 954
Worcester 102.8 1530
Red Dragon FM
Cardiff 103.2 Newport 97.4
Saxon Radio
Bury St. Edmunds 96.4 1251
Severn Sound
Cheltenham and Gloucester
102.4 774 Stroud 103.0 774
South Coast Radio
Portsmouth, Chichester
-/1170 Southampton -/1557
Brighton -/1323
Southern Sound
Brighton 103.5 Eastbourne
102 Hastings 97.5
Newhaven 96.9

Spire FM
Salisbury 102
Sunshine
Ludlow -/819
Swansea Sound
96.4 1170
Touch AM
Cardiff -/1359 Newport -/1305
Two Counties Radio
Bournemouth 102.3 828
Xtra AM
Birmingham -/1152 Coventry
-/1359

Mileage chart

Map symbols

MOTORING INFORMATION

M4	Motorway with number
	Motorway junction with and without number
	Motorway junction with limited access
S	Motorway service area
	Motorway and junction under construction
A4	Primary route single/dual carriageway
S	Primary route service area
BATH	Primary destination
A1123	Other A road single/dual carriageway
B2070	B road single/dual carriageway
	Unclassified road single/dual carriageway
	Road under construction
	Narrow primary, other A or B road with passing places (Scotland)
	Road tunnel
	Steep gradient (arrows point downhill)
Toll	Road toll
5	Distance in miles between symbols

V	Vehicle ferry – Great Britain
CHERBOURG V	Vehicle ferry – Continental
H	Hovercraft ferry
	Airport
H	Heliport
	Railway line/in tunnel
	Railway station and level crossing
	Tourist railway
AA	AA Shop full services
AA	AA Roadside Shop – limited services
AA	AA Port Shop open as season demands
	AA telephone
	BT telephone in isolated places
	Urban area/village
628	Spot height in metres
	River, canal, lake
	Sandy beach
	County/Regional boundary
	National boundary
88	Page overlap and number

TOURIST INFORMATION

	Tourist Information Centre
	Tourist Information Centre (seasonal)
	Abbey, cathedral or priory
	Ruined abbey, cathedral or priory
	Castle
	Historic house
M	Museum or art gallery
	Industrial interest
	Garden
	Arboretum
	Country park
	Agricultural showground
	Theme park
	Zoo
	Wildlife collection – mammals
	Wildlife collection – birds
	Aquarium
	Nature reserve
RSPB	RSPB site
	Nature trail
	Forest drive
	National trail
	Viewpoint
	Picnic site

	Hill fort
	Roman antiquity
	Prehistoric monument
1066	Battle site with year
	Steam centre (railway)
	Cave
	Windmill
	Golf course
	County cricket ground
	Rugby Union national ground
	International athletics stadium
	Horse racing
	Show jumping/equestrian circuit
	Motor racing circuit
	Coastal launching site
	Ski slope – natural
	Ski slope – artificial
NT	National Trust property
★	Other places of interest
	Boxed symbols indicate attractions within urban areas
	National Park (England & Wales)
	National Scenic Area (Scotland)
	Forest Park
	Heritage Coast

Isles of Scilly

SV

WHITE ISLAND

ST. MARTIN'S

St Martin's Head

Old Grimsby

BRYHER

King Charles

Old Blockhouse

Higher Town

New Grimsby

Lizard Point

GREAT GANILLY

Isles of Scilly Heritage Coast

GREAT ARTHUR

TRESCO

SAMSON

North West Channel

Bant's Carn Burial

ST. MARY'S

Harry's Walls

Deep Point

Hugh Town

Garrison Walls

Isles of Scilly (St Mary's)

Old Town

ANNET

Peninnis Head

(Summer only)

To Penzance

St Mary's Sound

Broad Sound

Middle Town

GUGH

ST AGNES

Horse Point

Smith Sound

Western Rocks

Crow Sound

SCALE

0 1 2 3 4 miles

0 1 2 3 4 5 kilometres

9

SW

Trevose Head

Towan Head

Newquay
Fistral Bay

Kelsey Head

Holywell Bay

West Pentire

Pentire

Crantock

Penhale Point

Holywell

Ligger Point

Tresean

Treval

Cubert

Ligger or Perran Bay

Rose

Perranporth

Cligga Point

Goonhavern

Bolingey

World in Miniature

St Agnes Heritage Coast

Trevellas Downs

Perranzabuloe

Penhallow

ST AGNES HEAD

St Agnes

Mithian

Wheal Coates

Barkla Shop

Maraz

Goonbell

Goonwrea

St Agnes Leisure Park

Callestick

Porthtowan

Mount Hawke

Shortlanesend

South West Coast Path

Mawla

Cambrose

Blackwater

A390 Kenwyn

Godrevy – Portreath Heritage Coast

Portreath

Bridge

Illogan

Higher Town

Godrevy Island

Navax Point

Tehidy Woods

Scorrier

Chacewater

Godrevy Point

Reskadinnick

Kehelland

Cornish Engines

Redruth

Mount Ambrose

St Day

Kea

Gwithian

Pool

Carn Brea

Twelveheads

Carharrack

Bissoe

Carn Naun Point

The Island or St Ives Head

Phillack

Connor Downs

Camborne

Lanner A393

Gwennap

Devoran

Carn Downs

St Ives

Hayle

Angarrack

Barripper

Penponds

Troon

Four Lanes

Perranwell

Perranarworthal

Zennor Head

Carbis Bay

Coppermouse

Gwinear

Carnhell Green

B3303

Penhalvean

Ponsanooth

Gurnards Head

Zennor

Halsetown

Lelant

Merlins Magic Land

High Lanes

Praze-an-Beeble

Carnkie

Longdowns

Burnthouse

Mylor

Towednack

Penhaveanel

Stithians

Maba

Pendeen Watch

South West Coast Path

Men-An-Tol

Mulfra Quoit

Chysauster

St Erth

St Erth Praze

B3280

Crowan

Porkellis

Rame

Penryn

Flu

Morvah

14

New Mill

Canonstown

A30

B3302

Townshend

Drym

Leedstown

Argal & College Water Park

Treverva

Pendeen

Great Bosullow

Lanyon Quoit

Ludgvan

Crowlas

St Hilary

Godolphin Cross

Prospidnick

Trenear

Budock Water

Botallack

Trengwainton Garden NT

Gulval

Longrock

St Hilary

Relubbus

Crowntown

Wendron

Seworgan

Penjerrick

Cape Cornwall

Newbridge

Madron

Penzance

Longrock

Trescowe

Carleen

Coverack Bridges

Brill

Constantine

Mawnan Smith

St Just

Heamoor

Chyandour

Marazion

Goldsithney

Ashton

Sithney

Helston

Porth Navas

ROSEMULLION HEAD

Kelynack

Sancreed

St Michael's Mount NT

Perranuthnoe

A394

Breage

Helford Passage

Durgan

Mawnan

Whitesand Bay

Drift

Catchall

Newlyn

Praa Sands

Gweek

Seal Sanctuary

Helford

St Anthony

Crows-an-Wra

Kerris

Paul

Cudden Point

Rinsey Head

Trewavas Head

Flambards

A3083

Mawgan

Manaccan

Nare Point

LAND'S END

Sennen

St Buryan

Mousehole

MOUNT'S BAY

Porthleven

Garras

Tregidden

Porthallow

Trevescan

Trethewey

Treen

Lamorna

Gunwalloe

Tregidden

Port

Porthgwarra

Porthcurno

Cribba Head

Merthen Point

Lamorna Cove

White Cross

Cury

Goonhilly Downs Earth Station

St Keverne

Gwennap Head

St Levan

Minack Open Air Theatre

To Isles of Scilly (Summer only)

Poldhu Point

Mullion

GOONHILLY DOWNS

Coverack

Mullion Cove

Mullion Island

Mullion Cove

Predannack Head

Ruan Major

Kuggar

Black Head

Vellan Head

South West Coast Path

Ruan Minor

Cadgwith

The Lizard Heritage Coast

Lizard Head

Landewednack

Hot Point

LIZARD

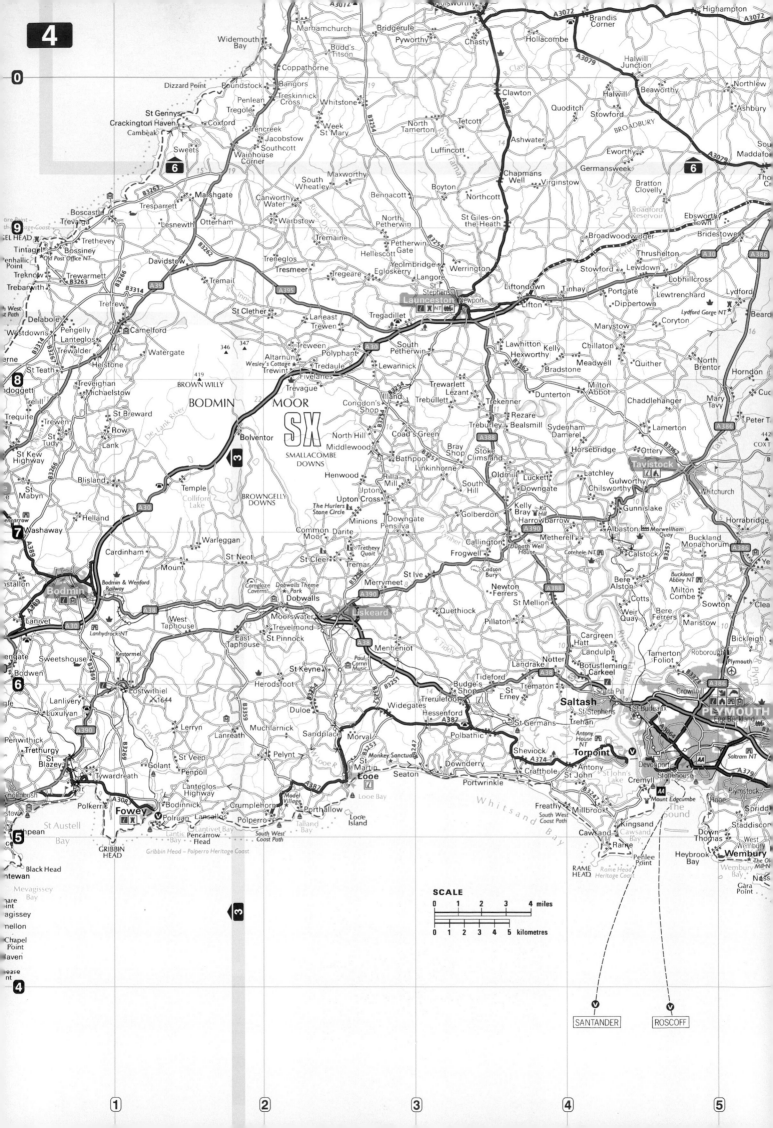

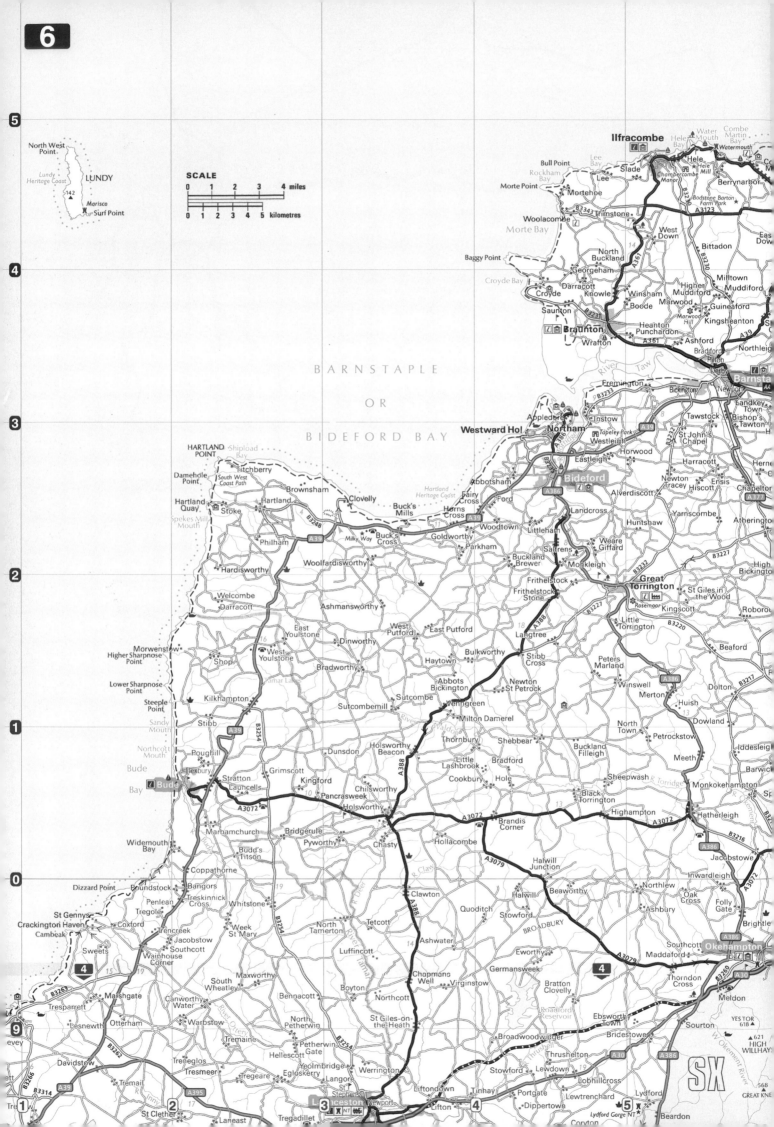

ST

SS

SV

BRI

Exmoor / North Devon region map

Foreland Point, Countisbury Cove, Lynmouth Bay, Lynton, Lynmouth, Countisbury, Brendon, Malmsmead, Exmoor Heritage Coast, Porlock Bay, West Porlock, Hurtstone Point, Bossington, Allerford, Woodcombe, SELWORTHY BEACON 308, Selworthy, Minehead, West Somerset Railway, Marsh Street, Blue Anchor Bay, Watchet

Woody Bay, Elwill Bay, Martinhoe, Trentishoe, Dean, Barbrook, Rockford, Watersmeet House NT, Tippacott, Oare, Porlock Weir, Porlock, Holnicote, Tivington, Knowle, Dunster, Butter Cross, Dunster Castle, Gallox Bridge, Carhampton, Old Cleeve, Washford, Tropiquaria, St Decumans, Five Bells, Williton, Doniford, Blue Anchor, Withycombe, Sampford Brett, Woolst, Kings

Parracombe, Kentisbury, Arlington, Arlington Court NT, Exmoor Bird Gardens, Loxhore, Lower Loxhore, Stoford, Barton Town, Challacombe, EXMOOR FOREST, HOAROAK HILL 474, SPAN HEAD 493, Simonsbath, Newland, River Exe, DRY HILL 444, DUNKERY HILL, DUNKERY BEACON 519, EXMOOR NATIONAL PARK, Wheddon Cross, Cutcombe, Luxborough, Rodhuish, Lower Roadwater, Stream, Capton, Monksilver, Sydenham Hall, Stogumber, Prest

Bratton Fleming, Benton, Brayford, High Bray, Charles, Bentwichen, North Radworthy, South Radworthy, Heasley Mill, WORTH HILL, Twitchen, Blackland, Withypool, Winsford, WINSFORD HILL, Knaplock, Liscombe, Tarr Steps, Tarr, Week, Exton, Bridgetown, Higher Combe, Hawkridge, North Quarme, Triscombe, Withiel Florey, Woolcotts, Brompton Regis, BRENDON HILLS, Treborough, Kingsbridge, Roadwater, Elworthy, Rooks Nest, Brompton Ralph, Gaulden Manor, Clatworthy, Whitefield, Langley Marsh, Langley, Willet

Goodleigh, Gunn, Accott, Stoke Rivers, Stoodleigh, East Buckland, West Buckland, Swimbridge, Newland, Filleigh, Castle Hill, South Molton, Quince Honey Farm, Aller, North Molton, Molland, Slade, West Anstey, East Anstey, Battleton, Dulverton, Brushford, Nightcott, Upcott, HADDON HILL, Bury, Skilgate, Chipstable, Upton, Coombe End, Maundown, Waterrow, Petton, Wiveliscombe, Huish Champflower, Clatworthy

Swimbridge Newland, Traveller's Rest, East Stowford, Filleigh, Bish Mill, Newtown, Ash Mill, Bishop's Nympton, Knowstone, Oakfordbridge, Oakford, Bampton, Clayhanger, Ashbrittle, Stawley, Kittisford, Budville, Appley, Thorne St Margaret, Runn, Bathealton, Langford

Umberleigh, Warkleigh, Satterleigh, Chittlehamholt, King's Nympton, Romansleigh, Marjansleigh, Yard, Meshaw, Rose Ash, George Nympton, Alswear, Creacombe, Rackenford, Loxbeare, Washfield, Hayne, Knightshayes Court NT, Chevithorne, Huntsham, Cove, Hockworthy, Staple Cross, Greenham, White Ball, Holcombe Rogus, Sampford Moor, Red Ball, Westleigh, Whitnage, Pitt, Burlescombe, Prescott, Uffculme, Ashford, Ayshford, Appledore

Burrington, Chittlehampton, Ashreigney, Chulmleigh, Elstone, Worlington, Cheldon, Chawleigh, Witheridge, Nomansland, Templeton, Withleigh, Calverleigh, Lurley, Bolham, Tiverton, Craze Lowman, Sampford Peverell, Halberton, Coldharbour Mill, Willand, Ashill, Bradfield, Kentisbeare, Blackborough, Craddock, Ashley, Eggesford, Filleigh, Eastington, Lapford, Woolfardisworthy, Morchard Bishop, Kennerleigh, Stockleigh English, East Village, Pennymoor, Washford Pyne, Puddington, Way Village, Cadeleigh, Upham, Bickleigh, Butterleigh, Cullompton, Knowle, Colebrook, Silverton, Bradninch, Westcott, Dulford, Kerswell, Colliton, Norman's Green, Luton, Plymtree

Hollocombe, Wembworthy, Brushford Barton, Coldridge, West Leigh, East Leigh, Zeal Monachorum, Down St Mary, Copplestone, Newbuildings, Sandford, West Sandford, Bow, Nymet Tracey, Coleford, Knowle, Shobrooke, Crediton, Cheriton Fitzpaine, Stockleigh Pomeroy, Cadbury, Fursdon, Little Silver, Upton Hellions, West Raddon, Thorverton, Nether Exe, Up Exe, Hele, Langford, Clyst Hydon, Payhembury, Plymtree, Talaton, Bucker

Ingleigh Green, Broadwood Kelly, Bondleigh, North Tawton, Sampford Courtenay, Yeoford, Uton, Hookway, Newton St Cyres, Cowley, Brampford Speke, Stoke Canon, Upton Pyne, Huxham, Poltimore, Killerton, Killerton NT, Rewe, Westwood, Broadclyst, Dog Village, Whimple, Fairmile, Cadhay, Hand-and-Pen, Allercombe, West Hill, Ottery St Mary, Talaford

Taw Green, Corscombe, Spreyton, Hittisleigh, Tedburn St Mary, Cheriton Bishop, Crockernwell, Drewsteignton, Longdown, Whitestone Cross, Ide, Exwick, Heavitree, EXETER, Pinhoe, Blackhorse, Whipton, Wonford, Sowton, Clyst Honiton, Marsh Green, Rockbeare, Tipton St John, Venn Ottery, Harpford

South Tawton, Sticklepath, South Zeal, East Week, Gooseford, Throwleigh, CAWSAND BEACON 548, Whiddon Down, Castle Drogo NT, Sandy Park, Murchington, Chagford, Great Weeke, Easton, Doccombe, Bridford, Dunsford, Doddiscombsleigh, Ashton, Kenn, Shillingford Abbot, Shillingford St George, Dunchideock, Alphington, Exminster, Kenford, Powderham, Countess Wear, Topsham, Exton, Woodbury, Woodbury Salterton, Clyst St George, Clyst St Mary, Farringdon, Aylesbeare, Yettington, Colaton Raleigh, Newton Poppleford, Southerton, Hardford, Bicton Park, BUTTERN HILL 414, WHITEHORSE HILL 605, 602, Throwleigh, Sloncombe, Moretonhampstead, Hayne, North Bovey, Christow

Roads: A39, A361, A377, A3072, A30, A396, A399, A3358, A3223, A3224, A3222, A3190, A3181, A373, A3052, A3179, A3180, A3052, M5, B3226, B3042, B3219, B3220, B3215, B3217, B3227, B3137

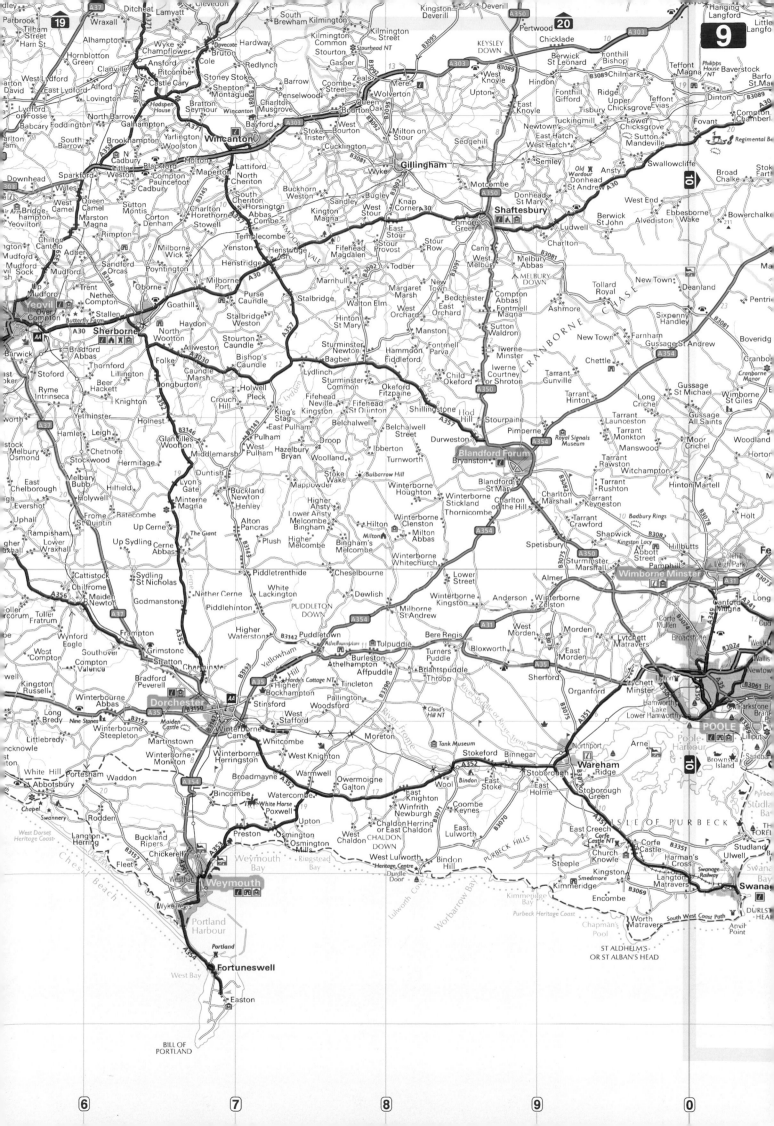

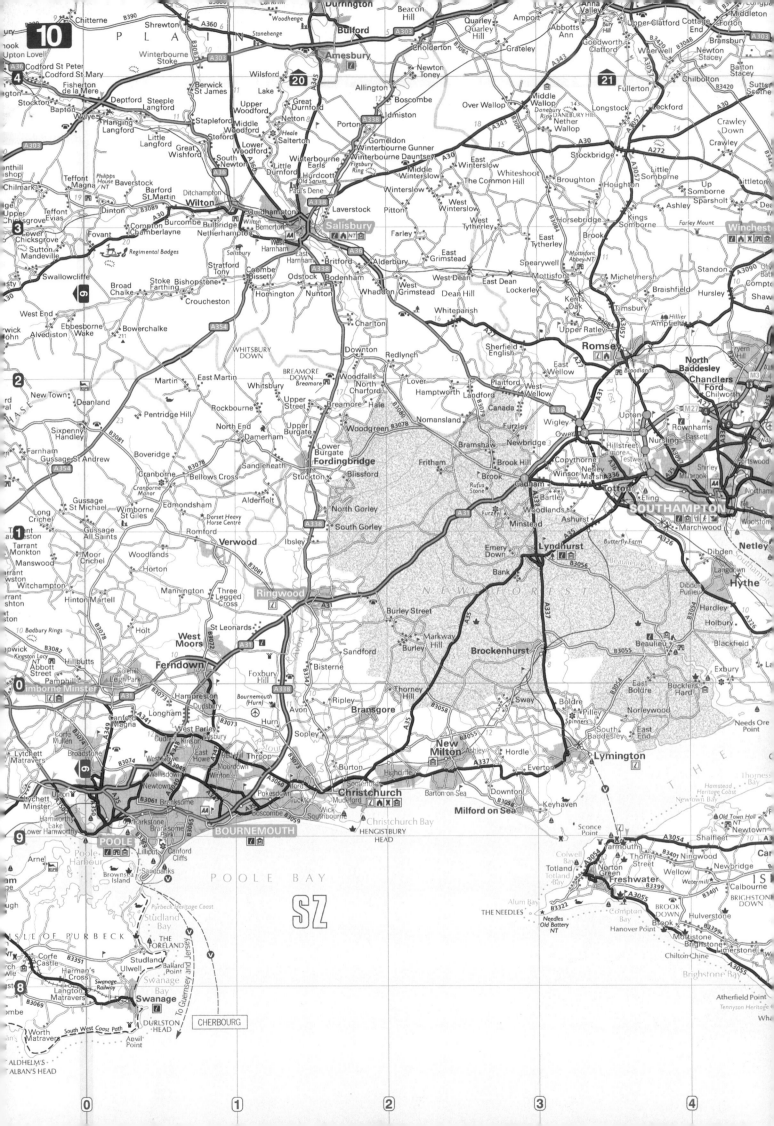

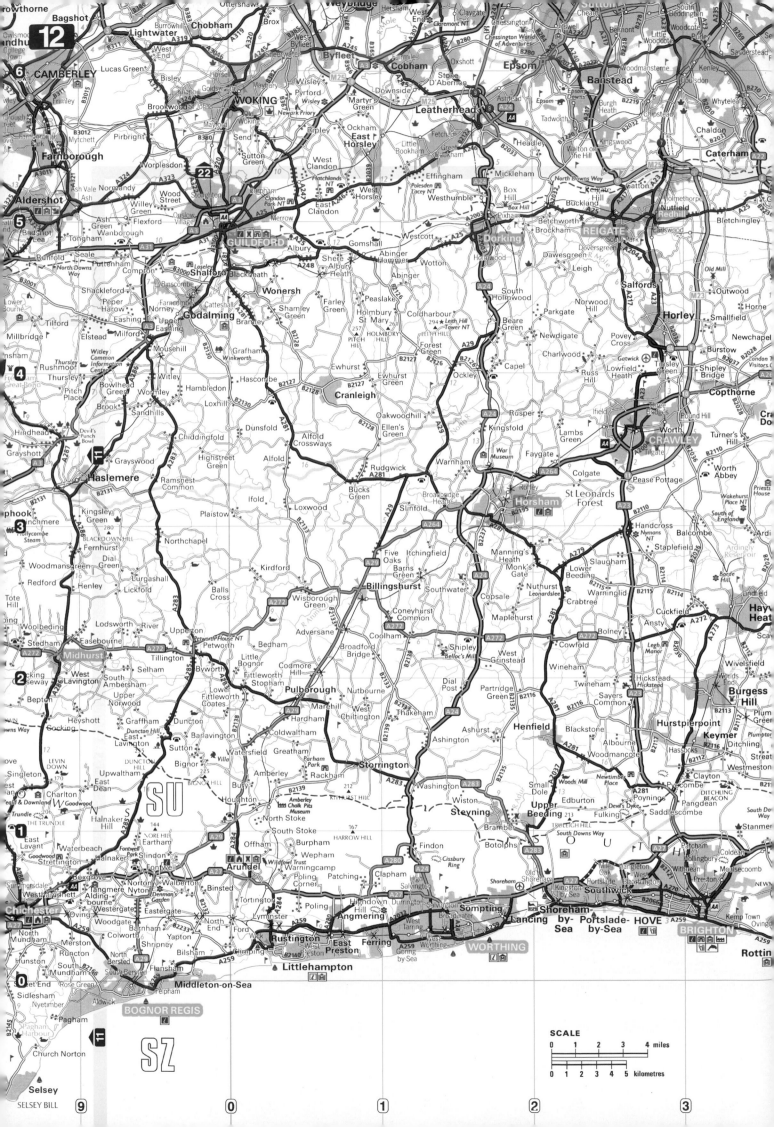

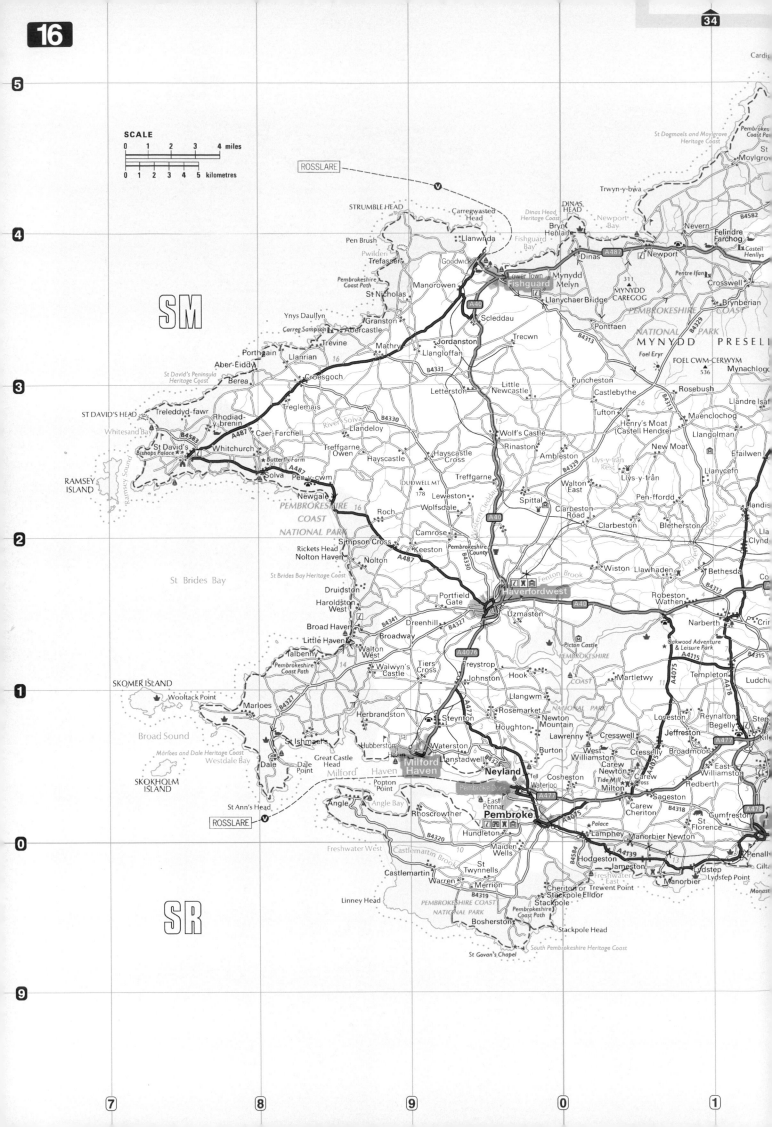

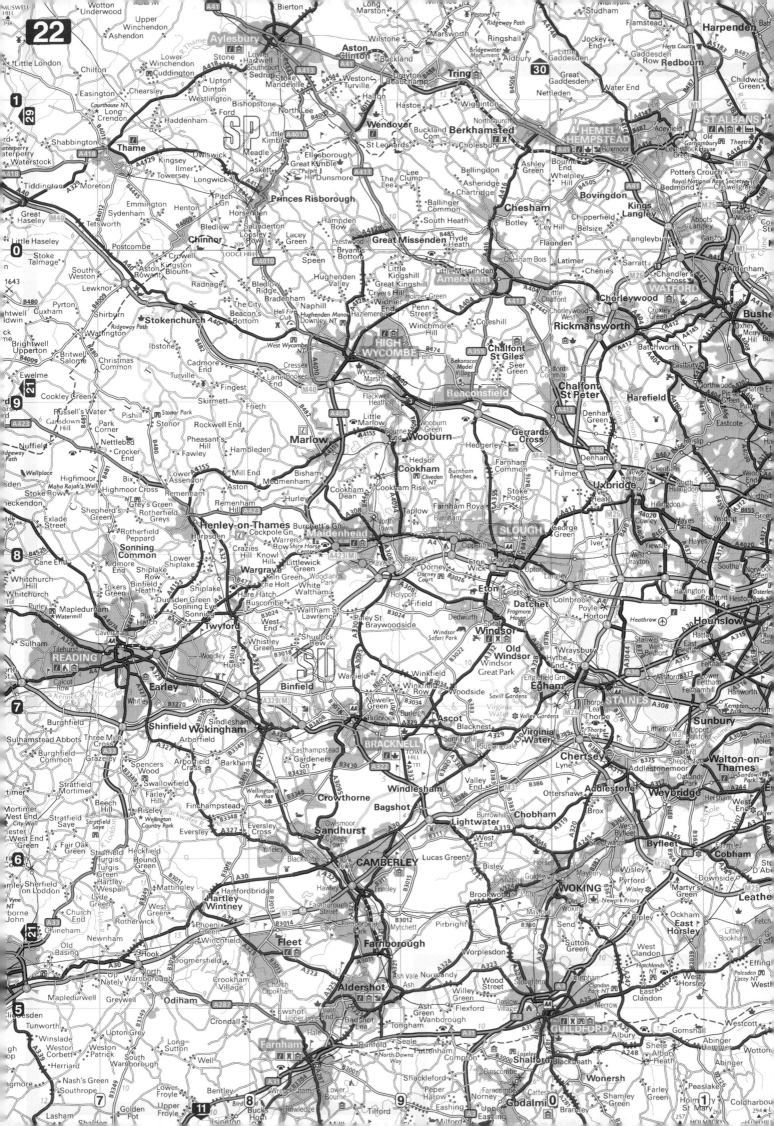

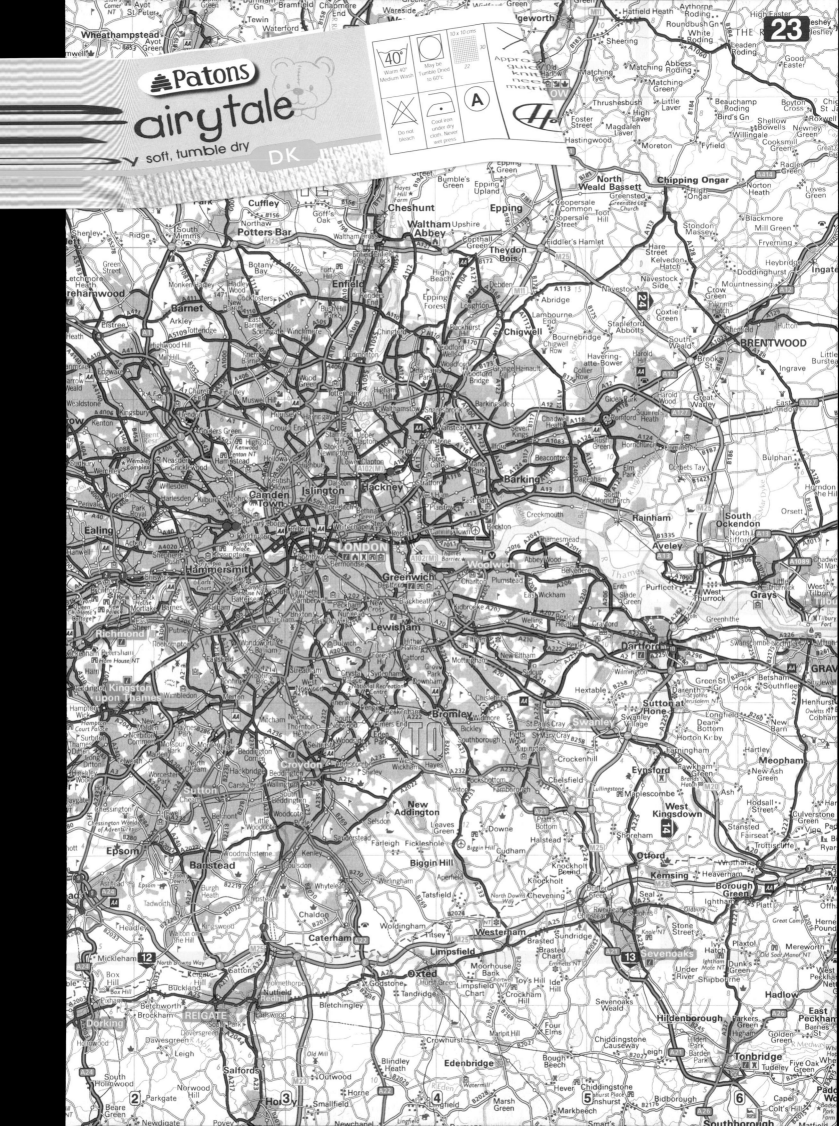

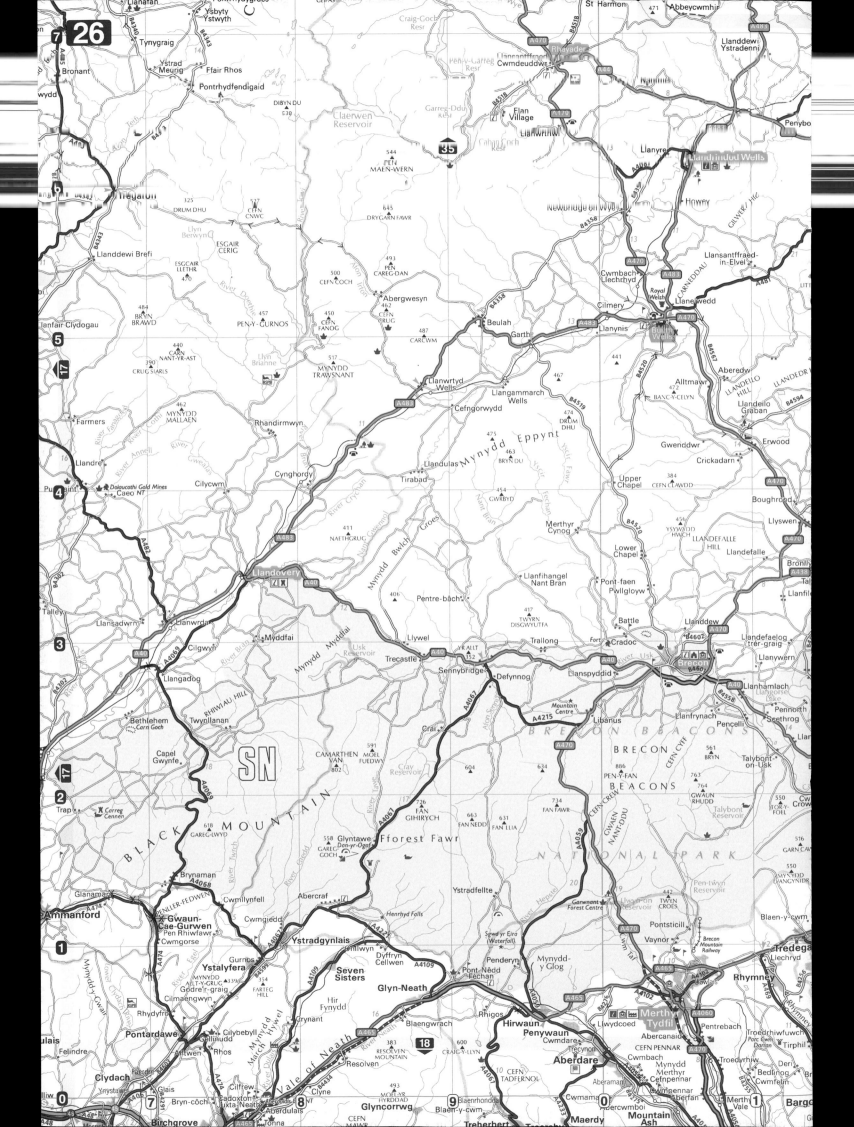

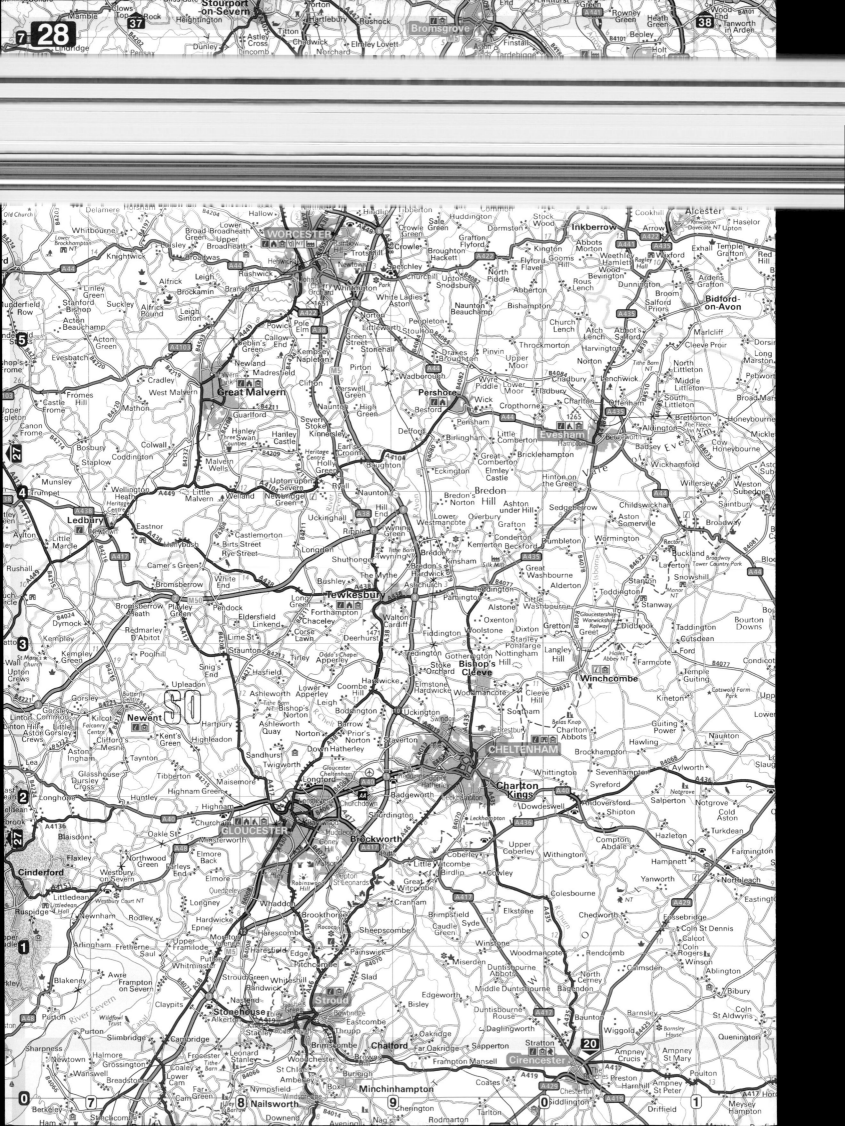

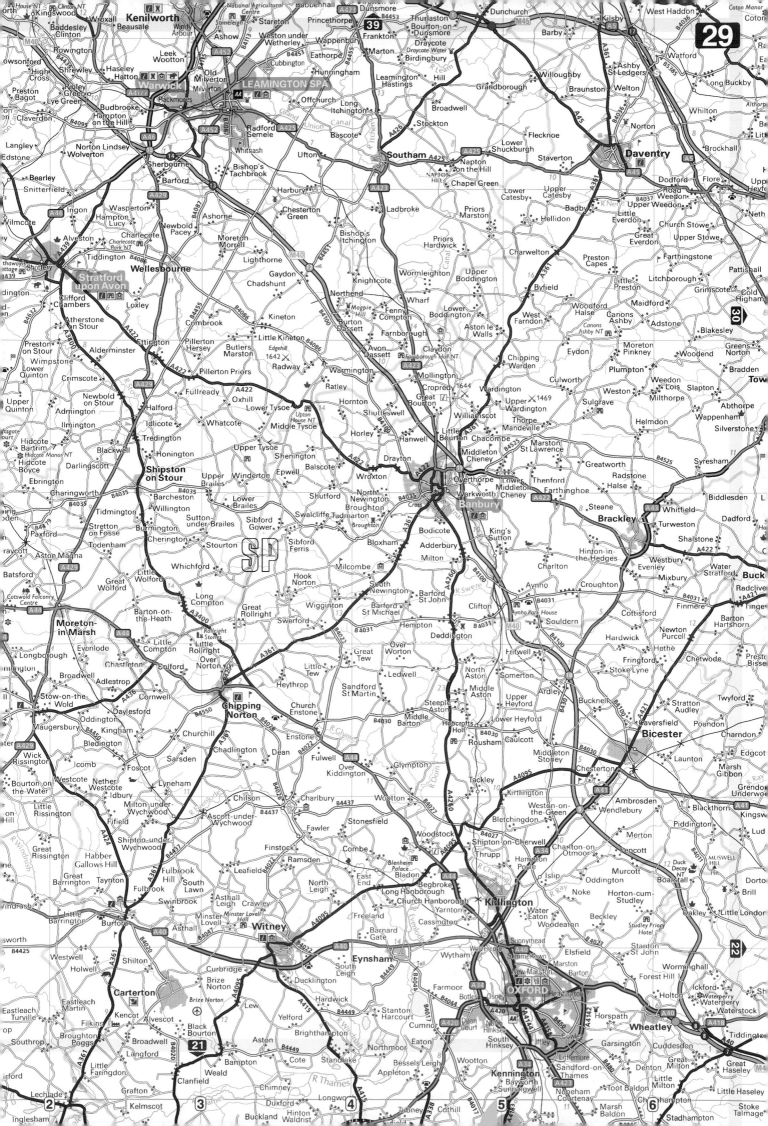

Clipston Arthingworth Rothwell A14 Sudborough Lowick Thorpe Waterville Clopton Winwick Stee
Kelmarsh Hall Harrington Weekley Warkton Grafton Underwood A605
Kelmarsh Orton Thorpe Kettering Cranford Slipton Islip Thrapston Twywell Titchmarsh B662 Hamerton 40

Pitsford Wellingborough Higham Ferrers Shelton A45 Upper Dean Kimbolton West Perry Gratham
Holdenby House Holdenby Chapel Brampton Moulton Sywell Wilby A510 Knuston Rushden Yielden B660
Long Buckby Church Brampton Boughton Mears Ashby Little Irchester Irchester Little Wymington Newton Bromswold Swineshead Staughton Green West Sta
Althorp Hall Harlestone A50 Overstone A573 Wymington A6 Pertenhall Great Staughton
Great Brington Kingsthorpe A4500 Earls Barton Great Doddington Farndish Knotting Riseley Keysoe Little Staughton
Little Brington New Duston Queen's Park Weston Favell Ecton A45 Wollaston Podington Knotting Green Keysoe Row Stap
Brockhall NORTHAMPTON Abington Great Billing Little Billing Strixton Hinwick Souldrop Sharnbrook Bolnhurst Thurleigh Eato
Harpole Duston Cogenhoe Whiston Grendon 9 Odell Colmworth Wyb
Upper Heyford St James End Far Cotton Little Houghton Castle Ashby Easton Maudit Bozeat Felmersham Radwell Milton Ernest Roothams Green
6 Delapre Abbey Brafield-on-the-Green Harrold Chellington Pavenham Ravensden
Nether Heyford Kislingbury Eleanor Cross Great Houghton Denton Yardley Hastings A509 Carlton Oakley Renhold A
M1 Hunsbury Hill Hardingstone A428 Lavendon West End Stevington Clapham BEDFORD Gr
Bugbrooke Wootton Cold Brayfield Turvey Bromham A6 Goldington Barf
Rothersthorpe Milton Malsor Collingtree Quinton Piddington Horton Warrington Olney Newton Blossomville A6 Biddenham AA
Pattishall Gayton Blisworth Courteenhall Ravenstone Weston Underwood Clifton Reynes Stagsden Willington
Eastcote A43 Roade 15 SP Kempston Mogerhanger Cople
Cold Higham Astcote Tiffield Stoke Bruerne Hartwell Emberton Moot Hall Elstow A600 Cardington
Greens Norton Shutlanger Ashton Long Street Stoke Goldington Filgrave Tyringham Sherington Astwood Marston Moretaine Northi
Towcester Alderton Grafton Regis Gayhurst Newport Pagnell Chicheley Bourne End Wootton Stewartby Wilstead Ickwell Green
Abthorpe Plumpton End Hanslope B526 Lathbury Chicheley Hall Upper Shelton Lower Shelton Silver End Swiss Garde
Silverstone Paulerspury Yardley Gobion Little Linford North Crawley Northwood End Ireland
Whittlebury Potterspury Castlethorpe Haversham Cranfield Millbrook Houghton Conquest Haynes A6
Lillingstone Lovell Old Stratford Cosgrove Great NewLinford Willen Moulsoe Salford West End Maulden Shefford
Lillingstone Dayrell Deanshanger Bradwell Broughton A421 Houghton House Farm A507
Chackmore Dadford Akeley Wicken Passenham Wolverton MILTON KEYNES Woolstone Lower End Lidlington Beadlow A507
Stowe House NT Leckhampstead Stony Stratford Calverton Bradwell Woughton on the Green Wavendon Ampthill Clophill Camp
Water Stratford Maids Moreton Thornton Beachampton Loughton Shenley Church End Simpson Walton Woburn Sands Aspley Guise Husborne Crawley Steppingley Upper Gravenhurst
Buckingham Shenley Brook End A5 Woburn Bow Brickhill Aspley Heath Ridgmont Flitton Silsoe Lwr Gravenhurst
Radclive Nash Whaddon A421 Far Bletchley Brickhill Flitwick Greenfield Wrest Park
Tingewick Gawcott Thornborough Bletchley Little Brickhill Woburn Abbey Tingrith Eversholt Pulloxhill Higham Gobion Apsley En
Barton Hartshorn Padbury Great Horwood Little Horwood Newton Longville Great Brickhill Milton Bryan Westoning A6
Preston Bissett Addington Adstock Drayton Parslow Stoke Hammond Potsgrove Harlington Barton-le-Clay Hexton
Twyford Hillesden A413 Mursley Winslow Hollingdon Heath and Reach A5 Toddington 12 Upper Sundon Sharpenhoe Barton Hills Wellbury
Steeple Claydon B4032 Soulbury Clipstone Hockliffe Tebworth Chalton Wingfield Ravensburgh Castle B655
Charndon Middle Claydon Swanbourne Stewkley Hoggeston Dunton Linslade Eggington Streatley Warden Hill Lilley A505
Edgcott Claydon NT East Claydon Granborough North Marston Burcott Leighton Buzzard Stanbridge Billington Houghton Regis Leagrave Limbury Mangrove Green Stopsley Cocke
Marsh Gibbon Botolph Claydon Oving Wing Little Billington Sewell A505 Luton Ramridge End
Grendon Underwood A41 QUAINTON HILL Pitchcott Whitchurch Ledburn Ascott NT Eaton Green Totternhoe Dunstable M1 AA Darleyhal
Kingswood Woodham Quainton 186 Aston Abbotts Slapton Eaton Bray Caddington Slip End Luton Hoo East Hy
Ludgershall Waddesdon Hardwick Wingrave Crafton Northall Kensworth A5 Markyate A1081
MUSWELL HILL Westcott Wotton Underwood Weedon Mentmore Horton Edlesborough Ivinghoe Whipsnade Kensworth Common Studham East Hy
Dorton A41 Bierton Rowsham Hulcott Cheddington Ivinghoe Aston Whipsnade Common Dagnall Markyate Flamstead Harpenden
Brill Upper Winchendon Long Marston Ivinghoe B489 Whipsnade NT Studham A5183 B487
Little London Chilton Ashendon Aylesbury Wilstone Marsworth Ringshall Jockey End Gaddesden Row Redbourn
Dorton Lower Winchendon Stone Lower Hartwell Aston Clinton Buckland Aldbury Little Gaddesden A414
Chearsley Upton Dinton Southcourt Sedrup Stoke Mandeville Weston Turville Drayton Beauchamp Tring 22 Great Gaddesden Childwick Green
Easington Cuddington Halton Nettleden Water End A5183
7 Long Crendon Haddenham Bishopstone North Lee Ford 8 Westlington 9 Wigginton Northchurch A41 A414 ST ALBANS 1
Wendover Buckland Berkhamsted HEMEL Adeyfield

Denver West Dereham Wereham Oxborough Boughton Gooderstone Great Cressingham Saham Toney Carbrooke Scoulton Deopham

32 Fordham Wretton Stoke Whittington Oxburgh Hall NT Little Cressingham Watton Griston Little Ellingham

Weeting Forest Santon Downham Croxton Quidenham East Harling Kenninghall Banham

Littleport Burnt Fen Hockwold Fens Hockwold cum Wilton Brandon Park Thetford Warren Lodge Thetford A134 Peddars Way Brettenham Shadwell Bridgham North Lopham South Lopham

Little Ouse River Town Street A1107 A11 A1075 Rushford R Thet Garboldisham Bress

Prickwillow 41 Lakenheath Elveden Euston A1066 Gasthorpe Smallworth Blo Norton

Queen Adelaide Kennyhill Barnham Coney Weston Hopton Thelnetham Redgrave Hinderclay

Middle Fen Mildenhall Fen Eriswell Market Weston Rickinghall Inferior Botesdale

Great Fen Thistley Green Beck Row Holywell Row Fakenham Magna Barningham Sapiston Honington Bardwell Hepworth Rickinghall Superior

Isleham Fen West Row Worlington Ixworth Thorpe Troston Stanton Walsham le Willows Gislingham Mill Street

Isleham Mildenhall AA Barton Mills Icklingham Anglo-Saxon Village Reconstruction West Stow Ampton Great Livermere Ixworth A143 Langham Four Ashes Finningham Wyverstone Street Wyverstone Bacton

Soham Wicken Fordham Freckenham Tuddenham Lackford Green Culford Ingham Timworth Conyer's Gn Upper Town Pakenham Bird Gardens Stanton Street Crowland

Chippenham Herringswell Cavenham Lackford Flempton Timworth Green Fornham St Martin Gt Barton Grimstone End Hunston Stowlangtoft Norton Little Green

Burwell A142 Snailwell A11 Kennett Hengrave Fornham All Saints R Lark Thurston Great Gn Norton Elmswell

Exning Kentford Risby Westley Bury St Edmunds A143 Beyton Green Kingshall Street Beyton Woolpit Wetherden Haughley

Newmarket Moulton Packhorse Bridge Higham Burthorpe Green Little Saxham Ickworth NT Horringer Blackthorpe Green Rushbrooke Rougham Hessett Drinkstone Harleston Stowupland Onehouse Stowmarket

Cheveley Gazeley Barrow Chevington Bradfield Combust Sicklesmere Bradfield St George Drinkstone Green Gedding Mill Green Buxhall Great Finborough Combs Combs Ford Needham Market

Ashley Dalham Denham Hargrave Green Broad Green Tan Office Green Whepstead Hawstead Mickley Green Maypole Green Rattlesden Felsham Hightown Green Brettenham Battisford Ringshall

Stetchworth Little Ditton Ditton Green Kirtling Lidgate Ousden Chedburgh A143 Rede Harrow Green Cross Green Windsor Green Oldhall Green Great Green Thorpe Green Cooks Green Cross Green Charles Tye Barking Tye

Dullingham Saxon Street Kirtling Green Cowlinge Attleton Green Thorns Wickhambrook Hawkedon Somerton Green Cross Green Lawshall Cockfield Thorpe Morieux Hitcham Causeway Hitcham Great Bricett Ringshall Stocks

Six Mile Bottom Dullingham Ley Burrough Green Great Bradley Lambfair Green Pound Green Wickham Street Denston Stansfield Audley End Shimpling Street Hitcham Street Nedging Tye Naughton Offton

Brinkley Willingham Green Carlton Farley Green Stradishall Hartest Shimpling Preston Kettlebaston Bildeston Nedging Wattisham

West Wratting Weston Green Carlton Green Little Bradley Little Thurlow Green Assington Green Upper Street Fenstead End Boxted Alpheton Lavenham Brent Eleigh Monks Eleigh Chelsworth Milden Ash Street Whatfield Elmset

Weston Colville 31 West Wickham Great Thurlow Thurlow Hundon Glemsford Stanstead Lavenham Guildhall NT Swingleton Green Lindsey Tye Lindsey Semer Aldham

Balsham 5 Withersfield Great Wratting Barnardiston Poslingford Brook Street Stanstead Street Bridge Street Little Waldingfield Rose Green Kersey A1071 Hadleigh

Streetly End Horseheath Mount Pleasant Nether Hall Cavendish Vineyards Pentlow Kentwell Hall Melford Hall NT Great Waldingfield Mill Green Wicker Street Green Groton

Cardinal's Green Haverhill Little Wratting Kedington Brockley Green Chilton Street Clare Ancient House River Stour Foxearth Long Melford Acton A1071

Bartlow Shudy Camps Sturmer Wixoe Stoke by Clare Ovington Belchamp St Paul Borley Green Borley Newman's Green Cornard Tye Newton Boxford A1071 Layham

Steventon End Ashdon Camps End Helions Bumpstead Birdbrook Baythorne End Ashen Belchamp Otten Belchamp Walter Bulmer Sudbury Great Cornard A1071 Stoke Street Shelley

Walden 4 Castle Camps Wiggens Green Steeple Bumpstead Ridgewell Tilbury Green Little Yeldham Bulmer Tye Middleton Little Cornard A134 Polstead Raydon

Wimbish Hempstead Spain's End Chapelend Way Stambourne Green Great Yeldham 24 Gestingthorpe Wickham St Paul Great Henny Henny Street Assington Rose Green Stoke by Nayland Lower Raydon

Tye Green Radwinter Great Sampford Toppesfield Pool Street Colne Valley Castle Hedingham Twinstead Lamarsh Leavenheath Honey Tye Thorington Street Stratford St Mary

Upper Green Wimbish Green Little Sampford Spains Hall Gainsford End Highstreet Green Sible Hedingham Lucking Street Little Maplestead Alphamstone Bures Nayland Boxted

Howlett End Thaxted Little Bardfield Great Bardfield Howe Street Great Maplestead Wissington Boxted Langham

Cutler's Green Monk Oxen Bardfield End Green Finchingfield Wethersfield Sible Hedingham A604 Booses Green Colne Engaine White Colne Mount Bures Little Horkesley Boxted Cross Castle House

3 6 7 Shalford Blackmore End Beazley Gosfield 8 Halstead Colne Engaine Wakes Colne 9 Fordham Horkesley Heath Great Horkesley 0 A12 Ardleigh

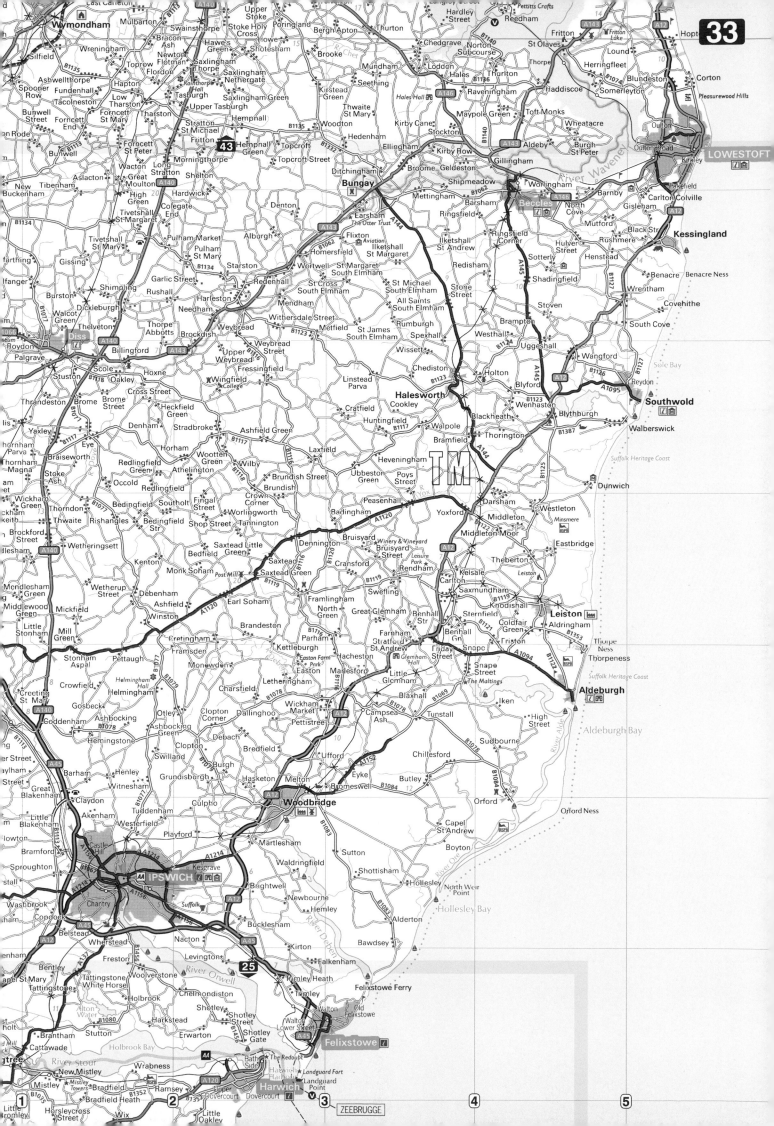

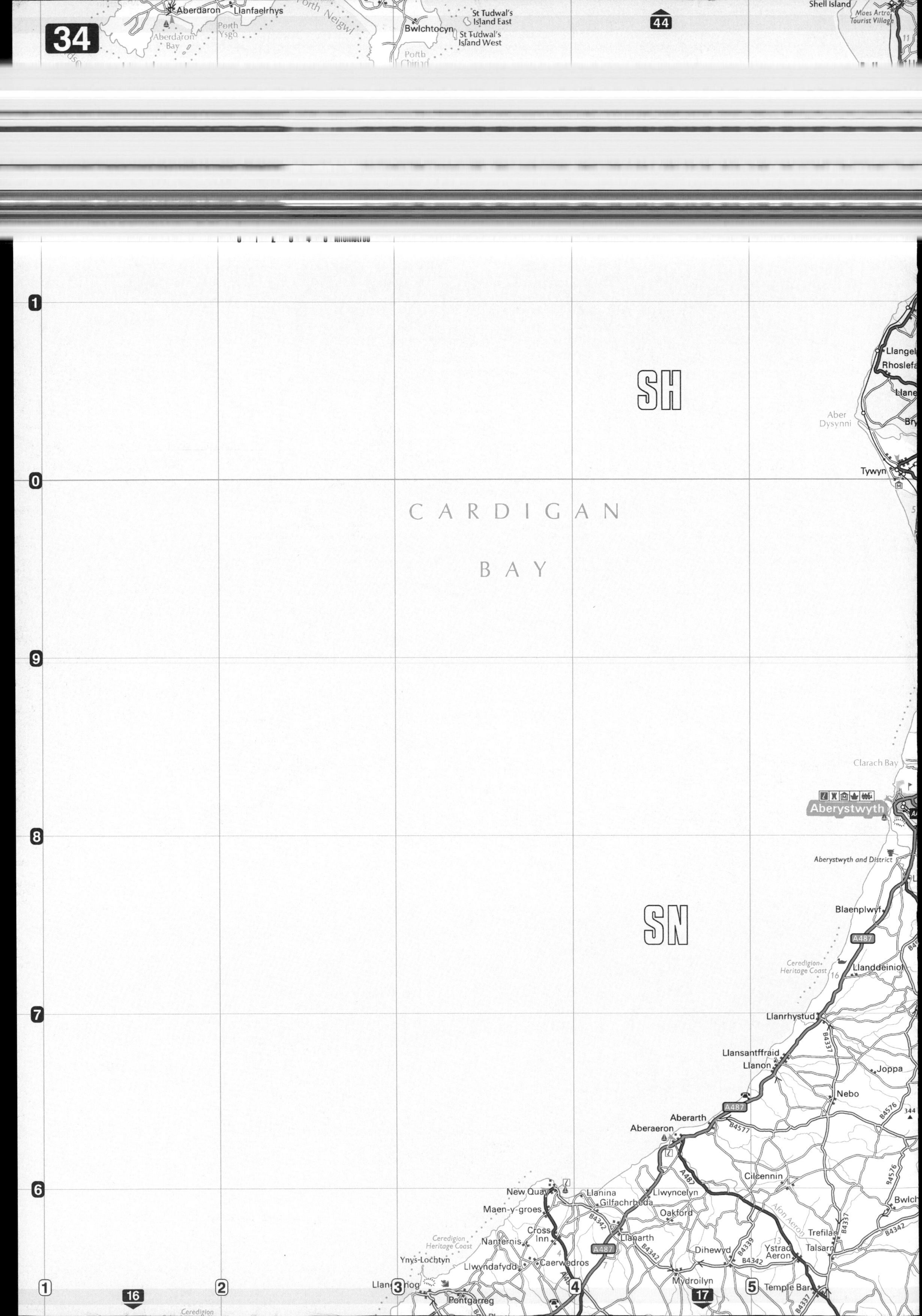

Aberdaron Llanfaelrhys orth Neigwl Bwlchtocyn St Tudwal's Island East St Tudwal's Island West **44** Shell Island Moes Artro Tourist Village

Aberdaron Bay Porth Ysgo Porth Chirlad

SH

Llangel Rhoslefa Llane

Aber Dysynni

Bry

Tywyn

C A R D I G A N

B A Y

Clarach Bay

Aberystwyth

Aberystwyth and District

SN

Blaenplwyf

A487

Ceredigion Heritage Coast 16 Llanddeiniol

Llanrhystud

Llansantffraid Llanon Joppa

Nebo

Aberarth A487 Aberaeron B4577

Cilcennin

New Quay Llanina Llwyncelyn Bwlch Gilfachrheda Maen-y-groes Oakford Trefila Cross B4342 Inn Llanarth Dihewyd Ystrad Talsarn Ceredigion Heritage Coast Nanternis A487 Aeron Ynys-Lochtyn Llwyndafydd Caerwedros Mydroilyn **17** Temple Bar Llan riog Ceredigion Pontgarreg

16 **2** **3** **4** **5**

1 **0** **9** **8** **7** **6**

A494

Y Maerdy Druid Corwen Cynwyd

Glyndyfrdwy Llangollen Railway Valle Crucis Abbey Trevor A539 Rhesymedre Cefn-Mawr Erbistock A525

Garth Aqueduct Llangollen A5 Tyn-dwr Cefn-Mawr Overton Horseman's Green

46 Overton

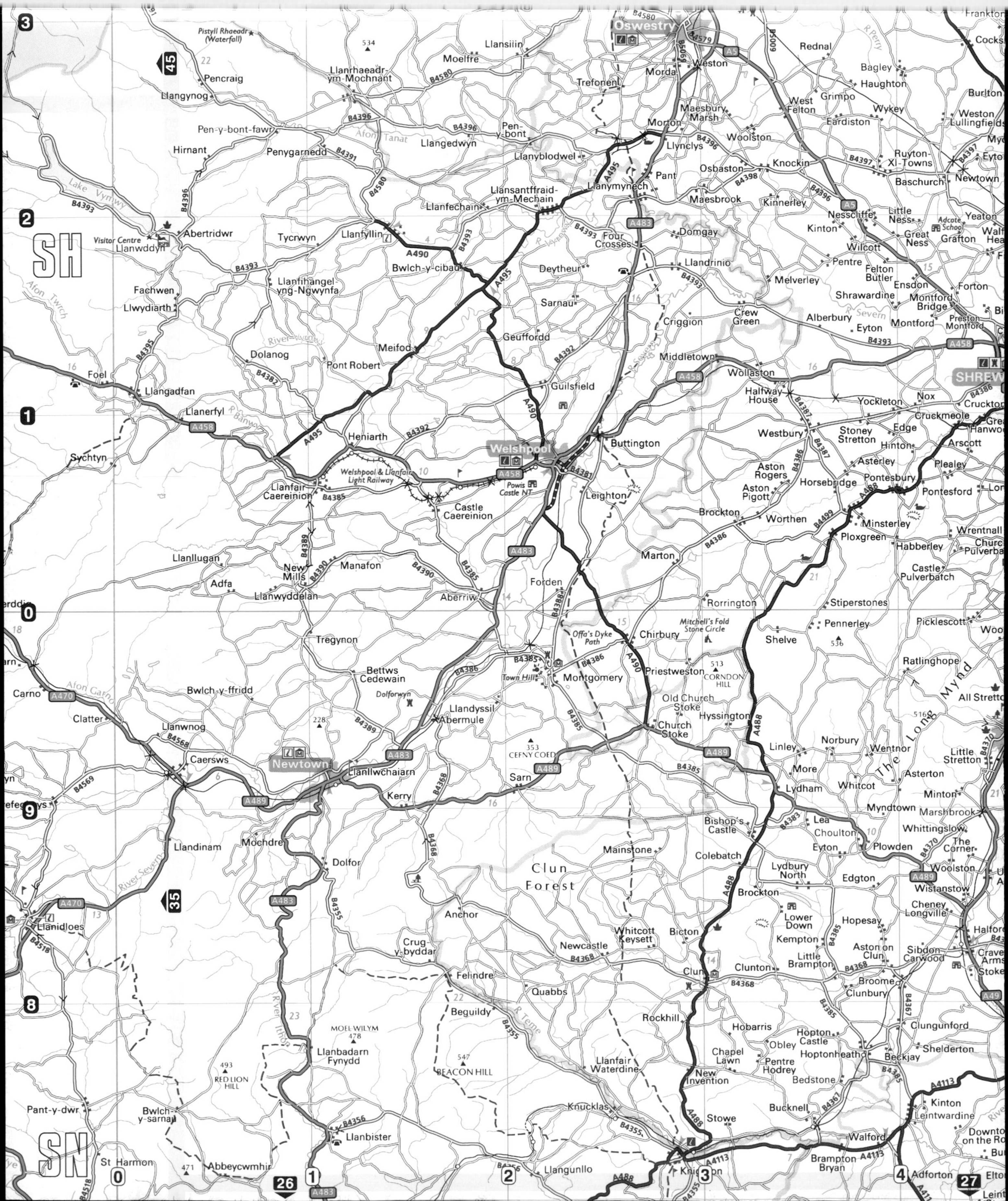

611 OEL GOC

SH

3

Pistyll Rhaeadr (Waterfall)
45 Pencraig
Llangynog
Pen-y-bont-fawr
Hirnant
Penygarnedd

534
Llanrhaeadr-ym-Mochnant
Moelfre Llansilin
B4580 B4396 Pen-y-bont
B4396 Llangedwyn Llanblodwel
Afon Tanat B4391 Llanfechain
B4396

Oswestry B4580 B4579 A5 Rednal Bagley Haughton Burlton
Weston Grimpo Wykey Weston Lullingfields
Morda Maesbury Marsh West Felton Eardiston Ruyton-XI-Towns Cockshu
Trefonen Morton Woolston B4397 Eyto Myd
Llynclys Osbaston Knockin Baschurch Newtown
Pant Maesbrook Kinnerley Nesscliffe Little Ness Yeaton Adcote School Grafton Walf Heat

Llanymynech A483 Four Crosses Domgay Kinton Wilcott Great Ness
Llansantffraid-ym-Mechain A493 Llandrinio Pentre Felton Butler Ensdon Forton
Deytheur Sarnau Melverley Shrawardine Montford Bridge Preston Montford Bi
Guilsford Crew Green Alberbury Eyton Montford
Criggion Severn
Middletown Wollaston A458 SHREW

2

Abertridwr Tycrwyn Llanfyllin A490 Bwlch-y-cibau
Fachwen Llwydiarth Llanfihangel-yng-Ngwynfa Meifod
Visitor Centre Llanwddyn
Lake Vyrnwy B4393 B4395 Foel Dolanog Pont Robert
Afon Twrch B4393

Geuffordd

SHREW

Welshpool Buttington Westbury Stoney Stretton Edge Cruckmeole
A458 Halfway House Yockleton Nox Cruckton Grea
Welshpool & Llanfair Light Railway B4381 Hinton Hanwo
Powis Castle NT Leighton Aston Rogers Horsebridge Asterley Pontesbury Plealey
Castle Caereinion Brockton Aston Pigott Worthen Minsterley Pontesford Lor
Llanfair Caereinion B4385 Marton B4386 Ploxgreen Habberley Wrentnal Church Pulverba
A495 Heniarth A458 Forden Rorrington Shelve Castle Pulverbatch
New Mills Manafon B4390 A483 Chirbury Stiperstones Picklescott Woo
Adfa Llanwyddelan Aberriw Mitchell's Fold Stone Circle Pennerley Ratlinghope
Offa's Dyke Path Priestweston CORNDON HILL All Stretto
Tregynon B4385 Montgomery Old Church Stoke Linley Norbury Wentnor Little Stretton The Long Mynd
Bettws Cedewain Dolforwyn Town Hill Hyssington More Asterton Whitcot Minton
Bwlch-y-ffridd Llandyssil Abermule Church Stoke Lydham Myndtown Marshbrook

1

Llangadfan Llanerfyl A458 Sychtyn
B4382 B4392 Llanllugan

0

Carno A470 Clatter Llanwnog B4568 Caersws B4569 Llandinam Mochdre Dolfor
Afon Carno

9

Newtown A483 Llanllwchaiarn Kerry B4368 Sarn A489
A489 Afon Severn

Clun Forest Mainstone Bishop's Castle Lea Choulton Eyton Plowden The Corner A489 Woolston Wistanstow
Colebatch Lydbury North Edgton Cheney Longville
Brockton Hopesay Halfor
Lower Down Kempton Aston on Clun Sibdon Carwood
Anchor Crug-y-byddar Felindre Quabbs Newcastle Whitcott Keysett Bicton Clun Clunton Little Brampton Broome Crave Stoke
Beguildy Rockhill Hobarris Clunbury A49
Hopton Castle Obley Hopton Heath Beckjay Shelderton

35

8

Llanidloes A470 Llanbadarn Fynydd MOEL WILYM 478
Felindre Quabbs BEACON HILL Llanfair Waterdine Chapel Lawn Pentre Hodrey Bucknell Clungunford
RED LION HILL 493 547 New Invention Leintwardine
Knucklas Stowe B4361 Kinton
Abbeycwmhir Llanbister Llangunllo Kn on A4113 Brampton Bryan Downto on the Ro
Pant-y-dwr Bwlch-y-sarnau B4356 Walford Adforton Elto
St Harmon A470 A4113 A4113

SN

26 1 2 3 4 27
A483 A488

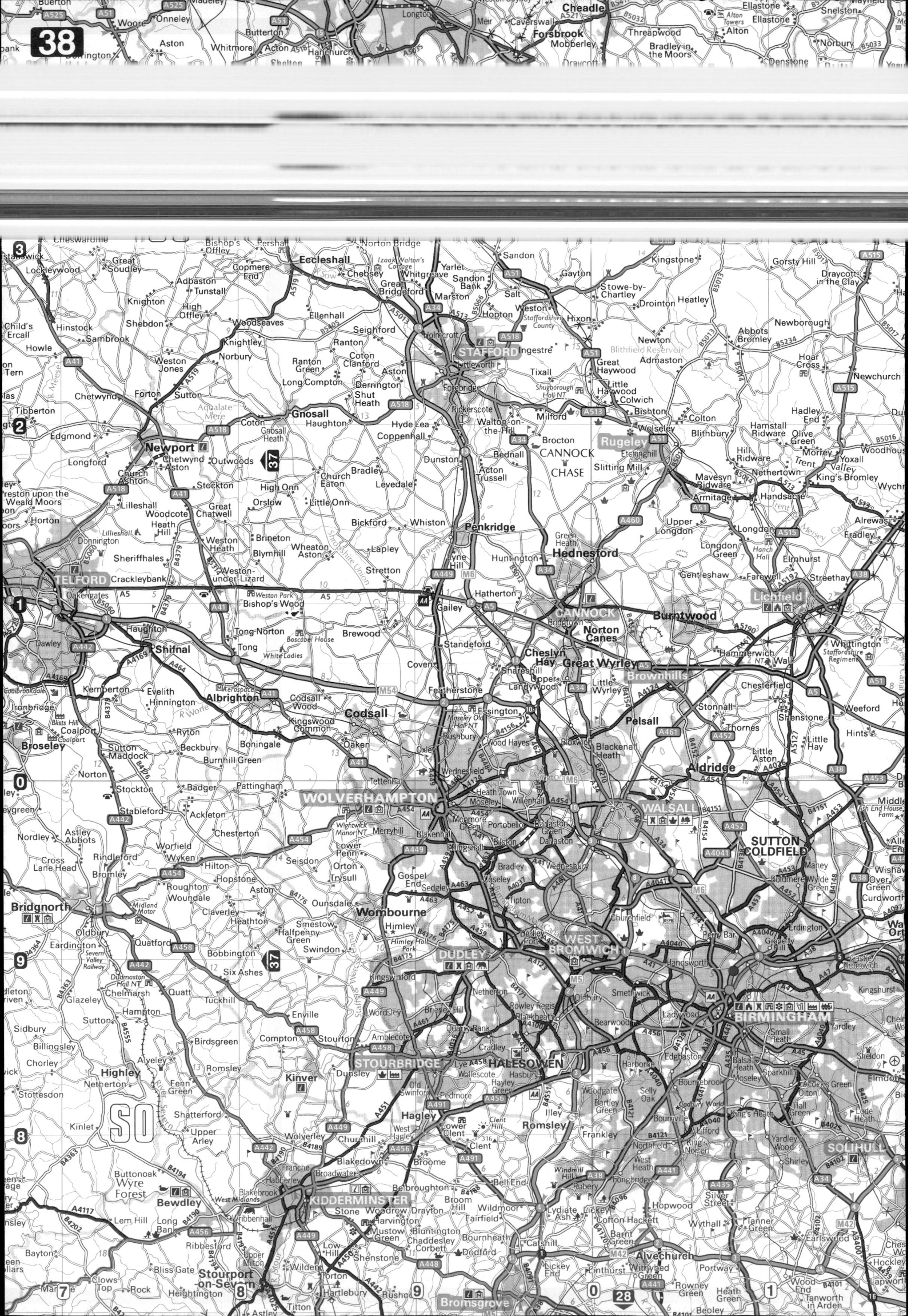

WOLVERHAMPTON

BIRMINGHAM

TELFORD

STAFFORD

WALSALL

SUTTON COLDFIELD

WEST BROMWICH

DUDLEY

STOURBRIDGE

HALESOWEN

KIDDERMINSTER

Lichfield

Rugeley

CANNOCK

Bridgnorth

Newport

Eccleshall

Shifnal

Broseley

Bewdley

Stourport-on-Severn

SOLIHULL

Highley

Kinver

Wombourne

Gnosall

Penkridge

Hednesford

Burntwood

Brownhills

Great Wyrley

Aldridge

Pelsall

Bromsgrove

Codsall

Albrighton

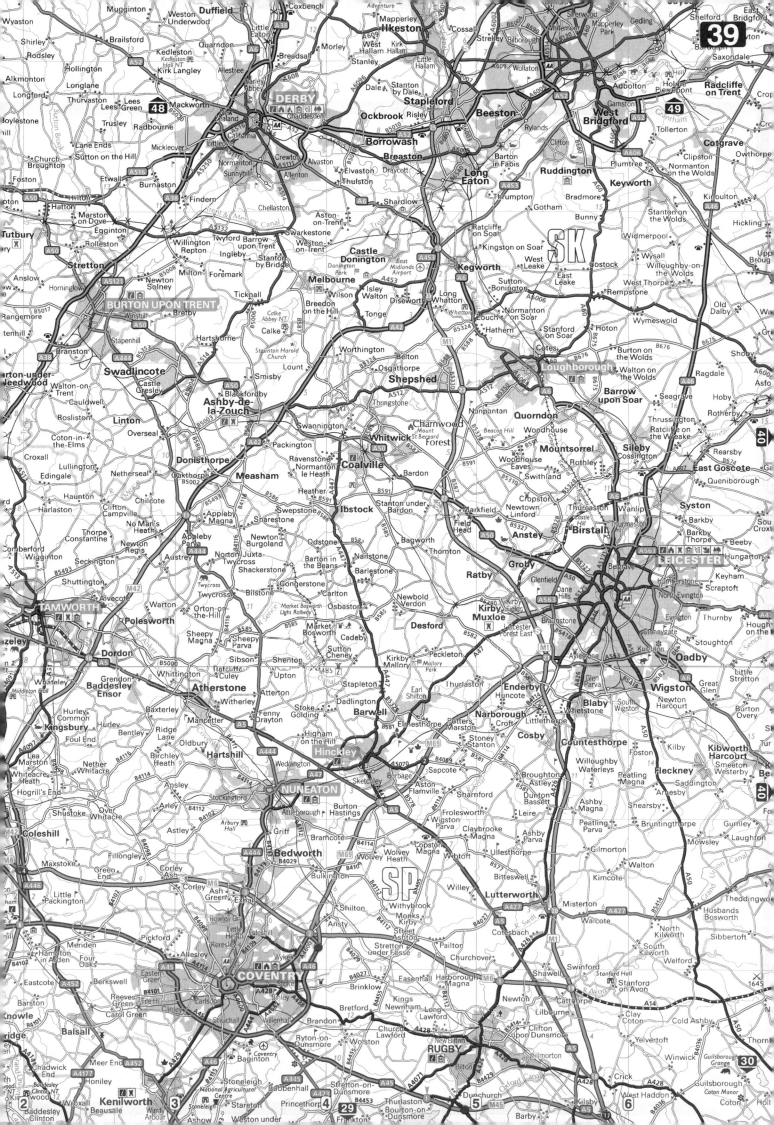

Grantham Melton Mowbray Oakham Stamford Bourne Market Deeping Deeping St James Corby Kettering Market Harborough Kibworth Beauchamp Desborough Rothwell Oundle

SK SP

Rutland Water

Vale of Catmose
Vale of Belvoir

ibraltar Point

Holme next
the Sea
Brancaster
Brancaster
Staithe
Stiffkey
Morston
Wells next
The Sea
Old Hunstanton
Thornham
Titchwell
Burnham
Norton
Carmelite Friary
Burnham Overy
A149
Warham St Mary
Warham
All Saints
Blakeney
Wiveton
Cockthorpe
Hunstanton
Ringstead
Burnham
Market
Burnham
Thorpe
Holkham
Hall
B1155
B1388
Langham
Glandford
Wighton
Westgate
Saxlingham
Heacham
Summerfield
B1153
New
Holkham
North Creake
Wells &
Walsingham
Light Railway
Great
Walsingham
Cross
Binham
Lower
Green
Field
Dalling
Sharrington
Bale
Norfolk
Lavender
Sedgeford
Docking
B1155
North
Creake
Little Walsingham
Copy's
Green
B1110
Thornag
Snettisham
Fring
Stanhoe
South
Creake
North
Barsham
Houghton St Giles
Thursford
Great
Snoring
Thursford
Stody Hunw
Brinton
Bircham
Newton
19
Barmer
West
Barsham
East
Barsham
Gunthorpe
Briningham
Ed
Ingoldisthorpe
Shernborne
Syderstone
A148
Little
Snoring
Barney
Croxton
Melton
Constable
Bris
Dersingham
Great Bircham
Bircham Tofts
Sculthorpe
B1105
Kettlestone
Swanton
Novers
Fulmodestone
Wolferton
Sandringham
Anmer
B1454
Tattersett
Coxford
Shereford
Dunton
Fakenham
Hempton
Little Ryburgh
B1110
Stibbard
Hindolveston
Thur
Castle
Rising
West Newton
New
Houghton
Houghton Hall
West
Rudham
East
Rudham
A1067
Flitcham
Helhoughton
Tatterford
Toftrees
Great
Ryburgh
A1065
Wood
Norton
Trinity Hospital
Hillington
Harpley
East
Raynham
Colkirk
Guestwick
North
Wootton
Congham
Little Massingham
West Raynham
South
Raynham
Gateley
Bintree
Foulsham
Roydon
Great
Massingham
Weasenham
St Peter
Horningtoft
North
Elmham
Twyford
South Wootton
Grimston
West Raynham
Wellingham
Whissonsett
Brisley
Billingford
Foxley
Theme
A149
Gaywood
B1145
Weasenham
All Saints
Tittleshall
Saxon Cathedral
Bawdeswe
Sparha
West
Lynn
King's Lynn
B1145
Gayton
B1145
Rougham
Stanfield
East Bilney
Beetley
Worthing
A1067
Tilney
All Saints
A17
Ashwicken
Gayton
Thorpe
TF
Mileham
Gressenhall
Hoe
Swanton
Morley
Elsing
A47
Saddle
Bow
West Winch
Middleton
East
Winch
West
Bilney
East
Walton
West
Acre
Castle Acre
Litcham
Beeston
Gressenhall
Green
Gressenhall
North
Tuddenham
Wiggenhall
St Germans
North
Runcton
Blackborough
End
Pentney
Newton
West
Lexham
East
Lexham
Longham
Wiggenhall
St Mary
the Virgin
Setchey
15
Bailey Gate
South Acre
Great
Dunham
7
B1147
A47
East Dereham
Mattisha
Burgh
Wiggenhall
St Mary
Magdalen
Watlington
9
Wormegay
River Nar
Narborough
A47
Sporle
Little Dunham
West
Fransham
Little Fransham
Great
Fransham
Wendling
Scarning
Mattishall
Clint
Green
South
Green
Runcton
Holme
Tottenhill
A134
Marham
A1065
Necton
East
Bradenham
Westfield
Yaxham
Stowbridge
South
Runcton
41
Shouldham
Swaffham
West
Bradenham
Shipdham
Whinburgh
Runhall
Stow
Bardolph
Shouldham
Thorpe
Barton
Bendish
Fincham
North
Pickenham
Holme
Hale
Garveston
Thuxton
Coston
Barr
Bro
Wimbotsham
A10
Stradsett
Beachamwell
South
Pickenham
Ashill
Cranworth
Southburgh
Reymerston
Downham
Market
Bexwell
Crimplesham
Boughton
Cockley
Cley
Saham
Hills
Ovington
Woodrising
Hardingham
Hingham
Hackford
14
Denver
West Dereham
Wereham
Oxborough
Gooderstone
B1077
Carbrooke
Wick
Fordham
Oxburgh Hall NT
Whittington
Great
Cressingham
Saham Toney
Watton
Deopham
St B
elph
Wretton
Stoke
Ferry
Little Cressingham
Griston
B1108
Little
Ellingham
Deopham
Green
Hilgay
TL
R Wissey
A134
Northwold
Merton
Rockland
St Peter
Ten Mile
Bank
B1106
Ickburgh
Caston
Great Ellingham
Hilgay Fen
B1386
Methwold Hythe
Methwold
Cranwich
Peddars Way
Thompson
Rockland
All Saints
Stow Bedon
Fen Street
Attleboro
Southery
Queens
Ground
B1112
Breckles
Lower Stow
Bedon
Shropham
Southery
Fens
Methwold Fens
Mundford
32
Great
Hockham
Feltwell
A1065
East Wretham
Eccles
Road
Banhan
Hockwold
Fens
Hockwold
cum Wilton
Weeting
Grime's
Graves
Thetford
Forest
Larling
Wilby
Littleport
A1101
Burnt Fen
Town
Street
Brandon
A134
Croxton
A11
Bridgham
East Harling
Kenninghall
Quidenham
B
North
6
7
8
9
0

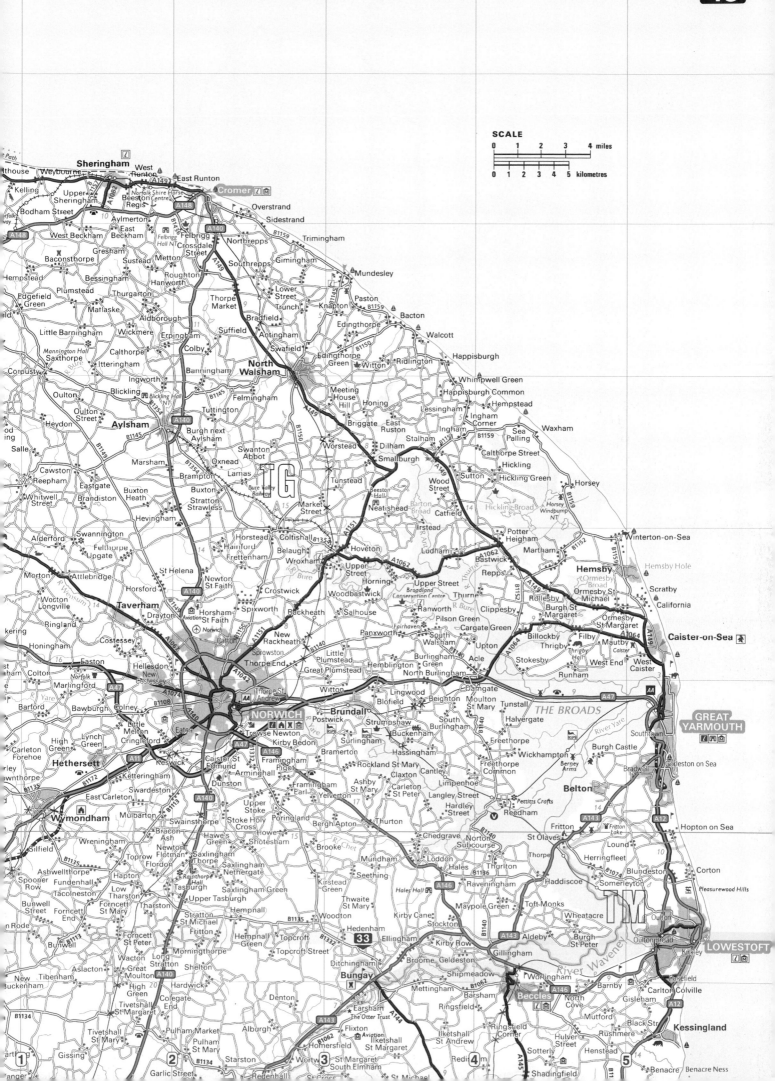

SCALE

0 1 2 3 4 miles

0 1 2 3 4 5 kilometres

Sheringham West Runton East Runton
Weybourne
Kelling
Upper Sheringham Beeston Regis Cromer
Bodham Street Aylmerton Overstrand
West Beckham East Beckham Sidestrand
Gresham Felbrigg Northrepps Trimingham
Baconsthorpe Sustead Metton
Hempstead Plumstead Thurgarton Roughton Hanworth Southrepps Gimingham Mundesley
Edgefield Green Matlaske Aldborough Thorpe Market Lower Street Knapton Paston Bacton
Little Barningham Erpingham Suffield Trunch
Saxthorpe Calthorpe Itteringham Colby Bradfield Edingthorpe Walcott
Corpusty Oulton Ingworth Banningham Antingham Swafield
Blickling North Walsham Edingthorpe Green Witton Ridlington Happisburgh
Heydon Felmingham Meeting House Hill Whimpwell Green
Aylsham Tuttington Honing Happisburgh Common
Whitwell Street Burgh next Aylsham Briggate Lessingham Hempstead
Cawston Eastgate Brandiston Swanton Abbot East Ruston Ingham Ingham Corner Sea Palling Waxham
Reepham Buxton Heath Oxnead Lamas Worstead Stalham Calthorpe Street
Salle Alderford Buxton Dilham Smallburgh Hickling Hickling Green Horsey
Felthorpe Stratton Strawless Market Street Wood Street Sutton
Swannington Upgate Hevingham Tunstead Beeston Hall Neatishead Barton Broad Catfield Hickling Broad
Morton Attlebridge St Helena Horstead Coltishall Irstead Potter Heigham Winterton-on-Sea
Wootton Longville Horsford Hautbois Frettenham Belaugh Hoveton Ludham Bastwick Martham
Ringland St Faith Newton Wroxham Upper Street Horning Repps Hemsby
Taverham Drayton Crostwick Woodbastwick Upper Street Thurne Clippesby Ormesby St Michael Scratby
Honingham Costessey Spixworth Rackheath Salhouse Ranworth Pilson Green Rollesby Ormesby St Margaret California
Easton Hellesdon New Rackheath Panxworth Cargate Green Burgh St Margaret Caister-on-Sea
Colton Marlingford New Costessey Catton Sprowston Thorpe End South Walsham Upton Billockby Filby Mautby
Bawburgh Colney Norwich Thorpe St Andrew Little Plumstead Hemblington Burlingham Green Acle Thrigby Stokesby West End West Caister
Barford Keswick Caister St Edmund Witton North Burlingham Runham
Little Melton Cringleford NORWICH Blofield Damgate THE BROADS
Carleton Forehoe High Green Eaton Brundall Beighton Moulton St Mary Tunstall
Hethersett Lynch Green Trowse Newton Postwick Strumpshaw South Burlingham Halvergate GREAT YARMOUTH
Ketteringham Kirby Bedon Surlingham Buckenham Freethorpe Southtown
Cranworthorpe East Carleton Armingham Bramerton Hassingham Wickhampton Burgh Castle Gorleston on Sea
Wymondham Swardeston Dunston Framingham Pigot Rockland St Mary Cantley Freethorpe Common Berney Arms Bradwell
Silfield Mulbarton Framingham Earl Ashby St Mary Claxton Limpenhoe Belton
Wreningham Bracon Ash Newton Flotman Yelverton Carleton St Peter Langley Street Hardley Street Reedham Pettitts Crafts
Ashwellthorpe Hapton Toprow Flordon Upper Stoke Howe Thurton Fritton Fritton Lake Hopton on Sea
Spooner Row Fundenhall Tacolneston Swainsthorpe Stoke Holy Cross Poringland Bergh Apton Chedgrave Norton Subcourse St Olaves Lound Blundeston Corton
Bunwell Street Rainthorpe Hall Saxlingham Nethergate Brooke Mundham Loddon Hales Thurlton Thorpe Herringfleet Somerleyton Pleasurewood Hills
Tasburgh Saxlingham Green Seething Ravingham Haddiscoe Oulton
Forncett St Mary Upper Tasburgh Hempnall Thwaite St Mary Kirby Cane Aldeby Burgh St Peter Wheatacre Oulton Broad
Bunwell Tharston Hempnall Green Woodton Stockton Maypole Green Toft Monks LOWESTOFT
New Buckenham Forncett End Stratton St Michael Hedenham Ellingham Kirby Row Gillingham Aldeby Carlton Colville
Tibenham Long Stratton Fritton Topcroft Ditchingham Broome Geldeston Barnby Gisleham
Aslacton Great Moulton Shelton Topcroft Street Bungay Shipmeadow Worlingham North Cove Black Str
Wacton Hardwick Morningthorpe Mettingham Barsham Beccles Mutford Kessingland
Tivetshall St Margaret Colegate End Denton Bunwell Redenhall Earsham The Otter Trust Ringsfield Ringsfield Corner Hulver Street Henstead
Tivetshall St Mary Pulham Market Alburgh Flixton Ilketshall St Andrew Sotterley Rushmere Benacre Benacre Ness
Gissing Pulham St Mary Homersfield Ilketshall St Margaret Redi Shadingfield
Garlic Street Starston St Margaret South Elmham St Michael
Redenhall Wortwell

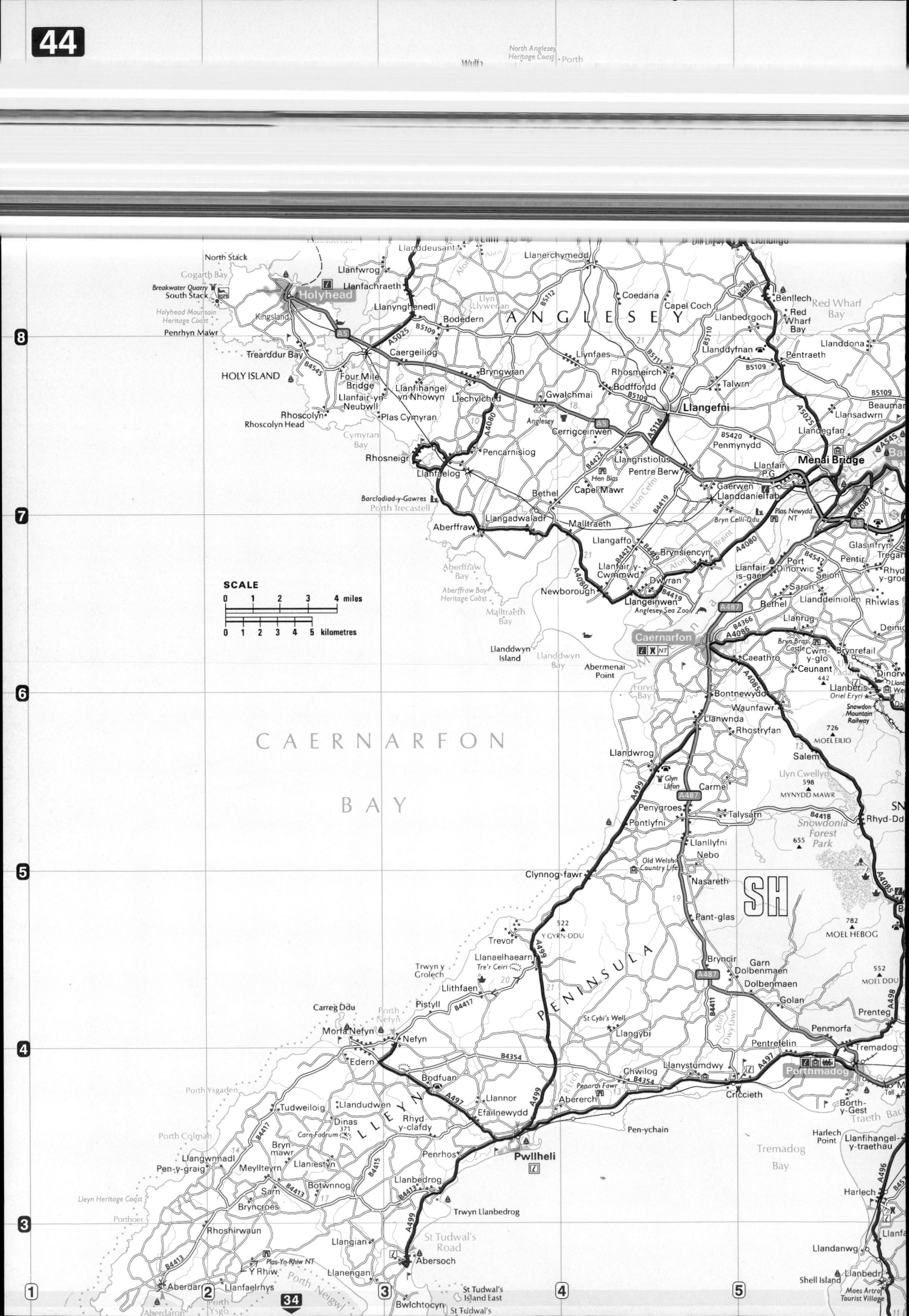

North Anglesey
Heritage Coast · Porth
Wulfa
Llandeusant
Dili Lligwy · Llanlingo
Llanerchymedd
Llanfwrog
North Stack
Gogarth Bay
Llanfachraeth
Coedana
Capel Coch
Benllech
Breakwater Quarry
South Stack
Holyhead
Llanynghenedl
Red Wharf
Bay
Llanbedrgoch
Red Wharf Bay
Holyhead Mountain
Heritage Coast
Kingsland
Bodedern
A N G L E S E Y
Llanddyfnan
Llanddona
Bryngwran
Llynfaes
Rhosmeirch
Bodffordd
Talwrn
Pentraeth
Trearddur Bay
HOLY ISLAND
Four Mile
Bridge
Gwalchmai
Llangefni
Beaumar
Llanfihangel
yn Nhowyn
Llechylched
Llansadwrn
Llanfair -yn-
Neubwll
Llandegfan
Plas Cymyran
Anglesey
Penmynydd
Menai Bridge
Rhoscolyn
Cerrigceinwen
Llanfair
P.G.
Bar
Rhoscolyn Head
Cymyran
Bay
Pencarnisiog
Langristiolus
Pentre Berw
Glasinfryn
Tregar
Rhosneigr
Llangristiolus
Hen Blas
Gaerwen
Llanddaniel fab
Port
Dinorwic
Pentir
Rhyd
y-groe
Llanfaelog
Bethel
Capel Mawr
Plas Newydd
NT
Seion
Barclodiad-y-Gawres
Llangadwaladr
Malltraeth
Bryn Celli-Ddu
Bethel
Deinio
Porth Trecastell
Aberffraw
Llangaffo
Brynsiencyn
Llanfair-y-
Cwmmwd
Llanrug
Rhiwlas
Aberffraw
Bay
Llangeinwen
Dwyran
Llanddeiniolen
Aberffraw Bay
Heritage Coast
Newborough
Port
is-gaer
Saron
Bryn Bras
Castle
Cwm-
y-glo
Brynrefail
Malltraeth
Bay
Langeinwen
Anglesey Sea Zoo
Caernarfon
Caeathro
Ceunant
Dinorw
SCALE
Llanddwyn
Island
Llanddwyn
Bay
Abermenai
Point
Bontnewydd
Llanberis
Oriel Eryri
We
0 1 2 3 4 miles
0 1 2 3 4 5 kilometres
Foryd
Bay
Waunfawr
Snowdon
Mountain
Railway
Llanddwyn
Island
8
7
6
5
4
3
Llanwnda
Rhostryfan
726
MOEL EILIO
C A E R N A R F O N
Llandwrog
Glyn
Llifon
Salem
Llyn Cwellyn
598
B A Y
Carmel
MYNYDD MAWR
Penygroes
13
Pontlyfni
Talysarn
Rhyd-Dd
B4418
Snowdonia
Forest
Park
655
Clynnog-fawr
Old Welsh
Country Life
Llanllyfni
Nebo
Nasareth
SH
Pant-glas
19
782
MOEL HEBOG
Trevor
522
Y GYRN-DDU
Bryncir
Garn
Dolbenmaen
552
MOEL DDU
Trwyn y
Grolech
Llanaelhaearn
Tre'r Ceiri
Dolbenmaen
Llithfaen
20
Golan
Pistyll
21
St Cybi's Well
Prenteg
Carreg Ddu
Porth
Nefyn
B4417
Llangybi
Penmorfa
Morfa Nefyn
Nefyn
St Tudwal's Well
Pentrefelin
Tremadog
Edern
B4354
Llanystumdwy
Porthmadog
Bodfuan
Chwilog
M
Porth Ysgaden
L L E Y N
A497
Llannor
Llanor
Penarth Fawr
Abererch
Criccieth
Borth-
y-Gest
Traeth Bach
Tudweiliog
Llandudwen
Efailnewydd
Pen-ychain
Tremadog
Bay
Harlech
Point
Llanfihangel-
y-traethau
Dinas
Carn Fadrun
Rhyd-
y-clafdy
Porth Colman
Bryn
mawr
Penrhos
Pwllheli
Langwnnadl
Llaniestyn
Meyllteyrn
Harlech
Pen-y-graig
Botwnnog
Llanbedrog
Lleyn Heritage Coast
Sarn
Bryncroes
Trwyn Llanbedrog
Llandanwg
Porthoer
Rhoshirwaun
Llangian
St Tudwal's
Road
Shell Island
Y Rhiw
Plas-Yn-Rhiw NT
Abersoch
Llandbedr
Maes Artro
Tourist Village
Aberdar
Llanfaelrhys
Llanengan
Porth Neigwl
St Tudwal's Island East
Aberdaron
Bwlchtocyn
St Tudwal's

1 2 34 3 4 5

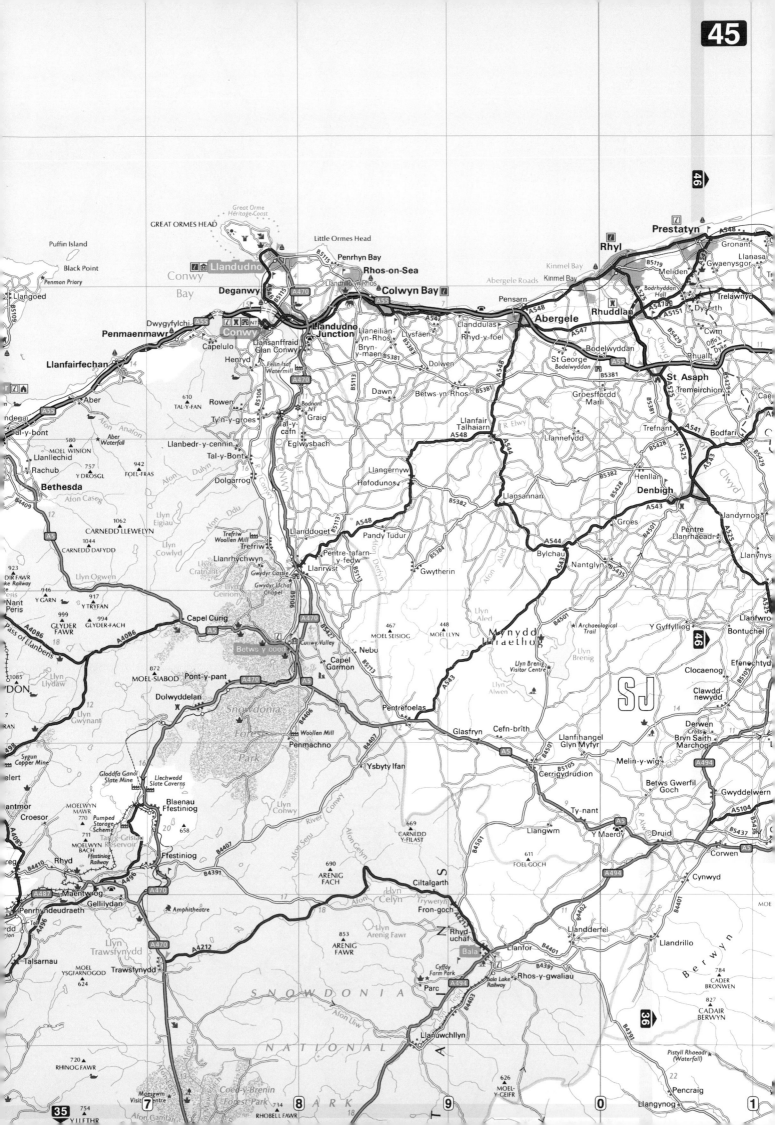

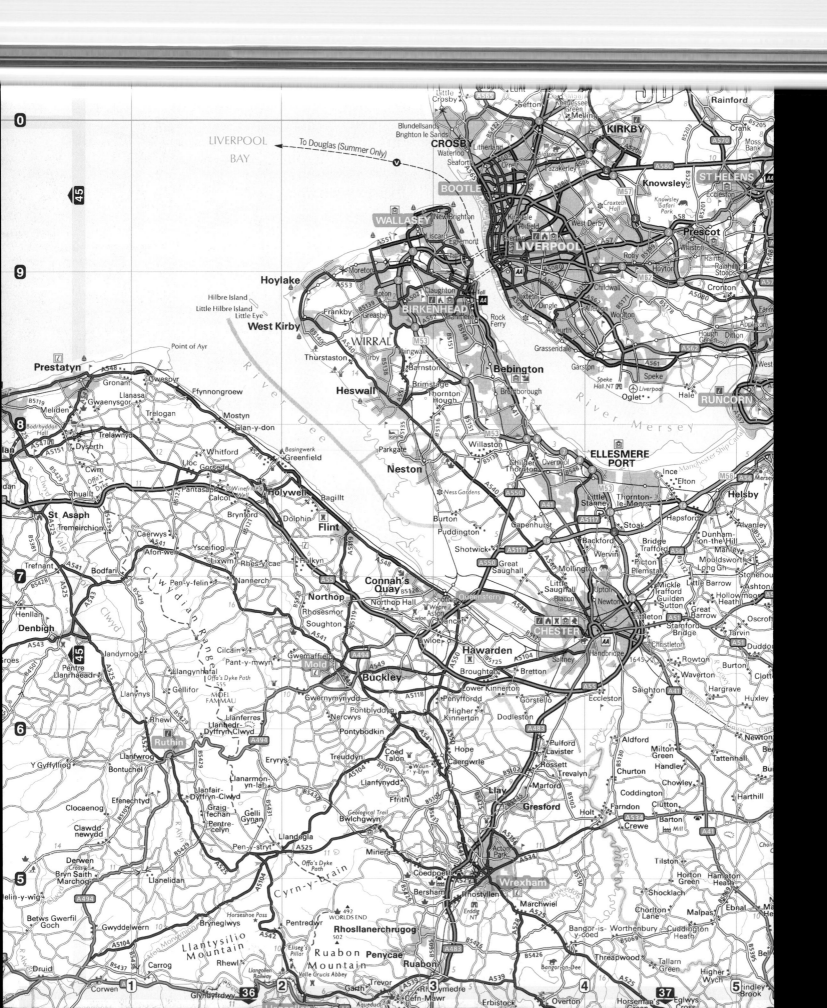

LIVERPOOL BAY

To Douglas (Summer Only)

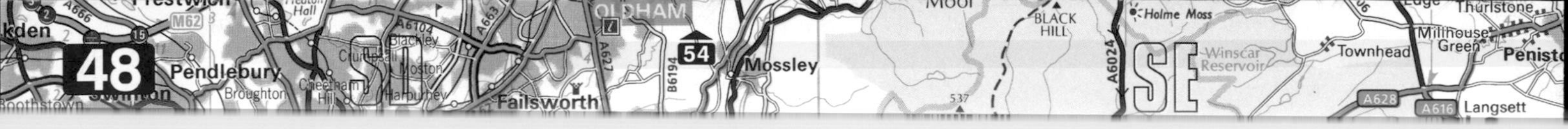

OLDHAM
Holme Moss
BLACK HILL
Winscar Reservoir
Townhead
Peniston
Mossley
A628 A616 Langsett

STOCKPORT
Brow
Rowarth
Brookhouses
THE PEAK
Ladybower Reservoir
Cheadle
Marple
Little Hayfield
Thornsett
Hayfield
Pennine Way
636
Edale
Altrincham
Gatley
Hazel Grove
Mellor
Birch Vale
New Mills
BROWN KNOLL
569
476
LOSE HILL
WIN HILL
HIGH NEB
Bowdon Hale
Dunham Town
High Lane
Disley
Mam Tor
Blue John Cavern
Hope
Aston
Thornhill
Bamford
Bramhall
Poynton
Furness Vale
Chinley
Whaley Bridge
Chapel-en-le-Frith
Speedwell Cavern
Peak Cavern
Castleton Peveril
Bradwell
Abney
Hath
Ashley
Rostherne
Bucklow Hill
Tatton Park NT
Styal
Woodford
Lyme Park
Taxal
Tunstead Milton
Cockyard
Sparrowpit
Peak Forest
Little Hucklow
Great Hucklow
Eyam Moor
Wilmslow
Mobberley
Knolls Green
Alderley Edge
Mottram St Andrew
Pott Shrigley
Kettleshulme
Fernilee
Combs
Dove Holes
HOB TOR
Wheston
Tideswell
Miller's Dale
Tunstead
Grindlow
Foolow
Eyam
Knutsford
Ollerton
Marthall
Watermill NT
Hare Hill NT
Prestbury
Rainow
SHINING TOR
Fairfield
Buxton
Wardlow
Stoney Middleton
Litton
Nether Alderley
Chelford
Monks Heath
Tytherington
Hurdsfield
Macclesfield
Poole's Cavern
Wormhill
Blackwell
Cressbrook
Little Longstone
Rowland
Lower Peover
Swan Green
Peover Heath
Copesthorne Hall
Siddington
Langley
Forest Chapel
Solomon's Temple
AXE EDGE
Taddington
Great Longstone
Ashford in the Water
Hassop
Pilsley
Goostrey
Twemlow Green
Withington
Warren
Gawsworth
Marton
Wildboarclough
Flash
Hollinsclough
Earl Sterndale
Chelmorton
Sheldon
Magpie Mine
Cranage
Holmes Chapel
Swettenham
North Rode
Bosley
Wincle
Danebridge
Allgreave
R Dove
Longnor
Crowdecote
Monyash
B5055
Over Haddon
Bakewell
Eaton
Key Green
Heaton
GUN HILL 373
Meerbrook
Upper Hulme
Brund
Sheen
Hartington
Heathcote
Youlgreave
Middleton
Birchover
Elton
Winster
Congleton
Hulme Walfield
Timbersbrook
Rushton Spencer
Newtown
Poolfold
Biddulph Grange NT
Rudyard Reservoir
Tittesworth Reservoir
Abbey Green
Thorncliff
Upper Elkstone
Warslow
Hulme End
Biggin
Brereton Green
Astbury
Little Moreton Hall NT
Biddulph
Lask Edge
Rudyard
Horton
Brindley Mill
Leek
Bradnop
Onecote
Wetton
Alstonefield
Alsop en le Dale
Longcliffe
Elworth
Sandbach
Wheelock
Mow Cop NT (folly)
Bradnop
Ford
Grindon
Hope
Milldale
Parwich
Brassing
Arclid Green
Brookhouse Green
Spen Gn
Butterton
Aldwark
Ballidon
Haslington
Alsager
Church Lawton
Kidsgrove
Latebrook
Brown Edge
Endon Bank
Longsdon
Endon
Stanley
Flint Mill
Cheddleton
Winkhill
Waterfall
Calton
Ilam
Thorpe
Tissington
Bradbourne
Carsing
Barthomley
Englesea-brook
Ravenscliffe
Wetley Rocks
Bagnall
Consall
Ipstones
Foxt
Cauldon
Waterhouses
Ilam Park NT
Fenny Bentley
Hognaston
Audley
Central Forest Park
STOKE-ON-TRENT
Burslem
Bucknall
Hulme
Cellarhead
Kingsley
Froghall
Whiston
Blore
Mapleton
Kniveton
Atlow
Betley
Wrinehill
Silverdale
May Bank
Hanley
Weston Coyney
Meir
Caverswall
Foxfield Light Railway
Dilhorne
Near Cotton
Stanton
Ramshorn
Wootton
Farley
Alton Towers
Swinscoe
Mayfield
Middle Mayfield
Ashbourne
Checkley
NEWCASTLE-UNDER-LYME
Keele
Madeley
Hartshill
Stoke-upon-Trent Fenton
Forsbrook
Mobberley
Cheadle
Oakamoor
Upper Ellastone
Ellastone
Church Mayfield
Clifton
Snelston
Bradley
Woore
Onneley
Butterton
Acton
Hanchurch
Trentham
Longton
Draycott in the Moors
Bradley in the Moors
Alton
Threapwood
Norbury
Roston
Yeaveley
Rodsley
Blackbrook
Hill Chorlton
Beech
Barlaston
Cresswell
Fulford
Upper Tean
Lower Tean
Checkley
Croxden
Hollington
Rocester
Denstone
Darley Moor
Wyaston
Osmaston
Pipe Aston
Whitmore
Maer
Chapel Chorlton
Tittensor
Knenhall
Fole
Marston Montgomery
Great Cubley
Little Cubley
Alkmonton
Longford
Loggerheads
Podmore
Cranberry
Bowers
Standon
Oulton
Moddershall
Hilderstone
Upper Leigh
Lower Leigh
Church Leigh
Withington
Upper Nobut
Stramshall
Somersal Herbert
Harehill
Boylestone
Broughton
Chatcull
Wetwood
Fairoak
Mill Meece
Yarnfield
Swynnerton
Stone
Garshall Green
Dod's Leigh
Uttoxeter
Doveridge
Church Broughton
Sugnall
Croxton
Slindon
Coldmeece
Milwich
Field
Bramshall
Sudbury
Scropton
Hatton
Bishop's
Aston
Frodswell
Birch Cross

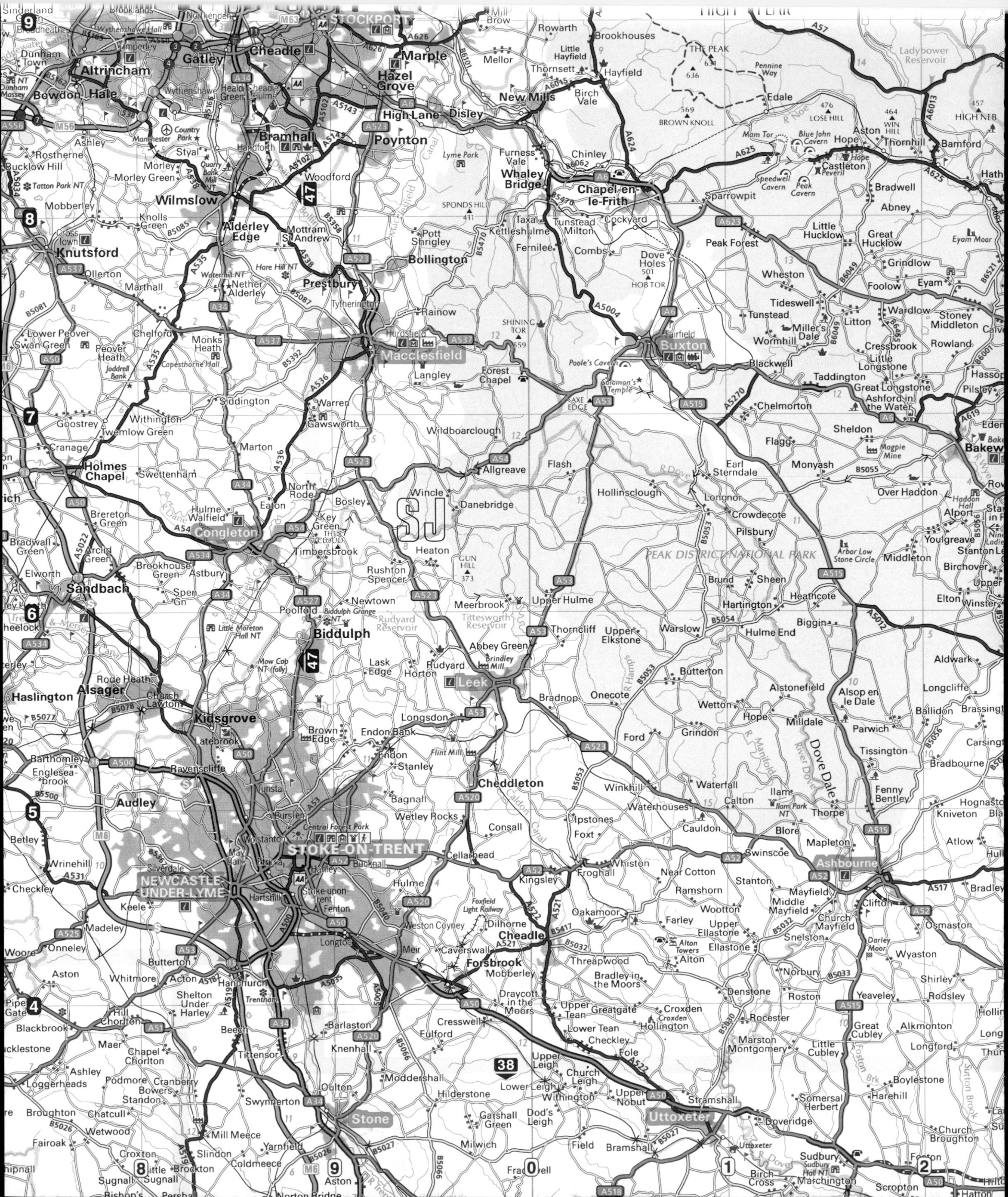

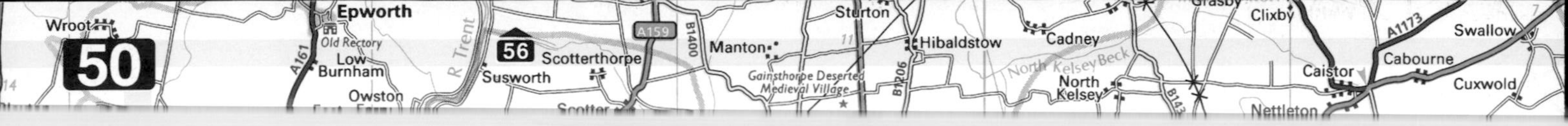

50
Epworth
56
Scotterthorpe
Hibaldstow
Caistor
Cabourne
Swallow
Cuxwold
Nettleton

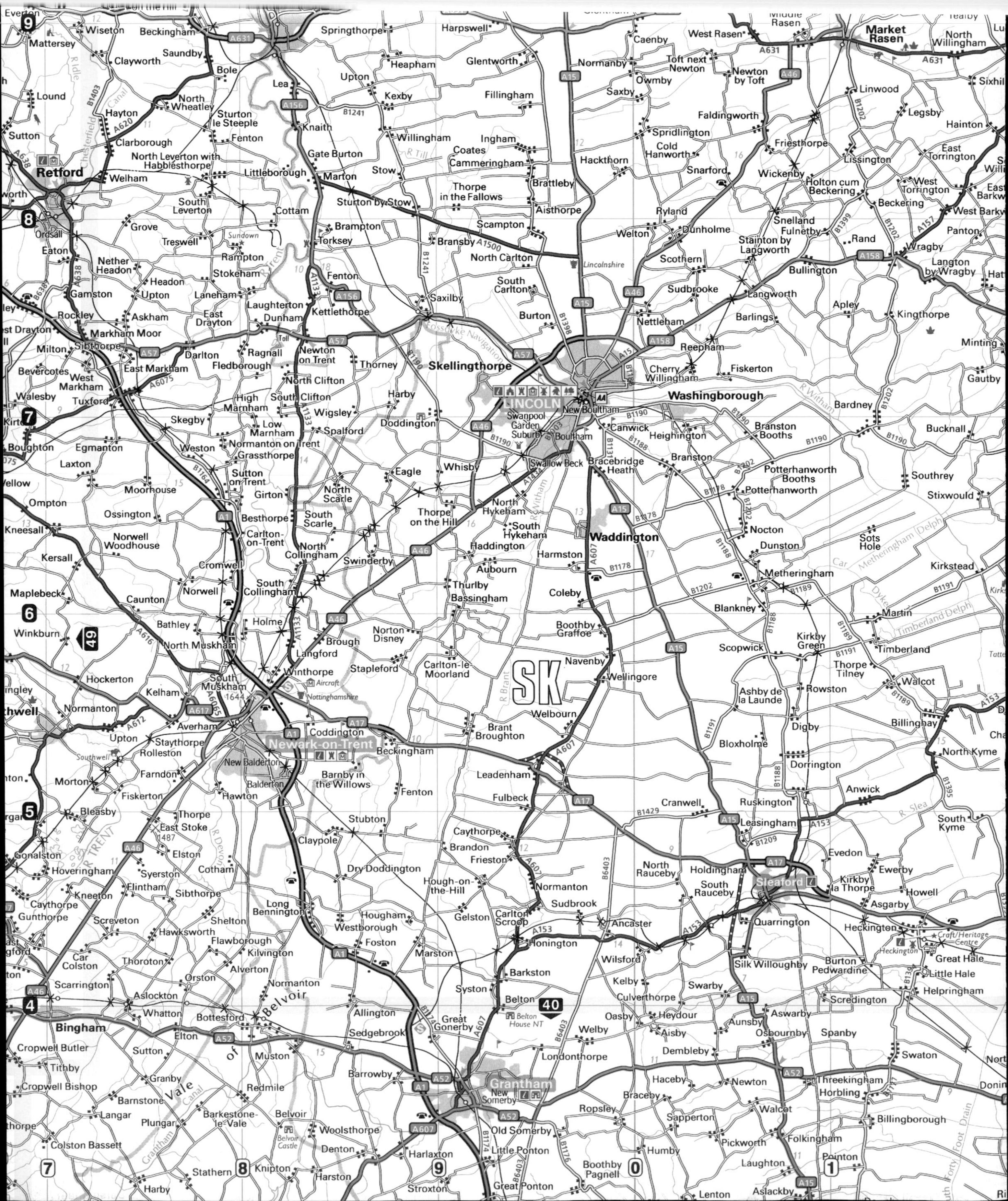

Retford
Market Rasen
Skellingthorpe
LINCOLN
Washingborough
Waddington
SK
Newark-on-Trent
Sleaford
Grantham
Bingham
Vale of Belvoir
49
40
Gainsborough
Tuxford
Metheringham
Saxilby
North Hykeham
Bracebridge Heath
Long Bennington
Ancaster
Heckington
Belton House NT

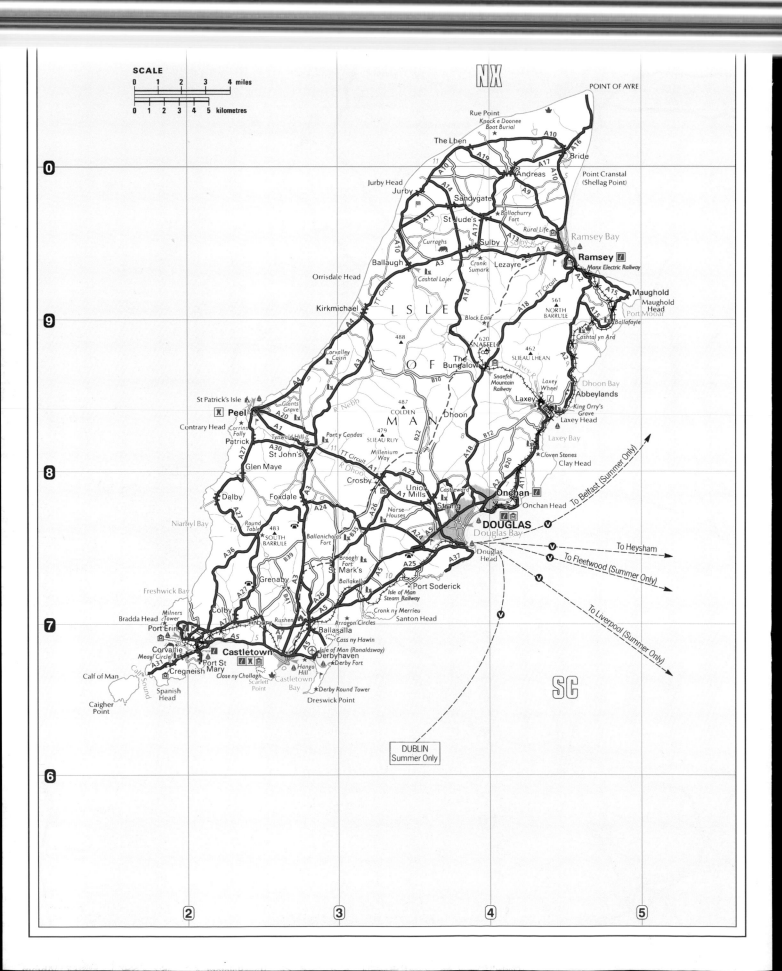

SCALE

0 1 2 3 4 miles

0 1 2 3 4 5 kilometres

NX

POINT OF AYRE

Rue Point

Knock e Doonee
Boat Burial

The Lhen

A10

A16

Bride

A19

A17

A10

Point Cranstal
(Shellag Point)

Jurby Head

Jurby

A14

Andreas

A9

Sandygate

A13

St Jude's

Ballachurry
Fort

Rural Life

Curraghs

A13

Sulby

Sulby

A3

Ramsey Bay

A10

Ballaugh

A3

Cronk
Sumark

Lezayre

Ramsey

Manx Electric Railway

Orrisdale Head

Cashtal Lajer

A14

A2

Maughold

Maughold
Head

A15

Kirkmichael

ISLE

A18

561
NORTH
BARRULE

Port Mooar

Cashtal yn Ard

Ballafayle

Block Eary

TT Circuit

488

OF

620
SNAEFELL

462
SLIEAU LHEAN

A9

St Patrick's Isle

Corvalley
Cairn

A4

The
Bungalow

Snaefell
Mountain
Railway

Laxey R

Dhoon Bay

Peel

Giants
Grave

A20

A9

MAN

B10

487
COLDEN

Laxey
Wheel

Laxey

Abbeylands

King Orry's
Grave

Laxey Head

Contrary Head

Corrins
Folly

Tynwald Hill

Port y Candas

479
SLIEAU RUY

B22

Dhoon

B12

Laxey Bay

To Belfast (Summer Only)

Patrick

A27

A30

St John's

A1

Millenium
Way

A18

Cloven Stones

Clay Head

Glen Maye

R Dhoo

TT Circuit

A1

A23

Crosby

Union
Mills

B20

A11

Dalby

Foxdale

A3

A26

Norse
Houses

Castleward

Strang

Onchan

Onchan Head

Niarbyl Bay

A27

Round
Table

16

483
SOUTH
BARRULE

B39

Ballanicholas
Fort

A5

A24

DOUGLAS

Douglas Bay

To Heysham

A36

Broogh
Fort

A5

A25

To Fleetwood (Summer Only)

Freshwick Bay

Grenaby

A27

A3

B41

St Mark's

Ballakell

A26

Isle of Man
Steam Railway

Port Soderick

Douglas
Head

To Liverpool (Summer Only)

Colby

A5

Cronk ny Merriu

Santon Head

Bradda Head

Milners
Tower

Port Erin

A7

Rushen

Arragon
Circles

A5

Cass ny Hawin

Ballasalla

SC

Corvalie

A31

A5

A7

Ballabeg

Isle of Man (Ronaldsway)

Meayl Circles

Castletown

Port St
Mary

Derbyhaven

Derby Fort

Calf of Man

Cregneish

Close ny Chollagh

Hango
Hill

Scarlett
Point

Castletown
Bay

Caigher
Point

Spanish
Head

Derby Round Tower

Dreswick Point

DUBLIN
Summer Only

0

9

8

7

6

2   3   4   5

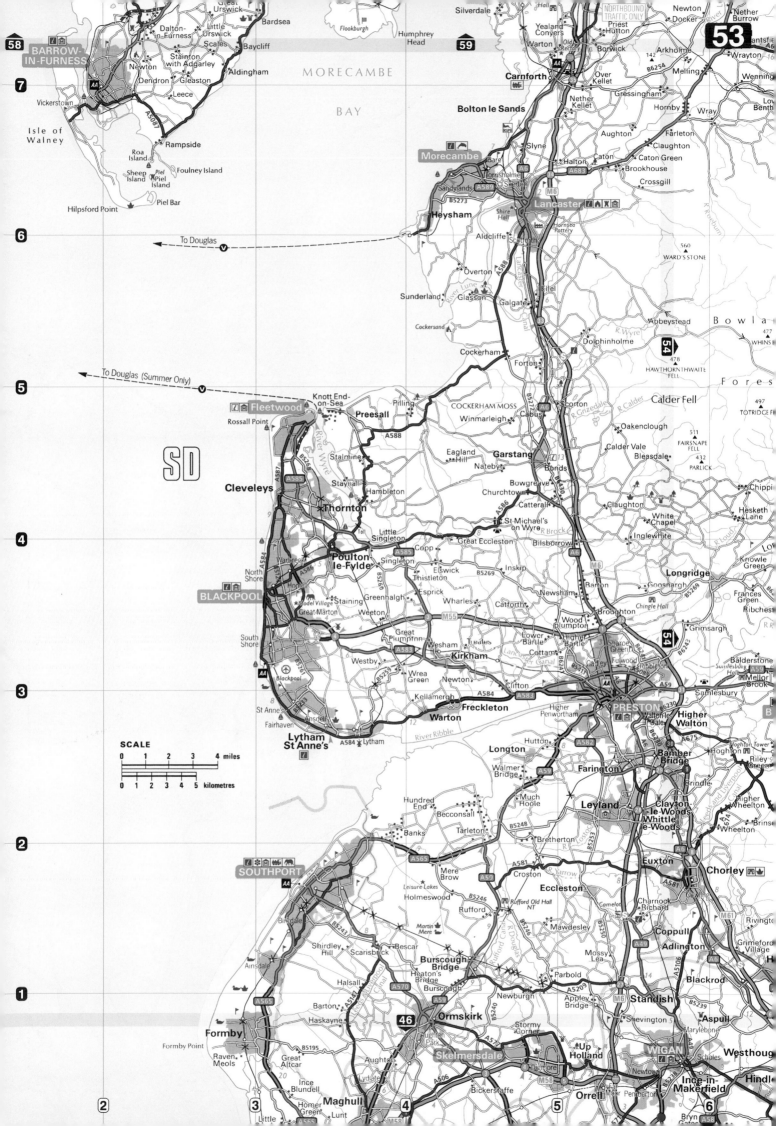

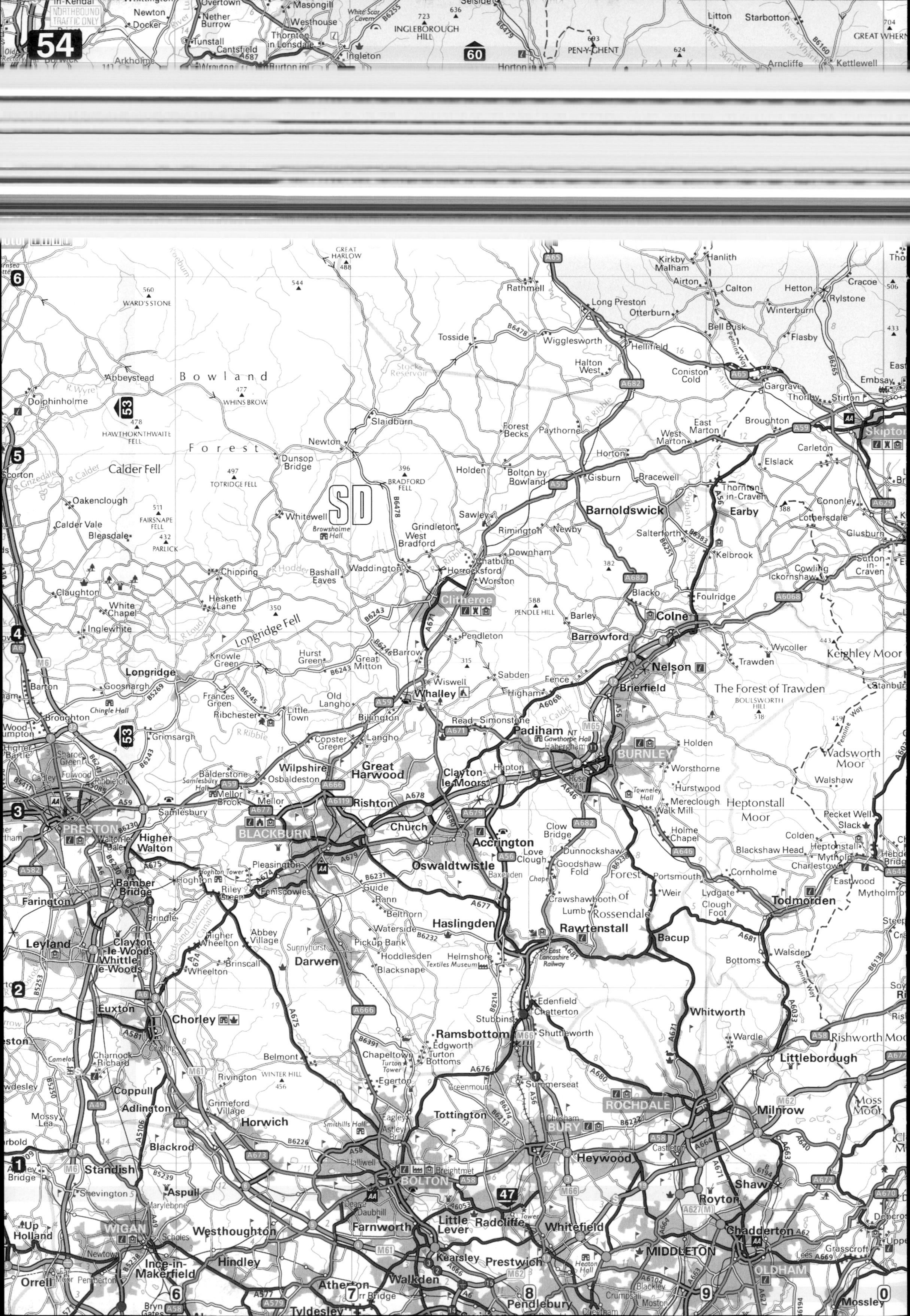

54
60
Newton
Docker
Nether Burrow
Tunstall
Cantsfield
Arkholme
Masongill
Westhouse
Thornton in Lonsdale
Ingleton
White Scar Cavern
INGLEBOROUGH HILL
723
636
PEN-Y-GHENT
693
Horton
Litton
Starbotton
624
Arncliffe
Kettlewell
GREAT WHERNSIDE
704
NORTHBOUND TRAFFIC ONLY
6
5
4
3
2
1
GREAT HARLOW
488
560
WARD'S STONE
544
Abbeystead
Bowland
Forest
477
WHINS BROW
Dolphinholme
53
478
HAWTHORNTHWAITE FELL
Calder Fell
497
TOTRIDGE FELL
Dunsop Bridge
Newton
Slaidburn
396
BRADFORD FELL
SD
B6478
Whitewell
Browsholme Hall
Oakenclough
Calder Vale
Bleasdale
511
FAIRSNAPE FELL
432
PARLICK
Chipping
Claughton
White Chapel
Inglewhite
Hesketh Lane
350
Longridge Fell
Longridge
Knowle Green
Hurst Green
Great Mitton
Goosnargh
Chingle Hall
Barton
Broughton
Frances Green
Ribchester
Little Town
Grimsargh
Bashall Eaves
Waddington
Grindleton
West Bradford
Rathmell
Tosside
Stocks Reservoir
Wigglesworth
Halton West
Long Preston
Otterburn
Hellifield
Kirkby Malham
Airton
Hanlith
Calton
Hetton
Cracoe
Rylstone
Winterburn
Bell Busk
Flasby
Coniston Cold
Gargrave
Thorlby
Stirton
Embsay
Skipton
Broughton
East Marton
West Marton
Carleton
Elslack
Forest Becks
Paythorne
Holden
Bolton by Bowland
Horton
Gisburn
Bracewell
Thornton-in-Craven
Earby
Cononley
Lothersdale
Glusburn
Sawley
Rimington
Newby
Barnoldswick
Salterforth
Kelbrook
Downham
Chatburn
Horrocksford
Worston
Clitheroe
588
PENDLE HILL
Barley
Blacko
Foulridge
Colne
Cowling
Ickornshaw
Sutton-in-Craven
Pendleton
Barrowford
Wycoller
Trawden
Keighley Moor
Nelson
Brierfield
The Forest of Trawden
BOULSWORTH HILL
518
Barrow
Wiswell
Whalley
315
Sabden
Fence
Higham
Old Langho
Billington
Read
Simonstone
Padiham
Gawthorpe Hall
Habergham
Burnley
Holden
Worsthorne
Wadsworth Moor
Walshaw
Hurstwood
Mereclough
Walk Mill
Heptonstall Moor
Pecket Well
Slack
Holme Chapel
Colden
Heptonstall
Mytholm
Charlestown
Blackshaw Head
Cornholme
Eastwood
Copster Green
Langho
Wilpshire
Osbaldeston
Great Harwood
Clayton-le-Moors
Hapton
Rose Hill
Balderstone
Samlesbury Hall
Mellor Brook
Mellor
Samlesbury
Rishton
Church
Accrington
Clow Bridge
Dunnockshaw
Love Clough
Goodshaw Fold
Forest of Rossendale
Crawshawbooth
Lumb
Portsmouth
Weir
Lydgate
Clough Foot
Todmorden
Baxenden
Oswaldtwistle
Blackburn
Preston
Fulwood
Ribbleton
Cadley
Sharoe Green
Higher Walton
Walton-le-Dale
Pleasington
Hoghton
Hoghton Tower
Riley Green
Feniscowles
Guide
Rann
Belthorn
Bamber Bridge
Farington
Brindle
Haslingden
Waterside
Pickup Bank
Hoddlesden
Blacksnape
Helmshore
Textiles Museum
Rawtenstall
East Lancashire Railway
Bacup
Walsden
Bottoms
Leyland
Clayton-le-Woods
Whittle-le-Woods
Higher Wheelton
Abbey Village
Sunnyhurst
Darwen
Brinscall
Wheelton
Euxton
Chorley
Edenfield
Chatterton
Stubbins
Shuttleworth
Whitworth
Wardle
Littleborough
Rishworth Moor
Ramsbottom
Edgworth
Chapeltown
Turton Tower
Turton Bottoms
Egerton
Belmont
Charnock Richard
Camelot
Rivington
WINTER HILL
456
Coppull
Adlington
Grimeford Village
Horwich
Greenmount
Summerseat
Tottington
Rochdale
Milnrow
Moss Moor
Mossy Lea
Blackrod
Standish
Eagley
Astley Br
Smithills Hall
Bury
Chesham
Heywood
Castleton
Shaw
Halliwell
Breightmet
Bolton
47
Aspull
Shevington
Marylebone
Daubhill
Royton
Up Holland
Wigan
Westhoughton
Farnworth
Little Lever
Radcliffe
Whitefield
Chadderton
Grasscroft
Lees
Scholes
Newtown
Orrell
Pemberton
Ince-in-Makerfield
Hindley
Kearsley
Prestwich
Heaton Hall
Middleton
Oldham
Atherton
Walkden
Pendlebury
Blackley
Crumpsall
Moston
Mossley
Tyldesley
Bryn Gates
6
7
8
9
0

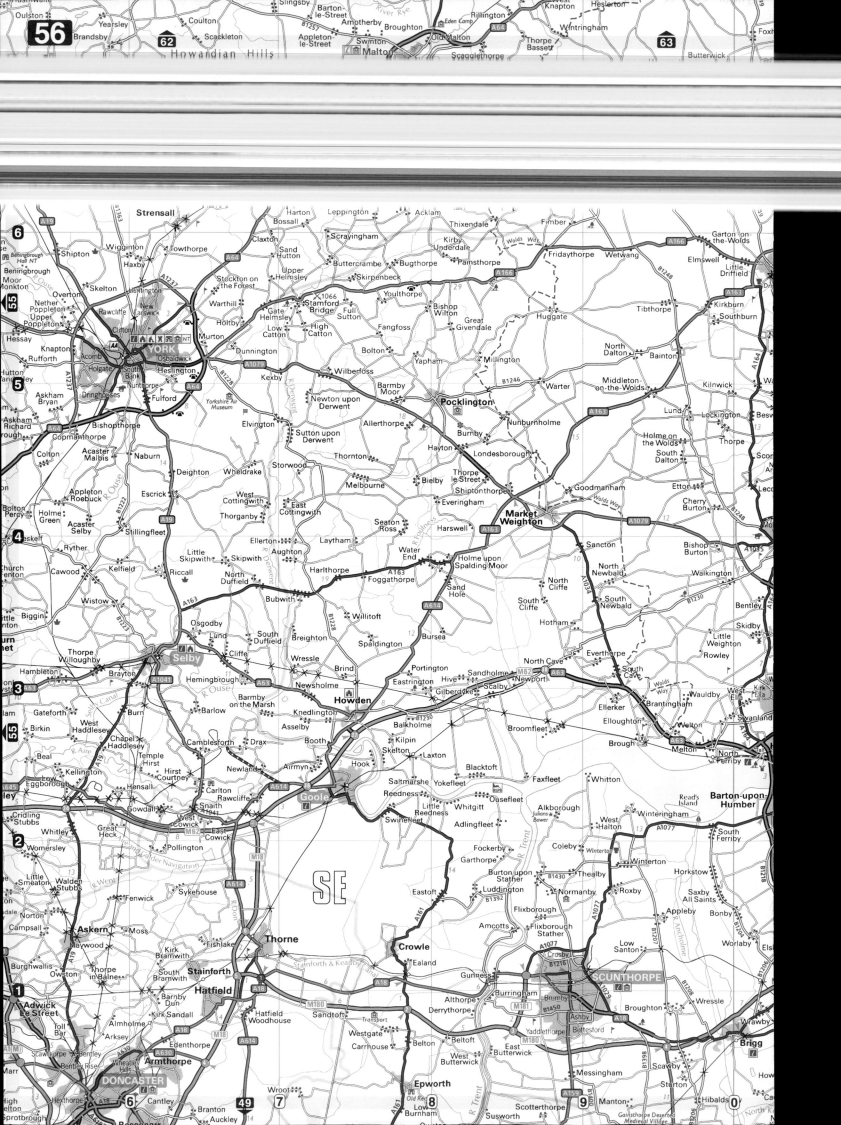

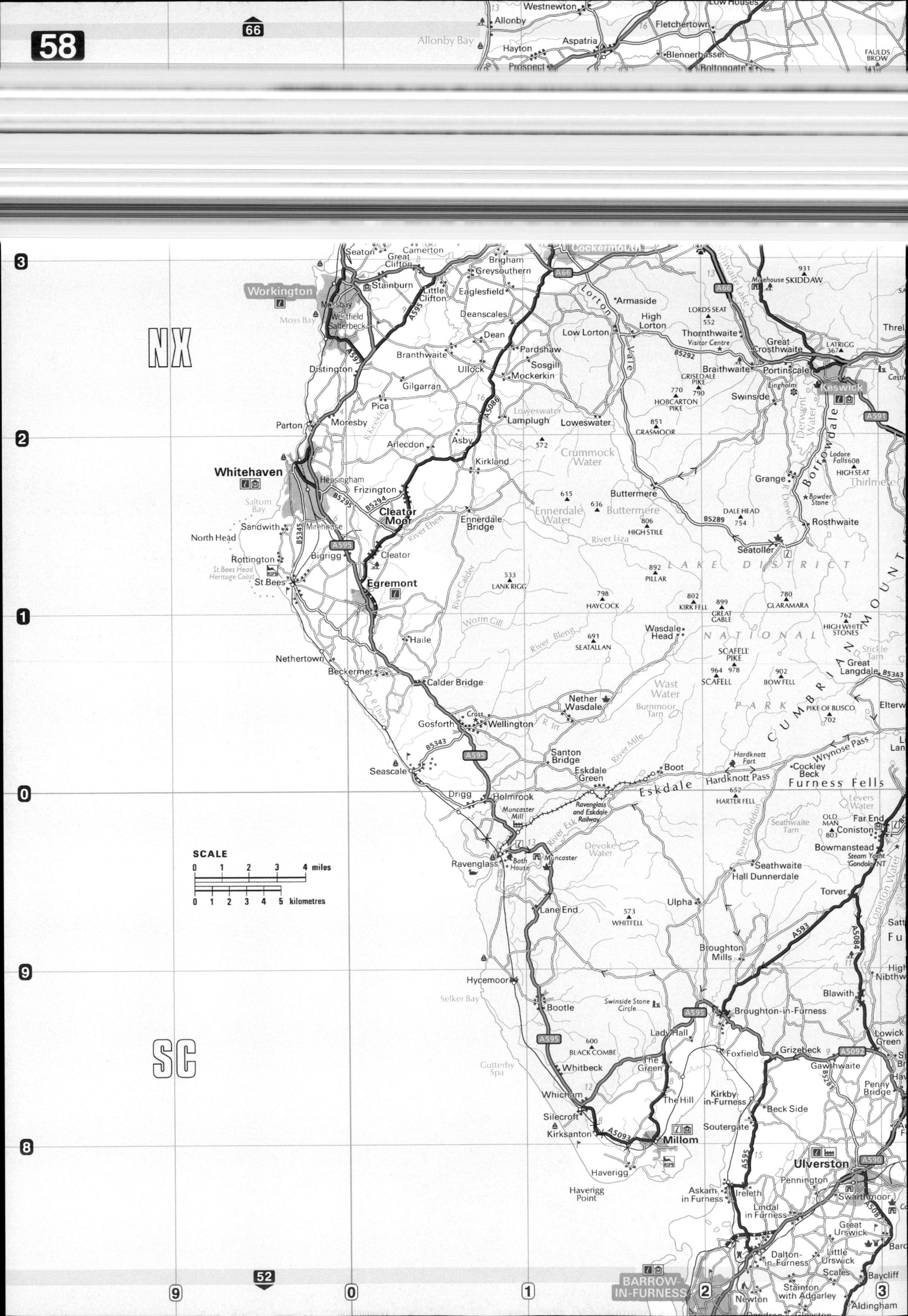

66

NX

SC

Workington
Moss Bay
Seaton
Great Clifton
Camerton
Stainburn
Little Clifton
Brigham
Greysouthen
Cockermouth
A66
Westnewton
Allonby
Allonby Bay
Hayton
Aspatria
Fletchertown
Blennerhasset
Prospect
Boltongate
FAULDS BROW
931
Mirehouse SKIDDAW
Threl
Westfield
Salterbeck
Distington
Eaglesfield
Deanscales
Dean
Pardshaw
Sosgill
Mockerkin
Armaside
High Lorton
Low Lorton
LORDS SEAT 552
Thornthwaite Visitor Centre
Great Crosthwaite
LATRIGG 367
A66
13
Branthwaite
Ullock
GRISEDALE PIKE 770
HOBCARTON PIKE 790
Braithwaite
Portinscale
Swinside
Keswick
A591
Gilgarran
Pica
Parton
Moresby
Arlecdon
Asby
Kirkland
Lamplugh
Loweswater
Loweswater
851
GRASMOOR
572
Crummock Water
Lingholm
Derwent Water
HIGH SEAT
Lodore Falls 608
A591
Whitehaven
Hensingham
Frizington
B5294
Cleator Moor
Ennerdale Bridge
Ennerdale Water
615
636
Buttermere
Buttermere
806
HIGH STILE
DALE HEAD 754
B5289
Grange
Bowder Stone
Thirlmere
Rosthwaite
Saltom Bay
B5295
Sandwith
Mirehouse
B5345
North Head
Bigrigg
Cleator
River Ehen
River Liza
PILLAR 892
Seatoller
LAKE DISTRICT
Rottington
St Bees Head Heritage Coast
St Bees
A595
Egremont
533
LANK RIGG
798
HAYCOCK
802
KIRK FELL
899
GREAT GABLE
780
GLARAMARA
762
HIGH WHITE STONES
Haile
River Calder
River Bleng
691
SEATALLAN
Wasdale Head
964 978
SCAFELL
SCAFELL PIKE
NATIONAL
Stickle Tarn
Great Langdale
B5343
Nethertown
Beckermet
Worm Gill
Wast Water
902
BOW FELL
PIKE OF BLISCO 702
Elterw
Lan
Calder Bridge
Cross
Nether Wasdale
Burnmoor Tarn
PARK
CUMBRIAN MOUNT
Gosforth
Wellington
River Irt
Santon Bridge
River Mite
Hardknott Fort
Wrynose Pass
Lan
La
B5343
Seascale
Eskdale Green
Boot
Hardknott Pass
Cockley Beck
Furness Fells
Drigg
Holmrook
Ravenglass and Eskdale Railway
Muncaster Mill
River Esk
Eskdale
652
HARTER FELL
Levers Water
Seathwaite Tarn
OLD MAN 803
Far End
Coniston
Ravenglass
Bath House
Muncaster
River Esk
13
Devoke Water
Seathwaite
Hall Dunnerdale
Bowmanstead
Steam Yacht Gondola NT
Coniston Water
Lane End
573
WHITFELL
Ulpha
Torver
A593
A5084
Fu
Satt
Broughton Mills
A593
Hycemoor
Selker Bay
Blawith
Lowick Green
High Nibthw
Bootle
Swinside Stone Circle
A595
Broughton-in-Furness
A595
BLACK COMBE 600
Lady Hall
Foxfield
Grizebeck
A5092
Gawthwaite
B5281
Penny Bridge
Whitbeck
The Green
Kirkby in-Furness
Beck Side
Whicham
Silecroft
Kirksanton
A5093
The Hill
Soutergate
Millom
Ulverston
A590
A595
Haverigg
Pennington
Askam in Furness
Ireleth
Lindal in Furness
Swarthmoor
Haverigg Point
Dalton-in-Furness
Little Urswick
Great Urswick
Bar
Scales
Baycliff
BARROW-IN-FURNESS
Stainton with Adgarley
Newton
Aldingham

SCALE
0 1 2 3 4 miles
0 1 2 3 4 5 kilometres

52

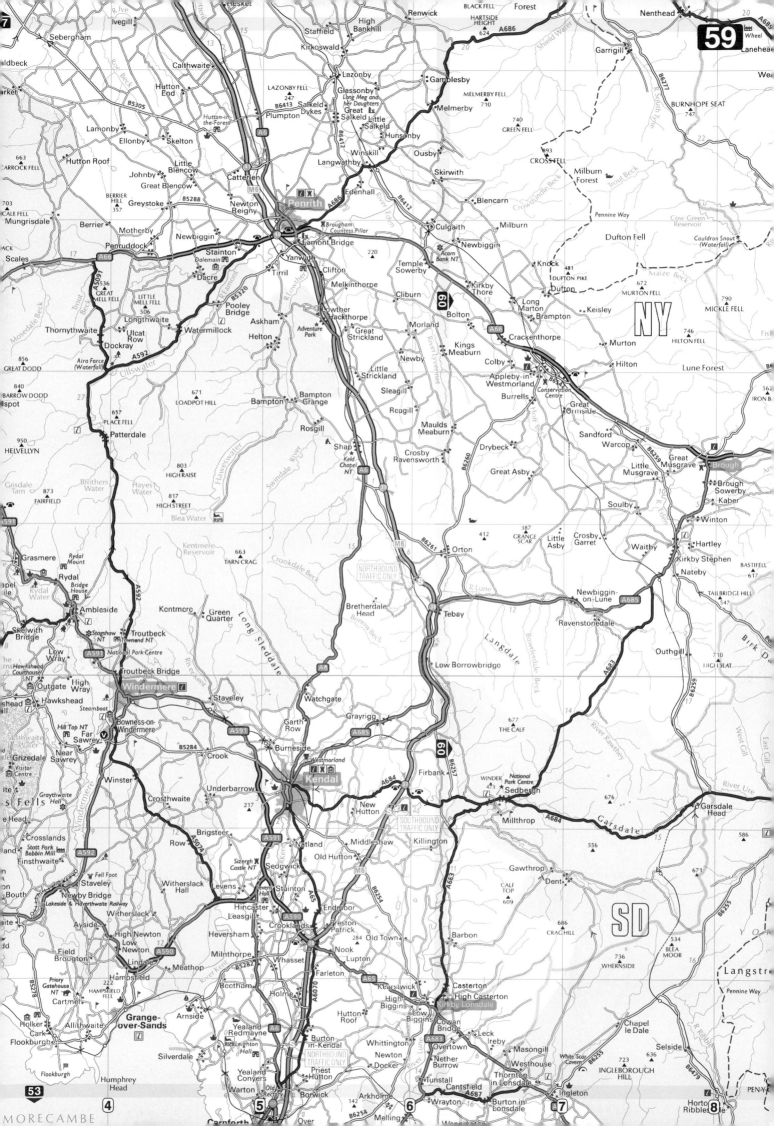

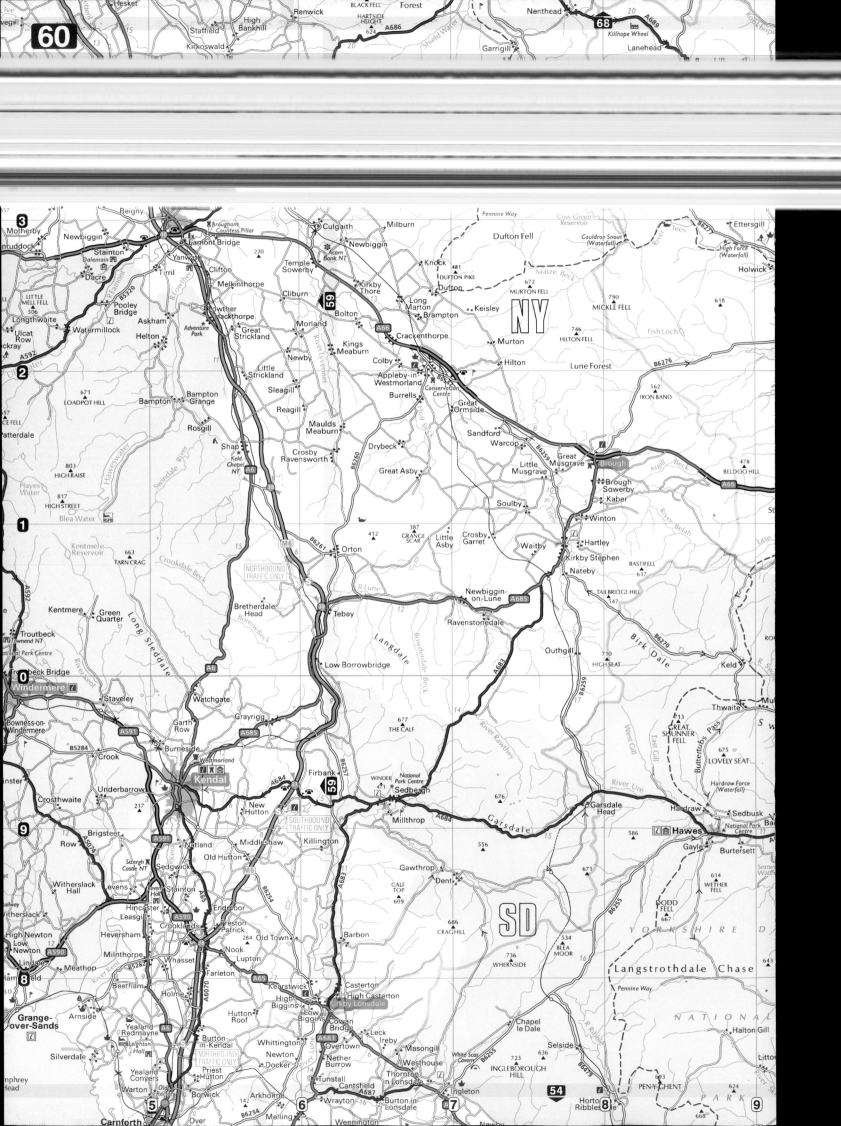

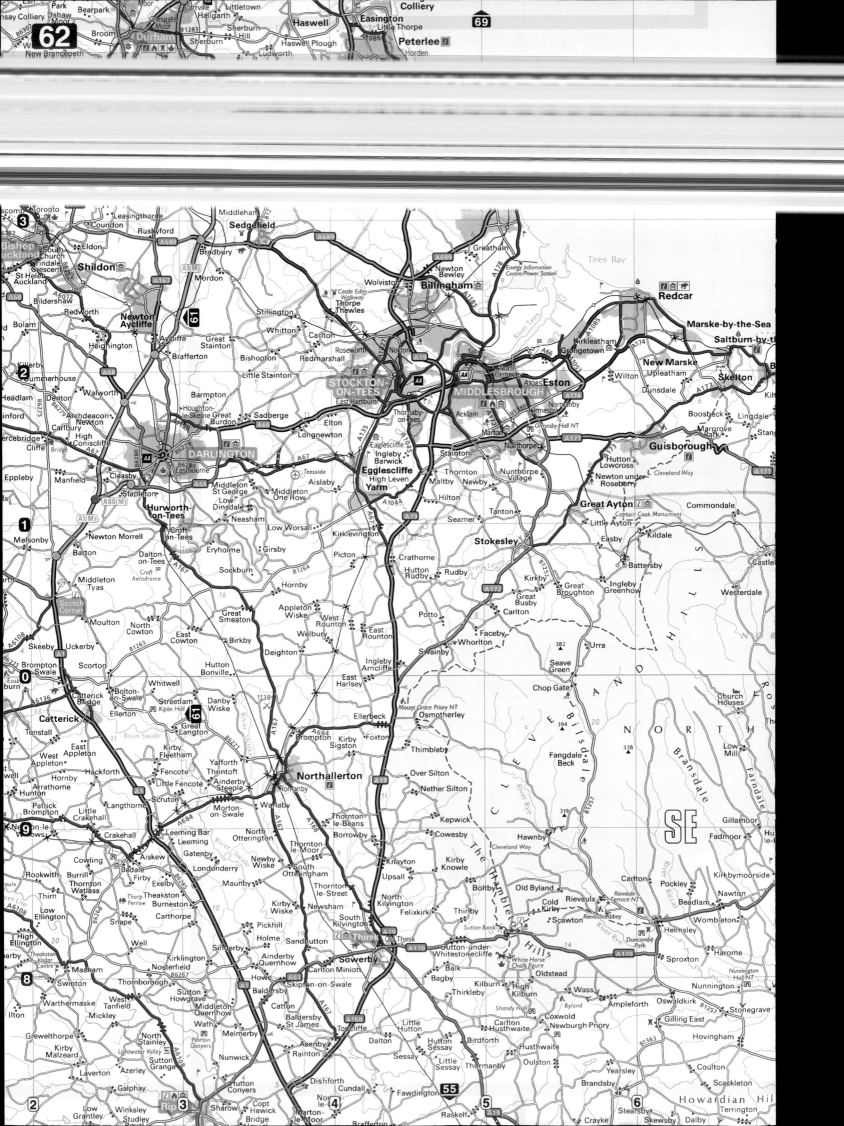

SCALE

0   1   2   3   4 miles

0 1 2 3 4 5 kilometres

Hummersea Scar

Loftus
Staithes
Easington
Hinderwell
Runswick
Goldsborough
Ellerby
Lythe
Scaling
B1266
A174
East Barnby
Sandsend
Mickleby
West Barnby
Dunsley
Whitby
Ugthorpe
Newholm
Saltwick Bay
North Yorkshire and Cleveland Heritage Coast
Overdale Wyke
Sandsend Wyke

The Moors Centre
301
A171
Ruswarp
Briggswath
Stainsacre
Aislaby
Sneaton
High Hawsker
Sleights
Ugglebarnby
Lealholm
Egton Dale
Iburndale
Ness Point or North Cheek
River Esk
Grosmont
Robin Hood's Bay
Glaisdale
Egton Bridge
Fylingthorpe
Robin Hood's Bay

YORKS MOORS
326
PIKE HILL
Goathland
Old Peak or South Cheek
Ravenscar
369
Wheeldale Roman Road
292
20
A171
Rosedale Abbey
Staintondale
290
Stape Riding
Hole of Horcum
Eller Beck
Harwood Dale
Hayburn Wyke
North Forest
North Yorkshire Moors Railway
Cloughton Wyke
Cloughton
Burniston
Cromer Point
Lastingham
Levisham
Bridestones (Rock formations)
Bickley
Broxa
Silpho
Cleveland Way
Spaunton
Lockton
239
Langdale End
Hackness
Suffield
Appleton-le-Moors
Cropton
North Riding Forest Park
Scalby
Wrelton
Aislaby
Middleton
Bee Dale
River Derwent
Sea Cut
Falsgrave
Scarborough
A170
Sinnington
13
Sawdon
Hutton Buscel
West Ayton
East Ayton
Oliver's Mount
Pickering
Wilton
Ebberston
Ruston
Wykeham
Seamer
Irton
Osgodby
AA
A165
Marton
Thornton Dale
Allerston
Brompton
B1261
Eastfield
Cayton
Cayton Bay
Normanby
Snainton
The Car
A170
17
A64
Lebberston
Gristhorpe
The Wyke
A1039
Kirby Misperton
Salton
Flamingo Land
Yedingham
Willerby
River Hertford
Folkton
Muston
Filey
Filey Brigg
Brawby
Great Barugh
Staxton
Flixton
A1039
Filey Bay
Great Habton
Knapton
Sherburn
Ganton
Hunmanby
A165
Scampston
East Heslerton
Potter Brompton
Reighton
Barton-le-Street
Amotherby
Rillington
West Knapton
West Heslerton
Fordon
B1249
Speeton
B1257
Broughton
Eden Camp
A64
Wintringham
Foxholes
Wold Newton
Burton Fleming
Buckton
Appleton-le-Street
A169
Bemp
Coneysthorpe
Swinton
Old Malton
Thorpe Bassett
Butterwick
Weaverthorpe
Grindale
Malton
8
Norton
Scagglethorpe
Settrington
Wolds Way
9
0
1
2
56
57
River Rye
River Derwent
B1258
B1248
B1229

TA

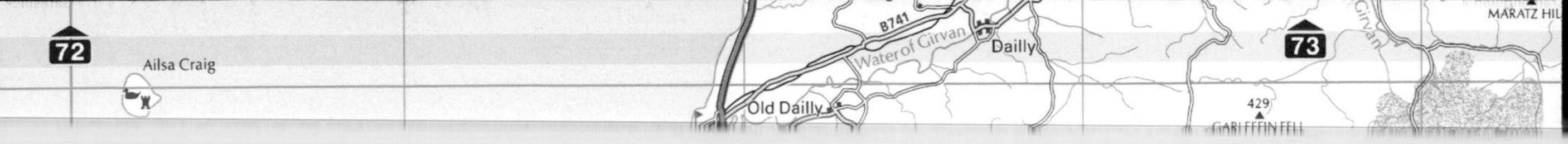

Ailsa Craig

Dailly
Old Dailly
MARATZ HILL
GARLEFFIN FELL

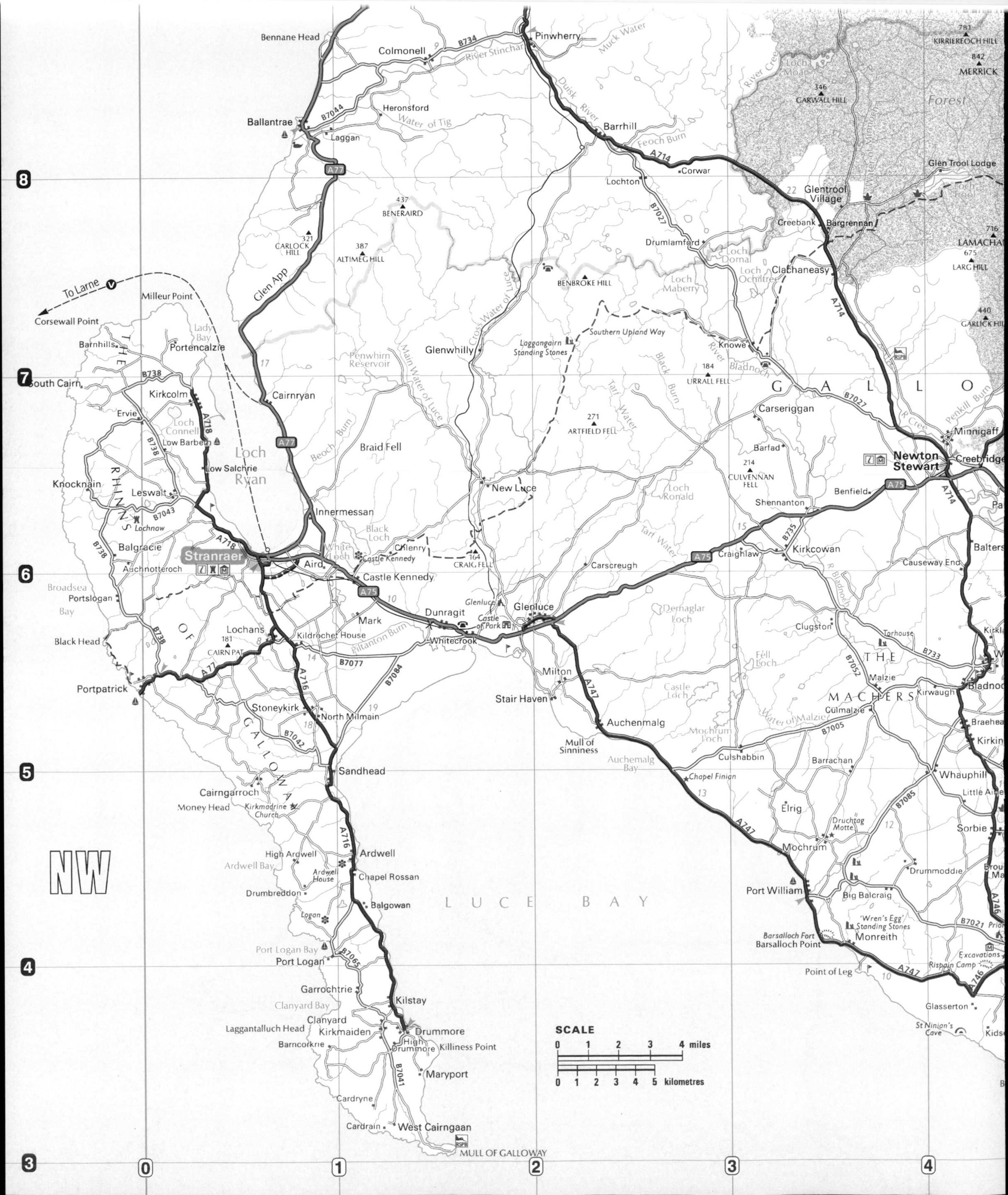

Bennane Head
Colmonell
B734
River Stinchar
Pinwherry
Muck Water
KIRRIEREOCH HILL 781
MERRICK 842
Heronsford
Water of Tig
Barrhill
River Cree
Loch Moan
CARWALL HILL 146
Forest
Ballantrae
B7044
Laggan
A77
A714
Corwar
Lochton
B7027
22 Glentrool Village
Glen Trool Lodge
Creebank
Bargrennan
LAMACHAN 716
LARG HILL 675
321 CARLOCK HILL
437 BENERAIRD
387 ALTIMEG HILL
Drumlamford
Loch Dornal
Loch Ochiltree
Clachaneasy
GARLICK HILL 440
Glen App
BENBROKE HILL
Loch Maberry
Laggangairn Standing Stones
Southern Upland Way
Knowe
River Bladnoch
GALLO
To Larne
Milleur Point
Corsewall Point
Lady Bay
Glenwhilly
Penwhirm Reservoir
Main Water of Luce
184 URRALL FELL
7
Barnhills
Portencalzie
17
Cairnryan
271 ARTFIELD FELL
Tarf Water
Black Burn
Carseriggan
B7027
Minnigaff
South Cairn
B738
Kirkcolm
Ervie
Loch Connell
Low Barbeth
A718
Low Salchrie
A77
Braid Fell
Beoch Burn
Loch Ryan
Barfad
214 CULVENNAN FELL
Newton Stewart
Creebridge
Knocknain
Leswalt
B7043
Lochnaw
New Luce
Loch Ronald
Shennanton
Benfield
A75
A714
Pa
Balgracie
A718
White Loch
Black Loch
Tarf Water
15
A75
Craighlaw
B735
Kirkcowan
Balters
Stranraer
Aird
A75
Chlenry
Castle Kennedy
Carscreugh
Causeway End
6
Broadsea
Auchnotteroch
10
Dunragit
Glenluce
164 CRAIG FELL
Demaglar Loch
Clugston
Tarhouse
B733
Kirk
Portslogan Bay
Lochans
181 CAIRN PAT
Kildrochet House
14
B7077
Whitecrook
Pilnanton Burn
B7084
Glenluce
Castle of Park
Fell Loch
Loch
B7052
THE MACHERS
Malzie
Kirwaugh
Bladnoc
W
Black Head
Stoneykirk
North Milmain
19
Milton
A747
Stair Haven
Mull of Sinniness
Auchenmalg
Castle Loch
Culmalzie
Braehea
Kirkin
Portpatrick
B7042
18
Sandhead
Mochrum Loch
Water of Malzie
B7005
Culshabbin
Barrachan
Whauphill
Little A
5
Cairngarroch
Money Head
Kirkmadrine Church
Auchenmalg Bay
13
Chapel Finian
Elrig
Druchtag Motte
B7085
12
Sorbie
NW
High Ardwell
Ardwell
Ardwell Bay
Ardwell House
Chapel Rossan
A716
A747
Mochrum
Drummoddie
Brou
Me
Drumbreddon
Balgowan
Logan
LUCE BAY
Port William
'Wren's Egg' Standing Stones
Monreith
B7021 Prior
A7
Port Logan Bay
Port Logan
B7065
Barsalloch Fort
Barsalloch Point
Excavations
Rispain Camp
A747
4
Garrochtrie
Kilstay
Point of Leg
10
A746
Clanyard Bay
Clanyard
Kirkmaiden
Drummore
High Drummore
Killiness Point
Glasserton
St Ninian's Cave
Kids
Laggantalluch Head
Barncorkrie
Maryport
B7041
Cardryne
Cardrain
West Cairngaan
MULL OF GALLOWAY

SCALE
0 1 2 3 4 miles
0 1 2 3 4 5 kilometres

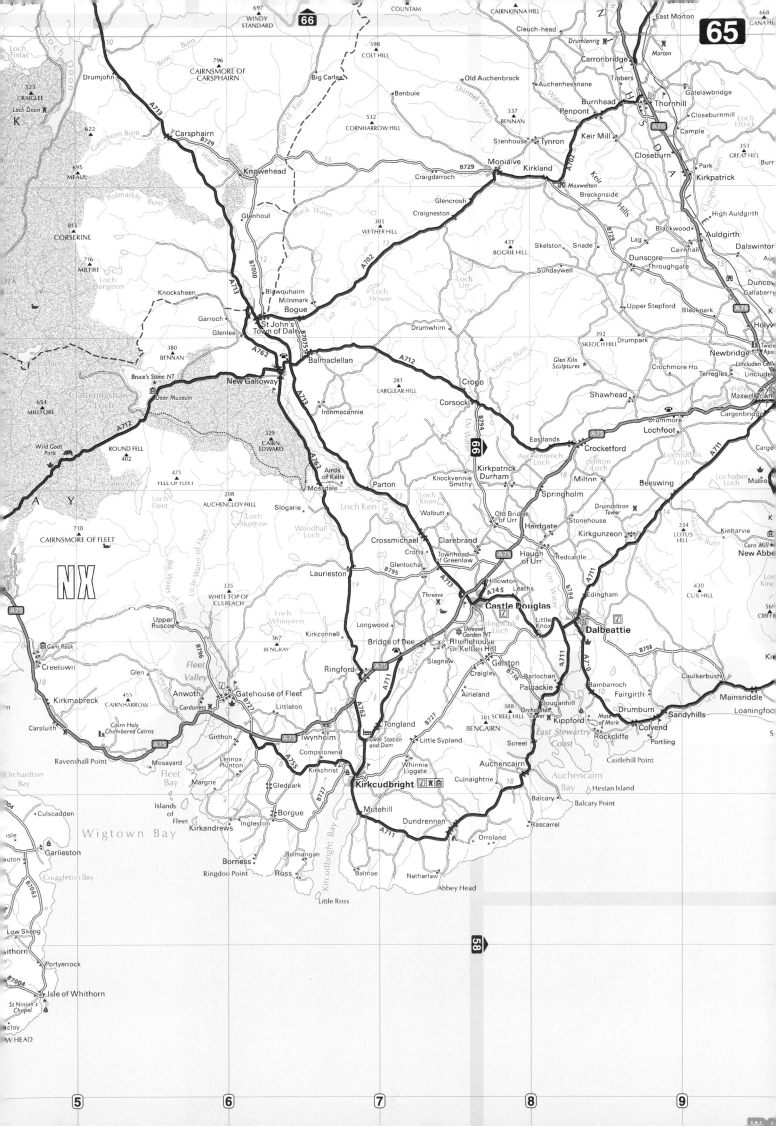

Pathhead • Mansfield • Afton Bridgend • Bankglen • New Cumnock • Upper Cairn • Kirkland • 74 • Kirkconnel • COCKER HILL 503 • Meikle Carco • Kirkland • Leadhills • March • 465 • Tweed's Well • Nether Howcleugh • Museum of Lead Mining • Wanlockhead Beam Engine • Wanlockhead 732 • Nunnerie 504 • A76

COUNTAM • CAIRNKINNA HILL 334 • Cleuch-head • Gateslack • East Morton • Kinnelhead • GANA HILL 668 • QUEENSBERRY 696 • Kinnelhead • Beattock • A7

697 WINDY STANDARD • 598 COLT HILL • Drumlanrig • Carronbridge • Morton • Gatelawbridge • Mitchellslacks • 512 • 399 • Lochwoo

0 • 796 CAIRNSMORE OF CARSPHAIRN • Big Carlae • Old Auchenbrack • Auchenhessnane • Burnhead • Thornhill • Closeburnmill • Loch Ettrick • St Ann's

B729 • Carsphairn • Benbuie • Shinnel Water • Burnhead • Penpont • A76 • Cample • 353 GREAT HILL • Burnfoot

537 CORNHARROW HILL • 337 BENNAN • Stenhouse • Tynron • Keir Mill • Closeburn • Kirkpatrick • Park • Kirkland • Courance • Grevrig

9 • Knowehead • Moniaive • B729 • Kirkland • A702 • Keir • Maxwelton • Breckonside • Closeburn • Ae • Townhead • Parkgate • Nethermill • A701

Glenhoul • Craigdarroch • Glencrosh • Kirkland • Hills • High Auldgirth • Ae Bridgend • 18 • Templar

B7000 • 532 • Glenhoul • Craigneston • 385 WETHER HILL • 65 • Skelston • Snade • Blackwood • Auldgirth • Dalswinton • Auchencairn • Shieldhill • Marjorieban

B713 • 12 • Blawquhairn • Milnmark • Bogue • A702 • 431 BOGRIE HILL • Sundaywell • Dunscore • Throughgate • Lag • Cairnhall • 15 • Duncow • Gallaberry • Amisfield Town • Tinwald

8 • Garroch • Glenlee • St John's Town of Dalry • Balmaclellan • Loch Urr • Loch Howie • 17 • A76 • Kirkton • Locharbriggs • 12

A762 • B7075 • Drumwhirn • 392 SKEOCH HILL • Drumpark • Glen Kiln Sculptures • Crochmore Ho. • Newbridge • Twelve Apostles • Lincluden College • Heathall • Torthorwald • Hig

New Galloway • A712 • 281 LARGLEAR HILL • Crogo • Corsock • 24 • Shawhead • Terregles • Lincluden • A75 • A709 • Roucan • CARTHAT HILL • 740 Ram

NX • A713 • Ironmacannie • B794 • Eastlands • Crocketford • Lochfoot • Drummore • Maxwelltown • Dumfries • Greenlea • Collin

325 CAIRN EDWARD • Airds of Kells • A762 • Mossdale • Parton • Knockvennie Smithy • Kirkpatrick Durham • 18 • Milton • Beeswing • Lochrutton Loch • Cargenbridge • AA • Kingholm Quay • Islesteps • B725 • Mouswald

7 • 208 AUCHENCLOY HILL • Slogarie • Loch Ken • Walbutt • Old Bridge of Urr • Springholm • Lochober Loch • Mabie • A710 • Conheath • Bankend • Comlongon Clarencef

Loch Skerrow • Woodhall Loch • Crossmichael • Clarebrand • Hardgate • Stonehouse • Kirkgunzeon • 334 • Kinharvie • LOTUS HILL • Glencaple • Kirconnel • Sweetheart • Shearington • Caerlaverock • Estuary • B725

335 WHITE TOP OF CULREACH • Laurieston • B795 • Glenlochar • Townhead of Greenlaw • A75 • Haugh of Urr • Redcastle • Drumcoltran Tower • 14 • Corn Mill • New Abbey • Blackshaw • Wildfowl Trust • Ingleston

Little Water of Fleet • Loch Whinyeon • Longwood • A713 • Hillowton • Leaths • Little Knox • Edingham • 430 CUIL HILL • 569 CRIFFELL • Loch Kindar • 16 • Carse Bay

6 • 367 BENGRAY • Kirkconnell • Bridge of Dee • A745 • Castle Douglas • Carlingwark Loch • Dalbeattie • B793 • Kirkbean • Carsethorn

Fleet Valley • Ringford • Rhonehouse or Kelton Hill • Threave Garden NT • Gelston • Barlochan • A711 • Barnbarroch • Fairgirth • Caulkerbush • Mainsriddle • Borron Point

Gatehouse of Fleet • B727 • Slagnaw • Craigley • B736 • Palnackie • A710 • Douganhill • 10 • Drumburn • Sandyhills • Loaningfoot • Southerness • Gill Foot Bay

Girthon • B721 • Littleton • Tongland • Airieland • 388 SCREEL HILL • Orchardton Tower • Kippford • Mote of Mark • Colvend • Southerness Point

Lennox Plunton • A75 • Twynholm • Compstonend • 381 SCREEL HILL • BENGAIRN • East Stewartry Coast • Rockcliffe • Portling • Castlehill Point

5 • Margrie • Power Station and Dam • Little Sypland • 65 • Screel • Auchencairn • Castlehill Point • Bec

Gledpark • B727 • Kirkchrist • Whinnie Liggate • Kirkcudbright • Culnaightrie • 18 • Auchencairn Bay • Hestan Island

Borgue • Ingleston • Mutehill • Dundrennan • Balcary • Balcary Point • N

Kirkandrews • A711 • Rascarrel • Holme S

Borness • Balmangan • Netherlaw • Orroland • Dubmill Point

Ringdoo Point • Ross • Balmae • Abbey Head • Allonby Bay

Little Ross • Kirkcudbright Bay

6 • 7 • 8 • 9 • 58 • 0

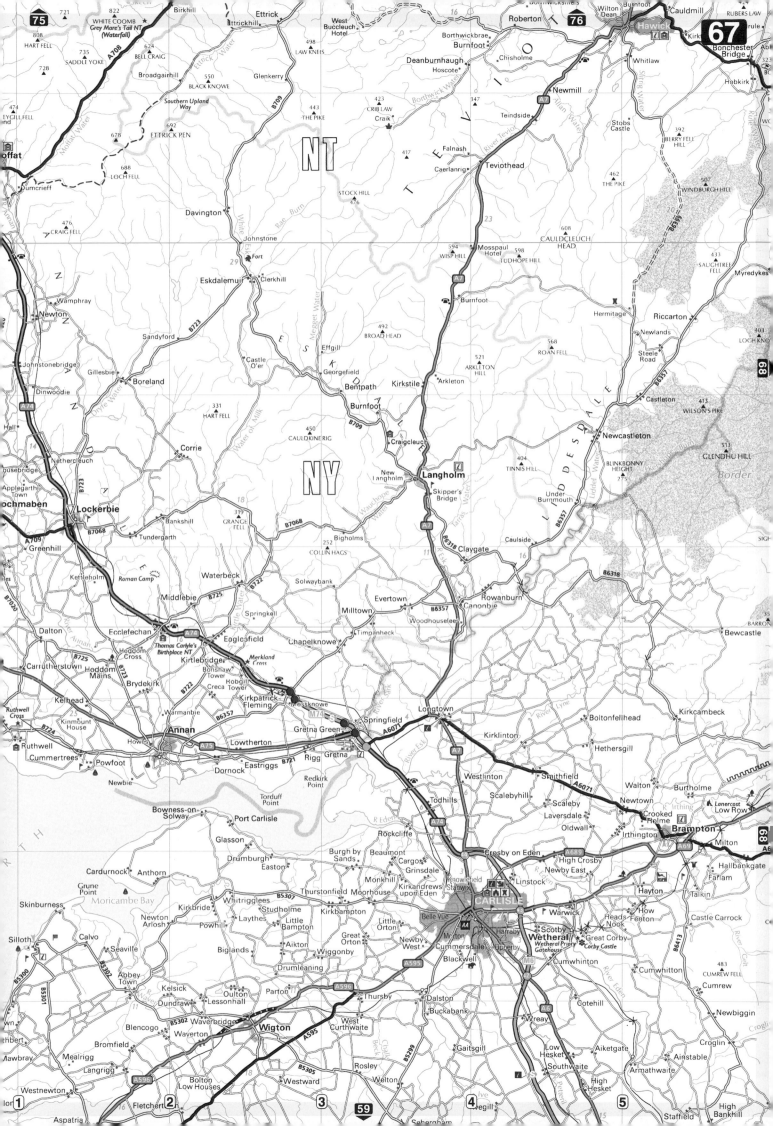

Bairnkine · Dolphinston · Ingram · Fawdon · Glanton
Camps · 76 · WINDYGATE HILL · 620 · CUSHAT LAW 616 · COCHRANE PIKE 334 · Great Ryle
Abbotrule · head · Camptown · Prendwick

Byrness · 368 CORBY PIKE · Hepple · Thropton · Rothbury · Great Tosson · Newtown · Whitton · Long

602 PEEL FELL · 551 · OH ME EDGE · 301 THE BEACON · 17
PEEL FELL · Camp Rochester · P A R K · 441 TOSSON HILL · ROTHBURY

513 MONKSIDE · 425 HINDHOPE LAW · Horsley · A68 · 391 DOUGH CRAG · 331 · Ewesley
KNOWE · Kielder · 1388 · Otterburn · Elsdon · B6341 · B6342
397 EARL'S SEAT · Troughend · B6342 · Netherwitton
67 · Kielder Water · 16
9 · Black Middens Bastle House · West Woodburn · East Woodburn · Ray Fell · A696 · High Hartlington · Longwitton · Hart Burn
307 WHITE HILL · Gatehouse · 14 · Scot's Gap · Hartburn
Falstone · Greenhaugh · Fort · Cambo · Middleton
Stannersburn · Hott · Charlton · Ridsdale · Kirkwhelpington · Wallington NT · R Wansbeck
Forest · Park · NORTHUMBERLAND · Bellingham · A68 · Sweethope Loughs · Kirkharle · Capheaton · 6
395 BOLT'S LAW · B6320 · Redesmouth · 15 · Great Bavington
519 SIGHTY CRAG · NATIONAL · PARK · Pennine Way · R North Tyne · Thockrington · Little Bavington · Kirkheaton
8 · 492 · BLACK KNOWE · Birtley · Crag Reservoir · Little Swinburne · Hallington Reservoir · Kearsley · Ingoe
335 · Chirdon · Wark · Great Swinburne · Colwell · Hallington · Ryal · Fenwick · B6309
PIKE · 325 ROUND TOP · Gunnerton · Barrasford
313 SPY RIGG · Wark's Burn · 12 · Simonburn · NY · Chollerton · Bingfield · Matten · Stamfordham · Heugh
Black Fell · GREEN RIGG · Humshaugh · Great Whittington · Clarewood
7 · Broomlee Lough · B6318 · Carrawburgh Temple of Mithras · Hadrian's Wall · Harlow Hi
67 · R Irthing · Greenlee Lough · Chesters Fort · Hadrian's Wall · B6318
Hadrian's Wall · Housesteads NT · Wall · Fallowfield · Halton · Halton Shields · B6318
Fort · Gilsland · Hadrian's Wall · Chesterholm (Vindolanda) · Newbrough · Fourstones · A6079 · Acomb · Sandhoe · Aydon · B6321
B6318 · Melkridge · Henshaw · Chesterwood · B6319 · Warden · A69 · Corbridge · Newton · Ovington · Ovingham · Horsley
Haltwhistle · A69 · Bardon Mill · R South Tyne · Haydon Bridge · Hexham · A695 Dilston · B6307 · Eltringham · Mickley Square · High M
Beltingham · Elrington · A695 · Broomhaugh · Bywell · High M
255 DENTON FELL · Park · Deanraw · Langley · B6305 · West Dipton Burn · Riding Mill · Stocksfield · Painshawfield
6 · Tindale · Rowfoot · Fellhouse Fell · Dye House · Ordley · New Ridley · Hedley on the H
te · Coanwood · Lambley · Whitfield · Steel · Slaley · Whitton
Halton Lea Gate · Wolf Hills · Bearsbridge · Catton · Whitley Chapel · B6309 · Ham
621 COLD FELL · Eals · Allendale · 357 DUKESFIELD FELL · B6306 · Kiln Pit Hill · Newlands · Ebchester
522 GLENDUE FELL · Knarsdale · R South Tyne · Ninebanks · R East Allen · Derwent Reservoir · 379 KILN PIT HILL · A68 · B6278
521 GELTSDALE MIDDLE · 584 THREE PIKES · Slaggyford · B6295 · 443 HANGMAN HILL · Blanchland · Edmundbyers · Blackhill · Cons
5 · Kirkhaugh · South Tynedale Railway · HARTLEY MOOR 572 · River Derwent · Muggleswick · Castleside
roglin Water · A689 · Carr Shield · 478 NOOKTON FELL · Hunstanworth · Healeyfield · A692
657 MIDDLE CARRICK · Alston · 540 BOLT'S LAW · 408 SKAYLOCK HILL · 379 CROSS RIGG · Ro
559 RENWICK FELL · 664 BLACK FELL · Gilderdale Forest · Dirt Pot · Allenheads
6 · wick · HARTSIDE HEIGHT 624 · A686 · 7 · Nenthead · 60 · 8 · 20 · A689 · 9 · 0
Killhope Wheel · Knope Burn · Rookhope

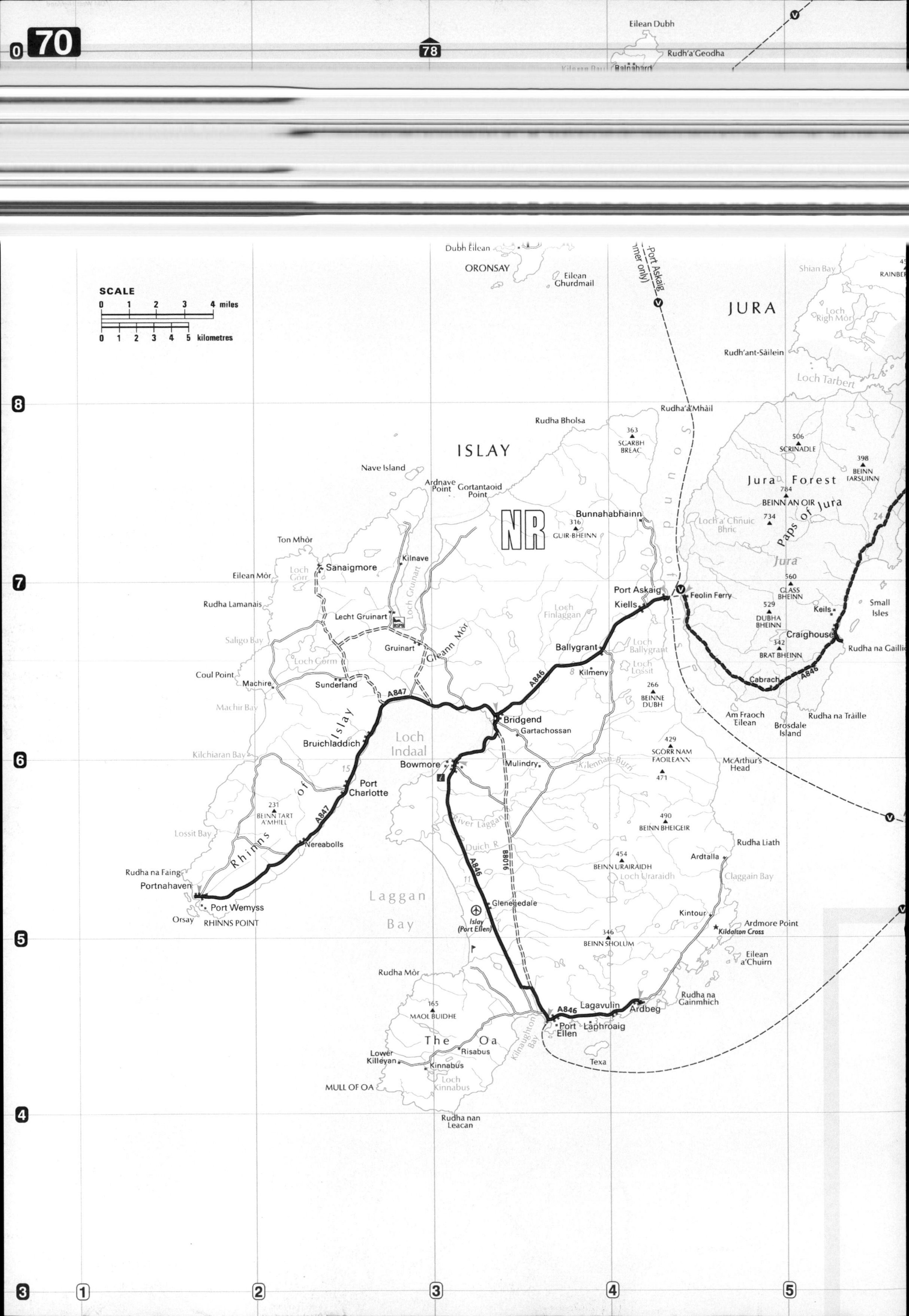

Eilean Dubh

Rudh'a'Geodha

Kilnave Paul (Balnahard)

V

ORONSAY

Dubh Eilean

Eilean Ghurdmail

Port Askaig (summer only)

Shian Bay

RAINBER

JURA

Loch Righ Mòr

SCALE

0 1 2 3 4 miles

0 1 2 3 4 5 kilometres

8

Rudha Bholsa

Rudha'a'Mhàil

Rudh'ant-Sàilein

Loch Tarbert

ISLAY

363
SGARBH
BREAC

506
SCRINADLE

398
BEINN
TARSUINN

Nave Island

Ardnave
Point

Gortantaoid
Point

Bunnahabhainn

316
GUIR-BHEINN

NR

Jura Forest

784
BEINN AN OIR Jura

734

Paps of Jura

24

Ton Mhòr

Kilnave

560
GLASS
BHEINN

Small
Isles

7

Eilean Mòr

Sanaigmore

Loch
Gorm

Loch
Finlaggan

Port Askaig V Feolin Ferry

Kiells

529
DUBHA
BHEINN

Keils

Rudha Lamanais

Lecht Gruinart

Loch Gruinart

342
BRAT BHEINN

Craighouse

Rudha na Gaillic

Saligo Bay

Gruinart

Gleann Mòr

Ballygrant

Loch
Ballygrant

Loch
Lossit

Cabrach

A846

Coul Point

Loch Gorm

A847

Kilmeny

266
BEINNE
DUBH

Machire

Sunderland

A846

Machir Bay

Bridgend

Am Fraoch
Eilean

Rudha na Tràille

Brosdale
Island

Kilchiaran Bay

Bruichladdich

Loch
Indaal

Gartachossan

429
SGÒRR NAM
FAOILEANN

McArthur's
Head

6

Bowmore

Mulindry

471

15

Port
Charlotte

231
BEINN TART
A'MHILL

A847

River Laggan

490
BEINN BHEIGEIR

Rudha Liath

Lossit Bay

Duich R.

Ardtalla

454
BEINN URAIRAIDH

Loch Uraraidh

Rudha na Faing

Rhinns of Islay

Nereabolls

A846

B8016

11

Claggain Bay

Portnahaven

Glenegedale

Kintour

Ardmore Point

Kildalton Cross

Port Wemyss

Laggan

Islay
(Port Ellen)

346

Kildalton Cross

Orsay RHINNS POINT

Bay

BEINN SHOLUM

Eilean
a'Chuirn

5

Rudha Mòr

165
MAOL BUIDHE

A846 Lagavulin Ardbeg

Rudha na
Gainmhich

Lower
Killeyan

The Oa

Risabus

Kinnabus

Kilnaughton Bay

Port
Ellen Laphroaig

Texa

MULL OF OA

Loch
Kinnabus

4

Rudha nan
Leacan

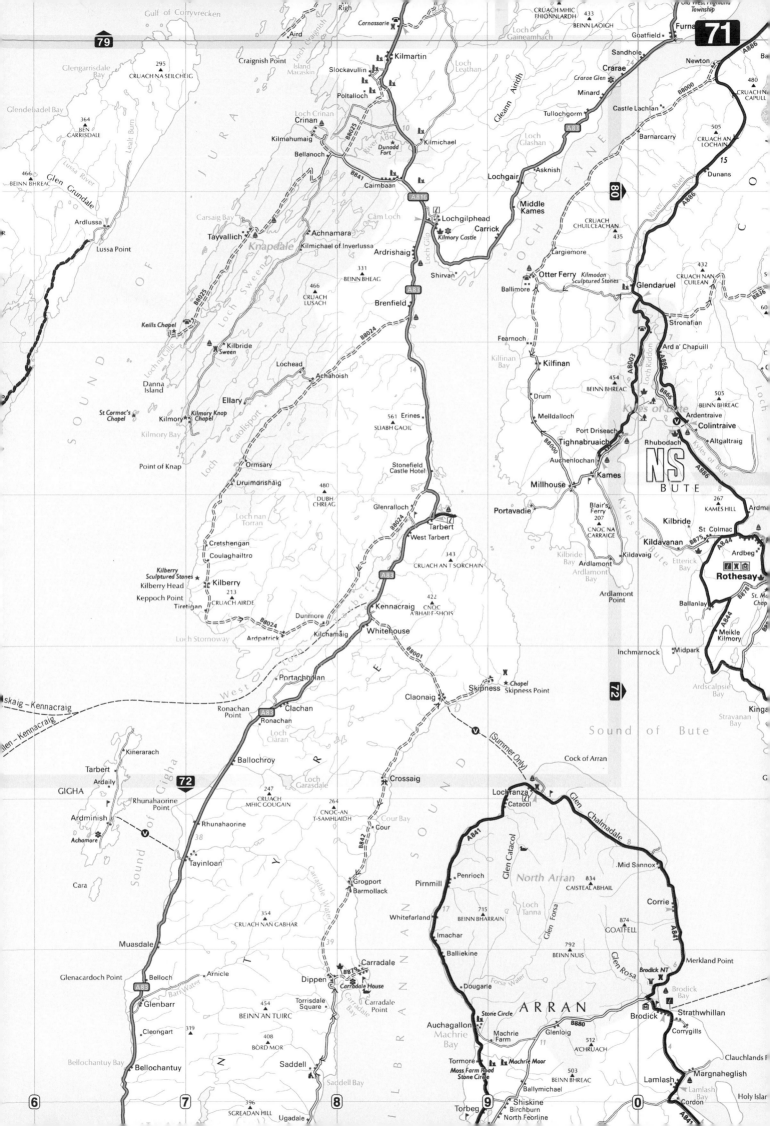

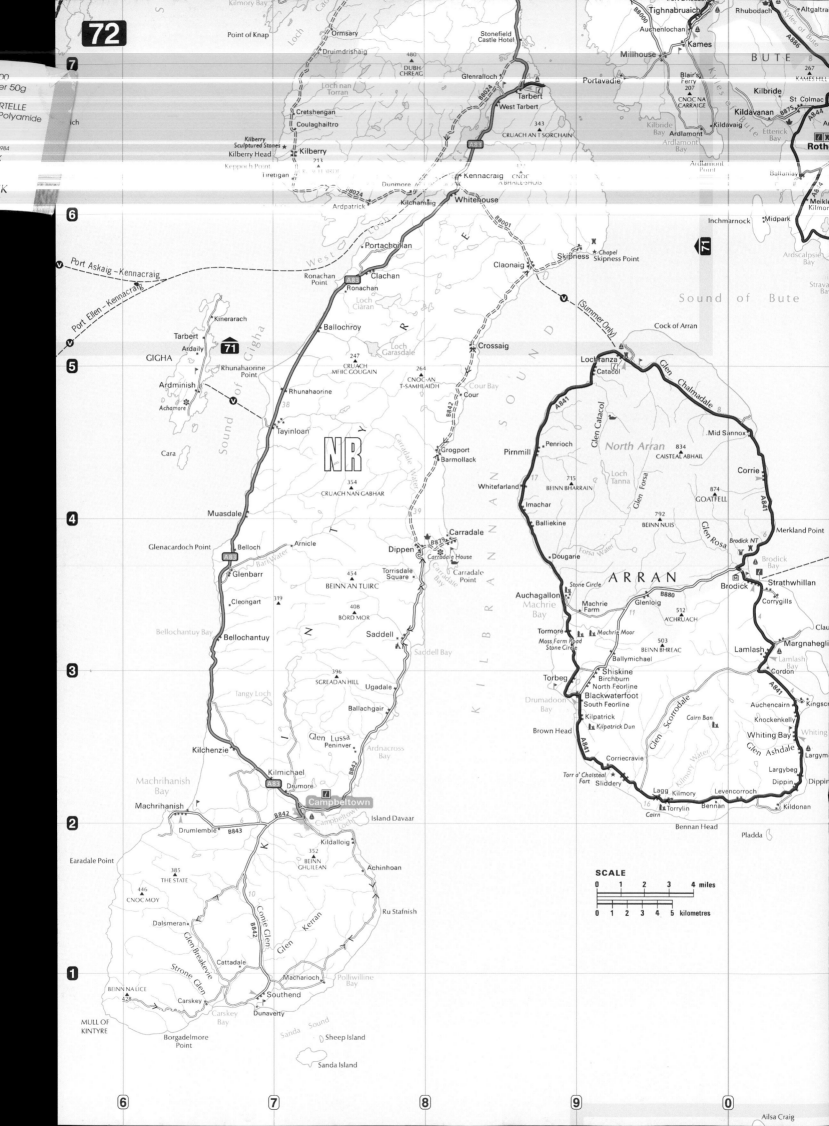

SCALE

0 1 2 3 4 miles

0 1 2 3 4 5 kilometres

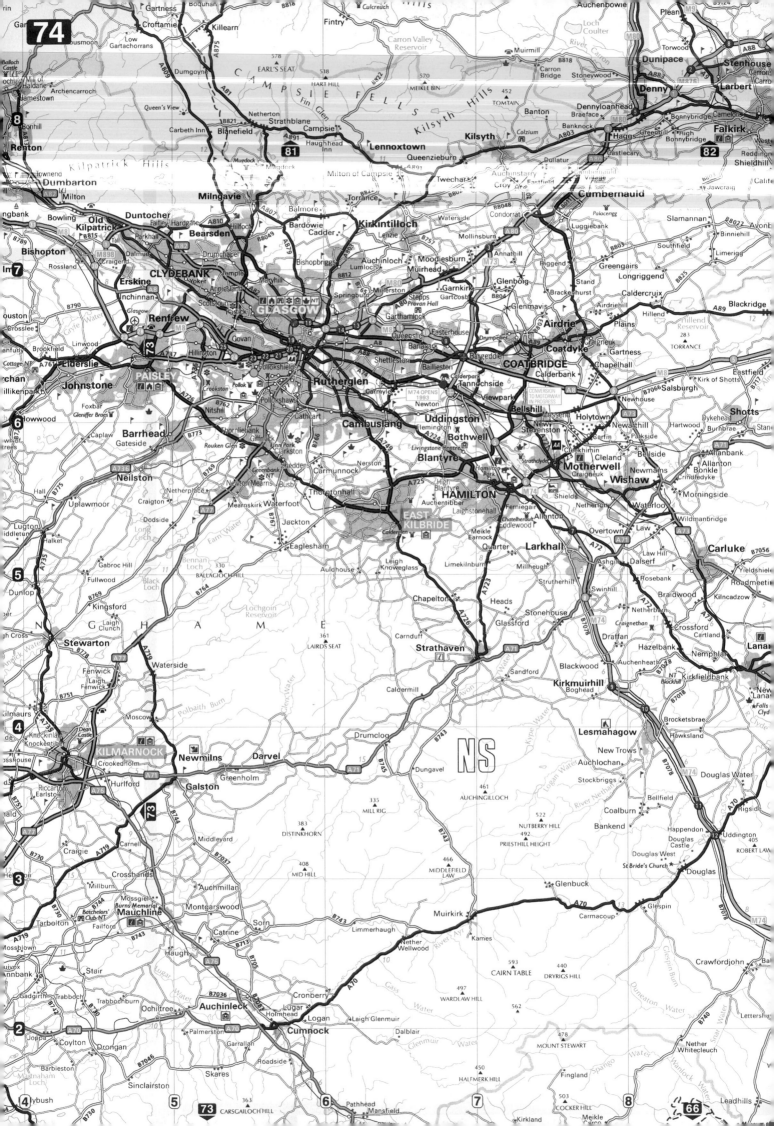

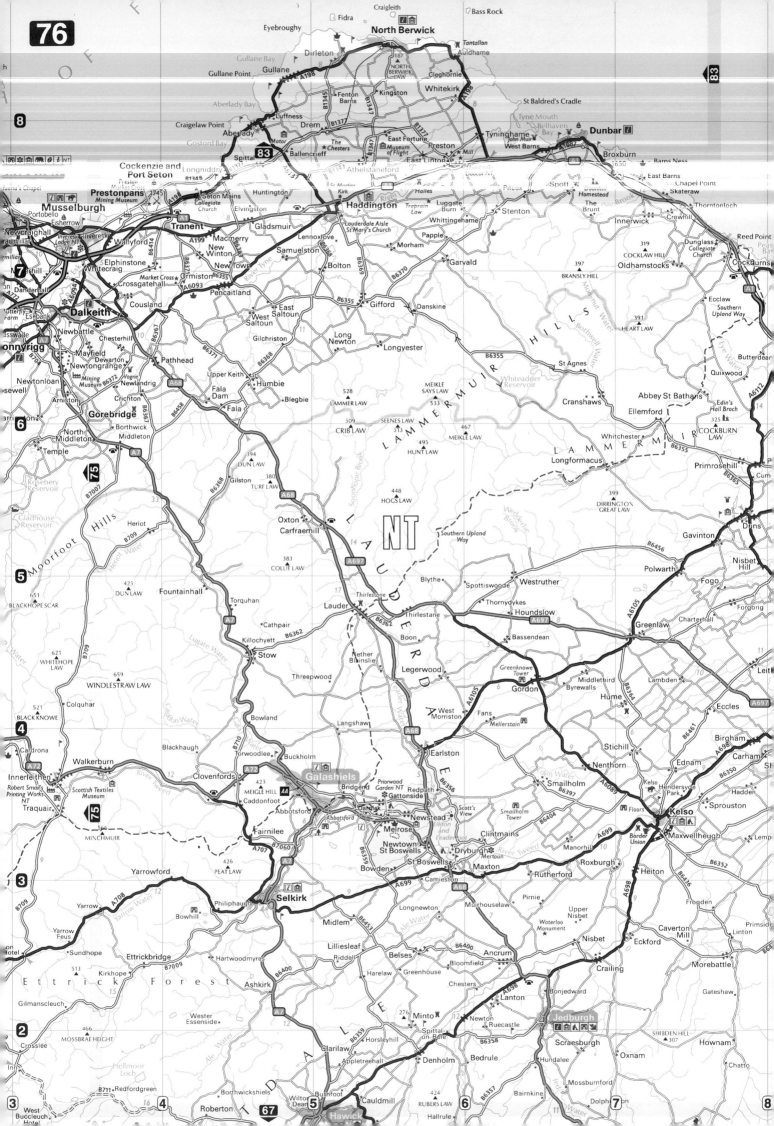

SCALE
0   1   2   3   4 miles
0 1 2 3 4 5 kilometres

car Point   Fast Castle Head

196
BROWN RIG
A1107
ST ABB'S HEAD

St Abbs

Coldingham
Coldingham Bay

shouse

Houndwood   22

Eyemouth

Heugh Head   Cairncross

21

262
HORSELEY HILL   Reston
B6438   A1
Auchencrow   Ayton   Burnmouth

Marygold

Lamberton

Chirnside   B6355   Marshall Meadows Bay

Edrom   B6437
Foulden   North Northumberland
Heritage Coast

Chirnsidebridge   Tithe Barn
Broadhaugh   1333
Edington   A6105
anderston   Whiteadder
umstane   Allanton   Hutton   Water   A6105
Barracks
Town Ramparts

Blackadder   B6460   Paxton   B6461
Tweedmouth   Berwick-upon-Tweed
Whitsome   Hilton   Sunwick   Spittal
Fishwick   A1167
13   A698

NU

B6461   Huds Head
B6470   Horndean
Ladykirk   Murton
B6437   Thornton
Norham
Swinton   Upsettlington   Scremerston

Simprim   Ladykirk   A698   Cheswick
Ho.   B6354

River Tweed   Ancroft   CAUSEWAY
FLOODED
AT HIGH TIDE
A6112   Duddo   Haggerston   HOLY ISLAND
The
A6112   Holy
The   Island
irsel   Lennel   Bowsden   Beal   Lindisfarne Castle NT
dstream   Lindisfarne   Castle Point
Cornhill-on-   Etal   Priory
Wark   Tweed   Heatherslaw   B6353   Lowick   Guile Point
Light Railway   East   Fenwick
Heatherslaw   Kyloe
Branxton   Mill   Buckton   North Northumberland
1513   Crookham   The Lady   Heritage Coast
Ford   Waterford Hall   EARNE
Staple   ISLANDS
A697   Sound
B6396   Fenton   St Cuthbert's   Inner
Howtel   Town   Cave NT   Sound
B6352   Milfield   Belford   Bamburgh
Thornington   Nesbit   B1342   B1340
Doddington   B6349   B1341
Lanton   Coupland   River Till
Yeavering   B6348   Lucker
B6351   Akeld   Warenford   Seahouses
Kirknewton   Chatton   A1   North
Kirk   Hethpool   Wooler   Sunderland   Beadnell
Yetholm   B6525   Ross Castle NT   Newstead   Chathill
Town   Newtown   Ellingham   Swinhoe
Yetholm   Chillingham   Preston   Tughall   Beadnell Bay
NORTHUMBERLAND   14   Brunton
Pennine   525   Christon   High Newton
Way   PRESTON HILL   North   Bank   by-the-Sea
564   CATERAN HILL   Charlton   Embleton
267   South   Embleton
NATIONAL   PARK   Falloden   Bay
816   Old Bewick   Charlton   Dunstanburgh
Mowhaugh   Sourhope   THE CHEVIOT   Ilderton   New   Ditchburn   Rock   Castle NT
Bewick   Eglingham   Dunstan
567   Rennington   Stamford   Craster
DUNMOOR HILL   Beanley   B6346   Howick   Howick
620   Powburn   Hall   Cullernose Point
WINDYGATE HILL   Hartside   Branton   B6341   B1339
Ingram   Glanton   Longhoughton
616   Fawdon   Denwick   Boulmer
334   River Aln
68   9   0   1   69   2   3

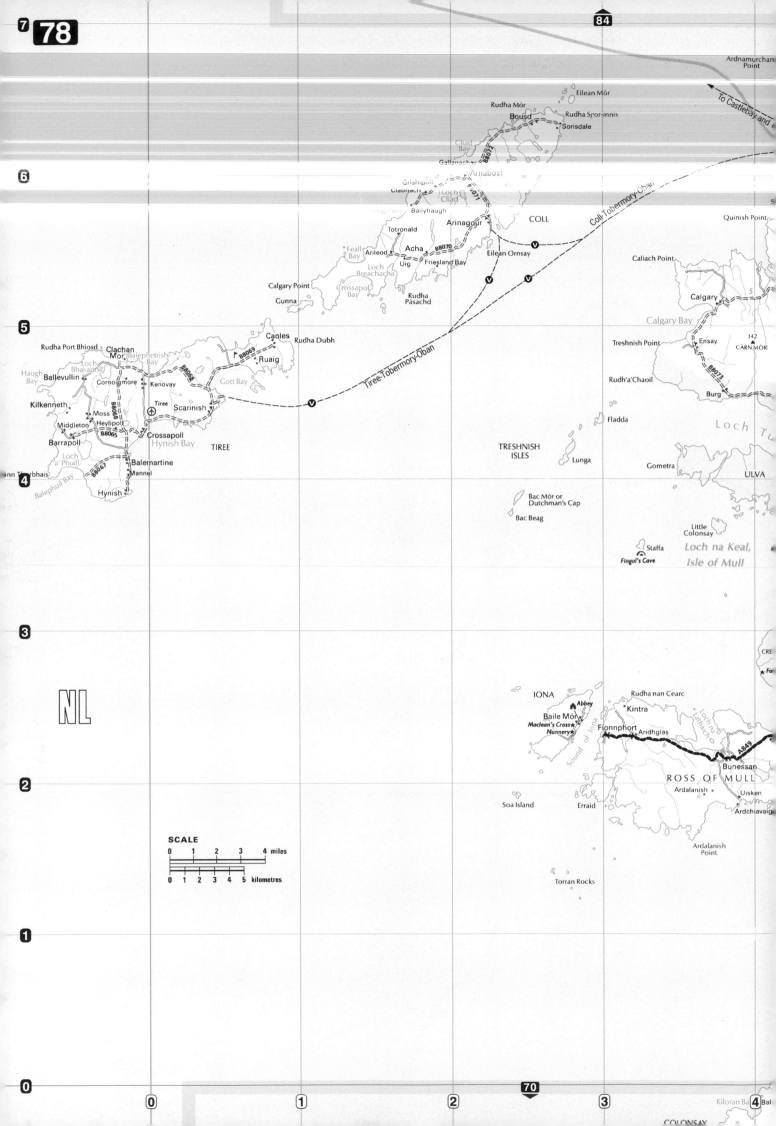

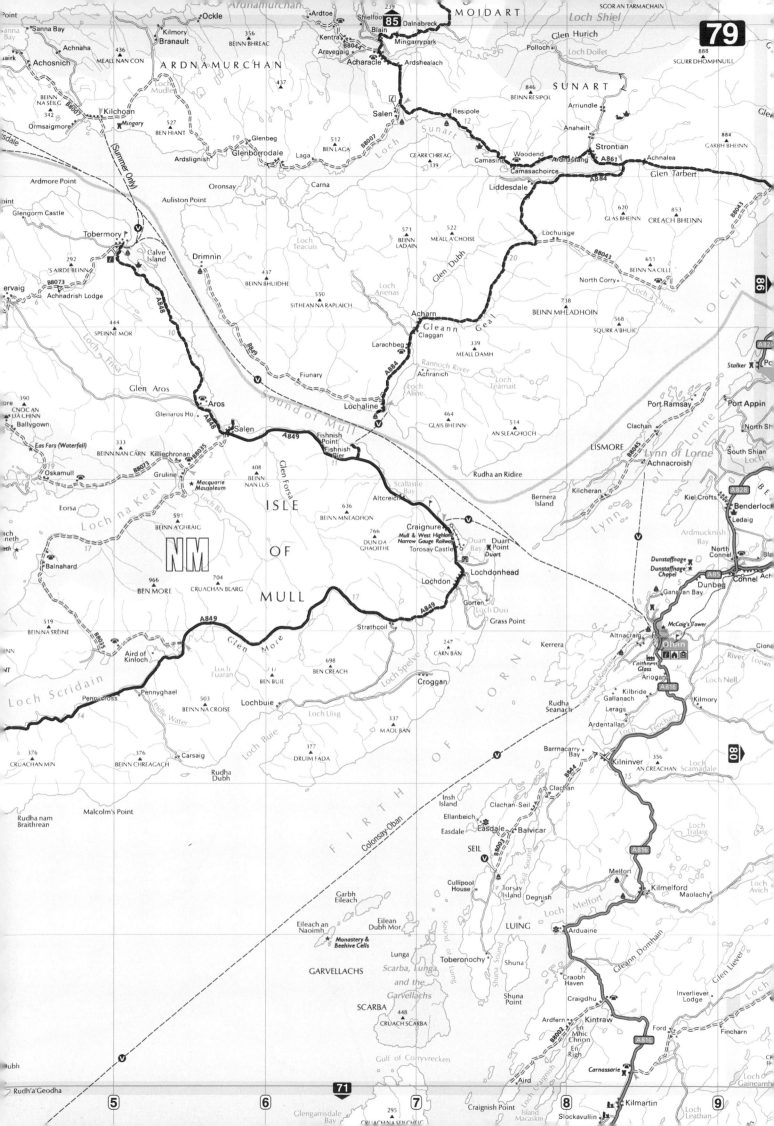

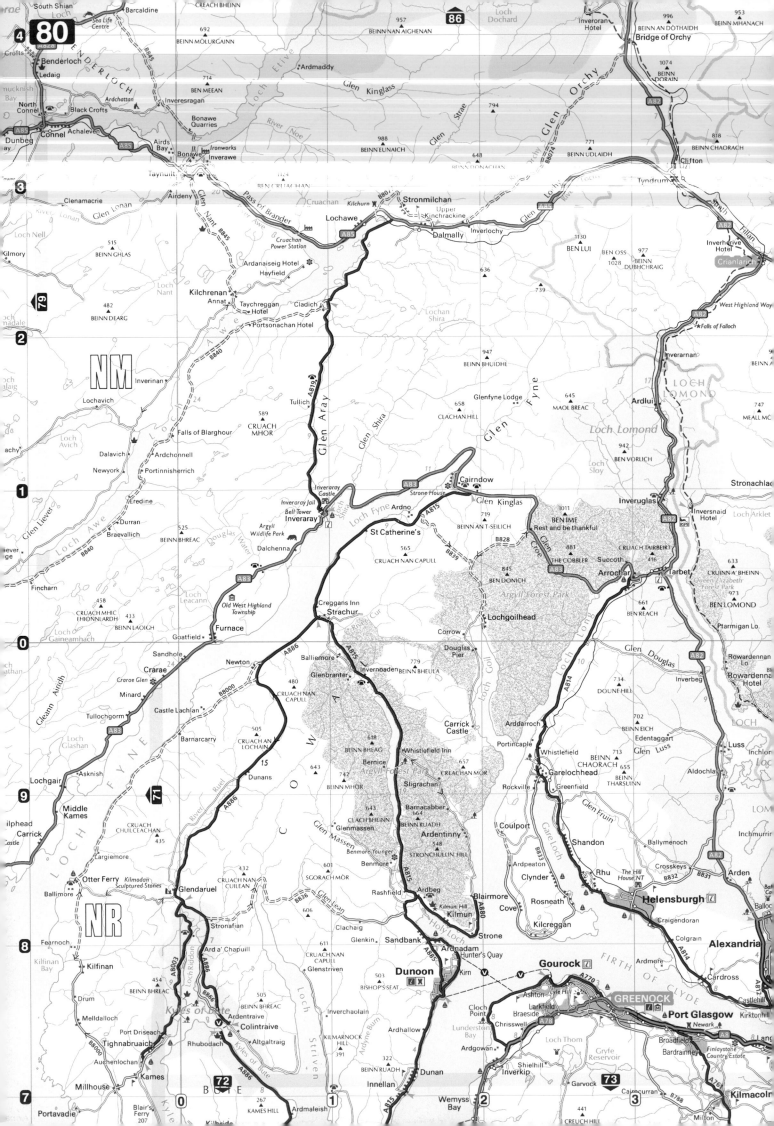

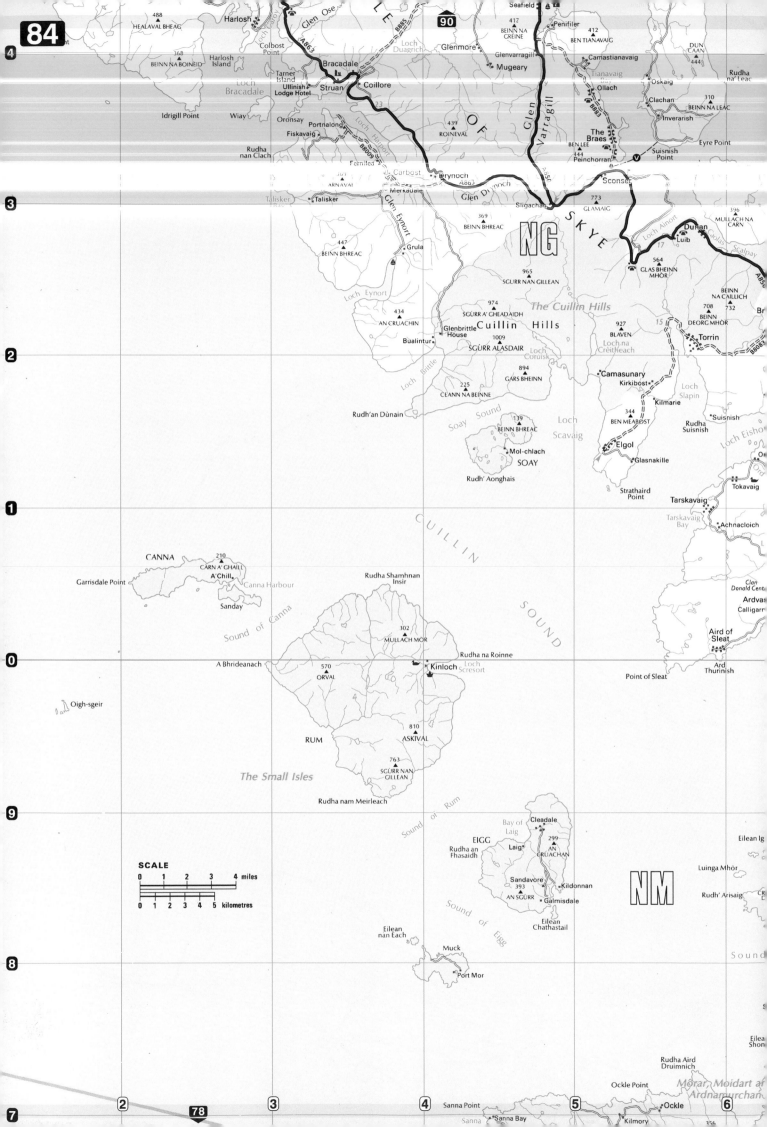

SCALE

0 1 2 3 4 miles

0 1 2 3 4 5 kilometres

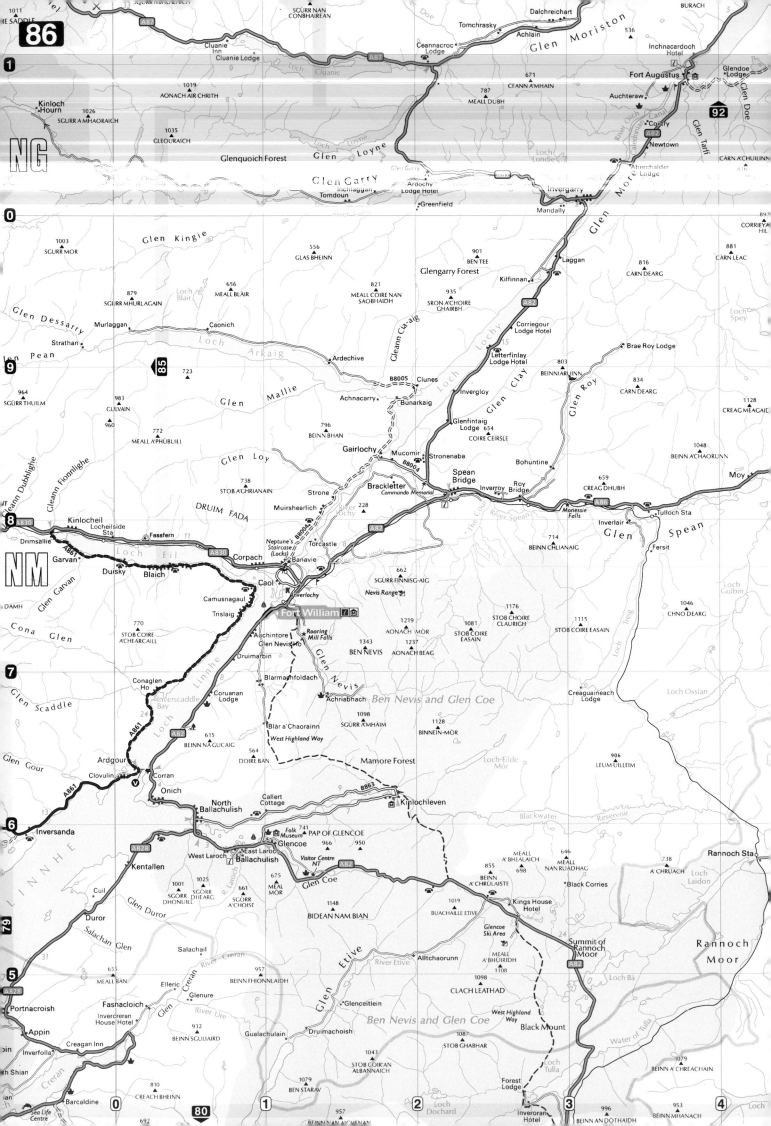

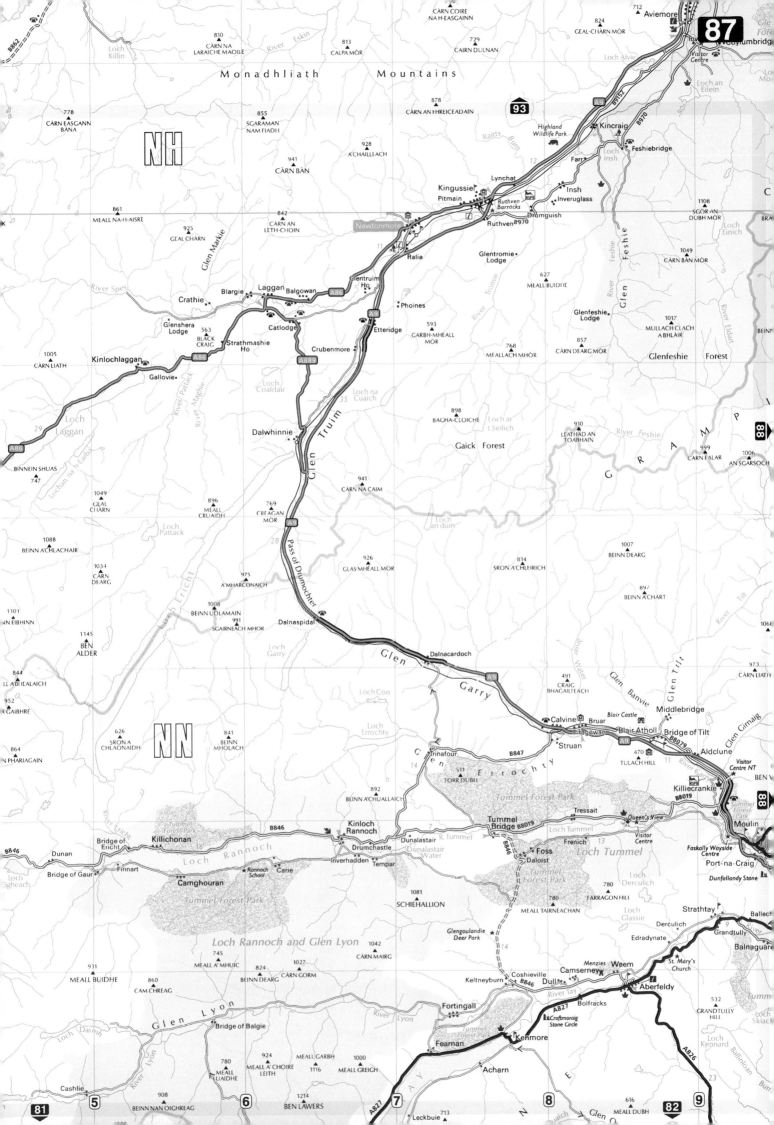

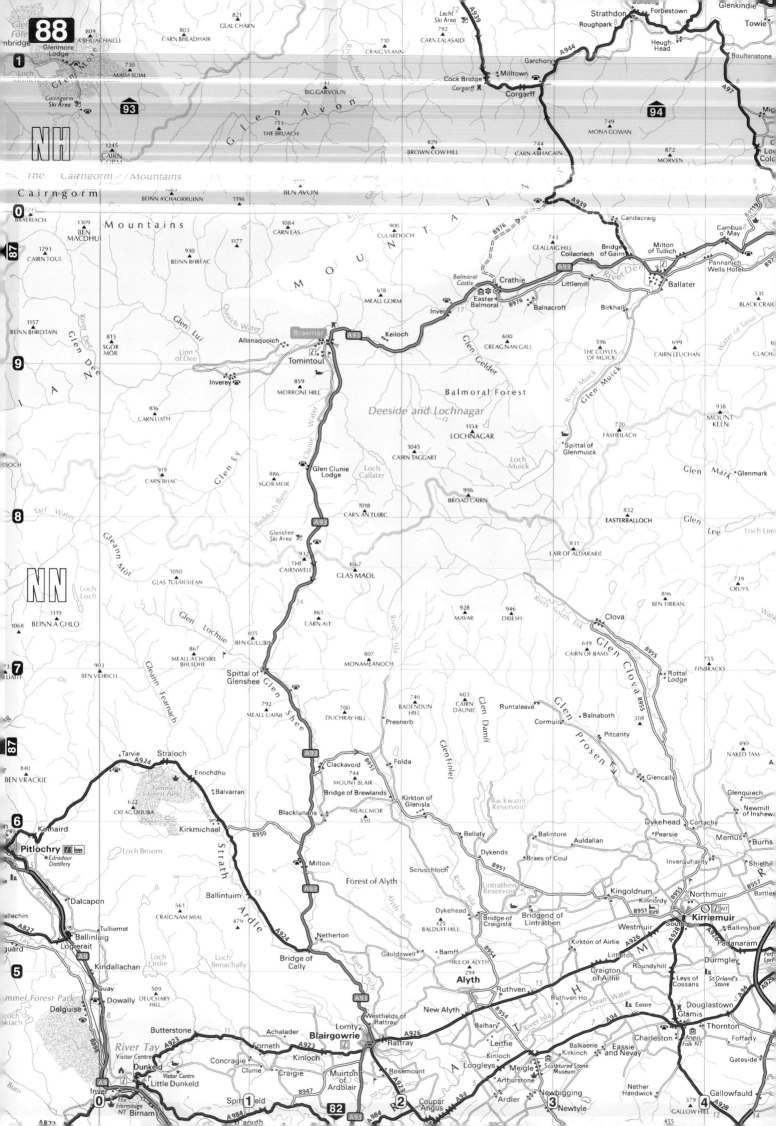

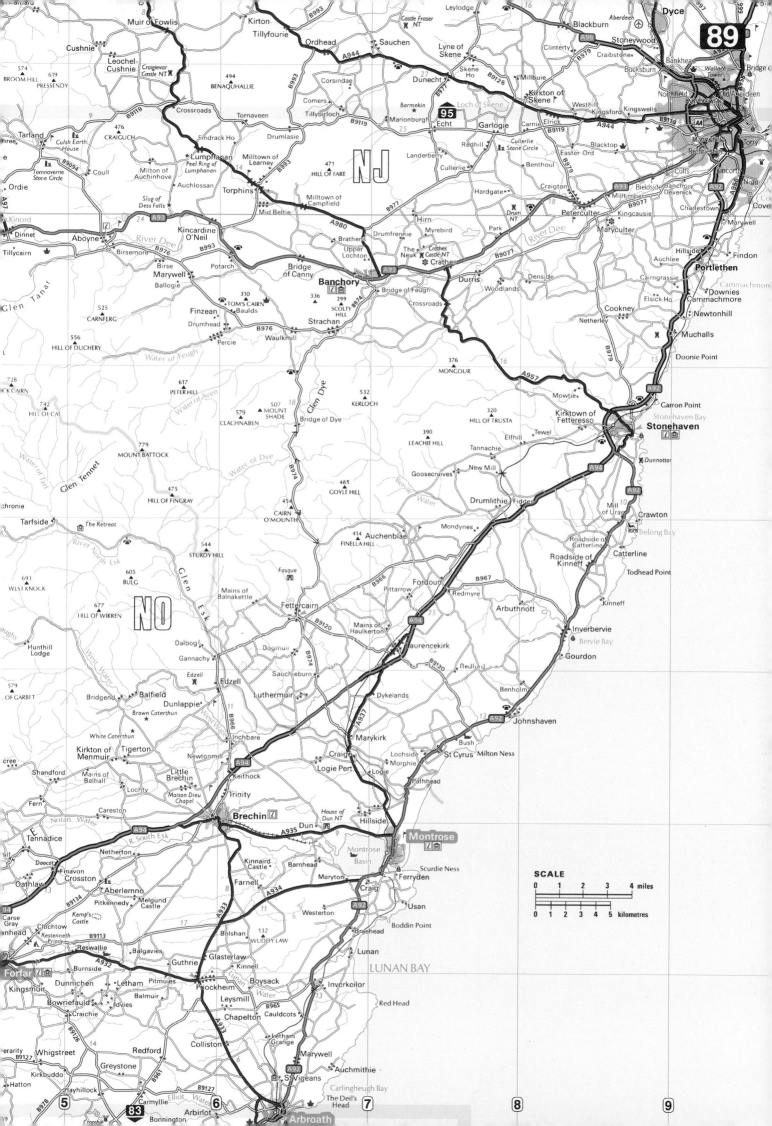

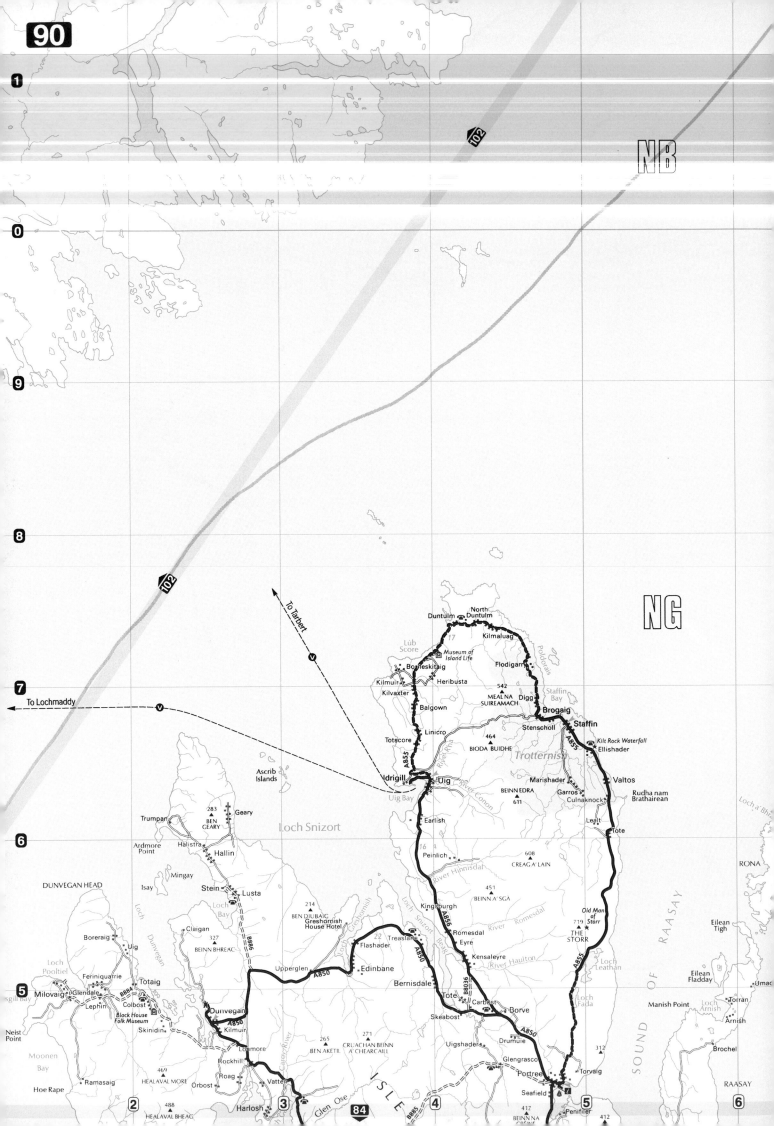

1

102

NB

0

9

8

102

To Tarbert

7

To Lochmaddy

6

5

NG

North
Duntulm   Duntulm
Kilmaluag
Lùb
Score   17   Flodigarry
Borneskitaig
Museum of
Island Life
Kilmuir   Heribusta
Kilvaxter   542
Balgown   MEAL NA   Digg
SUIREAMACH
Brogaig
Linicro   Stenscholl   Staffin
Totscore   464   A855
BIODA BUIDHE   Kilt Rock Waterfall
A855   Trotternish   Ellishader
River Rha

Idrigill   Uig   Marishader   Valtos
River Conon   BEINN EDRA   Garros
611   Culnaknock   Rudha nam
Brathairean
Loch a' Bhr

RONA

Ascrib
Islands

Earlish
Lealt
Tote

283   Geary
Trumpan   BEN   16   608
GEARY   Peinlich   CREAG A' LAIN
Ardmore   Halistra   River Hinnisdal
Point   Hallin   451
BEINN A' SGA

DUNVEGAN HEAD   Mingay   Stein   Lusta   Kingsburgh   Old Man
Isay   Loch   719   of Storr
Bay   214   THE
BEN DIUBAIG   Romesdal   STORR
Greshornish   Eyre
Claigan   House Hotel   River Romesdal
Boreraig   327   B886   22   Treaslane
BEINN BHREAC   Flashader   A850   Kensaleyre   Loch
Uig   Upperglen   A850   River Haulton   Leathan
Loch   Edinbane   A856   Eilean
Pooltiel   Bernisdale   B8036   Fladday
Feriniquarrie   Totaig   Tote   Manish Point   Loch
Milovaig   Glendale   B884   Skeabost   Carbost   Borve   Arnish   Torran
Lephin   Colbost   Skeabost   A850   Loch   Arnish
Black House   Fada
sgill Bay   Folk Museum   Dunvegan
Neist   Kilmuir   A850   Drumuie   312
Point   Skinidin   Uigshader   Portree   Brochel
Lonmore   Glengrasco   Torvaig
Moonen   Rockhill   265   271   B885   Seafield   SOUND OF RAASAY
Bay   469   BEN AKETIL   CRUACHAN BEINN
Ramasaig   HEALAVAL MORE   Roag   Orbost   A' CHEARCAILL   Penifiler   RAASAY
Hoe Rape   488   Vatten   417   412
HEALAVAL BHEAG   Harlosh   Glen Ose   84   BEINN NA
CROINE

2   3   4   5   6

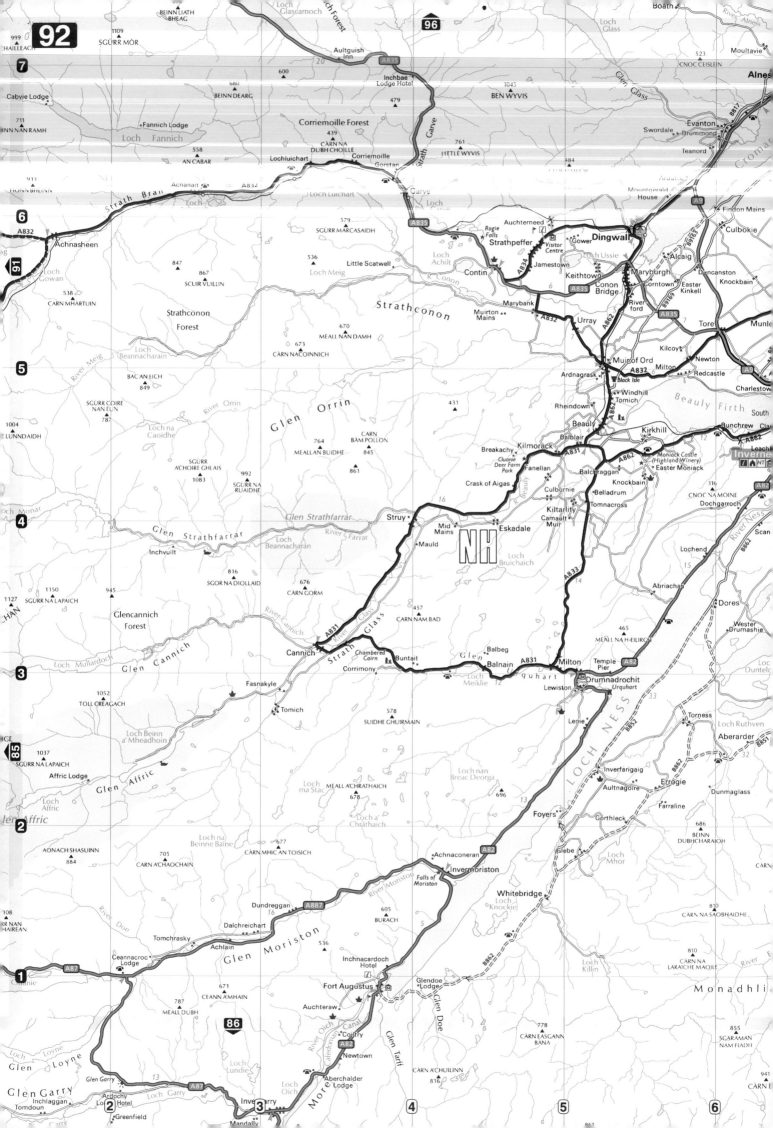

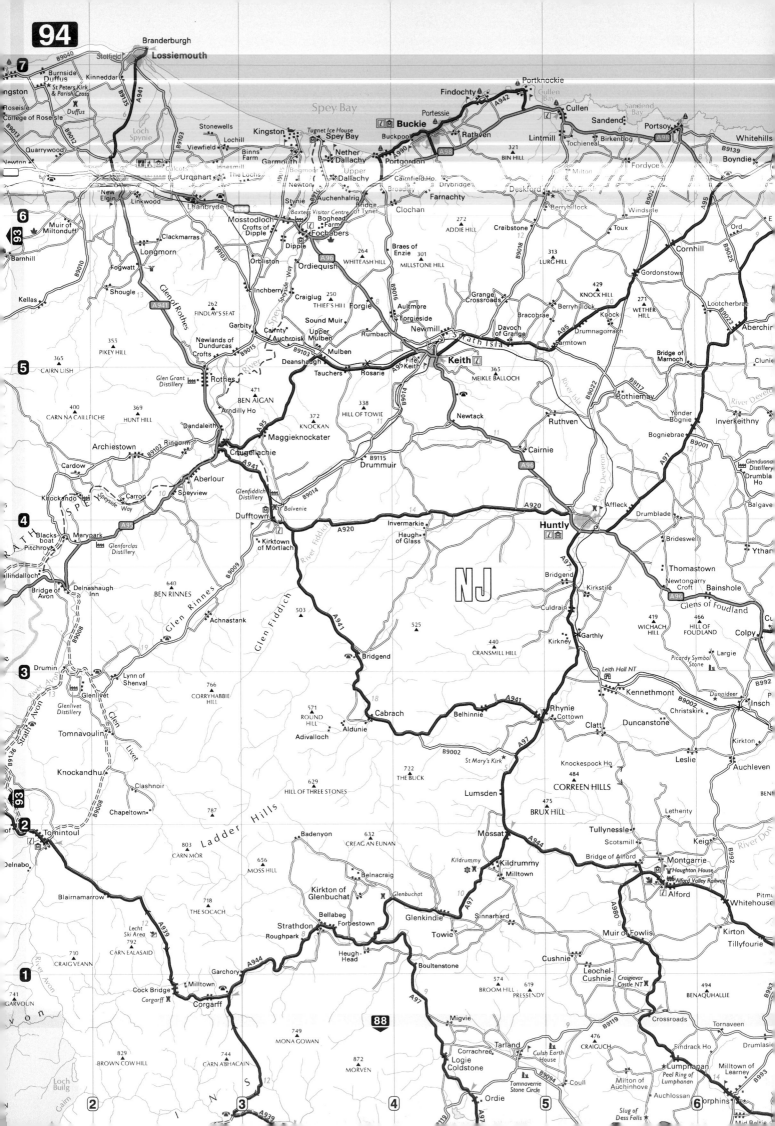

Troup Head
Rosehearty
Sandhaven
Kinnaird
Fraserburgh
Pittulie
Cullykhan Bay
Gamrie Bay
Crovie
Pennan
Craigiefold
Peathill
Percyhorner
Coburby
Kirktown
Fraserburgh Bay
Cairnbulg
Banff
Macduff
Gardenstown
Dubford
Protstonhill
Aberdour Bay
New Aberdour
Pitblae
Mid Ardlaw
Inverallochy
Banff Bay
Silverford
Longmanhill
Gamrie
B9031
Boyndlie
B9031
Memsie
St Combs
Duff House
A947
A98
Clenterty
Minnonie
Netherbrae
221
BRACKLAMORE HILL
B9032
Newburgh
A981
Rathen
Lonmay
Crofts of Savoch
Alvah
A98
Crimonmogate
Loch of Strathbeg
Rattray Head
234
WAUGHTON HILL
Strichen
A952
Crimond
Blackhill
Gorrachie
Danshillock
River Deveron
B9121
15
New Pitsligo
B9030
New Leeds
B9093
Blackhill
18
Muirden
Fintry
B9105
New Byth
Bonnykelly
Oldwhat
A950
Denhead
Leys
Backfolds
Kirktown
St Fergus
B9025
Garmond
B9027
Deer Abbey
Fetterangus
Rora
Turriff
Cuminestown
13
New Deer
B9170
Maud
B9106
Dunshillock
Mintlaw
River Ugie
Inverugie
A952
Muiresk
B9024
Darra
B9170
Howe of Teuchar
Maryhill
Blackhill of Clackriach
Old Deer
Aden Visitor Centre
Longside
Buchanhaven
Peterhead
Birkenhills
Millbrex
Kirkton
B9029
A948
Drymuir
Bulwark
Stuartfield
Inverquhomery
A950
Peterhead Bay
Fotrie
B992
Slacks of Cairnbanno
Nethermuir
B9030
Millbreck
Nether Kinmundy
Hillhead of Cocklaw
Burnhaven
Pitglassie
Dykeside
Knaven
Kinnadie
Clola
Little Dens
Boddam
Buchan Ness
Auchterless
Gourdas
Cottown
Cairnorrie
Auchnagatt
12
Kinknockie
Blackhill
NK
Stirling
Tifty
Lethenty
Brownhill
Inkhorn
Coldwells
Lendrum Terrace
Fyvie Castle NT
B9005
Woodhead
Haddo
Methlick
Arthrath
Muirtack
Hatton
Auchiries
Coldwells
A95
Gordonstown
Rothiebrisbane
Fyvie
River Ythan
Coldwells
A92
Bullers of Buchan
Badenscoth
B9001
Fisherford
B9005
14
Haddo House NT
Birness
17
North Haven
Cruden Bay
Rothienorman
Fisherford
St Katherines
Earlsford
Wedderlairs
Bogbrae
Chapel Hill
Whinnyfold
The Skares
Bay of Cruden
Rothmaise
Newseat
Cross of Jackston
Auchedly
Kinharrachie
Artrochie
A975
Tocher
A920
Meikle Wartle
Folla Rule
Tulloch
Medieval Tomb
Tarves
Ythsie
Ellon
Kirkton of Rayne
A947
Ythsie
Craigdam
Esslemont
Kirkton of Logie Buchan
Kirktown of Slains
Old Rayne
Loanhead Stone Circle
Daviot
Oldmeldrum
Tolquhon
10
B999
Collieston
Hillhead of Durno
Fingask
Pitmedden Garden NT
Pitmedden
B9000
32
Whiteford
Kirktown of Bourtie
Carnbrogie
Udny Green
Pitcaple
B9001
Housieside
Chapel of Garioch
518
Mither Tap
A96
Udny Station
Newburgh
Pittodrie House Hotel
Whiterashes
Woodland
Pettymuk
Cultercullen
Foveran
East Aquhorthies Stone Circle
Nether Crimond
Tillygreig
Inverurie
B993
Straloch
Reisque
Newmachar
Causeyend
17
Delfrigs
Port Elphinstone
Kinmuck
B979
Balmedie
Visitor Centre
Burnhervie
Kinkell Church
Whitecairns
Belhelvie
Balmedie
Pictillum
B993
Kinmundy
B977
Monymusk
B994
Kemnay
Cottown
Hatton of Fintray
Dyce Symbol Stones
18
Potterton
Craigearn
Kintore
B977
Overton
Parkhill Ho
B999
Leylodge
B977
16
Dyce
Blackdog
Castle Fraser NT
Blackburn
Aberdeen Airport
A92
Sauchen
Lyne of Skene
Stoneywood
A944
Clinterty
Craibstone
A96
Bankhead
To Stromness
To Lerwick
A944
Dunecht
Skene Ho
B9126
Millbuie
Bucksburn
Wallace Tower
Bridge of Don
ABERDEEN
89
Barmekin
B977
Kirkton of Skene
Westhill
Kingsford
Kingswells
Bucksburn
Old Aberdeen
Marionburgh
Echt
Garlogie
Carnie
Elrick
Northfield
B9119
AA
Corsindae
B9119
Redhill
Blacktop
Mannofield
Rubislaw
Torry
Nigg Bay
Landerberry
Cullerlie Stone Circle
Easter Ord
Cults
471
Benthoul
B979
Craigton
Milltimber
Bieldside
A93
Banchory
Kincorth
A956
Nigg
Hardgate
B9077
Charlestown
Altens Haven
Cove Bay
Cove
7
8
9
0
1

SCALE
0 1 2 3 4 miles
0 1 2 3 4 5 kilometres

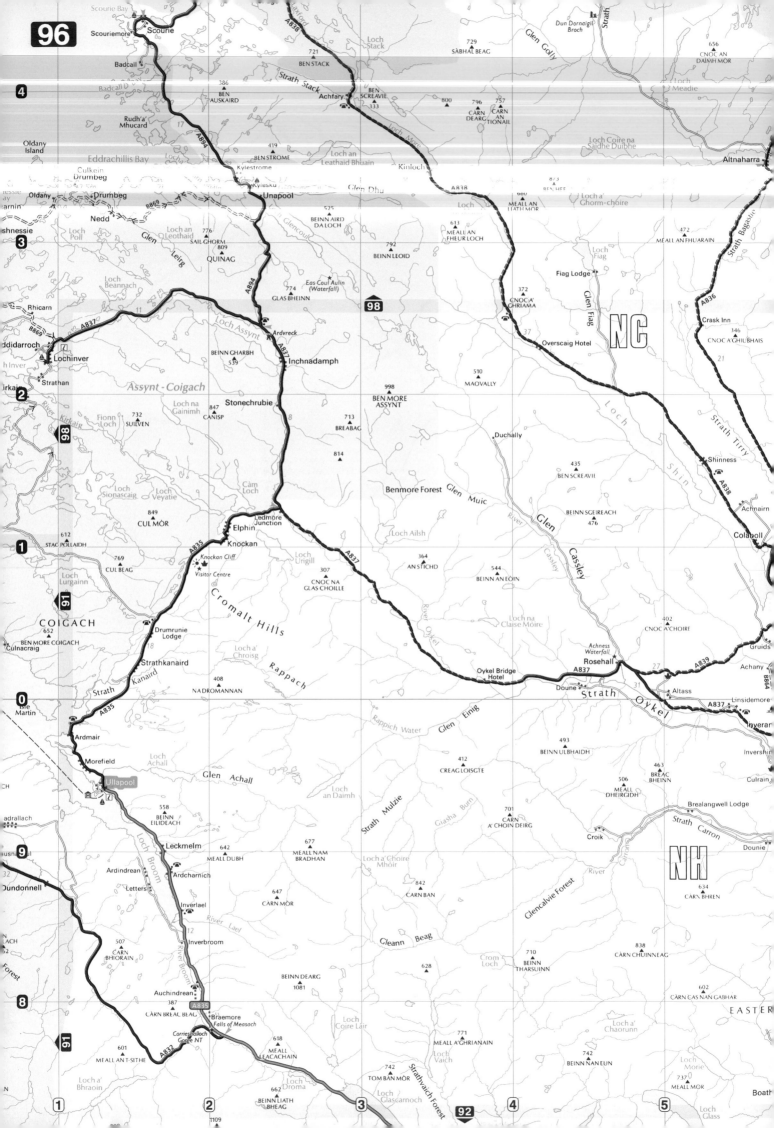

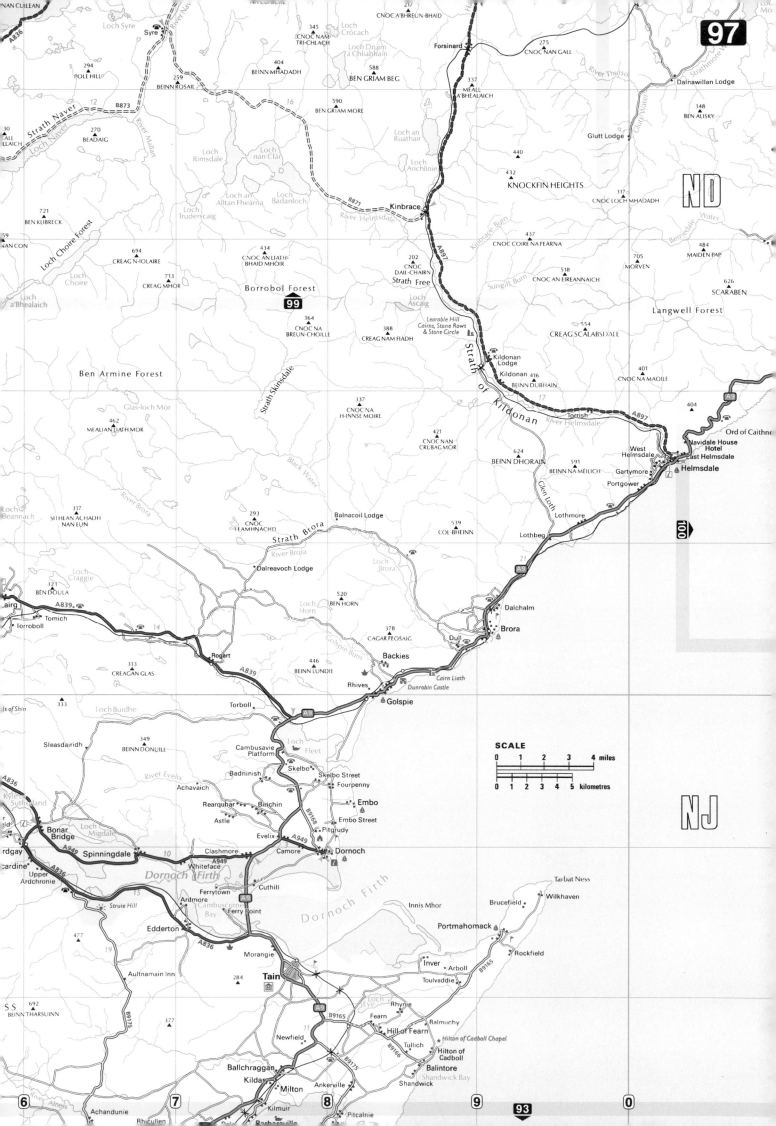

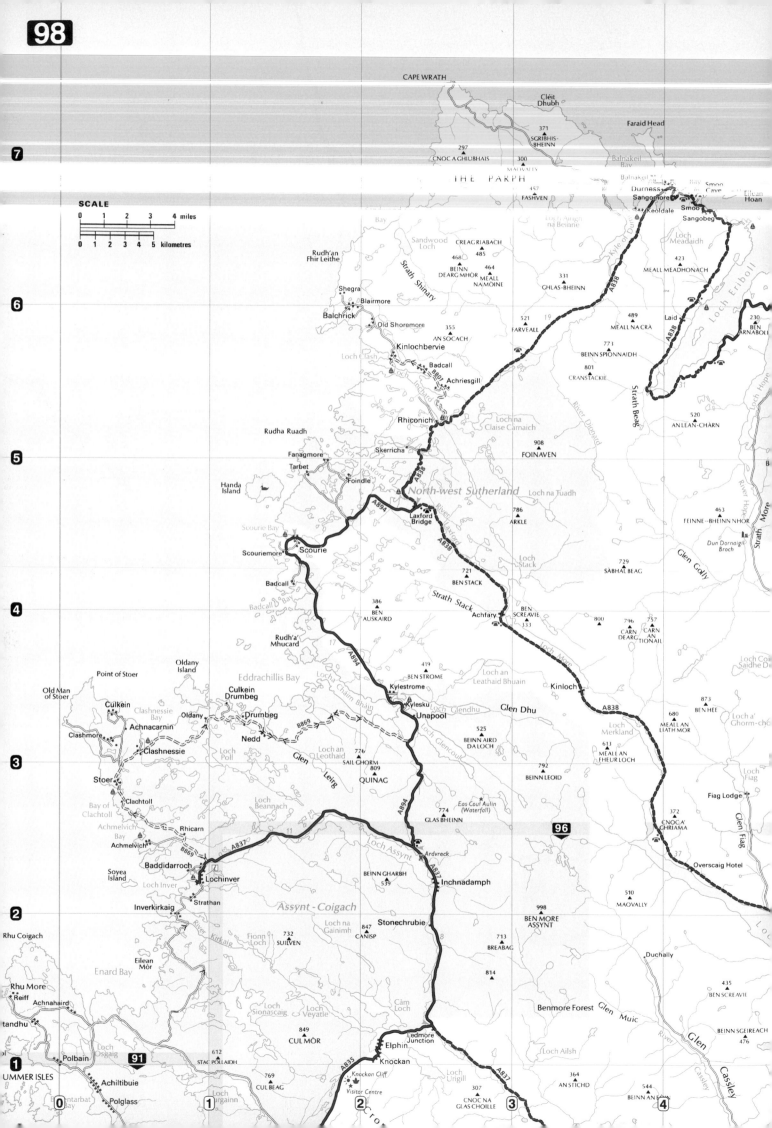

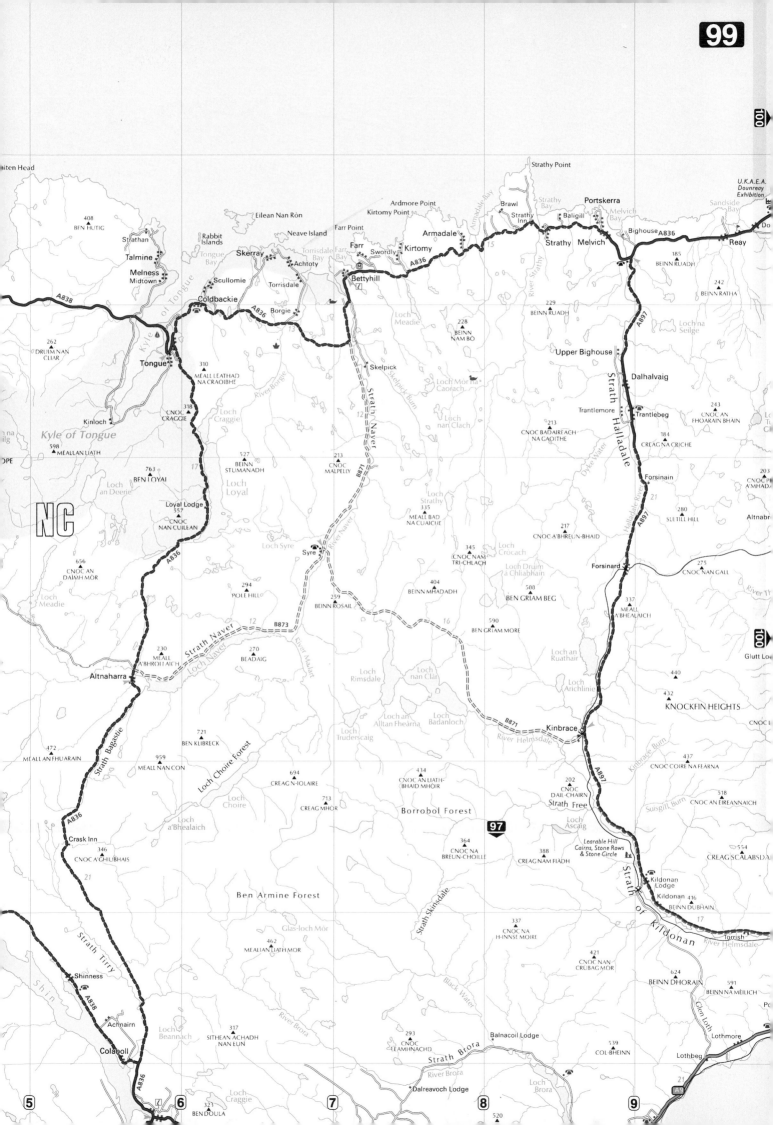

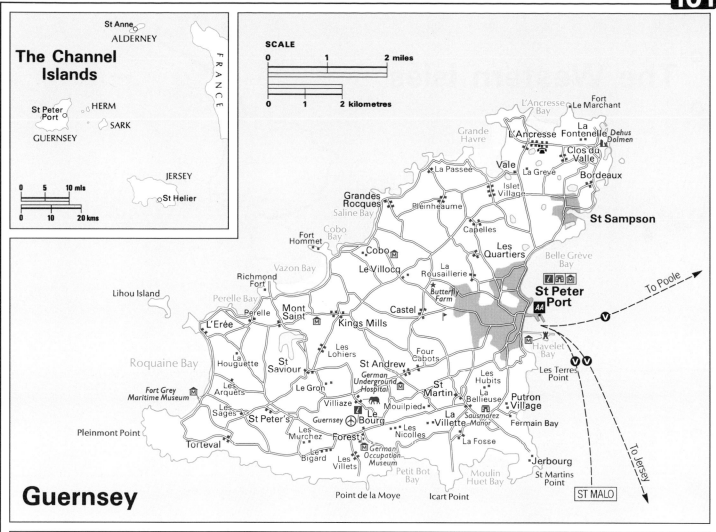

The Channel Islands

St Anne
ALDERNEY

F
R
A
N
C
E

HERM
St Peter
Port
SARK
GUERNSEY

JERSEY
St Helier

SCALE
0   1   2 miles
0   1   2 kilometres

0   5   10 mls
0   10   20 kms

L'Ancresse Bay   Fort Le Marchant
Grande Havre   L'Ancresse   La Fontenelle   Dehus Dolmen
La Passee   Clos du Valle
La Grève
Vale   Bordeaux
Islet Village
Grandes Rocques   Pleinheaume   St Sampson
Capelles
Cobo Bay
Fort Hommet   Les Quartiers
Cobo   La Rousaillerie   Belle Grève Bay
Vazon Bay   Le Villocq
Butterfly Farm   St Peter Port   To Poole
Richmond Fort   Castel
Lihou Island   Perelle Bay   Mont Saint   Four Cabots   AA
L'Erée   Perelle   Kings Mills   Havelet Bay
La Houguette   Les Lohiers   St Andrew   Les Hubits   Les Terres Point
Roquaine Bay   St Saviour   German Underground Hospital   La Bellieuse
Les Arquêts   Le Gron   St Martin   Putron Village   To Jersey
Fort Grey Maritime Museum   Villiaze   Mouilpied   La Villette   Fermain Bay
Les Sages   St Peter's   Le Bourg   Sausmarez Manor
Pleinmont Point   Les Murchez   Guernsey   Les Nicolles   La Fosse
Forest
Torteval   Le Bigard   Les Villets   German Occupation Museum   Jerbourg   ST MALO
Petit Bot Bay   St Martins Point
Point de la Moye   Icart Point   Moulin Huet Bay

Guernsey

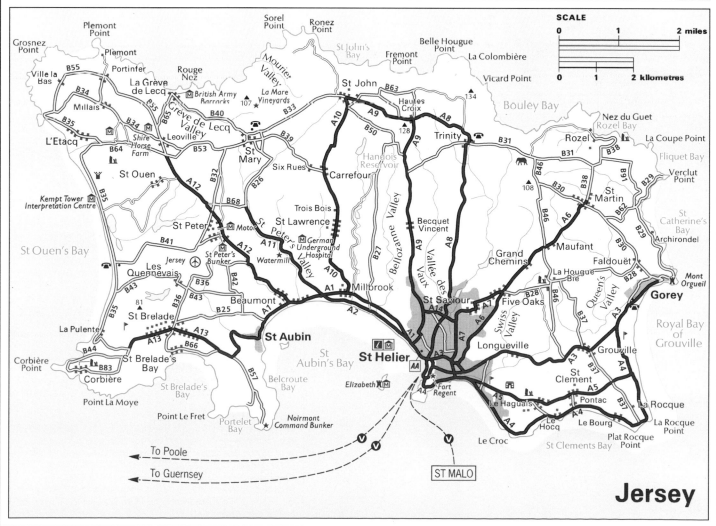

SCALE
0   1   2 miles
0   1   2 kilometres

Plemont Point
Grosnez Point   Plemont   Sorel Point   Ronez Point
Ville la Bas   B55   Portinfer   Rouge Nez   St John's Bay   Belle Hougue Point   La Colombière
B34   La Grève de Lecq   Mourier Valley   St John   Fremont Point   Vicard Point   Bouley Bay
Millais   B55   British Army Barracks   107   La Mare Vineyards   B63   Hautes Croix   Nez du Guet Rozel Bay
B35   B34   Grève de Lecq Valley   B40   B33   A10   A9   A8   La Coupe Point
L'Etacq   B64   Shire Horse Farm   B39   B50   128   Trinity   B31   Rozel   B38   Fliquet Bay
St Mary   Leoville   B53   St Mary   A9   B31   Verclut Point
St Ouen   A12   B32   Six Rues   Handois Reservoir   108   B30   St Martin   B29
Kempt Tower Interpretation Centre   B35   B26   Carrefour   B46   B62   St Catherine's Bay
B68   Trois Bois   Bellozanne Valley   Vallée des Vaux   A8   B46   A6   Archirondel
St Peter   Motor   St Peter's Bunker   St Lawrence   German Underground Hospital   Becquet Vincent   Grand Chemins   Maufant   La Hougue Bie   Faldouët   Mont Orgueil
St Ouen's Bay   B41   A12   A11   Watermill   St Peter's Valley   A10   A6   B28   Queen's Valley   B28   Gorey
Jersey   B36   A1   Millbrook   St Saviour   Five Oaks   B46   B37   B30   Royal Bay of Grouville
Les Quennevais   B43   B42   A14   A7   Swiss Valley   A3   Grouville
81   B36   B43   Beaumont   A1   A2   A1   A6   Longueville   B37   St Clement   A4
St Brelade   B25   A13   A7   A3   B31
La Pulente   A13   B66   St Aubin   St Helier   A3   A5   Pontac   B31   La Rocque
Corbière Point   B44   St Brelade's Bay   B57   St Aubin's Bay   AA   Le Haguais   A4   La Rocque Point
B83   Corbière   St Brelade's Bay   Belcroute Bay   Elizabeth   Fort Regent   A5   Le Bourg   Plat Rocque Point
Point La Moye   Noirmont Command Bunker   A4   Le Hocq
Point Le Fret   Portelet Bay   Le Croc   St Clements Bay
To Poole
To Guernsey   ST MALO

Jersey

The Western Isles

SCALE

0 5 10 miles

0 5 10 kilometres

NA **NB** **NF** **NG** **NL**

BUTT OF LEWIS

Lionel · Port of Ness
Skigersta
NESS
Borve
Shader
Cellar Head
A851
DIAVAL 158
Steinaclett Cairn & Stone Circle
Bragar · Arnol · Barvas
Black House
Tolsta
Shawbost
Carloway
Great Bernera
Gallan Head
Dun Carloway Broch
Coll
Tolsta Head
LEWIS
280 BEN BARVAS
ISLE OF LEWIS
Breasclete
Timsgarry
Valtos
Miavaig
Callanish
Laxdale
Stornoway
Portnaguran · Tiumpan Head
Aird · EYE PENINSULA
Broad Bay
Garrabost
Bayble
Uig
Callanish Standing Stones
233 EITSHAL
Sandwickhill A866 Knock
Chicken Head
Achmore
A859
Islivig
Aird Brenish
Brenish
496 TEINNASVAL
Leurbost
Grimshader
Crossbost
Cromore
Balallan
Laxay
Mealasta I
Kershader
Gravir
Loch Ouim
Kebock Head
Scarp
Aribruach
B8060
Loch Langavat
Loch Resort
Hushinish Point
TIRGA MORE 679
401 MÒR MHONADH
Seaforth Island 571
BEINN MHOR
Limervoy
To Ullapool
Ardvourlie
799 CLISHAM 37
PARK
Soay More
West Loch Tarbert
Ardhasig
Tarbert
Carnach
Loch Shell
OUTER HEBRIDES
Taransay
Rudha Sgeirigin
Sound of Taransay
Carnach
Scalpay
Shiant Islands
Toe Head
Borve
Grosebay
HARRIS
Manish
Rudha Bocaig
333 CHAIPAVAL 24
Shilldy
Pabbay
A859
Finsbay
Leverburgh
Rodel
Killegray
St Clements Church
Renish Point
Sound of Pabbay
Boreray
Berneray
Sound of Harris
Lochmaddy-Tarbert
The Little Minch
Griminish Pt
Vallay
Newton Ferry
Hermetray
Tigharry
Sollas
NORTH UIST
231 MARRIVAL
Weaver's Point
Lochmaddy-Uig
Bayhead
Rudha Port Scalpaig
Lochmaddy
Tarbert-Uig
Clachan-a-Luib
Locheport
Kirkibost Island
Carinish
147 EAVAL
Heisker or Monach Islands
Sound of Monach
Benbecula
Balivanich
Gramsdale
Ronay
RONA
BENBECULA
Hornish Point
Creagorry
Wiay
ISLE OF SKYE
Loch Bee
Grogarry
167 BEN TARBERT
Stilligarry
Howmore
Rudha Hallagro
RAASAY
227
Stoneybridge
606 HECLA
596 BEINN MHOR
SOUTH UIST
Rudha Ardvule
Rudha Bolum
South Uist Machair
Loch Eynort
374 STULAVAL · Stuley
Daliburgh
Lochboisdale
Kilbride
201 RONEVAL
Fiaray
185 BEN SCRIEN
Scurrival Pt
Eriskay
Castlebay Lochboisdale
Greian Head
BARRA
Borve
384 HEAVAL
Bruernish Point
Doirlinn Head
Kisimul
Castlebay
Vatersay
Muldoanich
Hellisay
Gighay
Sandray
Sound of Barra
SEA OF THE HEBRIDES
To Oban
Rosinish
Mingulay
Berneray
Barra Head

THE WESTERN ISLES

The Western Isles, na h-Eileanan Siar, stretch for 130 miles along the edge of the Atlantic, fringed on the west by mile after mile of clean, sandy beaches. The islands have a distinctive culture and Gaelic is the first language of the majority of islanders. Roadside placename signs are all in Gaelic, except in Stornoway (Steornabhagh) on Lewis, and Benbecula (Beinn na Faoghla), where they are bilingual. Although one island, Lewis (north) and Harris (south) are very different. Lewis is lowlying and covered with bleak peat moors, whereas Harris is rocky and mountainous, with fertile green 'machair' land to the West.

North Uist, Benbecula and South Uist offer beaches and lowlying 'machair' to the west and mountains and moorland to the east, while Barra has a rocky, broken east coast and fine-sand bays on the west, rising to a summit at Heaval.

Ferry Services

Lewis is linked by ferry to the mainland at Ullapool, with daily sailings (except Sun). Harris is linked to Skye at Uig, and North Uist at Lockmaddy in a triangular service. North Uist is served from Uig and Tarbert (Harris), also in a triangular service. South Uist is served from Oban (mainland), as is Barra, with the ferry arriving at Castlebay. Barra has an additional service from Mallaig from mid-June to the end of August.

Scottish Islands

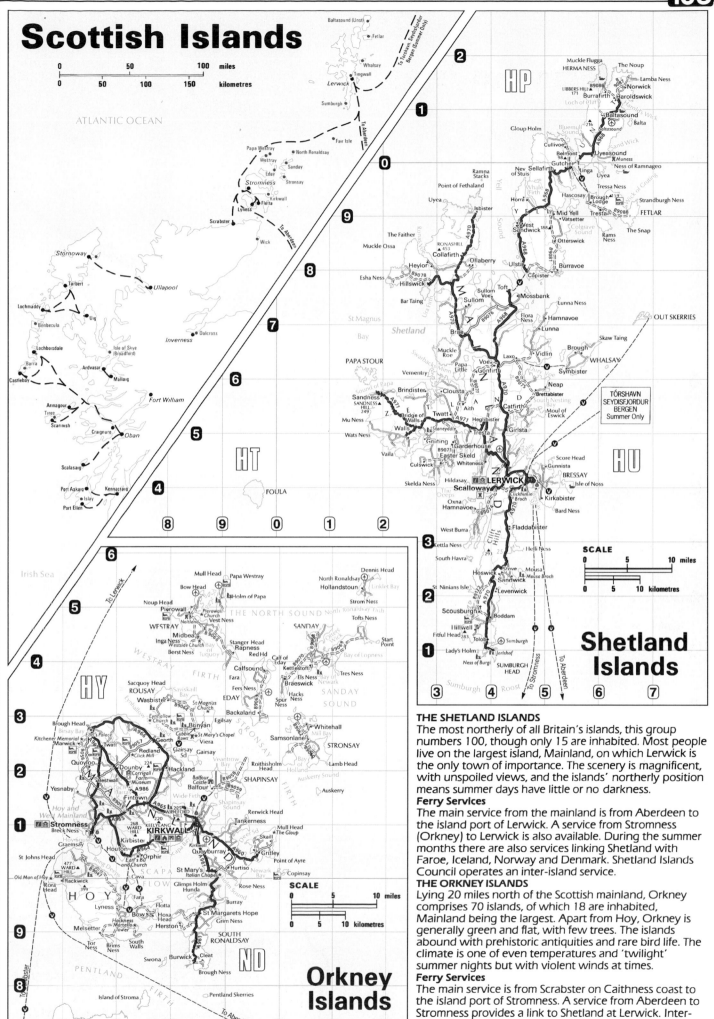

THE SHETLAND ISLANDS
The most northerly of all Britain's islands, this group numbers 100, though only 15 are inhabited. Most people live on the largest island, Mainland, on which Lerwick is the only town of importance. The scenery is magnificent, with unspoiled views, and the islands' northerly position means summer days have little or no darkness.

Ferry Services
The main service from the mainland is from Aberdeen to the island port of Lerwick. A service from Stromness (Orkney) to Lerwick is also available. During the summer months there are also services linking Shetland with Faroe, Iceland, Norway and Denmark. Shetland Islands Council operates an inter-island service.

THE ORKNEY ISLANDS
Lying 20 miles north of the Scottish mainland, Orkney comprises 70 islands, of which 18 are inhabited, Mainland being the largest. Apart from Hoy, Orkney is generally green and flat, with few trees. The islands abound with prehistoric antiquities and rare bird life. The climate is one of even temperatures and 'twilight' summer nights but with violent winds at times.

Ferry Services
The main service is from Scrabster on Caithness coast to the island port of Stromness. A service from Aberdeen to Stromness provides a link to Shetland at Lerwick. Inter-island services are also operated (advance reservations necessary).

Shetland Islands

Orkney Islands

Ireland

C

D

E

Bloc
Is

Aran Island

Rossan Point
Malin More
Glencolumbkille Folk Museum
Glencolumbkille
(Gleann Cholm Cille)
1972
Carrick
(An Charraig)
SLIEVE LEAGUE
Kilcar
(Cill Charthaigh)
Killybegs

St John's Point

Gweebarra B.

Donegal B
Bu

Inishmurray

R279
Grange
21
Cliffo
1722
Lissadell House
BENBULBE

Erris Head
Broad Haven
46
Downpatrick Head
Ballycastle
Killala Bay
Easky
Dromore West
Strandhill
Rosses Point
R29
N15
Sligo
R292

Belmullet
(Béal an Mhuirhead)
R314
R314
Killala
37
R297
Droma
Ballysada

Bunnahowen
R315
Killala
R312
Enniscrone
N59
32
N59

Inishkea
R313
Bangor Erris
N59
27
Ballina
Colloone
R290

Duvillaun More
Blacksod Bay
Carrowmore Lough
Crossmolina
Lough Conn
MTS
Bunnyconnellan
N17
R293

2204
SLIEVE MORE
2369
2646
NEPHIN
34
N57
20
O X
R294
Tobercurry
R296

Achill Head
Keel
R319
21
Connaught Regional Airport
Curry
Charlestown
Bo

Achill Island
Lough Feeagh
R317
Foxford
N57
Carracastle
R294

1
2
N59
Lough Cullin
23
Swinford
N5
R321
Kilkelly
R325
Frenchpark

Newport
R311
Turlough
N5
N60
R324
Kiltimagh
R293

Clew Bay
R335
Castlebar
N60
N17
N83
R325

Westport
Ballyhean
Balla

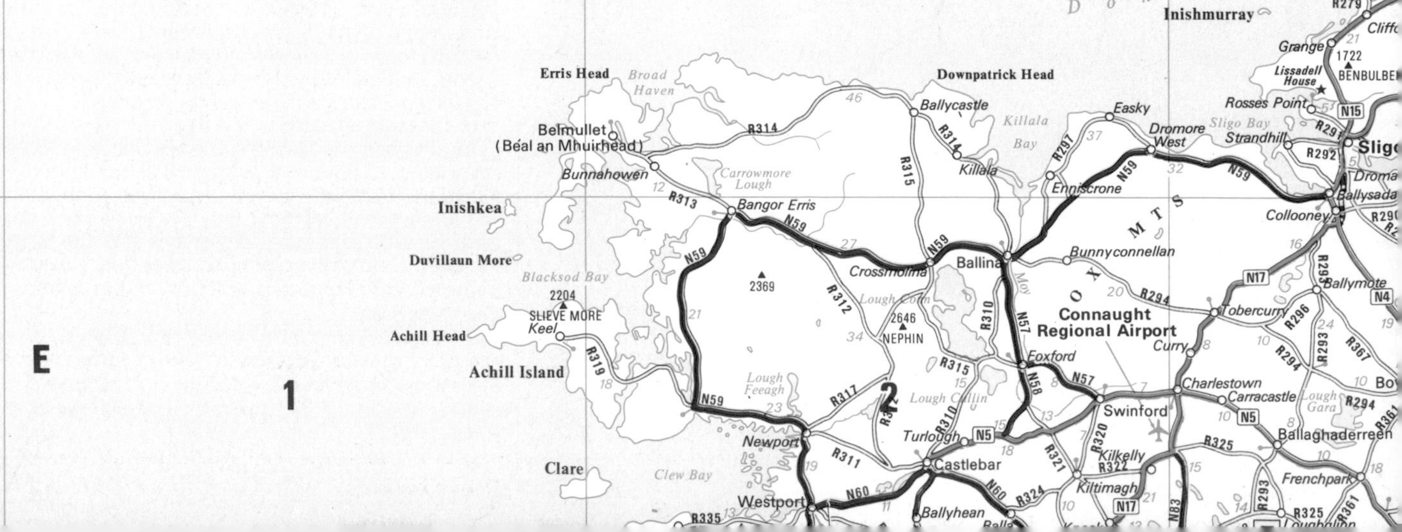

eath E5
G3
nmore F2
hterard F2
ns H2

asgreen G3
nasilla H1
ry E2
sage East H4
sage West H3
ickswell G2
stown G4
igo D3
nbridge D4
neroy D4
adown D4
aferry D5
arlington F4
avogie D5
glenone D4
Laoise F4
rmarnock F5
rane F5
troe G3
trush C4
stewart C4
umna F3
ntzpass D5

arney F4
dalstown D5
harkin C4
hangen F4
hcoole F4
ncormack H3
ndowney G3
hdrum G5
hfriland E5
hkeale G2
n Luric G2
arleville)
hmelton C4

Rathmolyon F4
Rathmore H2
Rathmullan C4
Rathnew F5
Rathowen E4
Rathvilty G4
Ratoath F4
Ray C4
Ring H3
(An Rinn)
Ringaskiddy H3
Riverstown F3
Rockcorry E4
Roosky E3
Rosapenna C3
Rosebercon G4
Roscommon E3
Roscrea F3
Ross Carberry J2
Rosscor D3
Rosses Point D3
Rosslare Harbour H4
Rosslea E4
Rostrevor E5
Roundstone F2
Roundwood F5
Rush F5

St Johnstown C4
Saintfield D5
Sallins F4
Scarriff G3
Scartaglen H2
Scarva D5
Schull J2
Scramoge E3
Scribbagh D3
Seskinore D4
Shanagolden G2
Shannon Airport G2
Shannonbridge F3
Shercock E4
Shillelagh G4

Shinrone F3
Shrule F2
Silvermines G3
Sion Mills D4
Sixmilebridge G2
Skerries F5
Skibbereen J2
Slane E4
Sligo D3
Smithborough E4
Sneem H1
Spiddal F2
(An Spideal)
Sporthouse Cross Roads H4
Stewartstown D4
Stonyford G4
Strabane D4
Stradbally F4
Stradone E4
Strandhill D3
Strangford D5
Stranorlar D3
Stratford F4
Strokestown E3
Summerbill F4
Swanlinbar E3
Swatragh D4
Swinford E2
Swords F5

Taghmon G4
Tagoat H4
Tahilla H1
Tallaght F5
Tallow H3
Tallowbridge H3
Tandragee D5
Tang F3
Tarbert G2
Templemore G3
Templepatrick D5
Templetouhy G3
Termonfeckin E5

Thomas Street F3
Thomastown G4
Thurles G3
Timahoe F4
Timoleague H2
Tinahely G4
Tipperary G3
Tobercurry E3
Tobermore D4
Togher F3
Toomyvara G3
Toormore J1
Tralee G2
Tramore H4
Trim F4
Tuam F2
Tuamgraney G3
Tulla G2
Tullamore F4
Tullow G4
Tulsk E3
Turlough E2
Tyholland D4
Tyrrellspass F4

Urlingford G3

Virginia E4
Waddington H4
Warrenpoint E5
Waterford H4
Watergrasshill H3
Waterville H1
Westport E2
Wexford G4
Whitegate H3
Whitehead D5
Wicklow F5
Woodenbridge G5
Woodford F3

Youghal H3

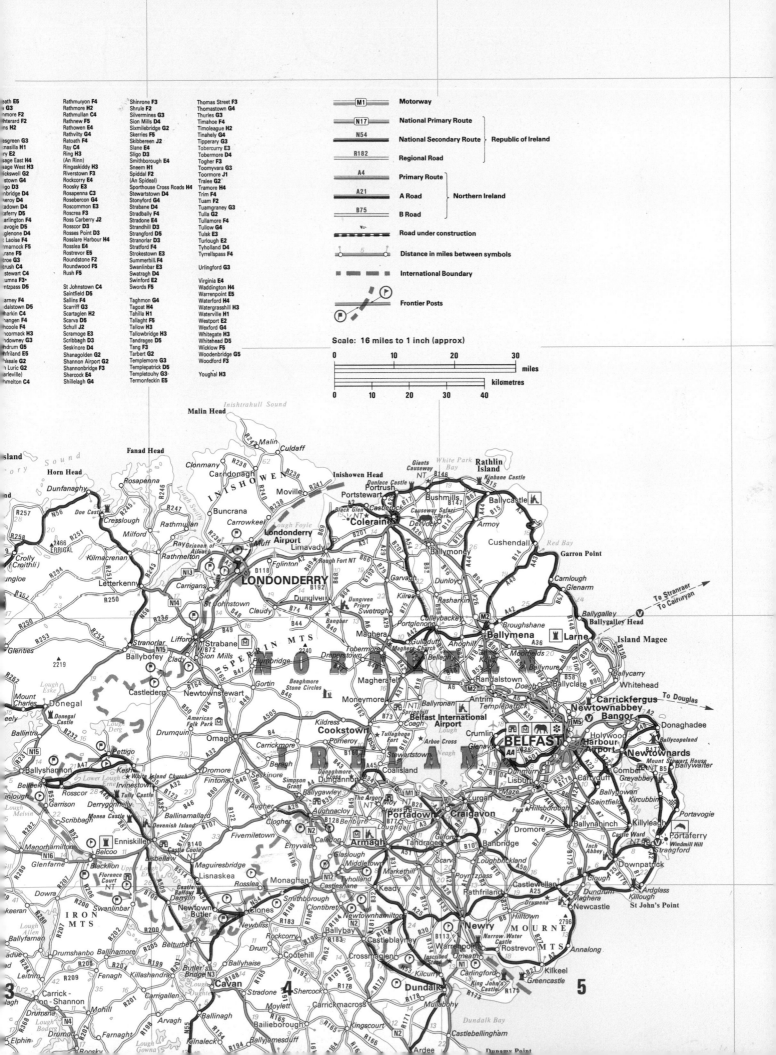

M1 Motorway
N17 National Primary Route — Republic of Ireland
N54 National Secondary Route — Republic of Ireland
R182 Regional Road — Republic of Ireland
A4 Primary Route — Northern Ireland
A21 A Road — Northern Ireland
B75 B Road — Northern Ireland
Road under construction
5 Distance in miles between symbols
International Boundary
Frontier Posts

Scale: 16 miles to 1 inch (approx)

miles: 0 10 20 30
kilometres: 0 10 20 30 40

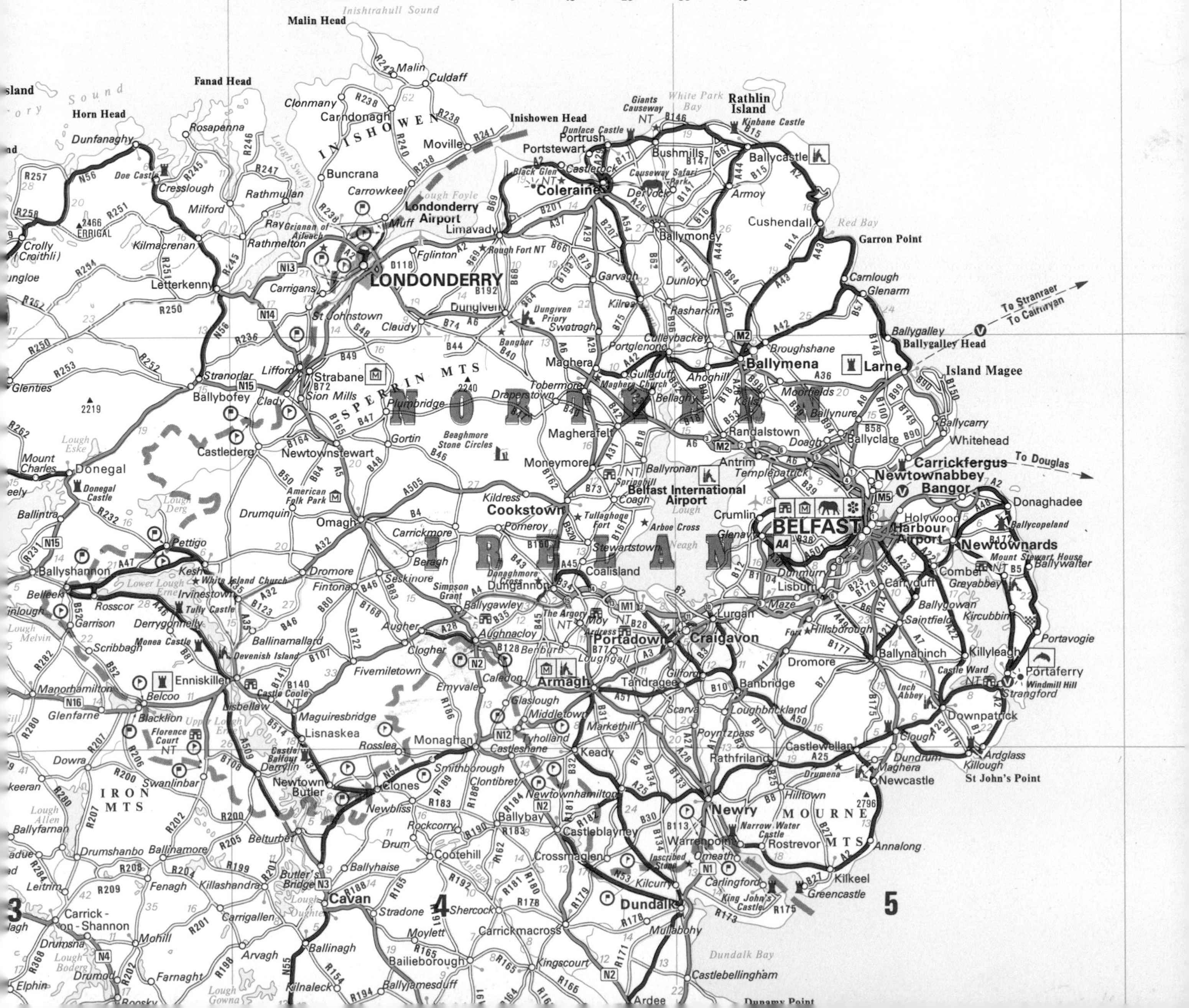
Malin Head
Inishtrahull Sound
Fanad Head
Horn Head
Inishowen Head
Giants Causeway
White Park Bay
Rathlin Island
Garron Point
Red Bay
Island Magee
Ballygalley Head
To Stranraer
To Cairnryan
To Douglas
LONDONDERRY
Londonderry Airport
Coleraine
Portrush
Portstewart
Ballycastle
Ballymoney
Ballymena
Larne
Carrickfergus
Newtownabbey
Bangor
BELFAST
Belfast International Airport
Harbour Airport
Newtownards
Donaghadee
Lisburn
Craigavon
Portadown
Lurgan
Armagh
Banbridge
Newry
Dundalk
Downpatrick
Newcastle
Portaferry
Strangford
Kilkeel
Warrenpoint
Enniskillen
Omagh
Cookstown
Dungannon
Strabane
Letterkenny
Donegal
Ballyshannon
Cavan
Monaghan
Carrickmacross
Clones
Lifford
Limavady
Magherafelt
Antrim
Dungiven
SPERRIN MTS
NORTHERN IRELAND
INISHOWEN
IRON MTS
MOURNE MTS
Lough Neagh
Lough Foyle
Lough Swilly
Lough Erne
Dundalk Bay
St John's Point
3
4
5

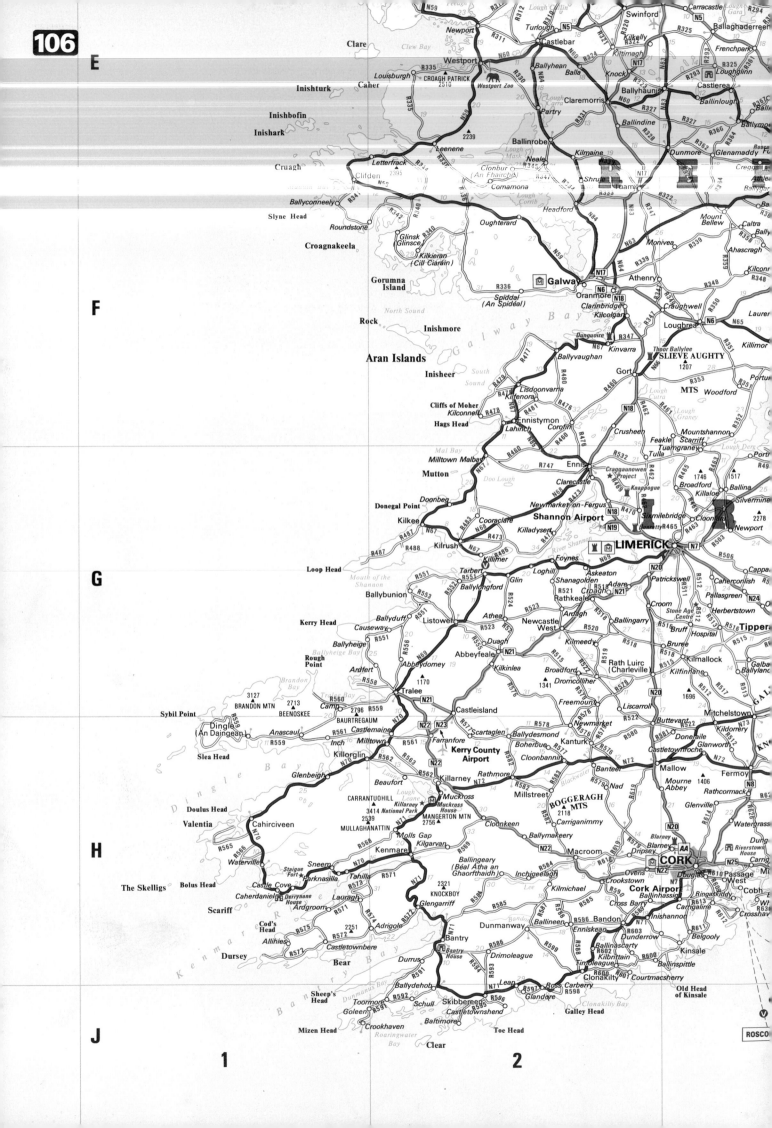

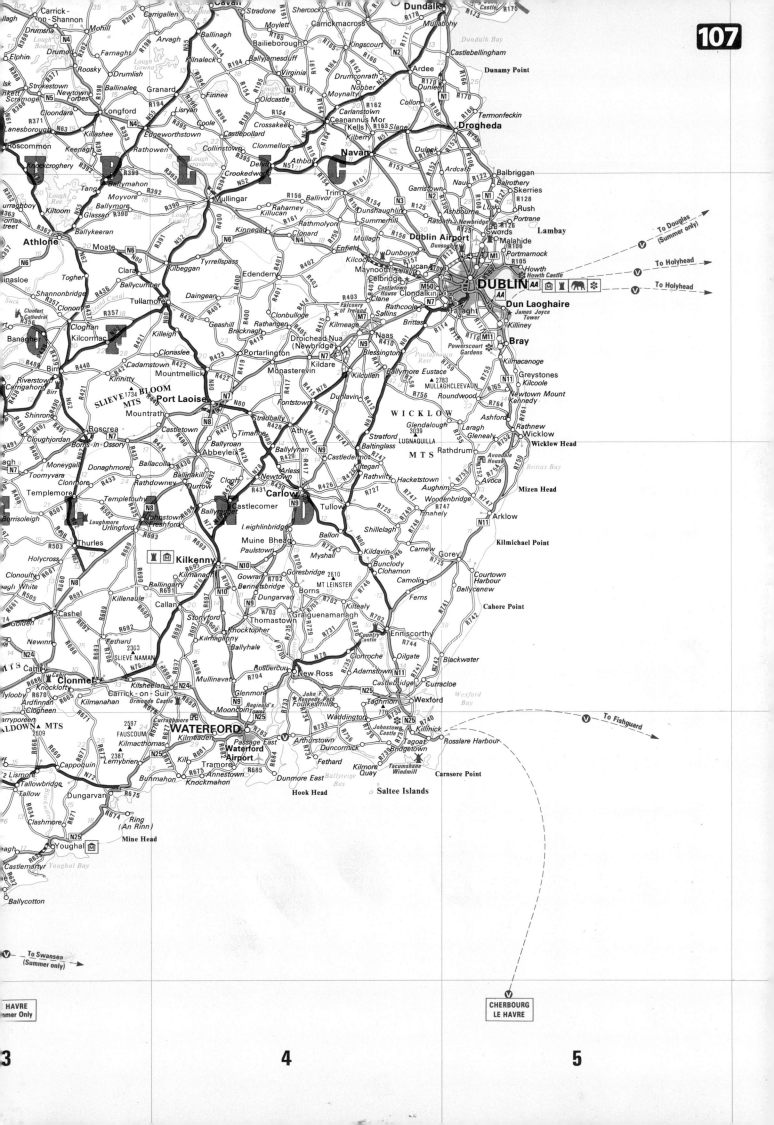

London

Scale 1:10,000
approx 6 inches to 1 mile

0	220	440	660	Yds
0	250	500	750 Mtrs

Legend

Symbol	Description
	Motorway
	Primary route single/dual
	Other A road single/dual
	B road single/dual
	Unclassified road single/dual
	Unclassified road wide/narrow
	Road under construction
	Road tunnel wide/narrow
	Restricted (access/private) road /Oxford St is closed to through traffic (except buses & taxis) 07.00-19.00 hrs Monday-Saturday
	Footpath
	Track
	Pedestrian street
	Railway line/in tunnel
↱	One way street/compulsory turn
↰	Banned turn
↰	Banned turn (restricted periods only)
⇄	British Rail station
⊖	London Regional Transport station
●	Docklands Light Railway station
Ⓟ	Parking
Ⓟ◯	Post Office

Symbol	Description	Symbol	Description
POL	Police Station	AA	AA Shop
†	Church	i	Tourist Information Centre
	Steps	i	Tourist Information Centre (summer only)
•	Mini-roundabout		

Royal Parks (Opening and closing times for traffic)

Green Park	Constitution Hill is always open *except* Sundays when it is closed 08.00 - dusk
Hyde Park	05.00 - Midnight
Regent's Park	05.00 - Dusk
St James's Park	The Mall is always open *except* on Sundays when it is closed 08.00 - dusk

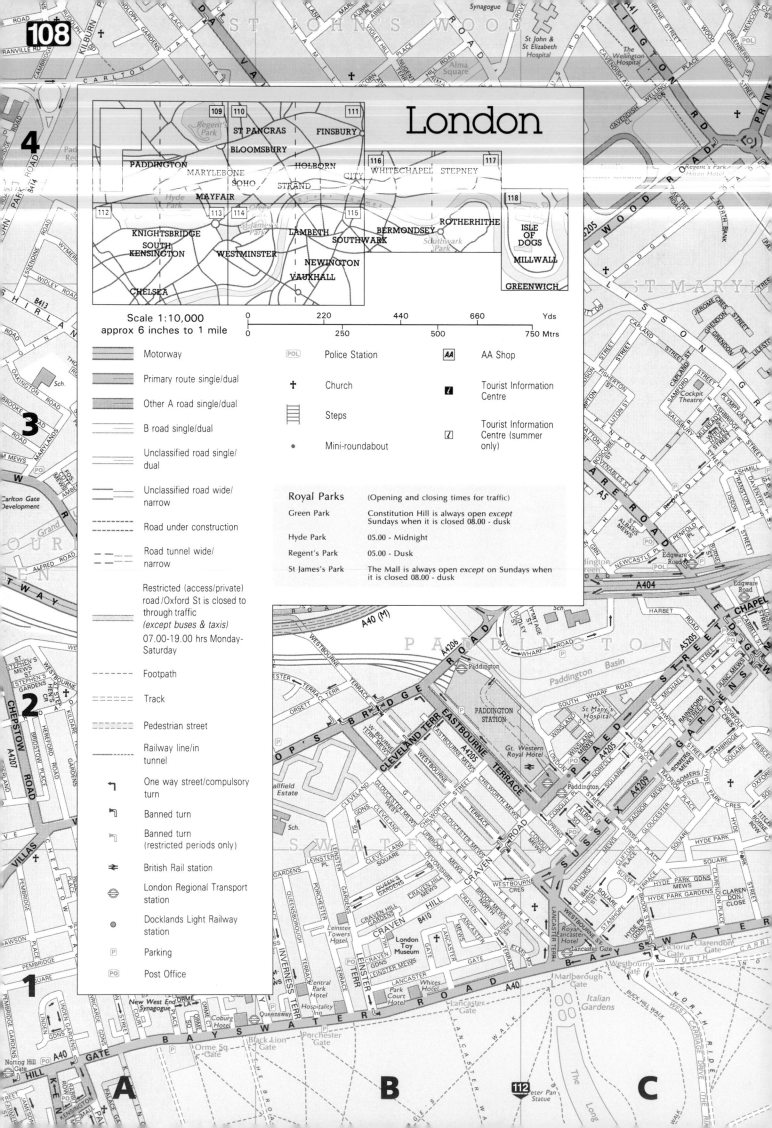

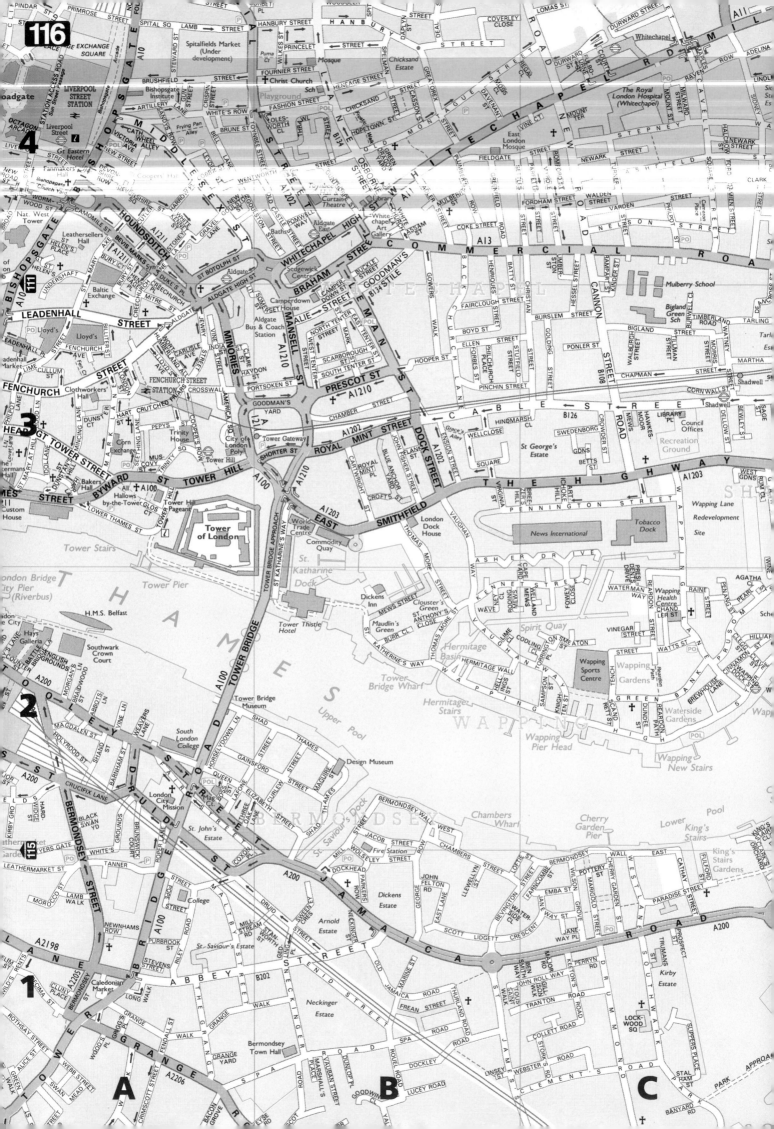

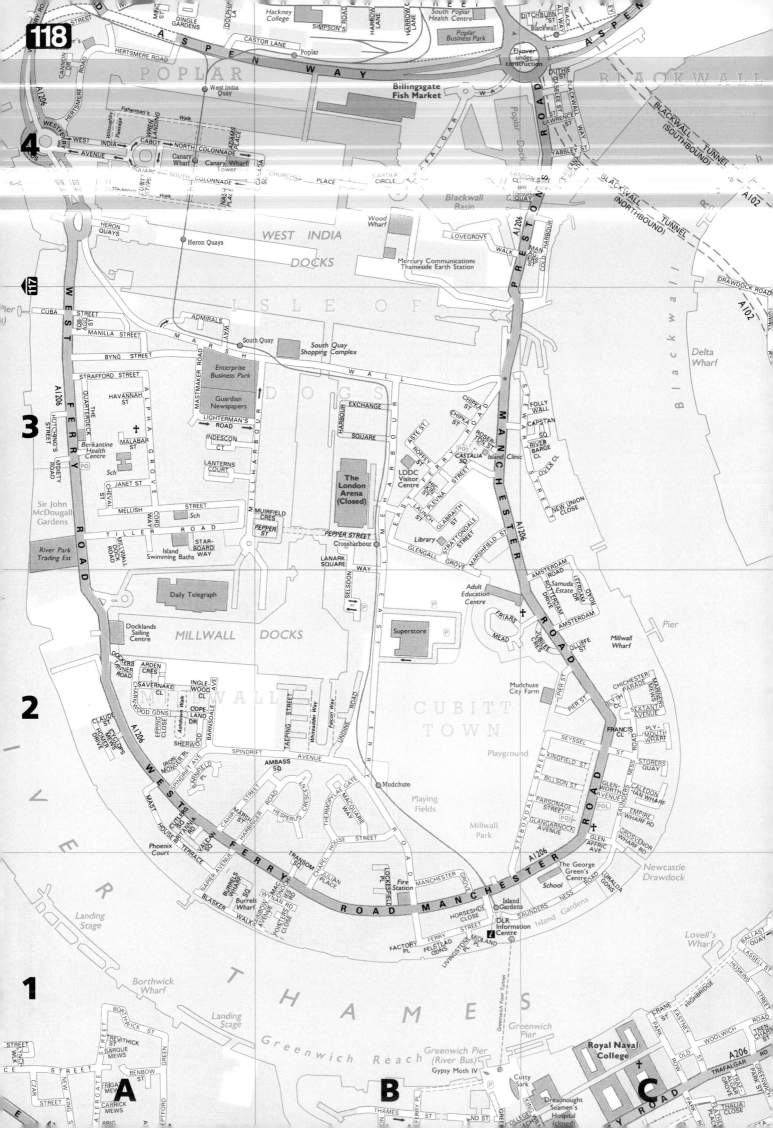

London street index

In the index, the street names are listed in alphabetical order and written in full, but may be abbreviated on the map. Postal codes are listed where information is available. Each entry is followed by its map page number in bold type and an arbitrary letter and figure grid reference eg Exhibition Road SW7 **112** C3. Turn to page '112'. The letter 'C' refers to the grid square located at the bottom of the page. The figure '3' refers to the grid square located at the lefthand side of the page. Exhibition Road is found within the intersecting square. SW7 refers to the postcode. A proportion of street names and their references are also followed by the name of another street in italics. These entries do not appear on the map due to insufficient space but can be located adjacent to the name of the road in italics.

119

Blackfriars Road Colworth Grove

Blackfriars Road SE1 115 D4
Blacklands Terrace SW3 113 D2
Blackwood Street SE17 115 F1
Blandford Square NW1 109 D3
Blandford Street W1 109 E2
Blasker Walk E14 118 A1
Bleeding Heart Yard EC1 111 D2
Greville Street
Blenheim Street W1 109 F1
New Bond Street
Bletchley Street N1 111 E4
Blithfield Street W8 112 A3
Blomfield Street EC2 111 F2
Blomfield Villas W2 108 B2
Bloomburg Street SW1 113 F2
Vauxhall Bridge Road
Bloomfield Place W1 109 F1
Bourdon Street
Bloomfield Terrace SW1 113 E2
Bloomsbury Court WC1 110 B2
High Holborn
Bloomsbury Place WC1 110 B3
Southampton Row
Bloomsbury Square WC1 110 B2
Bloomsbury Street WC1 110 B2
Bloomsbury Way WC1 110 B2
Blount Street E14 117 E4
Blue Anchor Yard E1 116 B3
Bolsover Street W1 109 F3
Bolt Court EC4 111 D2
Bolton Gardens Mews SW10 112 B1
Bolton Gardens SW5 112 A2
Bolton Street W1 113 F4
Bond Way SW8 114 B1
Bonding Yard Walk SE16 35 A2
Bonhill Street EC2 111 F3
Bonnington Square SW8 114 C1
Booker Close E14 117 F4
Boot Street N1 111 F4
Booth's Place W1 109 F2
Wells Street
Boreas Walk N1 111 E4
Nelson Place
Borough High Street SE1 115 E3
Borough Road SE1 115 E3
Borrett Close SE17 115 E1
Boscobel Place SW1 113 E2
Boscobel Street NW8 108 C3
Boss Street SE1 116 A2
Boston Place NW1 108 D3
Boswell Court WC1 110 B3
Boswell Street
Boswell Street WC1 110 B3
Botolph Lane EC3 111 F1
Boulcott Street E1 117 E3
Boundary Lane SE17 115 E1
Boundary Road SE1 115 D4
Bourdon Street W1 109 F1
Bourlet Close W1 109 F2
Bourne Street SW1 113 E2
Bouverie Street EC4 111 D1
Bow Lane EC4 111 E1
Bow Street WC2 110 B2
Bowden Street SE11 115 D1
Bower Street E1 117 D3
Bowling Green Lane EC1 111 D3
Bowling Green Place SE1 115 F4
Newcomen Street
Bowling Green Street SE11 114 C1
Bowling Green Walk N1 111 F4
Boyd Street E1 116 B3
Boyfield Street SE1 115 D3
Boyle Street W1 109 F1
Savile Row
Boyson Road SE17 115 E1
Brackley Street EC1 111 E3
Brad Street SE1 115 D4
Bradenham Close SE17 115 F1
Braganza Street SE17 115 D1
Braham Street E1 116 B3
Braidwood Street SE1 116 A2
Bramerton Street SW3 112 C1
Bramham Gardens SW5 112 A2
Branch Road E14 117 E3
Brandon Street SE17 115 E2
Brangton Road SE11 114 C1
Brass Tally Alley SE16 117 E1
Bray Crescent SE16 117 D2
Bray Place SW3 113 D2
Bread Street EC4 111 E1
Bream's Buildings EC 110 C2
Brechin Place SW7 112 B2
Breezer's Hill E1 116 C3
Bremner Road SW7 112 B3
Brendon Street W1 109 D2
Brenton Street E14 117 E4
Bressenden Place SW1 113 F3
Brettell Street SE17 115 F1
Brewer Street W1 110 A1
Brewer's Green SW1 114 A3
Caxton Street
Brewhouse Lane E1 116 C2
Brewhouse Walk SE16 117 E2
Brick Court EC4 110 C2
Middle Temple Lane
Brick Street W1 113 E4
Bride Lane EC4 111 D2
Bridewell Place EC4 111 D1
Bridford Mews W1 109 F3
Bridge Place SW1 113 F2
Bridge Street SW1 114 B3
Bridge Yard SE1 115 F4
Bridgeport Place E1 116 B2
Kennet Street
Bridgewater Street 111 E3
Beech Street
Bridgeway Street NW1 110 A2
Bridle Lane W1 110 A1
Brightlingsea Place E14 117 F3
Brill Place NW1 110 A4
Briset Street EC1 111 D3
Britannia Road E14 118 A2
Britannia Street WC1 110 C4
Britannia Walk N1 111 F4
Britten Street SW3 112 C1
Britton Street EC1 111 D3
Broad Court WC2 110 B2
Broad Sanctuary SW1 114 B3
Broad Walk W2 113 E4
Broadbent Street W1 109 F1
Broadley Street NW8 108 C4
Broadley Terrace NW1 109 D3
Broadstone Place W1 109 E2
Broadwall SE1 115 D4
Broadway SW1 114 A3
Broadwick Street W1 110 A1
Brockham Street SE1 115 E3
Brodlove Lane E1 117 D3
Bromley Street E1 117 E4
Brompton Place SW3 113 D3
Brompton Road SW3 113 D3
Brompton Square SW3 112 C3
Bronti Close SE17 115 E1
Brook Drive SE11 115 D2
Brook Gate W1 109 E1
Brook Mews North W2 108 B1
Brook Street W1 109 E1
Brook Street W2 108 C1
Brook's Mews W1 109 F1
Brooke Street EC1 111 D2
Brooke's Court EC1 110 C2
Brown Hart Gardens W1 109 E1
Brown Street W1 109 D2
Browning Street SE17 115 E2
Brownlow Mews WC1 110 C3
Brownlow Street WC1 110 C2
Brune Street E1 116 A4
Brunel Road SE16 117 D1
Brunswick Gardens W8 112 A4
Brunswick Mews W1 109 D2
Brunswick Place N1 111 F4
Brunswick Quay SE16 117 E1
Brunswick Square WC1 110 B3
Brunton Place E14 117 E3
Brushfield Street E1 116 A4
Bruton Lane W1 109 F1
Bruton Place W1 109 F1
Bruton Street W1 109 F1
Bryan Road SE16 117 F2
Bryanston Mews East W1 109 D2
Bryanston Mews West W1 109 D2
Bryanston Place W1 109 D2
Bryanston Square W1 109 D2
Bryanston Street W1 109 D2
Buck Hill Walk W2 108 C1
Buck Street WC2 110 B1
Buckingham Gate SW1 113 F3
Buckingham Palace Road SW1 113 F2
Buckingham Place SW1 113 F3
Buckland Street N1 111 F4
Buckle Street E1 116 B4
Bucklersbury EC4 111 E2
Bucknall Street WC2 110 B2
Buckters Rents SE16 117 E2
Budge's Walk W2 108 B4
Bulleid Way SW1 113 F2
Bulstrode Place W1 109 E2
Marylebone Lane
Bulstrode Street W1 109 E2
Bunhill Row EC1 111 F3
Bunhouse Place SW1 113 E2
Burbage Close SE1 115 F3
Burdett Street SE1 115 D3
Burgess Street E14 117 F4
Burgon Street EC4 111 E2
Carter Lane
Burleigh Street WC2 110 B1
Burlington Arcade W1 109 F1
Burlington Gardens W1 109 F1
Burne Street NW1 108 C3
Burnsall Street SW3 113 D1
Burnside Close SE16 117 E2
Burr Cose E1 116 B2
Burrell Street SE1 115 D4
Burrells Wharf Square E14 118 A1
Burrows Mews SE1 115 D4
Bursar Street SE1 116 A2
Tooley Street
Burslem Street E1 116 C3
Burton Grove SE17 115 F1
Burton Street WC1 110 B4
Burwell Close E1 116 C3
Burwood Place W2 109 D2
Bury Close SE16 117 E2
Bury Court EC3 116 A4
Bury Place WC1 110 B2
Bury Street EC3 116 A3
Bury Street SW1 114 A4
Bury Walk SW3 112 C2
Bush Lane EC4 111 E1
Bushell Street E1 116 B2
Wapping High Street
Butcher Row E1 117 E3
Bute Street SW7 112 C1
Butler Place SW1 113 F3
Buckingham Gate
Buttesland Street N1 111 F4
Byng Place WC1 110 A3
Byward Street EC3 116 A3
Bywater Place SE16 117 E2
Bywater Street SW3 113 D2
Cabbell Street NW1 108 C2
Cable Street E1 116 B3
Cabot Square E14 118 A4
Cadiz Street SE17 115 E1
Cadogan Gardens SW3 113 D2
Cadogan Gate SW1 113 D2
Cadogan Lane SW1 113 E3
Cadogan Place SW1 113 E2
Cadogan Square SW1 113 D2
Cadogan Street SW3 113 D2
Cahill Street EC1 111 E3
Dufferin Street
Cale Street SW3 112 C2
Caleb Street SE1 115 E4
Marshalsea Road
Caledonia Street N1 110 B4
Caledonian Road N1 & N7 110 B4
Callingham Close E14 117 F4
Callow Street SW3 112 B1
Calthorpe Street WC1 110 C3
Camberwell Road SE5 115 E1
Cambridge Circus WC2 110 B1
Cambridge Gate NW1 109 F3
Cambridge Gate Mews NW1 109 F4
Albany Street
Cambridge Place W8 112 B3
Cambridge Square W2 108 C2
Cambridge Street SW1 113 F2
Cambridge Terrace Mews NW1 110 F4
Chester Gate
Camdenhurst Street E14 117 E4
Camera Place SW10 112 B1
Cameron Place E1 116 C4
Camomile Street EC3 116 A4
Campden Grove W8 112 A4
Campden Hill Road W8 112 A3
Camperdown Street E1 116 B3
Canada Square E14 118 B4
Canada Street SE16 117 E1
Canal Street SE5 115 F1
Candover Street W1 109 F2
Foley Street
Canning Passage W8 112 B3
Canning Place W8 112 B3
Cannon Beck Road SE16 117 D2
Cannon Drive E14 117 F3
Cannon Row SW1 114 B3
Cannon Street EC4 111 E2
Cannon Street Road E1 116 C3
Canterbury Place SE17 115 E2
Canvey Street SE1 115 E4
Cape Yard E1 116 B3
Capland Street NW8 108 C3
Capper Street WC1 110 A3
Capstan Way SE16 117 E2
Carbis Road E14 117 F4
Carburton Street W1 109 F3
Cardale Street E14 118 B3
Plevina Street
Cardigan Street SE11 114 C1
Cardington Street NW1 110 A4
Carey Lane EC2 111 E2
Carey Street WC2 110 C2
Carlisle Avenue EC3 116 A3
Carlisle Lane SE1 114 C3
Carlisle Place SW1 113 F2
Carlisle Street W1 110 A2
Carlos Place W1 109 E1
Carlton Gardens SW1 114 A4
Carlton House Terrace SW17 114 A4
Carlyle Square SW3 112 C1
Carmelite Street EC4 111 D1
Carnaby Street W1 110 A1
Caroline Place Mews W2 108 A1
Caroline Street E1 117 E3
Caroline Terrace SW1 113 E2
Carpenter Street W1 109 E1
Carr Street E14 117 E4
Carrington Street W1 113 E4
Shepherd Street
Carter Lane EC4 111 E2
Carter Place SE17 115 E1
Carter Street SE17 115 E1
Caroline Street E1 117 E3
Caroline Terrace SW1 113 E2
Carpenter Street W1 109 E1
Carr Street E14 117 E4
Carter Lane EC4 111 E2
Carter Place SE17 115 E1
Carter Street SE17 115 E1
Carteret Street SW1 114 A3
Carthusian Street EC1 111 E3
Cartier Circle E14 118 B4
Carting Lane WC2 110 C1
Cartwright Gardens WC1 110 B4
Cartwright Street E1 116 B3
Casson Street E1 116 B4
Castalia Square E14 118 B3
Castle Baynard Street EC4 111 E1
Castle Lane SW1 114 A3
Castle Yard SE1 115 D4
Catesby Street SE17 115 F2
Cathay Street SE16 116 C1
Cathcart Road SW10 112 B1
Cathedral Piazza SW1 113 F3
Cathedral Street SE1 115 F4
Winchester Walk
Catherine Place SW1 113 F3
Catherine Street WC2 110 C1
Catherine Wheel Alley E1 116 A4
Catton Street WC1 110 C2
Causton Street SW1 114 B2
Cavaye Place SW10 112 B1
Cavell Street E1 116 C4
Cavendish Avenue NW8 108 C4
Cavendish Close NW8 108 C4
Cavendish Mews North W1 109 F3
Hallam Street
Cavendish Place W1 109 F2
Cavendish Square W1 109 F2
Caversham Street SW3 113 D1
Caxton Street SW1 114 A3
Cayton Place EC1 111 E4
Cayton Street
Cayton Street EC1 111 E4
Cecil Court WC2 110 B1
St Martin's Lane
Centaur Street SE1 114 C3
Central Street EC1 111 E4
Chadwell Street EC1 111 D4
Chadwick Street SW1 114 A3
Chagford Street NW1 109 D3
Chalton Street NW1 110 A4
Chamber Street E1 116 B3
Chambers Street SE16 116 B1
Chancel Street SE1 115 D4
Chancellor Passage E14 118 A4
South Colonnade
Chancery Lane WC2 110 C2
Chandler Street E1 116 C2
Chandos Place WC2 110 B1
Chandos Street W1 109 F2
Chantry Square W8 112 A3
Chapel Place W1 109 F2
Chapel Side W2 108 A1
Chapel Street NW1 108 C2
Chapel Street SW1 113 E3
Chapman Street E1 116 C3
Chapter Road SE17 115 E1
Chapter Street SW1 114 A2
Chapter Terrace SE17 115 D1
Chargrove Close SE16 117 D2
Charing Cross Road WC2 110 B2
Charles II Street SW1 114 A4
Charles Square N1 111 F4
Charles Street W1 113 F4
Charleston Street SE17 115 E2
Charlotte Place SW1 113 F2
Wilton Road
Charlotte Place W1 110 A2
Goodge Street
Charlotte Road EC2 111 F4
Charlotte Street W1 110 A3
Charlwood Street SW1 114 A1
Chart Street N1 111 F4
Charterhouse Square EC1 111 E2
Charterhouse Street EC1 111 D2
Chaseley Street E14 117 E4
Chatham Street SE17 115 F2
Cheapside EC2 111 E2
Chelsea Bridge Road SW1 113 E1
Chelsea Bridge SW1 & SW8 113 E1
Chelsea Embankment SW3 113 D1
Chelsea Manor Gardens SW3 113 D1
Chelsea Manor Street SW3 113 D1
Chelsea Park Gardens SW3 112 C1
Chelsea Square SW3 112 C1
Cheltenham Terrace SW3 113 D2
Chenies Mews WC1 110 A3
Chenies Street WC1 110 E3
Cheniston Gardens W8 112 A3
Chequer Street EC1 111 E3
Cherbury Street N1 111 F4
Cherry Garden Street SE16 116 C1
Chesham Place SW1 113 E3
Chesham Street SW1 113 E3
Chester Close South NW1 109 F4
Chester Court NW1 109 F4
Albany Street
Chester Gate NW1 109 F4
Chester Mews SW1 113 E3
Chester Place NW1 109 F4
Chester Row SW1 113 E2
Chester Square SW1 113 E2
Chester Street SW1 113 E3
Chester Terrace NW1 109 F4
Chester Way SE11 115 D2
Chesterfield Gardens W1 113 E4
Chesterfield Hill W1 109 E1
Chesterfield Street W1 113 E4
Cheval Place SW7 113 D3
Cheyne Gardens SW3 112 D1
Cheyne Walk SW3 & SW10 112 C1
Chicheley Street SE1 114 C4
Chichester Rents WC2 110 C2
Chancery Lane
Chichester Street SW1 114 A1
Chicksand Street E1 116 B4
Chigwell Hill E1 116 C3
The Highway
Child's Place SW5 112 A2
Child's Street SW5 112 A2
Chiltern Street W1 109 E3
Chilworth Mews W2 108 B2
Chilworth Street W2 108 B2
Chiswell Street EC1 111 E3
Chitty Street W1 110 A3
Christchurch Street SW3 113 D1
Christian Street E1 116 C3
Christopher Street EC2 111 F3
Chudleigh Street E1 117 E4
Chumleigh Street SE5 115 F1
Church Place SW1 113 F4
Piccadilly
Church Street NW8 108 C3
Church Yard Row SE11 115 D2
Churchill Gardens Road SW1 113 F1
Churchill Place E14 118 B4
Churchway NW1 110 A4
Churton Street SW1 114 A2
Cinnamon Street E1 116 C2
Circus Place EC2 111 F2
Finsbury Circus
Citadel Place SE11 114 C2
City Garden Row N1 111 E4
City Road EC1 111 F3
Clabon Mews SW1 113 D2
Clack Street SE16 117 D1
Clanricarde Gardens W2 108 A1
Clare Market WC2 110 C2
Claremont Close N1 111 D4
Claremont Square N1 111 D4
Clarence Gardens NW1 109 F4
Clarendon Close W2 108 C1
Clarendon Place W2 108 C1
Clarendon Street SW1 113 F1
Clareville Grove SW7 112 B2
Clareville Street SW7 112 B2
Clarges Mews W1 113 F4
Clarges Street W1 113 F4
Clark Street E1 116 C4
Clark's Orchard SE16 116 C1
Claude Street E14 118 A2
Clave Street E1 116 C2
Claverton Street SW1 114 A1
Clay Street W1 109 D2
Clayton Street SE11 114 C1
Clearbrook Way E1 117 D4
Cleaver Square SE11 115 D1
Cleaver Street SE11 115 D1
Clegg Street E1 116 C2
Clemence Street E14 117 F4
Clement's Inn WC2 110 C2
Clement's Road SE16 116 C1
Clements Lane EC4 111 F1
Clenston Mews W1 109 D2
Clere Street EC2 111 F3
Clerkenwell Close EC1 111 D3
Clerkenwell Green EC1 111 D3
Clerkenwell Road EC1 110 C3
Cleveland Gardens W2 108 B2
Cleveland Mews W1 109 F3
Cleveland Row SW1 114 A4
Cleveland Square W2 108 B2
Cleveland Street W1 109 F3
Cleveland Terrace W2 108 B2
Clifford Street W1 109 F1
Clifton Place W2 108 C1
Clifton Street EC2 111 F3
Clink Street SE1 115 E4
Clipper Close SE16 117 D2
Kinburn Street
Clipstone Mews W1 109 F3
Clipstone Street W1 109 F3
Cliveden Place SW1 113 E2
Cloak Lane EC4 111 E1
Cloth Fair EC1 111 E2
Cloth Street EC1 111 E3
Clunbury Street N1 111 F4
Cherbury Street
Cluny Place SE1 115 F3
Coach & Horses Yard W1 109 F1
Old Burlington Street
Cobb Street E1 116 A4
Cobourg Street NW1 110 A4
Cock Lane EC1 111 D2
Cockpit Yard WC1 110 C3
Cockspur Street SW1 114 B4
Codling Close E1 116 C1
Coin Street SE1 115 D4
Coke Street E1 116 B4
Colbeck Mews SW7 112 B2
Colchester Street 116 B4
Whitechapel High Street
Coldbath Square EC1 110 C3
Cole Street SE1 115 E3
Colebrooke Row N1 111 D1
Coleherne Mews SW10 114 A1
Coleherne Road SW10 112 A1
Coleman Street EC2 111 E2
Coley Street WC1 110 C3
College Hill EC4 111 E1
College Street
College Street EC4 111 E1
Collett Road SE16 116 C1
Collier Street N1 110 C4
Collingham Gardens SW5 112 A2
Collingham Place SW4 112 A2
Collingham Road SW5 112 A2
Collinson Street SE1 115 E3
Colnbrook Street SE1 115 D3
Colombo Street SE1 115 D4
Colonnade WC1 110 B3
Colworth Grove SE17 115 E2

Commercial Road — Fore Street Avenue

Commercial Road E1 & E14 **116** B4
Commercial Street E1 **116** A4
Compton Passage EC1 **111** D3
Compton Place WC1 **110** B3
Compton Street EC1 **111** D3
Comus Place SE17 **115** F2
Concert Hall Approach SE1 **114** C4
Conduit Mews W2 **108** C4
Conduit Place W2 **108** C2
Conduit Street W1 **109** F1
Congreve Street SE17 **115** F2
Connaught Place W2 **109** D1
Connaught Square W2 **109** D2
Connaught Street W2 **108** C2
Cons Street SE1 **115** D4
Constitution Hill SW1 **113** E3
Content Street SE17 **115** E2
Conway Street W1 **109** F3
Cook's Road SE17 **115** D1
Cookham Crescent SE16 **117** D2
Coombs Street N1 **111** E4
Cooper Close SE1 **115** D3
Cooper's Row EC3 **116** A3
Cope Place W8 **112** A3
Copenhagen Place E14 **117** F3
Copley Close SE17 **115** E1
Copperfield Street SE1 **115** E4
Copthall Avenue EC2 **111** F2
Coptic Street WC1 **110** B2
Coral Street SE1 **115** D3
Coram Street WC1 **110** B3
Cork Street W1 **109** F1
Corlett Street NW1 **108** C3
Bell Street
Corner House Street WC2 **114** B4
Northumberland Street
Cornhill EC3 **111** F2
Cornwall Gardens SW7 **112** B3
Cornwall Gardens Walk SW7 **112** A2
Cornwall Mews South SW7 **112** B2
Cornwall Mews West SW7 **112** A3
Cornwall Road SE1 **114** C4
Cornwall Street E1 **116** C3
Cornwall Terrace NW1 **109** D3
Cornwood Drive E1 **117** D4
Coronet Street N1 **111** F4
Corporation Row EC1 **111** D3
Corsham Street N1 **111** F4
Cosmo Place WC1 **110** B3
Cosser Street SE1 **114** C3
Cosway Street NW1 **109** D3
Cotham Street SE17 **115** E2
Cottesmore Gardens W8 **112** B3
Cottingham Close SE11 **115** D2
Cottington Street SE11 **115** D2
Cottons Lane SE1 **115** F4
Counter Street SE1 **115** F4
County Street SE1 **115** E2
Court Street E1 **116** C4
Courtenay Square SE11 **114** C1
Courtenay Street SE11 **114** C1
Courtfield Gardens SW5 **112** A2
Courtfield Road SW7 **112** B2
Cousin Lane EC4 **111** E1
Coventry Street W1 **110** A1
Coverley Close E1 **116** B4
Cowcross Street EC1 **111** D3
Cowley Street SW1 **114** B3
Cowper Street EC2 **111** F3
Coxon Place SE1 **116** A1
Crace Street NW1 **110** A4
Crail Row SE17 **115** F2
Cramer Street W1 **109** E2
Crampton Street SE17 **115** C2
Cranbourn Street WC2 **110** B1
Cranford Street E1 **117** E3
Cranley Gardens SW7 **112** B2
Cranley Mews SW7 **112** B2
Cranley Place SW7 **112** C2
Cranmer Court SW3 **113** D2
Cranwood Street EC1 **111** F4
Craven Hill Gardens W2 **108** B1
Craven Hill Mews W2 **108** B1
Craven Hill W2 **108** B1
Craven Road W2 **108** B1
Craven Street WC2 **110** B1
Craven Terrace W2 **108** B1
Crawford Passage EC1 **111** D3
Crawford Place W1 **109** D2
Crawford Street W1 **109** D2
Creasy Street SE1 **115** F3
Swan Mead
Creechurch Lane EC3 **116** A3
Creechurch Place EC3 **116** A3
Creed Lane EC4 **111** E2
Crescent EC3 **116** A3
America Square
Crescent Place SW3 **113** D2
Crescent Row EC1 **111** E3
Cresswell Place SW10 **112** B1
Cressy Place E1 **117** D4
Crestfield Street WC1 **110** B4
Cricketer's Court **115** D1
Kennington Park Road
Crimscott Street SE1 **116** A1
Cripplegate Street EC1 **109** E3
Viscount Street
Crispin Street E1 **116** A4
Crofts StreetE1 **116** B3
Cromer Street WC1 **110** B3
Cromwell Mews SW7 **112** C2
Cromwell Place SW7 **112** C2
Cromwell Road SW7 & SW5 **112** A1
Crondall Street N1 **111** F4
Crosby Row SE1 **115** F3
Cross Keys Close W1 **109** E2
Marylebone Lane
Cross Lane EC3 **116** A3
Harp Lane
Crosslet Street SE17 **115** F2
Crosswall EC3 **116** A3
Crowder Street E1 **116** C3
Crown Court WC2 **110** B2
Crown Office Row EC4 **111** D1
Crucifix Lane SE1 **116** A2
Cruikshank Street WC1 **110** C4
Crutched Friars EC3 **116** A3
Cuba Street E14 **117** F2
Cubitt Steps E14 **118** A4
Cubitt Street WC1 **110** C4
Culford Gardens SW3 **113** D2
Culling Road SE16 **117** D1
Cullum Street EC3 **116** A3
Culross Street W1 **109** E1
Culworth Street NW8 **108** C4
Cumberland Gardens WC1 **110** C4
Great Percy Street
Cumberland Gate W1 & W2 **109** D1
Cumberland Market NW1 **109** F4
Cumberland Street SW1 **113** F1
Cumberland Terrace NW1 **109** E4
Cumberland Terrace Mews NW1 **109** F4
Albany Street
Cumming Street N1 **110** C4
Cundy Street SW1 **113** E2
Cureton Street SW1 **114** B2
Curlew Street SE1 **116** B2
Cursitor Street EC4 **110** C2
Curzon Gate W1 **113** E4
Curzon Place W1 **113** E4
Curzon Street W1 **113** E4
Cuthbert Street W2 **108** C3
Cutlers Square E14 **118** A2
Cutler Street E1 **116** A4
Cyclops Mews E14 **118** A2
Cynthia Street N1 **110** C4
Cyrus Street EC1 **111** D3

D'arblay Street W1 **110** A2
D'oyley Street SW1 **113** E2
Dacre Street SW1 **114** A3
Dalgleish Street E14 **117** E4
Dallington Street EC1 **111** D3
Damien Street E1 **116** C4
Dane Street WC1 **110** C2
Dante Road SE11 **115** D2
Daplyn Street E1 **116** B4
Dartford Street SE17 **115** E1
Dartmouth Street SW1 **114** A3
Darwin Street SE17 **115** F2
Date Street SE17 **115** E1
Davenant Street E1 **116** B4
Daventry Street NW1 **108** C3
Davidge Street SE1 **115** D3
Davies Mews W1 **109** E1
Davies Street W1 **109** E1
Dawes Street SE17 **115** F2
De Laune Street SE17 **115** D1
De Vere Gardens W8 **112** B3
De Walden Street W1 **109** E2
Westmorland Street
Deacon Way SE17 **115** E2
Deal Porters Way SE16 **117** D1
Deal Street E1 **116** B4
Dean Bradley Street SW1 **114** B2
Dean Close SE16 **117** E2
Dean Farrar Street SW1 **114** A3
Dean Ryle Street SW1 **114** B2
Dean Stanley Street SW1 **114** B2
Millbank
Dean Street W1 **110** A2
Dean Trench Street SW1 **114** B3
Dean's Buildings SE17 **115** F2
Dean's Court EC4 **111** E2
Carter Lane
Dean's Mews W1 **109** F2
Deancross Street E1 **116** C3
Deanery Street W1 **113** E4
Decima Street SE1 **115** F3
Deck Close SE16 **117** E2
Defoe Close SE16 **117** F1
Dellow Street E1 **116** C3
Delverton Road SE17 **115** E1
Denbigh Street SW1 **114** A2
Denman Street W1 **110** A1
Denmark Place WC2 **110** B2
Charing Cross Road
Denmark Street WC2 **110** B2
Denny Crescent SE11 **115** D2
Denny Street SE11 **115** D2
Denyer Street SW3 **113** D2
Derby Gate SW1 **114** B3
Derby Street W1 **113** E4
Dering Street W1 **109** F2
Deverell Street SE1 **115** F3
Devereux Court WC2 **110** B1
Strand
Devonport Street E1 **117** D3
Devonshire Close W1 **109** F3
Devonshire Mews South W1 **109** E3
Devonshire Mews West W1 **109** E3
Devonshire Place Mews W1 **109** E3
Devonshire Place W1 **109** E3
Devonshire Place W8 **112** A3
St Mary's Place
Devonshire Row EC2 **116** A4
Devonshire Square EC2 **116** A4
Devonshire Street W1 **109** E3
Devonshire Terrace W2 **108** B1
Diadem Court W1 **110** A2
Dean Street
Diana Place NW1 **109** F3
Dickens Square SE1 **115** E3
Dilke Street SW3 **113** D1
Dingley Place EC1 **111** E4
Dingley Road EC1 **111** E4
Disney Place SE1 **115** E3
Redcross Way
Disney Street SE1 **115** E4
Distaff Lane EC4 **111** E1
Distin Street SE11 **114** C2
Dixon's Alley SE16 **116** C1
West Lane
Dock Hill Avenue SE16 **117** E2
Dock Street E1 **116** B3
Dockers Tanner Road E14 **118** A1
Dockhead SE1 **116** B1
Dockley Road SE16 **116** B1
Dod Street E14 **117** F4
Doddington Grove SE17 **115** D1
Doddington Place SE17 **115** D1
Dodson Street SE1 **115** D3
Dolben Street SE1 **115** D4
Dolland Street SE11 **114** C1
Dolphin Close SE16 **117** D2
Dombey Street WC1 **110** C3
Domingo Street EC1 **111** E3
Old Street
Dominion Street EC2 **111** F2
Donegal Street N1 **110** C4
Donne Place SW3 **113** D2
Doon Street SE1 **114** C4
Dora Street E14 **117** F4
Doric Way NW1 **110** A4
Dorrington Street EC1 **111** D3
Leather Lane
Dorset Close NW1 **109** D3
Dorset Mews SW1 **113** E3
Dorset Rise EC4 **111** D1
Dorset Square NW1 **109** D3
Dorset Street W1 **109** D2
Doughty Mews WC1 **110** C3
Doughty Street WC1 **110** C3
Douglas Place SW1 **114** A2
Douglas Street
Douglas Street SW1 **114** A2
Douro Place W8 **112** B3
Dove Mews SW5 **112** B2
Dove Walk SW1 **113** E2
Dovehouse Street SW3 **112** C1
Dover Street W1 **109** F1
Dowgate Hill EC4 **111** F1
Down Street W1 **113** E4
Downing Street SW1 **114** B4
Downton Road SE16 **117** E2
Draco Street SE17 **115** F1
Drake Street WC1 **110** C2
Draycott Avenue SW3 **113** D2
Draycott Place SW3 **113** D2
Draycott Terrace SW3 **113** D2
Drayson Mews W8 **112** A3
Drayton Gardens SW10 **112** B1
Druid Street SE1 **116** A2
Drummond Crescent NW1 **110** A4
Drummond Gate SW1 **114** A1
Drummond Road SE16 **116** C1
Drummond Street NW1 **109** F3
Drury Lane WC2 **110** B2
Dryden Court SE11 **115** D2
Duchess Mews W1 **109** F2
Duchess Street W1 **109** F2
Duchy Street SE1 **115** D4
Dudley Street W2 **108** B2
Dudmaston Mews SW3 **112** C2
Dufferin Street EC1 **111** E3
Dufour's Place W1 **110** A4
Duke Of Wellington Place SW1 **113** E3
Duke Of York Street SW1 **110** A1
Duke Street Hill SE1 **115** F4
Duke Street W1 **109** E2
Duke's Lane W8 **112** A4
Duke's Place EC3 **116** A4
Duke's Road WC1 **110** B4
Duke's Yard W1 **109** E2
Duke Street
Duncannon Street WC2 **110** B1
Dundee Street E1 **116** C2
Dunelm Street D1 **117** D4
Dunlop Place SE16 **116** B1
Dunraven Street W1 **109** E1
Dunstable Mews W1 **109** E3
Dunster Court EC3 **116** A3
Dunsterville Way SE1 **115** F3
Duplex Ride SW1 **113** E3
Dupont Street E14 **117** E4
Durham House Street WC2 **110** B1
Durham Row E1 **117** E4
Durham Street SE11 **114** C1
Durward Street E1 **116** C4
Durweston Street W1 **109** D2
Crawford Street
Dyott Street WC1 **110** B2
Dysart Street EC2 **111** F3

Eagle Court EC1 **111** D3
Eagle Street WC2 **110** C2
Eardley Crescent SW5 **112** A1
Earlstoke Street EC1 **111** D4
Spencer Street
Earl Street EC2 **111** F3
Earl's Court Gardens SW5 **112** A2
Earl's Court Square SW5 **112** A1
Earlham Street WC2 **110** B2
Earls Court Road W8 **112** A2
Earnshaw Street WC2 **110** B2
Easley's Mews W1 **109** E2
Wigmore Street
East Arbour Street E1 **117** D4
East Harding Street EC4 **111** D2
East India Dock Wall Road E14 **111** D2
East Lane SE16 **116** B1
East Road N1 **111** F4
East Smithfield E1 **116** B3
East Street SE17 **115** E1
East Tenter Street E1 **116** B3
Eastbourne Mews W2 **108** B2
Eastbourne Terrace W2 **108** B2
Eastcastle Street W1 **110** A2
Eastcheap EC3 **111** F1
Easton Street WC1 **110** C3
Eaton Gate SW1 **113** E2
Eaton Mews North SW1 **113** E2
Eaton Mews South SW1 **113** E2
Eaton Place SW1 **113** E2
Eaton Square SW1 **113** E2
Eaton Terrace SW1 **113** E2
Ebbisham Drive SW8 **114** C1
Ebenezer Street N1 **111** F4
Ebury Bridge Road SW1 **113** E1
Ebury Bridge SW1 **113** E2
Ebury Mews East SW1 **113** E2
Ebury Mews SW1 **113** E2
Ebury Square SW1 **113** E2
Ebury Street SW1 **113** E2
Eccleston Bridge SW1 **113** F2
Eccleston Mews SW1 **113** E3
Eccleston Place SW1 **113** E2
Eccleston Square Mews SW1 **113** F2
Eccleston Square SW1 **113** F2
Eccleston Street SW1 **113** E2
Edge Street W8 **112** A4
Edgware Road W2 **108** C3
Edward Mews W1 **109** E2
Edward Mews NW1 **109** F4
Egerton Crescent SW3 **113** D2
Egerton Gardens SW3 **112** C2
Egerton Terrace SW3 **113** D3
Elba Place SE17 **115** E2
Eldon Road W8 **112** B3
Eldon Street EC2 **111** F2
Elephant And Castle SE1 **115** E2
Elephant Lane SE16 **116** C2
Elephant Road SE17 **115** E2
Elf Row E1 **117** D3
Elgar Street SE16 **117** F1
Elia Street N1 **111** D4
Ellm Street SE1 **115** F3
Elizabeth Bridge SW1 **113** F2
Elizabeth Street SW1 **113** E2
Ellen Street E1 **116** B3
Elliott Road SE9 **115** D2
Ellis Street SW1 **113** E2
Elm Park Gardens SW10 **112** C1
Elm Park Lane SW3 **112** B1
Elm Park Road SW3 **112** B1
Elm Place SW7 **112** C1
Elm Street WC1 **110** C3
Elm Tree Close NW8 **108** C4
Elm Tree Road NW8 **108** C4
Elmos Road SE16 **117** E1
Elms Mews W2 **108** C1
Elsa Street E1 **117** E4
Elsted Street SE17 **115** F2
Elvaston Mews SW7 **112** B3
Elvaston Place SW7 **112** B3
Elverton Street SW1 **114** A2
Ely Place EC1 **111** D2
Elystan Place SW3 **113** D2
Elystan Street SW3 **112** C2
Emba Street SE16 **116** C1
Embankment Gardens SW3 **113** D1
Embankment Place WC2 **114** B4
Emerald Street WC1 **110** C3
Emerson Street SE1 **115** E4
Emery Hill Street SW1 **114** A2
Emery Street SE1 **115** D3
Emmett Street E14 **117** F3
Emperor's Gate SW7 **112** B2
Empress Place SW6 **112** A1
Empress Street SE17 **115** E1
Endell Street WC2 **110** B2
Endsleigh Gardens WC1 **110** A3
Endsleigh Place WC1 **110** A3
Endsleigh Street WC1 **110** A3
Enford Street W1 **109** D3
English Grounds SE1 **116** A2
Enid Street SE16 **116** B1
Ennismore Garden Mews SW7 **112** C3
Ennismore Gardens SW7 **112** C3
Ennismore Mews SW7 **112** C3
Ennismore Street SW7 **112** C3
Ensign Street E1 **116** B3
Ensor Mews SW7 **112** B1
Epworth Street EC2 **111** F3
Erasmus Street SW1 **114** B2
Errol Street EC1 **111** E3
Essex Street WC2 **110** C1
Esterbrooke Street SW1 **114** A2
Ethel Street SE17 **115** E2
Europa Place EC1 **111** E4
Euston Road NW1 **109** F3
Euston Square NW1 **110** A4
Euston Street NW1 **110** A4
Evelyn Gardens SW7 **114** B1
Evelyn Walk N1 **111** F4
Evelyn Yard W1 **110** A2
Gresse Street
Eversholt Street NW1 **110** A4
Ewer Street SE1 **115** E4
Exchange Place EC2 **116** A4
Exchange Square EC2 **116** A4
Exeter Street WC2 **110** B1
Exhibition Road SW7 **112** C3
Exmouth Market EC1 **111** D3
Exmouth Street E1 **117** D4
Exon Street SE17 **115** F2
Exton Street SE1 **114** C4
Eyre Street Hill EC1 **111** D3

Fair Street SE1 **116** A2
Fairclough Street E1 **116** B3
Falcon Close SE1 **115** E4
Falcon Way E14 **118** B2
Falmouth Road SE1 **115** E3
Fann Street EC1 **111** E3
Fanshaw Street N1 **111** F4
Fareham Street W1 **110** B1
Dean Street
Farm Street W1 **109** E1
Farmer Street W8 **112** A4
Farncombe Street SE16 **116** C1
Farnell Mews SW5 **112** A1
Farnham Place SE1 **115** E4
Farnham Royal SE11 **114** C1
Farrance Street E14 **117** F3
Farringdon Lane EC1 **111** D3
Farringdon Road EC1 **110** C3
Farringdon Street EC4 **111** D2
Farrins Rents SE16 **117** E2
Farrow Place SE16 **117** E1
Farthing Alley SE1 **116** B1
Wolseley Street
Farthing Fields E1 **116** C2
Fashion Street E1 **116** B4
Faunce Street SE17 **115** D1
Fawcett Street SW10 **112** B1
Featherstone Street EC1 **111** F3
Fen Court EC3 **116** A3
Fenchurch Avenue EC3 **116** A3
Fenchurch Buildings EC3 **111** F1
Fenchurch Street
Fenchurch Place EC3 **111** F1
Fenchurch Street
Fenchurch Street EC3 **111** F1
Fendall Street SE1 **116** A1
Fenning Street SE1 **115** F4
St Thomas Street
Fernsbury Street WC1 **110** C4
Fetter Lane EC4 **111** D2
Field Street WC1 **110** C4
Fieldgate Street E1 **116** B4
Fielding Street SE17 **115** E1
Finborough Road SW10 **112** A1
Finch Lane EC3 **111** F2
Finland Street SE16 **117** E1
Finsbury Avenue EC2 **111** F2
Finsbury Circus EC2 **111** F2
Finsbury Pavement EC2 **111** F3
Finsbury Square EC2 **111** F3
Finsbury Street EC2 **111** F3
First Street SW3 **113** D2
Firtree Close SE16 **117** E2
Fish Street Hill EC3 **111** F1
Fisher Street WC1 **110** C2
Fishermans Drive SE16 **117** E2
Fisherman's Walk E14 **118** A4
Fisherton Street NW8 **108** C3
Fitzalan Street SE11 **114** C2
Fitzhardinge Street W1 **109** E2
Fitzmaurice Place W1 **109** F1
Fitzroy Square W1 **109** F3
Fitzroy Street WC1 **109** F3
Flamborough Street E14 **117** E3
Flank Street E1 **116** B3
Flaxman Terrace WC1 **110** B4
Fleet Lane EC4 **111** D2
Fleet Square WC1 **110** C4
Fleet Street EC4 **111** D2
Fleming Road SE17 **115** D1
Fletcher Street E1 **116** B3
Cable Street
Flint Street SE17 **115** F2
Flitcroft Street WC2 **110** B2
Flood Street SW3 **113** D1
Flood Walk SW3 **113** D1
Floral Street WC2 **110** B1
Flower & Dean Walk E1 **116** B4
Thrawl Street
Foley Street W1 **109** F2
Forbes Street E1 **116** B3
Ford Square E1 **116** C4
Fordham Street E1 **116** C4
Fore Street Avenue EC2 **111** E2

Jubilee Street Muscovy Street

Jubilee Street E1 117 D4
Judd Street WC1 110 B4
Junction Mews W2 108 C2
Juxon Street SE11 114 C2

Kean Street WC2 110 C2
Keel Close SE16 117 E2
Keeley Street WC2 110 C2
Keeton's Road SE16 116 C1
Kelso Place W8 112 A3
Kemble Street WC2 110 C2
Kempsford Gardens SW5 112 A1
Kempsford Road SE11 115 D2
Kendal Street W2 109 C2
Kendall Place W1 109 D2
Kennet Street E1 116 B2
Kennet Wharf Lane EC4 111 E1
Kenning Street SE16 117 D2
Kennings Way SE11 115 B2
Kennington Green SE11 115 D1
Kennington Grove SE11 114 C1
Kennington Lane SE11 114 C1
Kennington Oval SE11 114 C1
Kennington Park Gardens SE11 115 D1
Kennington Park Place SE11 115 D1
Kennington Park Road SE11 115 D1
Kennington Road SE1 & SE11 114 C3
Kenrick Place W1 109 E2
Kensington Church Street W8 112 A4
Kensington Church Walk W8 112 A3
Kensington Court Place W8 112 A3
Kensington Court W8 112 A3
Kensington Gate W8 112 B3
Kensington Gore SW7 112 B3
Kensington High Street W8 & W14 112 A3
Kensington Mall W8 112 A4
Kensington Palace Gardens W8 112 A4
Kensington Road W8 & SW7 112 B3
Kensington Square W8 112 A3
Kent Passage NW1 109 D4
Kent Terrace NW1 109 D4
Kenton Street WC1 109 B3
Kenway Road SW5 111 A2
Keppel Row SE1 115 E4
Keppel Street WC1 110 B3
Keyse Road SE1 116 B1
Keystone Crescent N1 110 B4
Keyworth Street SE1 115 D3
Kinburn Street SE16 117 D2
Kinder Street E1 116 C3
King And Queen Street SE17 115 E2
King Charles Street SW1 114 B3
King David Lane E1 117 D3
King Edward Street EC1 111 E2
King Edward Walk SE1 115 D3
King James Street SE1 115 E3
King Square EC1 111 E4
King Street EC2 111 E2
King Street SW1 114 A4
King Street WC2 110 B1
King William Street EC4 111 F1
King's Bench Walk EC4 111 D1
King's Cross Road WC1 110 C4
King's Mews WC1 110 C3
King's Road SW3,SW6,SW10 113 D1
King's Stairs Close SE16 116 C2
Kinghorn Street EC1 111 E3
Kinglake Street SE17 115 F2
Kingly Street W1 109 F1
Kings Arms Yard EC2 111 F2
Kings Bench Street SE1 115 D3
Kingscote Street EC4 111 D1
Kingsway WC2 110 C2
Kinnerton Street SW1 113 E3
Kipling Street SE1 115 F4
Kirby Grove SE1 115 F3
Kirby Street EC1 111 D3
Knaresborough Place SW5 112 A2
Knightsbridge Green SW1 111 F3
Lamb's Passage
Knight's Walk SE11 115 D2
Knighten Street E1 116 C2
Knightrider Street EC4 111 E1
Knightsbridge SW1 & SW7 113 D3
Knox Street W1 109 D3
Kynance Mews SW7 112 B3
Kynance Place SW7 112 B3

Lackington Street EC2 111 F3
Lafone Street SE1 116 A2
Lagado Mews SE16 117 E2
Lamb Street E1 116 A4
Lamb Walk SE1 115 F3
Lamb's Conduit Street WC1 110 C3
Lamb's Passage EC1 111 F3
Lambeth Bridge SW1 & SE11 114 B2
Lambeth High Street SE1 114 C2
Lambeth Hill EC4 111 E1
Lambeth Palace Road SE1 114 C2
Lambeth Road SE1 114 C2
Lambeth Walk SE11 114 C2
Lamlash Street SE11 115 D2
Lanark Square E14 118 B3
Lancaster Gate W2 108 B1
Lancaster Mews W2 108 B1
Lancaster Place WC2 113 D3
Lancaster Street SE1 115 D3
Lancaster Terrace W2 108 C1
Lancaster Walk W2 108 B1
Lancelot Place SW7 113 D3
Lancing Street NW1 110 A4
Langdale Close SE17 115 E1
Langham Place W1 109 F2
Langham Street W1 109 F2
Langley Lane SW8 114 B1
Langley Street WC2 110 B1
Langton Close WC1 110 C3
Lansdowne Row W1 109 F1
Lansdowne Terrace WC1 110 B3
Lant Street SE1 115 E3
Larcom Street SE17 115 E2
Launcelot Street SE1 114 C3
Lower Marsh
Launceston Place W8 112 B3
Laurence Pountney Lane EC4 111 F1
Lavender Close SW3 112 C1
Lavender Road SE16 117 E2
Laverton Place SW5 112 A2
Lavington Street SE1 115 E4
Law Street SE1 115 F3
Lawn Lane SW8 114 B1
Lawrence Lane EC2 111 E2
Trump Street
Lawrence Street SW3 112 C1
Laxton Place NW1 109 F3
Laystall Street EC1 110 C3
Leadenhall Place EC3 111 F1
Leadenhall Street EC3 111 F2
Leake Street SE1 114 C3
Leather Lane EC1 111 D3
Leathermarket Street SE1 115 F3
Lecky Terrace SW7 112 C1
Lees Place W1 109 E1
Leicester Court WC2 110 B1
Cranbourn Street
Leicester Place WC2 110 A1
Lisle Street
Leicester Square WC2 110 B1
Leicester Street WC2 110 B1
Leigh Hunt Street SE1 115 E3
Leigh Street WC1 110 B4
Leinster Gardens W2 108 B1
Leinster Mews W2 108 B1
Leinster Place W2 108 B1
Leinster Terrace W2 108 B1
Leman Street E1 116 B3
Lennox Gardens Mews SW1 113 D2
Lennox Gardens SW1 113 D2
Leonard Street EC2 111 F3
Leopold Street E3 117 F4
Leroy Street SE1 116 F2
Lever Street EC1 111 E4
Leverett Street SW3 113 D2
Mossop Street
Lewisham Street SW1 114 B3
Lexham Gardens W8 112 A2
Lexham Mews W8 112 A2
Lexington Street W1 110 A1
Leyden Street E1 116 A4
Leydon Close SE16 117 E2
Library Place E1 116 C3
Library Street SE1 115 D3
Lilestone Street NW8 108 C3
Lillie Yard SW6 112 A1
Lime Close E1 116 B2
Lime Street EC3 111 F1
Limehouse Causeway E14 117 F3
Limerston Street SW10 112 B1
Lincoln Street SW3 113 D2
Lincoln's Inn Fields WC2 110 C2
Linden Gardens W2 108 A1
Lindley Street E1 116 C4
Lindsay Square SW1 114 B2
Lindsey Street EC1 111 E3
Linhope Street NW1 108 D3
Linsey Street SE16 116 B1
Lion Street E1 110 C2
Lipton Road E1 117 D3
Lisle Street W1 110 A1
Lisson Grove NW1 & NW8 108 C3
Lisson Street NW1 108 C3
Litchfield Street WC2 110 B1
Little Albany Street NW1 109 F4
Little Argyle Street W1 114 A2
Regent Street
Little Britain EC1 111 E2
Little Chester Street SW1 113 E3
Little College Street SW1 114 B3
Little Dorrit Close SE1 115 E4
Little Edward Street NW1 109 F4
Little George Street SW1 114 B3
Great George Street
Little Malborough Street W1 109 F1
Kingly Street
Little New Street EC4 111 D2
New Street Square
Little Newport Street WC2 110 B1
Little Portland Street W1 109 F2
Little Russell Street WC1 110 B2
Little Sanctuary SW1 114 B3
Broad Sanctuary
Little Smith Street SW1 114 B3
Little Somerset Street E1 114 A3
Little St James's Street SW1 114 A4
Little Titchfield Street W1 109 F2
Little Trinity Lane EC4 111 E1
Liverpool Grove SE17 115 E1
Liverpool Street EC2 111 F2
Livonia Street W2 110 A2
Lizard Street EC1 111 E4
Llewellyn Street SE16 116 B1
Lloyd Baker Street WC1 110 C4
Lloyd Square WC1 110 C4
Lloyd Street WC1 110 C4
Lloyd's Avenue EC3 116 A3
Lloyd's Row EC1 111 D4
Lockesfield Place E14 118 B1
Locksley Street E14 117 F4
Lockwood Square SE16 116 C1
Lodge Road NW8 108 C4
Loftie Street SE16 116 B1
Lolesworth Close E1 116 B4
Lollard Street SE11 114 C2
Loman Street SE1 115 E4
Lomas Street E1 116 C4
Lombard Lane EC4 111 A2
Temple Lane
London Bridge EC4 & SE1 111 F1
London Bridge Street SE1 115 F4
London Road SE1 115 D3
London Street EC3 116 A3
London Street W2 108 C2
London Wall EC2 111 E2
Long Acre WC2 110 B1
Long Lane EC1 111 E2
Long Lane SE1 115 F3
Long Walk SE1 116 A1
Long Yard WC1 110 C3
Longford Street NW1 109 F3
Longmoore Street SW1 113 F2
Longville Road SE11 115 D2
Lord North Street SW1 114 B3
Lordship Place SW3 112 C1
Lawrence Street
Lorenzo Street WC1 110 C4
Lorrimore Road SE7 115 E1
Lorrimore Square SE17 115 E1
Lothbury EC2 111 F2
Loughborough Street SE11 114 C1
Lovat Lane EC3 111 F1
Love Lane EC2 111 E2
Lovell Place SE16 117 E1
Lovers' Walk W1 113 C4
Lowell Street E14 117 E4
Lower Belgrave Street SW1 113 E3
Lower Grosvenor Place SW1 113 F3
Lower James Street W1 110 A1
Lower John Street W1 110 A1
Lower Marsh SE1 114 C3
Lower Road SE8 & SE16 117 D1
Lower Sloane Street SW1 113 E1
Lower Thames Street EC3 111 F1
Lowndes Place SW1 113 E3
Lowndes Square SW1 113 D3
Lowndes Street SW1 113 E3
Lowood Street E1 116 C3
Bewley Street
Loxham Street WC1 164 B3
Cromer Street
Lucan Place SW3 112 C2
Lucerne Mews W8 112 A4
Lucey Road SE16 116 B1
Ludgate Broadway EC4 111 D2
Pilgrim Street
Ludgate Circus EC4 111 D2
Luke Street EC2 111 F3
Lukin Street E1 117 D3
Lumley Street W1 109 E1
Brown Hart Garden
Lupus Street SW1 113 F1
Luton Street NW8 108 C3
Luxborough Street W1 109 E3
Lyall Street SW1 113 E3
Lygon Place SW1 113 F3
Lytham Street SE17 115 F1

Mabledon Place WC1 110 B4
Macclesfield Road EC1 111 E4
Mackenzie Walk E14 118 A4
Macklin Street WC2 110 B2
Mackworth Street NW1 109 F4
Macleod Street SE17 115 E1
Maddox Street SW1 109 F1
Magdalen Street SE1 116 A2
Magee Street SE11 115 D1
Maguire Street SE1 116 B2
Mahognay Close SE16 117 E2
Maiden Lane WC2 110 B1
Maiden Lane SE1 115 E4
Major Road SE16 116 C1
Makins Street SW3 116 D2
Malet Street WC1 110 A3
Mallord Street SW3 112 C1
Mallory Street NW8 108 C3
Mallow Street EC1 111 F3
Malta Street EC1 111 D3
Maltby Street SE1 116 A1
Maltravers Street WC2 110 C1
Manchester Square W1 109 E2
Manchester Street W1 109 E2
Manciple Street SE1 115 F3
Mandarin Street E14 117 F3
Mandeville Place W1 109 E2
Manette Street W1 110 B2
Manningford Close EC1 111 D4
Manningtree Strwwt E1 116 B4
Commercial Road
Manor Place SE17 115 E1
Manresa Road SW3 112 C1
Mansell Street E1 116 B3
Mansfield Mews W1 109 F2
Mansfield Street
Mansfield Street W1 109 F2
Mansion House Place EC4 111 A1
St Swithun's Lane
Manson Mews SW7 112 B2
Manson Place SW7 112 C2
Maple Leaf Square SE16 117 E2
Maple Street W1 109 F3
Maples Place E1 116 C4
Marble Arch W1 109 D1
Marchmont Street WC1 110 B3
Margaret Court W1 109 F2
Margaret Street
Margaret Street W1 109 F2
Margaretta Terrace SW3 112 C1
Margery Street WC1 110 C4
Marigold Street SE16 116 C1
Marjorie Mews E1 117 D4
Mark Lane EC3 116 A3
Market Court W1 109 E1
Oxford Street
Market Mews W1 113 E4
Market Place W1 109 F2
Markham Square SW3 113 D2
Markham Street SW3 113 D2
Marlborough Close SE17 115 E2
Marlborough Road SW1 114 A4
Marlborough Street SW3 112 C2
Marloes Road W8 112 A3
Marlow Way SE16 117 D2
Marne Street W10 116 B1
Maroon Street E14 117 E4
Marsh Wall E14 118 A3
Marshall Street W1 110 A1
Marshall's Place SE16 116 B1
Marshalsea Road SE1 115 E4
Marsham Street SW1 114 B3
Marsland Close SE17 115 E1
Martha Street E1 116 C3
Martin Lane EC4 111 F1
Martin's Street WC2 110 B1
Martlett Court WC2 110 B2
Bow Street
Marylebone High Street W1 109 E3
Marylebone Lane W1 109 E2
Marylebone Mews W1 109 E2
Marylebone Road NW1 109 D3
Marylebone Street W1 109 E2
Marylee Way SE11 114 C2
Mason Street SE17 115 F2
Mason's Arms Mews W1 109 F1
Maddox Street
Mason's Place EC1 111 E4
Mason's Yard SW1 109 E2
Duke Street St James's
Massinger Street SE17 115 F2
Mast House Terrace E14 118 A2
Master's Street E1 117 E4
Matlock Street E14 117 E4
Matthew Parker Street SW1 114 B3
Maunsel Street SW1 114 A2
Mayfair Place W1 113 F4
Mayflower Street SE16 117 D1
May's Court WC2 110 B1
St Martin's Lane
McAuley Close SE1 114 C3
McCleod's Mews SW7 112 B2
Mead Row SE1 115 D3
Meadcroft Road SE11 115 D1
Meadow Row SE1 115 E2
Meard Street W1 110 A2
Mecklenburgh Place WC1 110 C3
Mecklenburgh Square
Mecklenburgh Square WC1 110 C3
Mecklenburgh Street WC1 110 C3
Medway Street SW1 114 A2
Melbury Terrace NW1 109 D3
Melcombe Place NW1 109 D3
Melcombe Street NW1 109 D3
Melior Place SE1 115 F4
Snowsfields
Melton Street NW1 110 A4
Melon Place W8 112 A4
Memel Court EC1 111 E3
Baltic Street
Mepham Street SE1 114 C4
Mercer Street WC2 110 B1
Meredith Street EC1 111 D4
Merlin Street WC1 111 D4
Mermaid Court SE1 115 F4
Mermaid Row SE1 115 F3
Merrick Square SE1 115 E3
Merrington Road SW6 112 A1
Merrow Street SE17 115 E1
Methley Street SE11 115 D1
Mews Street E1 116 B2
Meymott Street SE1 115 D4
Micawber Street N1 111 E4
Midford Place W1 110 A3
Tottenham Court Road
Middle Street EC1 111 E2
Middle Temple Lane EC4 110 C2
Middle Yard SE1 115 F4
Middlesex Street E1 116 A4
Middleton Drive SE16 117 E2
Midhope Street WC1 110 B4
Midland Road NW1 110 B4
Midship Close SE16 117 E2
Milborne Grove SW10 112 B1
Milcote Street SE1 115 D3
Mile End Road E1 116 C4
Miles Street SW8 114 B1
Milford Lane WC2 110 C1
Milk Street EC2 111 E2
Milk Yard E1 117 D3
Mill Place E14 117 F3
Mill Street SE1 116 B1
Mill Street W1 109 F1
Millbank SW1 114 B2
Milligan Street E14 117 F3
Millman Street WC1 110 C3
Millstream Road SE1 116 A1
Milner Street SW3 113 D2
Milton Court EC2 111 F3
Milton Street EC2 111 F3
Milverton Street SE11 115 D1
Milward Street E1 116 C4
Mincing Lane EC3 116 A3
Minera Mews SW1 113 E2
Minories EC3 116 A3
Mint Street SE1 115 E3
Mitchell Street EC1 111 E3
Mitre Road SE1 115 D3
Mitre Street EC3 116 A3
Moiety Road E14 117 F1
Molyneux Street W1 109 D2
Monck Street SW1 114 B3
Moncorvo Close SW7 112 C3
Monkton Street SE11 115 D2
Monkwell Square EC2 111 E2
Monmouth Street WC2 110 B1
Montagu Mansions W1 109 D3
Montagu Mews North W1 109 D2
Montagu Mews South W1 109 D2
Montagu Mews West W1 109 D2
Montagu Place W1 109 D2
Montagu Row W1 109 D2
Montagu Square W1 109 D2
Montagu Street W1 109 D2
Montague Close SE1 115 F4
Montague Place WC1 110 D3
Montague Street WC1 110 B3
Montague Street EC1 111 E2
Montford Place SE11 114 C1
Montpelier Mews SW7 113 D3
Montpelier Place SW7 113 D3
Montpelier Square SW7 113 D3
Montpelier Street SW7 113 D3
Montpelier Walk SW7 113 D3
Montreal Place WC2 110 C1
Montrose Court SW7 112 C3
Montrose Place SW1 113 E3
Monument Street EC3 111 F1
Monza Street E1 117 D3
Moodkee Street SE16 117 D1
Moor Lane EC2 111 F2
Moore Street SW3 110 A1
Old Compton Street
Moorfields EC2 111 F2
Moorgate EC2 111 F2
Mora Street EC1 111 E4
Morecambe Close E1 117 D4
Morecambe Street SE17 115 E2
Moreland Street EC1 111 E4
Moreton Place SW1 114 A2
Moreton Street SW1 114 A2
Moreton Terrace SW1 114 A1
Morgan's Lane SE1 116 A2
Morley Street SE1 115 D3
Morocco Street SE1 115 F3
Morpeth Terrace SW1 113 F2
Morris Street E1 116 C3
Mortimer Market WC1 110 A3
Capper Street
Mortimer Street W1 109 F2
Morwell Street WC1 110 A2
Moss Close E1 116 B4
Mossop Street SW3 113 D2
Motcomb Street SW1 113 E3
Mount Pleasant WC1 110 C3
Mount Row W1 109 E1
Mount Street E1 116 C4
Mount Street W1 109 E1
Mount Terrace E1 116 C4
Moxon Street W1 109 E2
Mozart Terrace SW1 113 E2
Muirfield Crescent E14 118 B3
Mulberry Street E1 116 B4
Mulberry Walk SW3 112 C1
Mulready Street NW8 108 C3
Mulvaney Way SE1 115 F3
Mumford Court EC2 111 E2
Milk Street
Mundy Street N1 111 F4
Munster Square NW1 109 F4
Munton Road SE17 115 E2
Murphy Street SE1 114 C3
Murray Grove N1 111 E4
Musbury Street E1 117 D4
Muscovy Street EC3 116 A3

Museum Street Redriff Road

Museum Street WC1 110 B2
Myddelton Passage EC1 111 D4
Myddelton Square EC1 111 D4
Myddelton Street EC1 111 D4
Mylne Street EC1 111 D4
Myrdle Street E1 116 C4
Myrtle Walk N1 111 F4

Narrow Street E14 117 E3
Nash Place E14 118 A4
Nash Street NW1 109 F4
Nassau Street W1 109 F2
Nathanial Close E1 116 B4
Thrawl Street
Neal Street WC2 110 B2
Neathouse Place SW1 113 F2
Wilton Road
Nebraska Street SE1 115 E3
Neckinger SE1 116 B1
Neckinger Street SE1 116 B1
Nelson Passage EC1 111 E4
Mora Street
Nelson Place N1 111 E4
Nelson Square SE1 115 D4
Nelson Street E1 116 C4
Nelson Terrace N1 111 D4
Nelson Walk SE16 117 E2
Neptune Street SE16 117 D1
Neston Street SE16 117 D2
Netherton Grove SW10 112 B1
Netley Street NW1 109 F4
Nevern Place SW5 112 A2
Nevern Square SW5 112 A2
Neville Street SW7 112 C2
Neville Terrace SW7 112 C1
New Bond Street W1 109 F1
New Burlington Mews W1 116 A3
Hart Street
New Bridge Street EC4 111 D2
New Broad Street EC2 111 F2
New Burlington Place W1 109 F1
New Burlington Street W1 109 F1
New Cavendish Street W1 109 E2
New Change EC4 111 E2
New Compton Street WC2 110 B2
New Fetter Lane EC4 111 D2
New Goulston Street E1 116 A4
New Kent Road SE1 115 E2
New North Place EC2 111 F3
New North Road N1 111 F4
New North Street WC1 110 C3
New Oxford Street WC1 110 B2
New Quebec Street W1 109 D2
New Ride SW7 112 C3
New Road E1 116 C4
New Row WC2 110 B1
New Spring Gardens Walk SE11 114 B1
Goding Street
New Square WC2 110 C2
New Street EC2 116 A4
New Street Square EC4 111 D2
New Turnstile WC1 110 B2
High Holborn
Newark Street E1 116 C4
Newburgh Street W1 110 F1
Foubert's Place
Newburn Street SE11 114 C1
Newbury Street EC1 111 E2
Newcastle Place W2 108 C3
Newcomen Street SE1 115 F4
Newell Street E14 117 F3
Newgate Street EC1 111 D2
Newington Butts SE1 & SE11 115 D2
Newington Causeway SE1 115 E3
Newlands Quay E1 117 D3
Newman Street W1 110 A2
Newman's Row WC2 110 C2
Lincoln's Inn Fields
Newnham Terrace SE1 114 C3
Newnhams Row SE1 116 A1
Newport Place WC2 110 B1
Newport Street SE11 114 C2
Newton Street WC2 110 B2
Nicholas Lane EC4 111 F1
Nicholson Street SE1 115 D4
Nile Street N1 111 E4
Nine Elms Lane SW8 114 A1
Noble Street EC2 111 E2
Noel Street W1 110 A2
Norbiton Road E14 117 F4
Norfolk Crescent W2 108 C2
Norfolk Place W2 108 C2
Norfolk Square W2 108 C2
Norman Street EC1 111 E4
Norris Street SW1 110 A1
North Audley Street W1 109 E1
North Bank NW8 108 C4
North Colonnade E14 118 A4
North Crescent WC1 110 A3
North Flockton Street SE16 116 B1
Chambers Street
North Gower Street NW1 110 A4
North Mews WC1 110 C3
North Ride W2 108 C1
North Row W1 109 E1
North Tenter Street E1 116 B3
North Terrace SW3 112 C2
North Wharf Road W2 108 B2
Northampton Road EC1 111 D3
Northampton Row EC1 111 D3
Exmouth Market
Northampton Square EC1 111 D4
Northburgh Street EC1 111 D3
Northchurch SE17 115 F2
Northdown Street N1 110 C4
Northington Street WC1 110 C3
Northumberland Alley EC3 116 A3
Northumberland Avenue WC2 114 B4
Northumberland Street WC2 114 B4
Northy Street E14 117 E3
Norway Gate SE16 117 E1
Norway Place E14 117 F3
Norwich Street EC4 111 D2
Notting Hill Gate W11 108 A1
Nottingham Place W1 109 E3
Nottingham Street W1 109 E3

O'leary Square E1 117 D4
O'meara Street SE1 115 E4
Oak Lane E14 117 F3
Oak Tree Road NW8 108 C4
Oakden Street SE11 115 D2
Oakfield Street SW10 112 B1
Oakley Crescent EC1 111 E4
Oakley Gardens SW3 113 D1
Oakley Street SW3 112 C1
Oat Lane EC2 111 E2
Observatory Gardens W8 112 A4
Occupation Road SE17 115 E1
Ocean Street E1 117 E4
Octagon Arcade EC2 111 F2
Odessa Street SE16 117 F1
Ogle Street W1 109 F2
Old Bailey EC4 111 D2
Old Bond Street W1 109 F1
Old Broad Street EC2 111 F2
Old Brompton Road SW5 & SW7 112 A1
Old Burlington Street W1 109 F1
Old Castle Street E1 116 B4
Old Cavendish Street W1 109 F2
Old Church Road E1 117 D4
Old Church Street SW3 112 C1
Old Compton Street W1 110 A1
Old Court Place W8 112 A3
Old Gloucester Street WC1 110 B3
Old Jamaica Road SE16 116 B1
Old Jewry EC2 111 F2
Old Marylebone Road NW1 109 D2
Old Mitre Court EC4 111 D2
Fleet Street
Old Montagu Street E1 116 B4
Old North Street WC1 110 C3
Theobalds Road
Old Palace Yard SW1 114 B3
Old Paradise Street SE11 114 C2
Old Park Lane W1 113 E4
Old Pye Street SW1 114 A3
Old Quebec Street W1 109 D2
Old Queen Street SW1 114 A3
Old Square WC2 110 C2
Old Street EC1 111 E3
Oldbury Place W1 109 E3
Olivers Yard EC1 111 F3
Olney Road SE7 115 E1
Olympia Mews W2 108 B1
Onega Gate SE16 117 E1
Ongar Road SW6 112 A1
Onslow Gardens SW7 112 B2
Onslow Mews SW7 112 C2
Onslow Square SW7 112 C2
Onslow Street EC1 111 D3
Saffron Street
Ontario Street SE1 115 E3
Opal Street SE11 115 D2
Orange Place SE16 117 D1
Orange Street WC2 110 B1
Orb Street SE17 115 F2
Orchard Street W1 109 E2
Orchardson Street NW8 108 C3
Orde Hall Street WC1 110 C3
Orme Court W2 108 A1
Orme Lane W2 108 A1
Orme Square W2 108 A1
Ormond Yard SW1 110 A1
Ormonde Gate SW3 113 D1
Orsett Street SE11 114 C2
Orsett Terrace W2 108 B2
Orton Street E1 116 B2
Wapping High Street
Osbert Street SW1 114 A2
Osborne Street E1 116 B4
Oslo Square SE16 117 E1
Osnaburgh Street NW1 109 F3
Osnaburgh Terrace NW1 109 F4
Albany Street
Ossington Buildings W1 109 E2
Moxon Street
Ossington Street W2 108 A1
Ossulston Street NW1 110 A4
Osten Mews SW7 112 B2
Oswin Street SE11 115 D2
Othello Close SE1 115 D2
Otto Street SE17 115 D1
Oval Way SE11 114 C1
Ovington Gardens SW3 113 D3
Ovington Square SW3 113 D3
Ovington Street SW3 113 D2
Oxendon Street SW1 110 A1
Coventry Street
Owen Street EC1 111 D4
Oxford Square W2 108 C2
Oxford Street W1 109 E1

Paddington Green W2 108 C3
Paddington Street W1 109 E3
Page Street SW1 114 B2
Paget Street EC1 111 D4
Pakenham Street WC1 110 C3
Palace Avenue W8 112 A4
Palace Court W2 108 A1
Palace Gardens Mews W8 112 A4
Palace Gardens Terrace W8 112 A4
Palace Gate W8 112 B3
Palace Street SW1 113 F3
Pall Mall East SW1 110 B1
Pall Mall SW1 114 A4
Palmer Street SW1 114 A3
Pancras Lane EC4 111 E2
Panton Street SW1 110 A1
Paradise Street SE16 116 C1
Paradise Walk SW3 113 D1
Paragon Mews SE1 169 F2
Searles Road
Pardoner Street SE1 115 F3
Parfetts Street E1 116 C4
Paris Garden SE1 115 D4
Park Approach SE16 116 C1
Park Crescent Mews East W1 109 F3
Park Crescent Mews West W1 109 E3
Park Crescent W1 109 E3
Park Lane W1 109 E1
Park Place SW1 113 F4
Park Road NW1 & NW8 109 D4
Park Square East NW1 109 F3
Park Square Mews W1 109 E3
Harley Street
Park Square West NW1 109 E3
Park Street SE1 115 D4
Park Street W1 109 E1
Park Walk SW10 112 B1
Park West Place W2 109 D2
Parker Street WC2 110 B2
Parkers Row SE1 116 B1
Parliament Square SW1 114 B3
Parliament Street SW1 114 B4
Parnham Street E14 117 E4
Parry Street SW8 114 B1
Pasley Close SE17 115 E1
Passmore Street SW1 113 E2
Pastor Street SE11 115 D2
Pater Street W8 112 A3
Paternoster Row EC4 111 E2
Paternoster Square EC4 111 E2
Paul Street EC2 111 F3
Paultons Square SW3 112 C1
Paveley Street NW8 108 C4
Pavilion Road SW1 113 D2
Pavilion Street SW1 113 D3
Peabody Avenue SW1 113 F1
Peacock Street SE17 115 E2
Pear Tree Court EC1 111 D3
Pear Tree Street EC1 111 E3
Pearl Street E1 116 C2
Pearman Street SE1 115 D3
Peartree Lane E1 117 D3
Peerless Street EC1 111 E4
Pelham Crescent SW7 112 C2
Pelham Place SW7 112 C2
Pelham Street SW7 112 C2
Pelier Street SE17 115 E1
Pelling Street E14 117 F4
Pemberton Row EC4 111 D2
Pembridge Gardens W2 108 A1
Pembridge Road W11 108 A1
Pembridge Square W2 108 A1
Pembroke Mews W8 112 A2
Earls Court Road
Penang Street E1 116 C2
Penfold Place NW1 108 C3
Penfold Street NW1 & NW8 108 C3
Pennant Mews W8 112 A2
Pennington Street E1 116 C3
Penrose Grove SE17 115 E1
Penrose Street SE17 115 E1
Penryn Street NW1 112 A2
Penton Place SE17 115 D2
Penton Rise WC1 110 C4
Pentonville Road N1 110 C4
Pepper Street SE1 115 E4
Pepper Street E14 118 B3
Pepys Street EC3 116 A3
Percival Street EC1 111 D3
Percy Circus WC1 110 C4
Percy Street W1 110 A2
Perkin's Rents SW1 114 A3
Perkins Square SE1 115 E4
Perryn Road SE16 116 C1
Peter Street W1 110 A1
Peter's Hill EC4 111 E2
Carter Lane
Peter's Lane EC1 111 D3
Petersham Lane SW7 112 B3
Petersham Mews SW7 112 B3
Petersham Place SW7 112 B3
Peto Place NW1 109 F3
Petty France SW1 114 A3
Petyward SW3 113 D2
Phelp Street SE17 115 F1
Phene Street SW3 113 D1
Philchurch Place E1 116 B3
Phillimore Walk W8 112 A3
Philpot Lane EC3 111 F1
Philpot Street E1 116 C4
Phipp Street EC2 111 F3
Phoenix Place WC1 110 C3
Phoenix Road NW1 110 A4
Phoenix Street WC2 110 B2
Charing Cross Road
Piccadilly W1 113 F4
Pickard Street EC1 111 E4
Pickwick Street SE1 115 E3
Picton Place W1 109 E2
Piggot Street E14 117 F3
Pilgrim Street EC4 111 D2
Pilgrimage Street SE1 115 F3
Pimlico Road SW1 113 E2
Pinchin Street E1 116 B3
Pindar Street EC2 111 F3
Pine Street EC1 111 D3
Pitfield Street N1 111 F4
Pitsea Place E1 117 E3
Pitsea Street E1 117 E3
Pitt Street W8 112 A3
Pitt's Head Mews W1 113 E4
Pixley Street E14 117 F4
Platina Street EC2 111 F3
Playhouse Yard EC4 111 D1
Pleydell Street EC4 111 D1
Bouverie Street
Plough Place EC4 111 D2
Fetter Lane
Plover Way SE16 117 E1
Plumber's Row E1 117 B4
Plumtree Court EC4 111 D2
Plympton Place NW8 108 C3
Plympton Street
Plympton Street NW8 108 C3
Pocock Street SE1 115 D3
Poland Street W1 110 A2
Pollitt Drive NW8 108 C3
Polygon Road NW1 110 A4
Pomwell Way E1 116 B4
Pond Place SW3 112 C2
Ponler Street E1 116 C3
Ponsonby Place SW1 114 B2
Ponsonby Terrace SW1 114 B2
Pont Street Mews SW1 113 D3
Pont Street SW1 113 D3
Poolmans Street SE16 117 D2
Poonah Street E1 117 D3
Pope Street SE1 116 A1
Fleet Street
Poppins Court EC4 111 D2
Porchester Place W2 109 D2
Porchester Square W2 108 B2
Porchester Terrace W2 108 B1
Porchester Terrace W2 108 B2
Porlock Street SE1 115 F3
Porter Street W1 109 E3
Porter Street SE1 115 E4
Portland Place W1 109 F2
Portland Street SE17 115 F1
Portman Close W1 109 E2
Portman Mews South W1 109 E2
Portman Square W1 109 E2
Portman Street W1 109 E2
Portpool Lane EC1 110 C3
Portsea Place W2 109 D2
Portsmouth Street WC2 110 C2
Portugal Street
Portsoken Street EC3 116 B3
Portugal Street WC2 110 C2
Potier Street SE1 115 F3
Pottery Street SE16 116 C1
Poultry EC2 111 E2
Praed Street W2 108 C2
Pratt Walk SE11 114 C2
Prescot Street E1 116 B3
President Street EC1 111 E4
Central Street
Presidents Drive E1 116 C2
Prestwood Street N1 111 E4
Wenlock Road
Price's Street SE1 115 D4
Prideaux Place WC1 110 C4
Primrose Hill EC4 111 D1
Hutton Street
Primrose Street EC2 116 A4
Prince Albert Road NW1 & NW1 108 C4
Prince Consort Road SW7 112 C3
Prince of Wales Terrace W8 112 B1
Kensington Road
Prince's Gardens SW7 112 C3
Prince's Gate Mews SW7 112 C3
Prince's Gate SW7 112 C3
Princelet Street E1 116 B4
Princes Circus WC2 110 B2
Princes Street EC2 111 F2
Princes Street W1 109 F2
Princess Street SE1 115 D3
Princeton Street WC1 110 C2
Printer Street EC4 111 D2
Prioress Street SE1 115 F3
Priory Walk SW10 112 B1
Procter Street WC1 110 C2
Prospect Place E1 117 D2
Prospect Street SE16 116 C1
Providence Court W1 109 E1
Provost Street N1 111 F4
Prusom Street E1 116 C2
Pudding Lane EC3 111 F1
Puddle Dock EC4 110 D1
Pullen Street W1 109 F1
Puma Court E1 116 B4
Purbrook Street SE1 116 A1

Quarley Way SE15 109 D2
New Quebec Street
Quebec Way SE16 117 E1
Queen Anne Mews W1 109 F2
Chandos Street
Queen Anne Street W1 109 E2
Queen Anne's Gate SW1 114 A3
Queen Elizabeth Street SE1 116 A2
Queen Square WC1 110 B3
Queen Street EC4 111 E1
Queen Street Place EC4 111 E1
Queen Street W1 111 F4
Queen Victoria Street EC4 111 D1
Queen's Gardens SW1 113 F3
Queen's Gardens W2 108 B1
Queen's Gate Gardens SW7 112 B2
Queen's Gate Mews SW7 112 B3
Queen's Gate Place Mews SW7 112 B2
Queen's Gate Place SW7 112 B3
Queen's Gate SW7 112 B3
Queen's Gate Terrace SW7 112 B3
Queen's Row SE17 115 E1
Queen's Walk SW1 113 F4
Queenhithe EC4 111 E1
Queensberry Mews West SW7 112 B2
Queensberry Place SW7 109 F4
Harrington Street
Queensborough Terrace W2 108 B1
Queensway W2 108 A1
Quick Street N1 111 D4

Rabbit Row W8 112 A4
Radcot Street SE11 115 D1
Radley Court SE16 117 E2
Radley Mews W8 112 A2
Radnor Mews W2 108 C2
Radnor Place W2 108 C2
Radnor Street EC1 111 D3
Radnor Walk SW3 113 D1
Railway Approach SE1 115 F4
Railway Avenue SE16 117 D2
Raine Street E1 116 C2
Rainsford Street W2 108 C2
Ralston Street SW3 113 D1
Ramillies Place W1 109 F2
Ramillies Street W1 110 A2
Rampart Street E1 116 C4
Rampayne Street SW1 114 A2
Randall Road SE11 114 C2
Randall Row SE11 114 C2
Ranelagh Bridge W2 108 B2
Ranelagh Grove SW1 113 E2
Ranelagh Road SW1 114 A1
Ranston Street NW1 108 C3
Raphael Street SW7 113 D3
Ratcliff Grove EC1 111 E4
Ratcliffe Cross Street E1 117 E3
Ratcliffe Lane E14 117 E3
Rathbone Place W1 110 A2
Raven Row E1 116 C4
Ravensdon Street SE11 115 D1
Ravent Road SE11 114 C2
Ravey Street EC2 111 F3
Rawlings Street SW3 113 D2
Rawstorne Place EC1 111 D4
Rawstorne Street
Rawstorne Street EC1 111 D4
Ray Street EC1 111 D3
Reardon Path E1 116 C2
Reardon Street E1 116 C2
Rebecca Terrace SE16 117 D1
Rectory Square E1 117 E4
Red Lion Row SE17 115 E1
Red Lion Square WC1 110 C2
Red Lion Street WC1 110 C2
Redburn Street SW3 113 D1
Redcastle Close E1 117 D3
Redcliffe Gardens SW10 & SW5 112 A1
Redcliffe Mews SW10 112 B1
Redcliffe Place SW10 112 B1
Redcliffe Road SW10 112 B1
Redcliffe Square SW10 112 A1
Redcliffe Street SW10 112 A1
Redcross Way SE1 115 E4
Redesdale Street SW3 113 D1
Redfield Lane SW5 112 A2
Redhill Street NW1 109 F4
Redman's Road E1 117 D4
Redmead Lane E1 116 B2
Wapping High Street
Redriff Road SE16 117 E1

Town plans

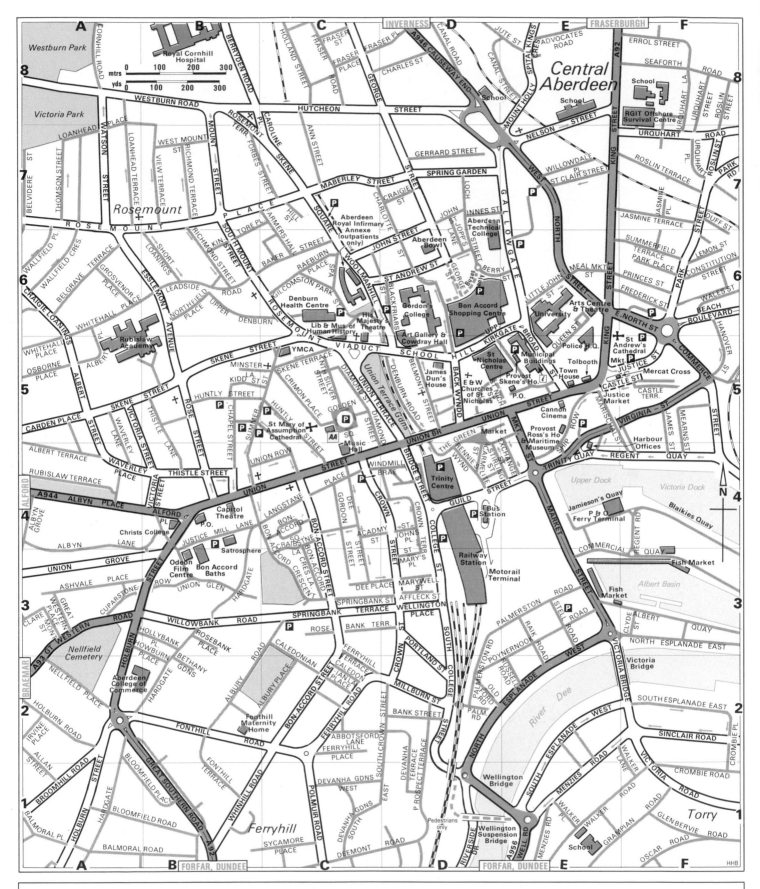

Aberdeen

Granite gives Aberdeen its especial character; but this is not to say that the city is a grim or a grey place, the granites used are of many hues – white, blue, pink and grey. Although the most imposing buildings date from the 19th century, granite has been used to dramatic effect since at least as early as the 15th century. From that time dates St Machar's Cathedral, originally founded in AD580,

but rebuilt several times, especially after a devasting fire started on the orders of Edward III of England in 1336. St Machar's is in Old Aberdeen, traditionally the ecclesiastical and educational hub of the city, while 'New' Aberdeen (actually no newer) has always been the commercial centre. Even that definition is deceptive, for although Old Aberdeen has King's College, founded in 1494, New Aberdeen has Marischal College, founded almost exactly a century later (but rebuilt in 1844)

and every bit as distinguished as a seat of learning. Both establishments functioned as independent universities until they were merged in 1860 to form Aberdeen University. The North Sea oil boom has brought many changes to the city, some of which threatened its character. But even though high-rise buildings are now common, the stately façades, towers and pillars of granite still reign supreme and Union Street remains one of the best thoroughfares in Britain.

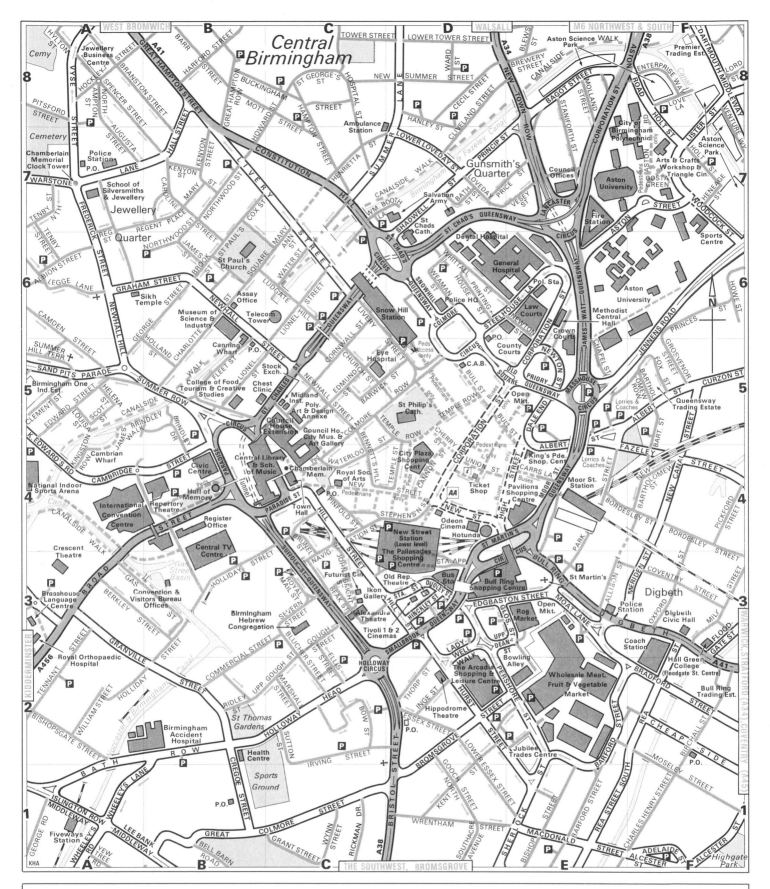

Birmingham

When the Romans were in Britain, Birmingham was little more than a staging post on Icknield Street. Throughout medieval times it was a minor agricultural centre in the middle of a heavily-forested region. Timbered houses clustered together round a green that was eventually to be called the Bull Ring. But by the 16th century, although still a tiny and unimportant village by today's standards, it had begun to gain a reputation as a manufacturing centre. Tens of thousands of sword blades were made here during the Civil War. Throughout the 18th century more and more land was built on. In 1770 the Birmingham Canal was completed, making trade very much easier and increasing the town's development dramatically. All of that pales into near insignificance compared with what happened in the 19th century. Birmingham was not represented in Parliament until 1832 and had no town council until 1838. Yet by 1889 it had already been made a city, and after only another 20 years it had become the second largest city in England. Many of Birmingham's most imposing public buildings date from the 19th century, when the city was growing rapidly. The International Convention Centre and National Indoor Sports Arena are two of the most recent developments. Surprisingly, the city has more miles of waterway than Venice.

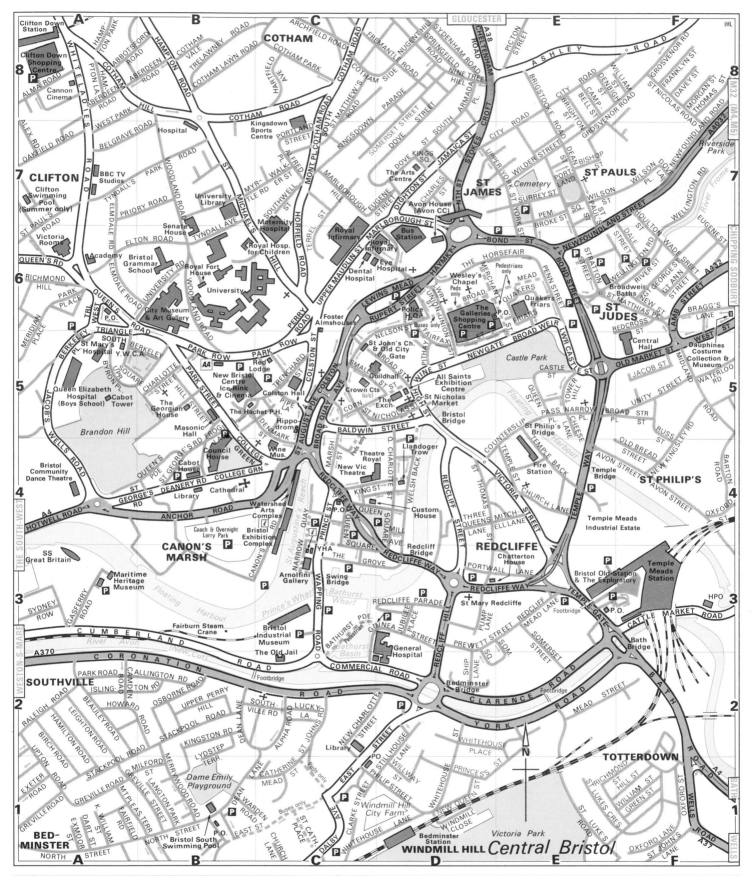

Bristol

One of Britain's most historic seaports, Bristol retains many of its visible links with the past, despite terrible damage inflicted during bombing raids in World War II. Most imposing is the cathedral, founded as an abbey church in 1140. Perhaps even more famous than the cathedral is the Church of St Mary Redcliffe. Ranking among the finest churches in the country, it owes much of its splendour to 14th- and 15th-century merchants who bestowed huge sums of money on it.

The merchant families brought wealth to the whole of Bristol, and their trading links with the world are continued in today's modern aerospace and technological industries. Much of the best of Bristol can be seen in the area of the Floating Harbour. Several of the old warehouses have been converted into museums, galleries and exhibition centres. Among them are genuinely picturesque old pubs, the best known which is the Llandoger Trow. It is a timbered 17th-century house, the finest of

its kind in Bristol. Further up the same street - King Street - is the Theatre Royal, built in 1766 and the oldest theatre in the country. In Corn Street, the heart of the business area, is a magnificent 18th-century corn exchange. In front of it are the four pillars known as the 'nails', on which merchants used to make cash transactions, hence to 'pay on the nail';

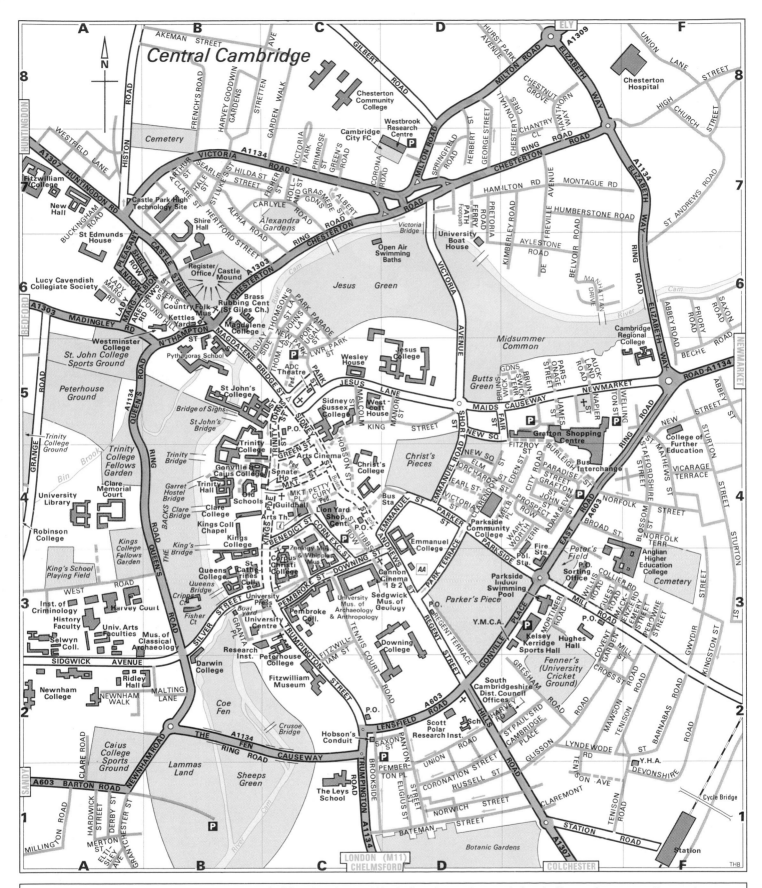

Cambridge

Few views in England, perhaps even in Europe, are as memorable as that from Cambridge's Backs towards the colleges. Dominating the scene, in every sense, is King's College Chapel. One of the finest Gothic buildings anywhere, it was built in three stages from 1446 to 1515.

No one would dispute that the chapel is Cambridge's masterpiece, but there are dozens of buildings here that would be the finest in any other town or city. Most are colleges, or are attached to colleges, and it is the university which permeates every aspect of Cambridge's landscape and life. In all there are 33 university colleges in the city, and nearly all have buildings and features of great interest. Guided tours of the colleges are available.

Cambridge can provide a complete history of English architecture. The oldest surviving building is the tower of St Benet's Church dating back to before the Norman Conquest, and its most famous church is the Church of the Holy Sepulchre, one of only four round churches of its kind.

Of the many notable museums in Cambridge, the Fitzwilliam Museum contains some of the best collections of ceramics, paintings, coins, medals and Egyptian, Greek and Roman antiquities outside London.

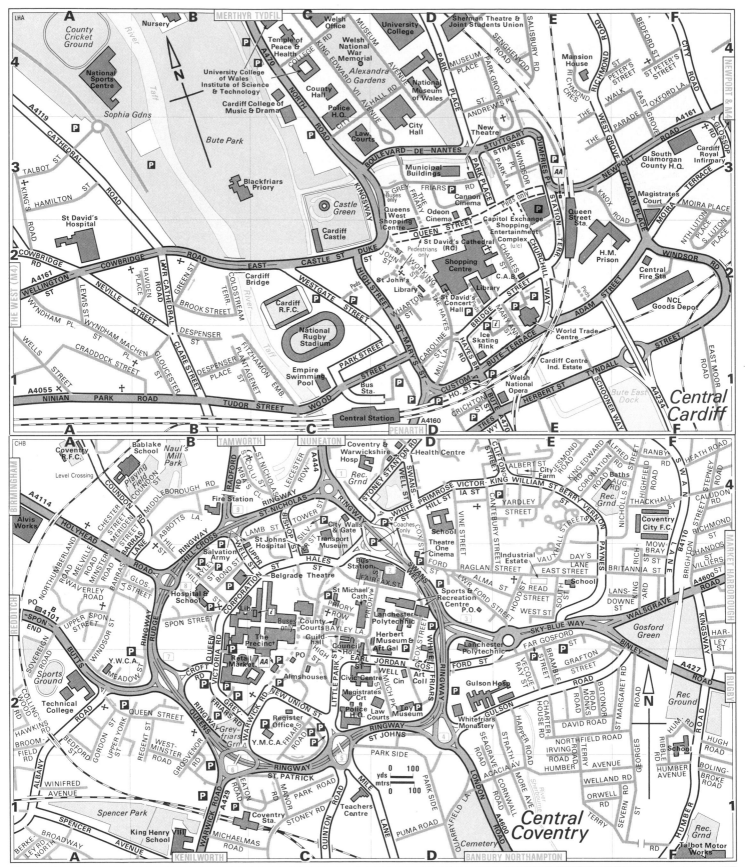

Central Cardiff

(Map labels, grid A–F / 1–4)

MERTHYR TYDFIL
LHA
County Cricket Ground
Nursery
River Taff
National Sports Centre
Temple of Peace & Health
Welsh Office
MUSEUM
University College
Sherman Theatre & Joint Students Union
SALISBURY RD
BEDFORD ST
CITY ROAD
Mansion House
ST PETER'S STREET
PETER'S STREET
Sophia Gdns
University College of Wales Institute of Science & Technology
Welsh National War Memorial
KING EDWARD VII AVENUE
Alexandra Gardens
PARK PLACE
PARK GROVE
SENGHENYDD RD
RICHMOND ROAD
THE WALK
THE PARADE
EAST GROVE
RICHMOND CRES
A4161
A4119
CATHEDRAL ROAD
Bute Park
University College of Music & Drama
County Hall
Police H.Q.
National Museum of Wales
PARK PLACE
ST. ANDREW'S PL.
New Theatre
WEST GROVE
NEWPORT ROAD
FITZALAN PLACE
South Glamorgan County H.Q.
Cardiff Royal Infirmary
NEWPORT & M4
A4161
GLOSSOP
TALBOT ST
KING'S ROAD
HAMILTON ST
St David's Hospital
NORTH ROAD
Law Courts
City Hall
BOULEVARD DE NANTES
STUTTGART STRASSE
WINDSOR
DUMFRIES PL.
PARK LA.
STATION TERR.
KNOX ROAD
AA
Magistrates Court
MOIRA TERRACE
MOIRA PLACE
Municipal Buildings
PARK PLACE
GREY FRIARS RD
Cannon Cinema
CHARLES
Queen Street Sta.
NTH.LUTON PLACE
S.LUTON PLACE
COWBRIDGE RD
WELLINGTON ST
NEVILLE STREET
COWBRIDGE ROAD EAST
LWR CATHEDRAL ROAD
GREEN ST
COLDSTREAM TERR.
Cardiff Bridge
CASTLE ST
KINGSWAY
Castle Green
Cardiff Castle
Blackfriars Priory
Queens West Shopping Centre
Odeon Cinema
St David's Cathedral (RC)
Capitol Exchange Shopping Entertainment Complex (u/c)
Shopping Centre
C.A.B.
Library
CHURCHILL WAY
ADAM STREET
H.M. Prison
Central Fire Sta
WINDSOR ROAD
NCL Goods Depot
A4161
WYNDHAM PL.
LEWIS ST
WYNDHAM MACHEN ST
RAWDEN PLACE
BROOK STREET
GLOUCESTER ST
CLARE STREET
DESPENSER ST
WESTGATE ST
HIGH STREET
DUKE ST
ST JOHN ST
Cardiff R.F.C.
St John's Library
St John's
QUEEN STREET
WHARTON ST
WORKING ST
St David's Concert Hall
BRIDGE ST
MARY ANN
HAYES BR.
CAROLINE ST
THE HAYES
MILL ST
CUSTOM HO. ST
World Trade Centre
Cardiff Centre Ind. Estate
BUTE TERRACE
SCHOONER WAY
TYNDALL STREET
EAST MOOR ROAD
A4234
WELLS STREET
CRADDOCK STREET
FITZHAMON EMB.
PLANTAGENET ST
DESPENSER PLACE
National Rugby Stadium
Empire Swimming Pool
PARK STREET
WOOD STREET
Bus Sta.
Ice Skating Rink
Welsh National Opera
HERBERT ST
CRICHTON ST
BUTE ST
Bute East Dock
A4055
WINIFRED AVENUE
NINIAN PARK ROAD
TUDOR STREET
Central Station
A4160
PENARTH
A4234
Central Cardiff

Central Coventry

CHB
BIRMINGHAM
REDDITCH
Coventry R.F.C.
Bablake School
Naul's Mill Park
TAMWORTH
NUNEATON
Coventry & Warwickshire Hosp
Health Centre
CLIFTON ST
ALBERT ST
City Farm
KING EDWARD RD
ALFRED RD
RANBY RD
HEATH ROAD
Level Crossing
Playing Field
COUNDON
MIDDLEBOROUGH RD
RADFORD RD
ST NICHOLAS
LEICESTER ROW
A4444
STONEY STANTON RD
SWANSWELL
VICTOR ST
PRIMROSE HILL ST
KING WILLIAM ST
CORONATION RD
BERRY ST
HIGHFIELD RD
THACKHALL ST
STEPNEY RD
CALUDON RD
RICHMOND ST
A4114
A4101
ALVIS WORKS
HOLYHEAD ROAD
CHESTER ST
MERIDEN ST
BARRAS LANE
ABBOTTS LA.
RINGWAY ST NICHOLAS
Fire Station
BISHOP ST
TOWER ST
City Walls & Gate
Transport Museum
Coaches only
School
VINE STREET
CANTERBURY STREET
YARDLEY STREET
RAGLAN STREET
Industrial Estate
VAUXHALL ST
DAY'S LANE
EAST STREET
Coventry City F.C.
CHANDOS ST
VILLIERS ST
MOWBRAY
A4600
NORTHUMBERLAND RD
MELVILLE RD
WAVERLEY ROAD
MINSTER RD
GLOS. ST
LA STREET
HILL CROSS
HILL ST
LAMB ST
WELL ST
UPPER HILL
RYLEY ST
BOND ST
St Johns Hospital
Salvation Army
HALES ST
Bus Station
FAIRFAX ST
Belgrade Theatre
COX ST
SWANS
Theatre One Cinema
FORD
Lanchester Polytechnic
ALMA ST
LWR FORD STREET
READ STREET
Sports & Recreation Centre
P.O.
WEST ST
School
BRITANNIA ST
LANSDOWNE ST
KING RICHARD ST
PAYNES LANE
A4600 ROAD
MARKET HARBOROUGH
KINGSWAY
UPPER SPON STREET
B4101
PO
SPON END
WINDSOR ST
RUDGE RD
CORPORATION ST
SPON STREET
Lib
Hospital & School
St Michael's Cath.
PRIORY ROW
PRIORY ST
Herbert Museum & Art Gal
COX ST
WHITEFRIARS ST
Lanchester Polytechnic
SKY-BLUE WAY
FAR GOSFORD ST
BINLEY ROAD
Gosford Green
A427
SOVEREIGN ROAD
BUTTS
Sports Ground
Y.W.C.A.
MEADOW
QUEEN VICTORIA RD
The Precinct
AA
Retail Market
County Courts
BAYLEY LA.
Guildhall
Council Ho.
EARL ST
JORDAN WELL
Lanchester Polytechnic
GOSFORD ST
FORD ST
VECQUE RAY ST
BRAMBLE ST
GRAFTON STREET
BOTONER ROAD
HARLEY ST
COLLINGWOOD RD
Technical College
QUEEN STREET
RINGWAY RUDGE
CROFT RD
GREY FRIARS RD
NEW UNION ST
WARWICK RD
LITTLE PARK ST
Civic Centre
Art Coll
MUCH PK. ST
Cin
Loy Museum
Gulson Hosp
Whitefriars Monastery
GULSON ROAD
HARPER ROAD
CHARTERHOUSE RD
DAVID ROAD
ST MARGARET RD
Rec Ground
HAWKINS RD
BROOMFIELD RD
BEDFORD ST
GORDON ST
UPPER YORK ST
REGENT ST
WESTMINSTER ROAD
GROSVENOR ROAD
Greyfriars Grn
Register Office
Y.M.C.A.
FRIARS RD
QUEENS ROAD
Magistrates Crt
Police H.Q.
Law Courts
RINGWAY ST JOHNS
PARK SIDE
EARL ST
SEAGRAVE ROAD
STRATHMORE AV
ACACIA AV.
CORNWALL RD
A4600 LONDON ROAD
NORTHFIELD ROAD
IRVING ROAD
HUMBER AVENUE
WELLAND RD
ORWELL RD
GEORGES RD
SEVERN RD
RIBBLE RD
TERRY RD
School
HUGH ROAD
HUMBER AVENUE
BOLINGBROKE ROAD
ALBANY ROAD
SPENCER AVENUE
Spencer Park
King Henry VIII School
WARWICK ROAD
A429
EATON RD
MICHAELMAS ROAD
Coventry Sta.
MANOR ROAD
STONEY RD
PARK ROAD
QUINTON ROAD
MILE LANE
Teachers Centre
PUMA ROAD
PARK SIDE
QUARRYFIELD LA.
River Sherbourne
Cemetery
KENILWORTH
BANBURY NORTHAMPTON
RUGBY
Talbot Motor Works
Rec. Grnd
Central Coventry

yds 0 100
mtrs 0 100
N

Cardiff

Strategically important to both the Romans and the Normans, Cardiff slipped from the prominence in medieval times and remained a quiet market town until it was transformed by the effects of the Industrial Revolution. The valleys of South Wales were a principal source of iron and coal — raw materials which helped to change the shape and course of the 19th-century world. Cardiff became a teeming export centre; by the end of the 19th-century it was the largest coal exporting city in the world.

Close to the Norman castle is the city's civic centre — a fine concourse of buildings dating largely from the early part of the 20th-century. Among them is the National Museum of Wales — a collection of art and antiquities from Wales and around the world.

Coventry Few British towns were as battered by the blitz as Coventry. The lovely old cathedral was bombed during an air raid in November 1940 which devastated the city. Rebuilding started almost immediately. Symbolising the creation of the new from the ashes of the old is Sir Basil Spence's cathedral, completed in 1962 beside the bombed ruins.

A few medieval buildings have survived intact in the city. St Mary's Guildhall is a finely restored 14th-century building with an attractive minstrels' gallery. Whitefriars Monastry now serves as a local museum. The Herbert Art Gallery and Museum has several notable collections. Coventry is an important manufacturing centre (most notably for cars) and some four miles out of the city is the fine campus of the University of Warwick.

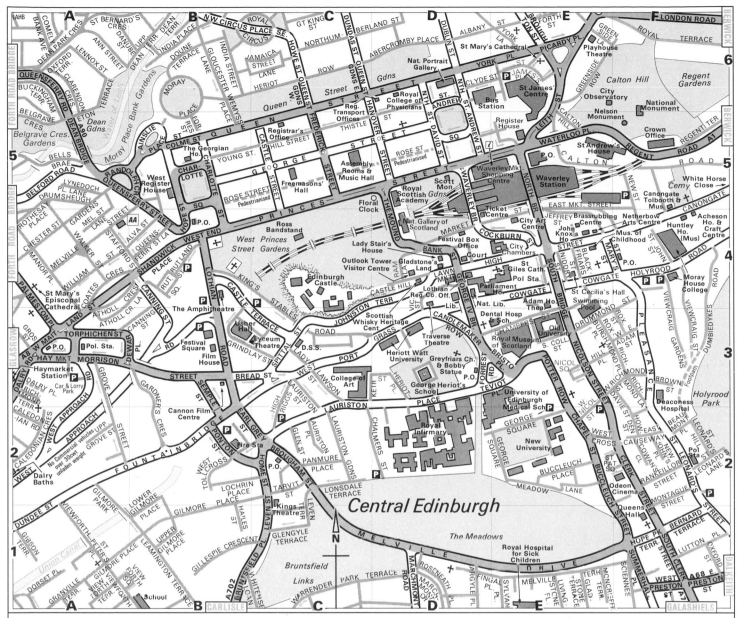

Edinburgh

Scotland's ancient capital, known as the 'Athens of the North', is one of the most beautiful cities in Europe, noted for its wealth of historical buildings, its scenic position on the Firth of Forth, backed by the Pentland Hills, and its famous festival which takes place each August. The Edinburgh Festival has more or less followed the same basic pattern since its inception in 1947, including opera, concerts covering a wide spectrum of different types of music, drama, dance and exhibitions of painting, sculpture etc. Subsequent additions are film and jazz festivals and the marvellously undisciplined 'fringe' performances which introduced the 'Beyond the Fringe' team to the international stage in the 1950s.

Edinburgh is dominated by the castle, perched on a volcanic crag above the Old Town. There has been a fortress on this spot since the 7th-century and parts of the present building date back to Norman times. The castle has featured prominently in Scottish history; James VI (James I of England), the son of Mary Queen of Scots, was born there in 1566, the Scottish Crown Jewels, last used at the coronation of Charles II in 1651 (10 years before his English coronation), are on display in the Crown Room, and the Casemates, beneath the Great Hall, contain graffiti carved by prisoners held there during the Napoleonic Wars. In modern times the Castle Esplanade

has become the venue for the floodlit Military Tattoo, an integral part of the Edinburgh Festival. There is still a strong military presence in the Castle and some parts are not open to visitors.

Below the Castle lies the Old Town with its narrow 'wynds' and alleys radiating from the famous Royal Mile, an area which was once a favourite drinking haunt of such literary figures as Robert Burns and Robert Fergusson. Here were Europe's first skyscrapers, a series of stark tenement buildings, some as high as 6 storeys, which housed many thousands of the city's inhabitants during the mid-18th century. Other notable buildings in this area include the Camera Obscura on Castle Hill which provides fine views over the city, and Lady Stair's House, off Lawnmarket, dating from the 17th-century and now a museum containing manuscripts and relics of Robert Burns, Sir Walter Scott and Robert Louis Stevenson. A sharp contrast is provided by the Georgian elegance of the New Town, constructed as a residential area for the city's merchants and aristocrats following the prosperity brought by the shipping trade during the 18th-century. Particularly notable is Charlotte Square, containing a fine example of Robert Adam's work at No. 7 which is open to the public. Princes Street, the main east-west thoroughfare, is noted for its fine shops and the pleasantly landscaped Princes Street Gardens with

their well known floral clock.

As befits such a splendid capital city, Edinburgh is filled with interesting buildings, museums and art galleries. The foremost, perhaps, is Holyroodhouse, at the opposite end of the Royal Mile to the castle, a 16th-century royal palace which was developed from the guesthouse of the old Abbey of Holyrood. Holyroodhouse was the seat of Mary Queen of Scots' court between 1561 and 1567 and the scene of the murder of her secretary, David Rizzio, in 1566. Bonnie Prince Charlie was resident there during his unsuccessful attempt to win the Crown in 1745. There are fine 17th-century state rooms and a picture gallery where the likenesses of Scottish monarchs (from as far back as 330bc) are on display, the work of Jacob de Wet in 1684 and 1685. It is now an official residence of the royal family, and royal garden parties are regularly held in its extensive grounds.

Other places of interest include: the house where John Knox, the Protestant reformer, is said to have died in 1572, noted for its magnificent Oak Room; the unusual Museum of Childhood, one of the first of its kind, devoted to toys, games etc throughout the years; the Royal Museum of Scotland, in Charles Street, which traces the history of the country from earliest times; and the royals, rebels, soldiers, scientists and writers, and featuring a display which traces the development of Highland dress.

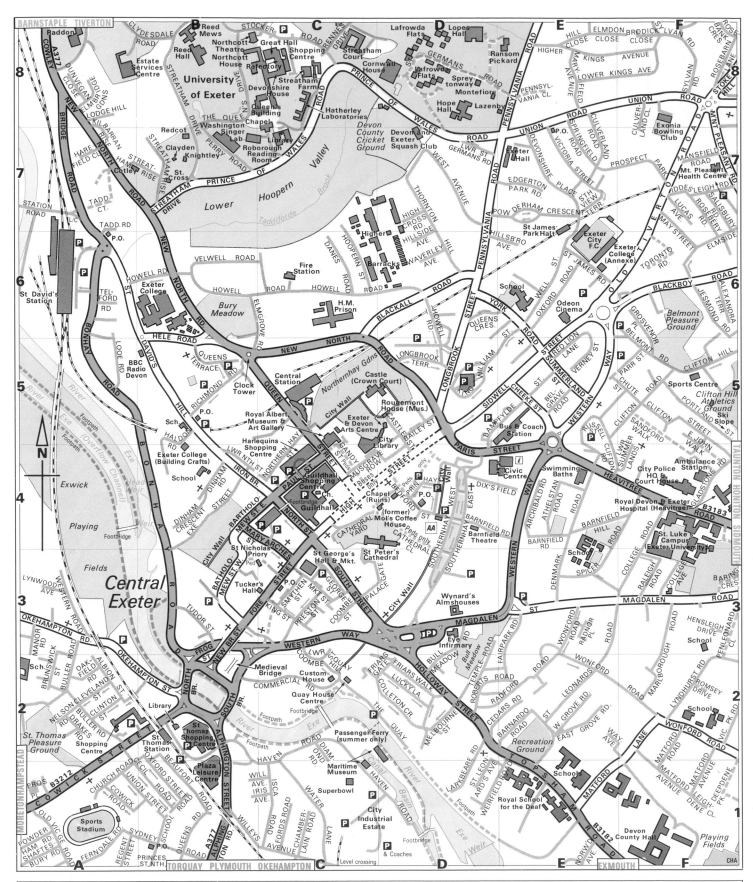

Exeter

The cathedral is Exeter's greatest treasure. Founded in 1050, but rebuilt by the Normans during the 12th-century and again at the end of the 13th-century, it has many beautiful and outstanding features - especially the exquisite rib-vaulting of the nave, the west face, which has the largest surviving array of 14th-century sculpture in Britain, the intricately decorated bishop's throne and the misericord carvings under the choir seats. Most remarkable, perhaps, is the fact that it still stood after much around it was flattened during the bombing raids in World War II.

There is still plenty of reminders of Old Exeter, which has been a city since Roman times: Roman and medieval walls encircle parts of the city; 14th-century underground passages which carried the city's water supply can be explored; the Guildhall is 15th-century and one of the oldest municipal buildings in the country; and Sir Francis Drake is said to have met his explorer companians at Mol's Coffee House. Exeter is famous for its extensive Maritime Museum, situated in the heart of the lively quay area, where there are over 130 boats from all over the world - some afloat, others ashore or under cover. Other museums include the Rougemont House, a Regency building now a museum of costume and lace, and the Royal Albert Memorial Museum and Art Gallery, displaying Exeter silver and regional archaeology.

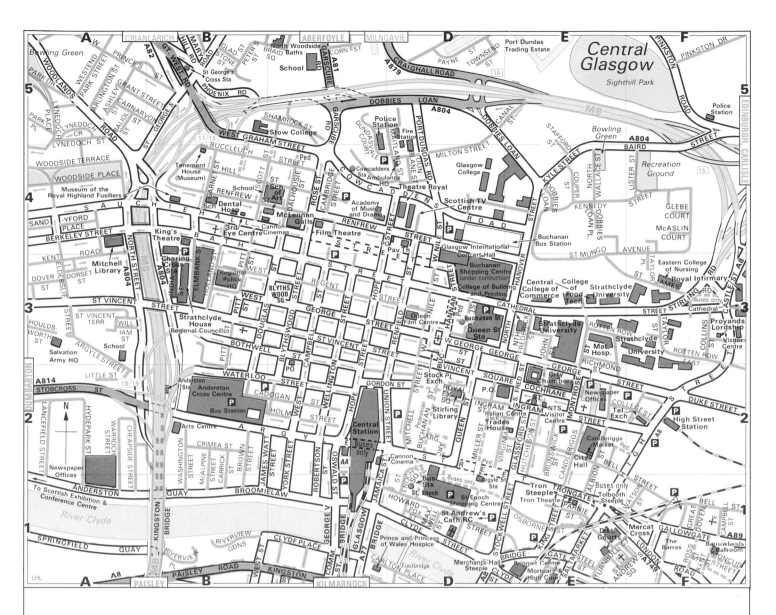

Glasgow

Scotland's largest city was founded in 543 when St Mungo built a church in what was then called Glasgu (meaning 'beloved green place'). The building of the present cathedral began in the 12th century and was completed during the 15th century. When Scotland's second university was established it brought renown to the city, and in 1454 it was made a royal burgh. Glasgow's commercial prosperity started in the 17th century when Port Glasgow, further down the River Clyde, began to import tobacco, sugar, cotton and other goods from the Americas. During the Industrial Revolution, ship building and heavy engineering made the city one of the great industrial centres of the world. The city rapidly expanded, producing areas of cheap housing that soon became notorious slums. Today these are being cleared and a great deal of the old city has now disappeared.

Although much of Glasgow is distinctly Victorian in character, its roots go back many centuries. The best link with the past is the cathedral, which was built on or near the site of St Mungo's church. It has features from many succeeding centuries, including an exceptional 13th century crypt. Nearby is Provand's Lordship, the city's oldest house. It dates from 1471 and has been carefully restored as a museum depicting various periods in the city's history. Two much larger museums are to be found a little out of the

centre. The Art Gallery and Museum in Kelvingrove Park contains one of the finest collections of British and European paintings in Britain, while the Hunterian Museum, attached to the university, covers archaeology, ethnography and a remarkable Coin Gallery. The Hunterian Gallery (also part of the university), is an ever growing collection, its core being paintings bequeathed in the 18th century by Dr William Hunter. The gallery's tower contains a remarkable re-creation of The home of Charles Rennie Mackintosh, the architect who at the end of the Victorian era led the way in making Glasgow a centre for Art Nouveau.

On Glasgow Green, the oldest of the city's parks, is People's Palace. Opened in 1898 as a cultural centre it concentrates on the ordinary folk of the city, recalling the city's many industries and also the political fight for trade unions and the causes of the suffragettes. Behind the main museum are the Winter Gardens, a huge conservatory containing tropical plants. Adjoining the green, the former Templeton carpet factory is modelled on the Doges' Palace in Venice. Most imposing of the Victorian buildings is City Chambers, it shows more clearly than anything else the opulance of Glasgow in its Victorian heyday. The building has an imposing arcaded entrance hall elaborately decorated with mosaics, marble and other stones. A marble staircase leads to a great banqueting hall decorated with murals showing the city's history. City Chambers overlooks the principal square, George Square,

which is noted for its 12 statues (including Queen Victoria, Prince Albert and James Watt).

Situated three miles south west of the city centre is Pollok Country Park. It covers an area of 370 acres and is truly a piece of countryside in the city. Two major museums are located within the park: Pollock House Museum contains the Stirling Maxwell collection of Spanish paintings and the Burrell Collection, a diverse assortment of objects amassed over some 80 years by Sir William Burrell and presented to the city of Glasgow in 1944. This is housed in a specially designed gallery.

Despite the multitude of historic buildings and museums Glasgow boasts more parks per head of population than any other European city. Over the past few years, a reviving prosperity has brought much environmental improvement.

The visual and performing arts have always been a tradition in Glasgow. It boasts a bewildering array of amateur choral societies as well as more famous ones. In the 1890s the Scottish National Orchestra was formed, and in 1950 it became the Scottish National Orchestra and has since gone from strength to strength. The BBC also has an orchestra based in Glasgow. Theatres include the Kings Theatre, the Pavilion, Citizens Theatre and the Theatre Royal, Scotland's only opera house and home of Scottish Opera. This wealth of achievement led to Glasgow being nominated European City of Culture in 1990.

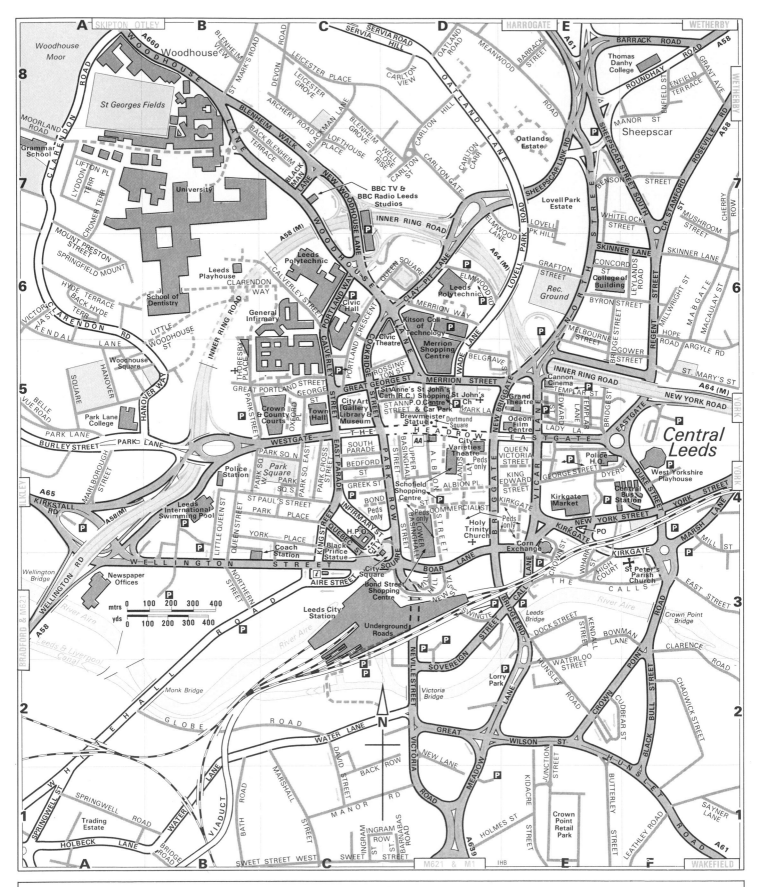

Leeds

In the centre of Leeds is its town hall – a monumental piece of architecture with a 225ft clock-tower. It was opened by Queen Victoria in 1858, and has been a kind of mascot for the city ever since. It exudes civic pride; such buildings could only have been created in the heyday of Victorian prosperity and confidence. Leeds' staple industry has always been the wool trade, but it only became a boom town towards the end of the 18th century, when textile mills were introduced. Today, the wool trade and ready-made clothing (Mr Hepworth and Mr Burton began their work here) are still important, though industries like paper, leather, furniture and electrical equipment are prominent.

Across Calverley Street from the town hall is the City Art Gallery, Library and Museum. Its collections include sculpture by Henry Moore, who was a student at Leeds School of Art. Nearby is the Headrow, Leeds' foremost shopping thoroughfare. On it is the City Varieties Theatre, venue for many years of the famous television programme 'The Good Old Days'. Off the Headrow are several shopping arcades, of which Leeds has many handsome examples. Leeds has a good number of interesting churches; perhaps the finest is St John's, unusual in that it dates from 1634, a time when few churches were built.

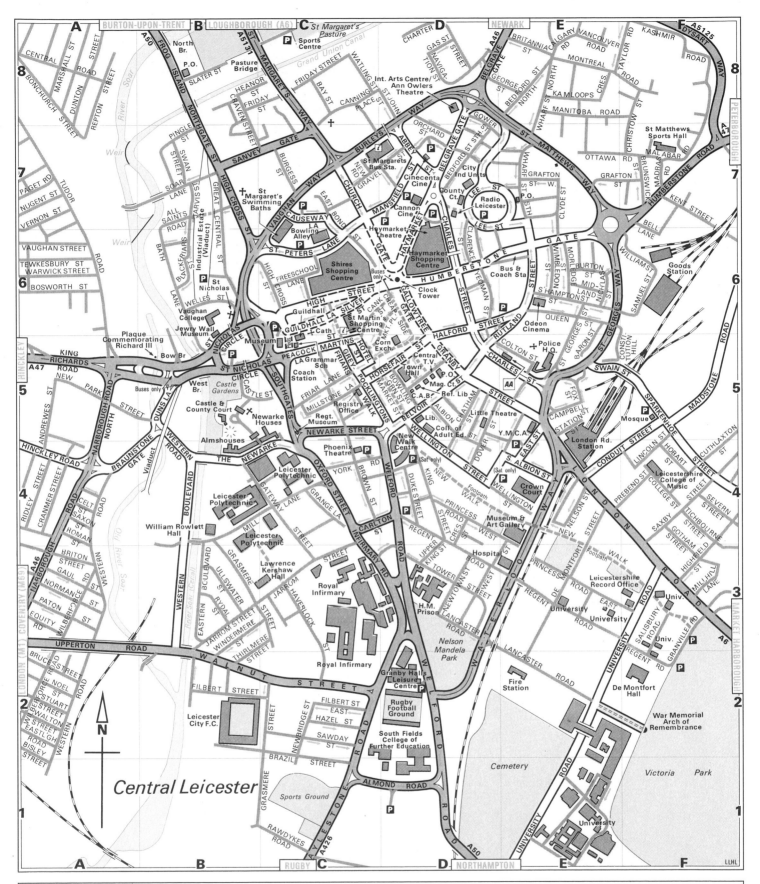

Central Leicester

Leicester

A regional capital in Roman times, Leicester has retained many buildings from its eventful and distinguished past. Today the city is a thriving contrast of heritage and modern amenities, including the modern Shires shopping mall, and one of Europe's largest permanent open-air markets. Among the most outstanding monuments from the past is the Jewry Wall, a great bastion of

Roman masonry. Close by are remains of the Roman baths and several other contemporary buildings. Attached is a musuem covering all periods from prehistoric times to 1500. Nine museums include the Wygston's House Museum of Costume, Newarke House, showing changing social conditions in Leicester through four hundred years; and Leicestershire Museum and Art Gallery, with collections of drawings, paintings, ceramics, geology and natural history.

The medieval Guildhall has many features of interest, including a great hall, library and police cells. Leicester's castle, although remodelled in the 17th century, retains a 12th-century great hall. The Church of St Mary de Castro, across the road from the castle, has features going back at least as far as Norman times; while St Nicholas's Church is even older, with Roman and Saxon foundations. St Martin's Cathedral dates mainly from the 13th- to 15th-centuries and has a notable Bishop's throne.

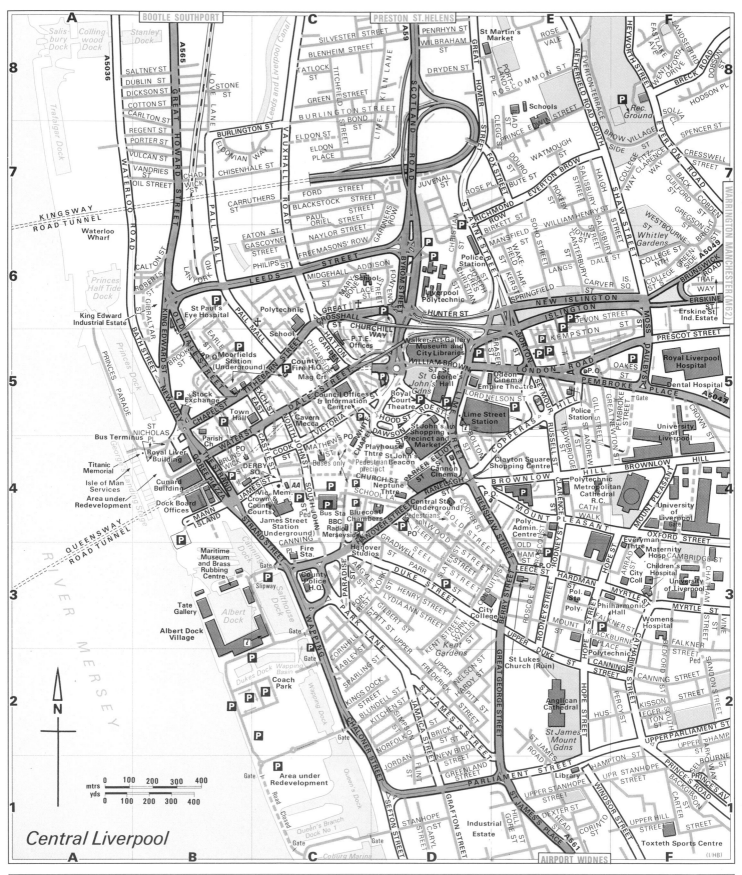

Central Liverpool

Liverpool

Although its dock area has been much reduced, Liverpool was at one time second only to London in pre-eminence as a port. Formerly the centrepiece of the docks area are three monumental buildings - the Dock Board Offices, built in 1907 with a huge copper-covered dome; the Cunard Building, dating from 1912 and decorated with an abundance of ornamental carving; and best-known of all, the world-famous Royal Liver Building, with the two 'liver birds' crowning its twin cupolas.

Some of the city's best industrial buildings have fallen into disuse in recent years, but some have been preserved as monuments of the idustrial age. One has become a maritime museum housing full-sized craft and a workshop where maritime crafts are demonstrated. Other museums and galleries include the Walker Art Gallery, with excellent collections of European painting and sculpture; Liverpool City Libraries, one of the oldest and largest public libraries in Britain, with a vast collection of books and manuscripts; and Bluecoat

Chambers, a Queen Anne building now used as a gallery and concert hall. Liverpool has two outstanding cathedrals: the Roman Catholic, completed in 1967 in an uncompromising controversial style; and the Protestant, constructed in the great tradition of Gothic architecture, but begun in 1904 and only recently completed.

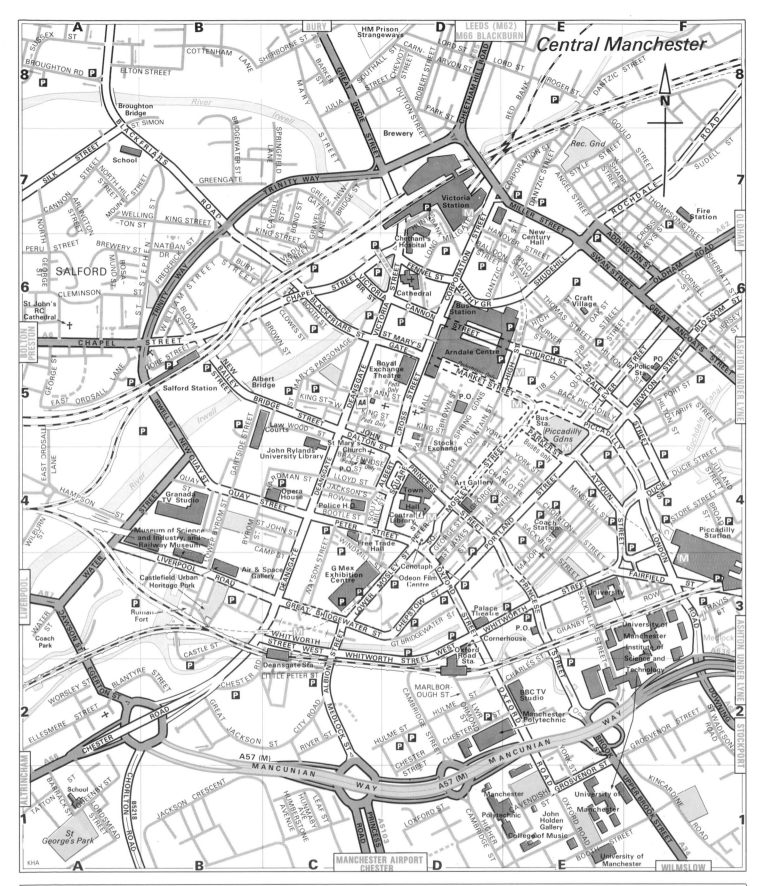

Manchester

Manchester is the regional centre for North-west England with a population of over half a million. Commerce and industry are vital aspects of the city's character, but it is also an important cultural centre – the Halle Orchestra has its home at the Free Trade Hall (a venue for many concerts besides classical music), there are several theatres, the John Rylands Library which houses one of the most important collections of books in the world, and a

number of museums and galleries, including the Whitworth Gallery with its lovely watercolours.

Like many great cities it suffered badly during World War II, but some older buildings remain including the massive Gothic-style town hall of 1877.

Manchester Cathedral dates mainly from the 15th century and is noted for its fine tower and outstanding carved woodwork. Nearby is Chetham's Hospital, also 15th-century and new housing has taken place, and more is planned. The massive Arndale Shopping Centre caters for the vast population, and there are

huge international-standard hotels. The Museum of Science and Industry in the Castlefield Urban Heritage Park contains exhibits from the Industrial Revolution to the Space Age and includes the world's first passenger railway station. Nearby are the Granada Television Studios where visitors can walk through the various film sets including the famous 'Coronation Street', and the impressive G-Mex exhibition centre. Manchester is also the first city in Britain to re-instate an on-street tramway system.

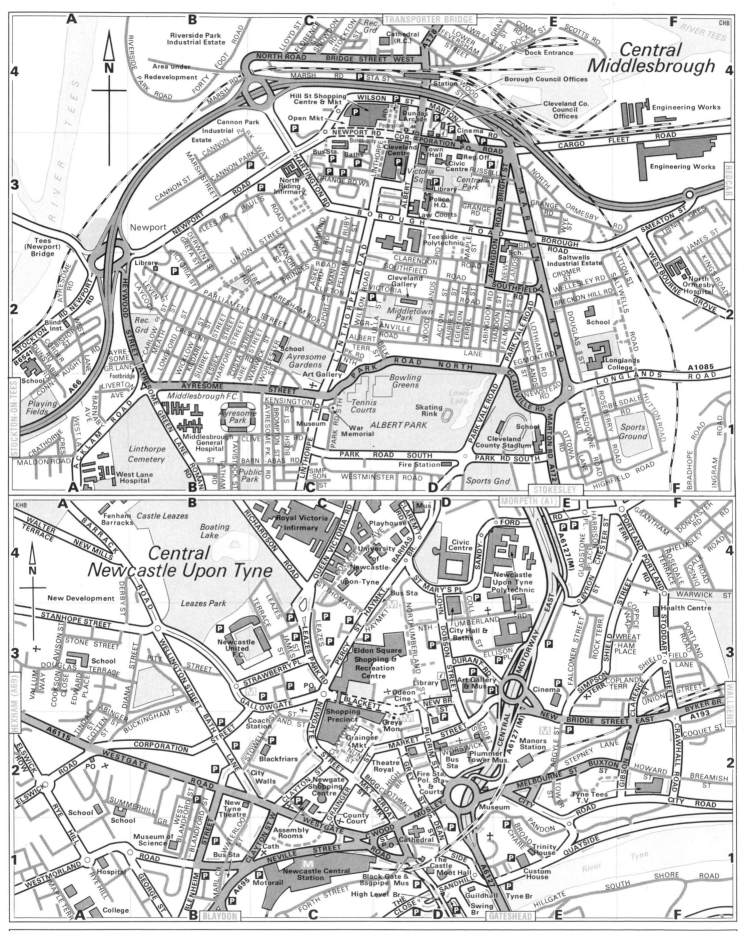

Middlesbrough

Once a quiet riverside village, Middlesbrough soon became a busy coal-exporting town when the Stockton and Darlington railway purchased land here. The Transporter Bridge, built in 1911, is Middlesbrough's most notable structure and one of only two such bridges in Britain. The local geology, natural history, social and industrial growth are all represented in the Dorman Museum. The Captain Cook Birthplace Museum, illustrates the life and discoveries of the famous voyager, born in the town in 1728. Middlesbrough also has two major art galleries.

Newcastle

The most impressive of Newcastle's six bridges is the High Level Bridge, built by Robert Stephenson between 1845 and 1849. Much of the city was replanned and rebuilt, including Grey Street, Newcastle's most handsome thoroughfare. The city's industrial background is traced in the Museum of Science and Engineering, while the Laing Art Gallery and Museum covers painting and costume. The Hancock Musum has an exceptional natural history collection. Town Moor is the city's largest open space: at nearly 1,000 acres, it is big enough to feel genuinely wild.

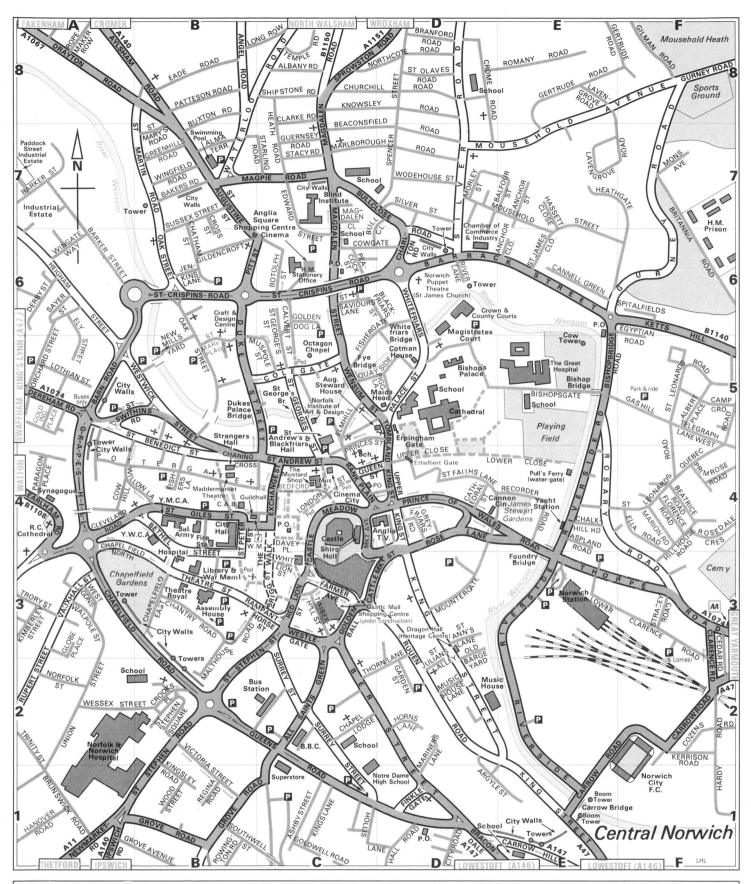

Norwich

Fortunately the heart has not been ripped out of Norwich to make way for some bland precinct, so its ancient character has been preserved. Narrow alleys run between the streets – sometimes opening out into quiet courtyards, sometimes into thoroughfares packed with people, sometimes into lanes which seem quite deserted. It is a unique place, with something of interest on every corner.

The cathedral was founded in 1096 by the city's first bishop, Herbert de Losinga. Among its most notable features are the nave, with its huge pillars, the bishop's throne (a Saxon survival unique in Europe) and the cloisters with their matchless collection of roof bosses. Across the city is the great stone keep of the castle, set on a mound and dominating all around it. It dates from Norman times, but was refaced in 1834. The keep now forms part of Norwich Castle Museum – an extensive and

fascinating collection. Other museums are Bridewell Museum – collections relating to local crafts and industries within a 14th-century building – and Strangers' Hall, a genuinely 'old world' house, rambling and full of surprises, both in its tumble of rooms and in the things which they contain. Especially picturesque parts of the city are Elm Hill – a street of ancient houses; Tombland – with two gateways into the Cathedral Close; and Pull's Ferry – a watergate by the river.

141

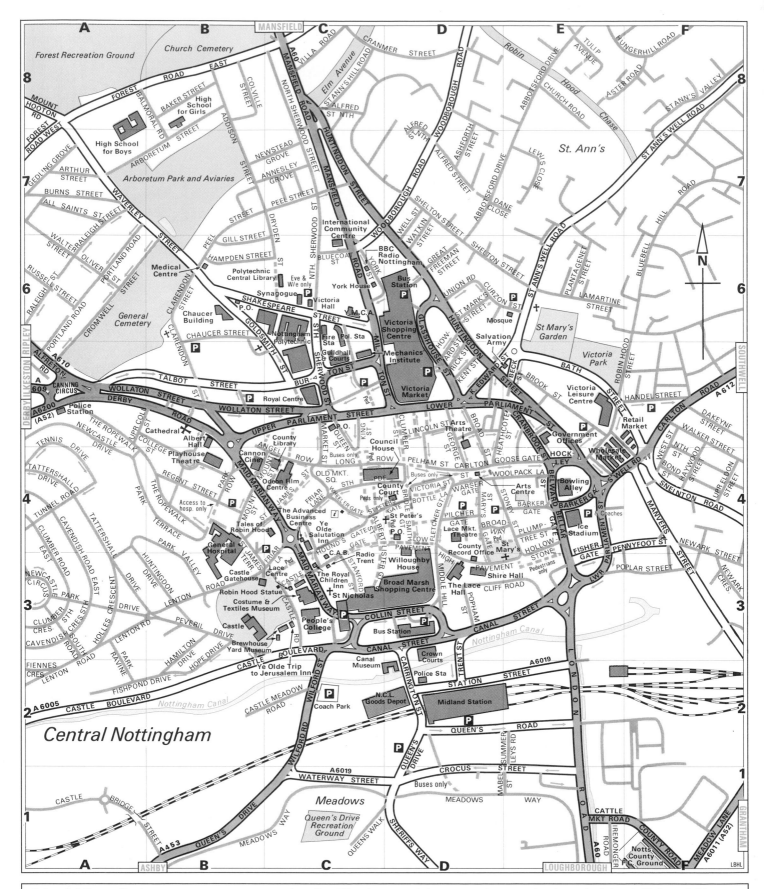

Nottingham

Hosiery and lace were the foundations upon which Nottingham's prosperity was built. The stockings came first – a knitting machine for these had been invented by a Nottinghamshire man as early as 1589 – but a machine called a 'tickler', which enabled simple patterns to be created in the stocking fabric, prompted the development of machine-made lace. The earliest fabric was produced in 1768, and an example from not much later than that is kept in the city's Castlegate Costume and Textile Museum. In fact, the entire history of lacemaking is beautifully explained in this converted row of Georgian terraces. The Industrial Museum at Wollaton Park has many other machines and exhibits tracing the development of the knitting industry, as well as displays on the other industries which have brought wealth to the city – tobacco, pharmaceuticals, engineering and printing. At Wollaton Hall is a natural history museum, while nearer the centre are the Canal Museum and the Brewhouse Yard Museum, a marvellous collection which shows items from daily life in the city up to the present day. Nottingham is not complete without mention of Robin Hood, the partly mythical figure whose statue is in the castle grounds. Although the castle itself has Norman foundations, the present structure is largely Victorian. It is now a museum.

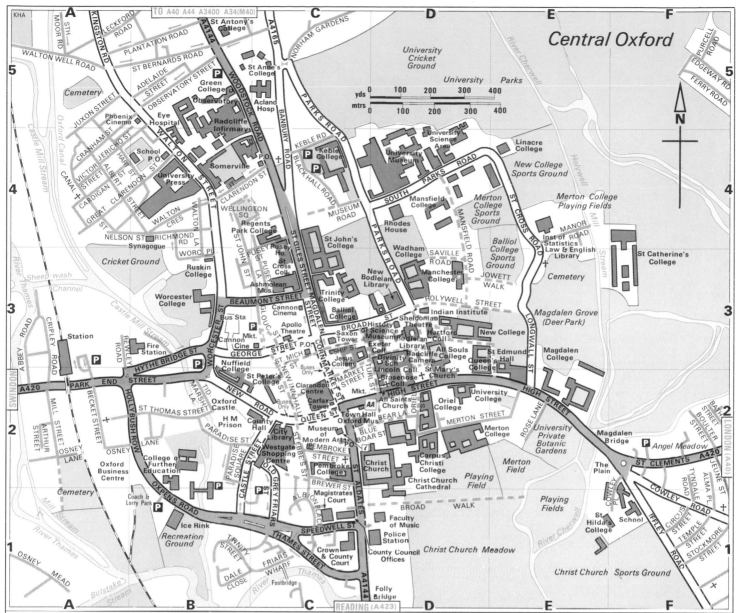

Oxford

At the centre of the city stands Carfax Tower, all that remains of the 14th century St Martin's Church. From Carfax to Magdalen Bridge stretches the High Street (also known simply as the 'High'), one of England's best and most interesting thoroughfares. A wide variety of shops intermingle with churches and colleges, ancient inns can be found in narrow alleyways and little streets (often suitable for cycles only) lead to views of the finest architecture. All around the area are eating establishments, some highly unusual, providing excellent resting places after a hard day's sightseeing. St Mary the Virgin Church (on the High) is the university church and has a magnificent tower, which visitors may climb, affording panoramic views of Oxford. Alongside the church runs Catte Street which opens out into Radcliffe Square, dominated by the Radcliffe Camera, an immense round structure built in the 18th century and now part of the four buildings that make up the Bodleian Library.

One of the world's most famous libraries, the Bodleian was established in the early 17th century by Sir Thomas Bodley. It is now the home for well over five million books, documents and manuscripts, and by law receives one copy of every book published in Britain. Close to the library in Broad Street is the Sheldonian Theatre, guarded by the sculptured head of Roman emperors posted on stone pillars, the theatre is probably one

of Oxford's most distinctive buildings. Built by Sir Christopher Wren, it is the venue for the annual prize giving ceremony and conferral of honorary degrees.

The University of Oxford comprises 36 colleges, the oldest of which are Balliol, Merton and University college, which date back to the mid-13th century. The remaining colleges were built over the following centuries, with some being constructed as recently as the late 1970s. Especially worthy of a visit is Magdalen College, close to Magdalen Bridge: just across the High Street are the Botanical Gardens. Founded in 1621, they are the oldest gardens in the country, displaying a collection of over 800 species of plants from all over the world and providing great botanical interest. Footpaths lead from here through Christ Church Meadow to Christ Church College and Cathedral. Dating back to 1525, it was founded by Cardinal Wolsey and called Cardinal College, but was given its present name by Henry VIII in 1546. Of particular note is the college's tower, designed by Christopher Wren and called Tom Tower, because of the bell 'Great Tom' that is housed here. The cathedral, which still functions as the college chapel, is the smallest in Britain. Other colleges that are undoubtedly worth visiting include All Souls, Brasenose and Trinity. Access to some colleges is restricted to certain times, although most are open in the afternoons. Details may be obtained from the Oxford

Information Centre at St Aldate's.

Located in Beaumont Street, to the north of the High is one of Oxford's greatest treasures, the Ashmolean Museum of Art and Archaeology. First opened in 1683, it is the oldest museum in the country, with the present building dating from 1845. Here, can be seen paintings by Italian, Dutch and French artists, drawings and miniatures, Indian sculpture, metalwork, as well as Chinese and Japanese porcelain. Archaeological exhibits from Britain, Europe, the Mediterrannean, Egypt and the Near East are on show and perhaps the loveliest exhibit is the 9th century Alfred Jewel. A more unusual attraction is the Oxford Story which gives the visitor a chance to experience the 800-year history of the city, using the latest video technology. This innovative exhibition in Broad Street, portrays its story with the help of mechanised, lifelike characters, sounds and even smells!

Oxford's two rivers, the Cherwell and the Isis (the Thames is known as the Isis here) have long played a part in the history of the city, formerly for commercial reasons but latterly as a place for recreation. Rowing has been traditionally associated with college life and in May, the Eights Week takes place, when college crews compete for the title of 'Head of the River'. Punting can be enjoyed by visitors and indeed simply strolling along the riverbank or meadows is a pleasurable means of passing the time.

143

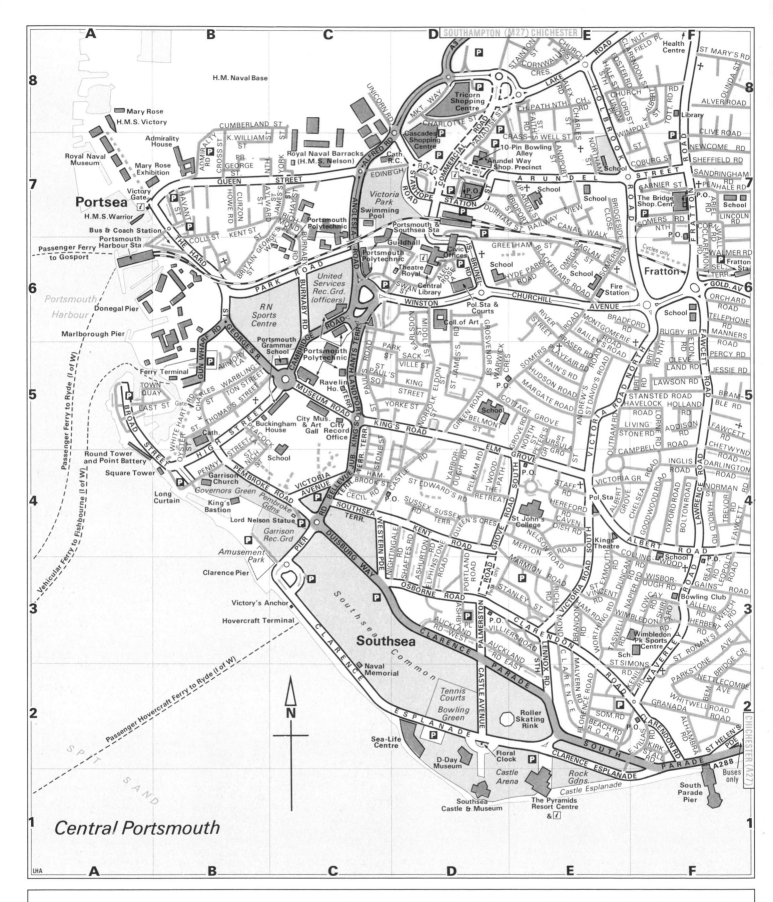

Portsmouth

Richard the Lionheart recognised the strategic importance of Portsea Island and ordered the first docks, and later the town to be built. Succeeding monarchs improved the defences and extended the docks which now cover some 300 acres – as befits Britain's premier naval base. Of the defensive fortifications, Fort Widley and the Round Tower are the best preserved remains. Three famous ships rest in Portsmouth; HMS Victory, the Mary Rose and HMS Warrior. The former; Lord Nelson's flagship, has been fully restored and the adjacent Royal Navy museum houses numerous relics of Trafalgar. The Mary Rose, built by Henry VIII, lay on the sea bed off Southsea until she was spectacularly raised in 1982. She has now been put on display and there is an exhibition of artefacts that have been recovered from her. HMS Warrior is the world's first iron hulled warship.

Portsmouth suffered greatly from bombing in World War II and the centre has been almost completely rebuilt. However, the old town clustered around the harbour mouth, escaped severe damage and, now restored, forms an attractive and fashionable area.

Southsea developed in the 19th century as an elegant seaside resort with fine houses and terraces, an esplanade and an extensive seafront common where the Sea-Life Centre, Southsea Castle & Museum, the D-Day Museum and the Pyramids Leisure Centre are to be found. Off shore, the restored Spit Bank Fort is worth a visit.

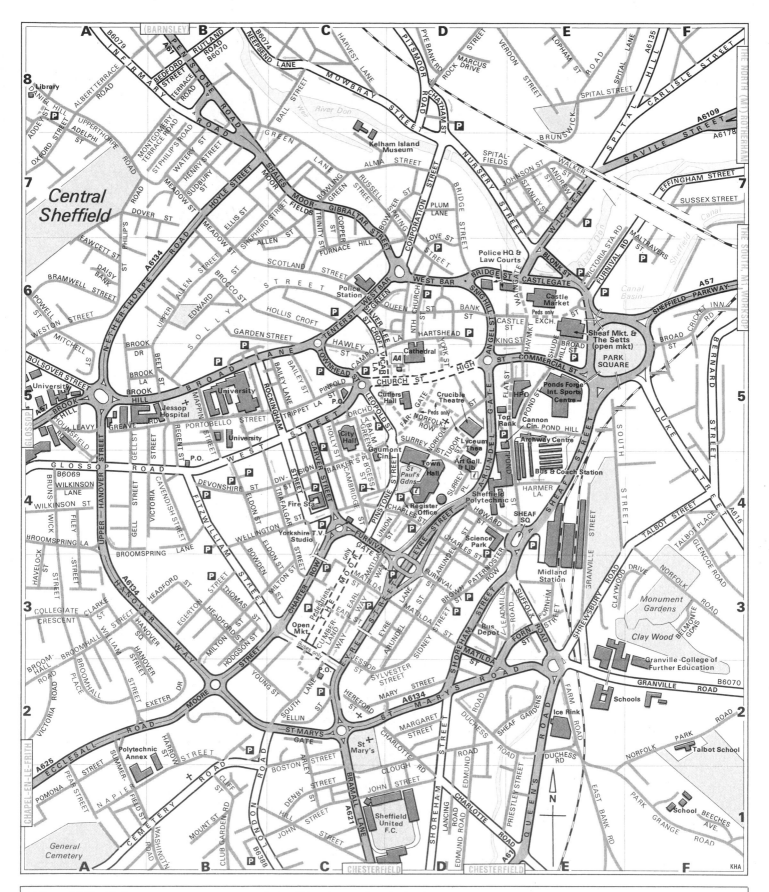

Sheffield

Cutlery – which has made the name of Sheffield famous throughout the world – has been manufactured here since at least as early as the time of Chaucer. The god of blacksmiths, Vulcan, is the symbol of the city's industry, and he crowns the town hall, which was opened in 1897 by Queen Victoria. At the centre of the industry, however, is Cutler's Hall, the headquarters of the Company of Cutlers. This society was founded in 1624 and has the right to grant trade marks to articles of a sufficiently high standard. In the hall is the company's collection of silver, with examples of craftsmanship dating back every year to 1773. A really large collection of cutlery is kept in the city museum. Steel production, a vital component of the industry, was greatly improved when the crucible process was invented here in 1740. At Abbeydale Industrial Hamlet, 3½ miles south-west of the city centre, is a complete restored site open as a museum and showing 18th-century methods of steel production. Sheffield's centre, transformed since World War II, is one of the finest and most modern in Europe. Modern developments include the Ponds Forge International Sports Centre and a few miles to the north east the Meadowhall Shopping Centre. Many parks are set in and around the city, and the Pennines are within easy reach.

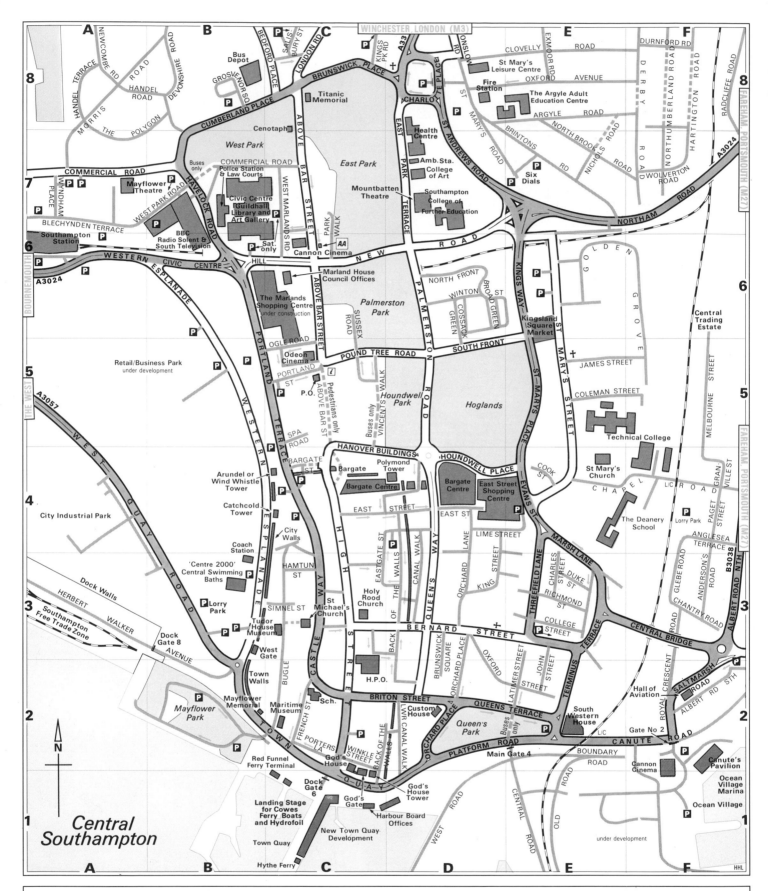

Southampton

In the days of the great ocean-going liners, Southampton was Britain's premier passenger port. Today container traffic is more important, but cruise liners still berth there. A unique double tide caused by the Solent waters, and protection from the open sea by the Isle of Wight, has meant that Southampton has always been a superb and important port. Like many great cities it was devastated by bombing raids during World War II. However, enough survives to make the city a fascinating place to explore. Outstanding are the town walls, which stand to their original height in some places, especially along Western Esplanade. The main landward entrance to the walled town was the Bargate – a superb medieval gateway with a Guildhall (now a museum) on its upper floor. The best place to appreciate old Southampton is in and around St Michael's Square. Here is St Michael's Church, oldest in the city and founded in 1070. Opposite is Tudor House Museum, a lovely gabled building housing much of interest. Down Bugle Street are old houses, with the town walls, pierced by the 13th-century West Gate, away to the right. At the corner of Bugle Street is the Wool House Maritime Museum, contained in a 14th-century warehouse. On the quayside is God's House Tower, part of the town's defences and now an archaeological museum.

146

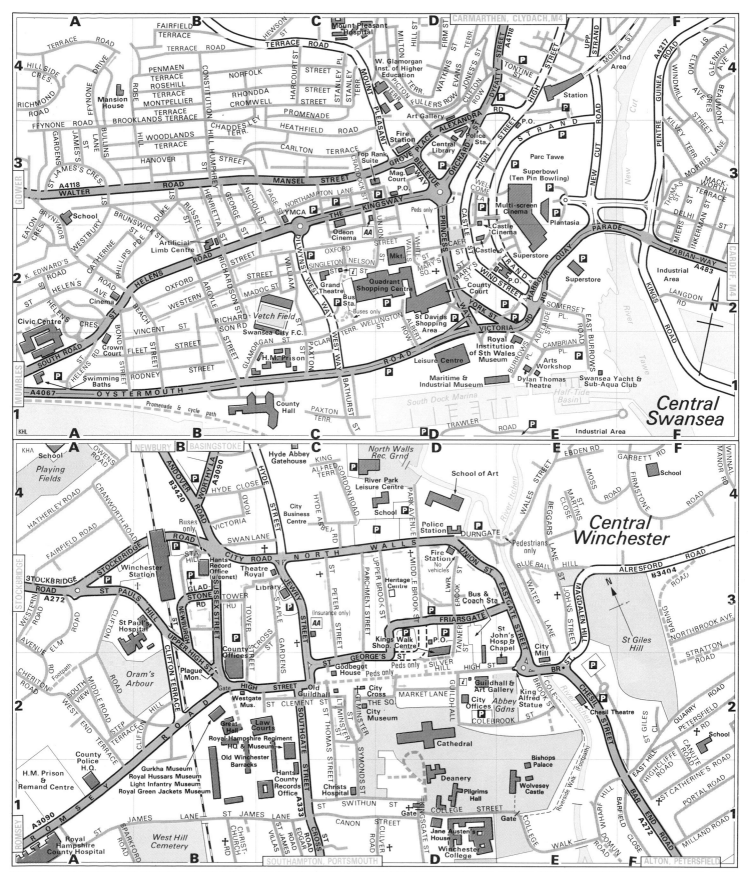

Swansea

Like nearly all towns in the valleys and along the coast of Glamorgan, Swansea grew at an amazing speed during the Industrial Revolution. Ironworks, smelting works, mills and factories of every kind were built to produce the goods which were exported from the city's docks. Heavy industry is still pre-eminent in the area, but commerce is of increasing importance and the university exerts a strong influence. Hundreds of acres of parkland lie in and around the city, and just to the west is the Gower, one of the most beautiful areas of Wales. The history of Swansea is traced in the Maritime and Industrial Museum and Royal Institution of South Wales Museum, while the Glynn Vivian Art Gallery contains notable paintings and porcelain.

Winchester The former capital of England has retained many reminders of its historical importance, notably the impressive Norman/Gothic cathedral, one of the longest in Europe which stands at the heart of the city. Nearby is Winchester College, the famous public school founded by William of Wykeham when he was Bishop of Winchester during the 14th-century. The Great Hall of the former Norman Castle, near the West Gate, is famous for its massive circle of oak, claimed to be King Arthur's Round Table. A modern shopping precinct has been recently opened, and the pedestrianised High Street retains a number of charming old buildings. A statue of King Alfred, who designated Winchester as his capital, stands in the High Street opposite the entrance to Abbey Gardens.

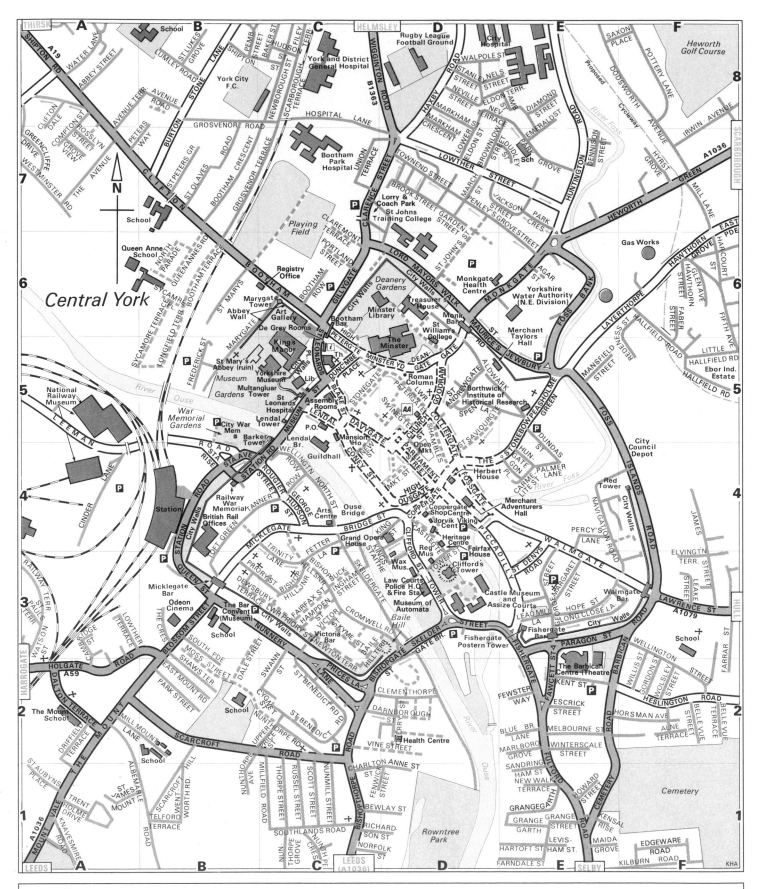

York

York Minster, unquestionably the city's outstanding glory, is considered to be one of the greatest cathedral churches in Europe. It is especially famous for its lovely windows which contain more than half the medieval stained glass in England.

Great medieval walls enclose the historic city centre and their three-mile circuit offers magnificent views of the Minster, York's numerous fine buildings, churches and the River Ouse. The ancient streets consist of a maze of alleys and lanes, some of them so narrow that the overhanging upper storeys of the houses almost touch. The most famous of these picturesque streets is The Shambles, formerly the butchers' quarter of the city, but now colonised by antique and tourist shops. York flourished throughout Tudor, Georgian and Victorian times and handsome buildings from these periods also feature throughout the city.

The Castle Museum gives a fascinating picture of York as it used to be and the Heritage Centre interprets the social and architectural history of the city. Other places of exceptional note in this city of riches include the Merchant Adventurer's Hall; the Treasurer's House, now owned by the National Trust and filled with fine paintings and furniture; the Jorvik Viking Centre, where there is an exciting restoration of the original Viking settlement at York, and the National Railway Museum.

Index to atlas

Each placename entry in this index is identified by its county or region name. These are shown in italics. A list of the abbreviated forms used is given below.

To locate a placename in the atlas turn to the map page number indicated in bold type in the index and use the 4 figure grid reference.

eg Hythe *Kent* **15** TR1634 is found on page **'15'**. The two letters 'TR' refer to the National Grid. To pin point our example the first bold figure **'1'** is found along the bottom edge of the page. The following figure **'6'** indicates how many imaginary tenths to move east of line **'1'**. The next bold figure **'3'** is found along the left hand side of the page. The last figure **'4'** shows how many imaginary tenths to move north of line **'3'**. You will locate Hythe where these two lines intersect.

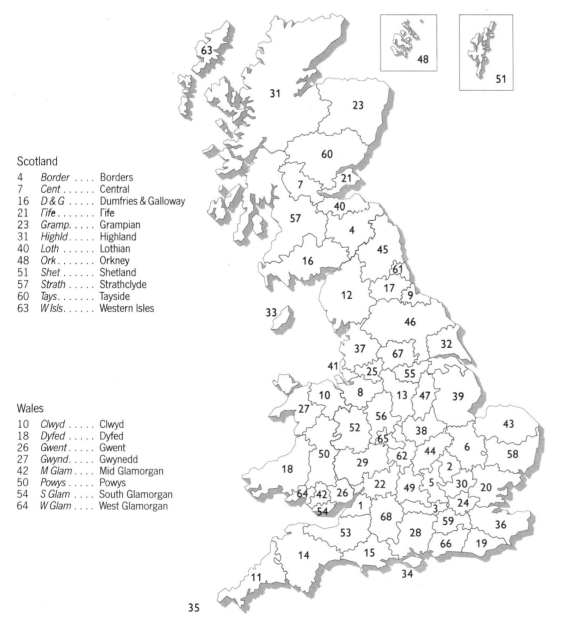

Scotland

4	*Border*	Borders
7	*Cent*	Central
16	*D & G*	Dumfries & Galloway
21	*Fife*	Fife
23	*Gramp.*	Grampian
31	*Highld.*	Highland
40	*Loth*	Lothian
48	*Ork*	Orkney
51	*Shet*	Shetland
57	*Strath*	Strathclyde
60	*Tays.*	Tayside
63	*W Isls.*	Western Isles

Wales

10	*Clwyd*	Clwyd
18	*Dyfed*	Dyfed
26	*Gwent*	Gwent
27	*Gwynd.*	Gwynedd
42	*M Glam*	Mid Glamorgan
50	*Powys*	Powys
54	*S Glam*	South Glamorgan
64	*W Glam*	West Glamorgan

England

1	*Avon*	Avon
2	*Beds*	Bedfordshire
3	*Berks*	Berkshire
5	*Bucks*	Buckinghamshire
6	*Cambs*	Cambridgeshire
8	*Ches*	Cheshire
9	*Cleve.*	Cleveland
11	*Cnwll.*	Cornwall
12	*Cumb*	Cumbria
13	*Derbys*	Derbyshire
14	*Devon.*	Devon
15	*Dorset.*	Dorset
17	*Dur.*	Durham
19	*E.Susx.*	East Sussex
20	*Essex*	Essex
22	*Gloucs.*	Gloucestershire
24	*Gt Lon.*	Greater London
25	*Gt Man*	Greater Manchester
28	*Hants*	Hampshire
29	*H & W*	Hereford & Worcester
30	*Herts.*	Hertfordshire
32	*Humb*	Humberside
33	*IOM*	Isle of Man
34	*IOW.*	Isle of Wight
35	*IOS*	Isles of Scilly
36	*Kent*	Kent
37	*Lancs*	Lancashire
38	*Leics*	Leicestershire
39	*Lincs*	Lincolnshire
41	*Mersyd*	Merseyside
43	*Norfk*	Norfolk
44	*Nhants*	Northamptonshire
45	*Nthumb.*	Northumberland
46	*N York.*	North Yorkshire
47	*Notts.*	Nottinghamshire
49	*Oxon.*	Oxfordshire
52	*Shrops*	Shropshire
53	*Somset.*	Somerset
55	*S York*	South Yorkshire
56	*Staffs*	Staffordshire
58	*Suffk.*	Suffolk
59	*Surrey*	Surrey
61	*T & W.*	Tyne & Wear
62	*Warwks*	Warwickshire
65	*W Mids*	West Midland
66	*W Susx*	West Sussex
67	*W York.*	West Yorkshire
68	*Wilts*	Wiltshire

A'Chill Applecross

A'Chill *Highld* 84 NG2705
Ab Kettleby *Leics* 40 SK7223
Abbas Combe *Somset* 9 ST7022
Abberley *H & W* 28 SO7567
Abberley Common *H & W* 28 SO7467
Abberton *Essex* 25 TM0019
Abberton *H & W* 28 SO9953
Abbess Roding *Essex* 24 TL5711
Abbey Dore *H & W* 27 SO3830
Abbey Green *Staffs* 48 SJ9757
Abbey St. Bathans *Border* 76 NT7661
Abbey Town *Cumb* 67 NY1750
Abbey Village *Lancs* 54 SD6422
Abbey Wood *Gt Lon* 23 TQ4779
Abbeydale *S York* 49 SK3281
Abbeylands *IOM* 52 SC4585
Abbeystead *Lancs* 53 SD5654
Abbot's Salford *Warwks* 28 SP0650
Abbotrule *Border* 68 NT6113
Abbots Bickington *Devon* 6 SS3813
Abbots Bromley *Staffs* 38 SK0724
Abbots Deuglie *Tays* 82 NO1111
Abbots Langley *Herts* 22 TL0901
Abbots Leigh *Avon* 19 ST5474
Abbots Morton *H & W* 28 SP0255
Abbots Ripton *Cambs* 31 TL2377
Abbots Worthy *Hants* 11 SU4932
Abbotsbury *Dorset* 9 SY5785
Abbotsford *Border* 76 NT5034
Abbotsham *Devon* 6 SS4226
Abbotskerswell *Devon* 5 SX8568
Abbotsley *Cambs* 31 TL2256
Abbott Street *Dorset* 9 ST9800
Abbotts Ann *Hants* 21 SU3243
Abdon *Shrops* 37 SO5786
Aber *Gwynd* 45 SH6572
Aberaeron *Dyfed* 34 SN4562
Aberaman *M Glam* 18 SO0100
Aberangell *Powys* 35 SH8410
Aberarder *Highld* 92 NH6225
Aberargie *Tays* 82 NO1615
Aberarth *Dyfed* 34 SN4763
Aberavon *W Glam* 18 SS7489
Abercairny *Tays* 82 NN9222
Abercanaid *M Glam* 18 SO0503
Abercarn *Gwent* 19 ST2194
Abercastle *Dyfed* 16 SM8533
Abercegir *Powys* 35 SH8001
Aberchalder Lodge *Highld* 86 NH3403
Aberchirder *Gramp* 94 NJ6252
Abercraf *Powys* 26 SN8212
Abercregan *W Glam* 18 SS8496
Abercrombie *Fife* 83 NO5102
Abercwmboi *M Glam* 18 ST0299
Abercych *Dyfed* 17 SN2441
Abercynon *M Glam* 18 ST0794
Aberdalgie *Tays* 82 NO0720
Aberdare *Powys* 18 SO0002
Aberdaron *Gwynd* 44 SH1726
Aberdeen *Gramp* 89 NJ9306
Aberdour *Fife* 82 NT1985
Aberdovey *Gwynd* 35 SN6196
Aberdulais *W Glam* 18 SS7799
Aberedw *Powys* 26 SO0847
Abereiddy *Dyfed* 16 SM7931
Abererch *Gwynd* 44 SH3936
Aberfan *M Glam* 18 SO0700
Aberfeldy *Tays* 87 NN8549
Aberffraw *Gwynd* 44 SH3569
Aberford *W York* 55 SE4337
Aberfoyle *Cent* 81 NN5200
Abergavenny *Gwent* 27 SO2914
Abergele *Clwyd* 45 SH9477
Abergorlech *Dyfed* 17 SN5833
Abergwesyn *Powys* 26 SN8552
Abergwili *Dyfed* 17 SN4320
Abergwynfi *W Glam* 18 SS8995
Aberkenfig *M Glam* 18 SS8984
Aberlady *Loth* 83 NT4679
Aberlemno *Tays* 89 NO5255
Aberllefenni *Gwynd* 35 SH7609
Aberllynfi *Powys* 27 SO1737
Aberlour *Gramp* 94 NJ2642
Abermule *Powys* 36 SO1694
Abernant *Dyfed* 17 SN3323
Abernethy *Tays* 82 NO1816
Abernyte *Tays* 83 NO2531
Aberporth *Dyfed* 17 SN2651
Aberriw *Powys* 36 SJ1801
Abersoch *Gwynd* 44 SH3127
Abersychan *Gwent* 19 SO2603
Aberthin *S Glam* 18 ST0074
Abertillery *Gwent* 27 SO2104
Abertridwr *M Glam* 18 ST1289
Abertridwr *Powys* 36 SJ0319
Aberuthven *Tays* 82 NN9815
Aberystwyth *Dyfed* 34 SN5881
Abingdon *Oxon* 21 SU4997
Abinger *Surrey* 12 TQ1145
Abinger Hammer *Surrey* 12 TQ0947
Abington *Nhants* 30 SP7861
Abington *Strath* 75 NS9323
Abington Pigotts *Cambs* 31 TL3044
Ablington *Gloucs* 28 SP1007
Abney *Derbys* 48 SK1980
Aboyne *Gramp* 89 NO5298
Abram *Gt Man* 47 SD6001
Abriachan *Highld* 92 NH5535
Abridge *Essex* 23 TQ4696
Abson *Avon* 20 ST7074
Abthorpe *Nhants* 29 SP6446
Aby *Lincs* 51 TF4078
Acaster Malbis *N York* 56 SE5845
Acaster Selby *N York* 56 SE5741
Accrington *Lancs* 54 SD7628
Acha *Strath* 78 NM1854
Achahoish *Strath* 71 NR7877
Achalader *Tays* 88 NO1245
Achaleven *Strath* 80 NM9233
Achanalt *Highld* 92 NH2661
Achandunie *Highld* 92 NH6472
Achany *Highld* 96 NC5602
Acharacle *Highld* 79 NM6767
Acharn *Tays* 87 NN7543
Achavanich *Highld* 100 ND1842
Achduart *Highld* 91 NC0403
Achfary *Highld* 98 NC2939
Achiltibuie *Highld* 91 NC0208
Achinhoan *Strath* 72 NR7516
Achintee *Highld* 85 NG9441
Achlain *Highld* 92 NH2812
Achmelvich *Highld* 98 NC0524
Achmore *Highld* 85 NG8533
Achmore *W Isls* 102 NB3029
Achnacarnin *Highld* 98 NC0432
Achnacarry *Highld* 86 NN1787
Achnacloich *Highld* 84 NG5908
Achnaconeran *Highld* 92 NH4118
Achnacroish *Strath* 79 NM8541
Achnadrish Lodge *Strath* 79 NM4652
Achnafauld *Tays* 82 NN8736
Achnagarron *Highld* 93 NH6870
Achnaha *Highld* 79 NM4668
Achnahaird *Highld* 98 NC0013
Achnairn *Highld* 96 NC5512
Achnalea *Highld* 79 NM8561
Achnamara *Strath* 71 NR7887
Achnasheen *Highld* 92 NH1658
Achnashellach Station *Highld* 91 NH0048
Achnastank *Gramp* 94 NJ2733
Achosnich *Highld* 79 NM4467
Achranich *Highld* 79 NM7047
Achreamie *Highld* 100 ND0166
Achriabhach *Highld* 86 NN1468
Achriesgill *Highld* 98 NC2554
Achtoty *Highld* 99 NC6762
Achurch *Nhants* 40 TL0283
Achvaich *Highld* 97 NH7194
Acklam *Cleve* 62 NZ4817
Acklam *N York* 56 SE7861
Ackleton *Shrops* 37 SO7698
Acklington *Nthumb* 69 NU2301
Ackton *W York* 55 SE4121
Ackworth Moor Top *W York* 55 SE4316
Acle *Norfk* 43 TG4010
Acock's Green *W Mids* 38 SP1283
Acol *Kent* 15 TR3067
Acomb *N York* 56 SE5651
Acomb *Nthumb* 68 NY9366
Aconbury *H & W* 27 SO5133
Acton *Ches* 47 SJ6352
Acton *Gt Lon* 23 TQ2080
Acton *H & W* 28 SO8467
Acton *Staffs* 38 SJ8241
Acton *Suffk* 32 TL8945
Acton Beauchamp *H & W* 28 SO6850
Acton Bridge *Ches* 47 SJ6075
Acton Burnell *Shrops* 37 SJ5302
Acton Green *H & W* 28 SO6950
Acton Park *Clwyd* 46 SJ3451
Acton Round *Shrops* 37 SO6395
Acton Scott *Shrops* 36 SO4589
Acton Trussell *Staffs* 38 SJ9318
Acton Turville *Avon* 20 ST8080
Adbaston *Staffs* 37 SJ7627
Adber *Dorset* 9 ST5920
Adbolton *Notts* 49 SK5938
Adderbury *Oxon* 29 SP4735
Adderley *Shrops* 37 SJ6640
Addiewell *Loth* 75 NS9962
Addingham *W York* 55 SE0749
Addington *Bucks* 30 SP7428
Addington *Kent* 14 TQ6559
Addiscombe *Gt Lon* 23 TQ3366
Addlestone *Surrey* 22 TQ0564
Addlestonemore *Surrey* 22 TQ0565
Addlethorpe *Lincs* 51 TF5468
Adeyfield *Herts* 22 TL0708
Adfa *Powys* 36 SJ0601
Adforton *H & W* 36 SO4071
Adisham *Kent* 15 TR2253
Adlestrop *Gloucs* 29 SP2426
Adlingfleet *Humb* 56 SE8421
Adlington *Lancs* 54 SD6013
Admaston *Shrops* 37 SJ6313
Admaston *Staffs* 38 SK0423
Admington *Warwks* 29 SP2045
Adsborough *Somset* 8 ST2729
Adscombe *Somset* 19 ST1837
Adstock *Bucks* 30 SP7329
Adversane *W Susx* 12 TQ0723
Advie *Highld* 93 NJ1234
Adwick Le Street *S York* 56 SE5308
Adwick upon Dearne *S York* 49 SE4701
Ae *D & G* 66 NX9889
Ae Bridgend *D & G* 66 NY0186
Affleck *Gramp* 94 NJ5540
Affpuddle *Dorset* 9 SY8093
Affric Lodge *Highld* 92 NH1822
Afon-wen *Clwyd* 46 SJ1371
Afton Bridgend *Strath* 66 NS6213
Agglethorpe *N York* 61 SE0885
Aigburth *Mersyd* 46 SJ3886
Aike *Humb* 57 TA0446
Aiketgate *Cumb* 67 NY4846
Aikton *Cumb* 67 NY2753
Ailey *H & W* 27 SO3348
Ailsworth *Cambs* 40 TL1198
Ainderby Quernhow *N York* 62 SE3480
Ainderby Steeple *N York* 62 SE3392
Aingers Green *Essex* 25 TM1120
Ainsdale *Mersyd* 53 SD3112
Ainstable *Cumb* 67 NY5246
Ainthorpe *N York* 62 NZ7007
Aird *D & G* 64 NX0960
Aird *Strath* 79 NM7600
Aird *W Isls* 102 NB5635
Aird of Kinloch *Strath* 79 NM5228
Aird of Sleat *Highld* 84 NG5900
Airdeny *Strath* 80 NM9929
Airdrie *Strath* 74 NS7565
Airdriehill *Strath* 74 NS7867
Airds Bay *Strath* 80 NM9932
Airds of Kells *D & G* 65 NX6770
Airieland *D & G* 65 NX7556
Airmyn *Humb* 56 SE7224
Airntully *Tays* 82 NO0935
Airor *Highld* 85 NG7205
Airth *Cent* 82 NS9087
Airton *N York* 54 SD9059
Aisby *Lincs* 50 SK8692
Aisby *Lincs* 40 TF0138
Aish *Devon* 5 SX6960
Aish *Devon* 5 SX8458
Aiskew *N York* 61 SE2788
Aislaby *Cleve* 62 NZ4012
Aislaby *N York* 63 NZ8608
Aislaby *N York* 63 SE7785
Aisthorpe *Lincs* 50 SK9480
Aith *Shet* 103 HU3455
Akeld *Nthumb* 77 NT9529
Akeley *Bucks* 30 SP7037
Akenham *Suffk* 33 TM1449
Albaston *Devon* 4 SX4270
Alberbury *Shrops* 36 SJ3614
Albourne *W Susx* 12 TQ2516
Albrighton *Shrops* 37 SJ4918
Albrighton *Shrops* 37 SJ8004
Alburgh *Norfk* 33 TM2687
Albury *Herts* 31 TL4324
Albury *Surrey* 12 TQ0447
Albury Heath *Surrey* 12 TQ0646
Alcaig *Highld* 92 NH5657
Alcaston *Shrops* 36 SO4587
Alcester *Warwks* 28 SP0857
Alciston *E Susx* 13 TQ5005
Alconbury *Cambs* 31 TL1875
Alconbury Weston *Cambs* 31 TL1777
Aldborough *N York* 55 SE4066
Aldborough *Norfk* 43 TG1834
Aldbourne *Wilts* 21 SU2676
Aldbrough *Humb* 57 TA2438
Aldbury *Herts* 30 SP9612
Aldcliffe *Lancs* 53 SD4660
Aldclune *Tays* 87 NN8964
Aldeburgh *Suffk* 33 TM4656
Aldeby *Norfk* 43 TM4493
Aldenham *Herts* 22 TQ1498
Alderbury *Wilts* 10 SU1827
Alderholt *Dorset* 10 SU1212
Alderley *Gloucs* 20 ST7690
Alderley Edge *Ches* 47 SJ8478
Aldermaston *Berks* 21 SU5965
Alderminster *Warwks* 29 SP2348
Aldershot *Hants* 22 SU8650
Alderton *Gloucs* 28 SP0033
Alderton *Nhants* 30 SP7446
Alderton *Suffk* 33 TM3441
Alderton *Wilts* 20 ST8482
Alderwasley *Derbys* 49 SK3053
Aldfield *N York* 55 SE2669
Aldford *Ches* 46 SJ4159
Aldgate *Leics* 40 SK9804
Aldham *Essex* 24 TL9126
Aldham *Suffk* 32 TM0545
Aldingbourne *W Susx* 12 SU9205
Aldingham *Cumb* 53 SD2870
Aldington *H & W* 28 SP0644
Aldington *Kent* 15 TR0736
Aldington Corner *Kent* 15 TR0636
Aldivalloch *Gramp* 94 NJ3526
Aldochlay *Strath* 80 NS3591
Aldreth *Cambs* 31 TL4473
Aldridge *W Mids* 38 SK0500
Aldringham *Suffk* 33 TM4461
Aldsworth *Gloucs* 28 SP1509
Aldunie *Gramp* 94 NJ3626
Aldwark *Derbys* 48 SK2257
Aldwark *N York* 55 SE4663
Aldwick *W Susx* 11 SZ9198
Aldwincle *Nhants* 40 TL0081
Aldworth *Berks* 21 SU5579
Alexandria *Strath* 80 NS3979
Aley *Somset* 19 ST1838
Alfington *Devon* 8 SY1197
Alfold *Surrey* 12 TQ0333
Alfold Crossways *Surrey* 12 TQ0335
Alford *Gramp* 94 NJ5715
Alford *Lincs* 51 TF4575
Alford *Somset* 9 ST6032
Alfreton *Derbys* 49 SK4155
Alfrick *H & W* 28 SO7453
Alfrick Pound *H & W* 28 SO7452
Alfriston *E Susx* 13 TQ5103
Algarkirk *Lincs* 41 TF2935
Alhampton *Somset* 9 ST6234
Alkborough *Humb* 56 SE8821
Alkerton *Gloucs* 28 SO7705
Alkham *Kent* 15 TR2542
Alkmonton *Derbys* 48 SK1838
All Cannings *Wilts* 20 SU0661
All Saints South Elmham *Suffk* 33 TM3482
All Stretton *Shrops* 36 SO4595
Allaleigh *Devon* 5 SX8053
Allanaquoich *Gramp* 88 NO1291
Allanbank *Strath* 74 NS8458
Allanton *Border* 77 NT8654
Allanton *Strath* 74 NS7454
Allanton *Strath* 74 NS8457
Allaston *Gloucs* 27 SO6304
Allbrook *Hants* 10 SU4521
Allen End *Warwks* 38 SP1696
Allen's Green *Herts* 31 TL4516
Allendale *Nthumb* 68 NY8355
Allenheads *Nthumb* 68 NY8645
Allensmore *H & W* 27 SO4635
Allenton *Derbys* 39 SK3732
Aller *Devon* 7 SS7625
Aller *Somset* 8 ST4029
Allerby *Cumb* 58 NY0839
Allercombe *Devon* 7 SY0494
Allerford *Somset* 7 SS9046
Allerston *N York* 63 SE8782
Allerthorpe *Humb* 56 SE7847
Allerton *Mersyd* 46 SJ3987
Allerton *W York* 55 SE1234
Allerton Bywater *W York* 55 SE4227
Allerton Mauleverer *N York* 55 SE4157
Allesley *W Mids* 39 SP3080
Allestree *Derbys* 49 SK3439
Allexton *Leics* 40 SK8100
Allgreave *Ches* 48 SJ9767
Allhallows *Kent* 24 TQ8377
Alligin Shuas *Highld* 91 NG8357
Allington *Dorset* 8 SY4693
Allington *Lincs* 50 SK8540
Allington *Wilts* 20 ST8975
Allington *Wilts* 20 SU0663
Allington *Wilts* 10 SU2039
Allithwaite *Cumb* 59 SD3876
Alloa *Cent* 82 NS8892
Allonby *Cumb* 58 NY0842
Alloway *Strath* 73 NS3318
Allowenshay *Somset* 8 ST3913
Alltchaorunn *Highld* 86 NN1951
Alltmawr *Powys* 26 SO0746
Alltwalis *Dyfed* 17 SN4431
Alltwen *W Glam* 18 SN7303
Alltyblaca *Dyfed* 17 SN5245
Allweston *Dorset* 9 ST6614
Almeley *H & W* 27 SO3351
Almeley Wooton *H & W* 27 SO3352
Almer *Dorset* 9 SY9199
Almholme *S York* 56 SE5808
Almington *Staffs* 37 SJ7034
Almondbank *Tays* 82 NO0625
Almondbury *W York* 55 SE1614
Almondsbury *Avon* 19 ST6084
Alness *Highld* 93 NH6569
Alnham *Nthumb* 68 NT9810
Alnmouth *Nthumb* 69 NU2410
Alnwick *Nthumb* 69 NU1813
Alperton *Gt Lon* 23 TQ1883
Alphamstone *Essex* 24 TL8735
Alpheton *Suffk* 32 TL8750
Alphington *Devon* 5 SX9190
Alport *Derbys* 48 SK2264
Alpraham *Ches* 47 SJ5859
Alresford *Essex* 25 TM0621
Alrewas *Staffs* 38 SK1614
Alsager *Ches* 47 SJ7955
Alshot *Somset* 8 ST1935
Alsop en le Dale *Derbys* 48 SK1554
Alston *Cumb* 68 NY7146
Alston *Devon* 8 ST3002
Alston Sutton *Somset* 19 ST4151
Alstone *Gloucs* 28 SO9832
Alstonefield *Staffs* 48 SK1355
Alswear *Devon* 7 SS7222
Altandhu *Highld* 98 NB9812
Altarnun *Cnwll* 4 SX2281
Altass *Highld* 96 NC5000
Altcreich *Strath* 79 NM6938
Altgaltraig *Strath* 80 NS0473
Althorne *Essex* 24 TQ9198
Althorpe *Humb* 56 SE8309
Altnabreac Station *Highld* 100 ND0045
Altnacraig *Strath* 79 NM8429
Altnaharra *Highld* 99 NC5635
Alton *Derbys* 49 SK3664
Alton *Hants* 11 SU7139
Alton *Staffs* 48 SK0741
Alton Barnes *Wilts* 20 SU1062
Alton Pancras *Dorset* 9 ST7002
Alton Priors *Wilts* 20 SU1162
Altrincham *Gt Man* 47 SJ7687
Alva *Cent* 82 NS8897
Alvah *Gramp* 95 NJ6760
Alvanley *Ches* 46 SJ4974
Alvaston *Derbys* 39 SK3833
Alvechurch *H & W* 38 SP0272
Alvecote *Warwks* 39 SK2404
Alvediston *Wilts* 9 ST9723
Alveley *Shrops* 37 SO7584
Alverdiscott *Devon* 6 SS5225
Alverstoke *Hants* 11 SZ6098
Alverstone *IOW* 11 SZ5785
Alverthorpe *W York* 55 SE3121
Alverton *Notts* 50 SK7942
Alves *Gramp* 93 NJ1362
Alvescot *Oxon* 29 SP2704
Alveston *Avon* 19 ST6388
Alveston *Warwks* 29 SP2356
Alvingham *Lincs* 51 TF3691
Alvington *Gloucs* 19 SO6000
Alwalton *Cambs* 40 TL1396
Alwinton *Nthumb* 68 NT9106
Alwoodley *W York* 55 SE2840
Alyth *Tays* 88 NO2448
Amberley *Gloucs* 20 SO8501
Amberley *W Susx* 12 TQ0213
Amble *Nthumb* 69 NU2604
Amblecote *W Mids* 38 SO8985
Ambler Thorn *W York* 55 SE0929
Ambleside *Cumb* 59 NY3704
Ambleston *Dyfed* 16 SN0025
Amcotts *Humb* 56 SE8514
Amersham *Bucks* 22 SU9597
Amesbury *Wilts* 20 SU1541
Amisfield Town *D & G* 66 NY0082
Amlwch *Gwynd* 44 SH4492
Ammanford *Dyfed* 17 SN6212
Amotherby *N York* 63 SE7473
Ampfield *Hants* 10 SU4023
Ampleforth *N York* 62 SE5878
Ampney Crucis *Gloucs* 20 SP0601
Ampney St. Mary *Gloucs* 20 SP0802
Ampney St. Peter *Gloucs* 20 SP0801
Amport *Hants* 21 SU3044
Ampthill *Beds* 30 TL0337
Ampton *Suffk* 32 TL8671
Amroth *Dyfed* 17 SN1608
Amwell *Herts* 31 TL1613
Anaheilt *Highld* 79 NM8162
Ancaster *Lincs* 50 SK9843
Anchor *Shrops* 36 SO1785
Ancroft *Nthumb* 77 NT9945
Ancrum *Border* 76 NT6224
Anderby *Lincs* 51 TF5275
Anderson *Dorset* 9 SY8897
Andover *Hants* 21 SU3645
Andoversford *Gloucs* 28 SP0219
Andreas *IOM* 52 SC4199
Anerley *Gt Lon* 23 TQ3369
Anfield *Mersyd* 46 SJ3692
Angarrack *Cnwll* 2 SW5838
Angelbank *Shrops* 37 SO5776
Angersleigh *Somset* 8 ST1918
Angle *Dyfed* 16 SM8603
Angmering *W Susx* 12 TQ0604
Angram *N York* 55 SE5248
Ankerville *Highld* 97 NH8174
Anlaby *Humb* 56 TA0328
Anmer *Norfk* 42 TF7429
Anmore *Hants* 11 SU6611
Anna Valley *Hants* 21 SU3543
Annan *D & G* 67 NY1966
Annat *Highld* 91 NG8954
Annat *Strath* 80 NN0322
Annathill *Strath* 74 NS7270
Annbank *Strath* 73 NS4023
Annesley *Notts* 49 SK5053
Annesley Woodhouse *Notts* 49 SK4953
Annfield Plain *Dur* 69 NZ1651
Anniesland *Strath* 74 NS5368
Ansdell *Lancs* 53 SD3428
Ansford *Somset* 9 ST6433
Ansley *Warwks* 39 SP3091
Anslow *Staffs* 39 SK2125
Anslow Gate *Staffs* 39 SK1924
Anstey *Herts* 31 TL4033
Anstey *Leics* 39 SK5508
Anstruther *Fife* 83 NO5703
Anstruther Easter *Fife* 83 NO5704
Ansty *W Susx* 12 TQ2923
Ansty *Warwks* 39 SP4083
Ansty *Wilts* 9 ST9526
Anthorn *Cumb* 67 NY1958
Antingham *Norfk* 43 TG2533
Antony *Cnwll* 4 SX4054
Antrobus *Ches* 47 SJ6480
Anwick *Lincs* 50 TF1150
Anwoth *D & G* 65 NX5856
Aperfield *Gt Lon* 23 TQ4158
Apethorpe *Nhants* 40 TL0295
Apley *Lincs* 50 TF1075
Apperknowle *Derbys* 49 SK3878
Apperley *Gloucs* 28 SO8628
Appin *Strath* 86 NM9346
Appleby *Humb* 56 SE9514
Appleby Magna *Leics* 39 SK3109
Appleby Parva *Leics* 39 SK3008
Appleby-in-Westmorland *Cumb* 60 NY6820
Applecross *Highld* 91 NG7144

Appledore Badcall

Appledore *Devon* 6 SS4630
Appledore *Devon* 7 ST0614
Appledore *Kent* 14 TQ9529
Appleford *Oxon* 21 SU5293
Applegarth Town *D & G* 67 NY1084
Appleshaw *Hants* 21 SU3048
Appleton *Ches* 46 SJ5186
Appleton *Oxon* 21 SP4401
Appleton Roebuck *N York* 56 SE5542
Appleton Wiske *N York* 62 NZ3804
Appleton-le-Moors *N York* 63 SE7387
Appleton-le-Street *N York* 63 SE7373
Appletreehall *Border* 76 NT5117
Appletreewick *N York* 55 SE0560
Appley *Somset* 8 ST0721
Appley Bridge *Lancs* 53 SD5209
Apse Heath *IOW* 11 SZ5683
Apsley End *Beds* 30 TL1232
Apuldram *W Susx* 11 SU8403
Arbirlot *Tays* 83 NO6040
Arboll *Highld* 97 NH8781
Arborfield *Berks* 22 SU7567
Arborfield Cross *Berks* 22 SU7666
Arbory *IOM* 52 SC2470
Arbroath *Tays* 89 NO6441
Arbuthnott *Gramp* 89 NO8074
Archdeacon Newton *Dur* 61 NZ2517
Archencarroch *Strath* 81 NS4182
Archiestown *Gramp* 94 NJ2244
Archirondel *Jersey* 101 JS2111
Arclid Green *Ches* 47 SJ7861
Ard a'Chapuill *Strath* 80 NS0179
Ardaily *Strath* 72 NR6450
Ardalanish *Strath* 78 NM3619
Ardanaiseig Hotel *Strath* 80 NN0824
Ardarroch *Highld* 85 NG8339
Ardarroch *Strath* 80 NS2494
Ardbeg *Strath* 70 NR4146
Ardbeg *Strath* 72 NS0766
Ardbeg *Strath* 80 NS1583
Ardcharnich *Highld* 96 NH1788
Ardchiavaig *Strath* 78 NM3818
Ardchonnel *Strath* 80 NM9812
Ardchullarie More *Cent* 81 NN5813
Ardechive *Highld* 86 NN1490
Ardeer *Strath* 73 NS2740
Ardeley *Herts* 31 TL3027
Ardelve *Highld* 85 NG8627
Arden *Strath* 80 NS3684
Ardens Grafton *Warwks* 28 SP1154
Ardentinny *Strath* 80 NS1887
Ardersier *Highld* 93 NH7855
Ardessie *Highld* 91 NH0689
Ardfern *Strath* 79 NM8004
Ardgay *Highld* 97 NH5990
Ardgour *Highld* 86 NN0163
Ardgowan *Strath* 80 NS2073
Ardhallow *Strath* 80 NS1674
Ardhasig *W Isls* 102 NB1202
Ardheslaig *Highld* 91 NG7855
Ardindrean *Highld* 96 NH1588
Ardingly *W Susx* 12 TQ3429
Ardington *Oxon* 21 SU4388
Ardlamont *Strath* 71 NR9865
Ardleigh *Essex* 25 TM0529
Ardleigh Heath *Essex* 25 TM0430
Ardler *Tays* 88 NO2642
Ardley *Oxon* 29 SP5427
Ardley End *Essex* 31 TL5214
Ardlui *Strath* 80 NN3115
Ardlussa *Strath* 71 NR6487
Ardmaddy *Strath* 80 NN0837
Ardmair *Highld* 96 NH1097
Ardmaleish *Strath* 72 NS0768
Ardminish *Strath* 72 NR6448
Ardmolich *Highld* 85 NM7172
Ardmore *Highld* 97 NH7086
Ardmore *Strath* 80 NS3178
Ardnadam *Strath* 80 NS1780
Ardnagrask *Highld* 92 NH5249
Ardnarff *Highld* 85 NG8935
Ardnastang *Highld* 79 NM8061
Ardno *Strath* 80 NN1508
Ardochy Lodge Hotel *Highld* 86 NH2002
Ardpatrick *Strath* 71 NR7660
Ardpeaton *Strath* 80 NS2185
Ardrishaig *Strath* 71 NR8585
Ardrossan *Strath* 73 NS2342
Ardshealach *Highld* 79 NM6867
Ardsley East *W York* 55 SE3025
Ardslignish *Highld* 79 NM5661
Ardtalla *Strath* 70 NR4654
Ardtoe *Highld* 79 NM6270
Arduaine *Strath* 79 NM7910
Ardvasar *Highld* 84 NG6303
Ardvorlich *Tays* 81 NN6322
Ardvourlie *W Isls* 102 NB1810
Ardwell *D & G* 64 NX1045
Ardwick *Gt Man* 47 SJ8597
Arevegaig *Highld* 79 NM6568
Arford *Hants* 11 SU8236
Argoed *Gwent* 19 ST1799
Aribruach *W Isls* 102 NB2417
Aridhglas *Strath* 78 NM3123
Arileod *Strath* 78 NM1655
Arinagour *Strath* 78 NM2257
Ariogan *Strath* 79 NM8627
Arisaig *Highld* 85 NM6586
Arisaig House *Highld* 85 NM6984
Arkendale *N York* 55 SE3861
Arkesden *Essex* 31 TL4834
Arkholme *Lancs* 54 SD5871
Arkleton *D & G* 67 NY3791
Arkley *Gt Lon* 23 TQ2295
Arksey *S York* 56 SE5807
Arkwright Town *Derbys* 49 SK4270
Arle *Gloucs* 28 SO9223
Arlecdon *Cumb* 58 NY0419
Arlesey *Beds* 31 TL1936
Arleston *Shrops* 37 SJ6609
Arley *Ches* 47 SJ6680
Arley *Warwks* 39 SP2890
Arlingham *Gloucs* 28 SO7010
Arlington *Devon* 7 SS6140
Arlington *E Susx* 13 TQ5407
Armadale *Highld* 99 NC7864
Armadale *Loth* 75 NS9368
Armaside *Cumb* 58 NY1527
Armathwaite *Cumb* 67 NY5046
Arminghall *Norfk* 43 TG2504
Armitage *Staffs* 38 SK0715
Armley *W York* 55 SE2833
Armston *Nhants* 40 TL0685
Armthorpe *S York* 56 SE6204
Arnabost *Strath* 78 NM2159
Arncliffe *N York* 54 SD9371
Arncroach *Fife* 83 NO5105
Arndilly House *Gramp* 94 NJ2847
Arne *Dorset* 9 SY9788
Arnesby *Leics* 39 SP6192
Arngask *Tays* 82 NO1410
Arnicle *Strath* 72 NR7138
Arnisdale *Highld* 85 NG8410
Arnish *Highld* 90 NG5948
Arniston *Loth* 75 NT3362
Arnol *W Isls* 102 NB3148
Arnold *Humb* 57 TA1241
Arnold *Notts* 49 SK5845
Arnprior *Cent* 81 NS6194
Arnside *Cumb* 59 SD4578
Aros *Strath* 79 NM5645
Arrad Foot *Cumb* 58 SD3080
Arram *Humb* 56 TA0344
Arrathorne *N York* 61 SE2093
Arreton *IOW* 11 SZ5386
Arrina *Highld* 91 NG7458
Arrington *Cambs* 31 TL3250
Ariundle *Highld* 79 NM8264
Arrochar *Strath* 80 NN2904
Arrow *Warwks* 28 SP0856
Arscott *Shrops* 36 SJ4307
Artafallie *Highld* 92 NH6349
Arthington *W York* 55 SE2644
Arthingworth *Nhants* 40 SP7581
Arthrath *Gramp* 95 NJ9636
Artrochie *Gramp* 95 NK0031
Arundel *W Susx* 12 TQ0106
Asby *Cumb* 58 NY0620
Ascog *Strath* 73 NS1062
Ascot *Berks* 22 SU9268
Ascott-under-Wychwood *Oxon* 29 SP3018
Asenby *N York* 62 SE3975
Asfordby *Leics* 40 SK7019
Asfordby Hill *Leics* 40 SK7219
Asgarby *Lincs* 50 TF1145
Asgarby *Lincs* 51 TF3366
Ash *Kent* 14 TQ6064
Ash *Kent* 15 TR2858
Ash *Somset* 8 ST4720
Ash *Surrey* 22 SU9051
Ash Green *Surrey* 22 SU9049
Ash Green *Warwks* 39 SP3384
Ash Magna *Shrops* 37 SJ5739
Ash Mill *Devon* 7 SS7823
Ash Parva *Shrops* 37 SJ5739
Ash Priors *Somset* 8 ST1529
Ash Street *Suffk* 32 TM0146
Ash Thomas *Devon* 7 ST0010
Ash Vale *Surrey* 22 SU8951
Ashampstead *Berks* 21 SU5676
Ashampstead Green *Berks* 21 SU5677
Ashbocking *Suffk* 33 TM1754
Ashbocking Green *Suffk* 33 TM1854
Ashbourne *Derbys* 48 SK1746
Ashbrittle *Somset* 7 ST0521
Ashburton *Devon* 5 SX7570
Ashbury *Devon* 6 SX5098
Ashbury *Oxon* 21 SU2685
Ashby *Humb* 56 SE8908
Ashby by Partney *Lincs* 51 TF4266
Ashby cum Fenby *Humb* 51 TA2500
Ashby de la Launde *Lincs* 50 TF0555
Ashby Folville *Leics* 40 SK7012
Ashby Magna *Leics* 39 SP5690
Ashby Parva *Leics* 39 SP5288
Ashby Puerorum *Lincs* 51 TF3271
Ashby St. Ledgers *Nhants* 29 SP5768
Ashby St. Mary *Norfk* 43 TG3202
Ashby-de-la-Zouch *Leics* 39 SK3516
Ashchurch *Gloucs* 28 SO9233
Ashcombe *Avon* 19 ST3361
Ashcombe *Devon* 5 SX9179
Ashcott *Somset* 19 ST4336
Ashdon *Essex* 31 TL5842
Ashe *Hants* 21 SU5350
Asheldham *Essex* 25 TL9701
Ashen *Essex* 32 TL7442
Ashendon *Bucks* 30 SP7014
Asheridge *Bucks* 22 SP9304
Ashfield *Cent* 81 NN7803
Ashfield *Suffk* 33 TM2062
Ashfield Green *Suffk* 33 TM2573
Ashford *Devon* 6 SS5335
Ashford *Devon* 5 SX6948
Ashford *Kent* 15 TR0142
Ashford *Surrey* 22 TQ0771
Ashford Bowdler *Shrops* 27 SO5170
Ashford Carbonel *Shrops* 27 SO5270
Ashford Hill *Hants* 21 SU5562
Ashford in the Water *Derbys* 48 SK1969
Ashgill *Strath* 74 NS7850
Ashill *Devon* 8 ST0811
Ashill *Norfk* 42 TF8804
Ashill *Somset* 8 ST3217
Ashingdon *Essex* 24 TQ8693
Ashington *Nthumb* 69 NZ2687
Ashington *Somset* 9 ST5621
Ashington *W Susx* 12 TQ1315
Ashkirk *Border* 76 NT4722
Ashleworth *Gloucs* 28 SO8125
Ashleworth Quay *Gloucs* 28 SO8125
Ashley *Cambs* 32 TL6961
Ashley *Ches* 47 SJ7784
Ashley *Devon* 7 SS6511
Ashley *Gloucs* 20 ST9394
Ashley *Hants* 10 SU3831
Ashley *Hants* 10 SZ2595
Ashley *Kent* 15 TR3048
Ashley *Nhants* 40 SP7990
Ashley *Staffs* 37 SJ7636
Ashley *Wilts* 20 ST8268
Ashley Green *Bucks* 22 SP9705
Ashmansworth *Hants* 21 SU4157
Ashmansworthy *Devon* 6 SS3418
Ashmore *Dorset* 9 ST9117
Ashmore Green *Berks* 21 SU5069
Ashorne *Warwks* 29 SP3057
Ashover *Derbys* 49 SK3463
Ashow *Warwks* 29 SP3170
Ashperton *H & W* 27 SO6441
Ashprington *Devon* 5 SX8157
Ashreigney *Devon* 7 SS6313
Ashtead *Surrey* 23 TQ1857
Ashton *Ches* 46 SJ5069
Ashton *Cnwll* 2 SW6028
Ashton *Devon* 5 SX8584
Ashton *H & W* 27 SO5164
Ashton *Nhants* 30 SP7649
Ashton *Nhants* 40 TL0588
Ashton Common *Wilts* 20 ST8958
Ashton Keynes *Wilts* 20 SU0494
Ashton under Hill *H & W* 28 SO9937
Ashton-in-Makerfield *Gt Man* 47 SJ5798
Ashton-under-Lyne *Gt Man* 48 SJ9399
Ashurst *Hants* 10 SU3310
Ashurst *Kent* 13 TQ5138
Ashurst *W Susx* 12 TQ1715
Ashurstwood *W Susx* 13 TQ4136
Ashwater *Devon* 6 SX3895
Ashwell *Herts* 31 TL2639
Ashwell *Leics* 40 SK8613
Ashwell End *Herts* 31 TL2540
Ashwellthorpe *Norfk* 43 TM1497
Ashwick *Somset* 19 ST6348
Ashwicken *Norfk* 42 TF7018
Askam in Furness *Cumb* 58 SD2177
Askern *S York* 56 SE5613
Askerswell *Dorset* 8 SY5292
Askett *Bucks* 22 SP8105
Askham *Cumb* 59 NY5123
Askham *Notts* 50 SK7374
Askham Bryan *N York* 56 SE5548
Askham Richard *N York* 56 SE5347
Asknish *Strath* 71 NR9391
Askrigg *N York* 61 SD9491
Askwith *N York* 55 SE1648
Aslackby *Lincs* 40 TF0830
Aslacton *Norfk* 33 TM1590
Aslockton *Notts* 50 SK7440
Aspatria *Cumb* 58 NY1441
Aspenden *Herts* 31 TL3528
Aspley Guise *Beds* 30 SP9335
Aspley Heath *Beds* 30 SP9334
Aspull *Gt Man* 47 SD6108
Asselby *Humb* 56 SE7127
Assington *Suffk* 25 TL9338
Assington Green *Suffk* 32 TL7751
Astbury *Ches* 47 SJ8461
Astcote *Nhants* 30 SP6753
Asterby *Lincs* 51 TF2679
Asterley *Shrops* 36 SJ3707
Asterton *Shrops* 36 SO3991
Asthall *Oxon* 29 SP2811
Asthall Leigh *Oxon* 29 SP3013
Astle *Highld* 97 NH7391
Astley *Gt Man* 47 SD7000
Astley *H & W* 28 SO7867
Astley *Shrops* 37 SJ5218
Astley *Warwks* 39 SP3189
Astley Abbots *Shrops* 37 SO7096
Astley Bridge *Gt Man* 54 SD7111
Astley Cross *H & W* 28 SO8069
Aston *Berks* 22 SU7884
Aston *Ches* 47 SJ5578
Aston *Ches* 47 SJ6146
Aston *Clwyd* 46 SJ3067
Aston *Derbys* 48 SK1783
Aston *H & W* 36 SO4671
Aston *Herts* 31 TL2722
Aston *Oxon* 21 SP3403
Aston *S York* 49 SK4685
Aston *Shrops* 37 SJ5328
Aston *Shrops* 37 SJ6109
Aston *Shrops* 37 SO8093
Aston *Staffs* 37 SJ7541
Aston *Staffs* 38 SJ8923
Aston *Staffs* 38 SJ9130
Aston Abbotts *Bucks* 30 SP8420
Aston Botterell *Shrops* 37 SO6384
Aston Cantlow *Warwks* 28 SP1460
Aston Clinton *Bucks* 30 SP8812
Aston Crews *H & W* 28 SO6723
Aston End *Herts* 31 TL2724
Aston Eyre *Shrops* 37 SO6594
Aston Fields *H & W* 28 SO9669
Aston Flamville *Leics* 39 SP4692
Aston Ingham *H & W* 28 SO6823
Aston le Walls *Nhants* 29 SP4950
Aston Magna *Gloucs* 29 SP1935
Aston Munslow *Shrops* 37 SO5186
Aston on Clun *Shrops* 36 SO3981
Aston Pigott *Shrops* 36 SJ3305
Aston Rogers *Shrops* 36 SJ3406
Aston Rowant *Oxon* 22 SU7299
Aston Somerville *H & W* 28 SP0438
Aston Subedge *Gloucs* 28 SP1441
Aston Tirrold *Oxon* 21 SU5586
Aston Upthorpe *Oxon* 21 SU5586
Aston-on-Trent *Derbys* 39 SK4129
Astwick *Beds* 31 TL2138
Astwood *Bucks* 30 SP9547
Astwood *H & W* 28 SO9365
Astwood Bank *H & W* 28 SP0462
Aswarby *Lincs* 40 TF0639
Aswardby *Lincs* 51 TF3770
Atch Lench *H & W* 28 SP0350
Atcham *Shrops* 37 SJ5409
Athelhampton *Dorset* 9 SY7694
Athelington *Suffk* 33 TM2171
Athelney *Somset* 8 ST3428
Athelstaneford *Loth* 76 NT5377
Atherington *Devon* 6 SS5922
Atherstone *Warwks* 39 SP3097
Atherstone on Stour *Warwks* 29 SP2051
Atherton *Gt Man* 47 SD6703
Atlow *Derbys* 48 SK2248
Attadale *Highld* 85 NG9238
Atterby *Lincs* 50 SK9792
Attercliffe *S York* 49 SK3788
Atterton *Leics* 39 SP3598
Attleborough *Norfk* 42 TM0495
Attleborough *Warwks* 39 SP3790
Attlebridge *Norfk* 43 TG1216
Attleton Green *Suffk* 32 TL7454
Atwick *Humb* 57 TA1850
Atworth *Wilts* 20 ST8565
Aubourn *Lincs* 50 SK9262
Auchagallon *Strath* 72 NR8934
Auchedly *Gramp* 95 NJ8933
Auchenblae *Gramp* 89 NO7279
Auchenbowie *Cent* 81 NS7987
Auchencairn *D & G* 66 NX7951
Auchencairn *D & G* 66 NX9884
Auchencrow *Border* 77 NT8560
Auchendinny *Loth* 75 NT2561
Auchengray *Strath* 75 NS9954
Auchenhalrig *Gramp* 94 NJ3761
Auchenheath *Strath* 74 NS8043
Auchenhessnane *D & G* 66 NX8096
Auchenlochan *Strath* 71 NR9772
Auchenmade *Strath* 73 NS3548
Auchenmalg *D & G* 64 NX2352
Auchentibber *Strath* 74 NS6755
Auchentiber *Strath* 73 NS3647
Auchentroig *Cent* 81 NS5493
Auchindrean *Highld* 96 NH1980
Auchininna *Gramp* 94 NJ6546
Auchinleck *Strath* 74 NS5521
Auchinloch *Strath* 74 NS6570
Auchinstarry *Strath* 74 NS7176
Auchintore *Highld* 86 NN0972
Auchiries *Gramp* 95 NK0737
Auchlee *Gramp* 89 NO8996
Auchleven *Gramp* 94 NJ6224
Auchlochan *Strath* 74 NS7937
Auchlossan *Gramp* 89 NJ5601
Auchlyne *Cent* 81 NN5129
Auchmillan *Strath* 74 NS5129
Auchmithie *Tays* 89 NO6743
Auchmuirbridge *Fife* 83 NO2101
Auchnacree *Tays* 89 NO4663
Auchnagatt *Gramp* 95 NJ9241
Auchnotteroch *D & G* 64 NW9960
Auchroisk *Gramp* 94 NJ3351
Auchronie *Tays* 88 NO4480
Auchterarder *Tays* 82 NN9412
Auchteraw *Highld* 92 NH3507
Auchterblair *Highld* 93 NH9222
Auchtercairn *Highld* 91 NG8077
Auchterhouse *Tays* 83 NO3337
Auchterless *Gramp* 95 NJ7141
Auchtermuchty *Fife* 83 NO2311
Auchterneed *Highld* 92 NH4959
Auchtertool *Fife* 82 NT2190
Auchtertyre *Highld* 85 NG8427
Auchtoo *Cent* 81 NN5520
Auckengill *Highld* 100 ND3663
Auckley *S York* 49 SE6400
Audenshaw *Gt Man* 48 SJ9197
Audlem *Ches* 47 SJ6543
Audley *Staffs* 47 SJ7950
Audley End *Essex* 31 TL5337
Audley End *Suffk* 32 TL8553
Aughertree *Cumb* 58 NY2538
Aughton *Humb* 56 SE7038
Aughton *Lancs* 46 SD3905
Aughton *Lancs* 53 SD5567
Aughton *S York* 49 SK4586
Aughton *Wilts* 21 SU2356
Aughton Park *Lancs* 46 SD4006
Auldallan *Tays* 88 NO3158
Auldearn *Highld* 93 NH9255
Aulden *H & W* 27 SO4654
Auldgirth *D & G* 66 NX9186
Auldhame *Loth* 83 NT5984
Auldhouse *Strath* 74 NS6250
Ault a' chruinn *Highld* 85 NG9420
Ault Hucknall *Derbys* 49 SK4665
Aultbea *Highld* 91 NG8789
Aultgrishin *Highld* 91 NG7485
Aultguish Inn *Highld* 92 NH3570
Aultmore *Gramp* 94 NJ4053
Aultnagoire *Highld* 92 NH5423
Aultnamain Inn *Highld* 97 NH6681
Aunsby *Lincs* 40 TF0438
Aust *Avon* 19 ST5788
Austerfield *Notts* 49 SK6694
Austrey *Warwks* 39 SK2906
Austwick *N York* 54 SD7668
Authorpe *Lincs* 51 TF3980
Avebury *Wilts* 20 SU1069
Aveley *Essex* 24 TQ5680
Avening *Gloucs* 20 ST8898
Averham *Notts* 50 SK7654
Aveton Gifford *Devon* 5 SX6947
Aviemore *Highld* 93 NH8913
Avington *Berks* 21 SU3767
Avoch *Highld* 93 NH7055
Avon *Dorset* 10 SZ1498
Avon Dassett *Warwks* 29 SP4150
Avonbridge *Cent* 75 NS9172
Avonmouth *Avon* 19 ST5178
Avonwick *Devon* 5 SX7158
Awbridge *Hants* 10 SU3224
Awliscombe *Devon* 8 ST1301
Awre *Gloucs* 28 SO7008
Awsworth *Notts* 49 SK4844
Axbridge *Somset* 19 ST4354
Axford *Hants* 21 SU6043
Axford *Wilts* 21 SU2370
Axminster *Devon* 8 SY2998
Axmouth *Devon* 8 SY2591
Aycliffe *Dur* 61 NZ2822
Aylburton *Gloucs* 19 SO6101
Aylesbeare *Devon* 5 SY0392
Aylesbury *Bucks* 30 SP8213
Aylesby *Humb* 57 TA2007
Aylesford *Kent* 14 TQ7359
Aylesham *Kent* 15 TR2452
Aylestone *Leics* 39 SK5700
Aylmerton *Norfk* 43 TG1839
Aylsham *Norfk* 43 TG1926
Aylton *H & W* 27 SO6537
Aylworth *Gloucs* 28 SP1021
Aymestrey *H & W* 27 SO4265
Aynho *Nhants* 29 SP5133
Ayot Green *Herts* 31 TL2214
Ayot St. Lawrence *Herts* 31 TL1916
Ayot St. Peter *Herts* 31 TL2115
Ayr *Strath* 73 NS3321
Aysgarth *N York* 61 SE0088
Ayshford *Devon* 7 ST0415
Ayside *Cumb* 59 SD3983
Ayston *Leics* 40 SK8600
Aythorpe Roding *Essex* 24 TL5815
Ayton *Border* 77 NT9260
Azerley *N York* 61 SE2574

B

Babbacombe *Devon* 5 SX9265
Babbs Green *Herts* 31 TL3916
Babcary *Somset* 9 ST5628
Babington *Somset* 20 ST7051
Babraham *Cambs* 31 TL5150
Babworth *Notts* 49 SK6880
Back of Keppoch *Highld* 85 NM6587
Backaland *Ork* 103 HY5630
Backfolds *Gramp* 95 NK0252
Backford *Ches* 46 SJ3971
Backies *Highld* 97 NC8302
Backlass *Highld* 100 ND2053
Backwell *Avon* 19 ST4968
Baconsthorpe *Norfk* 43 TG1236
Bacton *H & W* 27 SO3732
Bacton *Norfk* 43 TG3433
Bacton *Suffk* 32 TM0567
Bacup *Lancs* 54 SD8622
Badachro *Highld* 91 NG7873
Badbury *Wilts* 21 SU1980
Badby *Nhants* 29 SP5658
Badcall *Highld* 98 NC1541

Badcall Bedingfield Street

Badcall *Highld* 98 NC2455
Badcaul *Highld* 91 NH0291
Baddesley Clinton *Warwks* 29 SP2070
Baddesley Ensor *Warwks* 39 SP2798
Baddidarroch *Highld* 98 NC0822
Badenscoth *Gramp* 95 NJ6938
Badenyon *Gramp* 94 NJ3319
Badger *Shrops* 37 SO7699
Badgeworth *Gloucs* 28 SO9019
Badgworth *Somset* 19 ST3952
Badicaul *Highld* 85 NG7529
Badingham *Suffk* 33 TM3068
Badlesmere *Kent* 15 TR0153
Badlieu *Border* 75 NT0518
Badlipster *Highld* 100 ND2448
Badluachrach *Highld* 91 NG9994
Badninish *Highld* 97 NH7594
Badrallach *Highld* 91 NH0691
Badsey *H & W* 28 SP0743
Badshot Lea *Surrey* 22 SU8648
Badsworth *W York* 55 SE4614
Badwell Ash *Suffk* 32 TL9868
Bag Enderby *Lincs* 51 TF3571
Bagber *Dorset* 9 ST7513
Bagby *N York* 62 SE4680
Bagillt *Clwyd* 46 SJ2175
Baginton *Warwks* 39 SP3474
Baglan *W Glam* 18 SS7492
Bagley *Shrops* 36 SJ4027
Bagley *Somset* 19 ST4645
Bagmore *Hants* 21 SU6544
Bagnall *Staffs* 48 SJ9250
Bagot *Shrops* 37 SO5873
Bagshot *Surrey* 22 SU9063
Bagstone *Avon* 20 ST6987
Bagworth *Leics* 39 SK4408
Bagwy Llydiart *H & W* 27 SO4426
Baildon *W York* 55 SE1539
Baildon Green *W York* 55 SE1439
Baile Mor *Strath* 78 NM2824
Baillieston *Strath* 74 NS6764
Bainbridge *N York* 61 SD9390
Bainshole *Gramp* 94 NJ6035
Bainton *Cambs* 40 TF0906
Bainton *Humb* 56 SE9652
Baintown *Fife* 83 NO3503
Bairnkine *Border* 76 NT6515
Bakewell *Derbys* 48 SK2168
Bala *Gwynd* 45 SH9235
Balallan *W Isls* 102 NB2920
Balbeg *Highld* 92 NH4431
Balbeggie *Tays* 82 NO1629
Balblair *Highld* 92 NH5145
Balblair *Highld* 93 NH7066
Balby *S York* 49 SE5600
Balcary *D & G* 66 NX8149
Balchraggan *Highld* 92 NH5343
Balchrick *Highld* 98 NC1960
Balcombe *W Susx* 12 TQ3130
Balcomie Links *Fife* 83 NO6209
Balcurvie *Fife* 83 NO3400
Baldersby *N York* 62 SE3578
Baldersby St. James *N York* 62 SE3676
Balderstone *Lancs* 54 SD6332
Balderton *Notts* 50 SK8151
Baldinnie *Fife* 83 NO4211
Baldinnies *Tays* 82 NO0216
Baldock *Herts* 31 TL2434
Baldovie *Tays* 83 NO4533
Baldslow *E Susx* 14 TQ8013
Bale *Norfk* 42 TG0136
Baledgarno *Tays* 83 NO2730
Balemartine *Strath* 78 NL9841
Balerno *Loth* 75 NT1666
Balfarg *Fife* 83 NO2803
Balfield *Tays* 89 NO5468
Balfour *Ork* 103 HY4716
Balfron *Cent* 81 NS5489
Balgaveny *Gramp* 94 NJ6540
Balgavies *Tays* 89 NO5451
Balgonar *Fife* 82 NT0293
Balgowan *D & G* 64 NX1142
Balgowan *Highld* 87 NN6494
Balgown *Highld* 90 NG3868
Balgracie *D & G* 64 NW9860
Balgray *Tays* 83 NO4038
Balham *Gt Lon* 23 TQ2873
Balhary *Tays* 88 NO2646
Balholmie *Tays* 82 NO1436
Baligill *Highld* 99 NC8565
Balintore *Highld* 97 NH8675
Balintore *Tays* 88 NO2859
Balintraid *Highld* 93 NH7370
Balivanich *W Isls* 102 NF7755
Balk *N York* 62 SE4780
Balkeerie *Tays* 88 NO3244
Balkholme *Humb* 56 SE7828
Ballachgair *Strath* 72 NR7727
Ballachulish *Highld* 86 NN0858
Ballantrae *Strath* 64 NX0882
Ballasalla *IOM* 52 SC2870
Ballater *Gramp* 88 NO3695
Ballaugh *IOM* 52 SC3493
Ballchraggan *Highld* 97 NH7675
Ballechin *Tays* 87 NN9353
Ballencrieff *Loth* 83 NT4878
Ballevullin *Strath* 78 NL9546
Ballidon *Derbys* 48 SK2054
Balliekine *Strath* 72 NR8739
Balliemore *Strath* 80 NS1099
Balligmorrie *Strath* 64 NX2290
Ballimore *Cent* 81 NN5317
Ballimore *Strath* 71 NR9283
Ballindalloch *Gramp* 94 NJ1636
Ballindean *Tays* 83 NO2529
Ballinger Common *Bucks* 22 SP9103
Ballingham *H & W* 27 SO5731
Ballingry *Fife* 82 NT1797
Ballinluig *Tays* 88 NN9752
Ballinshoe *Tays* 88 NO4153
Ballintuim *Tays* 88 NO1055
Balloch *Highld* 93 NH7247
Balloch *Strath* 64 NX3295
Balloch *Tays* 82 NN8419
Ballochroy *Strath* 71 NR7352
Ballogie *Gramp* 89 NO5795
Balls Cross *W Susx* 12 SU9826
Balls Green *E Susx* 13 TQ4936
Ballygown *Strath* 79 NM4343
Ballygrant *Strath* 70 NR3966
Ballyhaugh *Strath* 78 NM1758
Ballymenoch *Strath* 80 NS3086
Ballymichael *Strath* 72 NR9231
Balmacara *Highld* 85 NG8028
Balmaclellan *D & G* 65 NX6579
Balmae *D & G* 65 NX6844
Balmaha *Cent* 81 NS4290
Balmalcolm *Fife* 83 NO3208
Balmangan *D & G* 65 NX6445
Balmedie *Gramp* 95 NJ9618
Balmerino *Fife* 83 NO3524
Balmore *Strath* 74 NS5973
Balmuchy *Highld* 97 NH8678
Balmuir *Tays* 89 NO5648
Balmule *Fife* 82 NT2088
Balmullo *Fife* 83 NO4220
Balnaboth *Tays* 88 NO3166
Balnacoil Lodge *Highld* 97 NC8011
Balnacroft *Gramp* 88 NO2894
Balnafoich *Highld* 93 NH6835
Balnaguard *Tays* 87 NN9451
Balnahard *Strath* 79 NM4534
Balnahard *Strath* 70 NR4199
Balnain *Highld* 92 NH4430
Balnakeil *Highld* 98 NC3968
Balnapaling *Highld* 93 NH7969
Balquharn *Tays* 82 NO0235
Balquhidder *Cent* 81 NN5320
Balsall *W Mids* 39 SP2376
Balsall Heath *W Mids* 38 SP0784
Balscote *Oxon* 29 SP3942
Balsham *Cambs* 31 TL5850
Baltasound *Shet* 103 HP6208
Baltersan *D & G* 64 NX4261
Baltonsborough *Somset* 8 ST5434
Balvicar *Strath* 79 NM7616
Balvraid *Highld* 85 NG8416
Balvraid *Highld* 93 NH8231
Bamber Bridge *Lancs* 53 SD5625
Bamber's Green *Essex* 24 TL5722
Bamburgh *Nthumb* 77 NU1734
Bamff *Tays* 88 NO2251
Bamford *Derbys* 48 SK2083
Bampton *Cumb* 59 NY5118
Bampton *Devon* 7 SS9522
Bampton *Oxon* 21 SP3103
Bampton Grange *Cumb* 59 NY5218
Banavie *Highld* 86 NN1177
Banbury *Oxon* 29 SP4540
Bancffosfelem *Dyfed* 17 SN4811
Banchory *Gramp* 89 NO6995
Banchory-Devenick *Gramp* 89 NJ9002
Bancycapel *Dyfed* 17 SN4214
Bancyfelin *Dyfed* 17 SN3218
Bandirran *Tays* 82 NO2030
Banff *Gramp* 95 NJ6863
Bangor *Gwynd* 44 SH5772
Bangor-is-y-coed *Clwyd* 46 SJ3845
Bangors *Cnwll* 6 SX2099
Banham *Norfk* 32 TM0687
Bank *Hants* 10 SU2807
Bankend *D & G* 66 NY0268
Bankend *Strath* 74 NS8033
Bankfoot *Tays* 82 NO0635
Bankglen *Strath* 66 NS5912
Bankhead *Gramp* 95 NJ9009
Bankhead *Strath* 73 NS3739
Banknock *Cent* 81 NS7779
Banks *Lancs* 53 SD3920
Bankshill *D & G* 67 NY1982
Banningham *Norfk* 43 TG2129
Bannister Green *Essex* 24 TL6920
Bannockburn *Cent* 82 NS8190
Banstead *Surrey* 23 TQ2559
Bantham *Devon* 5 SX6643
Banton *Strath* 81 NS7480
Banwell *Avon* 19 ST3959
Bapchild *Kent* 14 TQ9263
Bapton *Wilts* 20 ST9938
Bar Hill *Cambs* 31 TL3863
Barassie *Strath* 73 NS3232
Barbaraville *Highld* 93 NH7472
Barbieston *Strath* 73 NS4317
Barbon *Cumb* 60 SD6282
Barbrook *Devon* 18 SS7147
Barby *Nhants* 29 SP5470
Barcaldine *Strath* 86 NM9641
Barcheston *Warwks* 29 SP2639
Barcombe *E Susx* 13 TQ4114
Barcombe Cross *E Susx* 13 TQ4115
Barden *N York* 61 SE1493
Barden Park *Kent* 13 TQ5746
Bardfield End Green *Essex* 24 TL6231
Bardfield Saling *Essex* 24 TL6826
Bardney *Lincs* 50 TF1269
Bardon *Leics* 39 SK4412
Bardon Mill *Nthumb* 68 NY7764
Bardowie *Strath* 74 NS5873
Bardrainney *Strath* 80 NS3373
Bardsea *Cumb* 58 SD3074
Bardsey *W York* 55 SE3643
Bardwell *Suffk* 32 TL9473
Bare *Lancs* 53 SD4564
Barfad *D & G* 64 NX3266
Barford *Norfk* 43 TG1107
Barford *Warwks* 29 SP2760
Barford St. John *Oxon* 29 SP4433
Barford St. Martin *Wilts* 10 SU0531
Barford St. Michael *Oxon* 29 SP4332
Barfrestone *Kent* 15 TR2650
Bargeddie *Strath* 74 NS6964
Bargoed *M Glam* 19 ST1599
Bargrennan *D & G* 64 NX3577
Barham *Cambs* 30 TL1375
Barham *Kent* 15 TR2050
Barham *Suffk* 33 TM1451
Barholm *Lincs* 40 TF0810
Barkby *Leics* 39 SK6309
Barkby Thorpe *Leics* 39 SK6309
Barkestone-le-Vale *Leics* 40 SK7734
Barkham *Berks* 22 SU7766
Barking *Gt Lon* 23 TQ4484
Barking *Suffk* 32 TM0753
Barking Tye *Suffk* 32 TM0652
Barkingside *Gt Lon* 23 TQ4489
Barkisland *W York* 55 SE0519
Barkla Shop *Cnwll* 2 SW7350
Barkston *Lincs* 50 SK9341
Barkston Ash *N York* 55 SE4936
Barkway *Herts* 31 TL3835
Barlanark *Strath* 74 NS6664
Barlaston *Staffs* 48 SJ8938
Barlavington *W Susx* 12 SU9716
Barlborough *Derbys* 49 SK4777
Barlestone *Leics* 39 SK4205
Barley *Herts* 31 TL4038
Barley *Lancs* 54 SD8240
Barleythorpe *Leics* 40 SK8409
Barling *Essex* 25 TQ9389
Barlings *Lincs* 50 TF0774
Barlochan *D & G* 66 NX8157
Barlow *Derbys* 49 SK3474
Barlow *N York* 56 SE6428
Barlow *T & W* 69 NZ1561
Barmby Moor *Humb* 56 SE7748
Barmby on the Marsh *Humb* 56 SE6928
Barmer *Norfk* 42 TF8133
Barmollack *Strath* 72 NR8043
Barmouth *Gwynd* 35 SH6116
Barmpton *Dur* 62 NZ3118
Barmston *Humb* 57 TA1659
Barnacabber *Strath* 80 NS1789
Barnacarry *Strath* 80 NS0094
Barnack *Cambs* 40 TF0705
Barnard Castle *Dur* 61 NZ0516
Barnard Gate *Oxon* 29 SP4010
Barnardiston *Suffk* 32 TL7148
Barnbarroch *D & G* 66 NX8456
Barnburgh *S York* 55 SE4803
Barnby *Suffk* 33 TM4789
Barnby Dun *S York* 56 SE6109
Barnby in the Willows *Notts* 50 SK8552
Barnby Moor *Notts* 49 SK6684
Barncorkrie *D & G* 64 NX0935
Barnes *Gt Lon* 23 TQ2276
Barnes Street *Kent* 13 TQ6447
Barnet *Gt Lon* 23 TQ2496
Barnetby le Wold *Humb* 57 TA0509
Barney *Norfk* 42 TF9932
Barnham *Suffk* 32 TL8779
Barnham *W Susx* 12 SU9503
Barnham Broom *Norfk* 42 TG0807
Barnhead *Tays* 89 NO6657
Barnhill *Gramp* 93 NJ1457
Barnhill *Tays* 83 NO4731
Barnhills *D & G* 64 NW9871
Barningham *Dur* 61 NZ0810
Barningham *Suffk* 32 TL9676
Barnoldby le Beck *Humb* 57 TA2303
Barnoldswick *Lancs* 54 SD8746
Barns Green *W Susx* 12 TQ1226
Barnsley *Gloucs* 28 SP0704
Barnsley *S York* 55 SE3406
Barnsole *Kent* 15 TR2756
Barnstaple *Devon* 6 SS5633
Barnston *Essex* 24 TL6419
Barnston *Mersyd* 46 SJ2783
Barnstone *Notts* 40 SK7335
Barnt Green *H & W* 38 SP0173
Barnton *Ches* 47 SJ6375
Barnton *Loth* 75 NT1874
Barnwell All Saints *Nhants* 40 TL0484
Barnwell St. Andrew *Nhants* 40 TL0584
Barnwood *Gloucs* 28 SO8518
Barr *Strath* 64 NX2794
Barrachan *D & G* 64 NX3649
Barrapoll *Strath* 78 NL9442
Barrasford *Nthumb* 68 NY9173
Barrhead *Strath* 74 NS4958
Barrhill *Strath* 64 NX2382
Barrington *Cambs* 31 TL3849
Barrington *Somset* 8 ST3818
Barripper *Cnwll* 2 SW6338
Barrmill *Strath* 73 NS3651
Barrnacarry Bay *Strath* 79 NM8122
Barrock *Highld* 100 ND2570
Barrow *Gloucs* 28 SO8824
Barrow *Lancs* 54 SD7338
Barrow *Leics* 40 SK8815
Barrow *Somset* 9 ST7231
Barrow *Suffk* 32 TL7663
Barrow Burn *Nthumb* 68 NT8610
Barrow Gurney *Avon* 19 ST5268
Barrow Haven *Humb* 57 TA0622
Barrow upon Soar *Leics* 39 SK5717
Barrow upon Trent *Derbys* 39 SK3528
Barrow-in-Furness *Cumb* 53 SD2068
Barrow-upon-Humber *Humb* 57 TA0620
Barrowby *Lincs* 40 SK8736
Barrowden *Leics* 40 SK9400
Barrowford *Lancs* 54 SD8539
Barry *S Glam* 18 ST1268
Barry *Tays* 83 NO5334
Barsby *Leics* 40 SK6911
Barsham *Suffk* 33 TM3989
Barskimmings *Strath* 73 NS4825
Barston *W Mids* 39 SP2078
Bartestree *H & W* 27 SO5640
Barthol Chapel *Gramp* 95 NJ8133
Bartholomew Green *Essex* 24 TL7221
Barthomley *Ches* 47 SJ7652
Bartley *Hants* 10 SU3012
Bartley Green *W Mids* 38 SP0081
Bartlow *Cambs* 31 TL5845
Barton *Cambs* 31 TL4055
Barton *Ches* 46 SJ4454
Barton *Devon* 5 SX9167
Barton *Gloucs* 28 SP0925
Barton *Lancs* 53 SD3509
Barton *Lancs* 53 SD5137
Barton *N York* 61 NZ2208
Barton *Oxon* 29 SP5507
Barton Bendish *Norfk* 42 TF7105
Barton End *Gloucs* 20 ST8498
Barton Hartshorn *Bucks* 29 SP6430
Barton in Fabis *Notts* 39 SK5132
Barton in the Beans *Leics* 39 SK3906
Barton Mills *Suffk* 32 TL7173
Barton on Sea *Hants* 10 SZ2393
Barton Seagrave *Nhants* 30 SP8877
Barton St. David *Somset* 8 ST5432
Barton Stacey *Hants* 21 SU4341
Barton Town *Devon* 7 SS6840
Barton Waterside *Humb* 56 TA0222
Barton-le-Clay *Beds* 30 TL0830
Barton-le-Street *N York* 63 SE7274
Barton-le-Willows *N York* 56 SE7163
Barton-on-the-Heath *Warwks* 29 SP2532
Barton-Upon-Humber *Humb* 56 TA0221
Barton-under-Needwood *Staffs* 38 SK1818
Barvas *W Isls* 102 NB3649
Barway *Cambs* 31 TL5575
Barwell *Leics* 39 SP4496
Barwick *Devon* 6 SS5907
Barwick *Somset* 9 ST5513
Barwick in Elmet *W York* 55 SE4037
Baschurch *Shrops* 36 SJ4221
Bascote *Warwks* 29 SP4063
Bashall Eaves *Lancs* 54 SD6943
Basildon *Berks* 21 SU6078
Basildon *Essex* 24 TQ7189
Basingstoke *Hants* 21 SU6352
Baslow *Derbys* 48 SK2572
Bason Bridge *Somset* 19 ST3446
Bassaleg *Gwent* 19 ST2786
Bassendean *Border* 76 NT6245
Bassenthwaite *Cumb* 58 NY2332
Bassett *Hants* 10 SU4216
Bassingbourn *Cambs* 31 TL3343
Bassingham *Lincs* 50 SK9060
Bassingthorpe *Leics* 40 SK9628
Bassus Green *Herts* 31 TL3025
Baston *Lincs* 40 TF1113
Bastwick *Norfk* 43 TG4217
Batchworth *Herts* 22 TQ0694
Batcombe *Somset* 20 ST6938
Batecombe *Dorset* 9 ST6103
Batford *Herts* 30 TL1415
Bath *Avon* 20 ST7464
Bath Side *Essex* 25 TM2532
Bathampton *Avon* 20 ST7766
Bathealton *Somset* 8 ST0823
Batheaston *Avon* 20 ST7767
Bathford *Avon* 20 ST7866
Bathgate *Loth* 75 NS9768
Bathley *Notts* 50 SK7759
Bathpool *Cnwll* 4 SX2874
Bathpool *Somset* 8 ST2526
Bathville *Loth* 75 NS9367
Bathway *Somset* 19 ST5952
Batley *W York* 55 SE2224
Batsford *Gloucs* 29 SP1833
Battersby *N York* 62 NZ5907
Battersea *Gt Lon* 23 TQ2776
Battisford Tye *Suffk* 32 TM0354
Battle *E Susx* 14 TQ7515
Battle *Powys* 26 SO0130
Battledykes *Tays* 88 NO4555
Battlesbridge *Essex* 24 TQ7894
Battleton *Somset* 7 SS9127
Baughton *H & W* 28 SO8841
Baughurst *Hants* 21 SU5860
Baulds *Gramp* 89 NO6093
Baulking *Oxon* 21 SU3191
Baumber *Lincs* 51 TF2274
Baunton *H & W* 28 SP0104
Baverstock *Wilts* 10 SU0332
Bawburgh *Norfk* 43 TG1508
Bawdeswell *Norfk* 42 TG0420
Bawdrip *Somset* 19 ST3439
Bawdsey *Suffk* 33 TM3440
Bawtry *Notts* 49 SK6493
Baxenden *Lancs* 54 SD7726
Baxterley *Warwks* 39 SP2896
Bayble *W Isls* 102 NB5231
Baybridge *Hants* 11 SU5223
Baycliff *Cumb* 53 SD2872
Baydon *Wilts* 21 SU2878
Bayford *Herts* 23 TL3108
Bayford *Somset* 9 ST7229
Bayhead *W Isls* 102 NF7468
Baylham *Suffk* 33 TM1051
Baysham *H & W* 27 SO5727
Bayston Hill *Shrops* 37 SJ4808
Baythorne End *Essex* 32 TL7242
Bayton *H & W* 37 SO6973
Bayworth *Oxon* 21 SP4901
Beachampton *Bucks* 30 SP7736
Beachamwell *Norfk* 42 TF7505
Beacon *Devon* 8 ST1805
Beacon End *Essex* 25 TL9524
Beacon's Bottom *Bucks* 22 SU7895
Beaconsfield *Bucks* 22 SU9490
Beacontree *Gt Lon* 23 TQ4786
Beadlam *N York* 62 SE6584
Beadlow *Beds* 30 TL1038
Beadnell *Nthumb* 77 NU2229
Beaford *Devon* 6 SS5515
Beal *N York* 56 SE5325
Beal *Nthumb* 77 NU0642
Bealsmill *Cnwll* 4 SX3576
Beaminster *Dorset* 8 ST4701
Beamish *Dur* 69 NZ2253
Beamsley *N York* 55 SE0752
Beanacre *Wilts* 20 ST9066
Beanley *Nthumb* 77 NU0818
Beardon *Devon* 4 SX5184
Beare *Devon* 7 SS9901
Beare Green *Surrey* 12 TQ1742
Bearley *Warwks* 29 SP1860
Bearpark *Dur* 69 NZ2343
Bearsbridge *Nthumb* 68 NY7857
Bearsden *Strath* 74 NS5372
Bearstead *Kent* 14 TQ8055
Bearstone *Shrops* 37 SJ7239
Bearwood *W Mids* 38 SP0286
Beattock *D & G* 66 NT0802
Beauchamp Roding *Essex* 24 TL5809
Beaufort *Gwent* 27 SO1611
Beaulieu *Hants* 10 SU3802
Beauly *Highld* 92 NH5246
Beaumaris *Gwynd* 44 SH6076
Beaumont *Cumb* 67 NY3459
Beaumont *Essex* 25 TM1624
Beaumont *Jersey* 101 JS1109
Beausale *Warwks* 29 SP2470
Beauworth *Hants* 11 SU5726
Beaver Green *Kent* 15 TR0041
Beaworthy *Devon* 6 SX4699
Beazley End *Essex* 24 TL7429
Bebington *Mersyd* 46 SJ3383
Beccles *Suffk* 33 TM4289
Becconsall *Lancs* 53 SD4523
Beck Row *Suffk* 32 TL6977
Beck Side *Cumb* 58 SD2382
Beckbury *Shrops* 37 SJ7601
Beckenham *Gt Lon* 23 TQ3769
Beckering *Lincs* 50 TF1280
Beckermet *Cumb* 58 NY0106
Beckfoot *Cumb* 67 NY0949
Beckford *H & W* 28 SO9736
Beckhampton *Wilts* 20 SU0868
Beckingham *Lincs* 50 SK8753
Beckingham *Notts* 50 SK7789
Beckington *Somset* 20 ST8051
Beckjay *Shrops* 36 SO3977
Beckley *E Susx* 14 TQ8523
Beckley *Oxon* 29 SP5611
Beckton *Gt Lon* 23 TQ4381
Beckwithshaw *N York* 55 SE2653
Becquet Vincent *Jersey* 101 JS1411
Bedale *N York* 61 SE2688
Bedchester *Dorset* 9 ST8517
Beddau *M Glam* 18 ST0585
Beddgelert *Gwynd* 44 SH5948
Beddingham *E Susx* 13 TQ4407
Beddington *Gt Lon* 23 TQ3065
Beddington Corner *Gt Lon* 23 TQ2866
Bedfield *Suffk* 33 TM2166
Bedford *Beds* 30 TL0449
Bedham *W Susx* 12 TQ0122
Bedhampton *Hants* 11 SU7006
Bedingfield *Suffk* 33 TM1768
Bedingfield Street *Suffk* 33 TM1768

Branscombe Bucks Green

Branscombe Devon 8 SY1988
Bransford H & W 28 SO7952
Bransgore Hants 10 SZ1897
Bransley Shrops 37 SO6575
Branston Leics 40 SK8129
Branston Lincs 50 TF0166
Branston Staffs 39 SK2221
Branston Booths Lincs 50 TF0668
Branstone IOW 11 SZ5583
Brant Broughton Lincs 50 SK9154
Brantham Suffk 25 TM1034
Branthwaite Cumb 58 NY0525
Branthwaite Cumb 58 NY2937
Brantingham Humb 56 SE9429
Branton Nthumb 77 NU0416
Branton S York 49 SE6401
Branton Green N York 55 SE4362
Branxton Nthumb 77 NT8937
Brassington Derbys 48 SK2254
Brasted Kent 23 TQ4755
Brasted Chart Gt Lon 13 TQ4653
Brathens Gramp 89 NO6798
Bratoft Lincs 51 TF4764
Brattleby Lincs 50 SK9481
Bratton Wilts 20 ST9152
Bratton Clovelly Devon 4 SX4691
Bratton Fleming Devon 7 SS6437
Bratton Seymour Somset 9 ST6729
Braughing Herts 31 TL3925
Braunston Leics 40 SK8306
Braunston Nhants 29 SP5466
Braunstone Leics 39 SK5502
Braunton Devon 6 SS4836
Brawby N York 63 SE7378
Brawl Highld 99 NC8166
Brawlbin Highld 100 ND0757
Bray Berks 22 SU9079
Bray Shop Cnwll 4 SX3374
Braybrooke Nhants 40 SP7684
Brayford Devon 7 SS6834
Braythorn N York 55 SE2449
Brayton N York 56 SE6030
Braywick Berks 22 SU8979
Braywoodside Berks 22 SU8775
Breachwood Green Herts 30 TL1522
Breadsall Derbys 49 SK3639
Breadstone Gloucs 20 SO7000
Breage Cnwll 2 SW6128
Breakachy Highld 92 NH4644
Breamore Hants 10 SU1517
Brean Somset 19 ST2956
Brearton N York 55 SE3261
Breasclete W Isls 102 NB2135
Breaston Derbys 39 SK4533
Brechfa Dyfed 17 SN5230
Brechin Tays 89 NO6060
Breckles Norfk 42 TL9594
Breckonside D & G 66 NX8489
Brecon Powys 26 SO0428
Bredbury Gt Man 48 SJ9291
Brede E Susx 14 TQ8218
Bredenbury H & W 27 SO6056
Bredfield Suffk 33 TM2653
Bredgar Kent 14 TQ8860
Bredhurst Kent 14 TQ7962
Bredon H & W 28 SO9236
Bredon's Hardwick H & W 28 SO9135
Bredon's Norton H & W 28 SO9339
Bredwardine H & W 27 SO3344
Breedon on the Hill Leics 39 SK4022
Breich Loth 75 NS9560
Breightmet Gt Man 54 SD7409
Breighton Humb 56 SE7033
Breinton H & W 27 SO4739
Bremhill Wilts 20 ST9773
Brenchley Kent 14 TQ6741
Brendon Devon 18 SS7748
Brenfield Strath 71 NR8482
Brenish W Isls 102 NA9925
Brent Eleigh Suffk 32 TL9448
Brent Knoll Somset 19 ST3350
Brent Mill Devon 5 SX6959
Brent Pelham Herts 31 TL4330
Brentford Gt Lon 23 TQ1777
Brentingby Leics 40 SK7818
Brentwood Essex 24 TQ5993
Brenzett Kent 15 TR0027
Brenzett Green Kent 15 TR0128
Brereton Green Ches 47 SJ7764
Bressingham Norfk 32 TM0780
Bretby Derbys 39 SK2922
Bretford Warwks 39 SP4377
Bretforton H & W 28 SP0944
Bretherdale Head Cumb 59 NY5705
Bretherton Lancs 53 SD4720
Brettabister Shet 103 HU4857
Brettenham Norfk 32 TL9383
Brettenham Suffk 32 TL9654
Bretton Clwyd 46 SJ3563
Brewood Staffs 38 SJ8808
Briantspuddle Dorset 9 SY8193
Brick Houses S York 49 SK3081
Bricket Wood Herts 22 TL1202
Bricklehampton H & W 28 SO9742
Bride IOM 52 NX4401
Bridekirk Cumb 58 NY1133
Bridestowe Devon 4 SX5189
Brideswell Gramp 94 NJ5738
Bridford Devon 5 SX8186
Bridge Cnwll 2 SW6744
Bridge Kent 15 TR1854
Bridge Hewick N York 55 SE3370
Bridge of Alford Gramp 94 NJ5617
Bridge of Avon Gramp 94 NJ1835
Bridge of Avon Gramp 93 NJ1520
Bridge of Balgie Tays 87 NN5746
Bridge of Brewlands Tays 88 NO1961
Bridge of Brown Highld 93 NJ1120
Bridge of Cally Tays 88 NO1351
Bridge of Canny Gramp 89 NO6597
Bridge of Craigisla Tays 88 NO2553
Bridge of Dee D & G 65 NX7359
Bridge of Don Gramp 95 NJ9409
Bridge of Dulsie Highld 93 NH9341
Bridge of Dye Gramp 89 NO6586
Bridge of Earn Tays 82 NO1318
Bridge of Ericht Tays 87 NN5258
Bridge of Feugh Gramp 89 NO7094
Bridge of Forss Highld 100 ND0368
Bridge of Gairn Gramp 88 NO3597
Bridge of Gaur Tays 87 NN5056
Bridge of Marnoch Gramp 94 NJ5950
Bridge of Orchy Strath 80 NN2939
Bridge of Tilt Tays 87 NN8765
Bridge of Tynet Gramp 94 NJ3861
Bridge of Walls Shet 103 HU2752
Bridge of Weir Strath 73 NS3965
Bridge of Westfield Highld 100 ND0664
Bridge Sollers H & W 27 SO4142
Bridge Street Suffk 32 TL8749
Bridge Trafford Ches 46 SJ4571
Bridgehampton Somset 9 ST5624
Bridgehill Dur 68 NZ0951
Bridgemary Hants 11 SU5803
Bridgend Border 76 NT5235
Bridgend D & G 66 NT0708
Bridgend Devon 5 SX5548
Bridgend Fife 83 NO3911
Bridgend Gramp 94 NJ3731
Bridgend Gramp 94 NJ5135
Bridgend Loth 75 NT0475
Bridgend M Glam 18 SS9079
Bridgend Strath 70 NR3362
Bridgend Tays 82 NO1224
Bridgend Tays 89 NO5368
Bridgend of Lintrathen Tays 88 NO2854
Bridgerule Devon 6 SS2702
Bridgetown Somset 7 SS9233
Bridgham Norfk 32 TL9685
Bridgnorth Shrops 37 SO7193
Bridgtown Staffs 38 SJ9808
Bridgwater Somset 19 ST2937
Bridlington Humb 57 TA1866
Bridport Dorset 8 SY4692
Bridstow H & W 27 SO5824
Brierfield Lancs 54 SD8436
Brierley Gloucs 27 SO6215
Brierley W York 55 SE4010
Brierley Hill W Mids 28 SO9169
Brig o'Turk Cent 81 NN5306
Brigg Humb 56 TA0007
Briggate Norfk 43 TG3127
Briggswath N York 63 NZ8608
Brigham Cumb 58 NY0830
Brigham Humb 57 TA0753
Brighouse W York 55 SE1422
Brighstone IOW 10 SZ4282
Brighthampton Oxon 21 SP3803
Brightley Devon 6 SX6097
Brightling E Susx 14 TQ6820
Brightlingsea Essex 25 TM0817
Brighton E Susx 12 TQ3104
Brighton le Sands Mersyd 46 SJ3098
Brightons Cent 75 NS9277
Brightwalton Berks 21 SU4279
Brightwell Oxon 21 SU5790
Brightwell Suffk 33 TM2543
Brightwell Baldwin Oxon 21 SU6595
Brightwell Upperton Oxon 21 SU6594
Brignall Dur 61 NZ0712
Brigsley Humb 51 TA2501
Brigsteer Cumb 59 SD4889
Brigstock Nhants 40 SP9485
Brill Bucks 29 SP6513
Brill Cnwll 2 SW7229
Brilley H & W 27 SO2648
Brimfield H & W 27 SO5267
Brimfield Cross H & W 27 SO5368
Brimington Derbys 49 SK4073
Brimley Devon 5 SX8077
Brimpsfield Gloucs 28 SO9312
Brimpton Berks 21 SU5564
Brimscombe Gloucs 20 SO8702
Brimstage Mersyd 46 SJ3082
Brincliffe S York 49 SK3284
Brind Humb 56 SE7430
Brindister Shet 103 HU2857
Brindle Lancs 54 SD5924
Brineton Staffs 37 SJ8013
Bringhurst Leics 40 SP8492
Brington Cambs 30 TL0875
Briningham Norfk 42 TG0434
Brinkhill Lincs 51 TF3773
Brinkley Cambs 32 TL6354
Brinklow Warwks 39 SP4379
Brinkworth Wilts 20 SU0184
Brinscall Lancs 54 SD6221
Brinsley Notts 49 SK4548
Brinton Norfk 42 TG0335
Brinyan Ork 103 HY4327
Brisley Norfk 42 TF9421
Brislington Avon 19 ST6270
Brissenden Green Kent 14 TQ9439
Bristol Avon 19 ST5972
Briston Norfk 42 TG0632
Britford Wilts 10 SU1627
Brithdir Gwynd 35 SH7618
Brithdir M Glam 19 SO1401
British Legion Village Kent 14 TQ7257
Briton Ferry W Glam 18 SS7394
Britwell Salome Oxon 22 SU6792
Brixham Devon 5 SX9255
Brixton Devon 5 SX5552
Brixton Gt Lon 23 TQ3175
Brixton Deverill Wilts 20 ST8638
Brixworth Nhants 30 SP7470
Brize Norton Oxon 29 SP2907
Broad Alley H & W 28 SO8867
Broad Blunsdon Wilts 20 SU1491
Broad Campden Gloucs 28 SP1537
Broad Carr W York 55 SE0919
Broad Chalke Wilts 10 SU0325
Broad Green Essex 24 TL8823
Broad Green H & W 28 SO7756
Broad Green Suffk 32 TL7859
Broad Haven Dyfed 16 SM8613
Broad Hinton Wilts 20 SU1075
Broad Laying Hants 21 SU4362
Broad Marston H & W 28 SP1446
Broad Oak E Susx 14 TQ8219
Broad Oak H & W 27 SO4821
Broad Oak Mersyd 46 SJ5395
Broad Street E Susx 14 TQ8616
Broad Street Kent 15 TR1139
Broad Town Wilts 20 SU0977
Broad's Green Essex 24 TL6912
Broadbridge W Susx 11 SU8105
Broadbridge Heath W Susx 12 TQ1431
Broadclyst Devon 7 SX9897
Broadfield Strath 80 NS3373
Broadford Highld 85 NG6423
Broadford Bridge W Susx 12 TQ0921
Broadgairhill Border 67 NT2010
Broadgrass Green Suffk 32 TL9663
Broadhaugh Border 77 NT8655
Broadheath Gt Man 47 SJ7689
Broadhembury Devon 8 ST1004
Broadhempston Devon 5 SX8066
Broadland Row E Susx 14 TQ8319
Broadley Gramp 94 NJ3961
Broadmayne Dorset 9 SY7286
Broadmoor Dyfed 16 SN0906
Broadoak Dorset 8 SY4396
Broadoak E Susx 13 TQ6022
Broadoak Kent 15 TR1761
Broadstairs Kent 15 TR3967
Broadstone Dorset 10 SZ0095
Broadstone Shrops 37 SO5489
Broadwas H & W 28 SO7555
Broadwater Herts 31 TL2422
Broadwater W Susx 12 TQ1404
Broadwaters H & W 38 SO8477
Broadway H & W 28 SP0937
Broadway Somset 8 ST3215
Broadwell Gloucs 29 SP2027
Broadwell Oxon 29 SP2504
Broadwell Warwks 29 SP4565
Broadwindsor Dorset 8 ST4302
Broadwood Kelly Devon 7 SS6106
Broadwoodwidger Devon 4 SX4189
Brochel Highld 90 NG5846
Brockamin H & W 28 SO7753
Brockbridge Hants 11 SU6118
Brockdish Norfk 33 TM2179
Brockenhurst Hants 10 SU3002
Brocketsbrae Strath 74 NS8239
Brockford Street Suffk 33 TM1167
Brockhall Nhants 29 SP6362
Brockham Surrey 12 TQ1949
Brockhampton Gloucs 28 SP0322
Brockhampton H & W 27 SO5931
Brockholes W York 55 SE1510
Brocklesby Lincs 57 TA1311
Brockley Avon 19 ST4666
Brockley Suffk 32 TL8371
Brockley Green Suffk 32 TL7247
Brockley Green Suffk 32 TL8254
Brockton Shrops 36 SJ3104
Brockton Shrops 36 SO3285
Brockton Shrops 37 SO5794
Brockton Staffs 37 SJ8131
Brockweir Gwent 19 SO5401
Brockworth Gloucs 28 SO8916
Brocton Staffs 38 SJ9619
Brodick Strath 72 NS0135
Brodie Gramp 93 NH9757
Brodsworth S York 55 SE5007
Brogaig Highld 90 NG4767
Brokenborough Wilts 20 ST9189
Brokerswood Wilts 20 ST8352
Bromborough Mersyd 46 SJ3582
Brome Suffk 33 TM1376
Brome Street Suffk 33 TM1576
Bromeswell Suffk 33 TM3050
Bromfield Cumb 67 NY1746
Bromfield Shrops 37 SO4876
Bromham Beds 30 TL0051
Bromham Wilts 20 ST9665
Bromley Gt Lon 23 TQ4069
Bromley Shrops 37 SO7395
Brompton Kent 14 TQ7668
Brompton N York 62 SE3796
Brompton N York 63 SE9482
Brompton Ralph Somset 8 ST0832
Brompton Regis Somset 7 SS9531
Brompton-on-Swale N York 61 SE2199
Bromsberrow Gloucs 28 SO7433
Bromsberrow Heath Gloucs 28 SO7333
Bromsgrove H & W 28 SO9670
Bromyard H & W 27 SO6554
Bronant Dyfed 35 SN6467
Brongest Dyfed 17 SN3245
Bronington Clwyd 37 SJ4839
Bronllys Powys 26 SO1434
Bronwydd Arms Dyfed 17 SN4123
Bronygarth Shrops 36 SJ2637
Brook Hants 10 SU2714
Brook IOW 10 SZ3983
Brook Kent 15 TR0644
Brook Surrey 12 SU9237
Brook Hill Hants 10 SU2714
Brook Street Essex 24 TQ5793
Brook Street Kent 14 TQ9333
Brook Street Suffk 32 TL8248
Brooke Leics 40 SK8405
Brooke Norfk 43 TM2899
Brookfield Strath 73 NS4164
Brookhampton Hants 11 SU7106
Brookhampton Somset 9 ST6327
Brookhouse Lancs 53 SD5464
Brookhouse S York 49 SK5188
Brookhouse Green Ches 47 SJ8161
Brookhouses Derbys 48 SK0388
Brookland Kent 15 TQ9926
Brooklands Gt Man 47 SJ7890
Brookmans Park Herts 23 TL2404
Brookthorpe Gloucs 28 SO8312
Brookwood Surrey 22 SU9557
Broom Beds 31 TL1742
Broom S York 49 SK4491
Broom Warwks 28 SP0853
Broom Hill H & W 38 SO9175
Broom Hill Notts 49 SK5447
Broom Hill S York 49 SE4102
Broom Street Kent 15 TR0462
Broome H & W 38 SO9078
Broome Norfk 33 TM3591
Broome Shrops 36 SO4080
Broomedge Ches 47 SJ7085
Broomfield Essex 24 TL7010
Broomfield Kent 14 TQ8452
Broomfield Kent 15 TR1966
Broomfield Somset 8 ST2232
Broomfleet Humb 56 SE8727
Broomhaugh Nthumb 68 NZ0261
Broomhill Nthumb 69 NU2401
Brora Highld 97 NC9103
Broseley Shrops 37 SJ6701
Brotherlee Dur 60 NY9237
Brotherton N York 55 SE4825
Brotton Cleve 62 NZ6819
Broubster Highld 100 ND0359
Brough Cumb 60 NY7914
Brough Highld 100 ND2273
Brough Humb 56 SE9326
Brough Notts 50 SK8458
Brough Shet 103 HU5665
Brough Lodge Shet 103 HU5892
Brough Sowerby Cumb 60 NY7912
Broughall Shrops 37 SJ5741
Broughton Border 75 NT1136
Broughton Bucks 30 SP8939
Broughton Cambs 31 TL2878
Broughton Clwyd 46 SJ3363
Broughton Gt Man 47 SD8201
Broughton Hants 10 SU3033
Broughton Humb 56 SE9608
Broughton Lancs 53 SD5234
Broughton N York 54 SD9451
Broughton N York 63 SE7673
Broughton Nhants 30 SP8375
Broughton Oxon 29 SP4138
Broughton S Glam 18 SS9270
Broughton Staffs 37 SJ7634
Broughton Astley Leics 39 SP5292
Broughton Gifford Wilts 20 ST8763
Broughton Green H & W 28 SO9561
Broughton Hackett H & W 28 SO9254
Broughton Mains D & G 65 NX4545
Broughton Mills Cumb 58 SD2290
Broughton Moor Cumb 58 NY0533
Broughton Poggs Oxon 21 SP2303
Broughton-in-Furness Cumb 58 SD2187
Broughty Ferry Tays 83 NO4630
Brown Candover Hants 11 SU5739
Brown Edge Staffs 48 SJ9053
Brownhill Gramp 95 NJ8640
Brownhills Fife 83 NO5215
Brownhills W Mids 38 SK0405
Browninghill Green Hants 21 SU5859
Brownsham Devon 6 SS2826
Brownston Devon 5 SX6952
Brox Surrey 22 TQ0263
Broxa N York 63 SE9491
Broxbourne Herts 23 TL3606
Broxburn Loth 75 NT0872
Broxburn Loth 76 NT6977
Broxted Essex 24 TL5727
Broxwood H & W 27 SO3654
Bruan Highld 100 ND3139
Bruar Tays 87 NN8265
Brucefield Highld 97 NH9386
Bruchag Strath 73 NS1157
Bruisyard Suffk 33 TM3266
Bruisyard Street Suffk 33 TM3365
Brumby Humb 56 SE8909
Brund Staffs 48 SK1061
Brundall Norfk 43 TG3308
Brundish Suffk 33 TM2769
Brundish Street Suffk 33 TM2671
Brunthwaite W York 55 SE0546
Bruntingthorpe Leics 39 SP6089
Brunton Fife 83 NO3220
Brunton Nthumb 77 NU2024
Brunton Wilts 21 SU2456
Brushford Somset 7 SS9225
Brushford Barton Devon 7 SS6707
Bruton Somset 9 ST6835
Bryan's Green H & W 28 SO8868
Bryanston Dorset 9 ST8607
Bryant's Bottom Bucks 22 SU8599
Brydekirk D & G 67 NY1870
Brympton Somset 8 ST5115
Bryn W Glam 18 SS8192
Bryn Du Gwynd 44 SH3472
Bryn Gates Lancs 47 SD5901
Bryn Saith Marchog Clwyd 46 SJ0750
Bryn-coch W Glam 18 SS7499
Bryn henllan Dyfed 16 SN0139
Bryn-mawr Gwynd 44 SH2433
Bryn-y-maen Clwyd 45 SH8376
Brynaman Dyfed 26 SN7114
Brynberian Dyfed 16 SN1035
Bryncir Gwynd 44 SH4844
Bryncroes Gwynd 44 SH2231
Bryncrug Gwynd 35 SH6103
Bryneglwys Clwyd 46 SJ1447
Brynford Clwyd 46 SJ1774
Bryngwran Gwynd 44 SH3577
Bryngwyn Gwent 27 SO3909
Bryngwyn Powys 27 SO1849
Brynhoffnant Dyfed 17 SN3351
Brynithel Gwent 19 SO2101
Brynmawr Gwent 27 SO1911
Brynmenyn M Glam 18 SS9084
Brynmill W Glam 17 SS6392
Brynna M Glam 18 SS9883
Brynrefail Gwynd 44 SH5562
Brynsadler M Glam 18 ST0280
Brynsiencyn Gwynd 44 SH4867
Bualintur Highld 84 NG4020
Bubbenhall Warwks 39 SP3672
Bubwith Humb 56 SE7136
Buchanan Smithy Cent 81 NS4689
Buchanhaven Gramp 95 NK1247
Buchanty Tays 82 NN9328
Buchany Cent 81 NN7102
Buchlyvie Cent 81 NS5793
Buck's Cross Devon 6 SS3522
Buck's Mills Devon 6 SS3523
Buckabank Cumb 67 NY3749
Buckden Cambs 31 TL1967
Buckden N York 61 SD9477
Buckenham Norfk 43 TG3505
Buckerell Devon 8 ST1200
Buckfast Devon 5 SX7467
Buckfastleigh Devon 5 SX7366
Buckhaven Fife 83 NT3598
Buckholm Border 76 NT4738
Buckholt Gwent 27 SO5016
Buckhorn Weston Dorset 9 ST7524
Buckhurst Hill Essex 23 TQ4194
Buckie Gramp 94 NJ4265
Buckingham Bucks 30 SP6933
Buckland Bucks 30 SP8812
Buckland Devon 5 SX6743
Buckland Gloucs 28 SP0835
Buckland Herts 31 TL3533
Buckland Kent 15 TR3042
Buckland Oxon 21 SU3498
Buckland Surrey 12 TQ2150
Buckland Brewer Devon 6 SS4220
Buckland Common Bucks 22 SP9207
Buckland Dinham Somset 20 ST7551
Buckland Filleigh Devon 6 SS4609
Buckland in the Moor Devon 5 SX7273
Buckland Monachorum Devon 4 SX4968
Buckland Newton Dorset 9 ST6805
Buckland Ripers Dorset 9 SY6582
Buckland St. Mary Somset 8 ST2613
Buckland-Tout-Saints Devon 5 SX7645
Bucklebury Berks 21 SU5570
Bucklerheads Tays 83 NO4636
Bucklers Hard Hants 10 SU4000
Bucklesham Suffk 33 TM2441
Buckley Clwyd 46 SJ2763
Bucklow Hill Ches 47 SJ7383
Buckminster Leics 40 SK8722
Bucknall Lincs 50 TF1668
Bucknall Staffs 48 SJ9047
Bucknell Oxon 29 SP5625
Bucknell Shrops 36 SO3574
Buckpool Gramp 94 NJ4165
Bucks Green W Susx 12 TQ0833

Bucks Horn Oak Carfraemill

Bucks Horn Oak *Hants* 11 SU8041
Bucksburn *Gramp* 95 NJ8909
Buckton *Humb* 57 TA1872
Buckton *Nthumb* 77 NU0838
Buckworth *Cambs* 30 TL1476
Budbrooke *Warwks* 29 SP2665
Budby *Notts* 49 SK6169
Budd's Titson *Cnwll* 6 SS2401
Buddon *Tays* 83 NO5232
Bude *Cnwll* 6 SS2105
Budge's Shop *Cnwll* 4 SX3259
Budleigh Salterton *Devon* 8 SY0682
Budock Water *Cnwll* 2 SW7831
Buerton *Ches* 47 SJ6843
Bugbrooke *Nhants* 30 SP6757
Bugle *Cnwll* 3 SX0158
Bugley *Dorset* 9 ST7824
Bugthorpe *Humb* 56 SE7757
Buildwas *Shrops* 37 SJ6204
Builth Wells *Powys* 26 SO0350
Bulbridge *Wilts* 10 SU0830
Buldoo *Highld* 100 ND0067
Bulford *Wilts* 20 SU1643
Bulkeley *Ches* 46 SJ5354
Bulkington *Warwks* 39 SP3986
Bulkington *Wilts* 20 ST9458
Bulkworthy *Devon* 6 SS3914
Bull's Green *Herts* 31 TL2717
Bullbrook *Berks* 22 SU8869
Bullington *Hants* 21 SU4541
Bullington *Lincs* 50 TF0877
Bulmer *Essex* 32 TL8440
Bulmer *N York* 56 SE6967
Bulmer Tye *Essex* 24 TL8438
Bulphan *Essex* 24 TQ6385
Bulwark *Gramp* 95 NJ9345
Bulwell *Notts* 49 SK5343
Bulwick *Nhants* 40 SP9694
Bumble's Green *Essex* 23 TL4005
Bunacaimb *Highld* 85 NM6588
Bunarkaig *Highld* 86 NN1887
Bunbury *Ches* 47 SJ5657
Bunchrew *Highld* 92 NH6246
Bundalloch *Highld* 85 NG8927
Bunessan *Strath* 78 NM3821
Bungay *Suffk* 33 TM3389
Bunnahabhainn *Strath* 70 NR4173
Bunny *Notts* 39 SK5829
Buntait *Highld* 92 NH4030
Buntingford *Herts* 31 TL3629
Bunwell *Norfk* 33 TM1292
Bunwell Street *Norfk* 43 TM1193
Burbage *Leics* 39 SP4492
Burbage *Wilts* 21 SU2261
Burchett's Green *Berks* 22 SU8481
Burcombe *Wilts* 10 SU0730
Burcott *Bucks* 30 SP8823
Bures *Suffk* 24 TL9034
Burford *H & W* 27 SO5868
Burford *Oxon* 29 SP2512
Burg *Strath* 78 NM3845
Burgates *Hants* 11 SU7728
Burgess Hill *W Susx* 12 TQ3218
Burgh *Suffk* 33 TM2351
Burgh by Sands *Cumb* 67 NY3259
Burgh Castle *Norfk* 43 TG4805
Burgh Heath *Surrey* 23 TQ2457
Burgh Le Marsh *Lincs* 51 TF5065
Burgh next Aylsham *Norfk* 43 TG2125
Burgh on Bain *Lincs* 51 TF2186
Burgh St. Margaret *Norfk* 43 TG4413
Burgh St. Peter *Norfk* 43 TM4693
Burghclere *Hants* 21 SU4761
Burghead *Gramp* 93 NJ1168
Burghfield *Berks* 22 SU6668
Burghfield Common *Berks* 21 SU6566
Burghill *H & W* 27 SO4844
Burghwallis *S York* 56 SE5311
Burham *Kent* 14 TQ7262
Buriton *Hants* 11 SU7419
Burland *Ches* 47 SJ6153
Burlawn *Cnwll* 3 SW9970
Burleigh *Berks* 22 SU9169
Burleigh *Gloucs* 20 SO8601
Burlescombe *Devon* 8 ST0716
Burleston *Dorset* 9 SY7794
Burley *Hants* 10 SU2102
Burley *Leics* 40 SK8810
Burley Gate *H & W* 27 SO5947
Burley in Wharfedale *W York* 55 SE1646
Burley Street *Hants* 10 SU2004
Burley Wood Head *W York* 55 SE1544
Burleydam *Ches* 37 SJ6042
Burlingham Green *Norfk* 43 TG3610
Burlton *Shrops* 36 SJ4526
Burmarsh *Kent* 15 TR1032
Burmington *Warwks* 29 SP2637
Burn *N York* 56 SE5928
Burn of Cambus *Cent* 81 NN7102
Burnage *Gt Man* 47 SJ8692
Burnaston *Derbys* 39 SK2832
Burnbrae *Strath* 74 NS8759
Burnby *Humb* 56 SE8346
Burneside *Cumb* 59 SD5095
Burneston *N York* 61 SE3084
Burnett *Avon* 20 ST6665
Burnfoot *Border* 67 NT4113
Burnfoot *Border* 76 NT5116
Burnfoot *D & G* 66 NX9791
Burnfoot *D & G* 67 NY3388
Burnfoot *D & G* 67 NY3996
Burnfoot *Tays* 82 NN9904
Burnham *Bucks* 22 SU9282
Burnham Deepdale *Norfk* 42 TF8044
Burnham Green *Herts* 31 TL2616
Burnham Market *Norfk* 42 TF8342
Burnham Norton *Norfk* 42 TF8343
Burnham Overy *Norfk* 42 TF8442
Burnham Thorpe *Norfk* 42 TF8541
Burnham-on-Crouch *Essex* 25 TQ9496
Burnham-on-Sea *Somset* 19 ST3049
Burnhaven *Gramp* 95 NK1244
Burnhead *D & G* 66 NX8695
Burnhervie *Gramp* 95 NJ7319
Burnhill Green *Staffs* 37 SJ7800
Burnhope *Dur* 69 NZ1948
Burnhouse *Strath* 73 NS3850
Burniston *N York* 63 TA0193
Burnley *Lancs* 54 SD8432
Burnmouth *Border* 77 NT9560
Burnopfield *Dur* 69 NZ1757
Burnsall *N York* 55 SE0361
Burnside *Fife* 82 NO1608
Burnside *Fife* 75 NT0575
Burnside *Gramp* 94 NJ1769
Burnside *Tays* 88 NO4259
Burnside *Tays* 89 NO5050
Burnside of Duntrune *Tays* 83 NO4434
Burnt Hill *Berks* 21 SU5774
Burnt Yates *N York* 55 SE2561
Burntisland *Fife* 83 NT2385
Burntwood *Staffs* 38 SK0509
Burnworthy *Somset* 8 ST1915
Burpham *Surrey* 12 TQ0152
Burpham *W Susx* 12 TQ0308
Burradon *Nthumb* 68 NT9806
Burrafirth *Shet* 103 HP6113
Burravoe *Shet* 103 HU5180
Burrells *Cumb* 60 NY6718
Burrelton *Tays* 82 NO2037
Burridge *Devon* 8 ST3106
Burridge *Hants* 11 SU5110
Burrill *N York* 61 SE2387
Burringham *Humb* 56 SE8309
Burrington *Avon* 19 ST4859
Burrington *Devon* 7 SS6416
Burrington *H & W* 36 SO4472
Burrough Green *Cambs* 32 TL6355
Burrough on the Hill *Leics* 40 SK7510
Burrow *Somset* 7 SS9342
Burrow Bridge *Somset* 8 ST3530
Burrowhill *Surrey* 22 SU9762
Burry Port *Dyfed* 17 SN4400
Burrygreen *W Glam* 17 SS4591
Burscough *Lancs* 53 SD4310
Burscough Bridge *Lancs* 53 SD4412
Bursea *Humb* 56 SE8033
Bursledon *Hants* 11 SU4809
Burslem *Staffs* 47 SJ8649
Burstall *Suffk* 33 TM0944
Burstock *Dorset* 8 ST4202
Burston *Norfk* 33 TM1383
Burstow *Surrey* 12 TQ3141
Burstwick *Humb* 57 TA2227
Burtersett *N York* 60 SD8989
Burtholme *Cumb* 67 NY5463
Burthorpe Green *Suffk* 32 TL7764
Burtoft *Lincs* 41 TF2635
Burton *Ches* 46 SJ3174
Burton *Ches* 46 SJ5063
Burton *Dorset* 10 SZ1694
Burton *Dyfed* 16 SM9805
Burton *Lincs* 50 SK9574
Burton *Somset* 19 ST1944
Burton *Wilts* 20 ST8179
Burton Agnes *Humb* 57 TA1062
Burton Bradstock *Dorset* 8 SY4889
Burton Coggles *Lincs* 40 SK9725
Burton Dassett *Warwks* 29 SP3951
Burton End *Essex* 31 TL5323
Burton Fleming *Humb* 57 TA0871
Burton Hastings *Warwks* 39 SP4189
Burton in Lonsdale *N York* 54 SD6572
Burton Joyce *Notts* 49 SK6443
Burton Latimer *Nhants* 30 SP9074
Burton Lazars *Leics* 40 SK7716
Burton Leonard *N York* 55 SE3263
Burton Overy *Leics* 39 SP6798
Burton on the Wolds *Leics* 39 SK5821
Burton Pedwardine *Lincs* 50 TF1142
Burton Pidsea *Humb* 57 TA2431
Burton Salmon *N York* 55 SE4927
Burton upon Stather *Humb* 56 SE8717
Burton upon Trent *Staffs* 39 SK2323
Burton's Green *Essex* 24 TL8226
Burton-in-Kendal *Cumb* 59 SD5376
Burtonwood *Ches* 47 SJ5692
Burwardsley *Ches* 46 SJ5156
Burwarton *Shrops* 37 SO6185
Burwash *E Susx* 14 TQ6724
Burwash Common *E Susx* 13 TQ6323
Burwash Weald *E Susx* 13 TQ6523
Burwell *Cambs* 31 TL5866
Burwell *Lincs* 51 TF3579
Burwen *Gwynd* 44 SH4293
Burwick *Ork* 103 ND4484
Bury *Cambs* 41 TL2883
Bury *Gt Man* 54 SD8011
Bury *Somset* 7 SS9427
Bury *W Susx* 12 TQ0113
Bury Green *Herts* 31 TL4521
Bury St. Edmunds *Suffk* 32 TL8564
Burythorpe *N York* 56 SE7964
Busby *Strath* 74 NS5756
Buscot *Wilts* 21 SU2298
Bush *Gramp* 89 NO7565
Bush Bank *H & W* 27 SO4551
Bush Hill Park *Gt Lon* 23 TQ3395
Bushbury *W Mids* 38 SJ9202
Bushey *Herts* 22 TQ1395
Bushey Heath *Herts* 22 TQ1494
Bushley *H & W* 28 SO8734
Bushton *Wilts* 20 SU0677
Bussex *Somset* 8 ST3535
Butcher's Pasture *Essex* 24 TL6024
Butcombe *Avon* 19 ST5161
Butleigh *Somset* 8 ST5233
Butleigh Wootton *Somset* 8 ST5035
Butlers Marston *Warwks* 29 SP3250
Butley *Suffk* 33 TM3650
Buttercrambe *N York* 56 SE7358
Butterdean *Border* 76 NT7964
Butterknowle *Dur* 61 NZ1025
Butterleigh *Devon* 7 SS9708
Buttermere *Cumb* 58 NY1717
Buttershaw *W York* 55 SE1329
Butterstone *Tays* 88 NO0645
Butterton *Staffs* 38 SJ8242
Butterton *Staffs* 48 SK0756
Butterwick *Lincs* 51 TF3845
Butterwick *N York* 63 SE7277
Butterwick *N York* 56 SE9871
Buttington *Powys* 36 SJ2408
Buttonoak *Shrops* 37 SO7578
Buxhall *Suffk* 32 TM0057
Buxted *E Susx* 13 TQ4923
Buxton *Derbys* 48 SK0572
Buxton *Norfk* 43 TG2322
Buxton Heath *Norfk* 43 TG1821
Bwlch *Powys* 27 SO1522
Bwlch-y-cibau *Powys* 36 SJ1717
Bwlch-y-ffridd *Powys* 36 SO0795
Bwlch-y-groes *Dyfed* 17 SN2436
Bwlch-y-sarnau *Powys* 36 SO0374
Bwlchgwyn *Clwyd* 46 SJ2653
Bwlchllan *Dyfed* 34 SN5758
Bwlchtocyn *Gwynd* 34 SH3125
Byers Green *Dur* 61 NZ2233
Byfield *Nhants* 29 SP5152
Byfleet *Surrey* 22 TQ0661
Byford *H & W* 27 SO3942
Byker *T & W* 69 NZ2764
Bylchau *Clwyd* 45 SH9762
Byley *Ches* 47 SJ7269
Byrewalls *Border* 76 NT6642
Byrness *Nthumb* 68 NT7602
Bystock *Devon* 5 SY0283
Bythorn *Cambs* 30 TL0575
Byton *H & W* 27 SO3764
Bywell *Nthumb* 68 NZ0461
Byworth *W Susx* 12 SU9821

C

Cabourne *Lincs* 50 TA1401
Cabrach *Gramp* 94 NJ3826
Cabrach *Strath* 70 NR4964
Cabus *Lancs* 53 SD4948
Cabvie Lodge *Highld* 92 NH1567
Cadbury *Devon* 7 SS9105
Cadder *Strath* 74 NS6072
Caddington *Beds* 30 TL0619
Caddonfoot *Border* 76 NT4535
Cade Street *E Susx* 13 TQ6020
Cadeby *Leics* 39 SK4202
Cadeby *S York* 49 SE5100
Cadeleigh *Devon* 7 SS9108
Cadgwith *Cnwll* 2 SW7214
Cadham *Fife* 83 NO2801
Cadishead *Gt Man* 47 SJ7091
Cadle *W Glam* 17 SS6296
Cadley *Lancs* 53 SD5231
Cadley *Wilts* 21 SU2066
Cadley *Wilts* 21 SU2453
Cadmore End *Bucks* 22 SU7892
Cadnam *Hants* 10 SU3013
Cadney *Humb* 56 TA0103
Cadoxton *S Glam* 18 ST1269
Cadoxton Juxta-Neath *W Glam* 18 SS7598
Caeathro *Gwynd* 44 SH5061
Caenby *Lincs* 50 SK9989
Caeo *Dyfed* 26 SN6740
Caer Farchell *Dyfed* 16 SM7927
Caerau *M Glam* 18 SS8694
Caerau *S Glam* 18 ST1375
Caergeiliog *Gwynd* 44 SH3178
Caergwrle *Clwyd* 46 SJ3057
Caerlanrig *Border* 67 NT3904
Caerleon *Gwent* 19 ST3490
Caernarfon *Gwynd* 44 SH4862
Caerphilly *M Glam* 19 ST1587
Caersws *Powys* 36 SO0392
Caerwedros *Dyfed* 34 SN3755
Caerwent *Gwent* 19 ST4790
Caerwys *Clwyd* 46 SJ1272
Cairnbaan *Strath* 71 NR8390
Cairnbrogie *Gramp* 95 NJ8527
Cairnbulg *Gramp* 95 NK0365
Cairncross *Border* 77 NT8963
Cairncurran *Strath* 73 NS3170
Cairndow *Strath* 80 NN1810
Cairneyhill *Fife* 82 NT0486
Cairnfield House *Gramp* 94 NJ4162
Cairngarroch *D & G* 64 NX0549
Cairngrassie *Gramp* 89 NO9095
Cairnhall *D & G* 66 NX9086
Cairnie *Gramp* 94 NJ4844
Cairnorrie *Gramp* 95 NJ8641
Cairnryan *D & G* 64 NX0668
Cairnty *Gramp* 94 NJ3352
Caister-on-Sea *Norfk* 43 TG5112
Caistor *Lincs* 50 TA1101
Caistor St. Edmund *Norfk* 43 TG2303
Calbourne *IOW* 10 SZ4286
Calcot *Clwyd* 46 SJ1674
Calcot *Gloucs* 28 SP0810
Calcot Row *Berks* 22 SU6771
Calcots *Gramp* 94 NJ2563
Caldbeck *Cumb* 58 NY3240
Caldecote *Cambs* 40 TL1488
Caldecote *Cambs* 31 TL3456
Caldecote *Herts* 31 TL2338
Caldecote Highfields *Cambs* 31 TL3559
Caldecott *Leics* 40 SP8693
Caldecott *Nhants* 30 SP9868
Caldecott *Oxon* 21 SU4996
Calder Bridge *Cumb* 58 NY0306
Calder Grove *W York* 55 SE3016
Calder Vale *Lancs* 53 SD5345
Calderbank *Strath* 74 NS7663
Caldercruix *Strath* 74 NS8167
Caldermill *Strath* 74 NS6641
Caldicot *Gwent* 19 ST4888
Caldwell *N York* 61 NZ1613
Calfsound *Ork* 103 HY5738
Calgary *Strath* 78 NM3751
Califer *Gramp* 93 NJ0857
California *Cent* 74 NS9076
California *Derbys* 39 SK3335
California *Norfk* 43 TG5115
Calke *Derbys* 39 SK3721
Callakille *Highld* 91 NG6955
Callander *Cent* 81 NN6207
Callanish *W Isls* 102 NB2133
Callert Cottage *Highld* 86 NN1060
Callestick *Cnwll* 2 SW7750
Calligarry *Highld* 84 NG6203
Callington *Cnwll* 4 SX3669
Callow *H & W* 27 SO4934
Callow End *H & W* 28 SO8350
Callow Hill *Wilts* 20 SU0384
Calmore *Hants* 10 SU3414
Calmsden *Gloucs* 28 SP0508
Calne *Wilts* 20 ST9971
Calshot *Hants* 11 SU4701
Calstock *Cnwll* 4 SX4368
Calstone Wellington *Wilts* 20 SU0268
Calthorpe *Norfk* 43 TG1831
Calthorpe Street *Norfk* 43 TG4025
Calthwaite *Cumb* 59 NY4640
Calton *N York* 54 SD9059
Calton *Staffs* 48 SK1049
Calveley *Ches* 47 SJ5958
Calver *Derbys* 48 SK2374
Calverhall *Shrops* 37 SJ6037
Calverleigh *Devon* 7 SS9214
Calverton *Bucks* 30 SP7939
Calverton *Notts* 49 SK6149
Calvine *Tays* 87 NN8065
Calvo *Cumb* 67 NY1453
Calzeat *Border* 75 NT1135
Cam *Gloucs* 20 ST7599
Camas Luinie *Highld* 85 NG9428
Camasachoirce *Highld* 79 NM7660
Camasine *Highld* 79 NM7561
Camastianavaig *Highld* 84 NG5039
Camasunary *Highld* 84 NG5118
Camault Muir *Highld* 92 NH5040
Camber *E Susx* 15 TQ9618
Camberley *Surrey* 22 SU8860
Camberwell *Gt Lon* 23 TQ3276
Camblesforth *N York* 56 SE6425
Cambo *Nthumb* 68 NZ0285
Camborne *Cnwll* 2 SW6440
Cambridge *Cambs* 31 TL4558
Cambridge *Gloucs* 20 SO7403
Cambrose *Cnwll* 2 SW6845
Cambus *Cent* 82 NS8594
Cambus O' May *Gramp* 88 NO4198
Cambusavie Platform *Highld* 97 NH7696
Cambusbarron *Cent* 81 NS7792
Cambuskenneth *Cent* 81 NS8094
Cambusmoon *Strath* 81 NS4285
Cambuswallace *Strath* 75 NT0438
Camden Town *Gt Lon* 23 TQ2883
Cameley *Avon* 19 ST6157
Camelford *Cnwll* 3 SX1083
Camelon *Cent* 82 NS8680
Camer's Green *H & W* 28 SO7735
Camerory *Highld* 93 NJ0131
Camerton *Avon* 20 ST6857
Camerton *Cumb* 58 NY0330
Camghouran *Tays* 87 NN5556
Cammachmore *Gramp* 89 NO9195
Cammeringham *Lincs* 50 SK9482
Camore *Highld* 97 NH7889
Campbeltown *Strath* 72 NR7120
Cample *D & G* 66 NX8993
Campmuir *Tays* 82 NO2137
Camps *Loth* 75 NT0968
Camps End *Cambs* 31 TL6142
Campsall *S York* 56 SE5413
Campsie *Strath* 81 NS6079
Campsie Ash *Suffk* 33 TM3356
Campton *Beds* 30 TL1238
Camptown *Border* 68 NT6813
Camrose *Dyfed* 16 SM9220
Camserney *Tays* 87 NN8149
Camster *Highld* 100 ND2642
Camusnagaul *Highld* 91 NH0589
Camusnagaul *Highld* 86 NN0874
Camusteel *Highld* 91 NG7042
Camusterrach *Highld* 85 NG7141
Canada *Hants* 10 SU2818
Candacraig *Gramp* 88 NO3499
Candlesby *Lincs* 51 TF4567
Candyburn *Strath* 75 NT0741
Cane End *Oxon* 22 SU6779
Canewdon *Essex* 24 TQ9094
Canfield End *Essex* 24 TL5821
Canford Cliffs *Dorset* 10 SZ0589
Canford Magna *Dorset* 10 SZ0398
Canisbay *Highld* 100 ND3472
Canley *W Mids* 39 SP3077
Cann *Dorset* 9 ST8721
Cannich *Highld* 92 NH3331
Canning Town *Gt Lon* 23 TQ4081
Cannington *Somset* 19 ST2539
Cannock *Staffs* 38 SJ9810
Cannon Bridge *H & W* 27 SO4340
Canon Frome *H & W* 27 SO6443
Canon Pyon *H & W* 27 SO4548
Canonbie *D & G* 67 NY3976
Canons Ashby *Nhants* 29 SP5750
Canonstown *Cnwll* 2 SW5335
Canterbury *Kent* 15 TR1457
Cantley *Norfk* 43 TG3704
Cantley *S York* 49 SE6202
Canton *S Glam* 19 ST1676
Cantraywood *Highld* 93 NH7847
Cantsfield *Lancs* 54 SD6272
Canvey Island *Essex* 24 TQ7983
Canwick *Lincs* 50 SK9869
Canworthy Water *Cnwll* 4 SX2291
Caol *Highld* 86 NN1175
Caoles *Strath* 78 NM0848
Caonich *Highld* 86 NN0692
Capel *Kent* 13 TQ6344
Capel *Surrey* 12 TQ1740
Capel Bangor *Dyfed* 35 SN6580
Capel Betws Lleucu *Dyfed* 34 SN6058
Capel Coch *Gwynd* 44 SH4682
Capel Curig *Gwynd* 45 SH7258
Capel Dewi *Dyfed* 17 SN4542
Capel Dewi *Dyfed* 17 SN4720
Capel Garmon *Gwynd* 45 SH8155
Capel Gwynfe *Dyfed* 26 SN7222
Capel Hendre *Dyfed* 17 SN5911
Capel Iwan *Dyfed* 17 SN2936
Capel le Ferne *Kent* 15 TR2539
Capel Mawr *Gwynd* 44 SH4171
Capel Seion *Dyfed* 35 SN6379
Capel St. Andrew *Suffk* 33 TM3748
Capel St. Mary *Suffk* 25 TM0838
Capel-Dewi *Dyfed* 35 SN6282
Capelles *Guern* 101 GN5211
Capelulo *Gwynd* 45 SH7476
Capenhurst *Ches* 46 SJ3673
Capheaton *Nthumb* 68 NZ0380
Caplaw *Strath* 73 NS4458
Cappercleuch *Border* 75 NT2423
Capton *Devon* 5 SX8353
Capton *Somset* 18 ST0839
Caputh *Tays* 82 NO0840
Car Colston *Notts* 49 SK7142
Carbeth Inn *Cent* 81 NS5279
Carbis Bay *Cnwll* 2 SW5238
Carbost *Highld* 84 NG3731
Carbost *Highld* 90 NG4248
Carbrook *S York* 49 SK3889
Carbrooke *Norfk* 42 TF9402
Cardenden *Fife* 82 NT2195
Cardiff *S Glam* 19 ST1876
Cardigan *Dyfed* 17 SN1746
Cardinal's Green *Cambs* 31 TL6146
Cardington *Beds* 30 TL0847
Cardington *Shrops* 37 SO5095
Cardinham *Cnwll* 3 SX1268
Cardow *Gramp* 94 NJ1943
Cardrain *D & G* 64 NX1231
Cardrona *Border* 75 NT3038
Cardross *Strath* 80 NS3477
Cardryne *D & G* 64 NX1132
Cardurnock *Cumb* 67 NY1758
Careby *Lincs* 40 TF0216
Careston *Tays* 89 NO5260
Carew *Dyfed* 16 SN0403
Carew Cheriton *Dyfed* 16 SN0402
Carew Newton *Dyfed* 16 SN0404
Carey *H & W* 27 SO5730
Carfin *Strath* 74 NS7759
Carfraemill *Border* 76 NT5053

Cargate Green Childer Thornton

Cargate Green Norfk 43 TG3912
Cargen D & G 66 NX9672
Cargenbridge D & G 66 NX9575
Cargill Tays 82 NO1536
Cargo Cumb 67 NY3659
Cargreen Cnwll 4 SX4362
Carham Nthumb 76 NT7938
Carhampton Somset 7 ST0042
Carharrack Cnwll 2 SW7341
Carie Tays 87 NN6257
Carinish W Isls 102 NF8260
Carisbrooke IOW 11 SZ4888
Cark Cumb 59 SD3676
Carkeel Cnwll 4 SX4160
Carlbury Dur 61 NZ2115
Carlby Lincs 40 TF0413
Carlcroft Nthumb 68 NT8311
Carleen Cnwll 2 SW6130
Carleton N York 54 SD9749
Carleton Forehoe Norfk 43 TG0905
Carleton Rode Norfk 43 TM1093
Carleton St. Peter Norfk 43 TG3402
Carlincraig Gramp 95 NJ6743
Carlingcott Avon 20 ST6958
Carlisle Cumb 67 NY3956
Carlops Border 75 NT1656
Carloway W Isls 102 NB2043
Carlton Beds 30 SP9555
Carlton Cambs 32 TL6452
Carlton Cleve 62 NZ3921
Carlton Leics 39 SK3904
Carlton N York 42 NZ5004
Carlton N York 61 SE0684
Carlton N York 62 SE6086
Carlton N York 56 SE6423
Carlton Notts 49 SK6041
Carlton S York 55 SE3610
Carlton Suffk 33 TM3764
Carlton W York 55 SE3327
Carlton Colville Suffk 33 TM5189
Carlton Curlieu Leics 39 SP6997
Carlton Green Cambs 32 TL6451
Carlton Husthwaite N York 62 SE4976
Carlton in Lindrick Notts 49 SK5883
Carlton Miniott N York 62 SE3981
Carlton Scroop Lincs 50 SK9445
Carlton-le-Moorland Lincs 50 SK9058
Carlton-on-Trent Notts 50 SK7963
Carluke Strath 74 NS8450
Carmacoup Strath 74 NS7927
Carmarthen Dyfed 17 SN3919
Carmel Dyfed 17 SN5816
Carmel Gwynd 44 SH4954
Carmichael Strath 75 NS9238
Carmunnock Strath 74 NS5957
Carmyle Strath 74 NS6462
Carmyllie Tays 89 NO5442
Carn Brea Cnwll 2 SW6841
Carn-gorm Highld 85 NG9520
Carnaby Humb 57 TA1465
Carnach W Isls 102 NG2297
Carnbee Fife 83 NO5206
Carnbo Tays 82 NO0503
Carndu Highld 85 NG8827
Carnduff Strath 74 NS6646
Carnell Strath 73 NS4731
Carnforth Lancs 53 SD4970
Carnhell Green Cnwll 2 SW6137
Carnie Gramp 89 NJ8005
Carnkie Cnwll 2 SW7134
Carno Powys 35 SN9696
Carnoch Highld 85 NM8696
Carnock Fife 82 NT0489
Carnon Downs Cnwll 2 SW7940
Carnousie Gramp 94 NJ6650
Carnoustie Tays 83 NO5534
Carnwath Strath 75 NS9846
Carol Green W Mids 39 SP2577
Carperby N York 61 SE0089
Carr Gate W York 55 SE3123
Carr Shield Nthumb 68 NY8047
Carradale Strath 72 NR8138
Carrbridge Highld 93 NH9022
Carrefour Jersey 101 JS1213
Carreglefn Gwynd 44 SH3889
Carrhouse Humb 56 SE7706
Carrick Strath 71 NR9086
Carrick Castle Strath 80 NS1994
Carriden Cent 82 NT0181
Carrington Gt Man 47 SJ7492
Carrington Loth 75 NT3160
Carrog Clwyd 46 SJ1043
Carron Cent 82 NS8882
Carron Gramp 94 NJ2241
Carron Bridge Cent 81 NS7483
Carronbridge D & G 66 NX8698
Carronshore Cent 82 NS8983
Carruth House Strath 73 NS3566
Carrutherstown D & G 67 NY1071
Carrville Dur 69 NZ3043
Carsaig Strath 79 NM5421
Carscreugh D & G 64 NX2260
Carse Gray Tays 88 NO4553
Carseriggan D & G 64 NX3167
Carsethorn D & G 66 NX9959
Carshalton Gt Lon 23 TQ2764
Carsington Derbys 48 SK2553
Carskey Strath 72 NR6508
Carsluith D & G 65 NX4854
Carsphairn D & G 65 NX5693
Carstairs Strath 75 NS9345
Carstairs Junction Strath 75 NS9545
Carterton Oxon 29 SP2806
Carthew Cnwll 3 SX0056
Carthorpe N York 61 SE3083
Cartland Strath 74 NS8646
Cartmel Cumb 59 SD3878
Carway Dyfed 17 SN4606
Cashe's Green Gloucs 28 SO8205
Cassington Oxon 29 SP4511
Cassop Colliery Dur 62 NZ3438
Castel Guern 101 GN5108
Casterton Lancs 60 SD6279
Castle Acre Norfk 42 TF8115
Castle Ashby Nhants 30 SP8659
Castle Bolton N York 61 SE0391
Castle Bromwich W Mids 38 SP1489
Castle Bytham Lincs 40 SK9818
Castle Caereinion Powys 36 SJ1605
Castle Camps Cambs 32 TL6242
Castle Carrock Cumb 67 NY5455
Castle Cary Somset 9 ST6432
Castle Combe Wilts 20 ST8477
Castle Donington Leics 39 SK4427
Castle Douglas D & G 65 NX7662
Castle Eaton Wilts 20 SU1496
Castle Eden Dur 62 NZ4238
Castle Frome H & W 28 SO6645
Castle Gresley Derbys 39 SK2717
Castle Hedingham Essex 24 TL7835
Castle Hill Suffk 33 TM1446
Castle Kennedy D & G 64 NX1159
Castle Lachlan Strath 80 NS0195
Castle O'er D & G 67 NY2492
Castle Pulverbatch Shrops 36 SJ4202
Castle Rising Norfk 42 TF6624
Castle Stuart Highld 93 NH7449
Castlebay W Isls 102 NL6698
Castlebythe Dyfed 16 SN0229
Castlecary Strath 81 NS7878
Castlecraig Highld 93 NH8269
Castleford W York 55 SE4225
Castlehill Border 75 NT2135
Castlehill Highld 100 ND1968
Castlemartin Dyfed 16 SR9198
Castlemorton H & W 28 SO7937
Castleside Dur 68 NZ0748
Castlethorpe Bucks 30 SP8044
Castleton Border 67 NY5189
Castleton Derbys 48 SK1582
Castleton Gt Man 54 SD8810
Castleton Gwent 19 ST2583
Castleton N York 62 NZ6807
Castletown Highld 100 ND1967
Castletown IOM 52 SC2667
Castletown T & W 69 NZ3658
Castley N York 55 SE2646
Caston Norfk 42 TL9597
Castor Cambs 40 TL1298
Cat's Ash Gwent 19 ST3790
Catacol Strath 72 NR9149
Catchall Cnwll 2 SW4228
Catcliffe S York 49 SK4288
Catcomb Wilts 20 SU0076
Catcott Somset 19 ST3939
Catcott Burtle Somset 19 ST4043
Caterham Surrey 23 TQ3455
Catfield Norfk 43 TG3821
Catfirth Shet 103 HU4354
Catford Gt Lon 23 TQ3773
Catforth Lancs 53 SD4735
Cathcart Strath 74 NS5860
Cathedine Powys 26 SO1425
Catherington Hants 11 SU6914
Catherston Leweston Dorset 8 SY3694
Cathpair Border 76 NT4646
Catisfield Hants 11 SU5506
Catlodge Highld 87 NN6392
Catmere End Essex 31 TL4939
Catmore Berks 21 SU4580
Caton Lancs 53 SD5364
Caton Green Lancs 53 SD5565
Catrine Strath 74 NS5225
Catsfield E Susx 14 TQ7213
Catshill H & W 38 SO9573
Cattadale Strath 72 NR6710
Cattal N York 55 SE4454
Cattawade Suffk 25 TM1033
Catterall Lancs 53 SD4942
Catterick N York 61 SE2397
Catterick Bridge N York 61 SE2299
Catterlen Cumb 59 NY4833
Catterton N York 55 SE5145
Catteshall Surrey 12 SU9844
Catthorpe Leics 39 SP5578
Cattistock Dorset 9 SY5999
Catton Cumb 68 NY8257
Catton N York 62 SE3678
Catton Norfk 43 TG2312
Catwick Humb 57 TA1345
Catworth Cambs 30 TL0873
Caudle Green Gloucs 28 SO9410
Caulcott Oxon 29 SP5024
Cauldcots Tays 89 NO6547
Cauldhame Cent 81 NS6493
Cauldmill Border 76 NT5315
Cauldon Staffs 48 SK0749
Cauldwell Derbys 39 SK2517
Caulkerbush D & G 66 NX9257
Caulside D & G 67 NY4480
Caundle Marsh Dorset 9 ST6713
Caunton Notts 50 SK7460
Causeway End D & G 64 NX4260
Causeway End Essex 24 TL6819
Causewayend Strath 75 NT0336
Causewayhead Cent 81 NS8095
Causey Park Nthumb 69 NZ1794
Causeyend Gramp 95 NJ9419
Cavendish Suffk 32 TL8046
Cavenham Suffk 32 TL7670
Caversfield Oxon 29 SP5825
Caversham Berks 22 SU7274
Caverswall Staffs 48 SJ9542
Caverton Mill Border 76 NT7425
Cawdor Highld 93 NH8450
Cawood N York 56 SE5737
Cawsand Cnwll 4 SX4350
Cawston Norfk 43 TG1323
Cawthorne S York 55 SE2808
Caxton Cambs 31 TL3058
Caynham Shrops 37 SO5573
Caythorpe Lincs 50 SK9348
Caythorpe Notts 49 SK6845
Cayton N York 63 TA0583
Ceannacroc Lodge Highld 92 NH2211
Cefn Gwent 19 ST2788
Cefn Cribwr M Glam 18 SS8582
Cefn-brith Clwyd 45 SH9350
Cefn-mawr Clwyd 36 SJ2842
Cefn-y-pant Dyfed 17 SN1925
Cefngorwydd Powys 26 SN9045
Cellarhead Staffs 48 SJ9547
Cemaes Gwynd 44 SH3793
Cemmaes Powys 35 SH8406
Cemmaes Road Powys 35 SH8104
Cenarth Dyfed 17 SN2641
Ceres Fife 83 NO4011
Cerne Abbas Dorset 9 ST6601
Cerney Wick Gloucs 20 SU0796
Cerrigceinwen Gwynd 44 SH4274
Cerrigydrudion Clwyd 45 SH9548
Ceunant Gwynd 44 SH5361
Chaceley Gloucs 28 SO8530
Chacewater Cnwll 2 SW7544
Chackmore Bucks 30 SP6835
Chacombe Nhants 29 SP4944
Chadbury H & W 28 SP0146
Chadderton Gt Man 54 SD9005
Chaddesden Derbys 39 SK3836
Chaddesley Corbett H & W 38 SO8973
Chaddlehanger Devon 4 SX4678
Chaddleworth Berks 21 SU4178
Chadlington Oxon 29 SP3321
Chadshunt Warwks 29 SP3453
Chadwell Leics 40 SK7824
Chadwell Heath Gt Lon 23 TQ4888
Chadwell St. Mary Essex 24 TQ6478
Chadwick H & W 28 SO8369
Chadwick End W Mids 39 SP2073
Chaffcombe Somset 8 ST3510
Chagford Devon 5 SX7087
Chailey E Susx 13 TQ3919
Chainhurst Kent 14 TQ7248
Chaldon Surrey 23 TQ3155
Chaldon Herring or East Chaldon Dorset 9 SY7983
Chale IOW 11 SZ4877
Chale Green IOW 11 SZ4879
Chalfont Common Bucks 22 TQ0092
Chalfont St. Giles Bucks 22 SU9893
Chalfont St. Peter Bucks 22 TQ0090
Chalford Gloucs 20 SO8802
Chalford Wilts 20 ST8650
Chalgrove Oxon 21 SU6396
Chalk Kent 14 TQ6773
Chalkwell Kent 14 TQ8963
Challacombe Devon 7 SS6940
Challock Lees Kent 15 TR0050
Chalton Beds 30 TL0326
Chalton Hants 11 SU7315
Chalvey Berks 22 SU9679
Chalvington E Susx 13 TQ5109
Chandler's Cross Herts 22 TQ0698
Chandler's Ford Hants 10 SU4319
Chantry Somset 20 ST7146
Chantry Suffk 33 TM1443
Chapel Fife 83 NT2593
Chapel Allerton Somset 19 ST4050
Chapel Allerton W York 55 SE3037
Chapel Amble Cnwll 3 SW9975
Chapel Brampton Nhants 30 SP7266
Chapel Chorlton Staffs 37 SJ8137
Chapel Green Warwks 29 SP4660
Chapel Haddlesey N York 56 SE5826
Chapel Hill Gramp 95 NK0635
Chapel Hill Gwent 37 SO5399
Chapel Hill Lincs 51 TF2054
Chapel Hill N York 55 SE3446
Chapel Lawn Shrops 36 SO3176
Chapel Leigh Somset 8 ST1229
Chapel le Dale N York 60 SD7377
Chapel of Garioch Gramp 95 NJ7124
Chapel Rossan D & G 64 NX1044
Chapel Row Berks 21 SU5769
Chapel St. Leonards Lincs 51 TF5672
Chapel Stile Cumb 58 NY3205
Chapel-en-le-Frith Derbys 48 SK0580
Chapelend Way Essex 32 TL7039
Chapelhall Strath 74 NS7862
Chapelknowe D & G 67 NY3173
Chapelton Devon 6 SS5726
Chapelton Strath 74 NS6848
Chapelton Tays 89 NO6247
Chapeltown Gramp 94 NJ2320
Chapeltown Lancs 54 SD7315
Chapeltown S York 49 SK3596
Chapmans Well Devon 4 SX3593
Chapmanslade Wilts 20 ST8247
Chapmore End Herts 31 TL3216
Chappel Essex 24 TL8928
Chard Somset 8 ST3208
Chard Junction Somset 8 ST3404
Chardleigh Green Somset 8 ST3110
Chardstock Devon 8 ST3004
Charfield Avon 20 ST7292
Charing Kent 14 TQ9549
Charingworth Gloucs 29 SP1939
Charlbury Oxon 29 SP3519
Charlcombe Avon 20 ST7467
Charlcutt Wilts 20 ST9875
Charlecote Warwks 29 SP2656
Charles Devon 7 SS6832
Charles Tye Suffk 32 TM0252
Charleston Tays 88 NO3845
Charlestown Cnwll 3 SX0351
Charlestown Fife 82 NT0683
Charlestown Gramp 89 NJ9300
Charlestown Gt Man 47 SD8100
Charlestown Highld 91 NG8174
Charlestown Highld 92 NH6448
Charlestown W York 54 SD9726
Charlestown W York 55 SE1638
Charlesworth Derbys 48 SK0092
Charlinch Somset 19 ST2338
Charlton Gt Lon 23 TQ4178
Charlton H & W 28 SP0045
Charlton Nhants 29 SP5335
Charlton Nthumb 68 NY8184
Charlton Oxon 21 SU4088
Charlton Shrops 37 SJ5911
Charlton Somset 8 ST2926
Charlton W Susx 11 SU8812
Charlton Wilts 9 ST9022
Charlton Wilts 20 ST9588
Charlton Wilts 20 SU1156
Charlton Wilts 10 SU1723
Charlton Abbots Gloucs 28 SP0324
Charlton Adam Somset 8 ST5328
Charlton Horethorne Somset 9 ST6623
Charlton Kings Gloucs 28 SO9621
Charlton Mackrell Somset 8 ST5328
Charlton Marshall Dorset 9 ST9004
Charlton Musgrove Somset 9 ST7229
Charlton on the Hill Dorset 9 ST8903
Charlton-on-Otmoor Oxon 29 SP5616
Charlwood Hants 11 SU6731
Charlwood Surrey 12 TQ2441
Charminster Dorset 9 SY6792
Charmouth Dorset 8 SY3693
Charndon Bucks 30 SP6724
Charney Bassett Oxon 21 SU3894
Charnock Richard Lancs 53 SD5515
Charsfield Suffk 33 TM2556
Chart Sutton Kent 14 TQ8049
Charter Alley Hants 21 SU5958
Charterhall Border 76 NT7647
Charterhouse Somset 19 ST4955
Chartershall Cent 81 NS7990
Chartham Kent 15 TR1054
Chartham Hatch Kent 15 TR1056
Chartridge Bucks 22 SP9303
Charwelton Nhants 29 SP5356
Chastleton Oxon 29 SP2429
Chasty Devon 6 SS3402
Chatburn Lancs 54 SD7644
Chatcull Staffs 37 SJ7934
Chatham Kent 14 TQ7567
Chatham Green Essex 24 TL7115
Chathill Nthumb 77 NU1827
Chattenden Kent 14 TQ7572
Chatteris Cambs 41 TL3985
Chatterton Lancs 54 SD7918
Chattisham Suffk 33 TM0942
Chatto Border 76 NT7717
Chatton Nthumb 77 NU0528
Chawleigh Devon 7 SS7112
Chawton Hants 11 SU7037
Cheadle Gt Man 47 SJ8688
Cheadle Staffs 48 SK0043
Cheadle Hulme Gt Man 47 SJ8786
Cheam Gt Lon 23 TQ2463
Chearsley Bucks 22 SP7110
Chebsey Staffs 38 SJ8528
Checkendon Oxon 22 SU6683
Checkley Ches 47 SJ7346
Checkley Staffs 48 SK0237
Chedburgh Suffk 32 TL7957
Cheddar Somset 19 ST4553
Cheddington Bucks 30 SP9217
Cheddleton Staffs 48 SJ9752
Cheddon Fitzpaine Somset 8 ST2427
Chedgrave Norfk 43 TM3699
Chedington Dorset 8 ST4805
Chediston Suffk 33 TM3577
Chedworth Gloucs 28 SP0512
Chedzoy Somset 19 ST3437
Cheetham Hill Gt Man 47 SD8401
Cheetwood Gt Man 47 SJ8399
Cheldon Devon 7 SS7313
Chelford Ches 47 SJ8174
Chellaston Derbys 39 SK3730
Chellington Beds 30 SP9555
Chelmarsh Shrops 37 SO7288
Chelmondiston Suffk 25 TM2037
Chelmorton Derbys 48 SK1169
Chelmsford Essex 24 TL7007
Chelmsley Wood W Mids 38 SP1887
Chelsea Gt Lon 23 TQ2778
Chelsfield Gt Lon 23 TQ4864
Chelsworth Suffk 32 TL9748
Cheltenham Gloucs 28 SO9422
Chelveston Nhants 30 SP9969
Chelvey Avon 19 ST4668
Chelwood Avon 19 ST6361
Chelwood Gate E Susx 13 TQ4130
Chelworth Lower Green Wilts 20 SU0892
Chelworth Upper Green Wilts 20 SU0893
Cheney Longville Shrops 36 SO4284
Chenies Bucks 22 TQ0198
Chepstow Gwent 19 ST5393
Cherhill Wilts 20 SU0370
Cherington Gloucs 20 ST9098
Cherington Warwks 29 SP2936
Cheriton Hants 11 SU5828
Cheriton Kent 15 TR2037
Cheriton W Glam 17 SS4593
Cheriton Bishop Devon 5 SX7793
Cheriton Fitzpaine Devon 7 SS8606
Cheriton or Stackpole Elidor Dyfed 16 SR9897
Cherrington Shrops 37 SJ6619
Cherry Burton Humb 56 SE9841
Cherry Hinton Cambs 31 TL4856
Cherry Orchard H & W 28 SO8553
Cherry Willingham Lincs 50 TF0272
Chertsey Surrey 22 TQ0466
Cheselbourne Dorset 9 SY7699
Chesham Bucks 22 SP9601
Chesham Gt Man 54 SD8012
Chesham Bois Bucks 22 SU9699
Cheshunt Herts 23 TL3502
Cheslyn Hay Staffs 38 SJ9707
Chessetts Wood Warwks 38 SP1873
Chessington Surrey 23 TQ1863
Chester Ches 46 SJ4066
Chester Moor Dur 69 NZ2649
Chester-le-Street T & W 69 NZ2751
Chesterblade Somset 20 ST6641
Chesterfield Derbys 49 SK3871
Chesterhill Loth 76 NT3764
Chesters Border 76 NT6022
Chesters Border 68 NT6210
Chesterton Cambs 40 TL1295
Chesterton Cambs 31 TL4660
Chesterton Gloucs 20 SP0100
Chesterton Oxon 29 SP5621
Chesterton Shrops 37 SO7897
Chesterton Green Warwks 29 SP3558
Chesterwood Nthumb 68 NY8364
Chestfield Kent 15 TR1365
Cheston Devon 5 SX6858
Cheswardine Shrops 37 SJ7130
Cheswick Nthumb 77 NU0346
Chetnote Dorset 9 ST6008
Chettisham Cambs 41 TL5483
Chettle Dorset 9 ST9513
Chetton Shrops 37 SO6690
Chetwode Bucks 29 SP6429
Chetwynd Shrops 37 SJ7321
Chetwynd Aston Shrops 37 SJ7517
Cheveley Cambs 32 TL6861
Chevening Kent 23 TQ4857
Chevington Suffk 32 TL7859
Chevington Drift Nthumb 69 NZ2598
Chevithorne Devon 7 SS9715
Chew Magna Avon 19 ST5763
Chew Stoke Avon 19 ST5561
Chewton Keynsham Avon 19 ST6566
Chewton Mendip Somset 19 ST5953
Chicheley Bucks 30 SP9046
Chichester W Susx 11 SU8604
Chickerell Dorset 9 SY6480
Chicklade Wilts 9 ST9134
Chidden Hants 11 SU6517
Chiddingfold Surrey 12 SU9635
Chiddingly E Susx 13 TQ5414
Chiddingstone Kent 13 TQ5045
Chiddingstone Causeway Kent 13 TQ5246
Chideock Dorset 8 SY4292
Chidham W Susx 11 SU7903
Chidswell W York 55 SE2623
Chieveley Berks 21 SU4774
Chignall Smealy Essex 24 TL6611
Chignall St. James Essex 24 TL6610
Chigwell Essex 23 TQ4494
Chigwell Row Essex 23 TQ4693
Chilbolton Hants 21 SU3940
Chilcomb Hants 11 SU5028
Chilcombe Dorset 8 SY5291
Chilcompton Somset 19 ST6451
Chilcote Leics 39 SK2811
Child Okeford Dorset 9 ST8312
Child's Ercall Shrops 37 SJ6625
Childer Thornton Ches 46 SJ3677

Childrey Colerne

Childrey *Oxon*	21	SU3687
Childswickham *H & W*	28	SP0738
Childwall *Mersyd*	46	SJ4189
Childwick Green *Herts*	22	TL1410
Chilfrome *Dorset*	9	SY5898
Chilgrove *W Susx*	11	SU8314
Chilham *Kent*	15	TR0653
Chillaton *Devon*	4	SX4381
Chillenden *Kent*	15	TR2753
Chillerton *IOW*	11	SZ4883
Chillesford *Suffk*	33	TM3852
Chillingham *Nthumb*	77	NU0525
Chillington *Devon*	5	SX7942
Chillington *Somset*	8	ST3811
Chilmark *Wilts*	9	ST9732
Chilmington Green *Kent*	15	TQ9840
Chilson *Oxon*	29	SP3119
Chilsworthy *Cnwll*	4	SX4172
Chilsworthy *Devon*	6	SS3206
Chilthorne Domer *Somset*	8	ST5219
Chilton *Bucks*	22	SP6811
Chilton *Oxon*	21	SU4885
Chilton Candover *Hants*	21	SU5940
Chilton Cantelo *Somset*	9	ST5722
Chilton Foliat *Wilts*	21	SU3170
Chilton Polden *Somset*	19	ST3740
Chilton Street *Suffk*	32	TL7546
Chilton Trinity *Somset*	19	ST2939
Chilworth *Hants*	10	SU4018
Chimney *Oxon*	21	SP3501
Chineham *Hants*	21	SU6555
Chingford *Gt Lon*	23	TQ3894
Chinley *Derbys*	48	SK0482
Chinnor *Oxon*	22	SP7501
Chipnall *Shrops*	37	SJ7231
Chippenham *Cambs*	32	TL6669
Chippenham *Wilts*	20	ST9173
Chipperfield *Herts*	22	TL0401
Chipping *Herts*	31	TL3531
Chipping *Lancs*	54	SD6243
Chipping Campden *Gloucs*	28	SP1539
Chipping Norton *Oxon*	29	SP3127
Chipping Ongar *Essex*	24	TL5503
Chipping Sodbury *Avon*	20	ST7282
Chipping Warden *Nhants*	29	SP4948
Chipstable *Somset*	7	ST0427
Chipstead *Kent*	23	TQ5056
Chipstead *Surrey*	23	TQ2756
Chirbury *Shrops*	36	SO2698
Chirk *Clwyd*	36	SJ2837
Chirnside *Border*	77	NT8756
Chirnsidebridge *Border*	77	NT8556
Chirton *Wilts*	20	SU0757
Chisbury *Wilts*	21	SU2766
Chiselborough *Somset*	8	ST4614
Chiseldon *Wilts*	21	SU1880
Chisholme *Border*	67	NT4112
Chislehampton *Oxon*	21	SU5999
Chislehurst *Gt Lon*	23	TQ4470
Chislet *Kent*	15	TR2264
Chisley *W York*	54	SE0028
Chiswellgreen *Herts*	22	TL1304
Chiswick *Gt Lon*	23	TQ2078
Chisworth *Derbys*	48	SJ9991
Chithurst *W Susx*	11	SU8423
Chittering *Cambs*	31	TL4969
Chitterne *Wilts*	20	ST9843
Chittlehamholt *Devon*	7	SS6520
Chittlehampton *Devon*	7	SS6325
Chittlehampton *Devon*	7	SS6511
Chittoe *Wilts*	20	ST9566
Chivelstone *Devon*	5	SX7838
Chlenry *D & G*	64	NX1260
Chobham *Surrey*	22	SU9762
Cholderton *Wilts*	21	SU2242
Cholesbury *Bucks*	22	SP9307
Chollerton *Nthumb*	68	NY9372
Cholsey *Oxon*	21	SU5886
Cholstrey *H & W*	27	SO4659
Chop Gate *N York*	62	SE5599
Choppington *T & W*	69	NZ2484
Chopwell *T & W*	69	NZ1158
Chorley *Ches*	47	SJ5751
Chorley *Lancs*	54	SD5817
Chorley *Shrops*	37	SO6983
Chorleywood *Herts*	22	TQ0396
Chorleywood West *Herts*	22	TQ0296
Chorlton *Ches*	47	SJ7250
Chorlton Lane *Ches*	46	SJ4547
Chorlton-cum-Hardy *Gt Man*	47	SJ8193
Choulton *Shrops*	36	SO3788
Chowley *Ches*	46	SJ4756
Chrishall *Essex*	31	TL4439
Chrisswell *Strath*	80	NS2274
Christchurch *Cambs*	41	TL4996
Christchurch *Dorset*	10	SZ1592
Christian Malford *Wilts*	20	ST9678
Christleton *Ches*	46	SJ4465
Christmas Common *Oxon*	22	SU7193
Christon *Avon*	19	ST3757
Christon Bank *Nthumb*	77	NU2123
Christow *Devon*	5	SX8385
Christskirk *Gramp*	94	NJ6027
Chudleigh *Devon*	5	SX8679
Chudleigh Knighton *Devon*	5	SX8477
Chulmleigh *Devon*	7	SS6814
Church *Lancs*	54	SD7429
Church Ashton *Shrops*	37	SJ7317
Church Brampton *Nhants*	30	SP7165
Church Broughton *Derbys*	39	SK2033
Church Crookham *Hants*	22	SU8051
Church Eaton *Staffs*	38	SJ8417
Church End *Beds*	31	TL1937
Church End *Essex*	24	TL7228
Church End *Gt Lon*	23	TQ2490
Church End *Hants*	22	SU6756
Church End *Herts*	31	TL4422
Church Enstone *Oxon*	29	SP3725
Church Fenton *N York*	55	SE5136
Church Green *Devon*	8	SY1796
Church Hanborough *Oxon*	29	SP4213
Church Hill *Ches*	47	SJ6465
Church Houses *N York*	62	SE6697
Church Knowle *Dorset*	9	SY9481
Church Langton *Leics*	40	SP7293
Church Lawford *Warwks*	39	SP4576
Church Lawton *Staffs*	47	SJ8255
Church Leigh *Staffs*	38	SK0235
Church Lench *H & W*	28	SP0251
Church Mayfield *Staffs*	48	SK1544
Church Minshull *Ches*	47	SJ6660
Church Norton *W Susx*	11	SZ8795
Church Preen *Shrops*	37	SO5498
Church Pulverbatch *Shrops*	36	SJ4303
Church Stoke *Powys*	36	SO2794
Church Stowe *Nhants*	29	SP6357
Church Street *Kent*	14	TQ7174
Church Stretton *Shrops*	36	SO4593
Church Village *M Glam*	18	ST0885
Church Warsop *Notts*	49	SK5668
Churcham *Gloucs*	28	SO7618
Churchdown *Gloucs*	28	SO8819
Churchend *Essex*	25	TR0093
Churchfield *W Mids*	38	SP0192
Churchill *Avon*	19	ST4459
Churchill *Devon*	8	ST2902
Churchill *H & W*	38	SO8879
Churchill *H & W*	28	SO9253
Churchill *Oxon*	29	SP2824
Churchinford *Devon*	8	ST2112
Churchover *Warwks*	39	SP5180
Churchstanton *Somset*	8	ST1914
Churchstow *Devon*	5	SX7145
Churchtown *Derbys*	49	SK2662
Churchtown *Lancs*	53	SD4843
Churston Ferrers *Devon*	5	SX9056
Churt *Surrey*	11	SU8538
Churton *Ches*	46	SJ4156
Churwell *W York*	55	SE2729
Chwilog *Gwynd*	44	SH4338
Chyandour *Cnwll*	2	SW4731
Cilcain *Clwyd*	46	SJ1765
Cilcennin *Dyfed*	34	SN5260
Cilfrew *W Glam*	18	SN7700
Cilfynydd *M Glam*	18	ST0891
Cilgerran *Dyfed*	17	SN1942
Cilgwyn *Dyfed*	26	SN7429
Cilmaengwyn *W Glam*	26	SN7405
Cilmery *Powys*	26	SO0051
Cilrhedyn *Dyfed*	17	SN2834
Cilsan *Dyfed*	17	SN5922
Ciltalgarth *Gwynd*	45	SH8940
Cilycwm *Dyfed*	26	SN7539
Cimla *W Glam*	18	SS7696
Cinderford *Gloucs*	27	SO6514
Cippenham *Bucks*	22	SU9480
Cirencester *Gloucs*	20	SP0201
Clabhach *Strath*	78	NM1858
Clachaig *Strath*	80	NS1181
Clachan *Highld*	84	NG5436
Clachan *S Glam*	71	NR7656
Clachan *Strath*	79	NM7819
Clachan *Strath*	79	NM8543
Clachan Mor *Strath*	78	NL9847
Clachan-a-Luib *W Isls*	102	NF8163
Clachan-Seil *Strath*	79	NM7718
Clachaneasy *D & G*	64	NX3574
Clachnaharry *Highld*	92	NH6446
Clachtoll *Highld*	98	NC0427
Clackavoid *Tays*	88	NO1463
Clackmannan *Cent*	82	NS9191
Clackmarass *Gramp*	94	NJ2458
Clacton-on-Sea *Essex*	25	TM1715
Cladich *Strath*	80	NN0921
Cladswell *H & W*	28	SP0558
Claggan *Highld*	79	NM7049
Claigan *Highld*	90	NG2354
Clanfield *Hants*	11	SU6916
Clanfield *Oxon*	21	SP2801
Clanville *Hants*	21	SU3148
Clanville *Somset*	9	ST6233
Claonaig *Strath*	71	NR8656
Clapgate *Herts*	31	TL4424
Clapham *Beds*	30	TL0352
Clapham *Gt Lon*	23	TQ2975
Clapham *N York*	54	SD7469
Clapham *W Susx*	12	TQ0906
Clapton *Somset*	8	ST4106
Clapton *Somset*	19	ST6453
Clapton *Somset*	20	ST6852
Clapton-in-Gordano *Avon*	19	ST4773
Clapton-on-the-Hill *Gloucs*	28	SP1617
Claravale *T & W*	69	NZ1364
Clarbeston *Dyfed*	16	SN0521
Clarbeston Road *Dyfed*	16	SN0121
Clarborough *Notts*	50	SK7383
Clare *Suffk*	32	TL7745
Clarebrand *D & G*	65	NX7665
Clarencefield *D & G*	67	NY0968
Clarewood *Nthumb*	68	NZ0169
Clarilaw *Border*	76	NT5218
Clarkston *Strath*	74	NS5757
Clashmore *Highld*	98	NC0331
Clashmore *Highld*	97	NH7489
Clashnessie *Highld*	98	NC0530
Clashnoir *Gramp*	94	NJ2222
Clathy *Tays*	82	NN9920
Clathymore *Tays*	82	NO0121
Clatt *Gramp*	94	NJ5326
Clatter *Powys*	35	SN9994
Clatworthy *Somset*	7	ST0531
Claughton *Lancs*	53	SD5342
Claughton *Lancs*	53	SD5566
Claughton *Mersyd*	46	SJ3088
Claverdon *Warwks*	29	SP1965
Claverham *Avon*	19	ST4566
Clavering *Essex*	31	TL4731
Claverley *Shrops*	37	SO7993
Claverton *Avon*	20	ST7864
Clawdd-coch *S Glam*	18	ST0577
Clawdd-newydd *Clwyd*	46	SJ0852
Clawton *Devon*	6	SX3599
Claxby *Lincs*	50	TF1194
Claxton *N York*	56	SE6959
Claxton *Norfk*	43	TG3303
Clay Coton *Nhants*	39	SP5976
Clay Cross *Derbys*	49	SK3963
Clay End *Herts*	31	TL3024
Claybrooke Magna *Leics*	39	SP4988
Claydon *Oxon*	29	SP4549
Claydon *Suffk*	33	TM1349
Claygate *D & G*	67	NY3979
Claygate *Kent*	14	TQ7144
Claygate *Surrey*	22	TQ1563
Clayhanger *Devon*	7	ST0222
Clayhidon *Devon*	8	ST1615
Clayhill *E Susx*	14	TQ8323
Clayock *Highld*	100	ND1659
Claypits *Gloucs*	28	SO7606
Claypole *Lincs*	50	SK8449
Clayton *S York*	55	SE4507
Clayton *W Susx*	12	TQ2914
Clayton *W York*	55	SE1231
Clayton West *W York*	55	SE2510
Clayton-le-Moors *Lancs*	54	SD7530
Clayton-le-Woods *Lancs*	53	SD5622
Clayworth *Notts*	50	SK7387
Cleadale *Highld*	84	NM4789
Cleadon *T & W*	69	NZ3862
Clearbrook *Devon*	4	SX5265
Clearwell *Gloucs*	27	SO5608
Cleasby *N York*	61	NZ2512
Cleat *Ork*	103	ND4584
Cleatlam *Dur*	61	NZ1118
Cleator *Cumb*	58	NY0113
Cleator Moor *Cumb*	58	NY0115
Cleckheaton *W York*	55	SE1825
Clee St. Margaret *Shrops*	37	SO5684
Cleehill *Shrops*	37	SO5975
Cleekhimin *Strath*	74	NS7658
Cleethorpes *Humb*	57	TA3008
Cleeton St. Mary *Shrops*	37	SO6178
Cleeve *Avon*	19	ST4666
Cleeve *Oxon*	21	SU6081
Cleeve Hill *Gloucs*	28	SO9827
Cleeve Prior *H & W*	28	SP0849
Cleghornie *Loth*	83	NT5983
Clehonger *H & W*	27	SO4637
Cleish *Tays*	82	NT0998
Cleland *Strath*	74	NS7958
Clenamacrie *Strath*	80	NM9228
Clenchwarton *Norfk*	41	TF5920
Clent *H & W*	38	SO9279
Clenterty *Gramp*	95	NJ7760
Cleobury Mortimer *Shrops*	37	SO6775
Cleobury North *Shrops*	37	SO6286
Cleongart *Strath*	72	NR6734
Clephanton *Highld*	93	NH8150
Clerkhill *D & G*	67	NY2697
Cleuch Head *Border*	67	NT5910
Cleuch-head *D & G*	66	NS8200
Clevancy *Wilts*	20	SU0575
Clevedon *Avon*	19	ST4171
Cleveleys *Lancs*	53	SD3143
Cleverton *Wilts*	20	ST9785
Clewer *Somset*	19	ST4351
Cley next the Sea *Norfk*	42	TG0444
Cliburn *Cumb*	59	NY5824
Cliddesden *Hants*	21	SU6349
Cliff End *E Susx*	14	TQ8813
Cliffe *Dur*	61	NZ2115
Cliffe *Kent*	14	TQ7376
Cliffe *N York*	56	SE6631
Clifford *H & W*	27	SO2445
Clifford *W York*	55	SE4344
Clifford Chambers *Warwks*	29	SP1952
Clifford's Mesne *Gloucs*	28	SO7023
Clifton *Avon*	19	ST5773
Clifton *Beds*	31	TL1639
Clifton *Cent*	80	NN3231
Clifton *Cumb*	59	NY5326
Clifton *Derbys*	48	SK1644
Clifton *H & W*	28	SO8446
Clifton *Lancs*	53	SD4630
Clifton *N York*	56	SE5953
Clifton *Notts*	39	SK5434
Clifton *Oxon*	29	SP4931
Clifton *S York*	49	SK5296
Clifton *W York*	55	SE1622
Clifton *W York*	55	SE1948
Clifton Campville *Staffs*	39	SK2510
Clifton Hampden *Oxon*	21	SU5495
Clifton Reynes *Bucks*	30	SP9051
Clifton upon Dunsmore *Warwks*	39	SP5376
Clifton upon Teme *H & W*	28	SO7161
Cliftonville *Kent*	15	TR3771
Climping *W Susx*	12	SU9902
Clink *Somset*	20	ST7948
Clint *N York*	55	SE2659
Clint Green *Norfk*	42	TG0210
Clinterty *Gramp*	95	NJ8311
Clintmains *Border*	76	NT6132
Clippesby *Norfk*	43	TG4214
Clipsham *Leics*	40	SK9716
Clipston *Nhants*	40	SP7181
Clipston *Notts*	39	SK6334
Clipstone *Beds*	30	SP9426
Clitheroe *Lancs*	54	SD7441
Clive *Shrops*	37	SJ5124
Cloatley *Wilts*	20	ST9890
Clocaenog *Clwyd*	46	SJ0854
Clochan *Gramp*	94	NJ4060
Clochtow *Tays*	89	NO4852
Clodock *H & W*	27	SO3227
Clola *Gramp*	95	NK0043
Clophill *Beds*	30	TL0838
Clopton *Nhants*	40	TL0680
Clopton *Suffk*	33	TM2253
Clopton Corner *Suffk*	33	TM2254
Clos du Valle *Guern*	101	GN5412
Closeburn *D & G*	66	NX8992
Closeburnmill *D & G*	66	NX9094
Closworth *Somset*	9	ST5610
Clothall *Herts*	31	TL2731
Clotton *Ches*	46	SJ5264
Clough Foot *W York*	54	SD9123
Clough Head *W York*	55	SE0918
Cloughton *N York*	63	TA0194
Clousta *Shet*	103	HU3057
Clova *Tays*	88	NO3273
Clovelly *Devon*	6	SS3124
Clovenfords *Border*	76	NT4536
Clovulin *Highld*	86	NN0063
Clow Bridge *Lancs*	54	SD8228
Clowne *Derbys*	49	SK4875
Clows Top *H & W*	37	SO7172
Cluanie Inn *Highld*	85	NH0711
Cluanie Lodge *Highld*	85	NH0910
Clugston *D & G*	64	NX3557
Clun *Shrops*	36	SO3080
Clunas *Highld*	93	NH8846
Clunbury *Shrops*	36	SO3780
Clune *Highld*	93	NH7925
Clunes *Highld*	86	NN1988
Clungunford *Shrops*	36	SO3978
Clunie *Gramp*	94	NJ6350
Clunie *Tays*	88	NO1043
Clunton *Shrops*	36	SO3381
Clutton *Avon*	19	ST6259
Clutton *Ches*	46	SJ4654
Clutton Hill *Avon*	19	ST6359
Clydach *Gwent*	27	SO2213
Clydach *W Glam*	18	SN6800
Clydach Vale *M Glam*	18	SS9792
Clydebank *Strath*	74	NS4970
Clydey *Dyfed*	17	SN2535
Clyffe Pypard *Wilts*	20	SU0777
Clynder *Strath*	80	NS2484
Clynderwen *Dyfed*	16	SN1219
Clyne *W Glam*	18	SN8000
Clynnog-fawr *Gwynd*	44	SH4149
Clyro *Powys*	27	SO2143
Clyst Honiton *Devon*	5	SX9893
Clyst Hydon *Devon*	7	ST0301
Clyst St. George *Devon*	5	SX9888
Clyst St. Lawrence *Devon*	7	ST0200
Clyst St. Mary *Devon*	5	SX9791
Clyth *Highld*	100	ND2835
Cnwch Coch *Dyfed*	35	SN6774
Coad's Green *Cnwll*	4	SX2976
Coalburn *Strath*	74	NS8134
Coalburns *T & W*	69	NZ1260
Coaley *Gloucs*	20	SO7701
Coalhill *Essex*	24	TQ7597
Coalpit Heath *Avon*	20	ST6780
Coalport *Shrops*	37	SJ6902
Coalsnaughton *Cent*	82	NS9195
Coaltown of Balgonie *Fife*	83	NT2999
Coaltown of Wemyss *Fife*	83	NT3295
Coalville *Leics*	39	SK4214
Coanwood *Nthumb*	68	NY6859
Coat *Somset*	8	ST4520
Coatbridge *Strath*	74	NS7365
Coatdyke *Strath*	74	NS7465
Coate *Wilts*	20	SU0462
Coate *Wilts*	21	SU1882
Coates *Cambs*	41	TL3097
Coates *Gloucs*	20	SO9701
Coates *Lincs*	50	SK9083
Coates *W Susx*	12	SU9917
Cobbaton *Devon*	7	SS6126
Coberley *Gloucs*	28	SO9616
Cobham *Kent*	14	TQ6768
Cobham *Surrey*	22	TQ1060
Cobnash *H & W*	27	SO4560
Cobo *Guern*	101	GN4910
Coburby *Gramp*	95	NJ9164
Cock Bridge *Gramp*	94	NJ2509
Cock Clarks *Essex*	24	TL8102
Cock Green *Essex*	24	TL6919
Cock Marling *E Susx*	14	TQ8718
Cockayne Hatley *Beds*	31	TL2649
Cockburnspath *Border*	76	NT7770
Cockenzie and Port Seton *Loth*	76	NT4075
Cockerham *Lancs*	53	SD4651
Cockermouth *Cumb*	58	NY1230
Cockernhoe Green *Herts*	30	TL1223
Cockett *W Glam*	17	SS6394
Cockfield *Dur*	61	NZ1224
Cockfield *Suffk*	32	TL9054
Cockfosters *Gt Lon*	23	TQ2796
Cocking *W Susx*	11	SU8717
Cocking Causeway *W Susx*	11	SU8819
Cockington *Devon*	5	SX8963
Cocklake *Somset*	19	ST4449
Cockley Beck *Cumb*	58	NY2501
Cockley Cley *Norfk*	42	TF7904
Cockpole Green *Berks*	22	SU7981
Cockshutt *Shrops*	36	SJ4328
Cockthorpe *Norfk*	42	TF9842
Cockwood *Devon*	5	SX9780
Cockyard *Derbys*	48	SK0479
Coddenham *Suffk*	33	TM1354
Coddington *H & W*	28	SO7142
Coddington *Notts*	50	SK8354
Codford St. Mary *Wilts*	20	ST9739
Codford St. Peter *Wilts*	20	ST9639
Codicote *Herts*	31	TL2118
Codmore Hill *W Susx*	12	TQ0520
Codnor *Derbys*	49	SK4149
Codrington *Avon*	20	ST7278
Codsall *Staffs*	38	SJ8603
Codsall Wood *Staffs*	38	SJ8404
Coed Talon *Clwyd*	46	SJ2659
Coed-y-paen *Gwent*	19	ST3398
Coedana *Gwynd*	44	SH4382
Coedpoeth *Clwyd*	46	SJ2851
Coffinswell *Devon*	5	SX8968
Cofton Hackett *H & W*	38	SP0075
Cogan *S Glam*	19	ST1771
Cogenhoe *Nhants*	30	SP8260
Coggeshall *Essex*	24	TL8522
Coignafearn *Highld*	93	NH7018
Coilacriech *Gramp*	88	NO3296
Coilantogle *Cent*	81	NN5907
Coillore *Highld*	84	NG3537
Coiltry *Highld*	86	NH3506
Coity *M Glam*	18	SS9281
Col *W Isls*	102	NB4739
Colaboll *Highld*	96	NC5610
Colan *Cnwll*	3	SW8661
Colaton Raleigh *Devon*	8	SY0787
Colbost *Highld*	90	NG2148
Colburn *N York*	61	SE1999
Colby *Cumb*	60	NY6620
Colby *IOM*	52	SC2370
Colby *Norfk*	43	TG2231
Colchester *Essex*	25	TL9925
Cold Ash *Berks*	21	SU5169
Cold Ashby *Nhants*	39	SP6576
Cold Ashton *Avon*	20	ST7572
Cold Aston *Gloucs*	28	SP1219
Cold Brayfield *Bucks*	30	SP9252
Cold Hanworth *Lincs*	50	TF0383
Cold Hesledon *Dur*	69	NZ4146
Cold Hiendley *W York*	55	SE3714
Cold Higham *Nhants*	30	SP6653
Cold Kirby *N York*	62	SE5384
Cold Norton *Essex*	24	TL8500
Cold Overton *Leics*	40	SK8010
Coldbackie *Highld*	99	NC6160
Coldean *E Susx*	12	TQ3308
Coldeast *Devon*	5	SX8174
Colden *W York*	54	SD9628
Colden Common *Hants*	11	SU4822
Coldfair Green *Suffk*	33	TM4360
Coldharbour *Surrey*	12	TQ1443
Coldingham *Border*	77	NT9065
Coldmeece *Staffs*	38	SJ8532
Coldred *Kent*	15	TR2747
Coldridge *Devon*	7	SS6907
Coldstream *Border*	77	NT8439
Coldwaltham *W Susx*	12	TQ0216
Coldwell *H & W*	27	SO4235
Coldwells *Gramp*	95	NJ9538
Coldwells *Gramp*	95	NK1039
Cole *Somset*	9	ST6733
Cole Green *Herts*	23	TL2811
Colebatch *Shrops*	36	SO3187
Colebrook *Devon*	7	ST0006
Colebrooke *Devon*	7	SX7699
Coleby *Humb*	56	SE8919
Coleby *Lincs*	50	SK9760
Coleford *Devon*	7	SS7701
Coleford *Gloucs*	27	SO5710
Coleford *Somset*	20	ST6848
Coleford Water *Somset*	8	ST1133
Colegate End *Norfk*	33	TM1987
Colehill *Dorset*	10	SU0201
Coleman's Hatch *E Susx*	13	TQ4433
Colemere *Shrops*	36	SJ4332
Colemore *Hants*	11	SU7030
Colenden *Tays*	82	NO1029
Colerne *Wilts*	20	ST8271

Colesbourne Cretshengan

Colesbourne *Gloucs*	28	SP0013
Coleshill *Bucks*	22	SU9495
Coleshill *Oxon*	21	SU2393
Coleshill *Warwks*	39	SP2089
Coley *Avon*	19	ST5855
Colgate *W Susx*	12	TQ2332
Colgrain *Strath*	80	NS3280
Colinsburgh *Fife*	83	NO4703
Colinton *Loth*	75	NT2168
Colintraive *Strath*	80	NS0374
Colkirk *Norfk*	42	TF9126
Collace *Tays*	82	NO2032
Collafirth *Shet*	103	HU3482
Collaton *Devon*	5	SX7139
Collaton St. Mary *Devon*	5	SX8660
College of Roseisle *Gramp*	93	NJ1466
College Town *Berks*	22	SU8560
Collessie *Fife*	83	NO2813
Collier Row *Gt Lon*	23	TQ5091
Collier Street *Kent*	14	TQ7145
Collier's End *Herts*	31	TL3720
Collieston *Gramp*	95	NK0328
Collin *D & G*	66	NY0276
Collingbourne Ducis *Wilts*	21	SU2453
Collingbourne Kingston *Wilts*	21	SU2355
Collingham *W York*	55	SE3945
Collington *H & W*	27	SO6460
Collingtree *Nhants*	30	SP7555
Collins Green *Ches*	47	SJ5594
Colliston *Tays*	89	NO6045
Colliton *Devon*	8	ST0804
Collyweston *Nhants*	40	SK9902
Colmonell *Strath*	64	NX1485
Colmworth *Beds*	30	TL1058
Coln Rogers *Gloucs*	28	SP0809
Coln St. Aldwyns *Gloucs*	28	SP1405
Coln St. Dennis *Gloucs*	28	SP0810
Colnbrook *Gt Lon*	22	TQ0277
Colne *Cambs*	31	TL3775
Colne *Lancs*	54	SD8939
Colne Engaine *Essex*	24	TL8430
Colney *Norfk*	43	TG1807
Colney Heath *Herts*	23	TL2005
Colney Street *Herts*	22	TL1502
Colpy *Gramp*	94	NJ6432
Colquhar *Border*	75	NT3341
Colsterworth *Lincs*	40	SK9324
Colston Bassett *Notts*	40	SK7033
Colt's Hill *Kent*	13	TQ6443
Coltfield *Gramp*	93	NJ1163
Coltishall *Norfk*	43	TG2719
Colton *Cumb*	58	SD3185
Colton *N York*	56	SE5444
Colton *Norfk*	43	TG1009
Colton *Staffs*	38	SK0420
Colton *W York*	55	SE3732
Colva *Powys*	27	SO1952
Colvend *D & G*	66	NX8654
Colwall *H & W*	28	SO7542
Colwell *Nthumb*	68	NY9575
Colwich *Staffs*	38	SK0121
Colwinston *S Glam*	18	SS9375
Colworth *W Susx*	11	SU9103
Colwyn Bay *Clwyd*	45	SH8578
Colyford *Devon*	8	SY2592
Colyton *Devon*	8	SY2494
Combe *Berks*	21	SU3760
Combe *H & W*	27	SO3463
Combe *Oxon*	29	SP4116
Combe Fishacre *Devon*	5	SX8465
Combe Florey *Somset*	8	ST1531
Combe Hay *Avon*	20	ST7359
Combe Martin *Devon*	6	SS5846
Combe Moor *H & W*	27	SO3663
Combe Raleigh *Devon*	8	ST1502
Combe St. Nicholas *Somset*	8	ST3011
Combeinteignhead *Devon*	5	SX9071
Comberbach *Ches*	47	SJ6477
Comberford *Staffs*	39	SK1907
Comberton *Cambs*	31	TL3856
Comberton *H & W*	27	SO4968
Combrook *Warwks*	29	SP3051
Combs *Derbys*	48	SK0478
Combs *Suffk*	32	TM0456
Combs Ford *Suffk*	32	TM0457
Combwich *Somset*	19	ST2542
Comers *Gramp*	95	NJ6707
Comhampton *H & W*	28	SO8367
Commercial *Dyfed*	16	SN1416
Commins Coch *Powys*	35	SH8402
Common Moor *Cnwll*	4	SX2469
Common The *Wilts*	10	SU2432
Commondale *N York*	62	NZ6610
Compstall *Gt Man*	48	SJ9690
Compstonend *D & G*	65	NX6652
Compton *Berks*	21	SU5280
Compton *Devon*	5	SX8664
Compton *Hants*	10	SU4625
Compton *Staffs*	38	SO8284
Compton *Surrey*	12	SU9546
Compton *W Susx*	11	SU7714
Compton *Wilts*	20	SU1351
Compton Abbas *Dorset*	9	ST8618
Compton Abdale *Gloucs*	28	SP0516
Compton Bassett *Wilts*	20	SU0372
Compton Beauchamp *Oxon*	21	SU2786
Compton Bishop *Somset*	19	ST3955
Compton Chamberlayne *Wilts*	10	SU0229
Compton Dando *Avon*	19	ST6464
Compton Dundon *Somset*	8	ST4932
Compton Durville *Somset*	8	ST4117
Compton Greenfield *Avon*	19	ST5681
Compton Martin *Avon*	19	ST5457
Compton Pauncefoot *Somset*	9	ST6426
Compton Valence *Dorset*	9	SY5993
Comrie *Fife*	82	NT0289
Comrie *Tays*	81	NN7722
Conaglen House *Highld*	86	NN0268
Conchra *Highld*	85	NG8827
Concraigie *Tays*	88	NO0944
Conderton *H & W*	28	SO9637
Condicote *Gloucs*	28	SP1528
Condorrat *Strath*	74	NS7373
Condover *Shrops*	37	SJ4905
Coney Hill *Gloucs*	28	SO8517
Coney Weston *Suffk*	32	TL9578
Coneyhurst Common *W Susx*	12	TQ1023
Coneysthorpe *N York*	56	SE7171
Congdon's Shop *Cnwll*	4	SX2878
Congerstone *Leics*	39	SK3605
Congham *Norfk*	42	TF7123
Congleton *Ches*	47	SJ8562
Congresbury *Avon*	19	ST4363
Conheath *D & G*	66	NX9969
Conicavel *Gramp*	93	NH9853
Coningsby *Lincs*	51	TF2257
Conington *Cambs*	40	TL1885
Conington *Cambs*	31	TL3266
Conisbrough *S York*	49	SK5098
Conisholme *Lincs*	51	TF4095
Coniston *Cumb*	58	SD3097
Coniston *Humb*	57	TA1434
Coniston Cold *N York*	54	SD9054
Conistone *N York*	54	SD9867
Connah's Quay *Clwyd*	46	SJ2969
Connel *Strath*	80	NM9134
Connel Park *Strath*	66	NS6012
Connor Downs *Cnwll*	2	SW5939
Conon Bridge *Highld*	92	NH5455
Cononley *N York*	54	SD9846
Consall *Staffs*	48	SJ9848
Consett *Dur*	68	NZ1051
Constable Burton *N York*	61	SE1690
Constantine *Cnwll*	2	SW7329
Contin *Highld*	92	NH4556
Conwy *Gwynd*	45	SH7877
Conyer's Green *Suffk*	32	TL8867
Cooden *E Susx*	14	TQ7107
Cook's Green *Essex*	25	TM1818
Cookbury *Devon*	6	SS4006
Cookham *Berks*	22	SU8985
Cookham Dean *Berks*	22	SU8685
Cookham Rise *Berks*	22	SU8885
Cookhill *Warwks*	28	SP0558
Cookley *H & W*	38	SO8480
Cookley *Suffk*	33	TM3475
Cookley Green *Oxon*	22	SU6990
Cookney *Gramp*	89	NO8693
Cooks Green *Suffk*	32	TL9753
Cooksmill Green *Essex*	24	TL6306
Coolham *W Susx*	12	TQ1122
Cooling *Kent*	14	TQ7575
Coombe *Devon*	5	SX9373
Coombe *Devon*	8	SY1091
Coombe *Gloucs*	20	ST7694
Coombe *Hants*	11	SU6620
Coombe Bissett *Wilts*	10	SU1026
Coombe Cellars *Devon*	5	SX9072
Coombe End *Somset*	7	ST0329
Coombe Hill *Gloucs*	28	SO8826
Coombe Keynes *Dorset*	9	SY8484
Coombe Pafford *Devon*	5	SX9166
Coombe Street *Somset*	9	ST7631
Cooperhill *Gramp*	93	NH9953
Coopersale Common *Essex*	23	TL4702
Coopersale Street *Essex*	23	TL4701
Cop Street *Kent*	23	TQ2959
Copdock *Suffk*	33	TM1242
Copford Green *Essex*	24	TL9222
Copgrove *N York*	55	SE3463
Copister *Shet*	103	HU4879
Cople *Beds*	30	TL1048
Copley *Dur*	61	NZ0825
Copmanthorpe *N York*	56	SE5646
Copmere End *Staffs*	37	SJ8029
Copp *Lancs*	53	SD4239
Coppathorne *Cnwll*	6	SS2000
Coppenhall *Staffs*	38	SJ9019
Copperhouse *Cnwll*	2	SW5637
Coppingford *Cambs*	40	TL1679
Copplestone *Devon*	7	SS7702
Coppull *Lancs*	53	SD5614
Copsale *W Susx*	12	TQ1724
Copster Green *Lancs*	54	SD6733
Copston Magna *Warwks*	39	SP4588
Copt Hewick *N York*	55	SE3471
Copthall Green *Essex*	23	TL4201
Copthorne *W Susx*	12	TQ3139
Copy's Green *Norfk*	42	TF9439
Copythorne *Hants*	10	SU3014
Corbets Tay *Gt Lon*	24	TQ5685
Corbiere *Jersey*	101	JS0508
Corbridge *Nthumb*	68	NY9964
Corby *Nhants*	40	SP8988
Corby Glen *Lincs*	40	TF0024
Cordon *Strath*	72	NS0230
Coreley *Shrops*	37	SO6173
Corfe *Somset*	8	ST2319
Corfe Castle *Dorset*	9	SY9681
Corfe Mullen *Dorset*	9	SY9798
Corfton *Shrops*	37	SO4985
Corgarff *Gramp*	94	NJ2708
Corhampton *Hants*	11	SU6120
Corley *Warwks*	39	SP3085
Corley Ash *Warwks*	39	SP2986
Cormuir *Tays*	88	NO3066
Cornard Tye *Suffk*	32	TL9041
Cornforth *Dur*	62	NZ3134
Cornhill *Gramp*	94	NJ5858
Cornhill-on-Tweed *Nthumb*	77	NT8639
Cornholme *W York*	54	SD9126
Cornoigmore *Strath*	78	NL9846
Cornsay *Dur*	69	NZ1443
Cornsay Colliery *Dur*	69	NZ1643
Corntown *Highld*	92	NH5556
Corntown *M Glam*	18	SS9177
Cornwell *Oxon*	29	SP2727
Cornwood *Devon*	5	SX6059
Cornworthy *Devon*	5	SX8255
Corpach *Highld*	86	NN0976
Corpusty *Norfk*	43	TG1129
Corrachree *Gramp*	89	NJ4604
Corran *Highld*	85	NG8409
Corran *Highld*	86	NN0263
Corrie *D & G*	67	NY2086
Corrie *Strath*	72	NS0242
Corriecravie *Strath*	72	NR9223
Corriegour Lodge Hotel *Highld*	86	NN2692
Corriemoille *Highld*	92	NH3663
Corrimony *Highld*	92	NH3730
Corringham *Essex*	24	TQ7083
Corringham *Lincs*	50	SK8691
Corris *Gwynd*	35	SH7508
Corris Uchaf *Gwynd*	35	SH7408
Corrow *Strath*	80	NN1800
Corry *Highld*	85	NG6424
Corrygills *Strath*	72	NS0335
Corscombe *Devon*	7	SX6296
Corscombe *Dorset*	8	ST5105
Corse Lawn *Gloucs*	28	SO8330
Corsham *Wilts*	20	ST8770
Corsindae *Gramp*	95	NJ6808
Corsley *Wilts*	20	ST8246
Corsley Heath *Wilts*	20	ST8245
Corsock *D & G*	65	NX7675
Corston *Avon*	20	ST6965
Corston *Wilts*	20	ST9283
Corstorphine *Loth*	75	NT1972
Cortachy *Tays*	88	NO3959
Corton *Suffk*	43	TM5497
Corton *Wilts*	20	ST9340
Corton Denham *Somset*	9	ST6322
Coruanan Lodge *Highld*	86	NN0668
Corvallie *IOM*	52	SC1968
Corwar *Strath*	64	NX2780
Corwen *Clwyd*	46	SJ0743
Coryton *Devon*	4	SX4583
Coryton *Essex*	24	TQ7382
Cosby *Leics*	39	SP5495
Coseley *W Mids*	38	SO9494
Cosgrove *Nhants*	30	SP7942
Cosham *Hants*	11	SU6505
Cosheston *Dyfed*	16	SN0003
Coshieville *Tays*	87	NN7749
Cossall *Notts*	49	SK4842
Cossington *Leics*	39	SK6013
Cossington *Somset*	19	ST3540
Costessey *Norfk*	43	TG1711
Costock *Notts*	39	SK5726
Coston *Leics*	40	SK8422
Coston *Norfk*	42	TG0506
Cote *Oxon*	21	SP3502
Cotebrook *Ches*	47	SJ5765
Cotehill *Cumb*	67	NY4650
Cotes *Leics*	39	SK5520
Cotesbach *Leics*	39	SP5382
Cotgrave *Notts*	39	SK6435
Cotham *Notts*	50	SK7947
Cotherstone *Dur*	61	NZ0119
Cothill *Oxon*	21	SU4699
Cotleigh *Devon*	8	ST2002
Coton *Cambs*	31	TL4058
Coton *Nhants*	30	SP6771
Coton *Staffs*	37	SJ8120
Coton Clanford *Staffs*	38	SJ8723
Coton Hill *Shrops*	37	SJ4813
Coton in the Elms *Derbys*	39	SK2415
Cott *Devon*	5	SX7861
Cottage End *Hants*	21	SU4143
Cottam *Lancs*	53	SD5032
Cottam *Notts*	50	SK8179
Cottenham *Cambs*	31	TL4467
Cottered *Herts*	31	TL3129
Cotterstock *Nhants*	40	TL0490
Cottesbrooke *Nhants*	30	SP7173
Cottesmore *Leics*	40	SK9013
Cottingham *Humb*	57	TA0432
Cottingham *Nhants*	40	SP8490
Cottingley *W York*	55	SE1137
Cottisford *Oxon*	29	SP5831
Cotton *Suffk*	32	TM0666
Cottown *Gramp*	94	NJ5026
Cottown *Gramp*	95	NJ7615
Cottown *Gramp*	95	NJ8140
Cotts *Devon*	4	SX4365
Coughton *Warwks*	28	SP0860
Coulaghailtro *Strath*	71	NR7165
Coulags *Highld*	91	NG9645
Coull *Gramp*	89	NJ5102
Coulport *Strath*	80	NS2187
Coulsdon *Gt Lon*	23	TQ2959
Coulston *Wilts*	20	ST9554
Coulter *Strath*	75	NT0234
Coulton *N York*	62	SE6373
Coultra *Fife*	83	NO3523
Cound *Shrops*	37	SJ5505
Coundon *Dur*	61	NZ2329
Countersett *N York*	60	SD9187
Countess Wear *Devon*	5	SX9489
Countesthorpe *Leics*	39	SP5895
Countisbury *Devon*	18	SS7449
Coupar Angus *Tays*	82	NO2239
Coupland *Nthumb*	77	NT9330
Cour *Strath*	72	NR8248
Courance *D & G*	66	NY0590
Court Henry *Dyfed*	17	SN5522
Courteachan *Highld*	85	NM6897
Courteenhall *Nhants*	30	SP7653
Courtsend *Essex*	25	TR0293
Courtway *Somset*	8	ST2033
Cousland *Loth*	76	NT3768
Cousley Wood *E Susx*	13	TQ6533
Cove *Devon*	7	SS9619
Cove *Gramp*	89	NJ9501
Cove *Hants*	22	SU8555
Cove *Highld*	91	NG8191
Cove *Strath*	80	NS2282
Covehithe *Suffk*	33	TM5282
Coven *Staffs*	38	SJ9106
Coveney *Cambs*	41	TL4882
Covenham St. Bartholomew *Lincs*	51	TF3394
Covenham St. Mary *Lincs*	51	TF3394
Coventry *W Mids*	39	SP3378
Coverack *Cnwll*	2	SW7818
Coverack Bridges *Cnwll*	2	SW6630
Coverham *N York*	61	SE1086
Covington *Cambs*	30	TL0570
Cow Honeybourne *H & W*	28	SP1143
Cowan Bridge *Lancs*	60	SD6376
Cowbeech *E Susx*	13	TQ6114
Cowbit *Lincs*	41	TF2518
Cowbridge *S Glam*	18	SS9974
Cowden *Kent*	13	TQ4640
Cowdenbeath *Fife*	82	NT1691
Cowers Lane *Derbys*	49	SK3046
Cowes *IOW*	11	SZ4996
Cowesby *N York*	62	SE4689
Cowfold *W Susx*	12	TQ2122
Cowhill *Avon*	19	ST6091
Cowie *Cent*	82	NS8389
Cowley *Devon*	7	SX9095
Cowley *Gloucs*	28	SO9614
Cowley *Gt Lon*	22	TQ0582
Cowley *Oxon*	29	SP5304
Cowling *Lancs*	54	SD5917
Cowling *N York*	54	SD9643
Cowling *N York*	61	SE2387
Cowlinge *Suffk*	32	TL7154
Cowpen *Nthumb*	69	NZ2981
Cowplain *Hants*	11	SU6810
Cowshill *Dur*	60	NY8540
Cowslip Green *Avon*	19	ST4861
Cowthorpe *N York*	55	SE4252
Coxbank *Ches*	37	SJ6541
Coxbench *Derbys*	49	SK3743
Coxford *Cnwll*	6	SX1696
Coxford *Norfk*	42	TF8529
Coxheath *Kent*	14	TQ7451
Coxhoe *Dur*	62	NZ3136
Coxley *Somset*	19	ST5343
Coxley Wick *Somset*	19	ST5243
Coxtie Green *Essex*	24	TQ5696
Coxwold *N York*	62	SE5377
Coychurch *M Glam*	18	SS9379
Coylton *Strath*	73	NS4219
Coylumbridge *Highld*	93	NH9111
Coytrahen *M Glam*	18	SS8885
Crabbs Cross *H & W*	28	SP0465
Crabtree *W Susx*	12	TQ2125
Crackenthorpe *Cumb*	60	NY6622
Crackington Haven *Cnwll*	6	SX1496
Crackleybank *Shrops*	37	SJ7611
Cracoe *N York*	54	SD9760
Craddock *Devon*	8	ST0812
Cradley *H & W*	28	SO7347
Cradoc *Powys*	26	SO0130
Crafthole *Cnwll*	4	SX3654
Crafton *Bucks*	30	SP8819
Cragg *W York*	54	SE0023
Craggan *Highld*	93	NJ0226
Craghead *Dur*	69	NZ2150
Crai *Powys*	26	SN8924
Craibstone *Gramp*	94	NJ4959
Craibstone *Gramp*	95	NJ8710
Craichie *Tays*	89	NO5047
Craig *Tays*	89	NO6956
Craig Llangiwg *W Glam*	26	SN7204
Craigburn *Border*	75	NT2354
Craigcleuch *D & G*	67	NY3486
Craigdam *Gramp*	95	NJ8430
Craigdarroch *D & G*	65	NX7391
Craigdhu *Strath*	79	NM8205
Craigearn *Gramp*	95	NJ7214
Craigellachie *Gramp*	94	NJ2844
Craigend *Strath*	73	NS4670
Craigend *Tays*	82	NO1120
Craigendoran *Strath*	80	NS3181
Craigengillan *Strath*	73	NS4702
Craighlaw *D & G*	64	NX3061
Craigie *Strath*	73	NS4232
Craigie *Tays*	88	NO1143
Craigiefold *Gramp*	95	NJ9165
Craigley *D & G*	65	NX7658
Craiglockhart *Fife*	75	NT2271
Craiglug *Gramp*	94	NJ3355
Craigmillar *Loth*	75	NT3071
Craigneston *D & G*	65	NX7587
Craigneuk *Strath*	74	NS7765
Craignure *Strath*	79	NM7236
Craigo *Tays*	89	NO6864
Craigrothie *Fife*	83	NO3810
Craigruie *Cent*	81	NN4920
Craigton *Gramp*	89	NJ8301
Craigton *Strath*	74	NS4954
Craigton *Tays*	83	NO5138
Craigton of Airlie *Tays*	88	NO3250
Craik *Border*	67	NT3408
Crail *Fife*	83	NO6107
Crailing *Border*	76	NT6824
Crakehall *N York*	61	SE2489
Crambe *N York*	56	SE7364
Cramlington *Nthumb*	69	NZ2676
Cramond *Loth*	75	NT1976
Cramond Bridge *Loth*	75	NT1775
Cranage *Ches*	47	SJ7568
Cranberry *Staffs*	38	SJ8235
Cranborne *Dorset*	10	SU0513
Cranbrook *Kent*	14	TQ7736
Cranfield *Beds*	30	SP9542
Cranford *Gt Lon*	22	TQ1076
Cranford St. Andrew *Nhants*	30	SP9277
Cranford St. John *Nhants*	30	SP9276
Cranham *Gloucs*	28	SO8913
Crank *Mersyd*	46	SJ5099
Cranleigh *Surrey*	12	TQ0539
Cranmore *Somset*	20	ST6643
Cranoe *Leics*	40	SP7695
Cransford *Suffk*	33	TM3164
Cranshaws *Border*	76	NT6861
Crantock *Cnwll*	2	SW7960
Cranwell *Lincs*	50	TF0349
Cranwich *Norfk*	42	TL7794
Cranworth *Norfk*	42	TF9804
Craobh Haven *Strath*	79	NM7907
Crarae *Strath*	71	NR9897
Crask Inn *Highld*	96	NC5224
Crask of Aigas *Highld*	92	NH4642
Craster *Nthumb*	77	NU2519
Craswall *H & W*	27	SO2735
Cratfield *Suffk*	33	TM3175
Crathes *Gramp*	89	NO7596
Crathie *Gramp*	88	NO2695
Crathie *Highld*	87	NN5793
Crathorne *N York*	62	NZ4407
Craven Arms *Shrops*	36	SO4382
Crawford *Strath*	75	NS9520
Crawfordjohn *Strath*	74	NS8823
Crawick *D & G*	66	NS7811
Crawley *Hants*	10	SU4235
Crawley *Oxon*	29	SP3412
Crawley *W Susx*	12	TQ2636
Crawley Down *W Susx*	12	TQ3437
Crawshawbooth *Lancs*	54	SD8125
Crawton *Gramp*	89	NO8779
Cray *N York*	61	SD9479
Crayford *Gt Lon*	23	TQ5175
Crayke *N York*	56	SE5670
Crays Hill *Essex*	24	TQ7192
Craze Lowman *Devon*	7	SS9814
Crazies Hill *Oxon*	22	SU7980
Creacombe *Devon*	6	SS3219
Creagan Inn *Strath*	86	NM9744
Creagorry *W Isls*	102	NF7948
Creaguaineach Lodge *Highld*	86	NN3068
Creaton *Nhants*	30	SP7071
Creca *D & G*	67	NY2270
Credenhill *H & W*	27	SO4543
Crediton *Devon*	7	SS8300
Creebank *D & G*	64	NX3477
Creebridge *D & G*	64	NX4165
Creech Heathfield *Somset*	8	ST2727
Creech St. Michael *Somset*	8	ST2725
Creed *Cnwll*	3	SW9347
Creekmouth *Gt Lon*	23	TQ4581
Creeting St. Mary *Suffk*	33	TM0956
Creeton *Lincs*	40	TF0120
Creetown *D & G*	65	NX4759
Creggans Inn *Strath*	80	NN0902
Cregneish *IOM*	52	SC1867
Creich *Fife*	83	NO3221
Creigiau *M Glam*	18	ST0781
Cremyll *Cnwll*	4	SX4553
Cressage *Shrops*	37	SJ5904
Cressbrook *Derbys*	48	SK1673
Cresselly *Dyfed*	16	SN0606
Cressex *Bucks*	22	SU8492
Cressing *Essex*	24	TL7920
Cresswell *Dyfed*	16	SN0506
Cresswell *Nthumb*	69	NZ2993
Cresswell *Staffs*	48	SJ9739
Creswell *Derbys*	49	SK5274
Cretingham *Suffk*	33	TM2260
Cretshengan *Strath*	71	NR7166

D

Delnabo Duntisbourne Rouse

Delnabo *Gramp* **93** NJ1517
Delnashaugh Inn *Gramp* **94** NJ1835
Delny *Highld* **93** NH7372
Delves *Dur* **69** NZ1149
Delvine *Tays* **82** NO1240
Dembleby *Lincs* **40** TF0437
Denaby *S York* **49** SK4899
Denbigh *Clwyd* **45** SJ0566
Denbrae *Fife* **83** NO3818
Denbury *Devon* **5** SX8268
Denby *Derbys* **49** SK3946
Denby Dale *W York* **55** SE2208
Denchworth *Oxon* **21** SU3891
Dendron *Cumb* **53** SD2470
Denfield *Tays* **82** NN9517
Denford *Nhants* **30** SP9976
Dengie *Essex* **25** TL9802
Denham *Bucks* **22** TQ0487
Denham *Suffk* **32** TL7561
Denham *Suffk* **33** TM1974
Denham Green *Bucks* **22** TQ0488
Denhead *Fife* **83** NO4613
Denhead *Gramp* **95** NJ9952
Denhead of Gray *Tays* **83** NO3531
Denholm *Border* **76** NT5718
Denholme *W York* **55** SE0734
Denmead *Hants* **11** SU6512
Denmore *Gramp* **95** NJ9411
Dennington *Suffk* **33** TM2867
Denny *Cent* **81** NS8082
Dennyloanhead *Cent* **81** NS8080
Denside *Gramp* **89** NO8095
Densole *Kent* **15** TR2141
Denston *Suffk* **32** TL7652
Denstone *Staffs* **48** SK0940
Denstroude *Kent* **15** TR1061
Dent *Cumb* **60** SD7086
Dent-de-Lion *Kent* **15** TR3269
Denton *Cambs* **40** TL1587
Denton *Dur* **61** NZ2118
Denton *E Susx* **13** TQ4502
Denton *Gt Man* **48** SJ9295
Denton *Kent* **15** TR2147
Denton *Lincs* **40** SK8632
Denton *N York* **55** SE1448
Denton *Nhants* **30** SP8358
Denton *Norfk* **33** TM2788
Denver *Norfk* **41** TF6001
Denwick *Nthumb* **69** NU2014
Deopham *Norfk* **42** TG0400
Deopham Green *Norfk* **42** TM0499
Deptford *Gt Lon* **23** TQ3777
Deptford *Wilts* **10** SU0138
Derby *Derbys* **39** SK3536
Derbyhaven *IOM* **52** SC2867
Derculich *Tays* **87** NN8852
Deri *M Glam* **18** SO1201
Derringstone *Kent* **15** TR2049
Derrington *Staffs* **38** SJ8922
Derry Hill *Wilts* **20** ST9670
Derrythorpe *Humb* **56** SE8208
Dersingham *Norfk* **42** TF6830
Dervaig *Strath* **79** NM4352
Derwen *Clwyd* **46** SJ0750
Derwenlas *Powys* **35** SN7298
Desborough *Nhants* **40** SP8083
Desford *Leics* **39** SK4703
Deskford *Gramp* **94** NJ5061
Detling *Kent* **14** TQ7958
Devauden *Gwent* **19** ST4898
Devil's Bridge *Dyfed* **35** SN7376
Devizes *Wilts* **20** SU0061
Devonport *Devon* **4** SX4554
Devonside *Cent* **82** NS9196
Devoran *Cnwll* **2** SW7939
Dewarton *Loth* **76** NT3763
Dewlish *Dorset* **9** SY7798
Dewsbury *W York* **55** SE2421
Deytheur *Powys* **36** SJ2317
Dhoon *IOM* **52** SC3784
Dial Green *W Susx* **12** SU9227
Dial Post *W Susx* **12** TQ1519
Dibden *Hants* **10** SU4008
Dibden Purlieu *Hants* **10** SU4106
Dickleburgh *Norfk* **33** TM1682
Didbrook *Gloucs* **28** SP0531
Didcot *Oxon* **21** SU5290
Diddington *Cambs* **31** TL1965
Diddlebury *Shrops* **37** SO5085
Didling *W Susx* **11** SU8318
Didmarton *Gloucs* **20** ST8287
Didsbury *Gt Man* **47** SJ8491
Digby *Lincs* **50** TF0854
Digg *Highld* **90** NG4668
Diggle *Gt Man* **54** SE0007
Digmoore *Lancs* **46** SD4905
Dihewyd *Dyfed* **34** SN4855
Dilham *Norfk* **43** TG3325
Dilhorne *Staffs* **48** SJ9743
Dillington *Cambs* **30** TL1365
Dilston *Nthumb* **68** NY9763
Dilton *Wilts* **20** ST8548
Dilton Marsh *Wilts* **20** ST8449
Dilwyn *H & W* **27** SO4154
Dinas *Dyfed* **16** SN0138
Dinas *Gwynd* **44** SH2736
Dinas Powys *S Glam* **19** ST1571
Dinas-Mawddwy *Gwynd* **35** SH8515
Dinder *Somset* **19** ST5744
Dinedor *H & W* **27** SO5336
Dingle *Mersyd* **46** SJ3687
Dingley *Nhants* **40** SP7787
Dingwall *Highld* **92** NH5458
Dinnet *Gramp* **88** NO4598
Dinnington *S York* **49** SK5285
Dinnington *Somset* **8** ST4012
Dinnington *T & W* **69** NZ2073
Dinorwic *Gwynd* **44** SH5961
Dinton *Bucks* **22** SP7610
Dinton *Wilts* **10** SU0131
Dinwoodie *D & G* **67** NY1190
Dinworthy *Devon* **6** SS3015
Dipford *Somset* **8** ST2021
Dippen *Strath* **72** NR7937
Dippertown *Devon* **4** SX4284
Dippin *Strath* **72** NS0422
Dipple *Gramp* **94** NJ3258
Dipple *Strath* **73** NS2002
Diptford *Devon* **5** SX7256
Dipton *Dur* **69** NZ1554
Dirleton *Loth* **83** NT5184
Dirt Pot *Nthumb* **68** NY8545
Diseworth *Leics* **39** SK4524
Dishforth *N York* **62** SE3873
Disley *Ches* **48** SJ9784
Diss *Norfk* **33** TM1180
Distington *Cumb* **58** NY0023
Ditchampton *Wilts* **10** SU0831
Ditchburn *Nthumb* **77** NU1320
Ditcheat *Somset* **19** ST6236
Ditchingham *Norfk* **33** TM3391
Ditchling *E Susx* **12** TQ3215
Ditherington *Shrops* **37** SJ5014
Ditteridge *Wilts* **20** ST8169
Dittisham *Devon* **5** SX8655
Ditton *Ches* **46** SJ4986
Ditton *Kent* **14** TQ7158
Ditton Green *Cambs* **32** TL6558
Ditton Priors *Shrops* **37** SO6089
Dixton *Gloucs* **28** SO9830
Dixton *Gwent* **27** SO5113
Dobcross *Gt Man* **54** SD9906
Dobwalls *Cnwll* **4** SX2165
Doccombe *Devon* **5** SX7786
Dochgarroch *Highld* **92** NH6140
Docker *Lancs* **59** SD5774
Docking *Norfk* **42** TF7636
Docklow *H & W* **27** SO5657
Dockray *Cumb* **59** NY3921
Dod's Leigh *Staffs* **38** SK0134
Dodd's Green *Ches* **47** SJ6043
Doddinghurst *Essex* **24** TQ5999
Doddington *Cambs* **41** TL4090
Doddington *Kent* **14** TQ9357
Doddington *Lincs* **50** SK8970
Doddington *Nthumb* **77** NT9932
Doddington *Shrops* **37** SO6176
Doddiscombsleigh *Devon* **5** SX8586
Dodford *H & W* **38** SO9373
Dodford *Nhants* **29** SP6160
Dodington *Avon* **20** ST7580
Dodington *Somset* **19** ST1740
Dodleston *Ches* **46** SJ3661
Dodside *Strath* **74** NS5053
Dodworth *S York* **55** SE3105
Dog Village *Devon* **7** SX9896
Dogdyke *Lincs* **51** TF2055
Dogmersfield *Hants* **22** SU7852
Dolanog *Powys* **36** SJ0612
Dolbenmaen *Gwynd* **44** SH5043
Dolfor *Powys* **36** SO1087
Dolgarrog *Gwynd* **45** SH7767
Dolgellau *Gwynd* **35** SH7217
Doll *Highld* **97** NC8803
Dollar *Cent* **82** NS9698
Dollarfield *Cent* **82** NS9697
Dolphin *Clwyd* **46** SJ1973
Dolphinholme *Lancs* **53** SD5253
Dolphinston *Border* **76** NT6815
Dolphinton *Strath* **75** NT1046
Dolton *Devon* **6** SS5712
Dolwen *Clwyd* **45** SH8874
Dolwyddelan *Gwynd* **45** SH7352
Domgay *Powys* **36** SJ2818
Doncaster *S York* **56** SE5703
Donhead St. Andrew *Wilts* **9** ST9124
Donhead St. Mary *Wilts* **9** ST9024
Donibristle *Fife* **82** NT1688
Doniford *Somset* **18** ST0842
Donington *Lincs* **41** TF2035
Donington on Bain *Lincs* **51** TF2382
Donisthorpe *Leics* **39** SK3113
Donnington *Berks* **21** SU4668
Donnington *Gloucs* **29** SP1928
Donnington *Shrops* **37** SJ5708
Donnington *Shrops* **37** SJ7114
Donnington *W Susx* **11** SU8501
Donyatt *Somset* **8** ST3314
Doonfoot *Strath* **73** NS3219
Doonholm *Strath* **73** NS3317
Dorback Lodge *Highld* **93** NJ0716
Dorchester *Dorset* **9** SY6990
Dorchester *Oxon* **21** SU5794
Dordon *Warwks* **39** SK2500
Dore *S York* **49** SK3181
Dores *Highld* **92** NH5934
Dorking *Surrey* **12** TQ1649
Dormans Land *Surrey* **13** TQ4041
Dormington *H & W* **27** SO5840
Dormston *H & W* **28** SO9857
Dorney *Berks* **22** SU9378
Dornie *Highld* **85** NG8826
Dornoch *Highld* **97** NH7989
Dornock *D & G* **67** NY2366
Dorrery *Highld* **100** ND0754
Dorridge *W Mids* **38** SP1775
Dorrington *Lincs* **50** TF0852
Dorrington *Shrops* **37** SJ4702
Dorrington *Shrops* **37** SJ7340
Dorsington *Warwks* **28** SP1349
Dorstone *H & W* **27** SO3141
Dorton *Bucks* **30** SP6814
Douganhill *D & G* **66** NX8155
Dougarie *Strath* **72** NR8837
Douglas *IOM* **52** SC3775
Douglas *Strath* **74** NS8330
Douglas and Angus *Tays* **83** NO4233
Douglas Castle *Strath* **74** NS8431
Douglas Hill *Gwynd* **44** SH6065
Douglas Pier *Strath* **80** NS1999
Douglas Water *Strath* **74** NS8736
Douglas West *Strath* **74** NS8231
Douglastown *Tays* **88** NO4147
Dounby *Ork* **103** HY2920
Doune *Cent* **81** NN7201
Doune *Highld* **96** NC4400
Dounepark *Strath* **64** NX1897
Dounie *Highld* **96** NH5690
Dounreay *Highld* **100** ND0065
Dousland *Devon* **4** SX5369
Dove Holes *Derbys* **48** SK0777
Dovenby *Cumb* **58** NY0933
Dover *Kent* **15** TR3141
Dovercourt *Essex* **25** TM2431
Doverdale *H & W* **28** SO8666
Doveridge *Derbys* **38** SK1133
Doversgreen *Surrey* **12** TQ2548
Dowally *Tays* **88** NO0048
Dowdeswell *Gloucs* **28** SP0019
Dowhill *Strath* **73** NS2003
Dowlais *M Glam* **26** SO0607
Dowland *Devon* **6** SS5610
Dowlish Wake *Somset* **8** ST3712
Down Ampney *Gloucs* **20** SU0996
Down Hatherley *Gloucs* **28** SO8622
Down St. Mary *Devon* **7** SS7404
Down Thomas *Devon* **4** SX5050
Downderry *Cnwll* **4** SX3154
Downe *Gt Lon* **23** TQ4361
Downend *Avon* **19** ST6577
Downend *Gloucs* **20** ST8398
Downfield *Tays* **83** NO3932
Downgate *Cnwll* **4** SX2871
Downgate *Cnwll* **4** SX3672
Downham *Cambs* **41** TL5284
Downham *Essex* **24** TQ7296
Downham *Gt Lon* **23** TQ3871
Downham *Lancs* **54** SD7844
Downham Market *Norfk* **41** TF6103
Downhead *Somset* **9** ST5625
Downhead *Somset* **20** ST6945
Downhill *Tays* **82** NO0930
Downholme *N York* **61** SE1197
Downies *Gramp* **89** NO9294
Downley *Bucks* **22** SU8495
Downside *Surrey* **22** TQ1057
Downton *Hants* **10** SZ2693
Downton *Wilts* **10** SU1821
Downton on the Rock *H & W* **36** SO4273
Dowsby *Lincs* **40** TF1129
Doynton *Avon* **20** ST7274
Draethen *M Glam* **19** ST2287
Draffan *Strath* **74** NS7945
Drakeholes *Notts* **49** SK7090
Drakemyre *Strath* **73** NS2950
Drakes Broughton *H & W* **28** SO9248
Draughton *N York* **55** SE0352
Draughton *Nhants* **30** SP7676
Drax *N York* **56** SE6726
Draycote *Warwks* **29** SP4470
Draycott *Derbys* **39** SK4433
Draycott *Gloucs* **29** SP1835
Draycott *Somset* **19** ST4751
Draycott in the Clay *Staffs* **38** SK1528
Draycott in the Moors *Staffs* **48** SJ9840
Drayton *H & W* **38** SO8975
Drayton *Hants* **11** SU6705
Drayton *Leics* **40** SP8392
Drayton *Norfk* **43** TG1813
Drayton *Oxon* **29** SP4241
Drayton *Oxon* **21** SU4894
Drayton *Somset* **8** ST4024
Drayton Bassett *Staffs* **39** SK1900
Drayton Beauchamp *Bucks* **22** SP9011
Drayton Parslow *Bucks* **30** SP8328
Drayton St Leonard *Oxon* **21** SU5996
Dreenhill *Dyfed* **16** SM9214
Drefach *Dyfed* **17** SN3538
Drefach *Dyfed* **17** SN4945
Drefach *Dyfed* **17** SN5213
Dreghorn *Strath* **73** NS3538
Drellingore *Kent* **15** TR2441
Drem *Loth* **83** NT5079
Drewsteignton *Devon* **5** SX7391
Driffield *Gloucs* **20** SU0799
Driffield *Humb* **56** TA0257
Drift *Cnwll* **2** SW4328
Drigg *Cumb* **58** SD0699
Drighlington *W York* **55** SE2228
Drimnin *Highld* **79** NM5554
Drimpton *Dorset* **8** ST4104
Drimsallie *Highld* **85** NM9578
Dringhouses *N York* **56** SE5849
Drinkstone *Suffk* **32** TL9561
Drinkstone Green *Suffk* **32** TL9660
Driver's End *Herts* **31** TL2220
Drointon *Staffs* **38** SK0226
Droitwich *H & W* **28** SO8963
Dron *Tays* **82** NO1416
Dronfield *Derbys* **49** SK3578
Drongan *Strath* **73** NS4418
Dronley *Tays* **83** NO3435
Droop *Dorset* **9** ST7508
Droxford *Hants* **11** SU6018
Droylsden *Gt Man* **48** SJ9097
Druid *Clwyd* **45** SJ0443
Druidston *Dyfed* **16** SM8616
Druimachoish *Highld* **86** NN1246
Druimarbin *Highld* **86** NN0770
Druimdrishaig *Strath* **71** NR7370
Druimindarroch *Highld* **85** NM6884
Drum *Strath* **71** NR9276
Drum *Tays* **82** NO0400
Drumalbin *Strath* **74** NS9038
Drumbeg *Highld* **98** NC1232
Drumblade *Gramp* **94** NJ5840
Drumblair House *Gramp* **94** NJ6343
Drumbreddon *D & G* **64** NX0843
Drumbuie *Highld* **85** NG7730
Drumburgh *Cumb* **67** NY2659
Drumburn *D & G* **66** NX8854
Drumchapel *Strath* **74** NS5270
Drumchastle *Tays* **87** NN6858
Drumclog *Strath* **74** NS6438
Drumeldrie *Fife* **83** NO4403
Drumelzier *Border* **75** NT1334
Drumfearn *Highld* **85** NG6716
Drumfrennie *Gramp* **89** NO7298
Drumhead *Gramp* **89** NO6092
Drumin *Gramp* **94** NJ1830
Drumjohn *D & G* **65** NX5297
Drumlamford *Strath* **64** NX2876
Drumlasie *Gramp* **89** NJ6405
Drumleaning *Cumb* **67** NY2751
Drumlemble *Strath* **72** NR6619
Drumlithie *Gramp* **89** NO7880
Drummoddie *D & G* **64** NX3845
Drummond *Highld* **92** NH6065
Drummore *D & G* **64** NX1336
Drummore *D & G* **66** NX9074
Drummuir *Gramp* **94** NJ3843
Drumnadrochit *Highld* **92** NH5030
Drumnagorrach *Gramp* **94** NJ5252
Drumore *Strath* **72** NR7022
Drumpark *D & G* **66** NX8779
Drumrunie Lodge *Highld* **96** NC1604
Drumshang *Strath* **73** NS2514
Drumuie *Highld* **90** NG4546
Drumvaich *Cent* **81** NN6704
Drumvillie *Highld* **93** NH9420
Drumwalt *D & G* **64** NX3053
Drumwhirn *D & G* **65** NX7480
Drunzie *Tays* **82** NO1308
Dry Doddington *Lincs* **50** SK8546
Dry Drayton *Cambs* **31** TL3861
Drybeck *Cumb* **60** NY6615
Drybridge *Gramp* **94** NJ4362
Drybridge *Strath* **73** NS3536
Drybrook *Gloucs* **27** SO6417
Dryburgh *Border* **76** NT5932
Dryhope *Border* **75** NT2624
Drym *Cnwll* **2** SW6133
Drymen *Cent* **81** NS4788
Drymuir *Gramp* **95** NJ9046
Drynoch *Highld* **84** NG4031
Dryton *Shrops* **37** SJ5905
Dubford *Gramp* **95** NJ7963
Duchally *Highld* **96** NC3817
Ducklington *Oxon* **29** SP3507
Duddingston *Loth* **75** NT2872
Duddington *Nhants* **40** SK9800
Duddlestone *Somset* **8** ST2321
Duddlewick *Shrops* **37** SO6583
Duddo *Nthumb* **77** NT9342
Duddon *Ches* **46** SJ5164
Dudleston *Shrops* **36** SJ3438
Dudley *T & W* **69** NZ2573
Dudley *W Mids* **38** SO9490
Dudley Port *W Mids* **38** SO9691
Dudsbury *Dorset* **10** SZ0798
Duffield *Derbys* **49** SK3443
Duffryn *M Glam* **18** SS8495
Dufftown *Gramp* **94** NJ3240
Duffus *Gramp* **94** NJ1668
Dufton *Cumb* **60** NY6825
Duggleby *N York* **56** SE8767
Duirinish *Highld* **85** NG7831
Duisdalemore *Highld* **85** NG7013
Duisky *Highld* **85** NN0076
Duke Street *Suffk* **32** TM0742
Dukinfield *Gt Man* **48** SJ9397
Dulcote *Somset* **19** ST5644
Dulford *Devon* **8** ST0706
Dull *Tays* **87** NN8049
Dullatur *Strath* **74** NS7476
Dullingham *Cambs* **32** TL6357
Dullingham Ley *Cambs* **32** TL6456
Dulnain Bridge *Highld* **93** NH9925
Duloe *Beds* **30** TL1560
Duloe *Cnwll* **4** SX2358
Dulverton *Somset* **7** SS9127
Dulwich *Gt Lon* **23** TQ3373
Dumbarton *Strath* **80** NS3975
Dumbleton *Gloucs* **28** SP0135
Dumcrieff *D & G* **67** NT1003
Dumfries *D & G* **66** NX9776
Dumgoyne *Cent* **81** NS5283
Dummer *Hants* **21** SU5846
Dumpton *Kent* **15** TR3966
Dun *Tays* **89** NO6659
Dunalastair *Tays* **87** NN7158
Dunan *Highld* **84** NG5828
Dunan *Strath* **80** NS1571
Dunan *Tays* **87** NN4757
Dunans *Strath* **80** NS0491
Dunaverty *Strath* **72** NR6807
Dunball *Somset* **19** ST3141
Dunbar *Loth* **83** NT6778
Dunbeath *Highld* **100** ND1629
Dunbeg *Strath* **79** NM8833
Dunblane *Cent* **81** NN7801
Dunbog *Fife* **83** NO2817
Duncanston *Highld* **92** NH5856
Duncanstone *Gramp* **94** NJ5726
Dunchideock *Devon* **5** SX8787
Dunchurch *Warwks* **39** SP4871
Duncow *D & G* **66** NX9683
Duncrievie *Tays* **82** NO1309
Duncton *W Susx* **12** SU9617
Dundee *Tays* **83** NO4030
Dundon *Somset* **8** ST4832
Dundonald *Strath* **73** NS3634
Dundonnell *Highld* **91** NH0987
Dundraw *Cumb* **67** NY2149
Dundreggan *Highld* **92** NH3214
Dundrennan *D & G* **65** NX7447
Dundry *Avon* **19** ST5666
Dunecht *Gramp* **95** NJ7509
Dunfermline *Fife* **82** NT0987
Dunfield *Gloucs* **20** SU1497
Dungavel *Strath* **74** NS6537
Dunglass *Loth* **76** NT7671
Dunham *Notts* **50** SK8074
Dunham Town *Gt Man* **47** SJ7387
Dunham Woodhouses *Gt Man* **47** SJ7287
Dunham-on-the-Hill *Ches* **46** SJ4772
Dunhampton *H & W* **28** SO8466
Dunholme *Lincs* **50** TF0279
Dunino *Fife* **83** NO5311
Dunipace *Cent* **81** NS8083
Dunk's Green *Kent* **13** TQ6152
Dunkeld *Tays* **88** NO0242
Dunkerton *Avon* **20** ST7159
Dunkeswell *Devon* **8** ST1407
Dunkeswick *W York* **55** SE3047
Dunkirk *Avon* **20** ST7885
Dunkirk *Kent* **15** TR0759
Dunlappie *Tays* **89** NO5867
Dunley *H & W* **28** SO7869
Dunlop *Strath* **73** NS4049
Dunmaglass *Highld* **92** NH5922
Dunmore *Cent* **82** NS8989
Dunmore *Strath* **71** NR7961
Dunnet *Highld* **100** ND2171
Dunnichen *Tays* **89** NO5048
Dunning *Tays* **82** NO0114
Dunnington *Humb* **57** TA1551
Dunnington *N York* **56** SE6652
Dunnington *Warwks* **28** SP0654
Dunnockshaw *Lancs* **54** SD8127
Dunoon *Strath* **80** NS1776
Dunphail *Gramp* **93** NJ0048
Dunragit *D & G* **64** NX1557
Duns *Border* **76** NT7853
Duns Tew *Oxon* **29** SP4528
Dunsby *Lincs* **40** TF1026
Dunscore *D & G* **66** NX8684
Dunsdale *Cleve* **62** NZ6019
Dunsden Green *Oxon* **22** SU7377
Dunsdon *Devon* **6** SS3008
Dunsfold *Surrey* **12** TQ0035
Dunsford *Devon* **5** SX8189
Dunshelt *Fife* **83** NO2410
Dunshillock *Gramp* **95** NJ9848
Dunsill *Notts* **49** SK4661
Dunsley *N York* **63** NZ8511
Dunsley *Staffs* **38** SO8583
Dunsmore *Bucks* **22** SP8605
Dunsop Bridge *Lancs* **54** SD6649
Dunstable *Beds* **30** TL0122
Dunstall *Staffs* **38** SK1820
Dunstan *Nthumb* **77** NU2419
Dunster *Somset* **7** SS9943
Dunston *Lincs* **50** TF0662
Dunston *Norfk* **43** TG2202
Dunston *Staffs* **38** SJ9217
Dunston *T & W* **69** NZ2362
Dunstone *Devon* **5** SX5951
Dunstone *Devon* **5** SX7175
Dunswell *Humb* **57** TA0735
Dunsyre *Strath* **75** NT0748
Dunterton *Devon* **4** SX3779
Duntisbourne Abbots *Gloucs* **28** SO9607
Duntisbourne Rouse *Gloucs* **28** SO9805

Duntish
Elim

Duntish Dorset 9 ST6906
Duntocher Strath 74 NS4872
Dunton Beds 31 TL2344
Dunton Bucks 30 SP8224
Dunton Norfk 42 TF8830
Dunton Bassett Leics 39 SP5490
Dunton Green Kent 23 TQ5157
Duntulm Highld 90 NG4174
Dunure Strath 73 NS2515
Dunvant W Glam 17 SS5993
Dunvegan Highld 90 NG2547
Dunwich Suffk 33 TM4770
Durgan Cnwll 2 SW7727
Durham Dur 61 NZ2742
Durisdeer D & G 66 NS8903
Durisdeermill D & G 66 NS8804
Durleigh Somset 19 ST2736
Durley Hants 11 SU5116
Durley Wilts 21 SU2364
Durley Street Hants 11 SU5217
Durlock Kent 15 TR2757
Durlock Kent 15 TR3164
Durmgley Tays 88 NO4250
Durness Highld 98 NC4068
Duror Highld 86 NM9754
Durran Highld 100 ND1963
Durrington W Susx 12 TQ1105
Durrington Wilts 20 SU1544
Durris Gramp 89 NO7796
Dursley Gloucs 20 ST7598
Dursley Cross Gloucs 28 SO6920
Durston Somset 8 ST2928
Durweston Dorset 9 ST8508
Duston Nhants 30 SP7261
Duthil Highld 93 NH9324
Dutton Ches 47 SJ5779
Duxford Cambs 31 TL4846
Duxford Oxon 21 SP3600
Dwygyfylchi Gwynd 45 SH7376
Dwyran Gwynd 44 SH4465
Dyce Gramp 95 NJ8812
Dye House Nthumb 68 NY9358
Dyffryn Ardudwy Gwynd 34 SH5823
Dyffryn Cellwen W Glam 26 SN8510
Dyke Gramp 93 NH9858
Dyke Lincs 40 TF1022
Dykehead Cent 81 NS5997
Dykehead Strath 74 NS8759
Dykehead Tays 88 NO2453
Dykehead Tays 88 NO3859
Dykelands Gramp 89 NO7068
Dykends Tays 88 NO2557
Dykeside Gramp 95 NJ7243
Dymchurch Kent 15 TR1029
Dymock Gloucs 28 SO7031
Dyrham Avon 20 ST7475
Dysart Fife 83 NT3093
Dyserth Clwyd 45 SJ0578

E

Eagland Hill Lancs 53 SD4345
Eagle Lincs 50 SK8766
Eaglescliffe Cleve 62 NZ4215
Eaglesfield Cumb 58 NY0928
Eaglesfield D & G 67 NY2374
Eaglesham Strath 74 NS5751
Eagley Gt Man 54 SD7112
Eakring Notts 49 SK6762
Ealand Humb 56 SE7811
Ealing Gt Lon 23 TQ1780
Eals Nthumb 68 NY6756
Eamont Bridge Cumb 59 NY5228
Earby Lancs 54 SD9046
Eardington Shrops 37 SO7290
Eardisland H & W 27 SO4158
Eardisley H & W 27 SO3149
Eardiston H & W 28 SO6968
Eardiston Shrops 36 SJ3725
Earith Cambs 31 TL3875
Earl Shilton Leics 39 SP4697
Earl Soham Suffk 33 TM2363
Earl Sterndale Derbys 48 SK0966
Earl's Croome H & W 28 SO8642
Earlestown Mersyd 47 SJ5795
Earley Berks 22 SU7472
Earlish Highld 90 NG3861
Earls Barton Nhants 30 SP8563
Earls Colne Essex 24 TL8528
Earls Common H & W 28 SO9559
Earlsdon W Mids 39 SP3278
Earlsferry Fife 83 NO4800
Earlsfield Gt Lon 23 TQ2573
Earlsford Gramp 95 NJ8334
Earlsheaton W York 55 SE2621
Earlston Border 76 NT5738
Earlston Strath 73 NS4035
Earlswood Surrey 12 TQ2749
Earlswood Warwks 38 SP1174
Earnley W Susx 11 SZ8196
Earsdon Nthumb 69 NZ1993
Earsdon T & W 69 NZ3272
Earsham Norfk 33 TM3288
Eartham W Susx 12 SU9309
Easby N York 62 NZ5708
Easebourne W Susx 11 SU9023
Easenhall Warwks 39 SP4679
Eashing Surrey 12 SU9443
Easington Bucks 22 SP6810
Easington Cleve 63 NZ7417
Easington Dur 69 NZ4143
Easington Humb 57 TA3919
Easington Colliery Dur 69 NZ4344
Easingwold N York 55 SE5269
Eassie and Nevay Tays 88 NO3344
East Aberthaw S Glam 18 ST0366
East Allington Devon 5 SX7748
East Anstey Devon 7 SS8626
East Appleton N York 61 SE2395
East Ashey IOW 11 SZ5888
East Ashling W Susx 11 SU8107
East Ayton N York 63 SE9985
East Barkwith Lincs 50 TF1681
East Barming Kent 14 TQ7254
East Barnby N York 63 NZ8212
East Barnet Gt Lon 23 TQ2795
East Barns Loth 76 NT7176
East Barsham Norfk 42 TF9133
East Beckham Norfk 43 TG1639
East Bedfont Gt Lon 22 TQ0873
East Bergholt Suffk 25 TM0734
East Bilney Norfk 42 TF9519
East Blatchington E Susx 13 TQ4800
East Boldon T & W 69 NZ3661
East Boldre Hants 10 SU3700
East Bradenham Norfk 42 TF9308
East Brent Somset 19 ST3451
East Bridgford Notts 49 SK6943
East Buckland Devon 7 SS6831
East Budleigh Devon 8 SY0684
East Butterwick Humb 56 SE8306
East Calder Loth 75 NT0867
East Carleton Norfk 43 TG1701
East Carlton Nhants 40 SP8389
East Carlton W York 55 SE2143
East Challow Oxon 21 SU3888
East Charleton Devon 5 SX7642
East Chelborough Dorset 9 ST5505
East Chiltington E Susx 13 TQ3715
East Chinnock Somset 8 ST4913
East Chisenbury Wilts 20 SU1452
East Clandon Surrey 12 TQ0651
East Claydon Bucks 30 SP7325
East Coker Somset 8 ST5412
East Combe Somset 8 ST1631
East Compton Somset 19 ST6141
East Cornworthy Devon 5 SX8455
East Cottingwith Humb 56 SE7042
East Cowes IOW 11 SZ5095
East Cowick Humb 56 SE6620
East Cowton N York 61 NZ3003
East Cranmore Somset 20 ST6743
East Creech Dorset 9 SY9382
East Dean E Susx 13 TV5598
East Dean H & W 27 SO6520
East Dean Hants 10 SU2726
East Dean W Susx 11 SU9012
East Dereham Norfk 42 TF9913
East Down Devon 6 SS6041
East Drayton Notts 50 SK7775
East Dulwich Gt Lon 23 TQ3375
East Dundry Avon 19 ST5766
East Ella Humb 57 TA0529
East End Hants 21 SU4161
East End Hants 10 SZ3696
East End Kent 14 TQ8335
East End Oxon 29 SP3915
East End Somset 20 ST6746
East Everleigh Wilts 21 SU2053
East Farleigh Kent 14 TQ7353
East Farndon Nhants 40 SP7184
East Ferry Lincs 50 SK8199
East Fortune Loth 83 NT5479
East Garston Berks 21 SU3576
East Goscote Leics 39 SK6413
East Grafton Wilts 21 SU2560
East Grange Gramp 93 NJ0961
East Grimstead Wilts 10 SU2227
East Grinstead W Susx 13 TQ3938
East Guldeford E Susx 14 TQ9321
East Haddon Nhants 30 SP6668
East Hagbourne Oxon 21 SU5288
East Halton Humb 57 TA1319
East Ham Gt Lon 23 TQ4283
East Hanney Oxon 21 SU4193
East Hanningfield Essex 24 TL7701
East Hardwick W York 55 SE4618
East Harling Norfk 32 TL9986
East Harlsey N York 62 SE4299
East Harnham Wilts 10 SU1428
East Harptree Avon 19 ST5655
East Hartburn Cleve 62 NZ4217
East Hartford Nthumb 69 NZ2679
East Harting W Susx 11 SU7919
East Hatch Wilts 9 ST9228
East Hatley Cambs 31 TL2850
East Hauxwell N York 61 SE1693
East Haven Tays 83 NO5836
East Heckington Lincs 50 TF1944
East Hedleyhope Dur 61 NZ1540
East Helmsdale Highld 97 ND0315
East Hendred Oxon 21 SU4588
East Heslerton N York 63 SE9276
East Hewish Avon 19 ST4064
East Hoathly E Susx 13 TQ5216
East Holme Dorset 9 SY8986
East Horndon Essex 24 TQ6389
East Horrington Somset 19 ST5846
East Horsley Surrey 12 TQ0952
East Howe Dorset 10 SZ0795
East Huntspill Somset 19 ST3445
East Hyde Beds 30 TL1217
East Ilsley Berks 21 SU4980
East Keal Lincs 51 TF3863
East Kennett Wilts 20 SU1167
East Keswick W York 55 SE3644
East Kilbride Strath 74 NS6354
East Kirkby Lincs 51 TF3362
East Knighton Dorset 9 SY8185
East Knoyle Wilts 9 ST8830
East Kyloe Nthumb 77 NU0639
East Lambrook Somset 8 ST4318
East Langdon Kent 15 TR3346
East Langton Leics 40 SP7292
East Laroch Highld 86 NN0858
East Lavant W Susx 11 SU8608
East Lavington W Susx 12 SU9416
East Layton N York 61 NZ1609
East Leake Notts 39 SK5526
East Leigh Devon 7 SS6905
East Leigh Devon 5 SX7657
East Lexham Norfk 42 TF8517
East Linton Loth 76 NT5977
East Lockinge Oxon 21 SU4287
East Lound Humb 50 SK7899
East Lulworth Dorset 9 SY8682
East Lutton N York 56 SE9469
East Lydford Somset 9 ST5731
East Malling Kent 14 TQ7056
East Marden W Susx 11 SU8014
East Markham Notts 50 SK7373
East Martin Hants 10 SU0719
East Marton N York 54 SD9050
East Meon Hants 11 SU6822
East Mersea Essex 25 TM0414
East Molesey Surrey 22 TQ1467
East Morden Dorset 9 SY9194
East Morton D & G 66 NS8800
East Morton W York 55 SE0942
East Ness N York 62 SE6978
East Norton Leics 40 SK7800
East Ogwell Devon 5 SX8370
East Orchard Dorset 9 ST8317
East Peckham Kent 14 TQ6648
East Pennar Dyfed 16 SM9602
East Pennard Somset 19 ST5937
East Perry Cambs 30 TL1566
East Portlemouth Devon 5 SX7538
East Prawle Devon 5 SX7836
East Preston W Susx 12 TQ0602
East Pulham Dorset 9 ST7209
East Putford Devon 6 SS3616
East Quantoxhead Somset 18 ST1343
East Rainton T & W 69 NZ3347
East Ravendale Lincs 51 TF2399
East Raynham Norfk 42 TF8825
East Rigton W York 55 SE3743
East Rounton N York 62 NZ4203
East Rudham Norfk 42 TF8228
East Runton Norfk 43 TG1942
East Ruston Norfk 43 TG3427
East Saltoun Loth 76 NT4767
East Sheen Gt Lon 23 TQ2075
East Shefford Berks 21 SU3874
East Stockwith Lincs 50 SK7894
East Stoke Dorset 9 SY8686
East Stoke Notts 50 SK7549
East Stour Dorset 9 ST8022
East Stourmouth Kent 15 TR2662
East Stowford Devon 7 SS6326
East Stratton Hants 21 SU5440
East Taphouse Cnwll 3 SX1863
East Thirston Nthumb 61 NZ1900
East Tilbury Essex 24 TQ6877
East Tisted Hants 11 SU7032
East Torrington Lincs 50 TF1483
East Tuddenham Norfk 42 TG0711
East Tytherley Hants 10 SU2929
East Tytherton Wilts 20 ST9674
East Village Devon 7 SS8405
East Wall Shrops 37 SO5293
East Walton Norfk 42 TF7416
East Water Somset 19 ST5350
East Week Devon 5 SX6692
East Wellow Hants 10 SU3020
East Wemyss Fife 83 NT3497
East Whitburn Loth 75 NS9665
East Wickham Gt Lon 23 TQ4677
East Williamston Dyfed 16 SN0904
East Winch Norfk 42 TF6916
East Winterslow Wilts 10 SU2434
East Wittering W Susx 11 SZ7997
East Witton N York 61 SE1486
East Woodburn Nthumb 68 NY9086
East Woodhay Hants 21 SU4061
East Worldham Hants 11 SU7538
East Wretham Norfk 32 TL9190
East Youlstone Devon 6 SS2715
Eastbourne Dur 61 NZ3013
Eastbourne E Susx 13 TV6199
Eastbridge Suffk 33 TM4566
Eastburn W York 54 SE0144
Eastbury Berks 21 SU3477
Eastbury Herts 22 TQ1092
Eastby N York 54 SE0154
Eastchurch Kent 15 TQ9871
Eastcombe Gloucs 20 SO8904
Eastcote Gt Lon 22 TQ1088
Eastcote Nhants 30 SP6853
Eastcote W Mids 39 SP1979
Eastcott Wilts 20 SU0255
Eastcourt Wilts 20 ST9792
Eastcourt Wilts 21 SU2361
Eastend Essex 25 TQ9492
Eastend Strath 75 NS9537
Easter Balmoral Gramp 88 NO2694
Easter Compton Avon 19 ST5782
Easter Dalziel Highld 93 NH7550
Easter Howgate Loth 75 NT2463
Easter Kinkell Highld 92 NH5755
Easter Moniack Highld 92 NH5543
Easter Ord Gramp 89 NJ8304
Easter Pitkierie Fife 83 NO5606
Easter Skeld Shet 103 HU3144
Eastergate W Susx 12 SU9405
Easterhouse Strath 74 NS6865
Eastern Green W Mids 39 SP2879
Easterton Wilts 20 SU0254
Eastfield Cent 74 NS8964
Eastfield Strath 74 NS7475
Eastfiled N York 63 TA0484
Eastgate Dur 61 NY9538
Eastgate Norfk 43 TG1423
Easthampstead Berks 22 SU8667
Easthampton H & W 27 SO4063
Easthope Shrops 37 SO5695
Easthorpe Essex 24 TL9121
Eastington Devon 7 SS7408
Eastington Gloucs 28 SP1213
Eastlands D & G 66 NX8172
Eastleach Martin Gloucs 29 SP2004
Eastleach Turville Gloucs 29 SP1905
Eastleigh Devon 6 SS4827
Eastleigh Hants 10 SU4519
Eastling Kent 15 TQ9656
Eastney Hants 11 SZ6698
Eastnor H & W 28 SO7237
Eastoft Humb 56 SE8016
Easton Cambs 30 TL1371
Easton Cumb 67 NY2759
Easton Devon 5 SX7289
Easton Dorset 9 SY6971
Easton Hants 11 SU5132
Easton Lincs 40 SK9326
Easton Norfk 43 TG1310
Easton Somset 19 ST5147
Easton Suffk 33 TM2858
Easton Wilts 20 ST8970
Easton Grey Wilts 20 ST8887
Easton Maudit Nhants 30 SP8858
Easton on the Hill Nhants 40 TF0104
Easton Royal Wilts 21 SU2060
Easton-in-Gordano Avon 19 ST5175
Eastrea Cambs 41 TL2997
Eastriggs D & G 67 NY2466
Eastrington Humb 56 SE7929
Eastrop Wilts 21 SU2092
Eastry Kent 15 TR3054
Eastville Lincs 51 TF4056
Eastwell Leics 40 SK7728
Eastwick Herts 23 TL4311
Eastwood Essex 24 TQ8688
Eastwood Notts 49 SK4646
Eastwood W York 54 SD9726
Eathorpe Warwks 29 SP3969
Eaton Ches 47 SJ5763
Eaton Ches 47 SJ8765
Eaton Leics 40 SK7928
Eaton Norfk 43 TG2006
Eaton Notts 49 SK7077
Eaton Oxon 21 SP4403
Eaton Shrops 37 SO5089
Eaton Bray Beds 30 SP9720
Eaton Constantine Shrops 37 SJ5906
Eaton Green Beds 30 SP9621
Eaton Hastings Oxon 21 SU2598
Eaton Mascott Shrops 37 SJ5305
Eaton Socon Beds 31 TL1759
Eaton upon Tern Shrops 37 SJ6523
Ebberston N York 63 SE8982
Ebbesborne Wake Wilts 9 ST9924
Ebbw Vale Gwent 27 SO1609
Ebchester Dur 68 NZ1055
Ebford Devon 5 SX9887
Ebley Gloucs 28 SO8205
Ebnal Ches 46 SJ4948
Ebrington Gloucs 29 SP1840
Ebsworthy Town Devon 4 SX5090
Ecchinswell Hants 21 SU4959
Ecclaw Loth 76 NT7568
Ecclefechan D & G 67 NY1974
Eccles Border 76 NT7641
Eccles Gt Man 47 SJ7798
Eccles Kent 14 TQ7360
Eccles Road Norfk 32 TM0189
Ecclesall S York 49 SK3284
Ecclesfield S York 49 SK3593
Eccleshall Staffs 38 SJ8329
Eccleshill W York 55 SE1736
Ecclesmachan Loth 75 NT0573
Eccleston Ches 46 SJ4162
Eccleston Lancs 53 SD5217
Eccleston Mersyd 46 SJ4895
Echt Gramp 89 NJ7405
Eckford Border 76 NT7026
Eckington Derbys 49 SK4379
Eckington H & W 28 SO9241
Ecton Nhants 30 SP8263
Edale Derbys 48 SK1285
Edburton W Susx 12 TQ2311
Edderton Highld 97 NH7084
Eddleston Border 75 NT2447
Eddlewood Strath 74 NS7153
Eden Park Gt Lon 23 TQ3667
Edenbridge Kent 13 TQ4446
Edenfield Lancs 54 SD8019
Edenhall Cumb 59 NY5632
Edenham Lincs 40 TF0621
Edensor Derbys 48 SK2469
Edentaggart Strath 80 NS3293
Edenthorpe S York 56 SE6206
Edern Gwynd 44 SH2739
Edgbaston W Mids 38 SP0684
Edgcott Bucks 30 SP6722
Edgcott Devon 7 SS8438
Edge Gloucs 28 SO8409
Edge Shrops 36 SJ3908
Edgefield Norfk 43 TG0934
Edgefield Green Norfk 43 TG0934
Edgerton W York 55 SE1317
Edgeworth Gloucs 28 SO9406
Edgmond Shrops 37 SJ7119
Edgton Shrops 36 SO3885
Edgware Gt Lon 23 TQ1991
Edgworth Lancs 54 SD7416
Edinample Cent 81 NN6022
Edinbane Highld 90 NG3451
Edinburgh Loth 75 NT2573
Edingale Staffs 39 SK2111
Edingham D & G 66 NX8363
Edingley Notts 49 SK6655
Edingthorpe Norfk 43 TG3132
Edingthorpe Green Norfk 43 TG3031
Edington Border 77 NT8955
Edington Nthumb 69 NZ1582
Edington Somset 19 ST3839
Edington Wilts 20 ST9253
Edington Burtle Somset 19 ST3943
Edingworth Somset 19 ST3653
Edith Weston Leics 40 SK9205
Edithmead Somset 19 ST3249
Edlesborough Bucks 30 SP9719
Edlingham Nthumb 69 NU1109
Edlington Lincs 51 TF2371
Edmondsham Dorset 10 SU0611
Edmondsley Dur 69 NZ2349
Edmondthorpe Leics 40 SK8517
Edmonton Gt Lon 23 TQ3492
Edmundbyers Dur 68 NZ0150
Ednam Border 76 NT7337
Edradynate Tays 87 NN8751
Edrom Border 77 NT8255
Edstaston Shrops 37 SJ5132
Edstone Warwks 29 SP1861
Edwinstowe Notts 49 SK6266
Edworth Beds 31 TL2241
Edwyn Ralph H & W 27 SO6457
Edzell Tays 89 NO6068
Efail Isaf M Glam 18 ST0884
Efail-fach W Glam 18 SS7895
Efailnewydd Gwynd 44 SH3535
Efailwen Dyfed 16 SN1325
Efenechtyd Clwyd 46 SJ1155
Effgill D & G 67 NY3092
Effingham Surrey 12 TQ1153
Efford Devon 7 SS8901
Egerton Gt Man 54 SD7014
Egerton Kent 14 TQ9147
Eggesford Devon 7 SS6811
Eggington Beds 30 SP9525
Egginton Derbys 39 SK2628
Egglescliffe Cleve 62 NZ4113
Eggleston Dur 61 NY9923
Egham Surrey 22 TQ0071
Egleton Leics 40 SK8707
Eglingham Nthumb 77 NU1019
Egloshayle Cnwll 3 SX0072
Egloskerry Cnwll 4 SX2786
Eglwys Cross Clwyd 37 SJ4740
Eglwysbach Gwynd 45 SH8070
Eglwyswrw Dyfed 16 SN1438
Egmanton Notts 50 SK7368
Egremont Cumb 58 NY0110
Egremont Mersyd 46 SJ3192
Egton N York 63 NZ8006
Egton Bridge N York 63 NZ8004
Eight Ash Green Essex 25 TL9425
Eilanreach Highld 85 NG8018
Elan Village Powys 35 SN9364
Elberton Avon 19 ST6088
Elburton Devon 4 SX5353
Elcombe Wilts 20 SU1280
Eldersfield H & W 28 SO7931
Elderslie Strath 73 NS4463
Eldon Dur 61 NZ2328
Elfhill Gramp 89 NO8085
Elford Staffs 38 SK1810
Elgin Gramp 94 NJ2162
Elgol Highld 84 NG5213
Elham Kent 15 TR1744
Elie Fife 83 NO4900
Elim Gwynd 44 SH3584

F

G

Garlinge Green Great Casterton

Garlinge Green *Kent* 15 TR1152
Garlogie *Gramp* 89 NJ7805
Garmond *Gramp* 95 NJ8052
Garmouth *Gramp* 94 NJ3364
Garmston *Shrops* 37 SJ6006
Garn-Dolbenmaen *Gwynd* 44 SH4943
Garnkirk *Strath* 74 NS6768
Garrabost *W Isls* 102 NB5133
Garrallan *Strath* 74 NS5418
Garras *Cnwll* 2 SW7023
Garreg *Gwynd* 45 SH6141
Garrigill *Cumb* 60 NY7441
Garroch *D & G* 65 NX5981
Garrochtrie *D & G* 64 NX1138
Garrochty *Strath* 73 NS0953
Garros *Highld* 90 NG4962
Garsdale Head *Cumb* 60 SD7891
Garsdon *Wilts* 20 ST9687
Garshall Green *Staffs* 38 SJ9633
Garsington *Oxon* 21 SP5802
Garstang *Lancs* 53 SD4945
Garston *Herts* 22 TL1100
Garston *Mersyd* 46 SJ4084
Gartachossan *Strath* 70 NR3461
Gartcosh *Strath* 74 NS6967
Garth *Clwyd* 36 SJ2542
Garth *Powys* 26 SN9549
Garth Penrhyncoch *Dyfed* 35 SN6484
Garth Row *Cumb* 59 SD5297
Garthamlock *Strath* 74 NS6566
Garthorpe *Humb* 56 SE8418
Garthorpe *Leics* 40 SK8320
Gartly *Gramp* 94 NJ5232
Gartmore *Cent* 81 NS5297
Gartness *Cent* 81 NS5086
Gartness *Strath* 74 NS7864
Gartocharn *Strath* 81 NS4286
Garton *Humb* 57 TA2635
Garton-on-the-Wolds *Humb* 56 SE9759
Gartsherrie *Strath* 74 NS7265
Gartymore *Highld* 97 ND0114
Garvald *Loth* 76 NT5870
Garvan *Highld* 85 NM9777
Garvard *Strath* 70 NR3791
Garve *Highld* 92 NH3961
Garvestone *Norfk* 42 TG0207
Garvock *Strath* 73 NS2570
Garway *H & W* 27 SO4522
Garway Common *H & W* 27 SO4622
Gasper *Wilts* 9 ST7633
Gass *Strath* 73 NS4105
Gastard *Wilts* 20 ST8868
Gasthorpe *Norfk* 32 TL9781
Gaston Green *Essex* 31 TL4917
Gatcombe *IOW* 11 SZ4985
Gate Burton *Lincs* 50 SK8382
Gate Helmsley *N York* 56 SE6955
Gateforth *N York* 56 SE5628
Gatehead *Strath* 73 NS3936
Gatehouse *Nthumb* 68 NY7889
Gatehouse of Fleet *D & G* 65 NX5956
Gateley *Norfk* 42 TF9624
Gatenby *N York* 62 SE3287
Gateshaw *Border* 76 NT7722
Gateshead *T & W* 69 NZ2562
Gateside *Fife* 82 NO1809
Gateside *Strath* 73 NS3653
Gateside *Strath* 73 NS4858
Gateside *Tays* 88 NO4344
Gateslack *D & G* 66 NS8902
Gatley *Gt Man* 47 SJ8488
Gatton *Surrey* 12 TQ2752
Gattonside *Border* 76 NT5435
Gauldry *Fife* 83 NO3723
Gauldswell *Tays* 88 NO2151
Gaunt's End *Essex* 24 TL5525
Gautby *Lincs* 50 TF1772
Gavinton *Border* 76 NT7652
Gawcott *Bucks* 30 SP6831
Gawsworth *Ches* 48 SJ8969
Gawthrop *Cumb* 60 SD6987
Gawthwaite *Cumb* 58 SD2784
Gaydon *Warwks* 29 SP3653
Gayhurst *Bucks* 30 SP8446
Gayle *N York* 60 SD8688
Gayles *N York* 61 NZ1207
Gayton *Nhants* 30 SP7054
Gayton *Norfk* 42 TF7219
Gayton *Staffs* 38 SJ9828
Gayton le Marsh *Lincs* 51 TF4284
Gayton Thorpe *Norfk* 42 TF7418
Gaywood *Norfk* 41 TF6320
Gazeley *Suffk* 32 TL7264
Geary *Highld* 90 NG2661
Gedding *Suffk* 32 TL9457
Geddinge *Kent* 15 TR2346
Geddington *Nhants* 40 SP8983
Gedling *Notts* 49 SK6142
Gedney *Lincs* 41 TF4024
Gedney Broadgate *Lincs* 41 TF4022
Gedney Drove End *Lincs* 41 TF4629
Gedney Dyke *Lincs* 41 TF4126
Gedney Hill *Lincs* 41 TF3311
Geldeston *Norfk* 33 TM3991
Gelli Gynan *Clwyd* 46 SJ1854
Gellifor *Clwyd* 46 SJ1262
Gelligaer *M Glam* 18 ST1396
Gellilydan *Gwynd* 45 SH6839
Gellinudd *W Glam* 18 SN7303
Gellyburn *Tays* 82 NO0939
Gellywen *Dyfed* 17 SN2723
Gelston *D & G* 66 NX7758
Gelston *Lincs* 50 SK9145
Gembling *Humb* 57 TA1057
Gentleshaw *Staffs* 38 SK0511
George Green *Bucks* 22 SU9981
George Nympton *Devon* 7 SS7023
Georgefield *D & G* 67 NY2991
Georgeham *Devon* 6 SS4639
Georth *Ork* 103 HY3625
Germansweek *Devon* 6 SX4394
Gerrans *Cnwll* 3 SW8735
Gerrards Cross *Bucks* 22 TQ0088
Gerrick *Cleve* 62 NZ7012
Gestingthorpe *Essex* 24 TL8138
Geuffordd *Powys* 36 SJ2114
Gidea Park *Gt Lon* 23 TQ5290
Giffnock *Strath* 74 NS5658
Gifford *Loth* 76 NT5368
Giffordtown *Fife* 83 NO2811
Giggleswick *N York* 54 SD8063
Gilberdyke *Humb* 56 SE8329
Gilchriston *Loth* 76 NT4865
Gilcrux *Cumb* 58 NY1138
Gildersome *W York* 55 SE2429
Gildingwells *S York* 49 SK5585
Gilesgate Moor *Dur* 61 NZ2942
Gileston *S Glam* 18 ST0166
Gilfach *M Glam* 19 ST1598
Gilfach Goch *M Glam* 18 SS9790
Gilfachrheda *Dyfed* 34 SN4158
Gilgarran *Cumb* 58 NY0323
Gillamoor *N York* 62 SE6889
Gillesbie *D & G* 67 NY1691
Gilling *N York* 61 NZ1805
Gilling East *N York* 62 SE6176
Gillingham *Dorset* 9 ST8026
Gillingham *Kent* 14 TQ7768
Gillingham *Norfk* 33 TM4191
Gillock *Highld* 100 ND2159
Gills *Highld* 100 ND3272
Gilmanscleuch *Border* 75 NT3321
Gilmerton *Loth* 75 NT2868
Gilmerton *Tays* 82 NN8823
Gilmonby *Dur* 61 NY9912
Gilmorton *Leics* 39 SP5787
Gilsland *Nthumb* 68 NY6366
Gilwern *Gwent* 27 SO2414
Gimingham *Norfk* 43 TG2836
Gipping *Suffk* 32 TM0763
Gipsey Bridge *Lincs* 51 TF2849
Girdle Toll *Strath* 73 NS3440
Girlsta *Shet* 103 HU4250
Girsby *Cleve* 62 NZ3508
Girthon *D & G* 65 NX6053
Girton *Cambs* 31 TL4262
Girton *Notts* 50 SK8265
Girvan *Strath* 64 NX1897
Gisburn *Lancs* 54 SD8248
Gisleham *Suffk* 33 TM5188
Gislingham *Suffk* 32 TM0771
Gissing *Norfk* 33 TM1485
Gittisham *Devon* 8 SY1398
Gladestry *Powys* 27 SO2355
Gladsmuir *Loth* 76 NT4573
Glais *W Glam* 18 SN7000
Glaisdale *N York* 63 NZ7705
Glamis *Tays* 88 NO3846
Glan-y-don *Clwyd* 46 SJ1679
Glanaman *Dyfed* 26 SN6713
Glandford *Norfk* 42 TG0441
Glandwr *Dyfed* 17 SN1928
Glandyfi *Dyfed* 35 SN6996
Glanton *Nthumb* 68 NU0714
Glanvilles Wootton *Dorset* 9 ST6708
Glapthorn *Nhants* 40 TL0290
Glapwell *Derbys* 49 SK4766
Glasbury *Powys* 27 SO1739
Glascwm *Powys* 27 SO1552
Glasfryn *Clwyd* 45 SH9250
Glasgow *Strath* 74 NS5865
Glasinfryn *Gwynd* 44 SH5868
Glasnacardoch Bay *Highld* 85 NM6795
Glasnakille *Highld* 84 NG5313
Glasserton *D & G* 64 NX4237
Glassford *Strath* 74 NS7247
Glasshouse *Gloucs* 28 SO7021
Glasshouses *N York* 55 SE1764
Glasson *Cumb* 67 NY2560
Glasson *Lancs* 53 SD4456
Glassonby *Cumb* 59 NY5738
Glasterlaw *Tays* 89 NO5951
Glaston *Leics* 40 SK8900
Glastonbury *Somset* 19 ST5038
Glatton *Cambs* 40 TL1586
Glazebrook *Ches* 47 SJ6992
Glazebury *Ches* 47 SJ6797
Glazeley *Shrops* 37 SO7088
Gleaston *Cumb* 53 SD2570
Gledhow *W York* 55 SE3137
Gledpark *D & G* 65 NX6250
Gledrid *Shrops* 36 SJ3036
Glemsford *Suffk* 32 TL8348
Glen *D & G* 65 NX5457
Glen Clunie Lodge *Gramp* 88 NO1383
Glen Maye *IOM* 52 SC2379
Glen Nevis House *Highld* 86 NN1272
Glen Parva *Leics* 39 SP5798
Glen Trool Lodge *D & G* 64 NX4080
Glenancross *Highld* 85 NM6691
Glenaros House *Strath* 79 NM5544
Glenbarr *Strath* 72 NR6736
Glenbeg *Highld* 79 NM5862
Glenboig *Strath* 74 NS7268
Glenborrodale *Highld* 79 NM6061
Glenbranter *Strath* 80 NS1197
Glenbreck *Border* 75 NT0521
Glenbrittle House *Highld* 84 NG4121
Glenbuck *Strath* 74 NS7429
Glencally *Tays* 88 NO3562
Glencaple *D & G* 66 NX9968
Glencarron Lodge *Highld* 91 NH0650
Glencarse *Tays* 82 NO1921
Glenceitlein *Highld* 86 NN1548
Glencoe *Highld* 86 NN1058
Glencothe *Border* 75 NT0829
Glencraig *Fife* 82 NT1894
Glencrosh *D & G* 65 NX7689
Glendale *Highld* 90 NG1749
Glendaruel *Strath* 80 NR9983
Glendevon *Tays* 82 NN9904
Glendoe Lodge *Highld* 92 NH4009
Glendoick *Tays* 82 NO2022
Glenduckie *Fife* 83 NO2818
Gleneagles *Tays* 82 NN9208
Glenegedale *Strath* 70 NR3351
Glenelg *Highld* 85 NG8119
Glenerney *Gramp* 93 NJ0146
Glenfarg *Tays* 82 NO1310
Glenfeshie Lodge *Highld* 87 NN8493
Glenfield *Leics* 39 SK5406
Glenfinnan *Highld* 85 NM9080
Glenfinntaig Lodge *Highld* 86 NN2286
Glenfoot *Tays* 82 NO1815
Glenfyne Lodge *Strath* 80 NN2215
Glengarnock *Strath* 73 NS3252
Glengolly *Highld* 100 ND1065
Glengorm Castle *Strath* 79 NM4457
Glengrasco *Highld* 90 NG4444
Glenholm *Border* 75 NT1033
Glenhoul *D & G* 65 NX6187
Glenkerry *Border* 67 NT2710
Glenkin *Strath* 80 NS1280
Glenkindie *Gramp* 94 NJ4314
Glenlee *D & G* 65 NX6080
Glenlivet *Gramp* 94 NJ1929
Glenlochar *D & G* 65 NX7364
Glenloig *Strath* 72 NR9435
Glenlomond *Tays* 82 NO1704
Glenluce *D & G* 64 NX1957
Glenmark *Tays* 88 NO4183
Glenmassen *Strath* 80 NS1088
Glenmavis *Strath* 74 NS7467
Glenmore *Highld* 84 NG4340
Glenmore Lodge *Highld* 93 NH9709
Glenquiech *Tays* 88 NO4261
Glenralloch *Strath* 71 NR8569
Glenrothes *Fife* 83 NO2700
Glenshero Lodge *Highld* 87 NN5592
Glenstriven *Strath* 80 NS0878
Glentham *Lincs* 50 TF0090
Glentromie Lodge *Highld* 87 NN7897
Glentrool Village *D & G* 64 NX3578
Glentruim House *Highld* 87 NN6894
Glentworth *Lincs* 50 SK9488
Glenuig *Highld* 85 NM6677
Glenure *Strath* 86 NN0448
Glenurquhart *Highld* 93 NH7462
Glenvarragill *Highld* 84 NG4739
Glenwhilly *D & G* 64 NX1771
Glespin *Strath* 74 NS8127
Glewstone *H & W* 27 SO5521
Glinton *Cambs* 40 TF1505
Glooston *Leics* 40 SP7595
Glossop *Derbys* 48 SK0393
Gloster Hill *Nthumb* 69 NU2504
Gloucester *Gloucs* 28 SO8318
Glusburn *N York* 54 SE0045
Glutt Lodge *Highld* 100 ND0036
Gluvian *Cnwll* 3 SW9164
Glympton *Oxon* 29 SP4221
Glyn Ceiriog *Clwyd* 36 SJ2038
Glyn-Neath *W Glam* 26 SN8806
Glynarthen *Dyfed* 17 SN3148
Glyncorrwg *W Glam* 18 SS8798
Glynde *E Susx* 13 TQ4509
Glyndyfrdwy *Clwyd* 36 SJ1442
Glyntawe *Powys* 26 SN8416
Glynteg *Dyfed* 17 SN3538
Gnosall *Staffs* 38 SJ8220
Gnosall Heath *Staffs* 38 SJ8220
Goadby *Leics* 40 SP7598
Goadby Marwood *Leics* 40 SK7726
Goatacre *Wilts* 20 SU0276
Goatfield *Strath* 80 NN0100
Goathill *Dorset* 9 ST6717
Goathland *N York* 63 NZ8301
Goathurst *Somset* 8 ST2534
Gobowen *Shrops* 36 SJ3033
Godalming *Surrey* 12 SU9643
Goddard's Green *Kent* 14 TQ8134
Godmanchester *Cambs* 31 TL2470
Godmanstone *Dorset* 9 SY6697
Godmersham *Kent* 15 TR0550
Godney *Somset* 19 ST4842
Godolphin Cross *Cnwll* 2 SW6031
Godre'r-graig *W Glam* 26 SN7506
Godshill *IOW* 11 SZ5281
Godstone *Surrey* 12 TQ3551
Goetre *Gwent* 27 SO3206
Goff's Oak *Herts* 23 TL3202
Gofilon *Gwent* 27 SO2613
Gogar *Loth* 75 NT1672
Goginan *Dyfed* 35 SN6881
Golan *Gwynd* 44 SH5242
Golant *Cnwll* 3 SX1254
Golberdon *Cnwll* 4 SX3271
Golborne *Gt Man* 47 SJ6097
Golcar *W York* 55 SE0915
Goldcliff *Gwent* 19 ST3683
Golden Green *Kent* 13 TQ6348
Golden Pot *Hants* 11 SU7143
Golders Green *Gt Lon* 23 TQ2487
Goldhanger *Essex* 24 TL9008
Goldington *Beds* 30 TL0750
Goldsborough *N York* 63 NZ8314
Goldsborough *N York* 55 SE3856
Goldsithney *Cnwll* 2 SW5430
Goldsworth *Surrey* 22 SU9958
Goldthorpe *S York* 55 SE4604
Goldworthy *Devon* 6 SS3922
Gollanfield *Highld* 93 NH8053
Golspie *Highld* 97 NC8300
Gomeldon *Wilts* 10 SU1835
Gomshall *Surrey* 12 TQ0847
Gonalston *Notts* 49 SK6747
Gonfirth *Shet* 103 HU3661
Good Easter *Essex* 24 TL6212
Gooderstone *Norfk* 42 TF7602
Goodleigh *Devon* 6 SS6034
Goodmanham *Humb* 56 SE8843
Goodnestone *Kent* 15 TR0461
Goodnestone *Kent* 15 TR2554
Goodrich *H & W* 27 SO5719
Goodrington *Devon* 5 SX8958
Goodshaw Fold *Lancs* 54 SD8026
Goodwick *Dyfed* 16 SM9438
Goodworth Clatford *Hants* 21 SU3642
Goole *Humb* 56 SE7423
Goom's Hill *H & W* 28 SP0154
Goonbell *Cnwll* 2 SW7249
Goonhavern *Cnwll* 2 SW7853
Goonvrea *Cnwll* 2 SW7149
Goose Green *Avon* 20 ST6774
Goose Green *Essex* 25 TM1327
Goosecruives *Gramp* 89 NO7583
Gooseford *Devon* 5 SX6792
Goosey *Oxon* 21 SU3591
Goosnargh *Lancs* 53 SD5536
Goostrey *Ches* 47 SJ7770
Gordon *Border* 76 NT6443
Gordon Arms Hotel *Border* 75 NT3025
Gordonstown *Gramp* 94 NJ5656
Gordonstown *Gramp* 95 NJ7138
Gorebridge *Loth* 75 NT3461
Gores *Wilts* 20 SU1158
Gorey *Jersey* 101 SY2110
Goring *Oxon* 21 SU6080
Goring-by-Sea *W Susx* 12 TQ1102
Gorleston on Sea *Norfk* 43 TG5204
Gorrachie *Gramp* 95 NJ7358
Gorran *Cnwll* 3 SW9942
Gorran Haven *Cnwll* 3 SX0141
Gorse Hill *Wilts* 20 SU1586
Gorsedd *Clwyd* 46 SJ1576
Gorseinon *W Glam* 17 SS5998
Gorsgoch *Dyfed* 17 SN4850
Gorslas *Dyfed* 17 SN5713
Gorsley *Gloucs* 28 SO6925
Gorsley Common *Gloucs* 28 SO6825
Gorstan *Highld* 92 NH3862
Gorstello *Ches* 46 SJ3562
Gorsty Common *H & W* 27 SO4437
Gorsty Hill *Staffs* 38 SK1028
Gorten *Strath* 79 NM7432
Gorthleck *Highld* 92 NH5420
Gorton *Gt Man* 47 SJ8896
Gosbeck *Suffk* 33 TM1555
Gosberton *Lincs* 41 TF2331
Gosfield *Essex* 24 TL7829
Gosforth *Cumb* 58 NY0603
Gosforth *T & W* 69 NZ2368
Gospel End *Staffs* 38 SO8993
Gosport *Hants* 11 SZ6099
Gotham *Notts* 39 SK5330
Gotherington *Gloucs* 28 SO9529
Gotton *Somset* 8 ST2428
Goudhurst *Kent* 14 TQ7237
Goulceby *Lincs* 51 TF2579
Gourdas *Gramp* 95 NJ7741
Gourdie *Tays* 83 NO3532
Gourdon *Gramp* 89 NO8270
Gourock *Strath* 80 NS2477
Govan *Strath* 74 NS5465
Goveton *Devon* 5 SX7546
Gowdall *Humb* 56 SE6222
Gower *Highld* 92 NH5058
Gowerton *W Glam* 17 SS5896
Gowkhall *Fife* 82 NT0589
Goxhill *Humb* 57 TA1021
Goxhill *Humb* 57 TA1844
Graffham *W Susx* 12 SU9217
Grafham *Cambs* 31 TL1669
Grafham *Surrey* 12 TQ0241
Grafton *H & W* 28 SO9837
Grafton *N York* 55 SE4163
Grafton *Oxon* 21 SP2600
Grafton *Shrops* 36 SJ4319
Grafton Flyford *H & W* 28 SO9655
Grafton Regis *Nhants* 30 SP7546
Grafton Underwood *Nhants* 40 SP9280
Grafty Green *Kent* 14 TQ8748
Graig *Gwynd* 45 SH8071
Graig-fechan *Clwyd* 46 SJ1454
Grain *Kent* 14 TQ8876
Grainsby *Lincs* 51 TF2799
Grainthorpe *Lincs* 51 TF3896
Graizelound *Humb* 50 SK7698
Gramisdale *W Isls* 102 NF8155
Grampound *Cnwll* 3 SW9348
Grampound Road *Cnwll* 3 SW9150
Granborough *Bucks* 30 SP7625
Granby *Notts* 40 SK7536
Grand Chemins *Jersey* 101 JS1710
Grandborough *Warwks* 29 SP4966
Grandes Rocques *Guern* 101 GN5011
Grandtully *Tays* 87 NN9153
Grange *Cumb* 58 NY2517
Grange *Kent* 14 TQ7968
Grange *Tays* 83 NO2625
Grange Crossroads *Gramp* 94 NJ4754
Grange Hall *Gramp* 93 NJ0660
Grange Hill *Gt Lon* 23 TQ4492
Grange Lindores *Fife* 83 NO2516
Grange Moor *W York* 55 SE2215
Grange Villa *Dur* 69 NZ2352
Grange-over-Sands *Cumb* 59 SD4077
Grangehall *Strath* 75 NS9642
Grangemill *Derbys* 48 SK2457
Grangemouth *Cent* 82 NS9281
Grangepans *Cent* 82 NT0181
Grangetown *Cleve* 62 NZ5420
Gransmoor *Humb* 57 TA1259
Granston *Dyfed* 16 SM8934
Grantchester *Cambs* 31 TL4355
Grantham *Lincs* 40 SK9135
Granton *Fife* 75 NT2376
Grantown-on-Spey *Highld* 93 NJ0328
Grantshouse *Border* 76 NT8065
Grasby *Lincs* 57 TA0804
Grasmere *Cumb* 59 NY3307
Grasscroft *Gt Man* 54 SD9704
Grassendale *Mersyd* 46 SJ3985
Grassington *N York* 54 SE0063
Grassmoor *Derbys* 49 SK4067
Grassthorpe *Notts* 50 SK7967
Grateley *Hants* 21 SU2741
Graveley *Cambs* 31 TL2563
Graveley *Herts* 31 TL2327
Graveney *Kent* 15 TR0562
Gravesend *Kent* 14 TQ6571
Gravir *W Isls* 102 NB3915
Grayingham *Lincs* 50 SK9396
Grayrigg *Cumb* 59 SD5796
Grays *Essex* 24 TQ6177
Grayshott *Hants* 11 SU8735
Grayswood *Surrey* 11 SU9134
Grazeley *Berks* 22 SU6966
Greasbrough *S York* 49 SK4195
Greasby *Mersyd* 46 SJ2587
Greasley *Notts* 49 SK4846
Great Abington *Cambs* 31 TL5348
Great Addington *Nhants* 30 SP9675
Great Alne *Warwks* 28 SP1259
Great Altcar *Lancs* 46 SD3305
Great Amwell *Herts* 31 TL3712
Great Asby *Cumb* 60 NY6713
Great Ayton *N York* 62 NZ5610
Great Baddow *Essex* 24 TL7304
Great Badminton *Avon* 20 ST8082
Great Bardfield *Essex* 24 TL6730
Great Barford *Beds* 30 TL1351
Great Barrington *Gloucs* 29 SP2113
Great Barrow *Ches* 46 SJ4768
Great Barton *Suffk* 32 TL8967
Great Barugh *N York* 63 SE7479
Great Bavington *Nthumb* 68 NY9880
Great Bedwyn *Wilts* 21 SU2764
Great Bentley *Essex* 25 TM1021
Great Billing *Nhants* 30 SP8162
Great Bircham *Norfk* 42 TF7732
Great Blakenham *Suffk* 33 TM1150
Great Blencow *Cumb* 59 NY4532
Great Bolas *Shrops* 37 SJ6421
Great Bookham *Surrey* 22 TQ1354
Great Bosullow *Cnwll* 2 SW4133
Great Bourton *Oxon* 29 SP4545
Great Bowden *Leics* 40 SP7488
Great Bradley *Suffk* 32 TL6753
Great Braxted *Essex* 24 TL8614
Great Bricett *Suffk* 32 TM0350
Great Brickhill *Bucks* 30 SP9030
Great Bridgeford *Staffs* 38 SJ8827
Great Brington *Nhants* 30 SP6665
Great Bromley *Essex* 25 TM0826
Great Broughton *Cumb* 58 NY0731
Great Broughton *N York* 62 NZ5405
Great Budworth *Ches* 47 SJ6677
Great Burdon *Dur* 62 NZ3116
Great Burstead *Essex* 24 TQ6892
Great Busby *N York* 62 NZ5205
Great Canfield *Essex* 24 TL5918
Great Carlton *Lincs* 51 TF4085
Great Casterton *Leics* 40 TF0008

Great Chart

Hampton Poyle

Great Chart Kent 15 TQ9841
Great Chatfield Wilts 20 ST8563
Great Chatwell Staffs 37 SJ7914
Great Chesterford Essex 31 TL5042
Great Cheverell Wilts 20 ST9854
Great Chishill Cambs 31 TL4238
Great Clacton Essex 25 TM1716
Great Cliffe W York 55 SE3015
Great Clifton Cumb 58 NY0429
Great Coates Humb 57 TA2309
Great Comberton H & W 28 SO9542
Great Corby Cumb 67 NY4754
Great Cornard Suffk 32 TL8840
Great Cowden Humb 57 TA2342
Great Coxwell Oxon 21 SU2693
Great Cransley Nhants 30 SP8376
Great Cressingham Norfk 42 TF8501
Great Crosthwaite Cumb 58 NY2524
Great Cubley Derbys 48 SK1638
Great Dalby Leics 40 SK7414
Great Doddington Nhants 30 SP8864
Great Dunham Norfk 42 TF8714
Great Dunmow Essex 24 TL6222
Great Durnford Wilts 10 SU1338
Great Easton Essex 24 TL6025
Great Easton Leics 40 SP8492
Great Eccleston Lancs 53 SD4240
Great Ellingham Norfk 42 TM0196
Great Elm Somset 20 ST7449
Great Englebourne Devon 5 SX7756
Great Everdon Nhants 29 SP5957
Great Eversden Cambs 31 TL3653
Great Finborough Suffk 32 TM0158
Great Fransham Norfk 42 TF8913
Great Gaddesden Herts 22 TL0211
Great Gidding Cambs 40 TL1183
Great Givendale Humb 56 SE8153
Great Glemham Suffk 33 TM3361
Great Glen Leics 39 SP6597
Great Gonerby Lincs 40 SK8938
Great Gransden Cambs 31 TL2655
Great Green Cambs 31 TL2844
Great Green Suffk 32 TL9155
Great Green Suffk 32 TL9365
Great Habton N York 63 SE7576
Great Hale Lincs 50 TF1442
Great Hallingbury Essex 31 TL5119
Great Hanwood Shrops 36 SJ4409
Great Harrowden Nhants 30 SP8770
Great Harwood Lancs 54 SD7332
Great Haseley Oxon 21 SP6401
Great Hatfield Humb 57 TA1842
Great Haywood Staffs 38 SJ9922
Great Heck N York 56 SE5920
Great Henny Essex 24 TL8637
Great Hinton Wilts 20 ST9059
Great Hockham Norfk 32 TL9592
Great Holland Essex 25 TM2019
Great Horkesley Essex 25 TL9731
Great Hormead Herts 31 TL4029
Great Horton W York 55 SE1431
Great Horwood Bucks 30 SP7731
Great Houghton Nhants 30 SP7958
Great Houghton S York 55 SE4206
Great Hucklow Derbys 48 SK1777
Great Kelk Humb 57 TA1058
Great Kimble Bucks 22 SP8205
Great Kingshill Bucks 22 SU8797
Great Langdale Cumb 58 NY2906
Great Langton N York 61 SE2996
Great Leighs Essex 24 TL7217
Great Limber Lincs 57 TA1308
Great Linford Bucks 30 SP8542
Great Livermere Suffk 32 TL8871
Great Longstone Derbys 48 SK2071
Great Lumley T & W 69 NZ2949
Great Malvern H & W 28 SO7746
Great Maplestead Essex 24 TL8034
Great Marton Lancs 53 SD3235
Great Massingham Norfk 42 TF7922
Great Milton Oxon 21 SP6202
Great Missenden Bucks 22 SP8901
Great Mitton Lancs 54 SD7138
Great Mongeham Kent 15 TR3551
Great Moulton Norfk 33 TM1690
Great Musgrave Cumb 60 NY7613
Great Ness Shrops 36 SJ3919
Great Oak Gwent 27 SO3810
Great Oakley Essex 25 TM1927
Great Oakley Nhants 40 SP8785
Great Offley Herts 30 TL1427
Great Ormside Cumb 60 NY7017
Great Orton Cumb 67 NY3254
Great Ouseburn N York 55 SE4461
Great Oxendon Nhants 40 SP7383
Great Oxney Green Essex 24 TL6606
Great Paxton Cambs 31 TL2063
Great Plumpton Lancs 53 SD3833
Great Plumstead Norfk 43 TG3010
Great Ponton Lincs 40 SK9230
Great Preston W York 55 SE4029
Great Raveley Cambs 41 TL2581
Great Rissington Gloucs 29 SP1917
Great Rollright Oxon 29 SP3231
Great Ryburgh Norfk 42 TF9527
Great Ryle Nthumb 68 NU0212
Great Ryton Shrops 37 SJ4803
Great Saling Essex 24 TL6925
Great Salkeld Cumb 59 NY5536
Great Sampford Essex 24 TL6435
Great Saughall Ches 46 SJ3669
Great Shefford Berks 21 SU3875
Great Shelford Cambs 31 TL4651
Great Smeaton N York 62 NZ3404
Great Snoring Norfk 42 TF9434
Great Somerford Wilts 20 ST9682
Great Soudley Shrops 37 SJ7229
Great Stainton Dur 62 NZ3322
Great Stambridge Essex 24 TQ8991
Great Staughton Cambs 30 TL1264
Great Steeping Lincs 51 TF4364
Great Strickland Cumb 59 NY5522
Great Stukeley Cambs 31 TL2274
Great Sturton Lincs 51 TF2176
Great Swinburne Nthumb 68 NY9375
Great Tew Oxon 29 SP4028
Great Tey Essex 24 TL8925
Great Torrington Devon 6 SS4919
Great Tosson Nthumb 68 NU0200
Great Totham Essex 24 TL8611
Great Totham Essex 24 TL8713
Great Urswick Cumb 58 SD2674
Great Wakering Essex 25 TQ9487
Great Waldingfield Suffk 32 TL9144
Great Walsingham Norfk 42 TF9437
Great Waltham Essex 24 TL6913
Great Warley Essex 24 TQ5890
Great Washbourne Gloucs 28 SO9834
Great Weeke Devon 5 SX7187
Great Weldon Nhants 40 SP9289
Great Wenham Suffk 25 TM0738
Great Whittington Nthumb 68 NZ0070
Great Wigborough Essex 25 TL9615
Great Wilbraham Cambs 31 TL5557
Great Wishford Wilts 10 SU0735
Great Witcombe Gloucs 28 SO9114
Great Witley H & W 28 SO7566
Great Wolford Warwks 29 SP2534
Great Wratting Essex 32 TL6848
Great Wymondley Herts 31 TL2128
Great Wyrley Staffs 38 SJ9907
Great Yarmouth Norfk 43 TG5207
Great Yeldham Essex 24 TL7638
Greatford Lincs 40 TF0811
Greatgate Staffs 48 SK0539
Greatham Cleve 62 NZ4927
Greatham Hants 11 SU7730
Greatham W Susx 12 TQ0415
Greatstone-on-Sea Kent 15 TR0822
Greatworth Nhants 29 SP5542
Green End Herts 31 TL3222
Green End Herts 31 TL3333
Green End Warwks 39 SP2686
Green Hammerton N York 55 SE4556
Green Heath Staffs 38 SJ9913
Green Moor S York 49 SK2899
Green Ore Somset 19 ST5750
Green Quarter Cumb 59 NY4603
Green Street H & W 28 SO8749
Green Street Herts 31 TL4521
Green Street Herts 23 TQ1998
Green Street Green Kent 14 TQ5870
Green Tye Herts 31 TL4418
Greenburn Loth 75 NS9360
Greenfield Beds 30 TL0534
Greenfield Clwyd 46 SJ1977
Greenfield Highld 86 NH2000
Greenfield Strath 80 NS2490
Greenford Gt Lon 22 TQ1482
Greengairs Strath 74 NS7870
Greengates W York 55 SE1937
Greenhalgh Lancs 53 SD4035
Greenham Somset 8 ST0820
Greenhaugh Nthumb 68 NY7987
Greenhill Cent 82 NS8279
Greenhill D & G 67 NY1079
Greenhill Kent 15 TR1666
Greenhill Strath 75 NS9332
Greenhithe Kent 14 TQ5875
Greenholm Strath 74 NS5437
Greenhouse Border 76 NT5523
Greenhow Hill N York 55 SE1164
Greenland Highld 100 ND2367
Greenland S York 49 SK3988
Greenlaw Border 76 NT7146
Greenlea D & G 66 NY0375
Greenloaning Tays 82 NN8307
Greenmount Gt Man 54 SD7714
Greenock Strath 80 NS2876
Greenodd Cumb 58 SD3182
Greens Norton Nhants 30 SP6649
Greenside T & W 69 NZ1362
Greenside W York 55 SE1716
Greenstead Essex 25 TM0125
Greenstead Green Essex 24 TL8227
Greensted Essex 24 TL5403
Greenway Somset 8 ST3124
Greenwich Gt Lon 23 TQ3877
Greet Gloucs 28 SP0230
Greete Shrops 27 SO5770
Greetham Leics 40 SK9214
Greetham Lincs 51 TF3070
Greetland W York 55 SE0821
Greinton Somset 19 ST4136
Grenaby IOM 52 SC2672
Grendon Nhants 30 SP8760
Grendon Warwks 39 SP2799
Grendon Underwood Bucks 30 SP6820
Grenoside S York 49 SK3393
Gresford Clwyd 46 SJ3454
Gresham Norfk 43 TG1638
Greshornish House Hotel Highld 90 NG3454
Gressenhall Norfk 42 TF9615
Gressenhall Green Norfk 42 TF9616
Gressingham Lancs 53 SD5769
Greta Bridge Dur 61 NZ0813
Gretna D & G 67 NY3167
Gretna Green D & G 67 NY3168
Gretton Gloucs 28 SP0030
Gretton Nhants 40 SP8994
Gretton Shrops 37 SO5195
Grewelthorpe N York 61 SE2376
Grey's Green Oxon 22 SU7182
Greyrigg D & G 66 NY0888
Greysouthern Cumb 58 NY0729
Greystoke Cumb 59 NY4430
Greystone Tays 89 NO5343
Greywell Hants 22 SU7151
Griff Warwks 39 SP3689
Griffithstown Gwent 19 ST2998
Grimeford Village Lancs 54 SD6112
Grimesthorpe S York 49 SK3689
Grimethorpe S York 55 SE4109
Grimley H & W 28 SO8360
Grimmet Strath 73 NS3210
Grimoldby Lincs 51 TF3988
Grimpo Shrops 36 SJ3526
Grimsargh Lancs 54 SD5834
Grimsby Humb 57 TA2710
Grimscote Nhants 29 SP6553
Grimscott Cnwll 6 SS2606
Grimshader W Isls 102 NB4025
Grimsthorpe Lincs 40 TF0422
Grimston Leics 39 SK6821
Grimston Norfk 42 TF7222
Grimstone Dorset 9 SY6394
Grimstone End Suffk 32 TL9368
Grindale Humb 57 TA1271
Grindleford Derbys 48 SK2477
Grindleton Lancs 54 SD7545
Grindley Brook Shrops 37 SJ5242
Grindlow Derbys 48 SK1877
Grindon Staffs 48 SK0854
Gringley on the Hill Notts 50 SK7390
Grinsdale Cumb 67 NY3758
Grinshill Shrops 37 SJ5223
Grinton N York 61 SE0498
Grishipoll Strath 78 NM1859
Gristhorpe N York 63 TA0981
Griston Norfk 42 TL9499
Gritley Ork 103 HY5504
Grittenham Wilts 20 SU0382
Grittleton Wilts 20 ST8580
Grizebeck Cumb 58 SD2384
Grizedale Cumb 59 SD3394
Groby Leics 39 SK5207
Groes Clwyd 45 SJ0064
Groes-faen M Glam 18 ST0680
Groes-Wen M Glam 18 ST1286
Groesffordd Marli Clwyd 45 SJ0073
Grogport Strath 72 NR8144
Gronant Clwyd 46 SJ0983
Groombridge E Susx 13 TQ5337
Grosebay W Isls 102 NG1593
Grosmont Gwent 27 SO4024
Grosmont N York 63 NZ8305
Grossington Gloucs 20 SO7302
Groton Suffk 32 TL9641
Grouville Jersey 101 JS1908
Grove Notts 50 SK7479
Grove Oxon 21 SU4090
Grove Park Gt Lon 23 TQ4072
Grovesend W Glam 17 SN5900
Gruids Highld 96 NC5603
Gruinard Highld 91 NG9489
Gruinart Strath 70 NR2966
Grula Highld 84 NG3826
Gruline Strath 79 NM5440
Grundisburgh Suffk 33 TM2251
Gruting Shet 103 HU2749
Gualachulain Highld 86 NN1145
Guardbridge Fife 83 NO4518
Guarlford H & W 28 SO8145
Guay Tays 88 NN9948
Guestling Green E Susx 14 TQ8513
Guestling Thorn E Susx 14 TQ8516
Guestwick Norfk 42 TG0626
Guide Lancs 54 SD7025
Guilden Morden Cambs 31 TL2744
Guilden Sutton Ches 46 SJ4468
Guildford Surrey 12 SU9949
Guildtown Tays 82 NO1331
Guilsborough Nhants 30 SP6772
Guilsfield Powys 36 SJ2211
Guiltreehill Strath 73 NS3610
Guineaford Devon 6 SS5537
Guisborough Cleve 62 NZ6015
Guiseley W York 55 SE1942
Guist Norfk 42 TG0025
Guiting Power Gloucs 28 SP0924
Gullane Loth 83 NT4882
Gulval Cnwll 2 SW4831
Gulworthy Devon 4 SX4572
Gumfreston Dyfed 16 SN1001
Gumley Leics 39 SP6889
Gun Hill E Susx 13 TQ5614
Gunby Lincs 40 SK9121
Gunby Lincs 51 TF4666
Gundleton Hants 11 SU6133
Gunn Devon 7 SS6333
Gunnerside N York 61 SD9598
Gunnerton Nthumb 68 NY9074
Gunness Humb 56 SE8411
Gunnislake Devon 4 SX4371
Gunnista Shet 103 HU5043
Gunthorpe Norfk 42 TG0134
Gunthorpe Notts 49 SK6844
Gunwalloe Cnwll 2 SW6522
Gurnard IOW 11 SZ4795
Gurney Slade Somset 19 ST6249
Gurnos W Glam 26 SN7709
Gussage All Saints Dorset 10 SU0010
Gussage St. Michael Dorset 9 ST9811
Guston Kent 15 TR3244
Gutcher Shet 103 HU5499
Guthrie Tays 89 NO5650
Guyhirn Cambs 41 TF4003
Guyzance Nthumb 69 NU2103
Gwaenysgor Clwyd 46 SJ0781
Gwalchmai Gwynd 44 SH3876
Gwaun-Cae-Gurwen W Glam 26 SN6911
Gweek Cnwll 2 SW7026
Gwenddwr Powys 26 SO0643
Gwennap Cnwll 2 SW7340
Gwernaffield Clwyd 46 SJ2065
Gwernesney Gwent 19 SO4101
Gwernogle Dyfed 17 SN5333
Gwernymynydd Clwyd 46 SJ2162
Gwespyr Clwyd 46 SJ1183
Gwinear Cnwll 2 SW5937
Gwithian Cnwll 2 SW5841
Gwyddelwern Clwyd 46 SJ0746
Gwyddgrug Dyfed 17 SN4635
Gwytherin Clwyd 45 SH8761

H

Habberley H & W 37 SO8177
Habberley Shrops 36 SJ3903
Habergham Lancs 54 SD8033
Habertoft Lincs 51 TF5069
Habrough Humb 57 TA1413
Hacconby Lincs 40 TF1025
Haceby Lincs 40 TF0236
Hacheston Suffk 33 TM3059
Hackbridge Gt Lon 23 TQ2865
Hackenthorpe S York 49 SK4183
Hackford Norfk 42 TG0502
Hackforth N York 61 SE2492
Hackland Ork 103 HY3920
Hackleton Nhants 30 SP8055
Hacklinge Kent 15 TR3454
Hackness N York 63 SE9790
Hackney Gt Lon 23 TQ3484
Hackthorn Lincs 50 SK9982
Hackthorpe Cumb 59 NY5423
Hadden Border 76 NT7836
Haddenham Bucks 22 SP7308
Haddenham Cambs 31 TL4675
Haddington Lincs 50 SK9162
Haddington Loth 76 NT5173
Haddiscoe Norfk 43 TM4497
Haddo Gramp 95 NJ8337
Haddon Cambs 40 TL1392
Hadham Ford Herts 31 TL4321
Hadleigh Essex 24 TQ8187
Hadleigh Suffk 32 TM0242
Hadley H & W 28 SO8564
Hadley End Staffs 38 SK1320
Hadley Wood Gt Lon 23 TQ2698
Hadlow Kent 13 TQ6350
Hadlow Down E Susx 13 TQ5324
Hadnall Shrops 37 SJ5220
Hadstock Essex 31 TL5644
Hadzor H & W 28 SO9162
Hafodunos Clwyd 45 SH8666
Haggerston Nthumb 77 NU0443
Haggs Cent 81 NS7879
Hagley H & W 27 SO5641
Hagley H & W 38 SO9180
Hagworthingham Lincs 51 TF3469
Hail Weston Cambs 31 TL1662
Haile Cumb 58 NY0308
Hailsham E Susx 13 TQ5909
Hainault Gt Lon 23 TQ4591
Hainford Norfk 43 TG2218
Hainton Lincs 50 TF1884
Haisthorpe Humb 57 TA1264
Hakin Dyfed 16 SM8905
Halam Notts 49 SK6754
Halbeath Fife 82 NT1288
Halberton Devon 7 ST0112
Halcro Highld 100 ND2360
Hale Ches 46 SJ4782
Hale Cumb 59 SD5078
Hale Gt Man 47 SJ7786
Hale Hants 10 SU1818
Hale Surrey 22 SU8448
Hale Green E Susx 13 TQ5514
Hale Street Kent 14 TQ6749
Hales Norfk 43 TM3797
Hales Staffs 37 SJ7134
Hales Place Kent 15 TR1459
Halesowen W Mids 38 SO9683
Halesworth Suffk 33 TM3877
Halford Devon 5 SX8174
Halford Shrops 36 SO4383
Halford Warwks 29 SP2645
Halfpenny Green Staffs 38 SO8291
Halfway House Shrops 36 SJ3411
Halfway Houses Kent 14 TQ9372
Halifax W York 55 SE0925
Halistra Highld 90 NG2459
Halket Strath 73 NS4252
Halkirk Highld 100 ND1359
Halkyn Clwyd 46 SJ2171
Hall Strath 73 NS4154
Hall Dunnerdale Cumb 58 SD2195
Hall Green W Mids 38 SP1181
Hall's Green Herts 31 TL2728
Halland E Susx 13 TQ4916
Hallaton Leics 40 SP7896
Hallatrow Avon 19 ST6357
Hallbankgate Cumb 67 NY5859
Hallen Avon 19 ST5580
Hallgarth Dur 69 NZ3243
Hallin Highld 90 NG2558
Halling Kent 14 TQ7063
Hallington Lincs 51 TF3085
Hallington Nthumb 68 NY9875
Halliwell Gt Man 54 SD6910
Halloughton Notts 49 SK6951
Hallow H & W 28 SO8258
Hallrule Border 67 NT5914
Hallsands Devon 5 SX8138
Hallyne Border 75 NT1940
Halnaker W Susx 11 SU9007
Halsall Lancs 53 SD3710
Halse Nhants 29 SP5640
Halse Somset 8 ST1428
Halsetown Cnwll 2 SW5038
Halsham Humb 57 TA2727
Halstead Essex 24 TL8130
Halstead Kent 23 TQ4861
Halstead Leics 40 SK7505
Halstock Dorset 8 ST5308
Halsway Somset 18 ST1337
Haltham Lincs 51 TF2463
Halton Bucks 22 SP8710
Halton Clwyd 36 SJ3039
Halton Lancs 53 SD5064
Halton Nthumb 68 NY9967
Halton W York 55 SE3533
Halton East N York 55 SE0454
Halton Gill N York 60 SD8776
Halton Holegate Lincs 51 TF4165
Halton Lea Gate Nthumb 68 NY6458
Halton Shields Nthumb 68 NZ0168
Halton West N York 54 SD8454
Haltwhistle Nthumb 68 NY7064
Halvergate Norfk 43 TG4106
Halwell Devon 5 SX7753
Halwill Devon 6 SX4299
Halwill Junction Devon 6 SS4400
Ham Devon 8 ST2301
Ham Gloucs 20 ST6898
Ham Gt Lon 23 TQ1772
Ham Kent 15 TR3254
Ham Somset 8 ST2825
Ham Wilts 21 SU3262
Ham Green H & W 28 SP0163
Ham Street Somset 9 ST5534
Hamble Hants 11 SU4806
Hambleden Bucks 22 SU7886
Hambledon Hants 11 SU6414
Hambledon Surrey 12 SU9638
Hambleton Lancs 53 SD3742
Hambleton N York 56 SE5530
Hambridge Somset 8 ST3921
Hambrook W Susx 11 SU7806
Hamels Herts 31 TL3724
Hameringham Lincs 51 TF3167
Hamerton Cambs 40 TL1379
Hamilton Strath 74 NS7255
Hamlet Dorset 9 ST5908
Hammersmith Gt Lon 23 TQ2378
Hammerwich Staffs 38 SK0707
Hammoon Dorset 9 ST8114
Hamnavoe Shet 103 HU3735
Hamnavoe Shet 103 HU4971
Hampden Park E Susx 13 TQ6002
Hampden Row Bucks 22 SP8501
Hamperden End Essex 24 TL5730
Hampnett Gloucs 28 SP0915
Hampole S York 55 SE5010
Hampreston Dorset 10 SZ0598
Hampsfield Cumb 59 SD4080
Hampstead Gt Lon 23 TQ2685
Hampstead Norrey's Berks 21 SU5276
Hampsthwaite N York 55 SE2559
Hampton Gt Lon 22 TQ1369
Hampton H & W 28 SP0243
Hampton Kent 15 TR1568
Hampton Shrops 37 SO7486
Hampton Wilts 21 SU1892
Hampton Bishop H & W 27 SO5637
Hampton Heath Ches 46 SJ5049
Hampton in Arden W Mids 39 SP2080
Hampton Lovett H & W 28 SO8865
Hampton Lucy Warwks 29 SP2557
Hampton on the Hill Warwks 29 SP2564
Hampton Poyle Oxon 29 SP5015

Hampton Wick Hermitage

Hampton Wick *Gt Lon* 23 TQ1769
Hamptworth *Wilts* 10 SU2419
Hamsey *E Susx* 13 TQ4012
Hamstall Ridware *Staffs* 38 SK1019
Hamstead Marshall *Berks* 21 SU4165
Hamsterley *Dur* 69 NZ1156
Hamsterley *Dur* 61 NZ1231
Hamstreet *Kent* 15 TR0033
Hamworthy *Dorset* 9 SY9991
Hanbury *H & W* 28 SO9664
Hanbury *Staffs* 38 SK1727
Hanchurch *Staffs* 38 SJ8441
Hand and Pen *Devon* 7 SY0495
Handbridge *Ches* 46 SJ4065
Handcross *W Susx* 12 TQ2629
Handforth *Ches* 47 SJ8583
Handley *Ches* 46 SJ4657
Handley *Derbys* 49 SK3761
Handsworth *S York* 49 SK4186
Handsworth *W Mids* 38 SP0489
Hanging Langford *Wilts* 10 SU0337
Hangleton *E Susx* 12 TQ2607
Hanham *Avon* 19 ST6472
Hankelow *Ches* 47 SJ6645
Hankerton *Wilts* 20 ST9790
Hanley *Staffs* 47 SJ8847
Hanley Castle *H & W* 28 SO8442
Hanley Child *H & W* 27 SO6565
Hanley Swan *H & W* 28 SO8142
Hanley William *H & W* 28 SO6766
Hanlith *N York* 54 SD8961
Hanmer *Clwyd* 36 SJ4539
Hannaford *Devon* 6 SS6029
Hannington *Hants* 21 SU5355
Hannington *Nhants* 30 SP8170
Hannington *Wilts* 21 SU1793
Hannington Wick *Wilts* 21 SU1795
Hanslope *Bucks* 30 SP8046
Hanthorpe *Lincs* 40 TF0823
Hanwell *Gt Lon* 22 TQ1579
Hanwell *Oxon* 29 SP4343
Hanworth *Gt Lon* 22 TQ1271
Hanworth *Norfk* 43 TG1935
Happendon *Strath* 74 NS8533
Happisburgh *Norfk* 43 TG3831
Happisburgh Common *Norfk* 43 TG3728
Hapsford *Ches* 46 SJ4774
Hapton *Lancs* 54 SD7931
Hapton *Norfk* 43 TM1796
Harberton *Devon* 5 SX7758
Harbertonford *Devon* 5 SX7856
Harbledown *Kent* 15 TR1357
Harborne *W Mids* 38 SP0284
Harborough Magna *Warwks* 39 SP4778
Harbottle *Nthumb* 68 NT9304
Harbourneford *Devon* 5 SX7162
Harbury *Warwks* 29 SP3759
Harby *Leics* 40 SK7431
Harby *Notts* 50 SK8770
Harcombe *Devon* 5 SX8881
Harcombe *Devon* 8 SY1590
Harcombe Bottom *Devon* 8 SY3395
Harden *W York* 55 SE0838
Hardgate *D & G* 66 NX8167
Hardgate *Gramp* 89 NJ7901
Hardgate *Strath* 74 NS5072
Hardham *W Susx* 12 TQ0317
Hardingham *Norfk* 42 TG0403
Hardingstone *Nhants* 30 SP7657
Hardington *Somset* 20 ST7452
Hardington Mandeville *Somset* 8 ST5111
Hardington Marsh *Somset* 8 ST5009
Hardington Moor *Somset* 8 ST5112
Hardisworthy *Devon* 6 SS2320
Hardley *Hants* 10 SU4205
Hardley Street *Norfk* 43 TG3701
Hardraw *N York* 60 SD8691
Hardstoft *Derbys* 49 SK4363
Hardway *Hants* 11 SU6001
Hardway *Somset* 9 ST7234
Hardwick *Bucks* 30 SP8019
Hardwick *Cambs* 31 TL3758
Hardwick *Nhants* 30 SP8469
Hardwick *Norfk* 33 TM2289
Hardwick *Oxon* 29 SP3806
Hardwick *Oxon* 29 SP5729
Hardwicke *Gloucs* 28 SO7912
Hardwicke *Gloucs* 28 SO9027
Hardy's Green *Essex* 25 TL9320
Hare Croft *W York* 55 SE0835
Hare Green *Essex* 25 TM1025
Hare Hatch *Berks* 22 SU8077
Hare Street *Essex* 23 TL4209
Hare Street *Essex* 23 TL5300
Hare Street *Herts* 31 TL3929
Hareby *Lincs* 51 TF3365
Harefield *Gt Lon* 22 TQ0590
Harehill *Derbys* 38 SK1735
Harehills *W York* 55 SE3135
Harelaw *Border* 76 NT5323
Harescombe *Gloucs* 28 SO8310
Haresfield *Gloucs* 28 SO8010
Harestock *Hants* 10 SU4631
Harewood *W York* 55 SE3245
Harewood End *H & W* 27 SO5227
Harford *Devon* 5 SX6359
Hargrave *Ches* 46 SJ4862
Hargrave *Nhants* 30 TL0370
Hargrave Green *Suffk* 32 TL7759
Harkstead *Suffk* 25 TM1834
Harlaston *Staffs* 39 SK2110
Harlaxton *Lincs* 40 SK8832
Harlech *Gwynd* 44 SH5831
Harlescott *Shrops* 37 SJ4916
Harlesden *Gt Lon* 23 TQ2183
Harlesthorpe *Derbys* 49 SK4976
Harleston *Devon* 5 SX7945
Harleston *Norfk* 33 TM2483
Harleston *Suffk* 32 TM0160
Harlestone *Nhants* 30 SP7064
Harley *S York* 49 SK3698
Harlington *Beds* 30 TL0330
Harlington *Gt Lon* 22 TQ0877
Harlington *S York* 49 SE4802
Harlosh *Highld* 84 NG2841
Harlow *Essex* 23 TL4611
Harlow Hill *Nthumb* 68 NZ0768
Harlthorpe *Humb* 56 SE7337
Harlton *Cambs* 31 TL3852
Harlyn Bay *Cnwll* 3 SW8775
Harman's Cross *Dorset* 9 SY9880
Harmby *N York* 61 SE1289
Harmer Green *Herts* 31 TL2515
Harmer Hill *Shrops* 37 SJ4822
Harmston *Lincs* 50 SK9662
Harnage *Shrops* 37 SJ5604
Harnhill *Gloucs* 20 SP0600
Harold Hill *Gt Lon* 23 TQ5392
Harold Wood *Gt Lon* 24 TQ5590
Haroldston West *Dyfed* 16 SM8615
Haroldswick *Shet* 103 HP6312
Harome *N York* 62 SE6481
Harpenden *Herts* 30 TL1314
Harpford *Devon* 8 SY0990
Harpham *Humb* 57 TA0861
Harpley *H & W* 28 SO6861
Harpley *Norfk* 42 TF7825
Harpole *Nhants* 30 SP6961
Harpsdale *Highld* 100 ND1355
Harpsden *Oxon* 22 SU7680
Harpswell *Lincs* 50 SK9389
Harpurhey *Gt Man* 47 SD8501
Harraby *Cumb* 67 NY4154
Harracott *Devon* 6 SS5527
Harrapool *Highld* 85 NG6523
Harrietfield *Tays* 82 NN9829
Harrietsham *Kent* 14 TQ8652
Harringay *Gt Lon* 23 TQ3188
Harrington *Lincs* 51 TF3671
Harrington *Nhants* 40 SP7780
Harringworth *Nhants* 40 SP9197
Harrogate *N York* 55 SE3054
Harrold *Beds* 30 SP9457
Harrow *Gt Lon* 22 TQ1588
Harrow Green *Suffk* 32 TL8654
Harrow on the Hill *Gt Lon* 22 TQ1587
Harrow Weald *Gt Lon* 22 TQ1591
Harrowbarrow *Cnwll* 4 SX4070
Harston *Cambs* 31 TL4250
Harston *Leics* 40 SK8331
Harswell *Humb* 56 SE8240
Hart *Cleve* 62 NZ4734
Hartburn *Nthumb* 68 NZ0885
Hartest *Suffk* 32 TL8352
Hartfield *E Susx* 13 TQ4735
Hartford *Cambs* 31 TL2572
Hartford *Ches* 47 SJ6372
Hartford End *Essex* 24 TL6817
Hartfordbridge *Hants* 22 SU7757
Hartforth *N York* 61 NZ1606
Harthill *Ches* 46 SJ4955
Harthill *Loth* 74 NS9064
Harthill *S York* 49 SK4980
Hartington *Derbys* 48 SK1260
Hartland *Devon* 6 SS2524
Hartland Quay *Devon* 6 SS2224
Hartlebury *H & W* 38 SO8471
Hartlepool *Cleve* 62 NZ5032
Hartley *Cumb* 60 NY7808
Hartley *Kent* 14 TQ6066
Hartley *Kent* 14 TQ7634
Hartley Wespall *Hants* 22 SU6958
Hartley Wintney *Hants* 22 SU7656
Hartlip *Kent* 14 TQ8464
Harton *N York* 56 SE7061
Harton *T & W* 69 NZ3765
Hartpury *Gloucs* 28 SO7924
Hartshead *W York* 55 SE1822
Hartshill *Staffs* 47 SJ8546
Hartshill *Warwks* 39 SP3194
Hartshorne *Derbys* 39 SK3221
Hartside *Nthumb* 77 NT9716
Hartwell *Nhants* 30 SP7850
Hartwith *N York* 55 SE2161
Hartwood *Strath* 74 NS8459
Hartwoodmyres *Border* 76 NT4324
Harvel *Kent* 14 TQ6563
Harvington *H & W* 38 SO8775
Harvington *H & W* 28 SP0549
Harwell *Notts* 49 SK6891
Harwell *Oxon* 21 SU4989
Harwich *Essex* 25 TM2531
Harwood Dale *N York* 63 SE9695
Harworth *Notts* 49 SK6191
Hasbury *W Mids* 38 SO9582
Hascombe *Surrey* 12 TQ0039
Haselbeach *Nhants* 30 SP7177
Haselbury Plucknett *Somset* 8 ST4710
Haseley *Warwks* 29 SP2367
Haselor *Warwks* 28 SP1257
Hasfield *Gloucs* 28 SO8227
Haskayne *Lancs* 46 SD3508
Hasketon *Suffk* 33 TM2450
Haslemere *Surrey* 11 SU9032
Haslingden *Lancs* 54 SD7823
Haslingfield *Cambs* 31 TL4052
Haslington *Ches* 47 SJ7355
Hassingham *Norfk* 43 TG3605
Hassocks *W Susx* 12 TQ3015
Hassop *Derbys* 48 SK2272
Haster *Highld* 100 ND3251
Hastingleigh *Kent* 15 TR0945
Hastings *E Susx* 14 TQ8209
Hastingwood *Essex* 23 TL4807
Hastoe *Herts* 22 SP9209
Haswell *Dur* 69 NZ3743
Haswell Plough *Dur* 62 NZ3742
Hatch Beauchamp *Somset* 8 ST3020
Hatch End *Herts* 22 TQ1390
Hatchmere *Ches* 47 SJ5571
Hatcliffe *Humb* 51 TA2100
Hatfield *H & W* 27 SO5959
Hatfield *Herts* 23 TL2308
Hatfield *S York* 56 SE6609
Hatfield Broad Oak *Essex* 24 TL5416
Hatfield Heath *Essex* 31 TL5215
Hatfield Peverel *Essex* 24 TL7911
Hatfield Woodhouse *S York* 56 SE6708
Hatford *Oxon* 21 SU3395
Hatherden *Hants* 21 SU3450
Hatherleigh *Devon* 6 SS5404
Hathern *Leics* 39 SK5022
Hatherop *Gloucs* 28 SP1505
Hathersage *Derbys* 48 SK2381
Hathersage Booths *Derbys* 48 SK2480
Hatherton *Ches* 47 SJ6847
Hatherton *Staffs* 38 SJ9510
Hatley St. George *Cambs* 31 TL2751
Hatt *Cnwll* 4 SX4062
Hatton *Ches* 47 SJ5982
Hatton *Derbys* 39 SK2130
Hatton *Gramp* 95 NK0537
Hatton *Gt Lon* 22 TQ0975
Hatton *Lincs* 50 TF1776
Hatton *Shrops* 37 SO4790
Hatton *Tays* 89 NO4642
Hatton *Warwks* 29 SP2367
Hatton of Fintray *Gramp* 95 NJ8316
Haugh *Strath* 74 NS4925
Haugh of Glass *Gramp* 94 NJ4238
Haugh of Urr *D & G* 66 NX8066
Haugham *Lincs* 51 TF3381
Haughhead Inn *Strath* 81 NS6079
Haughley *Suffk* 32 TM0262
Haughley Green *Suffk* 32 TM0264
Haughton *Shrops* 36 SJ3726
Haughton *Shrops* 37 SJ7408
Haughton *Staffs* 38 SJ8620
Haughton le Skerne *Dur* 62 NZ3116
Haughton Moss *Ches* 47 SJ5756
Haultwick *Herts* 31 TL3323
Haunton *Staffs* 39 SK2310
Hautes Croix *Jersey* 101 JS1414
Hauxley *Nthumb* 69 NU2703
Hauxton *Cambs* 31 TL4452
Havant *Hants* 11 SU7106
Havenstreet *IOW* 11 SZ5690
Haverfordwest *Dyfed* 16 SM9515
Haverhill *Suffk* 32 TL6745
Haverigg *Cumb* 58 SD1578
Havering-atte-Bower *Essex* 23 TQ5193
Haversham *Bucks* 30 SP8242
Haverthwaite *Cumb* 59 SD3483
Havyat *Avon* 19 ST4761
Hawarden *Clwyd* 46 SJ3165
Hawbush Green *Essex* 24 TL7820
Hawe's Green *Norfk* 43 TM2399
Hawen *Dyfed* 17 SN3446
Hawes *N York* 60 SD8789
Hawford *H & W* 28 SO8460
Hawick *Border* 67 NT5014
Hawkchurch *Devon* 8 ST3400
Hawkedon *Suffk* 32 TL7953
Hawkeridge *Wilts* 20 ST8653
Hawkesbury *Avon* 20 ST7686
Hawkesbury Upton *Avon* 20 ST7786
Hawkhurst *Kent* 14 TQ7530
Hawkinge *Kent* 15 TR2139
Hawkley *Hants* 11 SU7429
Hawkridge *Devon* 7 SS8630
Hawkshead *Cumb* 59 SD3598
Hawkshead Hill *Cumb* 59 SD3398
Hawksland *Strath* 74 NS8439
Hawkspur Green *Essex* 24 TL6532
Hawkstone *Shrops* 37 SJ5830
Hawkswick *N York* 54 SD9570
Hawksworth *Notts* 50 SK7543
Hawksworth *W York* 55 SE1641
Hawkwell *Essex* 24 TQ8591
Hawley *Hants* 22 SU8657
Hawling *Gloucs* 28 SP0622
Hawnby *N York* 62 SE5489
Haworth *W York* 55 SE0337
Hawstead *Suffk* 32 TL8559
Hawthorn *Dur* 69 NZ4145
Hawthorn Hill *Lincs* 51 TF2155
Hawton *Notts* 50 SK7851
Haxby *N York* 56 SE6050
Haxey *Humb* 50 SK7799
Hay Green *Norfk* 41 TF5418
Hay Street *Herts* 31 TL3926
Hay-on-Wye *Powys* 27 SO2342
Haydock *Mersyd* 47 SJ5697
Haydon *Dorset* 9 ST6715
Haydon Bridge *Nthumb* 68 NY8464
Haydon Wick *Wilts* 20 SU1387
Hayes *Gt Lon* 22 TQ0980
Hayes *Gt Lon* 23 TQ4066
Hayes End *Gt Lon* 22 TQ0882
Hayfield *Derbys* 48 SK0386
Hayfield *Strath* 80 NN0723
Hayhillock *Tays* 89 NO5242
Hayle *Cnwll* 2 SW5537
Hayley Green *W Mids* 38 SO9582
Hayne *Devon* 7 SS9515
Hayne *Devon* 5 SX7685
Haynes *Beds* 30 TL0740
Haynes West End *Beds* 30 TL0640
Hayscastle *Dyfed* 16 SM8925
Hayscastle Cross *Dyfed* 16 SM9125
Hayton *Cumb* 58 NY1041
Hayton *Cumb* 67 NY5157
Hayton *Humb* 56 SE8245
Hayton *Notts* 49 SK7284
Haytor Vale *Devon* 5 SX7777
Haytown *Devon* 6 SS3814
Haywards Heath *W Susx* 12 TQ3324
Haywood *S York* 56 SE5812
Hazel Grove *Gt Man* 48 SJ9287
Hazelbank *Strath* 74 NS8345
Hazelbury Bryan *Dorset* 9 ST7408
Hazeleigh *Essex* 24 TL8203
Hazelton Walls *Fife* 83 NO3322
Hazelwood *Derbys* 49 SK3245
Hazlemere *Bucks* 22 SU8895
Hazleton *Gloucs* 28 SP0718
Heacham *Norfk* 42 TF6737
Headbourne Worthy *Hants* 11 SU4832
Headcorn *Kent* 14 TQ8344
Headingley *W York* 55 SE2836
Headington *Oxon* 29 SP5207
Headlam *Dur* 61 NZ1818
Headlesscross *Strath* 75 NS9158
Headley *Hants* 21 SU5162
Headley *Hants* 11 SU8236
Headley *Surrey* 23 TQ2054
Headon *Notts* 50 SK7476
Heads *Strath* 74 NS7247
Heads Nook *Cumb* 67 NY5054
Heage *Derbys* 49 SK3750
Healaugh *N York* 61 SE0199
Healaugh *N York* 55 SE5047
Heald Green *Gt Man* 48 SJ8485
Heale *Somset* 8 ST2420
Heale *Somset* 8 ST3825
Healey *N York* 61 SE1780
Healeyfield *Dur* 68 NZ0648
Healing *Humb* 57 TA2110
Heamoor *Cnwll* 2 SW4631
Heanor *Derbys* 49 SK4346
Heanton Punchardon *Devon* 6 SS5035
Heapham *Lincs* 50 SK8788
Heasley Mill *Devon* 7 SS7332
Heast *Highld* 85 NG6417
Heath *Derbys* 49 SK4567
Heath *W York* 55 SE3520
Heath and Reach *Beds* 30 SP9228
Heath End *Surrey* 22 SU8549
Heath Green *H & W* 38 SP0771
Heath Hill *Shrops* 37 SJ7613
Heath Town *W Mids* 38 SO9399
Heathcote *Derbys* 48 SK1460
Heather *Leics* 39 SK3910
Heathfield *E Susx* 13 TQ5821
Heathfield *Somset* 8 ST1626
Heathton *Shrops* 37 SO8192
Heatley *Staffs* 38 SK0626
Heaton *Staffs* 48 SJ9562
Heaton *T & W* 69 NZ2666
Heaton *W York* 55 SE1335
Heaton's Bridge *Lancs* 53 SD4011
Heaverham *Kent* 14 TQ5758
Heavitree *Devon* 5 SX9492
Hebburn *T & W* 69 NZ3164
Hebden *N York* 55 SE0263
Hebden Bridge *W York* 54 SD9927
Hebing End *Herts* 31 TL3122
Hebron *Dyfed* 17 SN1827
Hebron *Nthumb* 69 NZ1989
Heckfield *Hants* 22 SU7160
Heckfield Green *Suffk* 33 TM1875
Heckfordbridge *Essex* 25 TL9421
Heckington *Lincs* 50 TF1444
Heckmondwike *W York* 55 SE1824
Heddington *Wilts* 20 ST9966
Heddon-on-the-Wall *Nthumb* 69 NZ1366
Hedenham *Norfk* 43 TM3193
Hedge End *Hants* 11 SU4912
Hedgerley *Bucks* 22 SU9687
Hedging *Somset* 8 ST3029
Hedley on the Hill *Nthumb* 68 NZ0759
Hednesford *Staffs* 38 SJ9912
Hedon *Humb* 57 TA1928
Hedsor *Bucks* 22 SU9086
Heglibister *Shet* 103 HU3851
Heighington *Dur* 61 NZ2422
Heighington *Lincs* 50 TF0269
Heightington *H & W* 37 SO7671
Heiton *Border* 76 NT7130
Hele *Devon* 6 SS5347
Hele *Devon* 7 SS9902
Hele *Somset* 8 ST1824
Helensburgh *Strath* 80 NS2982
Helenton *Strath* 73 NS3830
Helford *Cnwll* 2 SW7526
Helford Passage *Cnwll* 2 SW7626
Helhoughton *Norfk* 42 TF8626
Helions Bumpstead *Essex* 32 TL6541
Helland *Cnwll* 3 SX0771
Hellescott *Cnwll* 4 SX2888
Hellesdon *Norfk* 43 TG2010
Hellidon *Nhants* 29 SP5158
Hellifield *N York* 54 SD8556
Hellingly *E Susx* 13 TQ5812
Helmdon *Nhants* 29 SP5943
Helme *W York* 55 SE0912
Helmingham *Suffk* 33 TM1857
Helmsdale *Highld* 97 ND0315
Helmshore *Lancs* 54 SD7821
Helmsley *N York* 62 SE6183
Helperby *N York* 55 SE4469
Helperthorpe *N York* 56 SE9570
Helpringham *Lincs* 50 TF1440
Helpston *Cambs* 40 TF1205
Helsby *Ches* 46 SJ4975
Helston *Cnwll* 2 SW6527
Helstone *Cnwll* 3 SX0881
Helton *Cumb* 59 NY5021
Hemblington *Norfk* 43 TG3411
Hemel Hempstead *Herts* 22 TL0507
Hemerdon *Devon* 5 SX5657
Hemingbrough *N York* 56 SE6730
Hemingby *Lincs* 51 TF2374
Hemingford Abbots *Cambs* 31 TL2871
Hemingford Grey *Cambs* 31 TL2970
Hemingstone *Suffk* 33 TM1454
Hemington *Nhants* 40 TL0985
Hemington *Somset* 20 ST7253
Hemley *Suffk* 33 TM2842
Hempnall *Norfk* 43 TM2494
Hempnall Green *Norfk* 43 TM2493
Hempriggs *Gramp* 93 NJ1063
Hempstead *Essex* 24 TL6338
Hempstead *Norfk* 43 TG1037
Hempstead *Norfk* 43 TG4028
Hempton *Norfk* 42 TF9129
Hempton *Oxon* 29 SP4431
Hemsby *Norfk* 43 TG4917
Hemswell *Lincs* 50 SK9290
Hemsworth *W York* 55 SE4213
Hemyock *Devon* 8 ST1313
Hendersyde Park *Border* 76 NT7435
Hendon *Gt Lon* 23 TQ2389
Hendy *Dyfed* 17 SN5803
Henfield *W Susx* 12 TQ2115
Hengoed *M Glam* 18 ST1494
Hengoed *Powys* 27 SO2253
Hengrave *Suffk* 32 TL8268
Henham *Essex* 24 TL5428
Henhurst *Kent* 14 TQ6669
Heniarth *Powys* 36 SJ1208
Henlade *Somset* 8 ST2623
Henley *Dorset* 9 ST6904
Henley *Somset* 8 ST4232
Henley *Suffk* 33 TM1551
Henley *W Susx* 11 SU8925
Henley's Down *E Susx* 14 TQ7312
Henley-in-Arden *Warwks* 28 SP1566
Henley-on-Thames *Oxon* 22 SU7682
Henllan *Clwyd* 45 SJ0268
Henllan *Dyfed* 17 SN3540
Henllys *Gwent* 19 ST2691
Henlow *Beds* 31 TL1738
Hennock *Devon* 5 SX8381
Henny Street *Essex* 24 TL8738
Henry's Moat (Castell Hendre) *Dyfed* 16 SN0427
Henryd *Gwynd* 45 SH7774
Hensall *N York* 56 SE5923
Henshaw *Nthumb* 68 NY7664
Hensingham *Cumb* 58 NX9816
Henstead *Suffk* 33 TM4885
Hensting *Hants* 11 SU4922
Henstridge *Somset* 9 ST7219
Henstridge Ash *Somset* 9 ST7220
Henton *Oxon* 22 SP7602
Henton *Somset* 19 ST4945
Henwick *H & W* 28 SO8355
Henwood *Cnwll* 4 SX2673
Heol-y-Cyw *M Glam* 18 SS9484
Hepple *Nthumb* 68 NT9901
Hepscott *Nthumb* 69 NZ2284
Heptonstall *W York* 54 SD9828
Hepworth *Suffk* 32 TL9874
Hepworth *W York* 55 SE1606
Herbrandston *Dyfed* 16 SM8707
Hereford *H & W* 27 SO5139
Hereson *Kent* 15 TR3865
Heribusta *Highld* 90 NG3970
Heriot *Loth* 76 NT3953
Hermiston *Loth* 75 NT1870
Hermitage *Berks* 21 SU5072
Hermitage *Border* 67 NY5095
Hermitage *Dorset* 9 ST6506

Iver Heath Kintra

Iver Heath *Bucks* 22 TQ0283
Iveston *Dur* 69 NZ1350
Ivinghoe *Bucks* 30 SP9416
Ivinghoe Aston *Bucks* 30 SP9517
Ivington *H & W* 27 SO4756
Ivington Green *H & W* 27 SO4656
Ivy Hatch *Kent* 14 TQ5854
Ivybridge *Devon* 5 SX6356
Ivychurch *Kent* 15 TR0327
Iwade *Kent* 14 TQ9067
Iwerne Courtney or Shroton *Dorset* 9 ST8512
Iwerne Minster *Dorset* 9 ST8614
Ixworth *Suffk* 32 TL9370
Ixworth Thorpe *Suffk* 32 TL9173

J

Jack-in-the-Green *Devon* 7 SY0195
Jackton *Strath* 74 NS5952
Jacobstow *Cnwll* 6 SX1995
Jacobstowe *Devon* 6 SS5801
Jameston *Dyfed* 16 SS0598
Jamestown *Highld* 92 NH4756
Jamestown *Strath* 80 NS3981
Janets-town *Highld* 100 ND3551
Janetstown *Highld* 100 ND1932
Jardine Hall *D & G* 67 NY1088
Jarrow *T & W* 69 NZ3364
Jasper's Green *Essex* 24 TL7226
Jawcraig *Cent* 74 NS8475
Jaywick *Essex* 25 TM1413
Jedburgh *Border* 76 NT6420
Jeffreston *Dyfed* 16 SN0906
Jemimaville *Highld* 93 NH7165
Jerbourg *Guern* 101 GN5305
Jesmond *T & W* 69 NZ2566
Jevington *E Susx* 13 TQ5601
Jockey End *Herts* 30 TL0413
John O'Groats *Highld* 100 ND3872
Johnby *Cumb* 59 NY4332
Johnshaven *Gramp* 89 NO7967
Johnston *Dyfed* 16 SM9310
Johnstone *Strath* 73 NS4263
Johnstonebridge *D & G* 67 NY1092
Joppa *Dyfed* 34 SN5666
Joppa *Strath* 73 NS4119
Jordanston *Dyfed* 16 SM9132
Juniper Green *Loth* 75 NT1968
Jurby *IOM* 52 SC3598

K

Kaber *Cumb* 60 NY7911
Kames *Strath* 71 NR9771
Kames *Strath* 74 NS6926
Kea *Cnwll* 2 SW8142
Keal Cotes *Lincs* 51 TF3660
Kearsley *Gt Man* 47 SD7504
Kearsney *Kent* 15 TR2844
Kearstwick *Cumb* 59 SD6079
Kedington *Suffk* 32 TL7046
Kedleston *Derbys* 49 SK3040
Keelby *Lincs* 57 TA1610
Keele *Staffs* 47 SJ8045
Keelham *W York* 55 SE0732
Keeston *Dyfed* 16 SM9019
Keevil *Wilts* 20 ST9258
Kegworth *Leics* 39 SK4826
Kehelland *Cnwll* 2 SW6241
Keig *Gramp* 94 NJ6119
Keighley *W York* 55 SE0541
Keillour *Tays* 82 NN9725
Keiloch *Gramp* 88 NO1891
Keils *Strath* 70 NR5268
Keinton Mandeville *Somset* 8 ST5430
Keir Mill *D & G* 66 NX8593
Keisley *Cumb* 60 NY7124
Keiss *Highld* 100 ND3461
Keith *Gramp* 94 NJ4250
Keithick *Tays* 82 NO2038
Keithock *Tays* 89 NO6063
Keithtown *Gramp* 92 NH5256
Kelbrook *Lancs* 54 SD9044
Kelburn *Strath* 73 NS2156
Kelby *Lincs* 50 TF0041
Keld *N York* 60 NY8900
Kelfield *N York* 56 SE5938
Kelham *Notts* 50 SK7755
Kelhead *D & G* 67 NY1469
Kellamergh *Lancs* 53 SD4029
Kellas *Gramp* 94 NJ1654
Kellas *Tays* 83 NO4535
Kellaton *Devon* 5 SX8039
Kelling *Norfk* 43 TG0942
Kellington *N York* 56 SE5524
Kelloe *Dur* 62 NZ3436
Kelly *Devon* 4 SX3981
Kelmarsh *Nhants* 40 SP7379
Kelmscot *Oxon* 21 SU2499
Kelsale *Suffk* 33 TM3865
Kelsall *Ches* 46 SJ5268
Kelshall *Herts* 31 TL3336
Kelsick *Cumb* 67 NY1950
Kelso *Border* 76 NT7234
Kelstedge *Derbys* 49 SK3363
Kelstern *Lincs* 51 TF2489
Kelston *Avon* 20 ST7067
Keltneyburn *Tays* 87 NN7749
Kelty *Fife* 82 NT1494
Kelvedon *Essex* 24 TL8619
Kelvedon Hatch *Essex* 24 TQ5698
Kelynack *Cnwll* 2 SW3729
Kemback *Fife* 83 NO4115
Kemberton *Shrops* 37 SJ7204
Kemble *Wilts* 20 ST9897
Kemerton *H & W* 28 SO9536
Kemeys Commander *Gwent* 27 SO3404
Kemnay *Gramp* 95 NJ7316
Kemp Town *E Susx* 12 TQ3303
Kempley *Gloucs* 28 SO6629
Kempley Green *Gloucs* 28 SO6728
Kempsey *H & W* 28 SO8549
Kempsford *Gloucs* 20 SU1696
Kempshott *Hants* 21 SU6050
Kempston *Beds* 30 TL0347
Kempton *Shrops* 36 SO3682
Kemsing *Kent* 23 TQ5558
Kenardington *Kent* 15 TQ9732
Kenchester *H & W* 27 SO4342
Kencot *Oxon* 29 SP2504
Kendal *Cumb* 59 SD5192
Kenilworth *Warwks* 39 SP2871
Kenley *Gt Lon* 23 TQ3260
Kenley *Shrops* 37 SJ5500
Kenmore *Highld* 91 NG7557
Kenmore *Tays* 87 NN7745
Kenn *Avon* 19 ST4268
Kenn *Devon* 5 SX9285
Kennacraig *Strath* 71 NR8262
Kennerleigh *Devon* 7 SS8107
Kennessee Green *Mersyd* 46 SD3801
Kennet *Cent* 82 NS9291
Kennethmont *Gramp* 94 NJ5428
Kennett *Cambs* 32 TL7068
Kennford *Devon* 5 SX9186
Kenninghall *Norfk* 32 TM0386
Kennington *Kent* 15 TR0245
Kennington *Oxon* 21 SP5201
Kennoway *Fife* 83 NO3502
Kenny *Somset* 8 ST3117
Kennyhill *Suffk* 32 TL6679
Kennythorpe *N York* 56 SE7865
Kenovay *Strath* 78 NL9946
Kensaleyre *Highld* 90 NG4151
Kensington *Gt Lon* 23 TQ2579
Kensworth *Beds* 30 TL0319
Kensworth Common *Beds* 30 TL0317
Kent's Green *Gloucs* 28 SO7423
Kent's Oak *Hants* 10 SU3224
Kentallen *Highld* 86 NN0057
Kentchurch *H & W* 27 SO4125
Kentford *Suffk* 32 TL7066
Kentisbeare *Devon* 7 ST0608
Kentisbury *Devon* 7 SS6243
Kentish Town *Gt Lon* 23 TQ2884
Kentmere *Cumb* 59 NY4504
Kenton *Devon* 5 SX9583
Kenton *Gt Lon* 23 TQ1788
Kenton *Suffk* 33 TM1965
Kenton *T & W* 69 NZ2267
Kentra *Highld* 79 NM6569
Kenwyn *Cnwll* 2 SW8145
Keoldale *Highld* 98 NC3866
Keppoch *Highld* 85 NG8924
Kepwick *N York* 62 SE4690
Keresley *W Mids* 39 SP3282
Kerris *Cnwll* 2 SW4427
Kerry *Powys* 36 SO1490
Kerrycroy *Strath* 73 NS1061
Kersall *Notts* 49 SK7162
Kersbrook *Devon* 8 SY0683
Kersey *Suffk* 32 TM0044
Kershader *W Isls* 102 NB3320
Kershopefoot *D & G* 67 NY4782
Kerswell *Devon* 8 ST0806
Kerswell Green *H & W* 28 SO8646
Kesgrave *Suffk* 33 TM2245
Kessingland *Suffk* 33 TM5286
Kestle *Cnwll* 3 SW9845
Kestle Mill *Cnwll* 3 SW8459
Keston *Gt Lon* 23 TQ4164
Keswick *Cumb* 58 NY2623
Keswick *Norfk* 43 TG2004
Ketsby *Lincs* 51 TF3676
Kettering *Nhants* 30 SP8678
Ketteringham *Norfk* 43 TG1603
Kettins *Tays* 83 NO2338
Kettlebaston *Suffk* 32 TL9650
Kettlebridge *Fife* 83 NO3007
Kettleburgh *Suffk* 33 TM2660
Kettleholm *D & G* 67 NY1577
Kettleshulme *Ches* 48 SJ9879
Kettlesing *N York* 55 SE2256
Kettlesing Bottom *N York* 55 SE2357
Kettlestoft *Ork* 103 HY6538
Kettlestone *Norfk* 42 TF9631
Kettlethorpe *Lincs* 50 SK8475
Kettlewell *N York* 54 SD9672
Ketton *Leics* 40 SK9704
Kew *Gt Lon* 23 TQ1876
Kexby *Lincs* 50 SK8785
Kexby *N York* 56 SE7050
Key Green *Ches* 48 SJ8963
Key Street *Kent* 14 TQ8764
Keyham *Leics* 39 SK6706
Keyhaven *Hants* 10 SZ3091
Keyingham *Humb* 57 TA2425
Keymer *W Susx* 12 TQ3115
Keynsham *Avon* 19 ST6568
Keysoe Row *Beds* 30 TL0861
Keyston *Cambs* 30 TL0475
Keyworth *Notts* 39 SK6130
Kibblesworth *T & W* 69 NZ2456
Kibworth Beauchamp *Leics* 39 SP6893
Kibworth Harcourt *Leics* 39 SP6894
Kidbrooke *Gt Lon* 23 TQ4176
Kidderminster *H & W* 38 SO8376
Kidlington *Oxon* 29 SP4913
Kidmore End *Oxon* 22 SU6979
Kidsdale *D & G* 64 NX4336
Kidsgrove *Staffs* 47 SJ8454
Kidwelly *Dyfed* 17 SN4006
Kiel Crofts *Strath* 79 NM9039
Kielder *Nthumb* 68 NY6293
Kiells *Strath* 70 NR4168
Kilbeg *Highld* 85 NG6506
Kilberry *Strath* 71 NR7164
Kilbirnie *Strath* 73 NS3154
Kilbride *Strath* 79 NM8525
Kilbride *Strath* 71 NR7279
Kilbride *Strath* 72 NS0367
Kilbride *W Isls* 102 NF7514
Kilburn *Derbys* 49 SK3845
Kilburn *Gt Lon* 23 TQ2483
Kilburn *N York* 62 SE5179
Kilby *Leics* 39 SP6295
Kilchamaig *Strath* 71 NR8060
Kilchattan *Strath* 70 NR3795
Kilchattan *Strath* 73 NS1054
Kilchenzie *Strath* 72 NR6724
Kilcheran *Strath* 79 NM8239
Kilchoan *Highld* 79 NM4863
Kilchrenan *Strath* 80 NN0322
Kilconquhar *Fife* 83 NO4802
Kilcot *Gloucs* 28 SO6925
Kilcoy *Highld* 92 NH5751
Kilcreggan *Strath* 80 NS2480
Kildale *N York* 62 NZ6009
Kildalloig *Strath* 72 NR7518
Kildary *Highld* 97 NH7674
Kildavanan *Strath* 72 NS0266
Kildonan *Highld* 97 NC9120
Kildonan *Strath* 72 NS0321
Kildonan Lodge *Highld* 97 NC9022
Kildonnan *Highld* 84 NM4885
Kildrochet House *D & G* 64 NX0856
Kildrummy *Gramp* 94 NJ4617
Kildwick *N York* 54 SE0046
Kilfinan *Strath* 71 NR9378
Kilfinnan *Highld* 86 NN2795
Kilgetty *Dyfed* 16 SN1207
Kilgrammie *Strath* 73 NS2502
Kilgwrrwg Common *Gwent* 19 ST4797
Kilham *Humb* 57 TA0664
Kilkenneth *Strath* 78 NL9444
Kilkhampton *Cnwll* 6 SS2511
Killamarsh *Derbys* 49 SK4581
Killay *W Glam* 17 SS6092
Killearn *Cent* 81 NS5286
Killen *Highld* 93 NH6758
Killerby *Dur* 61 NZ1919
Killerton *Devon* 7 SS9700
Killichonan *Tays* 87 NN5458
Killiechronan *Strath* 79 NM5441
Killiecrankie *Tays* 87 NN9162
Killilan *Highld* 85 NG9430
Killin *Cent* 81 NN5733
Killinghall *N York* 55 SE2858
Killington *Cumb* 59 SD6188
Killingworth *T & W* 69 NZ2770
Killochyett *Border* 76 NT4545
Kilmacolm *Strath* 73 NS3567
Kilmahog *Cent* 81 NN6108
Kilmahumaig *Strath* 71 NR7893
Kilmaluag *Highld* 90 NG4374
Kilmany *Fife* 83 NO3821
Kilmarie *Highld* 84 NG5517
Kilmarnock *Strath* 73 NS4237
Kilmartin *Strath* 71 NR8398
Kilmaurs *Strath* 73 NS4141
Kilmelford *Strath* 79 NM8512
Kilmeny *Strath* 70 NR3965
Kilmersdon *Somset* 20 ST6952
Kilmeston *Hants* 11 SU5825
Kilmichael *Strath* 71 NR8593
Kilmichael of Inverlussa *Strath* 71 NR7786
Kilmington *Devon* 8 SY2797
Kilmington *Wilts* 20 ST7736
Kilmington Common *Wilts* 9 ST7735
Kilmington Street *Wilts* 9 ST7835
Kilmorack *Highld* 92 NH4944
Kilmore *Highld* 85 NG6507
Kilmory *Highld* 79 NM5270
Kilmory *Strath* 79 NM8825
Kilmory *Strath* 71 NR7074
Kilmuir *Highld* 90 NG2547
Kilmuir *Highld* 90 NG3770
Kilmuir *Highld* 93 NH6749
Kilmuir *Highld* 97 NH7573
Kilmun *Strath* 80 NS1781
Kiln Green *Berks* 22 SU8178
Kiln Pit Hill *Nthumb* 68 NZ0355
Kilnave *Strath* 70 NR2871
Kilncadzow *Strath* 74 NS8848
Kilndown *Kent* 14 TQ7035
Kilninver *Strath* 79 NM8221
Kilnsea *Humb* 57 TA4115
Kilnsey *N York* 54 SD9767
Kilnwick *Humb* 56 SE9949
Kiloran *Strath* 70 NR3996
Kilpeck *H & W* 27 SO4430
Kilpin *Humb* 56 SE7726
Kilsby *Nhants* 39 SP5671
Kilspindie *Tays* 82 NO2125
Kilstay *D & G* 64 NX1238
Kilsyth *Strath* 81 NS7178
Kiltarlity *Highld* 92 NH5041
Kilton *Cleve* 62 NZ7018
Kilton Thorpe *Cleve* 62 NZ6917
Kilvaxter *Highld* 90 NG3869
Kilve *Somset* 18 ST1442
Kilvington *Notts* 50 SK8042
Kilwinning *Strath* 73 NS3043
Kimberley *Norfk* 42 TG0603
Kimberley *Notts* 49 SK4944
Kimberworth *S York* 49 SK4093
Kimblesworth *Dur* 69 NZ2547
Kimbolton *Cambs* 30 TL1067
Kimbolton *H & W* 27 SO5261
Kimcote *Leics* 39 SP5886
Kimmeridge *Dorset* 9 SY9179
Kimpton *Hants* 21 SU2746
Kimpton *Herts* 31 TL1718
Kinbrace *Highld* 99 NC8631
Kinbuck *Cent* 81 NN7905
Kincaple *Fife* 83 NO4618
Kincardine *Fife* 82 NS9387
Kincardine *Highld* 97 NH6089
Kincardine O'Neil *Tays* 89 NO5999
Kinclaven *Tays* 82 NO1538
Kincorth *Gramp* 89 NJ9403
Kincorth House *Gramp* 93 NJ0161
Kincraig *Highld* 87 NH8305
Kindallachan *Tays* 88 NN9949
Kinerarach *Strath* 71 NR6553
Kineton *Gloucs* 28 SP0926
Kineton *Warwks* 29 SP3350
Kinfauns *Tays* 82 NO1622
Kinfig *M Glam* 18 SS8081
King's Bromley *Staffs* 38 SK1216
King's Cliffe *Nhants* 40 TL0097
King's Coughton *Warwks* 28 SP0859
King's Heath *W Mids* 38 SP0781
King's Lynn *Norfk* 41 TF6120
King's Mills *Guern* 101 GN4808
King's Norton *Leics* 39 SK6800
King's Norton *W Mids* 38 SP0579
King's Nympton *Devon* 7 SS6819
King's Pyon *H & W* 27 SO4450
King's Somborne *Hants* 10 SU3531
King's Stag *Dorset* 9 ST7210
King's Stanley *Gloucs* 20 SO8103
King's Sutton *Oxon* 29 SP4936
King's Walden *Herts* 31 TL1623
Kingarth *Strath* 73 NS0956
Kingcausie *Gramp* 89 NO8699
Kingcoed *Gwent* 27 SO4305
Kingerby *Lincs* 50 TF0592
Kingford *Devon* 6 SS2806
Kingham *Oxon* 29 SP2624
Kingholm Quay *D & G* 66 NX9773
Kinglassie *Loth* 82 NT2298
Kingoldrum *Tays* 88 NO3355
Kingoodie *Tays* 83 NO3329
Kings Caple *H & W* 27 SO5528
Kings House Hotel *Highld* 86 NN2654
Kings Langley *Herts* 22 TL0702
Kings Meaburn *Cumb* 60 NY6221
Kings Muir *Border* 75 NT2539
Kings Newnham *Warwks* 39 SP4577
Kings Ripton *Cambs* 31 TL2676
Kings Weston *Avon* 19 ST5477
Kings Worthy *Hants* 11 SU4932
Kingsand *Cnwll* 4 SX4350
Kingsbarns *Fife* 83 NO5912
Kingsbridge *Devon* 5 SX7344
Kingsbridge *Somset* 7 SS9837
Kingsburgh *Highld* 90 NG3955
Kingsbury *Gt Lon* 23 TQ1988
Kingsbury *Warwks* 39 SP2196
Kingsbury Episcopi *Somset* 8 ST4321
Kingsclere *Hants* 21 SU5258
Kingscote *Gloucs* 20 ST8196
Kingscott *Devon* 6 SS5318
Kingscross *Strath* 72 NS0428
Kingsdon *Somset* 8 ST5126
Kingsdown *Kent* 15 TR3748
Kingsdown *Wilts* 20 ST8167
Kingsdown *Wilts* 20 SU1688
Kingseat *Fife* 82 NT1290
Kingsey *Bucks* 22 SP7406
Kingsfold *W Susx* 12 TQ1636
Kingsford *Strath* 73 NS4447
Kingsgate *Kent* 15 TR3970
Kingshall Street *Suffk* 32 TL9161
Kingsheanton *Devon* 6 SS5537
Kingshouse Hotel *Cent* 81 NN5620
Kingskerswell *Devon* 5 SX8767
Kingskettle *Fife* 83 NO3008
Kingsland *H & W* 27 SO4461
Kingsley *Ches* 47 SJ5574
Kingsley *Hants* 11 SU7838
Kingsley *Staffs* 48 SK0146
Kingsley Green *W Susx* 11 SU8930
Kingsley Park *Nhants* 30 SP7762
Kingsmuir *Fife* 83 NO5308
Kingsmuir *Tays* 89 NO4849
Kingsnorth *Kent* 15 TR0039
Kingsteignton *Devon* 5 SX8773
Kingsthorne *H & W* 27 SO4931
Kingsthorpe *Nhants* 30 SP7563
Kingston *Cambs* 31 TL3455
Kingston *Cnwll* 4 SX3675
Kingston *Devon* 5 SX6347
Kingston *Devon* 5 SY0687
Kingston *Dorset* 9 ST7509
Kingston *Dorset* 9 SY9579
Kingston *Gramp* 94 NJ3365
Kingston *IOW* 11 SZ4781
Kingston *Kent* 15 TR1950
Kingston *Loth* 83 NT5482
Kingston Bagpuize *Oxon* 21 SU4098
Kingston Blount *Oxon* 22 SU7399
Kingston by Sea *W Susx* 12 TQ2305
Kingston Deverill *Wilts* 20 ST8437
Kingston Lisle *Oxon* 21 SU3287
Kingston near Lewes *E Susx* 13 TQ3908
Kingston on Soar *Notts* 39 SK5027
Kingston Russell *Dorset* 9 SY5791
Kingston Seymour *Avon* 19 ST4066
Kingston St. Mary *Somset* 8 ST2229
Kingston upon Thames *Gt Lon* 23 TQ1869
Kingstone *H & W* 27 SO4235
Kingstone *Somset* 8 ST3713
Kingstone *Staffs* 38 SK0629
Kingswear *Devon* 5 SX8851
Kingswells *Gramp* 89 NJ8606
Kingswinford *W Mids* 38 SO8888
Kingswood *Avon* 19 ST6473
Kingswood *Bucks* 30 SP6919
Kingswood *Gloucs* 20 ST7491
Kingswood *Somset* 18 ST1037
Kingswood *Surrey* 23 TQ2455
Kingswood *Warwks* 38 SP1871
Kingswood Common *Staffs* 38 SJ8302
Kingthorpe *Lincs* 50 TF1275
Kington *Avon* 19 ST6290
Kington *H & W* 27 SO2956
Kington *H & W* 28 SO9956
Kington Langley *Wilts* 20 ST9276
Kington Magna *Dorset* 9 ST7622
Kington St. Michael *Wilts* 20 ST9077
Kingussie *Highld* 87 NH7500
Kingweston *Somset* 8 ST5230
Kinharrachie *Gramp* 95 NJ9231
Kinharvie *D & G* 66 NX9266
Kinkell Bridge *Tays* 82 NN9316
Kinknockie *Gramp* 95 NK0041
Kinleith *Loth* 75 NT1866
Kinlet *Shrops* 37 SO7180
Kinloch *Highld* 98 NC3434
Kinloch *Highld* 99 NC5552
Kinloch *Highld* 84 NM4099
Kinloch *Tays* 88 NO1444
Kinloch *Tays* 88 NO2644
Kinloch Hourn *Highld* 85 NG9506
Kinloch Rannoch *Tays* 87 NN6658
Kinlochard *Cent* 81 NN4502
Kinlochbervie *Highld* 98 NC2256
Kinlocheil *Highld* 85 NM9779
Kinlochewe *Highld* 91 NH0261
Kinlochlaggan *Highld* 87 NN5289
Kinlochleven *Highld* 86 NN1861
Kinlochmoidart *Highld* 85 NM7072
Kinlochnanuagh *Highld* 85 NM7384
Kinloss *Gramp* 93 NJ0661
Kinmel Bay *Clwyd* 45 SH9880
Kinmount House *D & G* 67 NY1368
Kinmuck *Gramp* 95 NJ8119
Kinmundy *Gramp* 95 NJ8817
Kinnadie *Gramp* 95 NJ9743
Kinnaird *Tays* 88 NN9559
Kinnaird *Tays* 83 NO2428
Kinnaird Castle *Tays* 89 NO6357
Kinneddar *Gramp* 94 NJ2269
Kinneff *Gramp* 89 NO8574
Kinnelhead *D & G* 66 NT0201
Kinnell *Tays* 89 NO6150
Kinnerley *Shrops* 36 SJ3320
Kinnersley *H & W* 27 SO3449
Kinnersley *H & W* 28 SO8743
Kinnerton *Powys* 27 SO2463
Kinnesswood *Tays* 82 NO1702
Kinninvie *Dur* 61 NZ0521
Kinnordy *Tays* 88 NO3655
Kinoulton *Notts* 39 SK6730
Kinross *Tays* 82 NO1102
Kinrossie *Tays* 82 NO1832
Kinsham *H & W* 27 SO3665
Kinsham *H & W* 28 SO9335
Kinsley *W York* 55 SE4114
Kinson *Dorset* 10 SZ0796
Kintbury *Berks* 21 SU3866
Kintessack *Gramp* 93 NJ0060
Kintillo *Tays* 82 NO1317
Kinton *H & W* 36 SO4174
Kinton *Shrops* 36 SJ3719
Kintore *Gramp* 95 NJ7916
Kintour *Strath* 70 NR4551
Kintra *Strath* 78 NM3125

Layer-de-la-Haye Little Yeldham

Layer-de-la-Haye *Essex* 25 TL9620
Layham *Suffk* 32 TM0240
Laymore *Dorset* 8 ST3804
Laytham *Humb* 56 SE7439
Laythes *Cumb* 67 NY2455
Lazonby *Cumb* 59 NY5439
Le Bigard *Guern* 101 GN4805
Le Bourg *Guern* 101 GN4905
Le Bourg *Jersey* 101 JS2006
Le Gron *Guern* 101 GN4807
Le Haquais *Jersey* 101 JS1807
Le Hocq *Jersey* 101 JS1806
Le Villocq *Guern* 101 GN5009
Lea *Derbys* 49 SK3257
Lea *H & W* 27 SO6521
Lea *Lincs* 50 SK8286
Lea *Shrops* 36 SO3589
Lea *Wilts* 20 ST9586
Lea Marston *Warwks* 39 SP2093
Leachkin *Highld* 92 NH6344
Leadburn *Loth* 75 NT2355
Leaden Roding *Essex* 24 TL5913
Leadenham *Lincs* 50 SK9452
Leadgate *Dur* 69 NZ1251
Leadhills *Strath* 74 NS8815
Leafield *Oxon* 29 SP3115
Leagrave *Beds* 30 TL0523
Leake Common Side *Lincs* 51 TF3952
Lealholm *N York* 63 NZ7607
Lealt *Highld* 90 NG5060
Leamington Hastings *Warwks* 29 SP4467
Leamington Spa *Warwks* 29 SP3265
Leasgill *Cumb* 59 SD4983
Leasingham *Lincs* 50 TF0548
Leasingthorne *Dur* 61 NZ2530
Leatherhead *Surrey* 23 TQ1656
Leathley *N York* 55 SE2347
Leaths *D & G* 66 NX7862
Leaton *Shrops* 36 SJ4618
Leaveland *Kent* 15 TR0053
Leavenheath *Suffk* 25 TL9537
Leavening *N York* 56 SE7863
Leaves Green *Gt Lon* 23 TQ4161
Lebberston *N York* 63 TA0782
Lechampstead Thicket *Berks* 21 SU4276
Lechlade *Wilts* 21 SU2199
Leck *Lancs* 60 SD6476
Leck Gruinart *Strath* 70 NR2768
Leckbuie *Tays* 81 NN7040
Leckford *Hants* 10 SU3737
Leckhampstead *Berks* 21 SU4375
Leckhampstead *Bucks* 30 SP7237
Leckhampton *Gloucs* 28 SO9419
Leckmelm *Highld* 96 NH1689
Leconfield *Humb* 56 TA0143
Ledaig *Strath* 79 NM9037
Ledburn *Bucks* 30 SP9021
Ledbury *H & W* 28 SO7137
Ledgemoor *H & W* 27 SO4150
Ledmore Junction *Highld* 96 NC2412
Ledsham *W York* 55 SE4529
Ledston *W York* 55 SE4328
Ledwell *Oxon* 29 SP4128
Lee *Devon* 6 SS4846
Lee *Gt Lon* 23 TQ3875
Lee Brockhurst *Shrops* 37 SJ5427
Lee Chapel *Essex* 24 TQ6987
Lee Clump *Bucks* 22 SP9004
Lee Mill *Devon* 5 SX5955
Lee-on-the-Solent *Hants* 11 SU5600
Leebotwood *Shrops* 37 SO4798
Leece *Cumb* 53 SD2469
Leeds *Kent* 14 TQ8253
Leeds *W York* 55 SE2932
Leedstown *Cnwll* 2 SW6034
Leek *Staffs* 48 SJ9856
Leek Wootton *Warwks* 29 SP2868
Leeming *N York* 61 SE2989
Leeming Bar *N York* 61 SE2889
Lees *Derbys* 49 SK2637
Lees *Gt Man* 54 SD9504
Lees Green *Derbys* 49 SK2637
Leesthorpe *Leics* 40 SK7813
Leetown *Tays* 82 NO2121
Leftwich *Ches* 47 SJ6672
Legbourne *Lincs* 51 TF3784
Legerwood *Border* 76 NT5843
Legsby *Lincs* 50 TF1385
Leicester *Leics* 39 SK5804
Leicester Forest East *Leics* 39 SK5202
Leigh *Dorset* 9 ST6108
Leigh *Gloucs* 28 SO8626
Leigh *Gt Man* 47 SJ6599
Leigh *H & W* 28 SO7853
Leigh *Kent* 13 TQ5446
Leigh *Surrey* 12 TQ2246
Leigh *Wilts* 20 SU0692
Leigh Beck *Essex* 24 TQ8183
Leigh Delamere *Wilts* 20 ST8879
Leigh Green *Kent* 14 TQ9033
Leigh Knoweglass *Strath* 74 NS6350
Leigh Sinton *H & W* 28 SO7750
Leigh upon Mendip *Somset* 20 ST6947
Leigh Woods *Avon* 19 ST5672
Leigh-on-Sea *Essex* 24 TQ8286
Leighterton *Gloucs* 20 ST8290
Leighton *Powys* 36 SJ2306
Leighton *Shrops* 37 SJ6105
Leighton Bromswold *Cambs* 30 TL1175
Leighton Buzzard *Beds* 30 SP9225
Leinthall Earls *H & W* 27 SO4467
Leinthall Starkes *H & W* 27 SO4369
Leintwardine *H & W* 36 SO4074
Leire *Leics* 39 SP5290
Leiston *Suffk* 33 TM4462
Leitfie *Tays* 88 NO2545
Leith *Loth* 75 NT2776
Leitholm *Border* 76 NT7944
Lelant *Cnwll* 2 SW5437
Lelley *Humb* 57 TA2032
Lem Hill *H & W* 37 SO7275
Lempitlaw *Border* 76 NT7832
Lemreway *W Isls* 102 NB3711
Lemsford *Herts* 31 TL2212
Lenchwick *H & W* 28 SP0347
Lendalfoot *Strath* 64 NX1390
Lendrick *Cent* 81 NN5506
Lendrum Terrace *Gramp* 95 NK1141
Lenham *Kent* 14 TQ8952
Lenham Heath *Kent* 14 TQ9149
Lenie *Highld* 92 NH5126
Lennel *Border* 77 NT8540
Lennox Plunton *D & G* 65 NX6051
Lennoxlove *Loth* 76 NT5172
Lennoxtown *Strath* 74 NS6277
Lenton *Lincs* 40 TF0230
Lenzie *Strath* 74 NS6572
Leochel-Cushnie *Gramp* 94 NJ5210
Leominster *H & W* 27 SO4959
Leonard Stanley *Gloucs* 20 SO8003
Leoville *Jersey* 101 JS0813
Lephin *Highld* 90 NG1749
Leppington *N York* 56 SE7661
Lepton *W York* 55 SE2015
Lerags *Strath* 79 NM8324
Lerryn *Cnwll* 3 SX1457
Lerwick *Shet* 103 HU4741
Les Arquets *Guern* 101 GN4607
Les Hubits *Guern* 101 GN5206
Les Lohiers *Guern* 101 GN4807
Les Murchez *Guern* 101 GN4805
Les Nicolles *Guern* 101 GN5005
Les Quartiers *Guern* 101 GN5210
Les Quennevais *Jersey* 101 JS0810
Les Sages *Guern* 101 GN4606
Les Villets *Guern* 101 GN4905
Lesbury *Nthumb* 69 NU2311
Leslie *Fife* 83 NO2501
Leslie *Gramp* 94 NJ5924
Lesmahagow *Strath* 74 NS8139
Lesnewth *Cnwll* 4 SX1390
Lessingham *Norfk* 43 TG3928
Lessonhall *Cumb* 67 NY2250
Leswalt *D & G* 64 NX0163
Letchmore Heath *Herts* 22 TQ1597
Letchworth *Herts* 31 TL2232
Letcombe Bassett *Oxon* 21 SU3784
Letcombe Regis *Oxon* 21 SU3886
Letham *Border* 68 NT6709
Letham *Fife* 83 NO3014
Letham *Tays* 89 NO5348
Letham Grange *Tays* 89 NO6345
Lethenty *Gramp* 94 NJ5820
Lethenty *Gramp* 95 NJ8140
Letheringham *Suffk* 33 TM2757
Letheringsett *Norfk* 42 TG0638
Letterfearn *Highld* 85 NG8823
Letterfinlay Lodge Hotel *Highld* 86 NN2491
Lettermorar *Highld* 85 NM7389
Letters *Highld* 96 NH1687
Lettershaw *Strath* 74 NS8920
Letterston *Dyfed* 16 SM9429
Lettoch *Highld* 93 NJ0219
Lettoch *Highld* 93 NJ1032
Letton *H & W* 27 SO3346
Letty Green *Herts* 23 TL2810
Letwell *S York* 49 SK5686
Leuchars *Fife* 83 NO4521
Leurbost *W Isls* 102 NB3725
Levedale *Staffs* 38 SJ8916
Level's Green *Essex* 31 TL4724
Leven *Fife* 83 NO3800
Leven *Humb* 57 TA1045
Levencorroch *Strath* 72 NS0021
Levens *Cumb* 59 SD4886
Levens Green *Herts* 31 TL3522
Levenshulme *Gt Man* 47 SJ8794
Levenwick *Shet* 103 HU4021
Leverburgh *W Isls* 102 NG0186
Leverington *Cambs* 41 TF4411
Leverstock Green *Herts* 22 TL0806
Leverton *Lincs* 51 TF4047
Levington *Suffk* 33 TM2339
Levisham *N York* 63 SE8390
Lew *Oxon* 29 SP3206
Lewannick *Cnwll* 4 SX2780
Lewdown *Devon* 4 SX4586
Lewes *E Susx* 13 TQ4110
Leweston *Dyfed* 16 SM9322
Lewisham *Gt Lon* 23 TQ3774
Lewiston *Highld* 92 NH5129
Lewknor *Oxon* 22 SU7197
Lewson Street *Kent* 15 TQ9661
Lewtrenchard *Devon* 4 SX4586
Lexworthy *Somset* 8 ST2535
Leybourne *Kent* 14 TQ6858
Leyburn *N York* 61 SE1190
Leygreen *Herts* 31 TL1624
Leyland *Lancs* 53 SD5422
Leylodge *Gramp* 95 NJ7613
Leys *Gramp* 95 NK0052
Leys *Tays* 83 NO2537
Leys of Cossans *Tays* 88 NO3849
Leysdown-on-Sea *Kent* 15 TR0370
Leysmill *Tays* 89 NO6047
Leysters *H & W* 27 SO5664
Leyton *Gt Lon* 23 TQ3786
Leytonstone *Gt Lon* 23 TQ3987
Lezant *Cnwll* 4 SX3479
Lezayre *IOM* 52 SC4294
Lhanbryde *Gramp* 94 NJ2761
Libanus *Powys* 26 SN9925
Libberton *Strath* 75 NS9943
Liberton *Loth* 75 NT2769
Lichfield *Staffs* 38 SK1109
Lickey *H & W* 38 SO9975
Lickey End *H & W* 38 SO9772
Lickfold *W Susx* 12 SU9226
Liddesdale *Highld* 79 NM7759
Liddington *Wilts* 21 SU2081
Lidgate *Suffk* 32 TL7258
Lidlington *Beds* 30 SP9939
Liff *Tays* 83 NO3332
Lifford *W Mids* 38 SP0580
Lifton *Devon* 4 SX3885
Liftondown *Devon* 4 SX3685
Lighthorne *Warwks* 29 SP3355
Lightwater *Surrey* 22 SU9362
Lilbourne *Nhants* 39 SP5676
Lilleshall *Shrops* 37 SJ7315
Lilley *Herts* 30 TL1126
Lilliesleaf *Border* 76 NT5325
Lillingstone Dayrell *Bucks* 30 SP7039
Lillingstone Lovell *Bucks* 30 SP7140
Lillington *Dorset* 9 ST6212
Lilliput *Dorset* 10 SZ0489
Lilstock *Somset* 19 ST1645
Limbury *Beds* 30 TL0724
Lime Street *H & W* 28 SO8130
Limekilnburn *Strath* 74 NS7050
Limekilns *Fife* 82 NT0883
Limerigg *Cent* 74 NS8571
Limerstone *IOW* 10 SZ4482
Limington *Somset* 8 ST5422
Limmerhaugh *Strath* 74 NS6127
Limpenhoe *Norfk* 43 TG3903
Limpley Stoke *Wilts* 20 ST7860
Limpsfield *Surrey* 13 TQ4053
Limpsfield Chart *Surrey* 13 TQ4251
Linby *Notts* 49 SK5351
Linchmere *W Susx* 11 SU8630
Lincluden *D & G* 66 NX9677
Lincoln *Lincs* 50 SK9771
Lincomb *H & W* 28 SO8268
Lindal in Furness *Cumb* 58 SD2475
Lindale *Cumb* 59 SD4180
Lindfield *W Susx* 12 TQ3425
Lindford *Hants* 11 SU8036
Lindley *W York* 55 SE1217
Lindley Green *N York* 55 SE2248
Lindores *Fife* 83 NO2616
Lindridge *H & W* 28 SO6769
Lindsell *Essex* 24 TL6427
Lindsey *Suffk* 32 TL9745
Lindsey Tye *Suffk* 32 TL9845
Lingdale *Cleve* 62 NZ6716
Lingen *H & W* 27 SO3667
Lingwood *Norfk* 43 TG3508
Linicro *Highld* 90 NG3966
Linkend *H & W* 28 SO8231
Linkenholt *Hants* 21 SU3657
Linkinhorne *Cnwll* 4 SX3173
Linktown *Fife* 83 NT2790
Linkwood *Gramp* 94 NJ2361
Linley *Shrops* 36 SO3592
Linley Green *H & W* 28 SO6953
Linleygreen *Shrops* 37 SO6898
Linlithgow *Loth* 75 NS9977
Linsidemore *Highld* 96 NH5499
Linslade *Beds* 30 SP9125
Linstead Parva *Suffk* 33 TM3377
Linstock *Cumb* 67 NY4258
Linthurst *H & W* 38 SO9972
Linthwaite *W York* 55 SE1014
Lintlaw *Border* 77 NT8258
Lintmill *Gramp* 94 NJ5165
Linton *Border* 76 NT7726
Linton *Cambs* 31 TL5646
Linton *Derbys* 39 SK2716
Linton *H & W* 28 SO6625
Linton *Kent* 14 TQ7550
Linton *N York* 54 SD9962
Linton *W York* 55 SE3946
Linton Hill *Gloucs* 28 SO6624
Linton-on-Ouse *N York* 55 SE4860
Linwood *Lincs* 50 TF1186
Linwood *Strath* 73 NS4464
Lionel *W Isls* 102 NB5263
Liphook *Hants* 11 SU8431
Liscard *Mersyd* 46 SJ2991
Liscombe *Devon* 7 SS8732
Liskeard *Cnwll* 4 SX2564
Liss *Hants* 11 SU7727
Lissett *Humb* 57 TA1458
Lissington *Lincs* 50 TF1083
Lisvane *S Glam* 19 ST1883
Litcham *Norfk* 42 TF8817
Litchborough *Nhants* 29 SP6354
Litchfield *Hants* 21 SU4653
Litherland *Mersyd* 46 SJ3397
Litlington *Cambs* 31 TL3142
Litlington *E Susx* 13 TQ5201
Little Abington *Cambs* 31 TL5349
Little Addington *Nhants* 30 SP9673
Little Airies *D & G* 64 NX4248
Little Alne *Warwks* 28 SP1461
Little Amwell *Herts* 23 TL3511
Little Asby *Cumb* 60 NY6909
Little Aston *Staffs* 38 SK0900
Little Ayton *N York* 62 NZ5610
Little Baddow *Essex* 24 TL7707
Little Badminton *Avon* 20 ST8084
Little Bampton *Cumb* 67 NY2755
Little Bardfield *Essex* 24 TL6531
Little Barford *Beds* 31 TL1756
Little Barningham *Norfk* 43 TG1333
Little Barrington *Gloucs* 29 SP2012
Little Barrow *Ches* 46 SJ4769
Little Bavington *Nthumb* 68 NY9878
Little Bedwyn *Wilts* 21 SU2866
Little Bentley *Essex* 25 TM1125
Little Berkhamsted *Herts* 23 TL2907
Little Billing *Nhants* 30 SP8061
Little Billington *Beds* 30 SP9322
Little Birch *H & W* 27 SO5130
Little Blakenham *Suffk* 33 TM1048
Little Blencow *Cumb* 59 NY4532
Little Bognor *W Susx* 12 TQ0020
Little Bolehill *Derbys* 49 SK2954
Little Bookham *Surrey* 22 TQ1254
Little Bourton *Oxon* 29 SP4544
Little Bradley *Suffk* 32 TL6852
Little Braxted *Essex* 24 TL8314
Little Brechin *Tays* 89 NO5862
Little Brickhill *Beds* 30 SP9132
Little Brington *Nhants* 30 SP6663
Little Bromley *Essex* 25 TM0928
Little Broughton *Cumb* 58 NY0731
Little Budworth *Ches* 47 SJ5965
Little Burstead *Essex* 24 TQ6692
Little Bytham *Lincs* 40 TF0118
Little Carlton *Lincs* 51 TF3985
Little Casterton *Leics* 40 TF0109
Little Cawthorpe *Lincs* 51 TF3583
Little Chalfont *Bucks* 22 SU9997
Little Chart *Kent* 14 TQ9446
Little Chesterford *Essex* 31 TL5141
Little Cheverell *Wilts* 20 ST9953
Little Chishill *Cambs* 31 TL4137
Little Clacton *Essex* 25 TM1618
Little Clifton *Cumb* 58 NY0528
Little Comberton *H & W* 28 SO9643
Little Common *E Susx* 14 TQ7107
Little Compton *Warwks* 29 SP2630
Little Cornard *Suffk* 32 TL9039
Little Cowarne *H & W* 27 SO6051
Little Coxwell *Oxon* 21 SU2893
Little Crakehall *N York* 61 SE2390
Little Cressingham *Norfk* 42 TF8700
Little Crosby *Mersyd* 46 SD3201
Little Cubley *Derbys* 48 SK1537
Little Dalby *Leics* 40 SK7714
Little Dens *Gramp* 95 NK0643
Little Dewchurch *H & W* 27 SO5231
Little Ditton *Cambs* 32 TL6658
Little Driffield *Humb* 56 TA0058
Little Dunham *Norfk* 42 TF8612
Little Dunkeld *Tays* 88 NO0342
Little Dunmow *Essex* 24 TL6521
Little Durnford *Wilts* 10 SU1234
Little Eaton *Derbys* 49 SK3641
Little Ellingham *Norfk* 42 TM0099
Little Everdon *Nhants* 29 SP5957
Little Eversden *Cambs* 31 TL3753
Little Faringdon *S York* 21 SP2201
Little Fencote *N York* 61 SE2893
Little Fenton *N York* 55 SE5235
Little Fransham *Norfk* 42 TF9011
Little Gaddesden *Herts* 30 SP9913
Little Glemham *Suffk* 33 TM3458
Little Gorsley *H & W* 28 SO6924
Little Gransden *Cambs* 31 TL2755
Little Green *Somset* 20 ST7248
Little Grimsby *Lincs* 51 TF3291
Little Hadham *Herts* 31 TL4322
Little Hale *Lincs* 50 TF1441
Little Hallam *Derbys* 49 SK4640
Little Hallingbury *Essex* 31 TL5017
Little Harrowden *Nhants* 30 SP8771
Little Haseley *Oxon* 21 SP6400
Little Hatfield *Humb* 57 TA1743
Little Haven *Dyfed* 16 SM8512
Little Hay *Staffs* 38 SK1102
Little Haywood *Staffs* 38 SK0021
Little Heath *W Mids* 39 SP3482
Little Hereford *H & W* 27 SO5568
Little Horkesley *Essex* 25 TL9532
Little Hormead *Herts* 31 TL4028
Little Horsted *E Susx* 13 TQ4718
Little Horton *W York* 55 SE1531
Little Horwood *Bucks* 30 SP7930
Little Houghton *Nhants* 30 SP8059
Little Houghton *S York* 55 SE4205
Little Hucklow *Derbys* 48 SK1678
Little Hutton *N York* 62 SE4576
Little Irchester *Nhants* 30 SP9066
Little Keyford *Somset* 20 ST7746
Little Kimble *Bucks* 22 SP8207
Little Kineton *Warwks* 29 SP3350
Little Kingshill *Bucks* 22 SU8999
Little Knox *D & G* 66 NX8060
Little Langdale *Cumb* 58 NY3103
Little Langford *Wilts* 10 SU0436
Little Lashbrook *Devon* 6 SS4007
Little Laver *Essex* 24 TL5409
Little Leigh *Ches* 47 SJ6175
Little Leighs *Essex* 24 TL7117
Little Lever *Gt Man* 47 SD7507
Little Linford *Bucks* 30 SP8444
Little Load *Somset* 8 ST4724
Little London *E Susx* 13 TQ5620
Little London *Essex* 31 TL4729
Little London *Hants* 21 SU3749
Little London *Hants* 21 SU6259
Little Longstone *Derbys* 48 SK1871
Little Malvern *H & W* 28 SO7640
Little Maplestead *Essex* 24 TL8234
Little Marcle *H & W* 28 SO6736
Little Marlow *Bucks* 22 SU8787
Little Massingham *Norfk* 42 TF7824
Little Melton *Norfk* 43 TG1607
Little Mill *Gwent* 19 SO3203
Little Milton *Oxon* 21 SP6100
Little Missenden *Bucks* 22 SU9299
Little Mongham *Kent* 15 TR3351
Little Musgrave *Cumb* 60 NY7612
Little Ness *Shrops* 36 SJ4019
Little Newcastle *Dyfed* 16 SM9829
Little Newsham *Dur* 61 NZ1217
Little Norton *Somset* 8 ST4715
Little Oakley *Essex* 25 TM2129
Little Oakley *Nhants* 40 SP8985
Little Onn *Staffs* 38 SJ8315
Little Orton *Cumb* 67 NY3555
Little Packington *Warwks* 39 SP2184
Little Pannell *Wilts* 20 SU0053
Little Paxton *Cambs* 31 TL1862
Little Petherick *Cnwll* 3 SW9172
Little Plumstead *Norfk* 43 TG3112
Little Ponton *Lincs* 40 SK9232
Little Preston *Nhants* 29 SP5854
Little Raveley *Cambs* 41 TL2579
Little Reedness *Humb* 56 SE8022
Little Ribston *N York* 55 SE3853
Little Rissington *Gloucs* 29 SP1819
Little Rollright *Oxon* 29 SP2930
Little Ryburgh *Norfk* 42 TF9628
Little Salkeld *Cumb* 59 NY5636
Little Sampford *Essex* 24 TL6533
Little Saughall *Ches* 46 SJ3768
Little Saxham *Suffk* 32 TL8063
Little Scatwell *Highld* 92 NH3856
Little Sessay *N York* 62 SE4674
Little Shelford *Cambs* 31 TL4551
Little Silver *Devon* 7 SS8601
Little Singleton *Lancs* 53 SD3739
Little Skipwith *N York* 56 SE6538
Little Smeaton *N York* 55 SE5216
Little Snoring *Norfk* 42 TF9532
Little Sodbury *Avon* 20 ST7582
Little Somborne *Hants* 10 SU3832
Little Somerford *Wilts* 20 ST9684
Little Soudley *Shrops* 37 SJ7128
Little Stainton *Dur* 62 NZ3420
Little Staughton *Beds* 30 TL1062
Little Steeping *Lincs* 51 TF4362
Little Stonham *Suffk* 33 TM1160
Little Stretton *Leics* 39 SK6600
Little Stretton *Shrops* 36 SO4491
Little Strickland *Cumb* 59 NY5619
Little Stukeley *Cambs* 31 TL2175
Little Sugnall *Staffs* 37 SJ8031
Little Sypland *D & G* 65 NX7253
Little Tew *Oxon* 29 SP3828
Little Tey *Essex* 24 TL8923
Little Thetford *Cambs* 31 TL5376
Little Thorpe *Dur* 62 NZ4242
Little Thurlow Green *Suffk* 32 TL6851
Little Thurrock *Essex* 24 TQ6277
Little Torrington *Devon* 6 SS4916
Little Town *Lancs* 54 SD6635
Little Wakering *Essex* 25 TQ9388
Little Walden *Essex* 31 TL5441
Little Waldingfield *Suffk* 32 TL9245
Little Walsingham *Norfk* 42 TF9337
Little Waltham *Essex* 24 TL7012
Little Washbourne *Gloucs* 28 SO9833
Little Weighton *Humb* 56 SE9833
Little Weldon *Nhants* 40 SP9289
Little Wenham *Suffk* 32 TM0839
Little Wenlock *Shrops* 37 SJ6406
Little Weston *Somset* 9 ST6225
Little Whitefield *IOW* 11 SZ5889
Little Wilbraham *Cambs* 31 TL5458
Little Witcombe *Gloucs* 28 SO9115
Little Witley *H & W* 28 SO7863
Little Wittenham *Oxon* 21 SU5693
Little Wolford *Warwks* 29 SP2635
Little Woodcote *Surrey* 23 TQ2861
Little Wratting *Suffk* 32 TL6847
Little Wymington *Beds* 30 SP9565
Little Wymondley *Herts* 31 TL2127
Little Wyrley *Staffs* 38 SK0105
Little Yeldham *Essex* 32 TL7839

Littleborough Longtown

Littleborough *Gt Man*	54	SD9316
Littleborough *Notts*	50	SK8282
Littlebourne *Kent*	15	TR2057
Littlebredy *Dorset*	9	SY5889
Littlebury *Essex*	31	TL5139
Littlebury Green *Essex*	31	TL4838
Littledean *Gloucs*	28	SO6713
Littleham *Devon*	6	SS4323
Littleham *Devon*	5	SY0381
Littlehampton *W Susx*	12	TQ0201
Littlehempston *Devon*	5	SX8162
Littlemill *Gramp*	88	NO3295
Littlemill *Highld*	93	NH9150
Littlemore *Oxon*	21	SP5302
Littleover *Derbys*	39	SK3334
Littleport *Cambs*	41	TL5686
Littlestone-on-Sea *Kent*	15	TR0824
Littlethorpe *Leics*	39	SP5496
Littlethorpe *N York*	55	SE3269
Littleton *Ches*	46	SJ4466
Littleton *D & G*	65	NX6355
Littleton *Hants*	10	SU4532
Littleton *Somset*	8	ST4930
Littleton *Surrey*	22	TQ0668
Littleton Drew *Wilts*	20	ST8380
Littleton-on-Severn *Avon*	19	ST5989
Littletown *Dur*	69	NZ3343
Littlewick Green *Berks*	22	SU8379
Littleworth *H & W*	28	SO8850
Littleworth *Oxon*	21	SU3197
Littleworth *Staffs*	38	SJ9323
Littley Green *Essex*	24	TL6917
Litton *Derbys*	48	SK1675
Litton *N York*	60	SD9074
Litton *Somset*	19	ST5954
Litton Cheney *Dorset*	8	SY5490
Liverpool *Mersyd*	46	SJ3490
Liversedge *W York*	55	SE1923
Liverton *Cleve*	63	NZ7115
Liverton *Devon*	5	SX8075
Livingston *Loth*	75	NT0668
Livingston Village *Loth*	75	NT0366
Lixton *Devon*	5	SX6950
Lixwm *Clwyd*	46	SJ1671
Lizard *Cnwll*	2	SW7012
Llanaelhaearn *Gwynd*	44	SH3844
Llanafan *Dyfed*	35	SN6872
Llanallgo *Gwynd*	44	SH5085
Llanarmon Dyffryn Ceiriog *Clwyd*	36	SJ1532
Llanarmon-yn-Ial *Clwyd*	46	SJ1956
Llanarth *Dyfed*	34	SN4257
Llanarth *Gwent*	27	SO3710
Llanarthne *Dyfed*	17	SN5320
Llanasa *Clwyd*	46	SJ1081
Llanbadarn Fawr *Dyfed*	34	SN6081
Llanbadarn Fynydd *Powys*	36	SO0977
Llanbadoc *Gwent*	19	ST3799
Llanbeder *Gwent*	19	ST3890
Llanbedr *Gwynd*	44	SH5826
Llanbedr *Powys*	27	SO2320
Llanbedr-Dyffryn-Clwyd *Clwyd*	46	SJ1459
Llanbedr-y-cennin *Gwynd*	45	SH7669
Llanbedrgoch *Gwynd*	44	SH5180
Llanbedrog *Gwynd*	44	SH3231
Llanberis *Gwynd*	44	SH5760
Llanbethery *S Glam*	18	ST0369
Llanbister *Powys*	36	SO1173
Llanblethian *S Glam*	18	SS9873
Llanboidy *Dyfed*	17	SN2123
Llanbradach *M Glam*	18	ST1490
Llanbrynmair *Powys*	35	SH8902
Llancarfan *S Glam*	18	ST0470
Llancloudy *H & W*	27	SO4921
Llandaf *S Glam*	19	ST1577
Llandanwg *Gwynd*	44	SH5728
Llanddanielfab *Gwynd*	44	SH4970
Llanddarog *Dyfed*	17	SN5016
Llanddeiniol *Dyfed*	34	SN5571
Llanddeiniolen *Gwynd*	44	SH5465
Llandderfel *Gwynd*	45	SH9837
Llanddeusant *Gwynd*	44	SH3485
Llanddew *Powys*	26	SO0530
Llanddewi *W Glam*	17	SS4588
Llanddewi Brefi *Dyfed*	26	SN6655
Llanddewi Rhydderch *Gwent*	27	SO3512
Llanddewi Velfrey *Dyfed*	16	SN1415
Llanddewi Ystradenni *Powys*	26	SO1068
Llanddoget *Gwynd*	45	SH8063
Llanddona *Gwynd*	44	SH5779
Llanddowror *Dyfed*	17	SN2514
Llanddulas *Clwyd*	45	SH9178
Llanddyfnan *Gwynd*	44	SH5078
Llandefaelogtrer-graig *Powys*	26	SO1229
Llandefalle *Powys*	26	SO1035
Llandegai *Gwynd*	44	SH5971
Llandegfan *Gwynd*	44	SH5674
Llandegla *Clwyd*	46	SJ2051
Llandegley *Powys*	26	SO1463
Llandegveth *Gwent*	19	ST3395
Llandeilo *Dyfed*	17	SN6222
Llandeilo Graban *Powys*	26	SO0944
Llandeloy *Dyfed*	16	SM8626
Llandenny *Gwent*	27	SO4104
Llandevaud *Gwent*	19	ST4090
Llandevenny *Gwent*	19	ST4186
Llandinam *Powys*	35	SO0288
Llandissilio *Dyfed*	16	SN1221
Llandogo *Gwent*	19	SO5203
Llandough *S Glam*	18	SS9972
Llandough *S Glam*	19	ST1673
Llandovery *Dyfed*	26	SN7634
Llandow *S Glam*	18	SS9473
Llandre *Dyfed*	35	SN6286
Llandre *Dyfed*	26	SN6741
Llandre Isaf *Dyfed*	16	SN1328
Llandrillo *Clwyd*	36	SJ0337
Llandrillo-yn-Rhos *Clwyd*	45	SH8380
Llandrindod Wells *Powys*	26	SO0561
Llandrinio *Powys*	36	SJ2817
Llandudno *Gwynd*	45	SH7882
Llandudno Junction *Gwynd*	45	SH7977
Llandudwen *Gwynd*	44	SH2736
Llandulas *Powys*	26	SN8841
Llandwrog *Gwynd*	44	SH4555
Llandybie *Dyfed*	17	SN6115
Llandyfaelog *Dyfed*	17	SN4111
Llandyfriog *Dyfed*	17	SN3341
Llandygwydd *Dyfed*	17	SN2443
Llandyrnog *Clwyd*	46	SJ1065
Llandyssil *Powys*	36	SO1995
Llandysul *Dyfed*	17	SN4140
Llanedeyrn *S Glam*	19	ST2181
Llanegryn *Gwynd*	34	SH6005
Llanegwad *Dyfed*	17	SN5221
Llaneilian *Gwynd*	44	SH4692
Llanelian-yn-Rhos *Clwyd*	45	SH8676
Llanelidan *Clwyd*	46	SJ1150
Llanelieu *Powys*	27	SO1834
Llanelli *Dyfed*	17	SN5000
Llanelltyd *Gwynd*	35	SH7119
Llanelwedd *Powys*	26	SO0451
Llanenddwyn *Gwynd*	34	SH5823
Llanengan *Gwynd*	44	SH2926
Llanerchymedd *Gwynd*	44	SH4184
Llanerfyl *Powys*	36	SJ0309
Llanfachraeth *Gwynd*	44	SH3182
Llanfachreth *Gwynd*	35	SH7522
Llanfaelog *Gwynd*	44	SH3373
Llanfaelrhys *Gwynd*	44	SH2026
Llanfaethlu *Gwynd*	44	SH3186
Llanfair *Gwynd*	44	SH5728
Llanfair Caereinion *Powys*	36	SJ1006
Llanfair Clydogau *Dyfed*	17	SN6251
Llanfair Dyffryn Clwyd *Clwyd*	46	SJ1355
Llanfair P G *Gwynd*	44	SH5271
Llanfair Talhaiarn *Clwyd*	45	SH9270
Llanfair Waterdine *Shrops*	36	SO2376
Llanfair-is-gaer *Gwynd*	44	SH5065
Llanfair-y-Cwmmwd *Gwynd*	44	SH4466
Llanfair-yn-Neubwll *Gwynd*	44	SH3076
Llanfairfechan *Gwynd*	45	SH6874
Llanfairynghornwy *Gwynd*	44	SH3290
Llanfallteg *Dyfed*	17	SN1520
Llanfallteg West *Dyfed*	16	SN1419
Llanfarian *Dyfed*	34	SN5877
Llanfechain *Powys*	36	SJ1920
Llanfechelli *Gwynd*	44	SH3791
Llanferres *Clwyd*	46	SJ1860
Llanfihangel ar-Arth *Dyfed*	17	SN4540
Llanfihangel Glyn Myfyr *Clwyd*	45	SH9849
Llanfihangel Nant Bran *Powys*	26	SN9434
Llanfihangel Rhydithon *Powys*	27	SO1566
Llanfihangel Rogiet *Gwent*	19	ST4587
Llanfihangel yn Nhowyn *Gwynd*	44	SH3277
Llanfihangel-y-Creuddyn *Dyfed*	35	SN6675
Llanfihangel-y-traethau *Gwynd*	44	SH5934
Llanfihangel-yng-Ngwynfa *Powys*	36	SJ0816
Llanfilo *Powys*	26	SO1132
Llanfoist *Gwent*	27	SO2813
Llanfor *Gwynd*	45	SH9336
Llanfrechfa *Gwent*	19	ST3293
Llanfrynach *Powys*	26	SO0725
Llanfwrog *Clwyd*	46	SJ1157
Llanfwrog *Gwynd*	44	SH3084
Llanfyllin *Powys*	36	SJ1419
Llanfynydd *Clwyd*	46	SJ2856
Llanfynydd *Dyfed*	17	SN5527
Llanfyrnach *Dyfed*	17	SN2231
Llangadfan *Powys*	35	SJ0110
Llangadog *Dyfed*	26	SN7028
Llangadwaladr *Gwynd*	44	SH3869
Llangaffo *Gwynd*	44	SH4468
Llangammarch Wells *Powys*	26	SN9346
Llangan *S Glam*	18	SS9577
Llangarron *H & W*	27	SO5220
Llangathen *Dyfed*	17	SN5822
Llangattock *Powys*	27	SO2117
Llangattock Lingoed *Gwent*	27	SO3620
Llangedwyn *Clwyd*	36	SJ1824
Llangefni *Gwynd*	44	SH4675
Llangeinor *M Glam*	18	SS9187
Llangeinwen *Gwynd*	44	SH4465
Llangeitho *Dyfed*	35	SN6259
Llangeler *Dyfed*	17	SN3739
Llangelynin *Gwynd*	34	SH5707
Llangendeirne *Dyfed*	17	SN4513
Llangennech *Dyfed*	17	SN5601
Llangernyw *Clwyd*	45	SH8767
Llanglan *Gwynd*	44	SH2928
Llangloffan *Dyfed*	16	SM9032
Llanglydwen *Dyfed*	17	SN1826
Llangoed *Gwynd*	44	SH6079
Llangollen *Clwyd*	36	SJ2141
Llangolman *Dyfed*	16	SN1127
Llangors *Powys*	26	SO1327
Llangower *Gwynd*	45	SH9032
Llangranog *Dyfed*	34	SN3154
Llangristiolus *Gwynd*	44	SH4373
Llangrove *H & W*	27	SO5219
Llangunllo *Powys*	36	SO2171
Llangunnor *Dyfed*	17	SN4320
Llangurig *Powys*	35	SN9079
Llangwm *Clwyd*	45	SH9644
Llangwm *Dyfed*	16	SM9909
Llangwm *Gwent*	19	ST4299
Llangwm-isaf *Gwent*	19	SO4300
Llangwyryfon *Dyfed*	34	SN5970
Llangybi *Dyfed*	17	SN6053
Llangybi *Gwent*	19	ST3796
Llangybi *Gwynd*	44	SH4341
Llangynhafal *Clwyd*	46	SJ1263
Llangynidr *Powys*	27	SO1519
Llangynin *Dyfed*	17	SN2517
Llangynog *Dyfed*	17	SN3314
Llangynog *Powys*	36	SJ0526
Llangynwyd *M Glam*	18	SS8588
Llanhamlach *Powys*	26	SO0926
Llanharan *M Glam*	18	ST0083
Llanharry *M Glam*	18	ST0080
Llanhennock *Gwent*	19	ST3592
Llanhilleth *Gwent*	19	SO2100
Llanidloes *Powys*	35	SN9584
Llaniestyn *Gwynd*	44	SH2733
Llanigon *Powys*	27	SO2139
Llanilar *Dyfed*	35	SN6275
Llanilid *M Glam*	18	SS9781
Llanina *Dyfed*	34	SN4059
Llanishen *Gwent*	19	SO4703
Llanishen *S Glam*	19	ST1781
Llanllechid *Gwynd*	45	SH6268
Llanllowell *Gwent*	19	ST3998
Llanllugan *Powys*	36	SJ0502
Llanllwch *Dyfed*	17	SN3818
Llanllwchaiarn *Powys*	36	SO1292
Llanllwni *Dyfed*	17	SN4741
Llanllyfni *Gwynd*	44	SH4751
Llanmadoc *W Glam*	17	SS4493
Llanmaes *S Glam*	18	SS9769
Llanmartin *Gwent*	19	ST3989
Llanmiloe *Dyfed*	17	SN2408
Llanmorlais *W Glam*	17	SS5294
Llannefydd *Clwyd*	45	SH9870
Llannon *Dyfed*	17	SN5308
Llannor *Gwynd*	44	SH3537
Llanon *Dyfed*	34	SN5166
Llanover *Gwent*	27	SO3109
Llanpumsaint *Dyfed*	17	SN4229
Llanrhaeadr-ym-Mochnant *Clwyd*	36	SJ1226
Llanrhidian *W Glam*	17	SS4992
Llanrhychwyn *Gwynd*	45	SH7761
Llanrhyddlad *Gwynd*	44	SH3389
Llanrhystud *Dyfed*	34	SN5369
Llanrian *Dyfed*	16	SM8231
Llanrothal *H & W*	27	SO4718
Llanrug *Gwynd*	44	SH5363
Llanrumney *S Glam*	19	ST2280
Llanrwst *Gwynd*	45	SH8061
Llansadurnen *Dyfed*	17	SN2810
Llansadwrn *Dyfed*	26	SN6931
Llansadwrn *Gwynd*	44	SH5575
Llansaint *Dyfed*	17	SN3808
Llansamlet *W Glam*	18	SS6897
Llansanffraid Glan Conwy *Gwynd*	45	SH8076
Llansannan *Clwyd*	45	SH9365
Llansantffraed *Powys*	26	SO1223
Llansantffraed-Cwmdeuddwr *Powys*	35	SN9667
Llansantffraed-in-Elvel *Powys*	26	SO0954
Llansantffraid *Dyfed*	34	SN5167
Llansantffraid-ym-Mechain *Powys*	36	SJ2220
Llansawel *Dyfed*	17	SN6136
Llansilin *Clwyd*	36	SJ2128
Llansoy *Gwent*	19	SO4402
Llanspyddid *Powys*	26	SO0128
Llanstadwell *Dyfed*	16	SM9404
Llansteffan *Dyfed*	17	SN3511
Llantarnam *Gwent*	19	ST3093
Llanteg *Dyfed*	17	SN1810
Llanthewy Skirrid *Gwent*	27	SO3416
Llanthony *Gwent*	27	SO2827
Llantilio Pertholey *Gwent*	27	SO3116
Llantrisant *Gwent*	19	ST3996
Llantrisant *M Glam*	18	ST0483
Llantrithyd *S Glam*	18	ST0472
Llantwit Fardre *M Glam*	18	ST0886
Llantwit Major *S Glam*	18	SS9668
Llanuwchllyn *Gwynd*	45	SH8730
Llanvaches *Gwent*	19	ST4391
Llanvair Discoed *Gwent*	19	ST4492
Llanvapley *Gwent*	27	SO3614
Llanvetherine *Gwent*	27	SO3617
Llanvihangel Crucorney *Gwent*	27	SO3220
Llanwddyn *Powys*	35	SJ0219
Llanwenog *Dyfed*	17	SN4945
Llanwern *Gwent*	19	ST3688
Llanwinio *Dyfed*	17	SN2626
Llanwnda *Dyfed*	16	SM9339
Llanwnda *Gwynd*	44	SH4758
Llanwnen *Dyfed*	17	SN5347
Llanwnog *Powys*	35	SO0293
Llanwrda *Dyfed*	26	SN7131
Llanwrin *Powys*	35	SH7803
Llanwrthwl *Powys*	35	SN9763
Llanwrtyd Wells *Powys*	26	SN8846
Llanwyddelan *Powys*	36	SJ0801
Llanyblodwel *Shrops*	36	SJ2323
Llanybri *Dyfed*	17	SN3312
Llanybydder *Dyfed*	17	SN5244
Llanycefn *Dyfed*	16	SN0923
Llanychaer Bridge *Dyfed*	16	SM9835
Llanymawddwy *Gwynd*	35	SH9019
Llanymynech *Shrops*	36	SJ2621
Llanynghenedl *Gwynd*	44	SH3181
Llanynis *Powys*	26	SN9950
Llanynys *Clwyd*	46	SJ1062
Llanyre *Powys*	26	SO0462
Llanystumdwy *Gwynd*	44	SH4738
Llanywern *Powys*	26	SO1028
Llawhaden *Dyfed*	16	SN0717
Llawnt *Shrops*	36	SJ2430
Llawryglyn *Powys*	35	SN9291
Llay *Clwyd*	46	SJ3355
Llechryd *Dyfed*	17	SN2143
Lledrod *Dyfed*	35	SN6470
Llithfaen *Gwynd*	44	SH3542
Llowes *Powys*	27	SO1941
Llwydcoed *M Glam*	26	SN9904
Llwydiarth *Powys*	36	SJ0315
Llwyncelyn *Dyfed*	34	SN4459
Llwyndafydd *Dyfed*	34	SN3755
Llwyngwril *Gwynd*	34	SH5909
Llwynmawr *Clwyd*	36	SJ2237
Llwynypia *M Glam*	18	SS9993
Llynclys *Shrops*	36	SJ2824
Llynfaes *Gwynd*	44	SH4178
Llys-y-fran *Dyfed*	16	SN0424
Llysfaen *Clwyd*	45	SH8977
Llyswen *Powys*	26	SO1337
Llysworney *S Glam*	18	SS9673
Llywel *Powys*	26	SN8630
Loan *Cent*	75	NS9675
Loanhead *Loth*	75	NT2865
Loaningfoot *D & G*	66	NX9655
Loans *Strath*	73	NS3431
Lobhillcross *Devon*	4	SX4686
Loch Katrine Pier *Cent*	81	NN4907
Loch Loyal Lodge *Highld*	99	NC6146
Loch Maree Hotel *Highld*	91	NG9170
Lochailort *Highld*	85	NM7682
Lochans *D & G*	64	NX0656
Locharbriggs *D & G*	66	NX9980
Lochavich *Strath*	80	NM9415
Lochawe *Strath*	80	NN1227
Lochboisdale *W Isls*	102	NF7919
Lochbuie *Strath*	79	NM6025
Lochcarron *Highld*	85	NG8939
Lochdon *Strath*	79	NM7233
Lochead *Strath*	71	NR7778
Lochearnhead *Cent*	81	NN5823
Lochee *Tays*	83	NO3731
Locheilside Station *Highld*	85	NM9978
Lochend *Highld*	92	NH5937
Locheport *W Isls*	102	NF8563
Lochfoot *D & G*	66	NX8973
Lochgair *Strath*	71	NR9290
Lochgelly *Fife*	82	NT1893
Lochgilphead *Strath*	71	NR8688
Lochgoilhead *Strath*	80	NN2001
Lochieheads *Fife*	83	NO2513
Lochill *Gramp*	94	NJ2964
Lochindorb Lodge *Highld*	93	NH9635
Lochinver *Highld*	98	NC0922
Lochluichart *Highld*	92	NH3363
Lochmaben *D & G*	66	NY0882
Lochmaddy *W Isls*	102	NF9169
Lochore *Fife*	82	NT1796
Lochranza *Strath*	72	NR9350
Lochside *Gramp*	89	NO7364
Lochside *Highld*	93	NH8152
Lochton *Strath*	64	NX2579
Lochty *Fife*	83	NO5208
Lochty *Tays*	89	NO5362
Lochuisge *Highld*	79	NM7955
Lochwinnoch *Strath*	73	NS3559
Lochwood *D & G*	66	NY0896
Lockengate *Cnwll*	3	SX0361
Lockerbie *D & G*	67	NY1381
Lockeridge *Wilts*	20	SU1467
Lockerley *Hants*	10	SU3025
Locking *Avon*	19	ST3659
Lockington *Humb*	56	SE9947
Lockleywood *Shrops*	37	SJ6928
Locksbottom *Gt Lon*	23	TQ4265
Lockton *N York*	63	SE8489
Loddington *Leics*	40	SK7902
Loddington *Nhants*	30	SP8178
Loddiswell *Devon*	5	SX7248
Loddon *Norfk*	43	TM3698
Lode *Cambs*	31	TL5362
Lode Heath *W Mids*	38	SP1580
Loders *Dorset*	8	SY4994
Lodsworth *W Susx*	12	SU9223
Lofhouse Gate *W York*	55	SE3324
Lofthouse *N York*	61	SE1073
Lofthouse *W York*	55	SE3325
Loftus *Cleve*	63	NZ7218
Logan *Strath*	74	NS5820
Loganlea *Loth*	75	NS9762
Loggerheads *Staffs*	37	SJ7336
Logie *Fife*	83	NO4020
Logie *Gramp*	93	NJ0150
Logie *Tays*	89	NO6963
Logie Coldstone *Gramp*	88	NJ4304
Logie Pert *Tays*	89	NO6664
Logierait *Tays*	88	NN9752
Login *Dyfed*	17	SN1623
Lolworth *Cambs*	31	TL3664
Lonbain *Highld*	91	NG6852
Londesborough *Humb*	56	SE8645
London *Gt Lon*	23	TQ2879
London Apprentice *Cnwll*	3	SX0049
London Colney *Herts*	23	TL1803
Londonderry *N York*	61	SE3087
Londonthorpe *Lincs*	40	SK9537
Londubh *Highld*	91	NG8680
Long Ashton *Avon*	19	ST5570
Long Bank *H & W*	37	SO7674
Long Bennington *Lincs*	50	SK8344
Long Bredy *Dorset*	9	SY5690
Long Buckby *Nhants*	29	SP6367
Long Clawson *Leics*	40	SK7227
Long Compton *Staffs*	38	SJ8522
Long Compton *Warwks*	29	SP2832
Long Crendon *Bucks*	22	SP6908
Long Crichel *Dorset*	9	ST9710
Long Ditton *Surrey*	23	TQ1766
Long Duckmanton *Derbys*	49	SK4471
Long Eaton *Derbys*	39	SK4833
Long Green *Ches*	46	SJ4770
Long Green *H & W*	28	SO8433
Long Itchington *Warwks*	29	SP4165
Long Lawford *Warwks*	39	SP4776
Long Load *Somset*	8	ST4623
Long Marston *Herts*	30	SP8915
Long Marston *N York*	55	SE5051
Long Marston *Warwks*	28	SP1548
Long Marton *Cumb*	60	NY6624
Long Melford *Suffk*	32	TL8645
Long Newnton *Gloucs*	20	ST9192
Long Newton *Loth*	76	NT5164
Long Preston *N York*	54	SD8358
Long Riston *Humb*	57	TA1242
Long Stratton *Norfk*	33	TM1992
Long Street *Bucks*	30	SP7947
Long Sutton *Hants*	22	SU7347
Long Sutton *Lincs*	41	TF4322
Long Sutton *Somset*	8	ST4725
Long Thurlow *Suffk*	32	TM0068
Long Waste *Shrops*	37	SJ6115
Long Whatton *Leics*	39	SK4723
Long Wittenham *Oxon*	21	SU5493
Longbenton *T & W*	69	NZ2668
Longborough *Gloucs*	29	SP1729
Longbridge *W Mids*	38	SP0177
Longbridge Deverill *Wilts*	20	ST8640
Longburton *Dorset*	9	ST6412
Longcliffe *Derbys*	48	SK2255
Longcombe *Devon*	5	SX8359
Longcot *Oxon*	21	SU2790
Longden *Shrops*	36	SJ4406
Longdon *H & W*	28	SO8336
Longdon *Staffs*	38	SK0714
Longdon Green *Staffs*	38	SK0813
Longdon upon Tern *Shrops*	37	SJ6115
Longdown *Devon*	5	SX8691
Longdowns *Cnwll*	2	SW7434
Longfield *Kent*	14	TQ6069
Longford *Derbys*	48	SK2137
Longford *Gloucs*	28	SO8320
Longford *Shrops*	37	SJ6434
Longford *Shrops*	37	SJ7218
Longforgan *Tays*	83	NO2929
Longformacus *Border*	76	NT6957
Longframlington *Nthumb*	69	NU1300
Longham *Dorset*	10	SZ0698
Longham *Norfk*	42	TF9416
Longhirst *Nthumb*	69	NZ2289
Longhope *Gloucs*	28	SO6918
Longhorsley *Nthumb*	69	NZ1494
Longhoughton *Nthumb*	77	NU2415
Longlane *Derbys*	48	SK2437
Longlevens *Gloucs*	28	SO8519
Longleys *Tays*	88	NO2643
Longmanhill *Gramp*	95	NJ7362
Longmoor Camp *Hants*	11	SU7931
Longmorn *Gramp*	94	NJ2358
Longnewton *Border*	76	NT5827
Longnewton *Cleve*	62	NZ3816
Longney *Gloucs*	28	SO7612
Longniddry *Loth*	76	NT4476
Longnor *Shrops*	37	SJ4800
Longnor *Staffs*	48	SK0864
Longparish *Hants*	21	SU4345
Longridge *Lancs*	54	SD6037
Longridge *Loth*	75	NS9462
Longriggend *Strath*	74	NS8270
Longrock *Cnwll*	2	SW5031
Longsdon *Staffs*	48	SJ9654
Longside *Gramp*	95	NK0347
Longstanton *Cambs*	31	TL3966
Longstock *Hants*	10	SU3537
Longstowe *Cambs*	31	TL3054
Longstreet *Wilts*	20	SU1451
Longthorpe *Cambs*	40	TL1698
Longthwaite *Cumb*	59	NY4323
Longton *Lancs*	53	SD4825
Longton *Staffs*	48	SJ9143
Longtown *Cumb*	67	NY3768
Longtown *H & W*	27	SO3229

Longueville Market Bosworth

Longueville Jersey 101 JS1708
Longville in the Dale Shrops 37 SO5393
Longwick Bucks 22 SP7905
Longwitton Nthumb 68 NZ0788
Longwood D & G 65 NX7060
Longworth Oxon 21 SU3899
Longyester Loth 76 NT5465
Lonmay Gramp 95 NK0159
Lonmore Highld 90 NG2646
Looe Cnwll 4 SX2553
Loose Kent 14 TQ7552
Loosley Row Bucks 22 SP8100
Lootcherbrae Gramp 94 NJ6053
Lopen Somset 8 ST4214
Loppington Shrops 36 SJ4629
Lornty Tays 88 NO1746
Loscoe Derbys 49 SK4247
Lossiemouth Gramp 94 NJ2370
Lostock Gralam Ches 47 SJ6974
Lostock Green Ches 47 SJ6973
Lostwithiel Cnwll 3 SX1059
Lothbeg Highld 97 NC9410
Lothersdale N York 54 SD9545
Lothmore Highld 97 NC9611
Loughborough Leics 39 SK5319
Loughor W Glam 17 SS5698
Loughton Bucks 30 SP8337
Loughton Essex 23 TQ4296
Loughton Shrops 37 SO6182
Lound Lincs 40 TF0618
Lound Notts 49 SK6986
Lound Suffk 43 TM5099
Lount Leics 39 SK3819
Louth Lincs 51 TF3287
Love Clough Lancs 54 SD8127
Lovedean Hants 11 SU6812
Lover Wilts 10 SU2120
Loversall S York 49 SK5798
Loves Green Essex 24 TL6404
Loveston Dyfed 16 SN0808
Lovington Somset 9 ST5930
Low Ackworth W York 55 SE4517
Low Barbeth D & G 64 NX0166
Low Bentham N York 54 SD6469
Low Biggins Cumb 59 SD6077
Low Borrowbridge Cumb 59 NY6101
Low Bradfield S York 49 SK2691
Low Bradley N York 54 SE0048
Low Burnham Humb 50 SE7802
Low Catton Humb 56 SE7053
Low Dinsdale Dur 62 NZ3411
Low Eggborough N York 56 SE5623
Low Ellington N York 61 SE1983
Low Gartachorrans Cent 81 NS4685
Low Grantley N York 55 SE2370
Low Ham Somset 8 ST4329
Low Harrogate N York 55 SE2955
Low Hesket Cumb 67 NY4646
Low Hill H & W 38 SO8473
Low Hutton N York 56 SE7667
Low Lorton Cumb 58 NY1525
Low Marnham Notts 50 SK8069
Low Mill N York 62 SE6795
Low Moorsley T & W 69 NZ3446
Low Mowthorpe N York 56 SE8966
Low Newton Cumb 59 SD4082
Low Row Cumb 67 NY5863
Low Row N York 61 SD9797
Low Salchrie D & G 64 NX0365
Low Santon Humb 56 SE9412
Low Skeog D & G 65 NX4540
Low Tharston Norfk 43 TM1895
Low Worsall N York 62 NZ3909
Low Wray Cumb 59 NY3701
Lowdham Notts 49 SK6646
Lower Aisholt Somset 8 ST2035
Lower Ansty Dorset 9 ST7603
Lower Apperley Gloucs 28 SO8527
Lower Arncott Oxon 29 SP6019
Lower Ashton Devon 5 SX8484
Lower Assendon Oxon 22 SU7484
Lower Bartle Lancs 53 SD4933
Lower Beeding W Susx 12 TQ2127
Lower Benefield Nhants 40 SP9988
Lower Bentley H & W 28 SO9865
Lower Boddington Nhants 29 SP4852
Lower Bourne Surrey 22 SU8444
Lower Brailes Warwks 29 SP3139
Lower Breakish Highld 85 NG6723
Lower Broadheath H & W 28 SO8157
Lower Bullingham H & W 27 SO5138
Lower Burgate Hants 10 SU1515
Lower Caldecote Beds 31 TL1746
Lower Cam Gloucs 20 SO7400
Lower Catesby Nhants 29 SP5159
Lower Chapel Powys 26 SO0235
Lower Chicksgrove Wilts 9 ST9729
Lower Chute Wilts 21 SU3153
Lower Clapton Gt Lon 23 TQ3485
Lower Clent H & W 38 SO9279
Lower Cumberworth W York 55 SE2209
Lower Dean Beds 30 TL0569
Lower Diabaig Highld 91 NG7960
Lower Dicker E Susx 13 TQ5511
Lower Down Shrops 36 SO3484
Lower Dunsforth N York 55 SE4464
Lower Egleton H & W 27 SO6245
Lower End Bucks 30 SP9238
Lower Eythorne Kent 15 TR2849
Lower Failand Avon 19 ST5173
Lower Farringdon Hants 11 SU7035
Lower Feltham Gt Lon 22 TQ0971
Lower Fittleworth W Susx 12 TQ0118
Lower Froyle Hants 22 SU7544
Lower Gabwell Devon 5 SX9169
Lower Gledfield Highld 96 NH5890
Lower Godney Somset 19 ST4742
Lower Gravenhurst Beds 30 TL1035
Lower Green Kent 13 TQ5640
Lower Green Kent 13 TQ6341
Lower Green Norfk 42 TF9837
Lower Halliford Surrey 22 TQ0866
Lower Halstow Kent 14 TQ8567
Lower Hamworthy Dorset 9 SY9990
Lower Hardres Kent 15 TR1553
Lower Hartwell Bucks 30 SP7912
Lower Hergest H & W 27 SO2755
Lower Heyford Oxon 29 SP4824
Lower Irlam Gt Man 47 SJ7193
Lower Killeyan Strath 70 NR2742
Lower Kinnerton Ches 46 SJ3462
Lower Langford Avon 19 ST4560
Lower Largo Fife 83 NO4102
Lower Leigh Staffs 38 SK0135
Lower Loxhore Devon 7 SS6137
Lower Lydbrook Gloucs 27 SO5916
Lower Lye H & W 27 SO4066
Lower Machen Gwent 19 ST2288
Lower Middleton Cheney Nhants 29 SP5041
Lower Moor W Mids 28 SO9747
Lower Morton Avon 19 ST6491
Lower Nazeing Essex 23 TL3906
Lower Penarth S Glam 19 ST1869
Lower Penn Staffs 38 SO8796
Lower Peover Ches 47 SJ7474
Lower Pond Street Essex 31 TL4537
Lower Quinton Warwks 29 SP1847
Lower Raydon Suffk 25 TM0338
Lower Roadwater Somset 7 ST0339
Lower Seagry Wilts 20 ST9580
Lower Shelton Beds 30 SP9942
Lower Shiplake Oxon 22 SU7679
Lower Shuckburgh Warwks 29 SP4862
Lower Slaughter Gloucs 28 SP1622
Lower Standen Kent 15 TR2340
Lower Stanton St. Quintin Wilts 20 ST9180
Lower Stoke Kent 14 TQ8375
Lower Stone Gloucs 20 ST6794
Lower Stow Bedon Norfk 42 TL9694
Lower Street Dorset 9 SY8399
Lower Street Norfk 43 TG2635
Lower Street Suffk 33 TM1052
Lower Sundon Beds 30 TL0526
Lower Swanwick Hants 11 SU4909
Lower Swell Gloucs 29 SP1725
Lower Tean Staffs 48 SK0138
Lower Town Devon 5 SX7172
Lower Town Dyfed 16 SM9637
Lower Tysoe Warwks 29 SP3445
Lower Upcott Devon 5 SX8880
Lower Upham Hants 11 SU5219
Lower Vexford Somset 8 ST1135
Lower Weare Somset 19 ST4053
Lower Westmancote H & W 28 SO9337
Lower Whatley Somset 20 ST7447
Lower Whitley Ches 47 SJ6179
Lower Wield Hants 21 SU6340
Lower Willingdon E Susx 13 TQ5803
Lower Winchendon Bucks 30 SP7312
Lower Woodford Wilts 10 SU1235
Lower Wraxhall Dorset 9 ST5700
Lowesby Leics 40 SK7207
Lowestoft Suffk 43 TM5493
Loweswater Cumb 58 NY1421
Lowfield Heath W Susx 12 TQ2739
Lowick Nhants 40 SP9881
Lowick Nthumb 77 NU0139
Lowick Green Cumb 58 SD2985
Lowsonford Warwks 29 SP1868
Lowther Cumb 59 NY5323
Lowtherton D & G 67 NY2466
Lowthorpe Humb 57 TA0860
Lowton Somset 8 ST1918
Loxbeare Devon 7 SS9116
Loxhill Surrey 12 TQ0038
Loxhore Devon 7 SS6138
Loxhore Cott Devon 7 SS6138
Loxley Warwks 29 SP2553
Loxton Avon 19 ST3755
Loxwood W Susx 12 TQ0331
Lubenham Nhants 40 SP7087
Lucas Green Surrey 22 SU9460
Luccombe Somset 7 SS9243
Luccombe Village IOW 11 SZ5879
Lucker Nthumb 77 NU1530
Luckett Cnwll 4 SX3873
Lucking Street Essex 24 TL8134
Luckington Wilts 20 ST8383
Lucklawhill Fife 83 NO4221
Luckwell Bridge Somset 7 SS9038
Lucton H & W 27 SO4364
Ludborough Lincs 51 TF2995
Ludbrook Devon 5 SX6654
Ludchurch Dyfed 16 SN1411
Luddenden W York 55 SE0426
Luddenden Foot W York 55 SE0325
Luddesdown Kent 14 TQ6666
Luddington Humb 56 SE8316
Luddington Warwks 28 SP1652
Luddington in the Brook Nhants 40 TL1083
Ludford Lincs 50 TF1989
Ludford Shrops 37 SO5174
Ludgershall Bucks 29 SP6517
Ludgershall Wilts 21 SU2650
Ludgvan Cnwll 2 SW5033
Ludham Norfk 43 TG3818
Ludlow Shrops 37 SO5175
Ludney Somset 8 ST3812
Ludwell Wilts 9 ST9122
Ludworth Dur 62 NZ3641
Luffincott Devon 6 SX3394
Luffness Loth 83 NT4780
Lugar Strath 74 NS5921
Luggate Burn Loth 76 NT5974
Luggiebank Strath 74 NS7672
Lugton Strath 73 NS4152
Lugwardine H & W 27 SO5540
Luib Highld 84 NG5627
Lulham H & W 27 SO4141
Lullington Derbys 39 SK2412
Lullington Somset 20 ST7851
Lulsgate Bottom Avon 19 ST5165
Lulsley H & W 28 SO7455
Lumb Lancs 54 SD8324
Lumb W York 55 SE0221
Lumby N York 55 SE4830
Lumloch Strath 74 NS6370
Lumphanan Gramp 89 NJ5804
Lumphinnans Fife 82 NT1792
Lumsden Gramp 94 NJ4722
Lunan Tays 89 NO6851
Lunanhead Tays 89 NO4752
Luncarty Tays 82 NO0929
Lund Humb 56 SE9647
Lund N York 56 SE6532
Lundford Magna Lincs 50 TF1989
Lundie Cent 81 NN7304
Lundie Tays 83 NO2836
Lundin Links Fife 83 NO4002
Lunna Shet 103 HU4869
Lunsford Kent 14 TQ6959
Lunsford's Cross E Susx 14 TQ7210
Lunt Mersyd 46 SD3402
Luppitt Devon 8 ST1606
Lupridge Devon 5 SX7153
Lupset W York 55 SE3119
Lupton Cumb 59 SD5581
Lurgashall W Susx 12 SU9326
Lurley Devon 7 SS9215
Luscombe Devon 5 SX7957
Luss Strath 80 NS3692
Lusta Highld 90 NG2656
Lustleigh Devon 5 SX7881
Luston H & W 27 SO4863
Luthermuir Gramp 89 NO6568
Luthrie Fife 83 NO3319
Luton Beds 30 TL0921
Luton Devon 8 ST0802
Luton Devon 5 SX9076
Luton Kent 14 TQ7766
Lutterworth Leics 39 SP5484
Lutton Devon 5 SX5959
Lutton Lincs 41 TF4325
Lutton Nhants 40 TL1187
Luxborough Somset 7 SS9738
Luxulyan Cnwll 3 SX0558
Lybster Highld 100 ND2435
Lydbury North Shrops 36 SO3486
Lydd Kent 15 TR0420
Lydden Kent 15 TR2645
Lydden Kent 15 TR3567
Lyddington Leics 40 SP8797
Lyde Green Hants 22 SU7057
Lydeard St. Lawrence Somset 8 ST1332
Lydford Devon 4 SX5185
Lydford on Fosse Somset 9 ST5630
Lydgate W York 54 SD9225
Lydham Shrops 36 SO3391
Lydiard Millicent Wilts 20 SU0986
Lydiard Tregoze Wilts 20 SU1085
Lydiate Mersyd 46 SD3604
Lydiate Ash H & W 38 SO9775
Lydlinch Dorset 9 ST7413
Lydney Gloucs 19 SO6303
Lydstep Dyfed 16 SS0898
Lye W Mids 38 SO9284
Lye Green E Susx 13 TQ5134
Lye Green Warwks 29 SP1965
Lye's Green Wilts 20 ST8146
Lyford Oxon 21 SU3994
Lymbridge Green Kent 15 TR1244
Lyme Border 75 NT2041
Lyme Regis Dorset 8 SY3492
Lyminge Kent 15 TR1641
Lymington Hants 10 SZ3295
Lyminster W Susx 12 TQ0204
Lymm Ches 47 SJ6887
Lympne Kent 15 TR1135
Lympsham Somset 19 ST3354
Lympstone Devon 5 SX9984
Lynch Green Norfk 43 TG1505
Lynchat Highld 87 NH7801
Lyndhurst Hants 10 SU3008
Lyndon Leics 40 SK9004
Lyne Surrey 22 TQ0166
Lyne Hill Staffs 38 SJ9212
Lyne of Skene Gramp 95 NJ7610
Lyneal Shrops 36 SJ4433
Lyneham Oxon 29 SP2720
Lyneham Wilts 20 SU0278
Lyness Ork 103 ND3094
Lyng Norfk 42 TG0617
Lyng Somset 8 ST3329
Lynmouth Devon 18 SS7249
Lynn of Shenval Gramp 94 NJ2129
Lynsted Kent 14 TQ9460
Lynton Devon 18 SS7249
Lyon's Gate Dorset 9 ST6505
Lyonshall H & W 27 SO3355
Lytchett Matravers Dorset 9 SY9495
Lytchett Minster Dorset 9 SY9693
Lyth Highld 100 ND2762
Lytham Lancs 53 SD3627
Lytham St. Anne's Lancs 53 SD3427
Lythe N York 63 NZ8413
Lythmore Highld 100 ND0566

M

Mabe Burnthouse Cnwll 2 SW7634
Mabie D & G 66 NX9570
Mablethorpe Lincs 51 TF5085
Macclesfield Ches 48 SJ9173
Macclesfield Forest Ches 48 SJ9772
Macduff Gramp 95 NJ7064
Macharioch Strath 72 NR7309
Machen M Glam 19 ST2189
Machire Strath 70 NR2164
Machrie Farm Strath 72 NR9033
Machrihanish Strath 72 NR6320
Machrins Strath 70 NR3693
Machynlleth Powys 35 SH7400
Machynys Dyfed 17 SS5198
Mackworth Derbys 49 SK3137
Macmerry Loth 76 NT4372
Maddaford Devon 6 SX5494
Madderty Tays 82 NN9522
Maddiston Cent 75 NS9476
Madeley Staffs 47 SJ7744
Madingley Cambs 31 TL3960
Madley H & W 27 SO4238
Madresfield H & W 28 SO8047
Madron Cnwll 2 SW4531
Maen-y-groes Dyfed 34 SN3858
Maenclochog Dyfed 16 SN0827
Maendy S Glam 18 ST0076
Maentwrog Gwynd 45 SH6640
Maer Staffs 37 SJ7938
Maerdy M Glam 18 SS9798
Maesbrook Shrops 36 SJ3021
Maesbury Marsh Shrops 36 SJ3125
Maesllyn Dyfed 17 SN3644
Maesteg M Glam 18 SS8590
Maesybont Dyfed 17 SN5616
Maesycwmmer M Glam 19 ST1594
Magdalen Laver Essex 23 TL5108
Maggieknockater Gramp 94 NJ3145
Maggots End Essex 31 TL4827
Magham Down E Susx 13 TQ6011
Maghull Mersyd 46 SD3703
Magor Gwent 19 ST4286
Maiden Bradley Wilts 20 ST8038
Maiden Head Avon 19 ST5666
Maiden Newton Dorset 9 SY5997
Maiden Wells Dyfed 16 SR9799
Maidencombe Devon 5 SX9268
Maidenhayne Devon 8 SY2795
Maidenhead Berks 22 SU8980
Maidens Strath 73 NS2107
Maidenwell Lincs 51 TF3179
Maidford Nhants 29 SP6052
Maids Moreton Bucks 30 SP7035
Maidstone Kent 14 TQ7555
Maidwell Nhants 30 SP7476
Mains of Bainakettle Gramp 89 NO6274
Mains of Balhall Tays 89 NO5163
Mains of Dalvey Highld 93 NJ1132
Mains of Haulkerton Gramp 89 NO7172
Mainsforth Dur 62 NZ3131
Mainsriddle D & G 66 NX9456
Mainstone Shrops 36 SO2787
Maisemore Gloucs 28 SO8121
Makeney Derbys 49 SK3544
Malborough Devon 5 SX7139
Malden Surrey 23 TQ2166
Maldon Essex 24 TL8506
Malham N York 54 SD9063
Mallaig Highld 85 NM6796
Mallaigvaig Highld 85 NM6897
Malleny Mills Loth 75 NT1665
Malltraeth Gwynd 44 SH4068
Mallwyd Gwynd 35 SH8612
Malmesbury Wilts 20 ST9387
Malmsmead Somset 18 SS7947
Malpas Ches 46 SJ4847
Malpas Cnwll 3 SW8442
Malpas Gwent 19 ST3090
Maltby Cleve 62 NZ4613
Maltby S York 49 SK5392
Maltby le Marsh Lincs 51 TF4681
Malting Green Essex 25 TL9720
Maltman's Hill Kent 14 TQ9043
Malton N York 56 SE7871
Malvern Link H & W 28 SO7947
Malvern Wells H & W 28 SO7742
Malzie D & G 64 NX3754
Mamble H & W 37 SO6871
Mamhilad Gwent 19 SO3003
Manaccan Cnwll 2 SW7624
Manafon Powys 36 SJ1102
Manaton Devon 5 SX7581
Manby Lincs 51 TF3986
Mancetter Warwks 39 SP3296
Manchester Gt Man 47 SJ8497
Mancot Clwyd 46 SJ3167
Mandally Highld 86 NH2900
Manea Cambs 41 TL4789
Maney W Mids 38 SP1195
Manfield N York 61 NZ2113
Mangotsfield Avon 20 ST6676
Mangrove Green Herts 30 TL1224
Manish W Isls 102 NG1089
Manley Ches 46 SJ5071
Manmoel Gwent 19 SO1803
Mannel Strath 78 NL9840
Manning's Heath W Susx 12 TQ2028
Manningford Bohune Wilts 20 SU1357
Manningford Bruce Wilts 20 SU1358
Manningham W York 55 SE1435
Mannington Dorset 10 SU0605
Manningtree Essex 25 TM1031
Mannofield Gramp 89 NJ9104
Manor Park Gt Lon 23 TQ4285
Manorbier Dyfed 16 SS0697
Manorbier Newton Dyfed 16 SN0400
Manorhill Border 76 NT6632
Manorowen Dyfed 16 SM9336
Mansell Gamage H & W 27 SO3944
Mansell Lacy H & W 27 SO4245
Mansfield Notts 49 SK5361
Mansfield Strath 66 NS6214
Mansfield Woodhouse Notts 49 SK5363
Manston Dorset 9 ST8115
Manston W York 55 SE3634
Manswood Dorset 9 ST9708
Manthorpe Lincs 40 TF0715
Manton Humb 50 SE9302
Manton Leics 40 SK8704
Manton Wilts 21 SU1768
Manuden Essex 31 TL4926
Maolachy Strath 79 NM8913
Maperton Somset 9 ST6726
Maplebeck Notts 49 SK7060
Mapledurham Oxon 22 SU6776
Mapledurwell Hants 22 SU6851
Maplehurst W Susx 12 TQ1824
Maplescombe Kent 14 TQ5664
Mapleton Derbys 48 SK1647
Mapperley Derbys 49 SK4342
Mapperley Park Notts 49 SK5842
Mapperton Dorset 8 SY5099
Mappleborough Green Warwks 28 SP0866
Mappleton Humb 57 TA2243
Mappowder Dorset 9 ST7306
Marazanvose Cnwll 2 SW7950
Marazion Cnwll 2 SW5130
Marbury Ches 47 SJ5645
March Cambs 41 TL4196
March Strath 66 NS9914
Marcham Oxon 21 SU4596
Marchamley Shrops 37 SJ5929
Marchington Staffs 38 SK1330
Marchwiel Clwyd 46 SJ3547
Marchwood Hants 10 SU3810
Marcross S Glam 18 SS9269
Marden H & W 27 SO5146
Marden Kent 14 TQ7444
Marden Wilts 20 SU0857
Marden Thorn Kent 14 TQ7642
Mardlebury Herts 31 TL2618
Mardy Gwent 27 SO3015
Mare Green Somset 8 ST3326
Mareham le Fen Lincs 51 TF2761
Mareham on the Hill Lincs 51 TF2867
Marehill W Susx 12 TQ0618
Maresfield E Susx 13 TQ4624
Marfleet Humb 57 TA1429
Marford Clwyd 46 SJ3556
Margam W Glam 18 SS7887
Margaret Marsh Dorset 9 ST8218
Margaretting Essex 24 TL6701
Margaretting Tye Essex 24 TL6800
Margate Kent 15 TR3571
Margnaheglish Strath 72 NS0332
Margrie D & G 65 NX5950
Margrove Park Cleve 62 NZ6515
Marham Norfk 42 TF7009
Marhamchurch Cnwll 6 SS2203
Marholm Cambs 40 TF1401
Mariansleigh Devon 7 SS7422
Marine Town Kent 14 TQ9274
Marionburgh Gramp 89 NJ7006
Marishader Highld 90 NG4963
Maristow Devon 4 SX4764
Marjoriebanks D & G 66 NY0883
Mark D & G 64 NX1157
Mark Somset 19 ST3847
Mark Cross E Susx 13 TQ5010
Mark Cross E Susx 13 TQ5831
Markbeech Kent 13 TQ4742
Markby Lincs 51 TF4878
Market Bosworth Leics 39 SK4002

Market Deeping Milton of Balgonie

Market Deeping *Lincs* 40 TF1310
Market Drayton *Shrops* 37 SJ6734
Market Harborough *Leics* 40 SP7387
Market Lavington *Wilts* 20 SU0154
Market Overton *Leics* 40 SK8816
Market Rasen *Lincs* 50 TF1089
Market Stainton *Lincs* 51 TF2279
Market Street *Norfk* 43 TG2921
Market Weighton *Humb* 56 SE8741
Market Weston *Suffk* 32 TL9877
Markfield *Leics* 39 SK4809
Markham *Gwent* 19 SO1601
Markham Moor *Notts* 49 SK7173
Markinch *Fife* 83 NO2901
Markington *N York* 55 SE2865
Marks Tey *Essex* 24 TL9023
Marksbury *Avon* 20 ST6662
Markshall *Essex* 24 TL8425
Markyate *Herts* 30 TL0616
Marlborough *Wilts* 21 SU1868
Marlcliff *Warwks* 28 SP0950
Marldon *Devon* 5 SX8663
Marlesford *Suffk* 33 TM3258
Marlingford *Norfk* 43 TG1309
Marloes *Dyfed* 16 SM7908
Marlow *Bucks* 22 SU8486
Marlpit Hill *Kent* 13 TQ4347
Marnhull *Dorset* 9 ST7818
Marple *Gt Man* 48 SJ9588
Marr *S York* 55 SE5105
Marrick *N York* 61 SE0798
Marsden *T & W* 69 NZ3964
Marsden *W York* 55 SE0411
Marsh Baldon *Oxon* 21 SU5699
Marsh Gibbon *Bucks* 29 SP6422
Marsh Green *Devon* 8 SY0493
Marsh Green *Kent* 13 TQ4344
Marsh Lane *Derbys* 49 SK4079
Marsh Street *Somset* 7 SS9944
Marshalswick *Herts* 23 TL1608
Marsham *Norfk* 43 TG1923
Marshborough *Kent* 15 TR3057
Marshbrook *Shrops* 36 SO4489
Marshchapel *Lincs* 51 TF3599
Marshfield *Avon* 20 ST7873
Marshfield *Gwent* 19 ST2582
Marshgate *Cnwll* 4 SX1592
Marshland St James *Norfk* 41 TF5209
Marshwood *Dorset* 8 SY3899
Marske *N York* 61 NZ1000
Marske-by-the-Sea *Cleve* 62 NZ6322
Marston *H & W* 27 SO3557
Marston *Lincs* 50 SK8943
Marston *Oxon* 29 SP5208
Marston *Staffs* 38 SJ9227
Marston *Wilts* 20 ST9656
Marston Green *W Mids* 38 SP1785
Marston Magna *Somset* 9 ST5922
Marston Meysey *Wilts* 20 SU1297
Marston Montgomery *Derbys* 48 SK1337
Marston Moretaine *Beds* 30 SP9941
Marston on Dove *Derbys* 39 SK2329
Marston St. Lawrence *Nhants* 29 SP5341
Marston Stannet *H & W* 27 SO5655
Marston Trussell *Nhants* 40 SP6985
Marstow *H & W* 27 SO5518
Marsworth *Bucks* 30 SP9114
Marten *Wilts* 21 SU2860
Marthall *Ches* 47 SJ7975
Martham *Norfk* 43 TG4518
Martin *Hants* 10 SU0619
Martin *Kent* 15 TR3447
Martin *Lincs* 50 TF1259
Martin *Lincs* 51 TF2466
Martin Hussingtree *H & W* 28 SO8860
Martinhoe *Devon* 18 SS6648
Martinstown *Dorset* 9 SY6489
Martlesham *Suffk* 33 TM2547
Martletwy *Dyfed* 16 SN0310
Martley *H & W* 28 SO7560
Martock *Somset* 8 ST4619
Marton *Ches* 47 SJ8560
Marton *Cleve* 62 NZ5115
Marton *Humb* 57 TA1739
Marton *Lincs* 50 SK8381
Marton *N York* 55 SE4162
Marton *N York* 63 SE7383
Marton *Shrops* 36 SJ2802
Marton *Warwks* 29 SP4068
Marton-le-Moor *N York* 55 SE3770
Martyr Worthy *Hants* 11 SU5132
Martyr's Green *Surrey* 22 TQ0857
Marwick *Ork* 103 HY2324
Marwood *Devon* 6 SS5437
Mary Tavy *Devon* 4 SX5079
Marybank *Highld* 92 NH4853
Maryburgh *Highld* 92 NH5456
Maryculter *Gramp* 89 NO8599
Maryhill *Gramp* 95 NJ8245
Maryhill *Strath* 74 NS5669
Marykirk *Gramp* 89 NO6865
Marylebone *Gt Man* 47 SD5807
Marypark *Gramp* 94 NJ1938
Maryport *Cumb* 58 NY0336
Maryport *D & G* 64 NX1434
Marystow *Devon* 4 SX4382
Maryton *Tays* 89 NO6856
Marywell *Gramp* 89 NO9399
Marywell *Tays* 89 NO5895
Marywell *Tays* 89 NO6544
Masham *N York* 61 SE2280
Masongill *N York* 60 SD6675
Mastin Moor *Derbys* 49 SK4575
Matching *Essex* 31 TL5212
Matching Green *Essex* 23 TL5311
Matching Tye *Essex* 23 TL5111
Matfen *Nthumb* 68 NZ0371
Matfield *Kent* 13 TQ6541
Mathern *Gwent* 19 ST5290
Mathon *H & W* 28 SO7346
Mathry *Dyfed* 16 SM8832
Matlaske *Norfk* 43 TG1534
Matlock *Derbys* 49 SK3059
Matlock Bank *Derbys* 49 SK3060
Matson *Gloucs* 28 SO8515
Mattersey *Notts* 49 SK6889
Mattingley *Hants* 22 SU7357
Mattishall *Norfk* 42 TG0511
Mattishall Burgh *Norfk* 42 TG0512
Mauchline *Strath* 74 NS4927
Maud *Gramp* 95 NJ9148
Maufant *Jersey* 101 JS1811
Maugersbury *Gloucs* 29 SP2025
Maughold *IOM* 52 SC4991
Mauld *Highld* 92 NH4038
Maulden *Beds* 30 TL0538
Maulds Meaburn *Cumb* 60 NY6216
Maunby *N York* 62 SE3586
Maund Bryan *H & W* 27 SO5650
Maundown *Somset* 7 ST0628
Mautby *Norfk* 43 TG4812
Mavesyn Ridware *Staffs* 38 SK0816
Mavis Enderby *Lincs* 51 TF3666
Mawbray *Cumb* 66 NY0846
Mawdesley *Lancs* 53 SD4914
Mawdlam *M Glam* 18 SS8081
Mawgan *Cnwll* 2 SW7025
Mawgan Porth *Cnwll* 3 SW8567
Mawla *Cnwll* 2 SW7045
Mawnan *Cnwll* 2 SW7827
Mawnan Smith *Cnwll* 2 SW7728
Maxey *Cambs* 40 TF1208
Maxstoke *Warwks* 39 SP2386
Maxted Street *Kent* 15 TR1244
Maxton *Border* 76 NT6130
Maxton *Kent* 15 TR3041
Maxwell Town *D & G* 66 NX9676
Maxwellheugh *Border* 76 NT7333
Maxworthy *Cnwll* 4 SX2593
May Bank *Staffs* 47 SJ8547
Maybole *Strath* 73 NS2909
Maybury *Surrey* 22 TQ0159
Mayfield *E Susx* 13 TQ5826
Mayfield *Loth* 75 NT3565
Mayfield *Staffs* 48 SK1545
Mayford *Surrey* 22 SU9956
Maynard's Green *E Susx* 13 TQ5818
Maypole Green *Norfk* 43 TM4195
Maypole Green *Suffk* 32 TL9159
Meadgate *Avon* 20 ST6758
Meadle *Bucks* 22 SP8005
Meadowfield *Dur* 61 NZ2439
Meadwell *Devon* 4 SX4081
Mealrigg *Cumb* 67 NY1345
Meamskirk *Strath* 74 NS5455
Meanwood *W York* 55 SE2837
Meare *Somset* 19 ST4541
Meare Green *Somset* 8 ST2922
Mears Ashby *Nhants* 30 SP8366
Measham *Leics* 39 SK3311
Meathop *Cumb* 59 SD4380
Meavy *Devon* 4 SX5467
Medbourne *Leics* 40 SP8093
Medmenham *Berks* 22 SU8084
Medomsley *Dur* 69 NZ1154
Medstead *Hants* 11 SU6537
Meer End *W Mids* 39 SP2474
Meerbrook *Staffs* 48 SJ9860
Meesden *Herts* 31 TL4332
Meeth *Devon* 6 SS5408
Meeting House Hill *Norfk* 43 TG3028
Meidrim *Dyfed* 17 SN2920
Meifod *Powys* 36 SJ1513
Meigle *Tays* 88 NO2844
Meikle Carco *D & G* 66 NS7813
Meikle Earnock *Strath* 74 NS7053
Meikle Kilmory *Strath* 72 NS0560
Meikle Obney *Tays* 82 NO0337
Meikle Wartle *Gramp* 95 NJ7230
Meikleour *Tays* 82 NO1539
Meinciau *Dyfed* 17 SN4610
Meir *Staffs* 48 SJ9342
Melbourn *Cambs* 31 TL3844
Melbourne *Derbys* 39 SK3825
Melbourne *Humb* 56 SE7543
Melbury Abbas *Dorset* 9 ST8820
Melbury Bubb *Dorset* 9 ST5906
Melbury Osmond *Dorset* 9 ST5707
Melchbourne *Beds* 30 TL0265
Melcombe Bingham *Dorset* 9 ST7602
Meldon *Devon* 5 SX5692
Meldon *Nthumb* 69 NZ1183
Meldreth *Cambs* 31 TL3746
Meldrum *Cent* 81 NS7299
Melfort *Strath* 79 NM8313
Melgund Castle *Tays* 89 NO5455
Meliden *Clwyd* 45 SJ0680
Melin-y-wig *Clwyd* 45 SJ0448
Melkinthorpe *Cumb* 59 NY5525
Melkridge *Nthumb* 68 NY7364
Melksham *Wilts* 20 ST9063
Melldalloch *Strath* 71 NR9374
Melling *Lancs* 54 SD5970
Melling *Mersyd* 46 SD3800
Mellis *Suffk* 33 TM0974
Mellon Charles *Highld* 91 NG8491
Mellon Udrigle *Highld* 91 NG8996
Mellor *Gt Man* 48 SJ9888
Mellor *Lancs* 54 SD6530
Mellor Brook *Lancs* 54 SD6431
Mells *Somset* 20 ST7248
Melmerby *Cumb* 59 NY6137
Melmerby *N York* 61 SE0785
Melmerby *N York* 62 SE3376
Melness *Highld* 99 NC5861
Melplash *Dorset* 8 SY4898
Melrose *Border* 76 NT5434
Melsetter *Ork* 103 ND2689
Melsonby *N York* 61 NZ1908
Meltham *W York* 55 SE1010
Melton *Humb* 56 SE9726
Melton *Suffk* 33 TM2850
Melton Constable *Norfk* 42 TG0432
Melton Mowbray *Leics* 40 SK7518
Melton Ross *Humb* 57 TA0610
Melvaig *Highld* 91 NG7486
Melverley *Shrops* 36 SJ3316
Melvich *Highld* 99 NC8764
Membury *Devon* 8 ST2803
Memsie *Gramp* 95 NJ9762
Menai Bridge *Gwynd* 44 SH5571
Mendham *Suffk* 33 TM2782
Mendlesham *Suffk* 33 TM1065
Mendlesham Green *Suffk* 33 TM0963
Menheniot *Cnwll* 4 SX2863
Mennock *D & G* 66 NS8107
Menston *W York* 55 SE1643
Menstrie *Cent* 82 NS8597
Mentmore *Bucks* 30 SP9019
Meoble *Highld* 85 NM7987
Meole Brace *Shrops* 37 SJ4810
Meonstoke *Hants* 11 SU6119
Meopham *Kent* 14 TQ6466
Mepal *Cambs* 41 TL4481
Meppershall *Beds* 30 TL1336
Mere *Ches* 47 SJ7281
Mere *Wilts* 9 ST8132
Mere Brow *Lancs* 53 SD4218
Mereclough *Lancs* 54 SD8730
Mereworth *Kent* 13 TQ6553
Meriden *W Mids* 39 SP2482
Merkadale *Highld* 84 NG3931
Merrion *Dyfed* 16 SR9397
Merriott *Somset* 8 ST4412
Merrow *Surrey* 12 TQ0250
Merry Hill *Herts* 22 TQ1394
Merryhill *W Mids* 38 SO8897
Merrymeet *Cnwll* 4 SX2766
Mersham *Kent* 15 TR0540
Merston *W Susx* 11 SU8902
Merstone *IOW* 11 SZ5285
Merther *Cnwll* 3 SW8644
Merthyr Cynog *Powys* 26 SN9837
Merthyr Mawr *M Glam* 18 SS8877
Merthyr Tydfil *M Glam* 26 SO0406
Merthyr Vale *M Glam* 18 ST0799
Merton *Devon* 6 SS5212
Merton *Gt Lon* 23 TQ2570
Merton *Norfk* 42 TL9098
Merton *Oxon* 29 SP5717
Meshaw *Devon* 7 SS7619
Messing *Essex* 24 TL8918
Messingham *Humb* 56 SE8904
Metfield *Suffk* 33 TM2980
Metherell *Cnwll* 4 SX4069
Metheringham *Lincs* 50 TF0661
Methil *Fife* 83 NT3799
Methley *W York* 55 SE3926
Methlick *Gramp* 95 NJ8537
Methven *Tays* 82 NO0225
Methwold *Norfk* 42 TL7394
Methwold Hythe *Norfk* 42 TL7194
Mettingham *Suffk* 33 TM3689
Metton *Norfk* 43 TG2037
Mevagissey *Cnwll* 3 SX0144
Mexborough *S York* 49 SE4700
Mey *Highld* 100 ND2872
Meyllteyrn *Gwynd* 44 SH2332
Meysey Hampton *Gloucs* 20 SP1100
Miavaig *W Isls* 102 NB0834
Michaelchurch *H & W* 27 SO5225
Michaelchurch Escley *H & W* 27 SO3134
Michaelston-le-Pit *S Glam* 19 ST1572
Michaelstone-y-Fedw *Gwent* 19 ST2484
Michaelstow *Cnwll* 3 SX0778
Micheldever *Hants* 11 SU5139
Micheldever Station *Hants* 21 SU5143
Michelmersh *Hants* 10 SU3426
Mickfield *Suffk* 33 TM1361
Mickle Trafford *Ches* 46 SJ4469
Micklebring *S York* 49 SK5194
Mickleby *N York* 63 NZ8012
Micklefield *W York* 55 SE4432
Mickleham *Surrey* 12 TQ1653
Mickleover *Derbys* 39 SK3033
Mickleton *Dur* 61 NY9623
Mickleton *Gloucs* 28 SP1643
Mickletown *W York* 55 SE4027
Mickley *N York* 61 SE2576
Mickley Green *Suffk* 32 TL8457
Mickley Square *Nthumb* 68 NZ0762
Mid Ardlaw *Gramp* 95 NJ9463
Mid Beltie *Gramp* 89 NJ6200
Mid Calder *Loth* 75 NT0767
Mid Clyth *Highld* 100 ND2937
Mid Lavant *W Susx* 11 SU8508
Mid Mains *Highld* 92 NH4239
Mid Sannox *Strath* 72 NS0145
Mid Yell *Shet* 103 HU5190
Midbea *Ork* 103 HY4444
Middle Aston *Oxon* 29 SP4726
Middle Barton *Oxon* 29 SP4325
Middle Chinnock *Somset* 8 ST4713
Middle Claydon *Bucks* 30 SP7225
Middle Duntisbourne *Gloucs* 28 SO9806
Middle Handley *Derbys* 49 SK4077
Middle Kames *Strath* 71 NR9189
Middle Mayfield *Staffs* 48 SK1444
Middle Rasen *Lincs* 50 TF0889
Middle Rocombe *Devon* 5 SX9069
Middle Stoke *Kent* 14 TQ8275
Middle Street *Essex* 23 TL4005
Middle Town *IOS* 2 SV8808
Middle Tysoe *Warwks* 29 SP3444
Middle Wallop *Hants* 10 SU2937
Middle Winterslow *Wilts* 10 SU2333
Middle Woodford *Wilts* 10 SU1136
Middlebie *D & G* 67 NY2176
Middlebridge *Tays* 87 NN8866
Middlegill *D & G* 66 NT0406
Middleham *N York* 61 SE1287
Middlehill *Wilts* 20 ST8168
Middlehope *Shrops* 37 SO4988
Middlemarsh *Dorset* 9 ST6707
Middlesbrough *Cleve* 62 NZ4919
Middleshaw *Cumb* 59 SD5588
Middlesmoor *N York* 61 SE0973
Middlestone *Dur* 61 NZ2531
Middlestown *W York* 55 SE2617
Middlethird *Border* 76 NT6843
Middleton *Cleve* 62 NZ5233
Middleton *Derbys* 48 SK1963
Middleton *Derbys* 49 SK2755
Middleton *Essex* 32 TL8639
Middleton *Gt Man* 47 SD8705
Middleton *H & W* 27 SO5469
Middleton *Hants* 21 SU4244
Middleton *Loth* 76 NT3758
Middleton *N York* 63 SE7885
Middleton *Nhants* 40 SP8489
Middleton *Norfk* 42 TF6616
Middleton *Nthumb* 68 NZ0584
Middleton *Shrops* 37 SO5477
Middleton *Strath* 78 NL9443
Middleton *Strath* 73 NS3952
Middleton *Suffk* 33 TM4267
Middleton *Tays* 82 NO1206
Middleton *W Glam* 17 SS4287
Middleton *W York* 55 SE1249
Middleton *W York* 55 SE3028
Middleton *Warwks* 38 SP1798
Middleton Cheney *Nhants* 29 SP4941
Middleton Moor *Suffk* 33 TM4167
Middleton One Row *Dur* 62 NZ3512
Middleton on the Hill *H & W* 27 SO5364
Middleton Quernhow *N York* 62 SE3378
Middleton Scriven *Shrops* 37 SO6887
Middleton St. George *Dur* 62 NZ3412
Middleton Stoney *Oxon* 29 SP5323
Middleton Tyas *N York* 61 NZ2205
Middleton-in-Teesdale *Dur* 61 NY9425
Middleton-on-Sea *W Susx* 12 SU9600
Middleton-on-the-Wolds *Humb* 56 SE9449
Middletown *Powys* 36 SJ3012
Middlewich *Ches* 47 SJ7066
Middlewood *Cnwll* 4 SX2775
Middlewood *H & W* 27 SO2844
Middlewood Green *Suffk* 33 TM0961
Middleyard *Strath* 74 NS5132
Middlezoy *Somset* 8 ST3733
Midford *Avon* 20 ST7660
Midgham *Berks* 21 SU5567
Midgley *W York* 55 SE0226
Midgley *W York* 55 SE2714
Midhopestones *S York* 48 SK2399
Midhurst *W Susx* 11 SU8821
Midlem *Border* 76 NT5227
Midpark *Strath* 72 NS0259
Midsomer Norton *Avon* 20 ST6654
Midtown *Highld* 99 NC5861
Midtown Brae *Highld* 91 NG8284
Migvie *Gramp* 88 NJ4306
Milborne Port *Somset* 9 ST6718
Milborne St. Andrew *Dorset* 9 SY8097
Milborne Wick *Somset* 9 ST6620
Milbourne *Nthumb* 69 NZ1175
Milbourne *Wilts* 20 ST9587
Milburn *Cumb* 60 NY6529
Milbury Heath *Avon* 20 ST6790
Milby *N York* 55 SE4067
Milcombe *Oxon* 29 SP4134
Milden *Suffk* 32 TL9546
Mildenhall *Suffk* 32 TL7174
Mildenhall *Wilts* 21 SU2069
Mile Oak *E Susx* 12 TQ2407
Mile Town *Kent* 14 TQ9274
Mileham *Norfk* 42 TF9119
Miles Hope *H & W* 27 SO5764
Miles Platting *Gt Man* 47 SJ8599
Milfield *Fife* 82 NT0688
Milfield *Nthumb* 77 NT9333
Milford *Derbys* 49 SK3545
Milford *Staffs* 38 SJ9720
Milford *Surrey* 12 SU9442
Milford Haven *Dyfed* 16 SM9005
Milford on Sea *Hants* 10 SZ2891
Milkwall *Gloucs* 27 SO5809
Mill Bank *W York* 55 SE0321
Mill Brow *Gt Man* 48 SJ9789
Mill End *Bucks* 22 SU7885
Mill End *Herts* 31 TL3332
Mill Green *Cambs* 32 TL6245
Mill Green *Essex* 24 TL6301
Mill Green *Lincs* 41 TF2223
Mill Green *Suffk* 32 TL9542
Mill Green *Suffk* 32 TL9957
Mill Green *Suffk* 33 TM1360
Mill Hill *Gt Lon* 23 TQ2292
Mill Meece *Staffs* 38 SJ8333
Mill of Drummond *Tays* 82 NN8315
Mill of Haldane *Strath* 80 NS3982
Mill of Uras *Gramp* 89 NO8680
Mill Street *Suffk* 32 TM0672
Millais *Jersey* 101 JS0615
Milland *W Susx* 11 SU8328
Millbreck *Gramp* 95 NK0044
Millbrex *Gramp* 95 NJ8144
Millbridge *Surrey* 11 SU8442
Millbrook *Beds* 30 TL0138
Millbrook *Cnwll* 4 SX4252
Millbrook *Hants* 10 SU3813
Millbrook *Jersey* 101 JS1210
Millbuie *Gramp* 95 NJ7909
Millburn *Strath* 73 NS4429
Millcorner *E Susx* 14 TQ8223
Millcraig *Highld* 93 NH6571
Milldale *Staffs* 48 SK1354
Miller's Dale *Derbys* 48 SK1473
Millerhill *Loth* 75 NT3269
Millerston *Strath* 74 NS6467
Millhalf *H & W* 27 SO2747
Millhouse *Strath* 71 NR9570
Millhouse Green *S York* 55 SE2203
Millhousebridge *D & G* 67 NY1085
Millhouses *S York* 49 SK3484
Millikenpark *Strath* 73 NS4162
Millington *Humb* 56 SE8351
Millisle *D & G* 65 NX4547
Millom *Cumb* 58 SD1780
Millport *Strath* 73 NS1654
Millthrop *Cumb* 60 SD6591
Milltimber *Gramp* 89 NJ8501
Milltown *D & G* 67 NY3375
Milltown *Devon* 6 SS5538
Milltown *Gramp* 94 NJ2609
Milltown *Gramp* 94 NJ4716
Milltown of Campfield *Gramp* 89 NJ6500
Milltown of Learney *Gramp* 89 NJ6303
Milnathort *Tays* 82 NO1204
Milngavie *Strath* 74 NS5574
Milnmark *D & G* 65 NX6582
Milnrow *Gt Man* 54 SD9212
Milnthorpe *Cumb* 59 SD4981
Milovaig *Highld* 90 NG1549
Milson *Shrops* 37 SO6472
Milsted *Kent* 14 TQ9058
Milston *Wilts* 20 SU1645
Milton *Avon* 19 ST3462
Milton *Cambs* 31 TL4762
Milton *Cent* 81 NN5001
Milton *Cumb* 67 NY5560
Milton *D & G* 64 NX2154
Milton *D & G* 66 NX8470
Milton *Derbys* 39 SK3126
Milton *Dyfed* 16 SN0403
Milton *Gramp* 94 NJ5163
Milton *Highld* 100 ND3451
Milton *Highld* 91 NG7043
Milton *Highld* 92 NH4930
Milton *Highld* 92 NH5749
Milton *Highld* 97 NH7674
Milton *Kent* 14 TQ6674
Milton *Notts* 49 SK7173
Milton *Oxon* 21 SU4892
Milton *Somset* 8 ST4621
Milton *Strath* 73 NS3569
Milton *Strath* 81 NS4274
Milton *Tays* 88 NO1357
Milton Abbas *Dorset* 9 ST8002
Milton Abbot *Devon* 4 SX4079
Milton Bridge *Loth* 75 NT2562
Milton Bryan *Beds* 30 SP9730
Milton Clevedon *Somset* 20 ST6637
Milton Combe *Devon* 4 SX4866
Milton Damerel *Devon* 6 SS3810
Milton Ernest *Beds* 30 TL0156
Milton Green *Ches* 46 SJ4658
Milton Hill *Oxon* 21 SU4790
Milton Keynes *Bucks* 30 SP8537
Milton Lilbourne *Wilts* 21 SU1960
Milton Malsor *Nhants* 30 SP7355
Milton Morenish *Tays* 81 NN6135
Milton of Auchinhove *Gramp* 89 NJ5503
Milton of Balgonie *Fife* 83 NO3200

Milton of Buchanan Netherhampton

Milton of Buchanan *Cent* 81 NS4490
Milton of Campsie *Strath* 74 NS6576
Milton of Leys *Highld* 93 NH6942
Milton of Tullich *Gramp* 88 NO3897
Milton on Stour *Dorset* 9 ST7928
Milton Regis *Kent* 14 TQ9064
Milton-under-Wychwood *Oxon* 29 SP2618
Milverton *Somset* 8 ST1225
Milverton *Warwks* 29 SP3166
Milwich *Staffs* 38 SJ9632
Minard *Strath* 71 NR9796
Minchinhampton *Gloucs* 20 SO8700
Minehead *Somset* 7 SS9646
Minera *Clwyd* 46 SJ2751
Minffordd *Gwynd* 44 SH5938
Mingarry Park *Highld* 79 NM6869
Miningsby *Lincs* 51 TF3264
Minions *Cnwll* 4 SX2671
Minishant *Strath* 73 NS3314
Minllyn *Gwynd* 35 SH8514
Minnigaff *D & G* 64 NX4166
Minnonie *Gramp* 95 NJ7760
Minskip *N York* 55 SE3864
Minstead *Hants* 10 SU2811
Minsted *W Susx* 11 SU8520
Minster *Kent* 14 TQ9573
Minster *Kent* 15 TR3064
Minster Lovell *Oxon* 29 SP3111
Minsterley *Shrops* 36 SJ3705
Minsterworth *Gloucs* 28 SO7817
Minterne Magna *Dorset* 9 ST6504
Minting *Lincs* 50 TF1873
Mintlaw *Gramp* 95 NJ9948
Minto *Border* 76 NT5620
Minton *Shrops* 36 SO4390
Mirehouse *Cumb* 58 NX9715
Mirfield *W York* 55 SE2019
Miserden *Gloucs* 28 SO9308
Miskin *M Glam* 18 ST0480
Misson *Notts* 49 SK6895
Misterton *Leics* 39 SP5583
Misterton *Notts* 50 SK7694
Misterton *Somset* 8 ST4508
Mistley *Essex* 25 TM1231
Mitcham *Gt Lon* 23 TQ2768
Mitchel Troy *Gwent* 27 SO4910
Mitcheldean *Gloucs* 28 SO6618
Mitchell *Cnwll* 3 SW8554
Mitchellslacks *D & G* 66 NX9696
Mitford *Nthumb* 69 NZ1786
Mithian *Cnwll* 2 SW7450
Mixbury *Oxon* 29 SP6033
Mobberley *Ches* 47 SJ7879
Mobberley *Staffs* 48 SK0041
Moccas *H & W* 27 SO3543
Mochdre *Powys* 36 SO0788
Mochrum *D & G* 64 NX3446
Mockbeggar *Kent* 14 TQ7146
Mockerkin *Cumb* 58 NY0923
Modbury *Devon* 5 SX6651
Moddershall *Staffs* 38 SJ9236
Moelfre *Clwyd* 36 SJ1828
Moelfre *Gwynd* 44 SH5186
Moffat *D & G* 66 NT0805
Mogerhanger *Beds* 30 TL1449
Mol-chlach *Highld* 84 NG4513
Molash *Kent* 15 TR0251
Mold *Clwyd* 46 SJ2363
Moldgreen *W York* 55 SE1516
Molehill Green *Essex* 24 TL5624
Molescroft *Humb* 56 TA0140
Molesworth *Cambs* 30 TL0775
Molland *Devon* 7 SS8028
Mollington *Ches* 46 SJ3870
Mollington *Oxon* 29 SP4447
Mollinsburn *Strath* 74 NS7171
Monachylemore *Cent* 81 NN4719
Mondynes *Gramp* 89 NO7779
Monewden *Suffk* 33 TM2358
Moneydie *Tays* 82 NO0629
Moniaive *D & G* 66 NX7890
Monifieth *Tays* 83 NO4932
Monikie *Tays* 83 NO4938
Monimail *Fife* 83 NO2914
Monk Fryston *N York* 55 SE5029
Monk Hesleden *Dur* 62 NZ4537
Monk Sherborne *Hants* 21 SU6056
Monk Soham *Suffk* 33 TM2165
Monk Street *Essex* 24 TL6128
Monk's Gate *W Susx* 12 TQ2027
Monken Hadley *Gt Lon* 23 TQ2497
Monkhide *H & W* 27 SO6144
Monkhill *Cumb* 67 NY3458
Monkhopton *Shrops* 37 SO6293
Monkland *H & W* 27 SO4557
Monkleigh *Devon* 6 SS4520
Monknash *S Glam* 18 SS9170
Monkokehampton *Devon* 6 SS5805
Monks Horton *Kent* 14 TQ8356
Monks Eleigh *Suffk* 32 TL9647
Monks Heath *Ches* 47 SJ8474
Monks Kirby *Warwks* 39 SP4683
Monkseaton *T & W* 69 NZ3472
Monksilver *Somset* 18 ST0737
Monksthorpe *Lincs* 51 TF4465
Monkswood *Gwent* 19 SO3402
Monkton *E Susx* 8 ST1803
Monkton *Kent* 15 TR2964
Monkton *Strath* 73 NS3527
Monkton *T & W* 69 NZ3363
Monkton Combe *Avon* 20 ST7762
Monkton Deverill *Wilts* 20 ST8537
Monkton Farleigh *Wilts* 20 ST8065
Monkton Heathfield *Somset* 8 ST2526
Monkton Wyld *Dorset* 8 SY3396
Monkwearmouth *T & W* 69 NZ3958
Monkwood *Hants* 11 SU6630
Monmore Green *W Mids* 38 SO9297
Monmouth *Gwent* 27 SO5012
Monnington on Wye *H & W* 27 SO3743
Monreith *D & G* 64 NX3541
Mont Saint *Guern* 101 GN4708
Montacute *Somset* 8 ST4916
Montford *Shrops* 36 SJ4114
Montford Bridge *Shrops* 36 SJ4215
Montgarrie *Gramp* 94 NJ5717
Montgarswood *Strath* 74 NS5227
Montgomery *Powys* 36 SO2296
Montgreenan *Strath* 73 NS3343
Montrose *Tays* 89 NO7157
Monxton *Hants* 21 SU3144
Monyash *Derbys* 48 SK1566
Monymusk *Gramp* 95 NJ6815
Monzie *Tays* 82 NN8725
Moodiesburn *Strath* 74 NS6970
Moonzie *Fife* 83 NO3317
Moor Allerton *W York* 55 SE3038
Moor Crichel *Dorset* 9 ST9908
Moor End *W York* 55 SE0528
Moor Green *Herts* 31 TL3226
Moor Head *W York* 55 SE1337
Moor Monkton *N York* 55 SE5156
Moorby *Lincs* 51 TF2964
Moordown *Dorset* 10 SZ0994
Moore *Ches* 47 SJ5784
Moorgreen *Notts* 49 SK4847
Moorhouse *Cumb* 67 NY3356
Moorhouse *Notts* 50 SK7566
Moorhouse Bank *Surrey* 13 TQ4353
Moorlinch *Somset* 19 ST3936
Moorsholm *Cleve* 62 NZ6814
Moorside *Dorset* 9 ST7919
Moorswater *Cnwll* 4 SX2364
Moorthorpe *W York* 55 SE4611
Moortown *Lincs* 50 TF0798
Moortown *W York* 55 SE2939
Morangie *Highld* 97 NH7683
Morar *Highld* 85 NM6793
Morborne *Cambs* 40 TL1391
Morchard Bishop *Devon* 7 SS7707
Morcombelake *Dorset* 8 SY4094
Morcott *Leics* 40 SK9200
Morda *Shrops* 36 SJ2827
Morden *Dorset* 9 SY9195
Morden *Gt Lon* 23 TQ2666
Mordiford *H & W* 27 SO5737
Mordon *Dur* 62 NZ3226
More *Shrops* 36 SO3491
Morebath *Devon* 7 SS9525
Morebattle *Border* 76 NT7724
Morecambe *Lancs* 53 SD4364
Moredon *Wilts* 20 SU1487
Morefield *Highld* 96 NH1195
Morehall *Kent* 15 TR2136
Moreleigh *Devon* 5 SX7652
Morenish *Tays* 81 NN6035
Moresby *Cumb* 58 NX9921
Morestead *Hants* 11 SU5025
Moreton *Dorset* 9 SY8089
Moreton *Essex* 23 TL5307
Moreton *H & W* 27 SO5064
Moreton *Mersyd* 46 SJ2689
Moreton *Oxon* 22 SP6904
Moreton Corbet *Shrops* 37 SJ5623
Moreton Jeffries *H & W* 27 SO6048
Moreton Morrell *Warwks* 29 SP3155
Moreton on Lugg *H & W* 27 SO5045
Moreton Pinkney *Nhants* 29 SP5749
Moreton Say *Shrops* 37 SJ6334
Moreton Valence *Gloucs* 28 SO7809
Moreton-in-Marsh *Gloucs* 29 SP2032
Moretonhampstead *Devon* 5 SX7586
Morfa Nefyn *Gwynd* 44 SH2840
Morham *Loth* 76 NT5571
Morland *Cumb* 59 NY6022
Morley *Ches* 47 SJ8282
Morley *Derbys* 49 SK3940
Morley *W York* 55 SE2627
Morley Green *Ches* 47 SJ8281
Morley St. Botolph *Norfk* 42 TM0799
Morningside *Loth* 75 NT2470
Morningside *Strath* 74 NS8355
Morningthorpe *Norfk* 33 TM2192
Morpeth *Nthumb* 69 NZ1986
Morphie *Gramp* 89 NO7164
Morrey *Staffs* 38 SK1218
Morriston *W Glam* 18 SS6697
Morston *Norfk* 42 TG0043
Mortehoe *Devon* 6 SS4545
Morthen *S York* 49 SK4788
Mortimer *Berks* 21 SU6564
Mortimer West End *Hants* 21 SU6363
Mortimer's Cross *H & W* 27 SO4263
Mortlake *Gt Lon* 23 TQ2075
Morton *Cumb* 67 NY3854
Morton *Derbys* 49 SK4060
Morton *Lincs* 50 SK8091
Morton *Lincs* 40 TF0923
Morton *Norfk* 43 TG1216
Morton *Notts* 49 SK7251
Morton *Shrops* 36 SJ2924
Morton Bagot *Warwks* 28 SP1164
Morton-on-Swale *N York* 62 SE3291
Morvah *Cnwll* 2 SW4035
Morval *Cnwll* 4 SX2556
Morvich *Highld* 85 NG9621
Morville *Shrops* 37 SO6794
Morwenstow *Cnwll* 6 SS2015
Mosborough *S York* 49 SK4281
Moscow *Strath* 73 NS4840
Moseley *H & W* 28 SO8159
Moseley *W Mids* 38 SO9498
Moseley *W Mids* 38 SP0783
Moss *S York* 56 SE5914
Moss *Strath* 78 NL9544
Moss Bank *Mersyd* 46 SJ5197
Moss-side *Highld* 93 NH8555
Mossat *Gramp* 94 NJ4719
Mossbank *Shet* 103 HU4575
Mossbay *Cumb* 58 NX9927
Mossblown *Strath* 73 NS3925
Mossburnford *Border* 76 NT6616
Mossdale *D & G* 65 NX6670
Mossdale *Strath* 73 NS4904
Mossend *Strath* 74 NS7460
Mossgiel *Strath* 73 NS4828
Mossknowe *D & G* 67 NY2769
Mossley *Gt Man* 48 SD9701
Mosspaul Hotel *Border* 67 NY3999
Mosstodloch *Gramp* 94 NJ3259
Mossy Lea *Lancs* 53 SD5312
Mossyard *D & G* 65 NX5451
Mosterton *Dorset* 8 ST4505
Moston *Gt Man* 47 SD8701
Mostyn *Clwyd* 46 SJ1580
Motcombe *Dorset* 9 ST8525
Mothecombe *Devon* 5 SX6047
Motherby *Cumb* 59 NY4228
Motherwell *Strath* 74 NS7457
Motspur Park *Gt Lon* 23 TQ2267
Mottingham *Gt Lon* 23 TQ4272
Mottisfont *Hants* 10 SU3226
Mottistone *IOW* 10 SZ4083
Mottram in Longdendale *Gt Man* 48 SJ9995
Mottram St Andrew *Ches* 47 SJ8778
Mouilpied *Guern* 101 GN5106
Mouldsworth *Ches* 46 SJ5071
Moulin *Tays* 87 NN9459
Moulsecoomb *E Susx* 12 TQ3307
Moulsford *Oxon* 21 SU5883
Moulsoe *Bucks* 30 SP9141
Moultavie *Highld* 92 NH6371
Moulton *Ches* 47 SJ6569
Moulton *Lincs* 41 TF3023
Moulton *N York* 61 NZ2303
Moulton *Nhants* 30 SP7866
Moulton *S Glam* 18 ST0770
Moulton *Suffk* 32 TL6964
Moulton Chapel *Lincs* 41 TF2918
Moulton Seas End *Lincs* 41 TF3227
Moulton St. Mary *Norfk* 43 TG3907
Mount *Cnwll* 3 SX1468
Mount Ambrose *Cnwll* 2 SW7043
Mount Bures *Essex* 24 TL9032
Mount Hawke *Cnwll* 2 SW7147
Mount Lothian *Loth* 75 NT2757
Mount Pleasant *Derbys* 49 SK3448
Mount Pleasant *Suffk* 32 TL7347
Mount Tabor *W York* 55 SE0527
Mountain *W York* 55 SE0930
Mountain Ash *M Glam* 18 ST0499
Mountain Cross *Border* 75 NT1547
Mountfield *E Susx* 14 TQ7320
Mountgerald House *Highld* 92 NH5661
Mountjoy *Cnwll* 3 SW8760
Mountnessing *Essex* 24 TQ6297
Mounton *Gwent* 19 ST5193
Mountsorrel *Leics* 39 SK5814
Mountstuart *Strath* 73 NS1159
Mousehill *Surrey* 12 SU9441
Mousehole *Cnwll* 2 SW4626
Mouswald *D & G* 66 NY0672
Mowhaugh *Border* 76 NT8120
Mowsley *Leics* 39 SP6489
Mowtie *Gramp* 89 NO8388
Moy *Highld* 93 NH7634
Moy *Highld* 86 NN4282
Moye *Highld* 85 NG8818
Moylgrove *Dyfed* 16 SN1144
Muasdale *Strath* 72 NR6840
Much Birch *H & W* 27 SO5030
Much Cowarne *H & W* 27 SO6147
Much Dewchurch *H & W* 27 SO4831
Much Hadham *Herts* 31 TL4219
Much Hoole *Lancs* 53 SD4723
Much Marcle *H & W* 27 SO6532
Much Wenlock *Shrops* 37 SO6299
Muchalls *Gramp* 89 NO9092
Muchelney *Somset* 8 ST4224
Muchelney Ham *Somset* 8 ST4423
Muchlarnick *Cnwll* 4 SX2156
Mucklestone *Staffs* 37 SJ7237
Muckton *Lincs* 51 TF3781
Mucomir *Highld* 86 NN1884
Muddiford *Devon* 6 SS5638
Muddles Green *E Susx* 13 TQ5413
Mudeford *Dorset* 10 SZ1892
Mudford *Somset* 9 ST5719
Mudford Sock *Somset* 9 ST5519
Mugdock *Cent* 74 NS5577
Mugeary *Highld* 84 NG4439
Mugginton *Derbys* 49 SK2842
Muggleswick *Dur* 68 NZ0449
Muir of Fowlis *Gramp* 94 NJ5612
Muir of Miltonduff *Gramp* 94 NJ1859
Muir of Ord *Highld* 92 NH5250
Muir of Thorn *Tays* 82 NO0637
Muirden *Gramp* 95 NJ7054
Muirdrum *Tays* 83 NO5637
Muiresk *Gramp* 95 NJ6948
Muirhead *Fife* 83 NO2805
Muirhead *Strath* 74 NS6869
Muirhead *Tays* 83 NO3434
Muirhouselaw *Border* 76 NT6328
Muirhouses *Cent* 82 NT0180
Muirkirk *Strath* 74 NS6927
Muirmill *Cent* 81 NS7283
Muirshearlich *Highld* 86 NN1380
Muirtack *Gramp* 95 NJ9937
Muirton *Tays* 82 NN9211
Muirton Mains *Highld* 92 NH4553
Muirton of Ardblair *Tays* 88 NO1643
Muker *N York* 60 SD9097
Mulbarton *Norfk* 43 TG1901
Mulben *Gramp* 94 NJ3550
Mulindry *Strath* 70 NR3659
Mullion *Cnwll* 2 SW6719
Mullion Cove *Cnwll* 2 SW6617
Mumby *Lincs* 51 TF5174
Muncher's Green *Herts* 31 TL3126
Munderfield Row *H & W* 27 SO6451
Munderfield Stocks *H & W* 27 SO6550
Mundesley *Norfk* 43 TG3136
Mundford *Norfk* 42 TL8093
Mundham *Norfk* 43 TM3397
Mundon Hill *Essex* 24 TL8602
Mungrisdale *Cumb* 59 NY3630
Munlochy *Highld* 92 NH6453
Munnoch *Strath* 73 NS2548
Munsley *H & W* 28 SO6640
Munslow *Shrops* 37 SO5287
Murchington *Devon* 5 SX6888
Murcott *Oxon* 29 SP5815
Murkle *Highld* 100 ND1668
Murlaggan *Highld* 85 NN0192
Murroes *Tays* 83 NO4635
Murrow *Cambs* 41 TF3707
Mursley *Bucks* 30 SP8128
Murthill *Tays* 89 NO4657
Murthly *Tays* 82 NO1038
Murton *Cumb* 60 NY7221
Murton *Dur* 69 NZ3847
Murton *N York* 56 SE6452
Murton *Nthumb* 77 NT9748
Musbury *Devon* 8 SY2794
Musselburgh *Loth* 75 NT3472
Muston *Leics* 40 SK8237
Muston *N York* 63 TA0979
Mustow Green *H & W* 38 SO8774
Muswell Hill *Gt Lon* 23 TQ2889
Mutehill *D & G* 65 NX6848
Mutford *Suffk* 33 TM4888
Muthill *Tays* 82 NN8717
Mybster *Highld* 100 ND1652
Myddfai *Dyfed* 26 SN7730
Myddle *Shrops* 36 SJ4623
Mydroilyn *Dyfed* 34 SN4555
Mylor *Cnwll* 2 SW8135
Mylor Bridge *Cnwll* 2 SW8036
Mynachlog ddu *Dyfed* 16 SN1430
Myndtown *Shrops* 36 SO3989
Mynydd-bach *Gwent* 19 ST4894
Mynydd-bach *W Glam* 18 SS6597
Myrebird *Gramp* 89 NO7398
Myredykes *Border* 67 NY5998
Mytchett *Surrey* 22 SU8855
Mytholm *W York* 54 SD9827
Mytholmroyd *W York* 54 SE0126
Myton-on-Swale *N York* 55 SE4366

N

Naast *Highld* 91 NG8283
Naburn *N York* 56 SE5945
Nackington *Kent* 15 TR1554
Nacton *Suffk* 33 TM2240
Nafferton *Humb* 57 TA0559
Nag's Head *Gloucs* 20 ST8898
Nailsbourne *Somset* 8 ST2128
Nailsea *Avon* 19 ST4770
Nailstone *Leics* 39 SK4106
Nailsworth *Gloucs* 20 ST8499
Nairn *Highld* 93 NH8856
Nannerch *Clwyd* 46 SJ1669
Nanpantan *Leics* 39 SK5017
Nanpean *Cnwll* 3 SW9556
Nanstallon *Cnwll* 3 SX0367
Nant Peris *Gwynd* 44 SH6058
Nant-y-moel *M Glam* 18 SS9392
Nanternis *Dyfed* 34 SN3756
Nantgaredig *Dyfed* 17 SN4921
Nantglyn *Clwyd* 45 SJ0061
Nantmel *Powys* 26 SO0366
Nantmor *Gwynd* 44 SH6046
Nantwich *Ches* 47 SJ6552
Naphill *Bucks* 22 SU8496
Napleton *H & W* 28 SO8648
Napton on the Hill *Warwks* 29 SP4661
Narberth *Dyfed* 16 SN1015
Narborough *Leics* 39 SP5497
Narborough *Norfk* 42 TF7412
Nasareth *Gwynd* 44 SH4749
Naseby *Nhants* 30 SP6978
Nash *Bucks* 30 SP7833
Nash *Gwent* 19 ST3483
Nash *Shrops* 37 SO6071
Nash's Green *Hants* 22 SU6745
Nassington *Nhants* 40 TL0696
Nasty *Herts* 31 TL3524
Nateby *Cumb* 60 NY7706
Nateby *Lancs* 53 SD4644
Natland *Cumb* 59 SD5289
Naughton *Suffk* 32 TM0249
Naunton *Gloucs* 28 SP1123
Naunton *H & W* 28 SO8645
Naunton *H & W* 28 SO8739
Naunton Beauchamp *H & W* 28 SO9652
Navenby *Lincs* 50 SK9858
Navestock *Essex* 23 TQ5397
Navestock Side *Essex* 24 TQ5697
Navidale House Hotel *Highld* 97 ND0316
Navity *Highld* 93 NH7864
Nawton *N York* 62 SE6584
Nayland *Suffk* 25 TL9734
Nazeing *Essex* 23 TL4106
Neap *Shet* 103 HU5058
Near Cotton *Staffs* 48 SK0646
Near Sawry *Cumb* 59 SD3795
Neasden *Gt Lon* 23 TQ2185
Neasham *Dur* 62 NZ3210
Neath *W Glam* 18 SS7597
Neatham *Hants* 11 SU7440
Neatishead *Norfk* 43 TG3420
Nebo *Dyfed* 34 SN5465
Nebo *Gwynd* 44 SH4850
Nebo *Gwynd* 45 SH8355
Necton *Norfk* 42 TF8709
Nedd *Highld* 98 NC1331
Nedging *Suffk* 32 TL9948
Nedging Tye *Suffk* 32 TM0149
Needham *Norfk* 33 TM2281
Needham Market *Suffk* 32 TM0855
Needingworth *Cambs* 31 TL3472
Neen Savage *Shrops* 37 SO6777
Neen Sollars *Shrops* 37 SO6672
Neenton *Shrops* 37 SO6387
Nefyn *Gwynd* 44 SH3040
Neilston *Strath* 73 NS4857
Nelson *Lancs* 54 SD8638
Nelson *M Glam* 18 ST1195
Nemphlar *Strath* 74 NS8544
Nempnett Thrubwell *Avon* 19 ST5260
Nenthead *Cumb* 68 NY7743
Nenthorn *Border* 76 NT6837
Nercwys *Clwyd* 46 SJ2360
Nereabolls *Strath* 70 NR2255
Nerston *Strath* 74 NS6456
Nesbit *Nthumb* 77 NT9833
Nesfield *N York* 55 SE0949
Nesscliffe *Shrops* 36 SJ3819
Neston *Ches* 46 SJ2977
Neston *Wilts* 20 ST8668
Netchwood *Shrops* 37 SO6291
Nether Alderley *Ches* 47 SJ8476
Nether Blainslie *Border* 76 NT5443
Nether Broughton *Notts* 40 SK6925
Nether Burrow *Lancs* 59 SD6174
Nether Cerne *Dorset* 9 SY6798
Nether Compton *Dorset* 9 ST5917
Nether Crimond *Gramp* 95 NJ8222
Nether Dallachy *Gramp* 94 NJ3563
Nether Exe *Devon* 7 SS9300
Nether Fingland *Strath* 66 NS9310
Nether Handwick *Tays* 88 NO3641
Nether Haugh *S York* 49 SK4196
Nether Headon *Notts* 50 SK7477
Nether Heage *Derbys* 49 SK3650
Nether Heyford *Nhants* 30 SP6658
Nether Howcleugh *Strath* 66 NT0312
Nether Kellet *Lancs* 53 SD5068
Nether Kinmundy *Gramp* 95 NK0543
Nether Moor *Derbys* 49 SK3866
Nether Padley *Derbys* 48 SK2478
Nether Poppleton *N York* 56 SE5654
Nether Silton *N York* 62 SE4592
Nether Stowey *Somset* 19 ST1939
Nether Wallop *Hants* 10 SU3036
Nether Wasdale *Cumb* 58 NY1204
Nether Wellwood *Strath* 74 NS6526
Nether Westcote *Oxon* 29 SP2220
Nether Whitacre *Warwks* 39 SP2392
Nether Whitecleuch *Strath* 74 NS8319
Netheravon *Wilts* 20 SU1448
Netherbrae *Gramp* 95 NJ7959
Netherburn *Strath* 74 NS7947
Netherbury *Dorset* 8 SY4799
Netherby *N York* 55 SE3346
Nethercleuch *D & G* 67 NY1186
Netherend *Gloucs* 19 SO5900
Netherfield *E Susx* 14 TQ7019
Netherfield Road *E Susx* 14 TQ7417
Netherhampton *Wilts* 10 SU1029

Netherhay North Shore

Netherhay *Dorset* 8 ST4105
Netherlaw *D & G* 65 NX7444
Netherley *Gramp* 89 NO8593
Nethermill *D & G* 66 NY0487
Nethermuir *Gramp* 95 NJ9044
Netherplace *Strath* 74 NS5255
Netherseal *Derbys* 39 SK2812
Netherthong *W York* 55 SE1309
Netherton *Cent* 81 NS5579
Netherton *Devon* 5 SX8971
Netherton *Nthumb* 68 NT9807
Netherton *Shrops* 37 SO7382
Netherton *Strath* 74 NS7854
Netherton *Tays* 88 NO1452
Netherton *Tays* 89 NO5457
Netherton *W Mids* 38 SO9488
Netherton *W York* 55 SE2816
Nethertown *Cumb* 58 NX9907
Nethertown *Highld* 100 ND3578
Nethertown *Staffs* 38 SK1017
Netherwitton *Nthumb* 68 NZ0990
Nethy Bridge *Highld* 93 NJ0020
Netley *Hants* 10 SU4508
Netley Marsh *Hants* 10 SU3313
Nettlebed *Oxon* 22 SU6986
Nettlebridge *Somset* 19 ST6448
Nettlecombe *Dorset* 8 SY5195
Nettleden *Herts* 22 TL0110
Nettleham *Lincs* 50 TF0075
Nettlestead *Kent* 14 TQ6852
Nettlestead Green *Kent* 14 TQ6850
Nettlestone *IOW* 11 SZ6290
Nettlesworth *Dur* 69 NZ2547
Nettleton *Lincs* 50 TA1100
Nettleton *Wilts* 20 ST8278
Netton *Wilts* 10 SU1336
Nevern *Dyfed* 16 SN0840
Nevill Holt *Leics* 40 SP8193
New Abbey *D & G* 66 NX9666
New Aberdour *Gramp* 95 NJ8863
New Addington *Gt Lon* 23 TQ3763
New Alresford *Hants* 11 SU5832
New Alyth *Tays* 88 NO2447
New Ash Green *Kent* 14 TQ6065
New Balderton *Notts* 50 SK8152
New Barn *Kent* 14 TQ6169
New Barnet *Gt Lon* 23 TQ2695
New Bewick *Nthumb* 77 NU0620
New Bilton *Warwks* 39 SP4875
New Bolingbroke *Lincs* 51 TF3057
New Boultham *Lincs* 50 SK9670
New Bradwell *Bucks* 30 SP8341
New Brampton *Derbys* 49 SK3771
New Brancepeth *Dur* 61 NZ2241
New Brighton *Mersyd* 46 SJ3093
New Buckenham *Norfk* 32 TM0890
New Byth *Gramp* 95 NJ8254
New Clipstone *Notts* 49 SK5963
New Costessey *Norfk* 43 TG1810
New Crofton *W York* 55 SE3817
New Cross *Gt Lon* 23 TQ3676
New Cross *Somset* 8 ST4119
New Cumnock *Strath* 66 NS6213
New Deer *Gramp* 95 NJ8847
New Denham *Bucks* 22 TQ0484
New Duston *Nhants* 30 SP7162
New Earswick *N York* 56 SE6155
New Edlington *S York* 49 SK5398
New Elgin *Gramp* 94 NJ2261
New Ellerby *Humb* 57 TA1639
New Eltham *Gt Lon* 23 TQ4472
New End *H & W* 28 SP0560
New Fletton *Cambs* 40 TL1997
New Galloway *D & G* 65 NX6377
New Gilston *Fife* 83 NO4208
New Grimsby *IOS* 2 SV8815
New Holkham *Norfk* 42 TF8839
New Holland *Humb* 57 TA0823
New Houghton *Derbys* 49 SK4965
New Houghton *Norfk* 42 TF7927
New Hutton *Cumb* 59 SD5691
New Inn *Dyfed* 17 SN4736
New Inn *Gwent* 19 ST3099
New Invention *Shrops* 36 SO2976
New Kelso *Highld* 91 NG9442
New Lanark *Strath* 74 NS8842
New Langholm *D & G* 67 NY3684
New Leake *Lincs* 51 TF4057
New Leeds *Gramp* 95 NJ9954
New Luce *D & G* 64 NX1764
New Malden *Gt Lon* 23 TQ2168
New Marston *Oxon* 29 SP5407
New Mill *Cnwll* 2 SW4534
New Mill *Gramp* 89 NO7883
New Mill *W York* 55 SE1609
New Mills *Cnwll* 3 SW8952
New Mills *Derbys* 48 SK0085
New Mills *Powys* 36 SJ0901
New Milton *Hants* 10 SZ2495
New Mistley *Essex* 25 TM1131
New Moat *Dyfed* 16 SN0625
New Ollerton *Notts* 49 SK6667
New Pitsligo *Gramp* 95 NJ8855
New Prestwick *Strath* 73 NS3424
New Quay *Dyfed* 34 SN3959
New Rackheath *Norfk* 43 TG2812
New Radnor *Powys* 27 SO2161
New Ridley *Nthumb* 68 NZ0559
New Romney *Kent* 15 TR0624
New Rossington *Notts* 49 SK6198
New Scone *Tays* 82 NO1326
New Sharlston *W York* 55 SE3819
New Silksworth *T & W* 69 NZ3853
New Somerby *Lincs* 40 SK9235
New Stevenston *Strath* 74 NS7659
New Town *Beds* 31 TL1945
New Town *Dorset* 9 ST8318
New Town *Dorset* 9 ST9515
New Town *Dorset* 9 ST9918
New Town *E Susx* 13 TQ4720
New Town *Loth* 76 NT4470
New Town *Somset* 8 ST2712
New Tredegar *M Glam* 18 SO1403
New Trows *Strath* 74 NS8038
New Walsoken *Cambs* 41 TF4609
New Waltham *Humb* 57 TA2804
New Wimpole *Cambs* 31 TL3549
New Winton *Loth* 76 NT4271
New York *Lincs* 51 TF2455
New Zealand *Derbys* 39 SK3336
Newall *W York* 55 SE1946
Newark *D & G* 66 NS7808
Newark-on-Trent *Notts* 50 SK7953
Newarthill *Strath* 74 NS7859
Newbattle *Loth* 75 NT3365
Newbie *D & G* 67 NY1764
Newbiggin *Cumb* 59 NY4729
Newbiggin *Cumb* 67 NY5549
Newbiggin *Cumb* 60 NY6228
Newbiggin *Dur* 60 NY9127
Newbiggin *N York* 61 SE0086
Newbiggin-by-the-Sea *Nthumb* 69 NZ3087
Newbiggin-on-Lune *Cumb* 60 NY7005
Newbigging *Strath* 75 NT0145
Newbigging *Tays* 88 NO2841
Newbigging *Tays* 83 NO4237
Newbold *Derbys* 49 SK3672
Newbold on Stour *Warwks* 29 SP2446
Newbold Pacey *Warwks* 29 SP2957
Newbold Verdon *Leics* 39 SK4403
Newborough *Cambs* 41 TF2005
Newborough *Gwynd* 44 SH4265
Newborough *Staffs* 38 SK1325
Newbourne *Suffk* 33 TM2743
Newbridge *Cnwll* 2 SW4231
Newbridge *D & G* 66 NX9479
Newbridge *Gwent* 19 ST2097
Newbridge *Hants* 10 SU2915
Newbridge *IOW* 10 SZ4187
Newbridge *Loth* 75 NT1272
Newbridge Green *H & W* 28 SO8439
Newbridge on Wye *Powys* 26 SO0158
Newbrough *Nthumb* 68 NY8767
Newbuildings *Devon* 7 SS7903
Newburgh *Fife* 83 NO2318
Newburgh *Gramp* 95 NJ9659
Newburgh *Gramp* 95 NJ9925
Newburgh *Lancs* 53 SD4810
Newburgh Priory *N York* 62 SE5476
Newburn *T & W* 69 NZ1665
Newbury *Berks* 21 SU4766
Newbury *Somset* 20 ST6949
Newby *Cumb* 59 NY5921
Newby *Lancs* 54 SD8146
Newby *N York* 62 NZ5012
Newby *N York* 54 SD7269
Newby Bridge *Cumb* 59 SD3686
Newby East *Cumb* 67 NY4758
Newby West *Cumb* 67 NY3753
Newby Wiske *N York* 62 SE3687
Newcastle *Gwent* 27 SO4417
Newcastle *Shrops* 36 SO2582
Newcastle Emlyn *Dyfed* 17 SN3040
Newcastle upon Tyne *T & W* 69 NZ2464
Newcastle-under-Lyme *Staffs* 47 SJ8445
Newcastleton *D & G* 67 NY4887
Newchapel *Dyfed* 17 SN2239
Newchapel *Surrey* 12 TQ3641
Newchurch *Gwent* 19 ST4597
Newchurch *IOW* 11 SZ5685
Newchurch *Kent* 15 TR0531
Newchurch *Powys* 27 SO2150
Newchurch *Staffs* 38 SK1423
Newcraighall *Loth* 75 NT3272
Newdigate *Surrey* 12 TQ1942
Newell Green *Berks* 22 SU8770
Newenden *Kent* 14 TQ8327
Newent *Gloucs* 28 SO7225
Newfield *Dur* 61 NZ2033
Newfield *Highld* 97 NH7877
Newgale *Dyfed* 16 SM8522
Newgate Street *Herts* 23 TL3005
Newhall *Ches* 47 SJ6145
Newhaven *E Susx* 13 TQ4401
Newholm *N York* 63 NZ8610
Newhouse *Strath* 74 NS7961
Newick *E Susx* 13 TQ4121
Newington *Kent* 14 TQ8564
Newington *Kent* 15 TR1837
Newington *Oxon* 21 SU6096
Newland *Gloucs* 27 SO5509
Newland *H & W* 28 SO7948
Newland *Humb* 57 TA0631
Newland *N York* 56 SE6824
Newland *Somset* 7 SS8238
Newlandrig *Loth* 76 NT3762
Newlands *Border* 67 NY5094
Newlands *Nthumb* 68 NZ0855
Newlands of Dundurcas *Gramp* 94 NJ2951
Newlyn *Cnwll* 2 SW4628
Newmachar *Gramp* 95 NJ8919
Newmains *Strath* 74 NS8256
Newman's Green *Suffk* 32 TL8843
Newmarket *Cumb* 59 NY3438
Newmarket *Suffk* 32 TL6463
Newmill *Border* 67 NT4510
Newmill *Gramp* 94 NJ4352
Newmill of Inshewan *Tays* 88 NO4260
Newmillerdam *W York* 55 SE3215
Newmills *Fife* 82 NT0186
Newmills *Gwent* 27 SO5107
Newmills *Loth* 75 NT1667
Newmiln *Tays* 82 NO1230
Newmilns *Strath* 74 NS5337
Newney Green *Essex* 24 TL6507
Newnham *Gloucs* 28 SO6911
Newnham *H & W* 27 SO6469
Newnham *Hants* 22 SU7053
Newnham *Herts* 31 TL2437
Newnham *Kent* 14 TQ9557
Newnham *Nhants* 29 SP5859
Newport *Devon* 6 SS5632
Newport *Dyfed* 16 SN0539
Newport *Essex* 31 TL5234
Newport *Gloucs* 20 ST7097
Newport *Gwent* 19 ST3188
Newport *Highld* 100 ND1324
Newport *Humb* 56 SE8530
Newport *IOW* 11 SZ5089
Newport *Shrops* 37 SJ7419
Newport Pagnell *Bucks* 30 SP8743
Newport-on-Tay *Fife* 83 NO4228
Newquay *Cnwll* 2 SW8161
Newseat *Gramp* 95 NJ7032
Newsham *Lancs* 53 SD5136
Newsham *N York* 61 NZ1010
Newsham *N York* 62 SE3784
Newsham *Nthumb* 69 NZ3080
Newsholme *Humb* 56 SE7129
Newstead *Border* 76 NT5634
Newstead *Notts* 49 SK5152
Newstead *Nthumb* 77 NU1527
Newtack *Gramp* 94 NJ4446
Newthorpe *N York* 55 SE4632
Newton *Beds* 31 TL2344
Newton *Border* 76 NT6020
Newton *Cambs* 41 TF4314
Newton *Cambs* 31 TL4349
Newton *Ches* 46 SJ4167
Newton *Ches* 46 SJ5059
Newton *Cumb* 53 SD2271
Newton *D & G* 67 NY1195
Newton *Derbys* 49 SK4459
Newton *Gramp* 94 NJ1663
Newton *Gramp* 94 NJ3362
Newton *H & W* 27 SO3432
Newton *H & W* 27 SO5153
Newton *Highld* 92 NH5850
Newton *Highld* 93 NH7448
Newton *Highld* 93 NH7866
Newton *Lancs* 53 SD4430
Newton *Lancs* 59 SD5974
Newton *Lancs* 54 SD6950
Newton *Lincs* 40 TF0436
Newton *Loth* 75 NT0977
Newton *M Glam* 18 SS8377
Newton *Nhants* 40 SP8883
Newton *Norfk* 42 TF8315
Newton *Notts* 49 SK6841
Newton *Nthumb* 68 NZ0364
Newton *Somset* 18 ST1038
Newton *Staffs* 38 SK0325
Newton *Strath* 80 NS0498
Newton *Strath* 74 NS6760
Newton *Strath* 75 NS9331
Newton *Suffk* 32 TL9240
Newton *Warwks* 39 SP5378
Newton Abbot *Devon* 5 SX8571
Newton Arlosh *Cumb* 67 NY2055
Newton Aycliffe *Dur* 61 NZ2724
Newton Bewley *Cleve* 62 NZ4626
Newton Blossomville *Bucks* 30 SP9251
Newton Bromswold *Beds* 30 SP9966
Newton Burgoland *Leics* 39 SK3708
Newton by Toft *Lincs* 50 TF0487
Newton Ferrers *Cnwll* 4 SX3466
Newton Ferrers *Devon* 5 SX5548
Newton Ferry *W Isls* 102 NF8978
Newton Flotman *Norfk* 43 TM2198
Newton Harcourt *Leics* 39 SP6497
Newton Heath *Gt Man* 47 SD8700
Newton Kyme *N York* 55 SE4644
Newton Longville *Bucks* 30 SP8431
Newton Mearns *Strath* 74 NS5355
Newton Morrell *N York* 61 NZ2309
Newton Mountain *Dyfed* 16 SM9808
Newton of Balcanquhal *Tays* 82 NO1610
Newton on Ouse *N York* 55 SE5159
Newton on Trent *Lincs* 50 SK8373
Newton Poppleford *Devon* 8 SY0889
Newton Purcell *Oxon* 29 SP6230
Newton Regis *Warwks* 39 SK2707
Newton Reigny *Cumb* 59 NY4731
Newton Row *Highld* 100 ND3449
Newton Solney *Derbys* 39 SK2825
Newton St. Cyres *Devon* 7 SX8898
Newton St. Faith *Norfk* 43 TG2217
Newton St. Loe *Avon* 20 ST7064
Newton St. Petrock *Devon* 6 SS4112
Newton Stacey *Hants* 21 SU4140
Newton Stewart *D & G* 64 NX4065
Newton Toney *Wilts* 21 SU2140
Newton Tracey *Devon* 6 SS5226
Newton under Roseberry *Cleve* 62 NZ5713
Newton upon Derwent *Humb* 56 SE7149
Newton Valence *Hants* 11 SU7232
Newton-le-Willows *Mersyd* 47 SJ5995
Newton-le-Willows *N York* 61 SE2189
Newton-on-the-Moor *Nthumb* 69 NU1705
Newtongarry Croft *Gramp* 94 NJ5735
Newtongrange *Loth* 75 NT3364
Newtonhill *Gramp* 89 NO9193
Newtonloan *Loth* 75 NT3362
Newtonmill *Tays* 89 NO6064
Newtonmore *Highld* 87 NN7098
Newtown *Ches* 47 SJ6247
Newtown *Ches* 48 SJ9060
Newtown *Cumb* 67 NY1048
Newtown *Cumb* 67 NY5062
Newtown *D & G* 66 NS7710
Newtown *Devon* 7 SS7625
Newtown *Dorset* 10 SZ0393
Newtown *Gloucs* 20 SO6702
Newtown *Gt Man* 47 SD5604
Newtown *H & W* 27 SO5333
Newtown *H & W* 27 SO6145
Newtown *H & W* 28 SO7037
Newtown *H & W* 28 SO8755
Newtown *Hants* 11 SU6013
Newtown *Highld* 86 NH3504
Newtown *IOW* 10 SZ4290
Newtown *Nthumb* 68 NU0300
Newtown *Powys* 36 SO1091
Newtown *Shrops* 36 SJ4222
Newtown *Shrops* 37 SJ4731
Newtown *Wilts* 9 ST9129
Newtown Linford *Leics* 39 SK5209
Newtown of Beltrees *Strath* 73 NS3758
Newtown St. Boswells *Border* 76 NT5732
Newtyle *Tays* 88 NO2941
Newyork *Strath* 80 NM9611
Neyland *Dyfed* 16 SM9605
Nicholashayne *Devon* 8 ST1016
Nicholaston *W Glam* 17 SS5288
Nidd *N York* 55 SE3060
Nigg *Gramp* 89 NJ9402
Nigg *Highld* 93 NH8071
Nightcott *Devon* 7 SS8925
Nine Elms *Wilts* 20 SU1085
Ninebanks *Nthumb* 68 NY7853
Nineveh *H & W* 27 SO6265
Ninfield *E Susx* 14 TQ7012
Ningwood *IOW* 10 SZ3989
Nisbet *Border* 76 NT6725
Nisbet Hill *Border* 76 NT7950
Niton *IOW* 11 SZ5076
Nitshill *Strath* 74 NS5260
No Man's Heath *Ches* 46 SJ5148
No Man's Heath *Warwks* 39 SK2808
Nocton *Lincs* 50 TF0564
Noke *Oxon* 29 SP5413
Nolton *Dyfed* 16 SM8618
Nolton Haven *Dyfed* 16 SM8618
Nomansland *Devon* 7 SS8313
Nomansland *Wilts* 10 SU2517
Noneley *Shrops* 37 SJ4828
Nonington *Kent* 15 TR2552
Nook *Cumb* 59 SD5481
Norbiton Common *Gt Lon* 23 TQ2067
Norbury *Ches* 47 SJ5547
Norbury *Derbys* 48 SK1241
Norbury *Gt Lon* 23 TQ3069
Norbury *Shrops* 36 SO3692
Norbury *Staffs* 37 SJ7823
Norchard *H & W* 28 SO8568
Nordelph *Norfk* 41 TF5501
Nordley *Shrops* 37 SO6996
Norham *Nthumb* 77 NT9047
Norland Town *W York* 55 SE0622
Norley *Ches* 47 SJ5772
Norleywood *Hants* 10 SZ3597
Norman's Green *Devon* 7 ST0503
Normanby *Cleve* 62 NZ5418
Normanby *Humb* 56 SE8816
Normanby *Lincs* 50 SK9988
Normanby *N York* 63 SE7381
Normanby le Wold *Lincs* 50 TF1295
Normandy *Surrey* 12 SU9351
Normanton *Derbys* 39 SK3433
Normanton *Leics* 50 SK8140
Normanton *Lincs* 50 SK9446
Normanton *Notts* 49 SK7054
Normanton *W York* 55 SE3822
Normanton le Heath *Leics* 39 SK3712
Normanton on Soar *Notts* 39 SK5122
Normanton on Trent *Notts* 50 SK7868
Normanton on the Wolds *Notts* 39 SK6232
Norney *Surrey* 12 SU9444
North Anston *S York* 49 SK5184
North Aston *Oxon* 29 SP4828
North Baddesley *Hants* 10 SU3920
North Ballachulish *Highld* 86 NN0560
North Barrow *Somset* 9 ST6129
North Barsham *Norfk* 42 TF9135
North Benfleet *Essex* 24 TQ7588
North Bersted *W Susx* 12 SU9201
North Berwick *Loth* 83 NT5485
North Boarhunt *Hants* 11 SU6010
North Bovey *Devon* 5 SX7484
North Bradley *Wilts* 20 ST8555
North Brentor *Devon* 4 SX4881
North Brewham *Somset* 20 ST7236
North Buckland *Devon* 6 SS4840
North Burlingham *Norfk* 43 TG3609
North Cadbury *Somset* 9 ST6327
North Carlton *Lincs* 50 SK9477
North Carlton *Notts* 49 SK5984
North Cave *Humb* 56 SE8932
North Cerney *Gloucs* 28 SP0107
North Charford *Hants* 10 SU1919
North Charlton *Nthumb* 77 NU1622
North Cheam *Gt Lon* 23 TQ2365
North Cheriton *Somset* 9 ST6925
North Chideock *Dorset* 8 SY4294
North Cliffe *Humb* 56 SE8736
North Clifton *Notts* 50 SK8272
North Cockerington *Lincs* 51 TF3790
North Collingham *Notts* 50 SK8362
North Common *E Susx* 13 TQ3921
North Connel *Strath* 79 NM9034
North Cornelly *M Glam* 18 SS8181
North Corry *Highld* 79 NM8353
North Cotes *Lincs* 51 TA3400
North Cove *Suffk* 33 TM4689
North Cowton *N York* 61 NZ2803
North Crawley *Bucks* 30 SP9244
North Creake *Norfk* 42 TF8538
North Curry *Somset* 8 ST3125
North Dalton *Humb* 56 SE9351
North Deighton *N York* 55 SE3951
North Duffield *N York* 56 SE6837
North Duntulm *Highld* 90 NG4274
North Elham *Kent* 15 TR1844
North Elmham *Norfk* 42 TF9820
North Elmsall *W York* 55 SE4712
North End *Essex* 24 TL6618
North End *Hants* 10 SU1016
North End *Hants* 11 SU6502
North End *Nhants* 30 SP9668
North End *W Susx* 12 SU9703
North Erradale *Highld* 91 NG7480
North Evington *Leics* 39 SK6204
North Fambridge *Essex* 24 TQ8597
North Feorline *Strath* 72 NR9029
North Ferriby *Humb* 56 SE9826
North Frodingham *Humb* 57 TA1053
North Gorley *Hants* 10 SU1611
North Green *Suffk* 33 TM3162
North Grimston *N York* 56 SE8467
North Hayling *Hants* 11 SU7303
North Hill *Cnwll* 4 SX2776
North Hillingdon *Gt Lon* 22 TQ0784
North Hinksey *Oxon* 29 SP4905
North Huish *Devon* 5 SX7156
North Hykeham *Lincs* 50 SK9465
North Kelsey *Humb* 50 TA0401
North Kessock *Highld* 93 NH6548
North Killingholme *Humb* 57 TA1417
North Kilvington *N York* 62 SE4285
North Kilworth *Leics* 39 SP6183
North Kyme *Lincs* 50 TF1552
North Landing *Humb* 57 TA2471
North Lee *Bucks* 22 SP8308
North Leigh *Oxon* 29 SP3813
North Leverton with Habblesthorpe *Notts* 50 SK7882
North Lopham *Norfk* 32 TM0382
North Luffenham *Leics* 40 SK9303
North Marden *W Susx* 11 SU8016
North Marston *Bucks* 30 SP7722
North Middleton *Loth* 75 NT3559
North Milmain *D & G* 64 NX0852
North Molton *Devon* 7 SS7329
North Moreton *Oxon* 21 SU5689
North Mundham *W Susx* 11 SU8702
North Muskham *Notts* 50 SK7958
North Newbald *Humb* 56 SE9136
North Newington *Oxon* 29 SP4240
North Newnton *Wilts* 20 SU1257
North Newton *Somset* 8 ST3031
North Nibley *Gloucs* 20 ST7495
North Ormsby *Lincs* 51 TF2893
North Otterington *N York* 62 SE3689
North Owersby *Lincs* 50 TF0594
North Perrott *Somset* 8 ST4709
North Petherton *Somset* 8 ST2833
North Petherwin *Cnwll* 4 SX2789
North Pickenham *Norfk* 42 TF8606
North Piddle *H & W* 28 SO9654
North Pool *Devon* 5 SX7741
North Poorton *Dorset* 8 SY5298
North Quarme *Somset* 7 SS9236
North Queensferry *Fife* 82 NT1380
North Radworthy *Devon* 7 SS7534
North Rauceby *Lincs* 50 TF0246
North Reston *Lincs* 51 TF3883
North Rigton *N York* 55 SE2749
North Rode *Ches* 47 SJ8866
North Runcton *Norfk* 42 TF6416
North Scarle *Lincs* 50 SK8466
North Shian *Strath* 79 NM9143
North Shields *T & W* 69 NZ3568
North Shoebury *Essex* 24 TQ9286
North Shore *Lancs* 53 SD3037

North Side Oxnead

North Side *Cambs* 41 TL2799
North Skirlaugh *Humb* 57 TA1439
North Somercotes *Lincs* 51 TF4296
North Stainley *N York* 61 SE2876
North Stifford *Essex* 24 TQ6080
North Stoke *Avon* 20 ST7069
North Stoke *Oxon* 21 SU6186
North Stoke *W Susx* 12 TQ0110
North Street *Berks* 21 SU6371
North Street *Kent* 15 TR0157
North Sunderland *Nthumb* 77 NU2131
North Tamerton *Cnwll* 6 SX3197
North Tawton *Devon* 7 SS6601
North Third *Cent* 81 NS7589
North Tidworth *Wilts* 21 SU2349
North Town *Berks* 22 SU8882
North Town *Devon* 6 SS5109
North Town *Somset* 19 ST5642
North Tuddenham *Norfk* 42 TG0314
North Walsham *Norfk* 43 TG2830
North Waltham *Hants* 21 SU5646
North Warnborough *Hants* 22 SU7351
North Weald Basset *Essex* 23 TL4904
North Wheatley *Notts* 50 SK7585
North Widcombe *Somset* 19 ST5758
North Willingham *Lincs* 50 TF1688
North Wingfield *Derbys* 49 SK4065
North Witham *Lincs* 40 SK9221
North Wootton *Dorset* 9 ST6514
North Wootton *Norfk* 42 TF6424
North Wootton *Somset* 19 ST5641
North Wraxall *Wilts* 20 ST8175
Northall *Bucks* 30 SP9520
Northallerton *N York* 62 SE3694
Northam *Devon* 6 SS4529
Northam *Hants* 10 SU4312
Northampton *H & W* 28 SO8365
Northampton *Nhants* 30 SP7560
Northaw *Herts* 23 TL2702
Northay *Somset* 8 ST2811
Northborough *Cambs* 40 TF1507
Northbourne *Kent* 15 TR3352
Northbrook *Hants* 11 SU5139
Northchapel *W Susx* 12 SU9529
Northchurch *Herts* 22 SP9708
Northcott *Devon* 4 SX3392
Northcourt *Oxon* 21 SU4998
Northdown *Kent* 15 TR3770
Northend *Warwks* 29 SP3952
Northenden *Gt Man* 47 SJ8289
Northfield *Gramp* 95 NJ9008
Northfield *Humb* 56 TA0326
Northfield *W Mids* 38 SP0279
Northfields *Lincs* 40 TF0208
Northfleet *Kent* 14 TQ6374
Northiam *E Susx* 14 TQ8324
Northill *Beds* 30 TL1446
Northington *Hants* 11 SU5637
Northlands *Lincs* 51 TF3453
Northleach *Gloucs* 28 SP1114
Northleigh *Devon* 6 SS6034
Northleigh *Devon* 8 SY1995
Northlew *Devon* 6 SX5099
Northmoor *Oxon* 21 SP4202
Northmuir *Tays* 88 NO3854
Northney *Hants* 11 SU7303
Northolt *Gt Lon* 22 TQ1384
Northop *Clwyd* 46 SJ2468
Northop Hall *Clwyd* 46 SJ2667
Northorpe *Lincs* 50 SK8997
Northorpe *Lincs* 41 TF2036
Northowram *W York* 55 SE1126
Northport *Dorset* 9 SY9288
Northrepps *Norfk* 43 TG2439
Northway *Somset* 8 ST1329
Northwich *Ches* 47 SJ6673
Northwick *H & W* 28 SO8458
Northwold *Norfk* 42 TL7597
Northwood *Gt Lon* 22 TQ0990
Northwood *IOW* 11 SZ4992
Northwood *Shrops* 36 SJ4633
Northwood End *Beds* 30 TL0941
Northwood Green *Gloucs* 28 SO7216
Norton *Cleve* 62 NZ4421
Norton *E Susx* 13 TQ4701
Norton *Gloucs* 28 SO8524
Norton *H & W* 28 SO8751
Norton *H & W* 28 SP0447
Norton *N York* 56 SE7971
Norton *Nhants* 29 SP5963
Norton *Notts* 49 SK5771
Norton *Powys* 27 SO3067
Norton *S York* 56 SE5415
Norton *Shrops* 37 SJ7200
Norton *Suffk* 32 TL9565
Norton *W Susx* 12 SU9206
Norton *Wilts* 20 ST8884
Norton Bavant *Wilts* 20 ST9043
Norton Bridge *Staffs* 38 SJ8630
Norton Canes *Staffs* 38 SK0107
Norton Canon *H & W* 27 SO3847
Norton Disney *Lincs* 50 SK8859
Norton Fitzwarren *Somset* 8 ST1925
Norton Green *IOW* 10 SZ3488
Norton Hawkfield *Avon* 19 ST5964
Norton Heath *Essex* 24 TL6004
Norton in Hales *Shrops* 37 SJ7038
Norton Lindsey *Warwks* 29 SP2263
Norton Little Green *Suffk* 32 TL9766
Norton Malreward *Avon* 19 ST6064
Norton St. Philip *Somset* 20 ST7755
Norton Subcourse *Norfk* 43 TM4198
Norton sub Hamdon *Somset* 8 ST4615
Norton Wood *H & W* 27 SO3648
Norton-Juxta-Twycross *Leics* 39 SK3207
Norton-le-Clay *N York* 55 SE4071
Norwell *Notts* 50 SK7761
Norwell Woodhouse *Notts* 50 SK7362
Norwich *Norfk* 43 TG2308
Norwick *Shet* 103 HP6414
Norwood *Cent* 82 NS8793
Norwood Green *Gt Lon* 22 TQ1378
Norwood Hill *Surrey* 12 TQ2343
Noseley *Leics* 40 SP7398
Noss Mayo *Devon* 5 SX5547
Nosterfield *N York* 61 SE2780
Nostie *Highld* 85 NG8527
Notgrove *Gloucs* 28 SP1020
Nottage *M Glam* 18 SS8177
Notter *Cnwll* 4 SX3960
Nottingham *Notts* 49 SK5739
Notton *W York* 55 SE3413
Notton *Wilts* 20 ST9169
Noutard's Green *H & W* 28 SO8066
Nox *Shrops* 36 SJ4110
Nuffield *Oxon* 22 SU6687
Nun Monkton *N York* 55 SE5057
Nunburnholme *Humb* 56 SE8447
Nuneaton *Warwks* 39 SP3691
Nuneham Courtenay *Oxon* 21 SU5599
Nunhead *Gt Lon* 23 TQ3475
Nunkeeling *Humb* 57 TA1449
Nunnerie *Strath* 66 NS9612
Nunney *Somset* 20 ST7345
Nunnington *N York* 62 SE6679
Nunsthorpe *Humb* 57 TA2607
Nunthorpe *Cleve* 62 NZ5314
Nunthorpe *N York* 56 SE6050
Nunthorpe Village *Cleve* 62 NZ5413
Nunton *Wilts* 10 SU1526
Nunwick *N York* 62 SE3274
Nupend *Gloucs* 28 SO7806
Nursling *Hants* 10 SU3716
Nutbourne *W Susx* 11 SU7705
Nutbourne *W Susx* 12 TQ0718
Nutfield *Surrey* 12 TQ3050
Nuthall *Notts* 49 SK5243
Nuthampstead *Herts* 31 TL4034
Nuthurst *W Susx* 12 TQ1925
Nutley *E Susx* 13 TQ4427
Nybster *Highld* 100 ND3663
Nyetimber *W Susx* 11 SZ8998
Nyewood *W Susx* 11 SU8021
Nymet Rowland *Devon* 7 SS7108
Nymet Tracey *Devon* 7 SS7200
Nympsfield *Gloucs* 20 SO8000
Nyton *W Susx* 12 SU9305

O

Oad Street *Kent* 14 TQ8762
Oadby *Leics* 39 SK6200
Oak Cross *Devon* 6 SX5399
Oakamoor *Staffs* 48 SK0444
Oakbank *Loth* 75 NT0766
Oakdale *Gwent* 19 ST1898
Oake *Somset* 8 ST1525
Oaken *Staffs* 38 SJ8602
Oakenclough *Lancs* 53 SD5447
Oakengates *Shrops* 37 SJ7010
Oakenshaw *Dur* 61 NZ1937
Oakenshaw *W York* 55 SE1727
Oaker Side *Derbys* 49 SK2760
Oakford *Devon* 7 SS9121
Oakford *Dyfed* 34 SN4558
Oakfordbridge *Devon* 7 SS9122
Oakham *Leics* 40 SK8608
Oakhanger *Hants* 11 SU7635
Oakhill *Somset* 19 ST6347
Oakington *Cambs* 31 TL4164
Oakle Street *Gloucs* 28 SO7517
Oakley *Beds* 30 TL0153
Oakley *Bucks* 29 SP6412
Oakley *Hants* 21 SU5650
Oakley *Suffk* 33 TM1677
Oakridge *Gloucs* 20 SO9103
Oaksey *Wilts* 20 ST9993
Oakthorpe *Leics* 39 SK3212
Oakwoodhill *Surrey* 12 TQ1337
Oakworth *W York* 55 SE0338
Oare *Kent* 15 TR0063
Oare *Somset* 18 SS7947
Oare *Wilts* 20 SU1563
Oasby *Lincs* 40 TF0039
Oath *Somset* 8 ST3827
Oathlaw *Tays* 89 NO4756
Oatlands Park *Surrey* 22 TQ0865
Oban *Strath* 79 NM8629
Obley *Shrops* 36 SO3377
Obney *Tays* 82 NO0237
Oborne *Dorset* 9 ST6518
Occlestone Green *Ches* 47 SJ6962
Occold *Suffk* 33 TM1570
Ochiltree *Strath* 74 NS5021
Ockbrook *Derbys* 39 SK4235
Ockham *Surrey* 22 TQ0756
Ockle *Highld* 79 NM5570
Ockley *Surrey* 12 TQ1440
Ocle Pychard *H & W* 27 SO5945
Odcombe *Somset* 8 ST5015
Odd Down *Avon* 20 ST7462
Oddingley *H & W* 28 SO9159
Oddington *Gloucs* 29 SP2225
Oddington *Oxon* 29 SP5515
Odell *Beds* 30 SP9657
Odiham *Hants* 22 SU7451
Odsal *W York* 55 SE1529
Odsey *Herts* 31 TL2938
Odstock *Wilts* 10 SU1426
Odstone *Leics* 39 SK3907
Offchurch *Warwks* 29 SP3565
Offenham *H & W* 28 SP0546
Offham *E Susx* 13 TQ4012
Offham *Kent* 14 TQ6557
Offham *W Susx* 12 TQ0208
Offord Cluny *Cambs* 31 TL2267
Offord Darcy *Cambs* 31 TL2266
Offton *Suffk* 32 TM0649
Offwell *Devon* 8 SY1999
Ogbourne Maizey *Wilts* 21 SU1871
Ogbourne St. Andrew *Wilts* 21 SU1872
Ogbourne St. George *Wilts* 21 SU2074
Ogle *Nthumb* 69 NZ1378
Oglet *Mersyd* 46 SJ4481
Ogmore *M Glam* 18 SS8876
Ogmore Vale *M Glam* 18 SS9390
Ogmore-by-Sea *M Glam* 18 SS8675
Okeford Fitzpaine *Dorset* 9 ST8010
Okehampton *Devon* 6 SX5995
Old *Nhants* 30 SP7872
Old Aberdeen *Gramp* 95 NJ9407
Old Alresford *Hants* 11 SU5834
Old Auchenbrack *D & G* 65 NX7597
Old Basford *Notts* 49 SK5543
Old Basing *Hants* 22 SU6652
Old Bewick *Nthumb* 77 NU0621
Old Bolingbroke *Lincs* 51 TF3565
Old Bramhope *W York* 55 SE2343
Old Brampton *Derbys* 49 SK3371
Old Bridge of Urr *D & G* 66 NX7767
Old Buckenham *Norfk* 32 TM0691
Old Burghclere *Hants* 21 SU4657
Old Byland *N York* 62 SE5585
Old Church Stoke *Powys* 36 SO2894
Old Clee *Humb* 57 TA2808
Old Cleeve *Somset* 7 ST0441
Old Clipstone *Notts* 49 SK6064
Old Dailly *Strath* 64 NX2299
Old Dalby *Leics* 39 SK6723
Old Deer *Gramp* 95 NJ9747
Old Edington *S York* 49 SK5397
Old Ellerby *Humb* 57 TA1637
Old Felixstowe *Suffk* 25 TM3135
Old Fletton *Cambs* 40 TL1997
Old Forge *H & W* 27 SO5518
Old Grimsby *IOS* 2 SV8915
Old Hall Green *Herts* 31 TL3722
Old Harlow *Essex* 23 TL4711
Old Hunstanton *Norfk* 42 TF6842
Old Hutton *Cumb* 59 SD5688
Old Kea *Cnwll* 3 SW8441
Old Kilpatrick *Strath* 81 NS4672
Old Knebworth *Herts* 31 TL2320
Old Langho *Lancs* 54 SD7035
Old Leake *Lincs* 51 TF4050
Old Malton *N York* 56 SE7972
Old Micklefield *W York* 55 SE4433
Old Milverton *Warwks* 29 SP2967
Old Newton *Suffk* 32 TM0562
Old Radnor *Powys* 27 SO2558
Old Rayne *Gramp* 95 NJ6728
Old Romney *Kent* 15 TR0325
Old Shoreham *W Susx* 12 TQ2006
Old Shoremore *Highld* 98 NC2058
Old Sodbury *Avon* 20 ST7581
Old Somerby *Lincs* 40 SK9633
Old Stratford *Nhants* 30 SP7741
Old Sunnford *W Mids* 38 SO9083
Old Thirsk *N York* 62 SE4382
Old Town *Cumb* 59 SD5982
Old Town *E Susx* 13 TV5999
Old Town *IOS* 2 SV9110
Old Trafford *Gt Man* 47 SJ8196
Old Warden *Beds* 30 TL1343
Old Weston *Cambs* 30 TL0977
Old Wick *Highld* 100 ND3649
Old Windsor *Berks* 22 SU9874
Old Wives Lees *Kent* 15 TR0754
Old Woking *Surrey* 22 TQ0157
Oldany *Highld* 98 NC0932
Oldberrow *Warwks* 28 SP1265
Oldbury *Shrops* 37 SO7192
Oldbury *W Mids* 38 SO9888
Oldbury *Warwks* 39 SP3194
Oldbury on the Hill *Gloucs* 20 ST8188
Oldbury-on-Severn *Avon* 19 ST6092
Oldcastle *Gwent* 27 SO3224
Oldcotes *Notts* 49 SK5888
Oldfield *H & W* 28 SO8464
Oldford *Somset* 20 ST7850
Oldhall Green *Suffk* 32 TL8956
Oldham *Gt Man* 54 SD9204
Oldhamstocks *Loth* 76 NT7470
Oldhurst *Cambs* 31 TL3077
Oldland *Avon* 20 ST6771
Oldmeldrum *Gramp* 95 NJ8127
Oldmill *Cnwll* 4 SX3673
Oldmixon *Avon* 19 ST3358
Oldstead *N York* 62 SE5379
Oldwall *Cumb* 67 NY4761
Oldwalls *W Glam* 17 SS4891
Oldwhat *Gramp* 95 NJ8651
Olive Green *Staffs* 38 SK1118
Oliver *Border* 75 NT0924
Oliver's Battery *Hants* 10 SU4527
Ollaberry *Shet* 103 HU3680
Ollach *Highld* 84 NG5137
Ollerton *Ches* 47 SJ7776
Ollerton *Notts* 49 SK6567
Ollerton *Shrops* 37 SJ6425
Olney *Bucks* 30 SP8951
Olrig House *Highld* 100 ND1866
Olton *W Mids* 38 SP1382
Olveston *Avon* 19 ST6086
Ombersley *H & W* 28 SO8463
Ompton *Notts* 49 SK6865
Onchan *IOM* 52 SC3978
Onecote *Staffs* 48 SK0455
Onibury *Shrops* 36 SO4579
Onich *Highld* 86 NN0261
Onllwyn *W Glam* 26 SN8410
Onneley *Staffs* 37 SJ7542
Onslow Village *Surrey* 12 SU9849
Onston *Ches* 47 SJ5873
Opinan *Highld* 91 NG7472
Orbliston *Gramp* 94 NJ3057
Orbost *Highld* 90 NG2543
Orby *Lincs* 51 TF4967
Orchard Portman *Somset* 8 ST2421
Orcheston *Wilts* 20 SU0545
Orcop *H & W* 27 SO4726
Orcop Hill *H & W* 27 SO4727
Ord *Gramp* 94 NJ6258
Ord *Highld* 84 NG6113
Ordhead *Gramp* 94 NJ6610
Ordie *Gramp* 88 NJ4501
Ordiequish *Gramp* 94 NJ3357
Ordley *Nthumb* 68 NY9459
Ordsall *Notts* 49 SK7079
Ore *E Susx* 14 TQ8311
Orford *Ches* 47 SJ6190
Orford *Suffk* 33 TM4250
Organford *Dorset* 9 SY9392
Orlestone *Kent* 15 TR0034
Orleton *H & W* 27 SO4967
Orleton *H & W* 28 SO7067
Orlingbury *Nhants* 30 SP8572
Ormesby *Cleve* 62 NZ5317
Ormesby St. Margaret *Norfk* 43 TG4914
Ormesby St. Michael *Norfk* 43 TG4714
Ormiscaig *Highld* 91 NG8590
Ormiston *Loth* 76 NT4169
Ormsaigmore *Highld* 79 NM4763
Ormsary *Strath* 71 NR7472
Ormskirk *Lancs* 46 SD4108
Oronsay *Strath* 70 NR3588
Orphir *Ork* 103 HY3404
Orpington *Gt Lon* 23 TQ4666
Orrell *Gt Man* 46 SD5303
Orrell *Mersyd* 46 SJ3496
Orroland *D & G* 65 NX7746
Orsett *Essex* 24 TQ6482
Orslow *Staffs* 37 SJ8015
Orston *Notts* 50 SK7740
Orton *Cumb* 60 NY6208
Orton *Nhants* 40 SP8079
Orton *Staffs* 38 SO8795
Orton Longueville *Cambs* 40 TL1796
Orton Waterville *Cambs* 40 TL1595
Orton-on-the-Hill *Leics* 39 SK3003
Orwell *Cambs* 31 TL3650
Osbaldeston *Lancs* 54 SD6431
Osbaldwick *N York* 56 SE6251
Osbaston *Leics* 39 SK4204
Osbaston *Shrops* 36 SJ3222
Osbournby *Lincs* 40 TF0638
Oscroft *Ches* 46 SJ5067
Osgathorpe *Leics* 39 SK4319
Osgodby *Lincs* 50 TF0792
Osgodby *N York* 56 SE6433
Osgodby *N York* 63 TA0584
Oskaig *Highld* 84 NG5438
Oskamull *Strath* 79 NM4540
Osmanthorpe *W York* 55 SE3333
Osmaston *Derbys* 38 SK1943
Osmington *Dorset* 9 SY7283
Osmington Mills *Dorset* 9 SY7381
Osmotherley *N York* 62 SE4596
Osney *Oxon* 29 SP4906
Ospringe *Kent* 15 TR0060
Ossett *W York* 55 SE2720
Ossington *Notts* 50 SK7564
Oswaldkirk *N York* 62 SE6278
Oswaldtwistle *Lancs* 54 SD7327
Oswestry *Shrops* 36 SJ2929
Otford *Kent* 23 TQ5359
Otham *Kent* 14 TQ7953
Othery *Somset* 8 ST3831
Otley *Suffk* 33 TM2055
Otley *W York* 55 SE2045
Otter Ferry *Strath* 71 NR9384
Otterbourne *Hants* 10 SU4522
Otterburn *N York* 54 SD8857
Otterburn *Nthumb* 68 NY8893
Otterham *Cnwll* 4 SX1690
Otterhampton *Somset* 19 ST2443
Ottershaw *Surrey* 22 TQ0263
Otterswick *Shet* 103 HU5285
Otterton *Devon* 8 SY0684
Ottery *Devon* 4 SX4475
Ottery St. Mary *Devon* 8 SY1095
Ottinge *Kent* 15 TR1642
Ottringham *Humb* 57 TA2624
Oughterside *Cumb* 58 NY1140
Oughtibridge *S York* 49 SK3093
Oughtrington *Ches* 47 SJ6987
Oulston *N York* 62 SE5474
Oulton *Cumb* 67 NY2450
Oulton *Norfk* 43 TG1328
Oulton *Staffs* 38 SJ9035
Oulton *Suffk* 43 TM5294
Oulton Broad *Suffk* 33 TM5192
Oulton Street *Norfk* 43 TG1527
Oundle *Nhants* 40 TL0388
Ounsdale *Staffs* 38 SO8693
Ousby *Cumb* 59 NY6134
Ousden *Suffk* 32 TL7459
Ousefleet *Humb* 56 SE8323
Ouston *Dur* 69 NZ2554
Outgate *Cumb* 59 SD3599
Outhgill *Cumb* 60 NY7801
Outhill *Warwks* 28 SP1066
Outlane *W York* 55 SE0817
Outwell *Norfk* 41 TF5103
Outwood *Surrey* 12 TQ3145
Outwoods *Staffs* 37 SJ7817
Ouzlewell Green *W York* 55 SE3326
Over *Cambs* 31 TL3770
Over Compton *Dorset* 9 ST5816
Over Green *Warwks* 38 SP1694
Over Haddon *Derbys* 48 SK2066
Over Kellet *Lancs* 53 SD5169
Over Kiddington *Oxon* 29 SP4021
Over Norton *Oxon* 29 SP3128
Over Silton *N York* 62 SE4493
Over Stenton *Fife* 83 NT2799
Over Stowey *Somset* 19 ST1838
Over Stratton *Somset* 8 ST4315
Over Wallop *Hants* 10 SU2838
Over Whitacre *Warwks* 39 SP2590
Over Worton *Oxon* 29 SP4329
Overbury *H & W* 28 SO9537
Overleigh *Somset* 8 ST4835
Overpool *Ches* 46 SJ3877
Overscaig Hotel *Highld* 96 NC4123
Overseal *Derbys* 39 SK2915
Oversland *Kent* 15 TR0557
Overstone *Nhants* 30 SP7966
Overstrand *Norfk* 43 TG2440
Overthorpe *Nhants* 29 SP4840
Overton *Clwyd* 36 SJ3741
Overton *Gramp* 95 NJ8714
Overton *Hants* 21 SU5149
Overton *Lancs* 53 SD4358
Overton *N York* 56 SE5555
Overton *Shrops* 37 SO5072
Overton *W Glam* 17 SS4685
Overton *W York* 55 SE2516
Overtown *Lancs* 60 SD6275
Overtown *Strath* 74 NS8053
Overy Staithe *Norfk* 42 TF8444
Oving *Bucks* 30 SP7821
Oving *W Susx* 11 SU9004
Ovingdean *E Susx* 12 TQ3503
Ovingham *Nthumb* 68 NZ0863
Ovington *Dur* 61 NZ1314
Ovington *Essex* 32 TL7642
Ovington *Hants* 11 SU5631
Ovington *Norfk* 42 TF9202
Ovington *Nthumb* 68 NZ0663
Ower *Hants* 10 SU3215
Owermoigne *Dorset* 9 SY7685
Owlerton *S York* 49 SK3389
Owlsmoor *Berks* 22 SU8462
Owlswick *Bucks* 22 SP7806
Owmby *Lincs* 57 TA0704
Owmby *Lincs* 50 TF0087
Owslebury *Hants* 11 SU5123
Owston *Leics* 40 SK7707
Owston *S York* 56 SE5511
Owston Ferry *Humb* 50 SE8000
Owstwick *Humb* 57 TA2732
Owthorne *Humb* 57 TA3328
Owthorpe *Notts* 39 SK6733
Oxborough *Norfk* 42 TF7401
Oxbridge *Dorset* 8 SY4797
Oxcombe *Lincs* 51 TF3177
Oxen End *Essex* 24 TL6629
Oxen Park *Cumb* 58 SD3187
Oxenhope *W York* 55 SE0334
Oxenpill *Somset* 19 ST4441
Oxenton *Gloucs* 28 SO9531
Oxenwood *Wilts* 21 SU3058
Oxford *Oxon* 29 SP5106
Oxhey *Herts* 22 TQ1295
Oxhill *Warwks* 29 SP3146
Oxley *W Mids* 38 SJ9001
Oxley Green *Essex* 24 TL9014
Oxley's Green *E Susx* 14 TQ6921
Oxlode *Cambs* 41 TL4886
Oxnam *Border* 76 NT6918
Oxnead *Norfk* 43 TG2224

Oxshott Plumtree

Oxshott *Surrey* 22 TQ1460
Oxspring *S York* 49 SE2601
Oxted *Surrey* 13 TQ3852
Oxton *Border* 76 NT4953
Oxton *N York* 55 SE5043
Oxton *Notts* 49 SK6351
Oxwich *W Glam* 17 SS4986
Oxwich Green *W Glam* 17 SS4985
Oykel Bridge Hotel *Highld* 96 NC3801
Oyne *Gramp* 95 NJ6725
Oystermouth *W Glam* 17 SS6187

P

Packington *Leics* 39 SK3614
Padanaram *Tays* 88 NO4251
Padbury *Bucks* 30 SP7230
Paddington *Gt Lon* 23 TQ2681
Paddlesworth *Kent* 14 TQ6862
Paddlesworth *Kent* 15 TR1939
Paddock Wood *Kent* 14 TQ6744
Padiham *Lancs* 54 SD7933
Padside *N York* 55 SE1659
Padstow *Cnwll* 3 SW9175
Padworth *Berks* 21 SU6166
Pagham *W Susx* 11 SZ8897
Paglesham *Essex* 24 TQ9293
Paignton *Devon* 5 SX8860
Pailton *Warwks* 39 SP4781
Painscastle *Powys* 27 SO1646
Painshawfield *Nthumb* 68 NZ0560
Painsthorpe *Humb* 56 SE8158
Painswick *Gloucs* 28 SO8609
Painter's Forstal *Kent* 15 TQ9958
Paisley *Strath* 73 NS4864
Pakefield *Suffk* 33 TM5390
Pakenham *Suffk* 32 TL9267
Paley Street *Berks* 22 SU8776
Palgrave *Suffk* 33 TM1178
Pallington *Dorset* 9 SY7891
Palmerston *Strath* 74 NS5019
Palnackie *D & G* 66 NX8157
Palnure *D & G* 65 NX4563
Palterton *Derbys* 49 SK4768
Pamber End *Hants* 21 SU6158
Pamber Green *Hants* 21 SU6159
Pamber Heath *Hants* 21 SU6162
Pamington *Gloucs* 28 SO9433
Pamphill *Dorset* 9 ST9900
Pampisford *Cambs* 31 TL4948
Panbride *Tays* 83 NO5635
Pancrasweek *Devon* 6 SS2905
Pandy *Gwent* 27 SO3322
Pandy Tudur *Clwyd* 45 SH8564
Panfield *Essex* 24 TL7325
Pangbourne *Berks* 21 SU6376
Pangdean *W Susx* 12 TQ2911
Pannal *N York* 55 SE3051
Pannal Ash *N York* 55 SE2953
Pannanich Wells Hotel *Gramp* 88 NO4097
Pant *Shrops* 36 SJ2722
Pant-glas *Gwynd* 44 SH4747
Pant-y-dwr *Powys* 35 SN9874
Pant-y-mwyn *Clwyd* 46 SJ1964
Pantasaph *Clwyd* 46 SJ1675
Pantglas *Powys* 35 SN7797
Panton *Lincs* 50 TF1778
Panxworth *Norfk* 43 TG3513
Papcastle *Cumb* 58 NY1031
Papigoe *Highld* 100 ND3851
Papple *Loth* 76 NT5972
Papplewick *Notts* 49 SK5451
Papworth Everard *Cambs* 31 TL2862
Papworth St. Agnes *Cambs* 31 TL2664
Par *Cnwll* 3 SX0753
Parbold *Lancs* 53 SD4011
Parbrook *Somset* 19 ST5736
Parc *Gwynd* 45 SH8834
Parc Seymour *Gwent* 19 ST4091
Pardshaw *Cumb* 58 NY0924
Parham *Suffk* 33 TM3060
Park *D & G* 66 NX9091
Park *Gramp* 89 NO7898
Park *Nthumb* 68 NY6861
Park Corner *Oxon* 22 SU6988
Park Gate *Hants* 11 SU5108
Park Gate *W York* 55 SE1841
Park Royal *Gt Lon* 23 TQ1982
Parkend *Gloucs* 27 SO6108
Parkers Green *Kent* 13 TQ6148
Parkgate *Ches* 46 SJ2878
Parkgate *D & G* 66 NY0288
Parkgate *Surrey* 12 TQ2043
Parkhall *Strath* 81 NS4871
Parkham *Devon* 6 SS3921
Parkhill House *Gramp* 95 NJ8914
Parkmill *W Glam* 17 SS5489
Parkside *Dur* 69 NZ4248
Parkstone *Dorset* 10 SZ0391
Parndon *Essex* 23 TL4308
Parr Bridge *Gt Man* 47 SD7001
Parracombe *Devon* 7 SS6745
Parson Drove *Cambs* 41 TF3708
Parson's Heath *Essex* 25 TM0226
Partick *Strath* 74 NS5467
Partington *Gt Man* 47 SJ7191
Partney *Lincs* 51 TF4068
Parton *Cumb* 58 NX9820
Parton *D & G* 65 NX6970
Partridge Green *W Susx* 12 TQ1919
Parwich *Derbys* 48 SK1854
Passenham *Nhants* 30 SP7839
Passfield *Hants* 11 SU8234
Paston *Norfk* 43 TG3234
Patcham *E Susx* 12 TQ3008
Patching *W Susx* 12 TQ0806
Patchway *Avon* 19 ST6082
Pateley Bridge *N York* 55 SE1565
Path of Condie *Tays* 82 NO0711
Pathhead *Fife* 83 NT2992
Pathhead *Gramp* 89 NO7263
Pathhead *Loth* 76 NT3964
Pathhead *Strath* 66 NS6114
Patna *Strath* 73 NS4110
Patney *Wilts* 20 SU0758
Patrick *IOM* 52 SC2482
Patrick Brompton *N York* 61 SE2190
Patricroft *Gt Man* 47 SJ7597
Patrington *Humb* 57 TA3122
Patrixbourne *Kent* 15 TR1855
Patterdale *Cumb* 59 NY3915
Pattingham *Staffs* 38 SO8299
Pattishall *Nhants* 30 SP6754
Pattiswick Green *Essex* 24 TL8124
Paul *Cnwll* 2 SW4627
Paul's Dene *Wilts* 10 SU1432
Paulerspury *Bucks* 30 SP7145
Paull *Humb* 57 TA1626
Paulton *Avon* 19 ST6556
Pauperhaugh *Nthumb* 68 NZ1099
Pavenham *Beds* 30 SP9955
Pawlett *Somset* 19 ST2942
Paxford *Gloucs* 29 SP1837
Paxton *Border* 77 NT9353
Payhembury *Devon* 8 ST0901
Paythorne *Lancs* 54 SD8251
Peacehaven *E Susx* 13 TQ4101
Peak Forest *Derbys* 48 SK1179
Peakirk *Cambs* 40 TF1606
Pean *Kent* 15 TR1837
Peanmeanach *Highld* 85 NM7180
Pearsie *Tays* 88 NO3659
Pease Pottage *W Susx* 12 TQ2633
Peasedown St. John *Avon* 20 ST7057
Peaseland Green *Norfk* 42 TG0516
Peasemore *Berks* 21 SU4577
Peasenhall *Suffk* 33 TM3569
Peaslake *Surrey* 12 TQ0844
Peasley Cross *Mersyd* 46 SJ5294
Peasmarsh *E Susx* 14 TQ8822
Peat Inn *Fife* 83 NO4509
Peathill *Gramp* 95 NJ9366
Peatling Magna *Leics* 39 SP5992
Peatling Parva *Leics* 39 SP5889
Pebmarsh *Essex* 24 TL8533
Pebworth *H & W* 28 SP1347
Pecket Well *W York* 54 SD9929
Peckforton *Ches* 46 SJ5356
Peckham *Gt Lon* 23 TQ3476
Peckleton *Leics* 39 SK4701
Pedlinge *Kent* 15 TR1335
Pedmore *W Mids* 38 SO9182
Pedwell *Somset* 19 ST4236
Peebles *Border* 75 NT2540
Peel *IOM* 52 SC2483
Pegsdon *Beds* 30 TL1130
Pegswood *Nthumb* 69 NZ2287
Pegwell *Kent* 15 TR3664
Peinchorran *Highld* 84 NG5233
Peinlich *Highld* 90 NG4158
Pelaw *T & W* 69 NZ3061
Peldon *Essex* 25 TL9816
Pelsall *W Mids* 38 SK0203
Pelton *Dur* 69 NZ2553
Pelynt *Cnwll* 4 SX2055
Pemberton *Dyfed* 17 SN5300
Pemberton *Gt Man* 47 SD5503
Pembrey *Dyfed* 17 SN4301
Pembridge *H & W* 27 SO3958
Pembroke *Dyfed* 16 SM9801
Pembroke Dock *Dyfed* 16 SM9603
Pembury *Kent* 13 TQ6240
Pen Rhiwfawr *W Glam* 26 SN7410
Pen-bont Rhydybeddau *Dyfed* 35 SN6783
Pen-ffordd *Dyfed* 16 SN0722
Pen-rhiw *Dyfed* 17 SN2440
Pen-twyn *Gwent* 27 SO5209
Pen-y-Bont-Fawr *Powys* 36 SJ0824
Pen-y-bont *Clwyd* 36 SJ2123
Pen-y-bryn *Dyfed* 17 SN1742
Pen-y-clawdd *Gwent* 27 SO4507
Pen-y-coedcae *M Glam* 18 ST0587
Pen-y-cwn *Dyfed* 16 SM8523
Pen-y-felin *Clwyd* 46 SJ1569
Pen-y-graig *Gwynd* 44 SH2033
Pen-y-stryt *Clwyd* 46 SJ1952
Penallt *Gwent* 27 SO5210
Penally *Dyfed* 16 SS1199
Penalt *H & W* 27 SO5629
Penarth *S Glam* 19 ST1871
Penbryn *Dyfed* 17 SN2951
Pencader *Dyfed* 17 SN4436
Pencaitland *Loth* 76 NT4468
Pencarnisiog *Gwynd* 44 SH3573
Pencarreg *Dyfed* 17 SN5445
Pencelli *Powys* 26 SO0925
Penclawdd *W Glam* 17 SS5495
Pencoed *M Glam* 18 SS9581
Pencombe *H & W* 27 SO5952
Pencraig *H & W* 27 SO5620
Pencraig *Powys* 36 SJ0426
Pendeen *Cnwll* 2 SW3834
Penderyn *M Glam* 26 SN9408
Pendine *Dyfed* 17 SN2208
Pendlebury *Gt Man* 47 SD7802
Pendleton *Lancs* 54 SD7539
Pendock *H & W* 28 SO7832
Pendoggett *Cnwll* 3 SX0279
Pendomer *Somset* 8 ST5210
Pendoylan *S Glam* 18 ST0576
Penegoes *Powys* 35 SH7600
Pengam *Gwent* 19 ST1597
Pengam *S Glam* 19 ST2177
Penge *Gt Lon* 23 TQ3570
Pengelly *Cnwll* 3 SX0783
Pengrugla *Cnwll* 3 SW9947
Penhallow *Cnwll* 2 SW7651
Penhalvean *Cnwll* 2 SW7038
Penhill *Wilts* 20 SU1588
Penhow *Gwent* 19 ST4290
Penifiler *Highld* 84 NG4841
Peninver *Strath* 72 NR7524
Penistone *S York* 55 SE2403
Penkill *Strath* 64 NX2398
Penkridge *Staffs* 38 SJ9213
Penlean *Cnwll* 6 SX2098
Penley *Clwyd* 36 SJ4040
Penllyn *S Glam* 18 SS9775
Penmachno *Gwynd* 45 SH7950
Penmaen *Gwent* 19 ST1897
Penmaen *W Glam* 17 SS5288
Penmaenmawr *Gwynd* 45 SH7276
Penmaenpool *Gwynd* 35 SH6918
Penmark *S Glam* 18 ST0568
Penmorfa *Gwynd* 44 SH5540
Penmynydd *Gwynd* 44 SH5074
Penn *Bucks* 22 SU9193
Penn Street *Bucks* 22 SU9295
Pennal *Gwynd* 35 SH6900
Pennan *Gramp* 95 NJ8465
Pennant *Powys* 35 SN8897
Pennard *W Glam* 17 SS5688
Pennerley *Shrops* 36 SO3599
Pennington *Cumb* 58 SD2677
Pennorth *Powys* 26 SO1125
Penny Bridge *Cumb* 58 SD3083
Penny Hill *Lincs* 41 TF3526
Pennycross *Strath* 79 NM5025
Pennyghael *Strath* 79 NM5125
Pennyglen *Strath* 73 NS2710
Pennymoor *Devon* 7 SS8611
Penparc *Dyfed* 17 SN2047
Penperlleni *Gwent* 27 SO3204
Penpoll *Cnwll* 3 SX1454
Penponds *Cnwll* 2 SW6339
Penpont *D & G* 66 NX8494
Penrhiwceiber *M Glam* 18 ST0597
Penrhiwllan *Dyfed* 17 SN3641
Penrhiwpal *Dyfed* 17 SN3445
Penrhos *Gwent* 27 SO4111
Penrhos *Gwynd* 44 SH3433
Penrhyn Bay *Gwynd* 45 SH8281
Penrhyncoch *Dyfed* 35 SN6384
Penrhyndeudraeth *Gwynd* 45 SH6139
Penrice *W Glam* 17 SS4987
Penrioch *Strath* 72 NR8744
Penrith *Cumb* 59 NY5130
Penrose *Cnwll* 3 SW8770
Penruddock *Cumb* 59 NY4227
Penryn *Cnwll* 2 SW7834
Pensarn *Clwyd* 45 SH9578
Pensax *H & W* 28 SO7269
Penselwood *Somset* 9 ST7531
Pensford *Avon* 19 ST6263
Pensham *H & W* 28 SO9444
Penshurst *Kent* 13 TQ5243
Pensilva *Cnwll* 4 SX2970
Pentewan *Cnwll* 3 SX0147
Pentir *Gwynd* 44 SH5766
Pentire *Cnwll* 2 SW7961
Pentlow *Essex* 32 TL8146
Pentney *Norfk* 42 TF7214
Penton Mewsey *Hants* 21 SU3247
Pentraeth *Gwynd* 44 SH5278
Pentre *M Glam* 18 SS9696
Pentre *Shrops* 36 SJ3617
Pentre Berw *Gwynd* 44 SH4772
Pentre Hodrey *Shrops* 36 SO3277
Pentre Llanrhaeadr *Clwyd* 46 SJ0863
Pentre Meyrick *S Glam* 18 SS9675
Pentre-bach *Powys* 26 SN9132
Pentre-celyn *Clwyd* 46 SJ1453
Pentre-celyn *Powys* 35 SH8905
Pentre-chwyth *W Glam* 18 SS6794
Pentre-cwrt *Dyfed* 17 SN3838
Pentre-Gwenlais *Dyfed* 17 SN6016
Pentre-tafarn-y-fedw *Gwynd* 45 SH8162
Pentrebach *M Glam* 26 SO0604
Pentredwr *Clwyd* 46 SJ1946
Pentrefelin *Gwynd* 44 SH5239
Pentrefoelas *Clwyd* 45 SH8751
Pentregat *Dyfed* 17 SN3551
Pentrich *Derbys* 49 SK3852
Pentridge Hill *Dorset* 10 SU0317
Pentyrch *M Glam* 18 ST1081
Penwithick *Cnwll* 3 SX0256
Penybanc *Dyfed* 17 SN6123
Penybont *Powys* 26 SO1164
Penycae *Clwyd* 46 SJ2745
Penyffordd *Clwyd* 46 SJ3061
Penygarnedd *Powys* 36 SJ1023
Penygraig *M Glam* 18 ST0090
Penygroes *Dyfed* 17 SN5813
Penygroes *Gwynd* 44 SH4752
Penysarn *Gwynd* 44 SH4590
Penywaun *M Glam* 26 SN9804
Penzance *Cnwll* 2 SW4730
Peopleton *H & W* 28 SO9350
Peover Heath *Ches* 47 SJ7973
Peper Harow *Surrey* 12 SU9344
Peplow *Shrops* 37 SJ6224
Pepperstock *Beds* 30 TL0817
Percie *Gramp* 89 NO5992
Percyhorner *Gramp* 95 NJ9665
Perelle *Guern* 101 GN4608
Periton *Somset* 7 SS9545
Perivale *Gt Lon* 23 TQ1682
Perkins Village *Devon* 5 SY0291
Perlethorpe *Notts* 49 SK6470
Perranarworthal *Cnwll* 2 SW7738
Perranporth *Cnwll* 2 SW7554
Perranuthnoe *Cnwll* 2 SW5329
Perranwell *Cnwll* 2 SW7739
Perranzabuloe *Cnwll* 2 SW7752
Perry Barr *W Mids* 38 SP0791
Perry Green *Wilts* 20 ST9689
Pershall *Staffs* 37 SJ8129
Pershore *H & W* 28 SO9446
Perth *Tays* 82 NO1123
Perthy *Shrops* 36 SJ3633
Pertwood *Wilts* 20 ST8936
Peter Tavy *Devon* 4 SX5177
Peter's Green *Herts* 30 TL1419
Peterborough *Cambs* 40 TL1998
Peterchurch *H & W* 27 SO3438
Peterculter *Gramp* 89 NJ8300
Peterhead *Gramp* 95 NK1246
Peterlee *Dur* 62 NZ4241
Peters Marland *Devon* 6 SS4713
Petersfield *Hants* 11 SU7423
Petersham *Gt Lon* 23 TQ1873
Peterston-Super-Ely *S Glam* 18 ST0876
Peterstone Wentlooge *Gwent* 19 ST2679
Peterstow *H & W* 27 SO5624
Petham *Kent* 15 TR1251
Petherwin Gate *Cnwll* 4 SX2889
Petrockstow *Devon* 6 SS5109
Pett *E Susx* 14 TQ8714
Pettaugh *Suffk* 33 TM1659
Petterden *Tays* 83 NO4240
Pettinain *Strath* 75 NS9543
Pettistree *Suffk* 33 TM3055
Petton *Devon* 7 ST0124
Petts Wood *Gt Lon* 23 TQ4567
Pettycur *Fife* 83 NT2686
Pettymuk *Gramp* 95 NJ9023
Petworth *W Susx* 12 SU9721
Pevensey *E Susx* 13 TQ6405
Pewsey *Wilts* 20 SU1660
Pheasant's Hill *Bucks* 22 SU7887
Phepson *H & W* 28 SO9459
Philham *Devon* 6 SS2522
Philiphaugh *Border* 76 NT4327
Phillack *Cnwll* 2 SW5638
Philleigh *Cnwll* 3 SW8639
Philpot End *Essex* 24 TL6118
Philpstoun *Loth* 75 NT0577
Phoenix Green *Hants* 22 SU7555
Phoines *Highld* 87 NN7093
Pibsbury *Somset* 8 ST4426
Pica *Cumb* 58 NY0222
Pickering *N York* 63 SE7984
Pickford *W Mids* 39 SP2881
Pickhill *N York* 62 SE3483
Picklescott *Shrops* 36 SO4399
Pickmere *Ches* 47 SJ6977
Pickney *Somset* 8 ST1929
Pickup Bank *Lancs* 54 SD7122
Pickwell *Leics* 40 SK7811
Pickworth *Leics* 40 SK9913
Pickworth *Lincs* 40 TF0433
Pictillum *Gramp* 95 NJ7317
Picton *Ches* 46 SJ4371
Picton *N York* 62 NZ4107
Piddinghoe *E Susx* 13 TQ4303
Piddington *Nhants* 30 SP8054
Piddington *Oxon* 29 SP6317
Piddlehinton *Dorset* 9 SY7197
Piddletrenthide *Dorset* 9 SY7099
Pidley *Cambs* 31 TL3377
Piercebridge *Dur* 61 NZ2115
Pierowall *Ork* 103 HY4348
Pilgrims Hatch *Essex* 24 TQ5895
Pilham *Lincs* 50 SK8693
Pillaton *Cnwll* 4 SX3664
Pillerton Hersey *Warwks* 29 SP2948
Pillerton Priors *Warwks* 29 SP2947
Pilley *Hants* 10 SZ3298
Pilley *S York* 49 SE3300
Pillgwenlly *Gwent* 19 ST3186
Pilling *Lancs* 53 SD4048
Pilning *Avon* 19 ST5684
Pilsbury *Derbys* 48 SK1163
Pilsdon *Dorset* 8 SY4199
Pilsley *Derbys* 48 SK2371
Pilsley *Derbys* 49 SK4262
Pilson Green *Norfk* 43 TG3713
Piltdown *E Susx* 13 TQ4422
Pilton *Leics* 40 SK9102
Pilton *Nhants* 40 TL0284
Pilton *Somset* 19 ST5941
Pimperne *Dorset* 9 ST9009
Pin Green *Herts* 31 TL2525
Pinchbeck *Lincs* 41 TF2425
Pinhoe *Devon* 7 SX9694
Pinley Green *Warwks* 29 SP2066
Pinminnoch *Strath* 64 NX1993
Pinmore *Strath* 64 NX2091
Pinner *Gt Lon* 22 TQ1289
Pinner Green *Gt Lon* 22 TQ1289
Pinvin *H & W* 28 SO9549
Pinwherry *Strath* 64 NX2086
Pinxton *Derbys* 49 SK4554
Pipe and Lyde *H & W* 27 SO5043
Pipe Gate *Shrops* 37 SJ7340
Piperhill *Highld* 93 NH8650
Pipewell *Nhants* 40 SP8485
Pirbright *Surrey* 22 SU9455
Pirnie *Border* 76 NT6528
Pirton *H & W* 28 SO8847
Pirton *Herts* 30 TL1431
Pishill *Oxon* 22 SU7389
Pistyll *Gwynd* 44 SH3241
Pitagowan *Tays* 87 NN8165
Pitblae *Gramp* 95 NJ9864
Pitcairngreen *Tays* 82 NO0627
Pitcalnie *Highld* 93 NH8072
Pitcaple *Gramp* 95 NJ7225
Pitcarity *Tays* 88 NO3365
Pitch Green *Bucks* 22 SP7703
Pitch Place *Surrey* 11 SU8839
Pitchcombe *Gloucs* 28 SO8508
Pitchcott *Bucks* 30 SP7720
Pitchford *Shrops* 37 SJ5303
Pitchroy *Gramp* 94 NJ1738
Pitcombe *Somset* 9 ST6732
Pitcox *Loth* 76 NT6475
Pitchie *Gramp* 95 NJ6716
Pitglassie *Gramp* 95 NJ6943
Pitgrudy *Highld* 97 NH7991
Pitkennedy *Tays* 89 NO5454
Pitlessie *Fife* 83 NO3309
Pitlochry *Tays* 87 NN9458
Pitmachie *Gramp* 95 NJ6728
Pitmain *Highld* 87 NH7400
Pitmedden *Gramp* 95 NJ8827
Pitmuies *Tays* 89 NO5649
Pitmunie *Gramp* 94 NJ6614
Pitney *Somset* 8 ST4528
Pitroddie *Tays* 82 NO2125
Pitscottie *Fife* 83 NO4112
Pitsea *Essex* 24 TQ7488
Pitsford *Nhants* 30 SP7567
Pitt *Devon* 7 ST0316
Pittarrow *Gramp* 89 NO7274
Pittenweem *Fife* 83 NO5502
Pitteuchar *Fife* 83 NT2899
Pittington *Dur* 69 NZ3244
Pittodrie House Hotel *Gramp* 95 NJ6924
Pitton *Wilts* 10 SU2131
Pittulie *Gramp* 95 NJ9567
Pity Me *Dur* 69 NZ2645
Pixham *Surrey* 12 TQ1750
Plains *Strath* 74 NS7966
Plaish *Shrops* 37 SO5296
Plaistow *Derbys* 49 SK3456
Plaistow *Gt Lon* 23 TQ4082
Plaistow *W Susx* 12 TQ0030
Plaitford *Hants* 10 SU2719
Plastow Green *Hants* 21 SU5361
Platt *Kent* 14 TQ6257
Plawsworth *Dur* 69 NZ2647
Plaxtol *Kent* 13 TQ6053
Play Hatch *Oxon* 22 SU7376
Playden *E Susx* 14 TQ9221
Playford *Suffk* 33 TM2147
Playing Place *Cnwll* 2 SW8141
Playley Green *Gloucs* 28 SO7631
Plealey *Shrops* 36 SJ4206
Plean *Cent* 82 NS8386
Pleasance *Fife* 82 NO2312
Pleasington *Lancs* 54 SD6426
Pleasley *Derbys* 49 SK5064
Pleinheaume *Guern* 101 GN5111
Plemont *Jersey* 101 JS0616
Plemstall *Ches* 46 SJ4570
Pleshey *Essex* 24 TL6614
Plockton *Highld* 85 NG8033
Ploughfield *H & W* 27 SO3841
Plowden *Shrops* 36 SO3887
Ploxgreen *Shrops* 36 SJ3604
Pluckley *Kent* 14 TQ9245
Pluckley Thorne *Kent* 14 TQ9244
Plumbland *Cumb* 58 NY1539
Plumley *Ches* 47 SJ7274
Plumpton *Cumb* 59 NY4937
Plumpton *E Susx* 12 TQ3613
Plumpton End *Nhants* 30 SP7245
Plumpton Green *E Susx* 12 TQ3616
Plumstead *Gt Lon* 23 TQ4478
Plumstead *Norfk* 43 TG1334
Plumtree *Notts* 39 SK6132

Plungar Rathen

Plungar *Leics* 40 SK7634
Plurenden *Kent* 14 TQ9337
Plush *Dorset* 9 ST7102
Plwmp *Dyfed* 17 SN3652
Plymouth *Devon* 4 SX4754
Plympton *Devon* 4 SX5456
Plymstock *Devon* 4 SX5152
Plymtree *Devon* 7 ST0502
Pockley *N York* 62 SE6385
Pocklington *Humb* 56 SE8048
Podimore *Somset* 8 ST5424
Podington *Beds* 30 SP9462
Podmore *Staffs* 37 SJ7835
Pointon *Lincs* 40 TF1131
Pokesdown *Dorset* 10 SZ1292
Polbain *Highld* 91 NB9910
Polbathic *Cnwll* 4 SX3456
Polbeth *Loth* 75 NT0264
Pole Elm *H & W* 28 SO8450
Polebrook *Nhants* 40 TL0686
Polegate *E Susx* 13 TQ5804
Polesworth *Warwks* 39 SK2602
Polglass *Highld* 91 NC0307
Polgooth *Cnwll* 3 SW9950
Polgown *D & G* 66 NS7103
Poling *W Susx* 12 TQ0404
Poling Corner *W Susx* 12 TQ0405
Polkerris *Cnwll* 3 SX0952
Pollington *Humb* 56 SE6119
Polloch *Highld* 79 NM7668
Pollokshaws *Strath* 74 NS5661
Pollokshields *Strath* 74 NS5763
Polmassick *Cnwll* 3 SW9745
Polmont *Cent* 82 NS9378
Polnish *Highld* 85 NM7582
Polperro *Cnwll* 4 SX2051
Polruan *Cnwll* 3 SX1250
Polstead *Suffk* 25 TL9938
Poltalloch *Strath* 71 NR8196
Poltimore *Devon* 7 SX9696
Polton *Loth* 75 NT2864
Polwarth *Border* 76 NT7450
Polyphant *Cnwll* 4 SX2682
Polzeath *Cnwll* 3 SW9378
Pomathorn *Loth* 75 NT2459
Ponders End *Gt Lon* 23 TQ3596
Pondersbridge *Cambs* 41 TL2692
Ponsanooth *Cnwll* 2 SW7537
Ponsworthy *Devon* 5 SX7073
Pont Robert *Powys* 36 SJ1012
Pont-ar-gothi *Dyfed* 17 SN5021
Pont-faen *Powys* 26 SN9934
Pont-Nedd-Fechan *Powys* 26 SN9007
Pont-rhyd-y-fen *W Glam* 18 SS7994
Pont-y-pant *Gwynd* 45 SH7554
Pontac *Jersey* 101 JS1807
Pontantwn *Dyfed* 17 SN4412
Pontardawe *W Glam* 26 SN7204
Pontarddulais *W Glam* 17 SN5903
Pontarsais *Dyfed* 17 SN4428
Pontblyddyn *Clwyd* 46 SJ2760
Pontefract *W York* 55 SE4521
Ponteland *Nthumb* 69 NZ1672
Ponterwyd *Dyfed* 35 SN7481
Pontesford *Shrops* 36 SJ4106
Pontfadog *Clwyd* 36 SJ2338
Pontfaen *Dyfed* 16 SN0234
Pontgarreg *Dyfed* 17 SN3353
Ponthenry *Dyfed* 17 SN4709
Ponthir *Gwent* 19 ST3292
Ponthirwaun *Dyfed* 17 SN2645
Pontllanfraith *Gwent* 19 ST1895
Pontlliw *W Glam* 35 SN6199
Pontlyfni *Gwynd* 44 SH4352
Pontnewydd *Gwent* 19 ST2896
Pontop *Dur* 69 NZ1453
Pontrhydfendigaid *Dyfed* 35 SN7366
Pontrhydygroes *Dyfed* 35 SN7472
Pontrilas *H & W* 27 SO3927
Ponts Green *E Susx* 14 TQ6715
Pontshaen *Dyfed* 17 SN4446
Pontshill *H & W* 27 SO6421
Pontsticill *M Glam* 26 SO0511
Pontwelly *Dyfed* 17 SN4140
Pontyates *Dyfed* 17 SN4708
Pontyberem *Dyfed* 17 SN5010
Pontybodkin *Clwyd* 46 SJ2759
Pontyclun *M Glam* 18 ST0381
Pontycymer *M Glam* 18 SS9091
Pontypool *Gwent* 19 SO2800
Pontypridd *M Glam* 18 ST0789
Pontywaun *Gwent* 19 ST2292
Pool *Cnwll* 2 SW6641
Pool *W York* 55 SE2445
Pool o'Muckhart *Cent* 82 NO0000
Pool Street *Essex* 24 TL7636
Poole *Dorset* 10 SZ0090
Poole Keynes *Wilts* 20 ST9995
Poolewe *Highld* 91 NG8580
Pooley Bridge *Cumb* 59 NY4724
Poolfold *Staffs* 48 SJ8959
Poolhill *Gloucs* 28 SO7229
Popham *Hants* 21 SU5543
Poplar *Gt Lon* 23 TQ3780
Porchfield *IOW* 10 SZ4491
Poringland *Norfk* 43 TG2701
Porkellis *Cnwll* 2 SW6933
Porlock *Somset* 7 SS8846
Porlock Weir *Somset* 18 SS8647
Port Appin *Strath* 79 NM9045
Port Askaig *Strath* 70 NR4369
Port Bannatyne *Strath* 72 NS0767
Port Carlisle *Cumb* 67 NY2461
Port Charlotte *Strath* 70 NR2558
Port Dinorwic *Gwynd* 44 SH5267
Port Driseach *Strath* 80 NR9973
Port Einon *W Glam* 17 SS4685
Port Ellen *Strath* 70 NR3645
Port Elphinstone *Gramp* 95 NJ7720
Port Erin *IOM* 52 SC1969
Port Gaverne *Cnwll* 3 SX0080
Port Glasgow *Strath* 80 NS3274
Port Henderson *Highld* 91 NG7573
Port Isaac *Cnwll* 3 SW9980
Port Logan *D & G* 64 NX0940
Port Mor *Highld* 84 NM4279
Port Na Craig *Tays* 87 NN9357
Port of Menteith *Cent* 81 NN5801
Port of Ness *W Isls* 102 NB5363
Port Quin *Cnwll* 3 SW9780
Port Ramsay *Strath* 79 NM8845
Port Soderick *IOM* 52 SC3472
Port St. Mary *IOM* 52 SC2067
Port Talbot *W Glam* 18 SS7689
Port Wemyss *Strath* 70 NR1651
Port William *D & G* 64 NX3343
Port-an-Eorna *Highld* 85 NG7732
Portachoillan *Strath* 71 NR7557
Portavadie *Strath* 71 NR9369
Portbury *Avon* 19 ST5075
Portchester *Hants* 11 SU6105
Portencalzie *D & G* 64 NX0171
Portencross *Strath* 73 NS1748
Portesham *Dorset* 9 SY6085
Portessie *Gramp* 94 NJ4366
Portfield Gate *Dyfed* 16 SM9215
Portgate *Devon* 4 SX4285
Portgordon *Gramp* 94 NJ3964
Portgower *Highld* 97 ND0013
Porth *Cnwll* 3 SW8362
Porth *M Glam* 18 ST0291
Porth Navas *Cnwll* 2 SW7527
Porthallow *Cnwll* 2 SW7923
Porthallow *Cnwll* 4 SX2251
Porthcawl *M Glam* 18 SS8177
Porthcothan *Cnwll* 3 SW8672
Porthcurno *Cnwll* 2 SW3822
Porthgain *Dyfed* 16 SM8132
Porthgwarra *Cnwll* 2 SW3721
Porthkerry *S Glam* 18 ST0866
Porthleven *Cnwll* 2 SW6225
Porthmadog *Gwynd* 44 SH5638
Porthoustock *Cnwll* 2 SW8021
Porthpean *Cnwll* 3 SX0250
Porthtowan *Cnwll* 2 SW6947
Porthyrhyd *Dyfed* 17 SN5215
Portincaple *Strath* 80 NS2393
Portinfer *Jersey* 101 JS0615
Portington *Humb* 56 SE7831
Portinnisherrich *Strath* 80 NM9711
Portinscale *Cumb* 58 NY2523
Portishead *Avon* 19 ST4675
Portknockie *Gramp* 94 NJ4868
Portlethen *Gramp* 89 NO9196
Portling *D & G* 66 NX8753
Portloe *Cnwll* 3 SW9339
Portmahomack *Highld* 97 NH9184
Portmellon *Cnwll* 3 SX0144
Portnacroish *Strath* 79 NM9247
Portnaguiran *W Isls* 102 NB5537
Portnahaven *Strath* 70 NR1652
Portnalong *Highld* 84 NG3434
Portobello *Loth* 75 NT3073
Portobello *W Mids* 38 SO9598
Porton *Wilts* 10 SU1836
Portpatrick *D & G* 64 NW9954
Portreath *Cnwll* 2 SW6545
Portree *Highld* 90 NG4843
Portrye *Strath* 73 NS1757
Portscatho *Cnwll* 3 SW8735
Portsea *Hants* 11 SU6300
Portskerra *Highld* 99 NC8765
Portskewett *Gwent* 19 ST4988
Portslade *E Susx* 12 TQ2506
Portslade-by-Sea *E Susx* 12 TQ2605
Portslogan *D & G* 64 NW9858
Portsmouth *Hants* 11 SU6400
Portsmouth *W York* 54 SD9026
Portsoy *Gramp* 94 NJ5866
Portswood *Hants* 10 SU4214
Portuairk *Highld* 79 NM4368
Portwrinkle *Cnwll* 4 SX3553
Portyerrock *D & G* 65 NX4738
Poslingford *Suffk* 32 TL7648
Posso *Border* 75 NT2033
Postbridge *Devon* 5 SX6579
Postcombe *Oxon* 22 SP7000
Postling *Kent* 15 TR1439
Postwick *Norfk* 43 TG2907
Potsgrove *Beds* 30 SP9530
Pott Shrigley *Ches* 48 SJ9479
Potter Brompton *N York* 63 SE9777
Potter Heigham *Norfk* 43 TG4119
Potter's Green *Herts* 31 TL3520
Potterhanworth *Lincs* 50 TF0566
Potterhanworth Booths *Lincs* 50 TF0767
Potterne *Wilts* 20 ST9958
Potterne Wick *Wilts* 20 ST9957
Potters Bar *Herts* 23 TL2401
Potters Crouch *Herts* 22 TL1105
Potters Marston *Leics* 39 SP4996
Pottersheath *Herts* 31 TL2318
Potterspury *Nhants* 30 SP7543
Potto *N York* 62 NZ4703
Potton *Beds* 31 TL2249
Poughill *Cnwll* 6 SS2207
Poughill *Devon* 7 SS8508
Poulshot *Wilts* 20 ST9659
Poulton *Gloucs* 20 SP0901
Poulton-le-Fylde *Lancs* 53 SD3439
Pound Green *E Susx* 13 TQ5123
Pound Green *Suffk* 32 TL7153
Pound Hill *W Susx* 12 TQ2937
Poundffald *W Glam* 17 SS5694
Poundon *Bucks* 29 SP6425
Poundsgate *Devon* 5 SX7072
Poundstock *Cnwll* 6 SX2099
Pouton *D & G* 65 NX4645
Povey Cross *Surrey* 12 TQ2642
Powburn *Nthumb* 77 NU0616
Powderham *Devon* 5 SX9684
Powerstock *Dorset* 8 SY5196
Powfoot *D & G* 67 NY1465
Powhill *Cumb* 67 NY2355
Powick *H & W* 28 SO8351
Powmill *Tays* 82 NT0297
Poxwell *Dorset* 9 SY7384
Poyle *Gt Lon* 22 TQ0376
Poynings *W Susx* 12 TQ2611
Poyntington *Dorset* 9 ST6520
Poynton *Ches* 48 SJ9283
Poynton Green *Shrops* 37 SJ5618
Poys Street *Suffk* 33 TM3570
Praa Sands *Cnwll* 2 SW5828
Pratt's Bottom *Gt Lon* 23 TQ4762
Praze-an-Beeble *Cnwll* 2 SW6335
Prees *Shrops* 37 SJ5533
Prees Green *Shrops* 37 SJ5531
Preesall *Lancs* 53 SD3647
Pren-gwyn *Dyfed* 17 SN4244
Prendwick *Nthumb* 68 NU0012
Prenteg *Gwynd* 44 SH5841
Prescot *Mersyd* 46 SJ4692
Prescott *Devon* 8 ST0814
Presnerb *Tays* 88 NO1866
Prestatyn *Clwyd* 45 SJ0682
Prestbury *Ches* 48 SJ8976
Prestbury *Gloucs* 28 SO9723
Presteigne *Powys* 27 SO3164
Prestleigh *Somset* 19 ST6340
Preston *Border* 76 NT7957
Preston *Devon* 5 SX8574
Preston *Devon* 5 SX8962
Preston *Dorset* 9 SY7083
Preston *E Susx* 12 TQ3106
Preston *Gloucs* 20 SP0400
Preston *Herts* 31 TL1824
Preston *Humb* 57 TA1830
Preston *Kent* 15 TR0260
Preston *Kent* 15 TR2460
Preston *Lancs* 53 SD5329
Preston *Leics* 40 SK8602
Preston *Loth* 76 NT5977
Preston *Nthumb* 77 NU1825
Preston *Somset* 8 ST0935
Preston *Suffk* 32 TL9450
Preston *Wilts* 21 SU2774
Preston Bagot *Warwks* 29 SP1765
Preston Bissett *Bucks* 29 SP6529
Preston Bowyer *Somset* 8 ST1326
Preston Brook *Ches* 47 SJ5680
Preston Candover *Hants* 21 SU6041
Preston Capes *Nhants* 29 SP5754
Preston Green *Warwks* 28 SP1665
Preston Gubbals *Shrops* 37 SJ4919
Preston on Stour *Warwks* 29 SP2049
Preston on the Hill *Ches* 47 SJ5780
Preston on Wye *H & W* 27 SO3842
Preston Patrick *Cumb* 59 SD5483
Preston Plucknett *Somset* 8 ST5316
Preston upon the Weald Moors *Shrops* 37 SJ6815
Preston Wynne *H & W* 27 SO5546
Preston-under-Scar *N York* 61 SE0691
Prestonpans *Loth* 76 NT3874
Prestwich *Gt Man* 47 SD8104
Prestwick *Strath* 73 NS3525
Prestwood *Bucks* 22 SP8700
Prickwillow *Cambs* 41 TL5982
Priddy *Somset* 19 ST5250
Priest Hutton *Lancs* 59 SD5273
Priestweston *Shrops* 36 SO2997
Primrosehill *Border* 76 NT7857
Primsidemill *Border* 76 NT8126
Princes Risborough *Bucks* 22 SP8003
Princethorpe *Warwks* 29 SP4070
Princetown *Devon* 5 SX5873
Priors Hardwick *Warwks* 29 SP4756
Priors Marston *Warwks* 29 SP4957
Priors Norton *Gloucs* 28 SO8624
Priston *Avon* 20 ST6960
Prittlewell *Essex* 24 TQ8687
Privett *Hants* 11 SU6727
Probus *Cnwll* 3 SW8947
Prospect *Cumb* 58 NY1140
Prospidnick *Cnwll* 2 SW6431
Protstonhill *Gramp* 95 NJ8163
Prudhoe *Nthumb* 68 NZ0962
Ptarmigan Lodge *Cent* 80 NN3500
Publow *Avon* 19 ST6264
Puckeridge *Herts* 31 TL3823
Puckington *Somset* 8 ST3718
Pucklechurch *Avon* 20 ST6976
Puddington *Ches* 46 SJ3273
Puddington *Devon* 7 SS8310
Puddletown *Dorset* 9 SY7594
Pudsey *W York* 55 SE2232
Pulborough *W Susx* 12 TQ0418
Pulford *Ches* 46 SJ3758
Pulham *Dorset* 9 ST7008
Pulham Market *Norfk* 33 TM1986
Pulham St. Mary *Norfk* 33 TM2085
Pulloxhill *Beds* 30 TL0634
Pumpherston *Loth* 75 NT0669
Pumsaint *Dyfed* 26 SN6540
Puncheston *Dyfed* 16 SN0129
Puncknowle *Dorset* 8 SY5388
Punnett's Town *E Susx* 13 TQ6220
Purbrook *Hants* 11 SU6707
Purfleet *Essex* 24 TQ5578
Puriton *Somset* 19 ST3241
Purleigh *Essex* 24 TL8402
Purley *Berks* 22 SU6675
Purley *Gt Lon* 23 TQ3161
Purse Caundle *Dorset* 9 ST6917
Purtington *Somset* 8 ST3908
Purton *Gloucs* 28 SO6904
Purton *Gloucs* 28 SO6705
Purton *Wilts* 20 SU0987
Purton Stoke *Wilts* 20 SU0990
Pury End *Nhants* 30 SP7145
Pusey *Oxon* 21 SU3596
Putley *H & W* 27 SO6337
Putley Green *H & W* 27 SO6437
Putloe *Gloucs* 28 SO7709
Putney *Gt Lon* 23 TQ2374
Putron Village *Guern* 101 GN5306
Puttenham *Surrey* 12 SU9247
Puxley *Nhants* 30 SP7542
Puxton *Avon* 19 ST4063
Pwll *Dyfed* 17 SN4801
Pwll Trap *Dyfed* 17 SN2616
Pwll-du *Gwent* 27 SO2411
Pwll-y-glaw *W Glam* 18 SS7993
Pwllgloyw *Powys* 26 SO0333
Pwllheli *Gwynd* 44 SH3735
Pwllmeyric *Gwent* 19 ST5292
Pye Bridge *Derbys* 49 SK4452
Pye Corner *Herts* 31 TL4412
Pyecombe *W Susx* 12 TQ2813
Pyle *M Glam* 18 SS8282
Pyleigh *Somset* 8 ST1330
Pylle *Somset* 19 ST6038
Pymore *Cambs* 41 TL4986
Pymore *Dorset* 8 SY4694
Pyrford *Surrey* 22 TQ0358
Pyrton *Oxon* 22 SU6896
Pytchley *Nhants* 30 SP8574
Pyworthy *Devon* 6 SS3102

Q

Quabbs *Shrops* 36 SO2180
Quadring *Lincs* 41 TF2233
Quainton *Bucks* 30 SP7420
Quarley *Hants* 21 SU2743
Quarndon *Derbys* 49 SK3340
Quarrier's Homes *Strath* 73 NS3666
Quarrington *Lincs* 50 TF0544
Quarrington Hill *Dur* 62 NZ3337
Quarry Bank *W Mids* 38 SO9386
Quarrywood *Gramp* 94 NJ1763
Quarter *Strath* 74 NS7251
Quatford *Shrops* 37 SO7391
Quatt *Shrops* 37 SO7588
Quebec *Dur* 69 NZ1743
Quedgeley *Gloucs* 28 SO8014
Queen Adelaide *Cambs* 41 TL5681
Queen Camel *Somset* 9 ST5924
Queen Charlton *Avon* 19 ST6367
Queen Oak *Dorset* 9 ST7831
Queen Street *Kent* 14 TQ6845
Queen's Bower *IOW* 11 SZ5684
Queenborough *Kent* 14 TQ9172
Queenhill *H & W* 28 SO8537
Queensbury *W York* 55 SE1030
Queensferry *Clwyd* 46 SJ3168
Queenslie *Strath* 74 NS6565
Queenzieburn *Strath* 74 NS6977
Quendon *Essex* 31 TL5130
Queniborough *Leics* 39 SK6412
Quenington *Gloucs* 28 SP1404
Quethiock *Cnwll* 4 SX3164
Quidenham *Norfk* 32 TM0287
Quidhampton *Wilts* 10 SU1030
Quinton *Nhants* 30 SP7754
Quintrell Downs *Cnwll* 3 SW8460
Quither *Devon* 4 SX4481
Quixwood *Border* 76 NT7863
Quoditch *Devon* 6 SX4097
Quorndon *Leics* 39 SK5616
Quothquan *Strath* 75 NS9939
Quoyburray *Ork* 103 HY5005
Quoyloo *Ork* 103 HY2420

R

Rableyheath *Herts* 31 TL2319
Rachan Mill *Border* 75 NT1134
Rachub *Gwynd* 45 SH6267
Rackenford *Devon* 7 SS8518
Rackham *W Susx* 12 TQ0413
Rackheath *Norfk* 43 TG2814
Rackwick *Ork* 103 ND2099
Radbourne *Derbys* 39 SK2836
Radcliffe *Gt Man* 47 SD7806
Radcliffe *Nthumb* 69 NU2602
Radcliffe on Trent *Notts* 49 SK6439
Radclive *Bucks* 30 SP6734
Radernie *Fife* 83 NO4609
Radford Semele *Warwks* 29 SP3464
Radlett *Herts* 23 TL1600
Radley *Oxon* 21 SU5398
Radley Green *Essex* 24 TL6205
Radnage *Bucks* 22 SU7897
Radstock *Avon* 20 ST6854
Radstone *Nhants* 29 SP5840
Radway *Warwks* 29 SP3648
Radwell *Beds* 30 TL0057
Radwell *Herts* 31 TL2335
Radwinter *Essex* 24 TL6037
Radyr *S Glam* 18 ST1280
Raecleugh *D & G* 66 NT0311
Rafford *Gramp* 93 NJ0556
Ragdale *Leics* 39 SK6619
Raglan *Gwent* 27 SO4107
Ragnall *Notts* 50 SK8073
Raigbeg *Highld* 93 NH8128
Rainbow Hill *H & W* 28 SO8555
Rainford *Mersyd* 46 SD4700
Rainham *Gt Lon* 23 TQ5282
Rainham *Kent* 14 TQ8165
Rainhill *Mersyd* 46 SJ4991
Rainhill Stoops *Mersyd* 46 SJ5090
Rainow *Ches* 48 SJ9475
Rainton *N York* 62 SE3675
Rainworth *Notts* 49 SK5858
Raisthorpe *N York* 56 SE8561
Rait *Tays* 82 NO2226
Raithby *Lincs* 51 TF3084
Raithby *Lincs* 51 TF3766
Rake *W Susx* 11 SU8027
Ralia *Highld* 87 NN7097
Ramasaig *Highld* 90 NG1644
Rame *Cnwll* 2 SW7233
Rame *Cnwll* 4 SX4249
Rampisham *Dorset* 9 ST5602
Rampside *Cumb* 53 SD2366
Rampton *Cambs* 31 TL4267
Rampton *Notts* 50 SK8078
Ramridge End *Beds* 30 TL1023
Ramsbottom *Gt Man* 54 SD7916
Ramsbury *Wilts* 21 SU2771
Ramscraigs *Highld* 100 ND1427
Ramsdean *Hants* 11 SU7022
Ramsdell *Hants* 21 SU5857
Ramsden *Oxon* 29 SP3515
Ramsden Bellhouse *Essex* 24 TQ7194
Ramsey *Cambs* 41 TL2885
Ramsey *Essex* 25 TM2130
Ramsey *IOM* 52 SC4594
Ramsey Forty Foot *Cambs* 41 TL3087
Ramsey Heights *Cambs* 41 TL2484
Ramsey Island *Essex* 25 TL9405
Ramsey Mereside *Cambs* 41 TL2889
Ramsey St. Mary's *Cambs* 41 TL2587
Ramsgate *Kent* 15 TR3865
Ramsgill *N York* 55 SE1170
Ramshope *Nthumb* 68 NT7304
Ramshorn *Staffs* 48 SK0845
Ramsnest Common *Surrey* 12 SU9432
Ranby *Lincs* 51 TF2278
Ranby *Notts* 49 SK6580
Rand *Lincs* 50 TF1078
Randwick *Gloucs* 28 SO8306
Ranfurly *Strath* 73 NS3865
Rangemore *Staffs* 38 SK1822
Rangeworthy *Avon* 20 ST6986
Rankinston *Strath* 73 NS4513
Rann *Lancs* 54 SD7124
Rannoch Station *Tays* 86 NN4257
Ranochan *Highld* 85 NM8282
Ranscombe *Somset* 7 SS9443
Ranskill *Notts* 49 SK6587
Ranton *Staffs* 38 SJ8524
Ranton Green *Staffs* 38 SJ8423
Ranworth *Norfk* 43 TG3514
Raploch *Cent* 81 NS7894
Rapness *Ork* 103 HY5141
Rapps *Somset* 8 ST3316
Rascarrel *D & G* 66 NX7948
Rashfield *Strath* 80 NS1483
Rashwood *H & W* 28 SO9165
Raskelf *N York* 55 SE4971
Ratagan *Highld* 85 NG9119
Ratby *Leics* 39 SK5105
Ratcliffe Culey *Leics* 39 SP3299
Ratcliffe on Soar *Notts* 39 SK4928
Ratcliffe on the Wreake *Leics* 39 SK6314
Rathen *Gramp* 95 NJ9960

Rathillet Ruckinge

Rathillet *Fife* 83 NO3620
Rathmell *N York* 54 SD8059
Ratho *Loth* 75 NT1370
Rathven *Gramp* 94 NJ4465
Ratley *Warwks* 29 SP3847
Ratling *Kent* 15 TR2453
Ratlinghope *Shrops* 36 SO4096
Rattar *Highld* 100 ND2673
Rattery *Devon* 5 SX7461
Rattlesden *Suffk* 32 TL9758
Ratton Village *E Susx* 13 TQ5901
Rattray *Tays* 88 NO1845
Raunds *Nhants* 30 SP9972
Raven Meols *Mersyd* 46 SD2905
Ravenfield *S York* 49 SK4895
Ravenglass *Cumb* 58 SD0896
Raveningham *Norfk* 43 TM3996
Ravenscar *N York* 63 NZ9801
Ravenscliffe *Staffs* 47 SJ8452
Ravensden *Beds* 30 TL0754
Ravenshead *Notts* 49 SK5654
Ravensthorpe *Nhants* 30 SP6670
Ravensthorpe *W York* 55 SE2220
Ravenstone *Bucks* 30 SP8451
Ravenstone *Leics* 39 SK4013
Ravenstonedale *Cumb* 60 NY7203
Ravenstruther *Strath* 75 NS9245
Ravensworth *N York* 61 NZ1308
Rawcliffe *Humb* 56 SE6822
Rawcliffe *N York* 56 SE5854
Rawling Street *Kent* 14 TQ9059
Rawmarsh *S York* 49 SK4396
Rawreth *Essex* 24 TQ7893
Rawridge *Devon* 8 ST2006
Rawtenstall *Lancs* 54 SD8123
Raydon *Suffk* 25 TM0438
Rayleigh *Essex* 24 TQ8090
Rayne *Essex* 24 TL7222
Raynes Park *Gt Lon* 23 TQ2368
Reach *Cambs* 31 TL5666
Read *Lancs* 54 SD7634
Reading *Berks* 22 SU7173
Reading Street *Kent* 14 TQ9230
Reading Street *Kent* 15 TR3869
Reagill *Cumb* 59 NY6017
Rearquhar *Highld* 97 NH7492
Rearsby *Leics* 39 SK6514
Reay *Highld* 99 NC9664
Reculver *Kent* 15 TR2269
Red Ball *Devon* 8 ST0917
Red Hill *Dorset* 10 SZ0995
Red Hill *Warwks* 28 SP1356
Red Roses *Dyfed* 17 SN2011
Red Row *T & W* 69 NZ2599
Red Wharf Bay *Gwynd* 44 SH5281
Redberth *Dyfed* 16 SN0804
Redbourn *Herts* 30 TL1012
Redbourne *Lincs* 50 SK9799
Redbrook *Clwyd* 37 SJ5041
Redbrook *Gloucs* 27 SO5309
Redbrook Street *Kent* 14 TQ9336
Redburn *Highld* 93 NH9447
Redcar *Cleve* 62 NZ6024
Redcastle *D & G* 66 NX8165
Redcastle *Highld* 92 NH5849
Redding *Cent* 82 NS9278
Reddingmuirhead *Cent* 75 NS9177
Redditch *H & W* 28 SP0467
Rede *Suffk* 32 TL8055
Redenhall *Norfk* 33 TM2684
Redesmouth *Nthumb* 68 NY8682
Redford *Gramp* 89 NO7570
Redford *Tays* 89 NO5644
Redford *W Susx* 11 SU8626
Redfordgreen *Border* 76 NT3616
Redgorton *Tays* 82 NO0828
Redgrave *Suffk* 32 TM0477
Redhill *Avon* 19 ST4962
Redhill *Gramp* 89 NJ7704
Redhill *Herts* 31 TL3033
Redhill *Surrey* 12 TQ2750
Redisham *Suffk* 33 TM4084
Redland *Avon* 19 ST5775
Redland *Ork* 103 HY3724
Redlingfield *Suffk* 33 TM1870
Redlingfield Green *Suffk* 33 TM1871
Redlynch *Somset* 9 ST7033
Redlynch *Wilts* 10 SU2021
Redmarley *H & W* 28 SO7666
Redmarley D'Abitot *Gloucs* 28 SO7531
Redmarshall *Cleve* 62 NZ3821
Redmile *Leics* 40 SK7935
Redmire *N York* 61 SE0491
Redmyre *Gramp* 89 NO7575
Rednal *Shrops* 36 SJ3628
Redpath *Border* 76 NT5835
Redruth *Cnwll* 2 SW6942
Redstone *Tays* 82 NO1834
Redwick *Avon* 19 ST5486
Redwick *Gwent* 19 ST4184
Redworth *Dur* 61 NZ2423
Reed *Herts* 31 TL3636
Reedham *Norfk* 43 TG4201
Reedness *Humb* 56 SE7923
Reepham *Lincs* 50 TF0473
Reepham *Norfk* 43 TG1022
Reeth *N York* 61 SE0399
Reeves Green *W Mids* 39 SP2677
Reiff *Highld* 98 NB9614
Reigate *Surrey* 12 TQ2550
Reighton *N York* 63 TA1375
Reisque *Gramp* 95 NJ8819
Reiss *Highld* 100 ND3354
Relubbus *Cnwll* 2 SW5631
Relugas *Gramp* 93 NH9948
Remenham *Berks* 22 SU7684
Remenham Hill *Berks* 22 SU7882
Rempstone *Notts* 39 SK5724
Rendcomb *Gloucs* 28 SP0209
Rendham *Suffk* 33 TM3464
Renfrew *Strath* 74 NS5067
Renhold *Beds* 30 TL0852
Renishaw *Derbys* 49 SK4577
Rennington *Nthumb* 77 NU2118
Renton *Strath* 80 NS3877
Renwick *Cumb* 67 NY5943
Repps *Norfk* 43 TG4217
Repton *Derbys* 39 SK3026
Resaurie *Highld* 93 NH7045
Rescassa *Cnwll* 3 SW9842
Resipole *Highld* 79 NM7264
Reskadinnick *Cnwll* 2 SW6341
Resolis *Highld* 93 NH6765
Resolven *W Glam* 18 SN8302
Rest and be Thankful *Strath* 80 NN2307
Reston *Border* 77 NT8862
Reswallie *Tays* 89 NO5051
Retford *Notts* 49 SK7081
Rettendon *Essex* 24 TQ7698
Revesby *Lincs* 51 TF2961
Rew Street *IOW* 11 SZ4794
Rewe *Devon* 7 SX9499
Reydon *Suffk* 33 TM4977
Reymerston *Norfk* 42 TG0206
Reynalton *Dyfed* 16 SN0908
Reynoldston *W Glam* 17 SS4889
Rezare *Cnwll* 4 SX3677
Rhandirmwyn *Dyfed* 26 SN7843
Rhayader *Powys* 35 SN9768
Rheindown *Highld* 92 NH5147
Rhes-y-cae *Clwyd* 46 SJ1871
Rhewl *Clwyd* 46 SJ1060
Rhewl *Clwyd* 46 SJ1744
Rhicarn *Highld* 98 NC0825
Rhiconich *Highld* 98 NC2552
Rhicullen *Highld* 93 NH6971
Rhigos *M Glam* 26 SN9205
Rhireavach *Highld* 91 NH0295
Rhives *Highld* 97 NC8200
Rhiwbina *S Glam* 19 ST1682
Rhiwderyn *Gwent* 19 ST2687
Rhiwlas *Gwynd* 44 SH5765
Rhoden Green *Kent* 14 TQ6845
Rhodes Minnis *Kent* 15 TR1542
Rhodiad-y-brenin *Dyfed* 16 SM7627
Rhonehouse or Kelton Hill *D & G* 65 NX7459
Rhoose *S Glam* 18 ST0666
Rhos *Dyfed* 17 SN3835
Rhos *W Glam* 18 SN7302
Rhos-hill *Dyfed* 17 SN1940
Rhos-on-Sea *Clwyd* 45 SH8480
Rhos-y-gwaliau *Gwynd* 45 SH9434
Rhoscolyn *Gwynd* 44 SH2267
Rhoscrowther *Dyfed* 16 SM9002
Rhosesmor *Clwyd* 46 SJ2168
Rhosgoch *Powys* 27 SO1847
Rhoshirwaun *Gwynd* 44 SH2029
Rhosllanerchrugog *Clwyd* 46 SJ2946
Rhosmeirch *Gwynd* 44 SH4677
Rhosneigr *Gwynd* 44 SH3173
Rhossili *W Glam* 17 SS4187
Rhostryfan *Gwynd* 44 SH4957
Rhostyllen *Clwyd* 46 SJ3148
Rhosybol *Gwynd* 44 SH4288
Rhosymedre *Clwyd* 36 SJ2842
Rhu *Strath* 80 NS2684
Rhuallt *Clwyd* 46 SJ0775
Rhubodach *Strath* 80 NS0273
Rhuddlan *Clwyd* 45 SJ0278
Rhunahaorine *Strath* 72 NR7048
Rhyd *Gwynd* 45 SH6341
Rhyd-Ddu *Gwynd* 44 SH5652
Rhyd-uchaf *Gwynd* 45 SH9037
Rhyd-y pennau *Dyfed* 35 SN6385
Rhyd-y-clafdy *Gwynd* 44 SH3234
Rhyd-y-foel *Clwyd* 45 SH9176
Rhyd-y-groes *Gwynd* 44 SH5867
Rhydargaeau *Dyfed* 17 SN4326
Rhydcymerau *Dyfed* 17 SN5738
Rhydlewis *Dyfed* 17 SN3447
Rhydowen *Dyfed* 17 SN4445
Rhydyfro *W Glam* 26 SN7105
Rhyl *Clwyd* 45 SJ0081
Rhymney *M Glam* 26 SO1107
Rhynd *Tays* 82 NO1520
Rhynie *Gramp* 94 NJ4927
Rhynie *Highld* 97 NH8479
Ribbesford *H & W* 37 SO7874
Ribbleton *Lancs* 53 SD5631
Ribchester *Lancs* 54 SD6535
Riby *Lincs* 57 TA1807
Riccall *N York* 56 SE6237
Riccarton *Border* 67 NY5494
Riccarton *Strath* 73 NS4236
Richards Castle *H & W* 27 SO4969
Richmond *N York* 61 NZ1701
Richmond *S York* 49 SK4085
Richmond Fort *Guern* 101 GN4609
Richmond upon Thames *Gt Lon* 23 TQ1774
Rickerscote *Staffs* 38 SJ9220
Rickford *Avon* 19 ST4859
Rickham *Devon* 5 SX7537
Rickinghall Inferior *Suffk* 32 TM0475
Rickinghall Superior *Suffk* 32 TM0375
Rickling *Essex* 31 TL4931
Rickling Green *Essex* 31 TL5129
Rickmansworth *Herts* 22 TQ0694
Riddell *Border* 76 NT5124
Riddlecombe *Devon* 7 SS6113
Riddlesden *W York* 55 SE0742
Ridge *Dorset* 9 SY9386
Ridge *Herts* 23 TL2100
Ridge *Wilts* 9 ST9531
Ridge Lane *Warwks* 39 SP2994
Ridgehill *Avon* 19 ST5462
Ridgeway *Derbys* 49 SK4081
Ridgewell *Essex* 32 TL7340
Ridgewood *E Susx* 13 TQ4719
Ridgmont *Beds* 30 SP9736
Riding Mill *Nthumb* 68 NZ0161
Ridlington *Leics* 40 SK8402
Ridlington *Norfk* 43 TG3430
Ridsdale *Nthumb* 68 NY9084
Rievaulx *N York* 62 SE5785
Rigg *D & G* 67 NY2966
Riggend *Strath* 74 NS7670
Righoul *Highld* 93 NH8851
Rigsby *Lincs* 51 TF4375
Rigside *Strath* 74 NS8735
Riley Green *Lancs* 54 SD6225
Rilla Mill *Cnwll* 4 SX2973
Rillington *N York* 63 SE8574
Rimington *Lancs* 54 SD8045
Rimpton *Somset* 9 ST6121
Rimswell *Humb* 57 TA3128
Rinaston *Dyfed* 16 SM9825
Rindleford *Shrops* 37 SO7395
Ringford *D & G* 65 NX6957
Ringland *Norfk* 43 TG1313
Ringmer *E Susx* 13 TQ4412
Ringmore *Devon* 5 SX6546
Ringmore *Devon* 5 SX9272
Ringorm *Gramp* 94 NJ2644
Ringsfield *Suffk* 33 TM4088
Ringsfield Corner *Suffk* 33 TM4087
Ringshall *Bucks* 30 SP9814
Ringshall *Suffk* 32 TM0452
Ringshall Stocks *Suffk* 32 TM0551
Ringstead *Nhants* 30 SP9875
Ringstead *Norfk* 42 TF7040
Ringwood *Hants* 10 SU1505
Ringwould *Kent* 15 TR3548
Ripe *E Susx* 13 TQ5110
Ripley *Derbys* 49 SK3950
Ripley *Hants* 10 SZ1698
Ripley *N York* 55 SE2860
Ripley *Surrey* 22 TQ0556
Riplington *Hants* 11 SU6623
Ripon *N York* 55 SE3171
Rippingale *Lincs* 40 TF0927
Ripple *H & W* 28 SO8737
Ripple *Kent* 15 TR3550
Ripponden *W York* 55 SE0319
Risabus *Strath* 70 NR3143
Risbury *H & W* 27 SO5455
Risby *Suffk* 32 TL8066
Risca *Gwent* 19 ST2391
Rise *Humb* 57 TA1542
Risegate *Lincs* 41 TF2129
Riseley *Beds* 30 TL0462
Riseley *Berks* 22 SU7263
Rishangles *Suffk* 33 TM1668
Rishton *Lancs* 54 SD7230
Rishworth *W York* 55 SE0318
Risley *Ches* 47 SJ6592
Risley *Derbys* 39 SK4535
Risplith *N York* 55 SE2468
River *Kent* 15 TR2943
River *W Susx* 12 SU9323
Riverford *Highld* 92 NH5454
Riverhead *Kent* 23 TQ5156
Rivington *Lancs* 54 SD6214
Road Weedon *Nhants* 29 SP6359
Roade *Nhants* 30 SP7651
Roadmeetings *Strath* 74 NS8649
Roadside *Highld* 100 ND1560
Roadside *Strath* 74 NS5717
Roadside of Catterline *Gramp* 89 NO8579
Roadside of Kinneff *Gramp* 89 NO8477
Roadwater *Somset* 7 ST0338
Roag *Highld* 90 NG2744
Roan of Craigoch *Strath* 73 NS2904
Roast Green *Essex* 31 TL4632
Roath *S Glam* 19 ST1977
Roberton *Border* 67 NT4214
Roberton *Strath* 75 NS9428
Robertsbridge *E Susx* 14 TQ7423
Roberttown *W York* 55 SE1922
Robeston Wathen *Dyfed* 16 SN0815
Robgill Tower *D & G* 67 NY2471
Robin Hood's Bay *N York* 63 NZ9505
Roborough *Devon* 6 SS5717
Roby *Mersyd* 46 SJ4390
Rocester *Staffs* 48 SK1039
Roch *Dyfed* 16 SM8821
Rochdale *Gt Man* 54 SD8913
Roche *Cnwll* 3 SW9860
Rochester *Kent* 14 TQ7468
Rochester *Nthumb* 68 NY8298
Rochford *Essex* 24 TQ8790
Rochford *H & W* 27 SO6268
Rochville *Strath* 80 NS2390
Rock *Cnwll* 3 SW9375
Rock *H & W* 37 SO7371
Rock *Nthumb* 77 NU2020
Rock Ferry *Mersyd* 46 SJ3386
Rockbeare *Devon* 7 SY0194
Rockbourne *Hants* 10 SU1118
Rockcliffe *Cumb* 67 NY3561
Rockcliffe *D & G* 66 NX8454
Rockfield *Gwent* 27 SO4814
Rockfield *Highld* 97 NH9282
Rockford *Devon* 18 SS7547
Rockhampton *Gloucs* 19 ST6593
Rockhill *Shrops* 36 SO2978
Rockingham *Nhants* 40 SP8691
Rockland All Saints *Norfk* 42 TL9996
Rockland St. Mary *Norfk* 43 TG3104
Rockland St. Peter *Norfk* 42 TL9897
Rockley *Notts* 49 SK7174
Rockley *Wilts* 20 SU1571
Rockwell End *Bucks* 22 SU7988
Rodborough *Gloucs* 28 SO8404
Rodborough *Wilts* 20 SU1485
Rodbourne *Wilts* 20 ST9383
Rodden *Dorset* 9 SY6184
Rode *Somset* 20 ST8053
Rode Heath *Ches* 47 SJ8056
Rodel *W Isls* 102 NG0483
Roden *Shrops* 37 SJ5716
Rodhuish *Somset* 7 ST0139
Rodington *Shrops* 37 SJ5814
Rodington Heath *Shrops* 37 SJ5814
Rodley *Gloucs* 28 SO7411
Rodmarton *Gloucs* 20 ST9498
Rodmell *E Susx* 13 TQ4106
Rodmersham *Kent* 14 TQ9261
Rodmersham Green *Kent* 14 TQ9161
Rodney Stoke *Somset* 19 ST4849
Rodono Hotel *Border* 75 NT2321
Rodsley *Derbys* 48 SK2040
Roe Green *Herts* 23 TL2107
Roe Green *Herts* 31 TL3133
Roecliffe *N York* 55 SE3765
Roehampton *Gt Lon* 23 TQ2273
Roffey *W Susx* 12 TQ1932
Rogart *Highld* 97 NC7202
Rogate *W Susx* 11 SU8023
Rogerstone *Gwent* 19 ST2787
Rogiet *Gwent* 19 ST4587
Roke *Oxon* 21 SU6293
Roker *T & W* 69 NZ4058
Rollesby *Norfk* 43 TG4416
Rolleston *Leics* 40 SK7300
Rolleston *Staffs* 39 SK2327
Rolston *Humb* 57 TA2144
Rolvenden *Kent* 14 TQ8431
Rolvenden Layne *Kent* 14 TQ8530
Romaldkirk *Dur* 61 NY9922
Romanby *N York* 62 SE3693
Romanno Bridge *Border* 75 NT1647
Romansleigh *Devon* 7 SS7220
Romesdal *Highld* 90 NG4053
Romford *Dorset* 10 SU0709
Romford *Gt Lon* 23 TQ5188
Romiley *Gt Man* 48 SJ9490
Romsey *Hants* 10 SU3521
Romsley *H & W* 38 SO9680
Romsley *Shrops* 37 SO7883
Ronachan *Strath* 71 NR7454
Rookhope *Dur* 61 NY9342
Rookley *IOW* 11 SZ5084
Rooks Bridge *Somset* 19 ST3652
Rooks Nest *Somset* 8 ST0933
Rookwith *N York* 61 SE2086
Roos *Humb* 57 TA2830
Roothams Green *Beds* 30 TL0957
Ropley *Hants* 11 SU6431
Ropley Dean *Hants* 11 SU6232
Ropsley *Lincs* 40 SK9933
Rora *Gramp* 95 NK0650
Rorrington *Shrops* 36 SJ3000
Rosarie *Gramp* 94 NJ3850
Rose *Cnwll* 2 SW7754
Rose Ash *Devon* 7 SS7921
Rose Green *Essex* 24 TL9028
Rose Green *Suffk* 25 TL9337
Rose Green *Suffk* 32 TL9744
Rose Green *W Susx* 11 SZ9099
Rose Hill *Lancs* 54 SD8231
Rose Lands *E Susx* 13 TQ6200
Rosebank *Strath* 74 NS8049
Rosebush *Dyfed* 16 SN0729
Rosedale Abbey *N York* 63 SE7296
Rosehall *Highld* 96 NC4702
Rosehearty *Gramp* 95 NJ9267
Roseisle *Gramp* 93 NJ1466
Rosemarket *Dyfed* 16 SM9508
Rosemarkie *Highld* 93 NH7357
Rosemary Lane *Devon* 8 ST1514
Rosemount *Tays* 88 NO1843
Rosenannon *Cnwll* 3 SW9566
Rosewell *Loth* 75 NT2862
Roseworth *Cleve* 62 NZ4221
Rosgill *Cumb* 59 NY5316
Roshven *Highld* 85 NM7078
Roskhill *Highld* 90 NG2744
Rosley *Cumb* 67 NY3245
Roslin *Loth* 75 NT2763
Rosliston *Derbys* 39 SK2416
Rosneath *Strath* 80 NS2583
Ross *D & G* 65 NX6444
Ross-on-Wye *H & W* 27 SO5923
Rossett *Clwyd* 46 SJ3657
Rossett Green *N York* 55 SE2952
Rossington *Notts* 49 SK6298
Rosskeen *Highld* 93 NH6869
Rossland *Strath* 73 NS4370
Roster *Highld* 100 ND2639
Rostherne *Ches* 47 SJ7483
Rosthwaite *Cumb* 58 NY2514
Roston *Derbys* 48 SK1340
Rosyth *Loth* 82 NT1082
Rothbury *Nthumb* 68 NU0501
Rotherby *Leics* 39 SK6716
Rotherfield *E Susx* 13 TQ5529
Rotherfield Greys *Oxon* 22 SU7282
Rotherfield Peppard *Oxon* 22 SU7182
Rotherham *S York* 49 SK4392
Rothersthorpe *Nhants* 30 SP7156
Rotherwick *Hants* 22 SU7156
Rothes *Gramp* 94 NJ2749
Rothesay *Strath* 73 NS0864
Rothiebrisbane *Gramp* 95 NJ7437
Rothiemay *Gramp* 94 NJ5548
Rothienorman *Gramp* 95 NJ7235
Rothley *Leics* 39 SK5812
Rothmaise *Gramp* 95 NJ6832
Rothwell *Lincs* 50 TF1499
Rothwell *Nhants* 40 SP8181
Rothwell *W York* 55 SE3428
Rottal Lodge *Tays* 88 NO3769
Rottingdean *E Susx* 12 TQ3602
Rottington *Cumb* 58 NX9613
Roucan *D & G* 66 NY0277
Rough Common *Kent* 15 TR1259
Rougham *Norfk* 42 TF8320
Rougham Green *Suffk* 32 TL9061
Roughpark *Gramp* 94 NJ3412
Roughton *Lincs* 51 TF2464
Roughton *Norfk* 43 TG2136
Roughton *Shrops* 37 SO7594
Roundbush Green *Essex* 24 TL5814
Roundham *Somset* 8 ST4209
Roundhay *W York* 55 SE3337
Roundway *Wilts* 20 SU0163
Roundyhill *Tays* 88 NO3750
Rous Lench *H & W* 28 SP0153
Rousdon *Devon* 8 SY2991
Rousham *Oxon* 29 SP4724
Routenburn *Strath* 73 NS1961
Routh *Humb* 57 TA0942
Row *Cnwll* 3 SX0976
Row *Cumb* 59 SD4589
Row Green *Essex* 24 TL7420
Rowanburn *D & G* 67 NY4177
Rowardennan Hotel *Cent* 80 NS3698
Rowarth *Derbys* 48 SK0189
Rowberrow *Somset* 19 ST4558
Rowde *Wilts* 20 ST9762
Rowen *Gwynd* 45 SH7671
Rowfoot *Nthumb* 68 NY6860
Rowington *Warwks* 29 SP2069
Rowland *Derbys* 48 SK2172
Rowland's Castle *Hants* 11 SU7310
Rowland's Gill *T & W* 69 NZ1658
Rowledge *Surrey* 11 SU8243
Rowley *Dur* 68 NZ0848
Rowley *Humb* 56 SE9732
Rowley Green *W Mids* 39 SP3483
Rowley Regis *W Mids* 38 SO9787
Rowlstone *H & W* 27 SO3727
Rowner *Hants* 11 SU5801
Rowney Green *H & W* 38 SP0471
Rownhams *Hants* 10 SU3817
Rowsham *Bucks* 30 SP8417
Rowsley *Derbys* 48 SK2565
Rowston *Lincs* 50 TF0856
Rowton *Ches* 46 SJ4564
Rowton *Shrops* 37 SJ6119
Roxburgh *Border* 76 NT6930
Roxby *Humb* 56 SE9116
Roxton *Beds* 30 TL1554
Roxwell *Essex* 24 TL6408
Roy Bridge *Highld* 86 NN2681
Roydon *Essex* 23 TL4010
Roydon *Norfk* 42 TF7023
Roydon *Norfk* 33 TM1080
Roydon Hamlet *Essex* 23 TL4107
Royston *Herts* 31 TL3540
Royston *S York* 55 SE3611
Royton *Gt Man* 54 SD9107
Rozel *Jersey* 101 JS1914
Ruabon *Clwyd* 46 SJ3043
Ruaig *Strath* 78 NM0747
Ruan Lanihorne *Cnwll* 3 SW8942
Ruan Major *Cnwll* 2 SW7016
Ruan Minor *Cnwll* 2 SW7115
Ruardean *Gloucs* 27 SO6217
Ruardean Hill *Gloucs* 27 SO6317
Ruardean Woodside *Gloucs* 27 SO6216
Rubery *H & W* 38 SO9977
Ruckinge *Kent* 15 TR0233

Ruckley Scofton

Ruckley Shrops 37 SJ5300
Rudby N York 62 NZ4706
Rudchester Nthumb 69 NZ1167
Ruddington Notts 39 SK5732
Rudge Somset 20 ST8251
Rudgeway Avon 19 ST6386
Rudgwick W Susx 12 TQ0834
Rudheath Ches 47 SJ6772
Rudley Green Essex 24 TL8303
Rudloe Wilts 20 ST8470
Rudry M Glam 19 ST2086
Rudston Humb 57 TA0967
Rudyard Staffs 48 SJ9557
Ruecastle Border 76 NT6120
Rufford Lancs 53 SD4615
Rufforth N York 55 SE5251
Rugby Warwks 39 SP5075
Rugeley Staffs 38 SK0418
Ruishton Somset 8 ST2625
Ruislip Gt Lon 22 TQ0987
Ruletown Head Border 68 NT6113
Rumbach Gramp 94 NJ3852
Rumbling Bridge Tays 82 NT0199
Rumburgh Suffk 33 TM3481
Rumford Cent 75 NS9377
Rumford Cnwll 3 SW8970
Rumney S Glam 19 ST2178
Runcorn Ches 46 SJ5182
Runcton W Susx 11 SU8802
Runcton Holme Norfk 41 TF6109
Runfold Surrey 22 SU8647
Runhall Norfk 42 TG0507
Runham Norfk 43 TG4610
Runnington Somset 8 ST1221
Runswick N York 63 NZ8016
Runtaleave Tays 88 NO2867
Runwell Essex 24 TQ7594
Ruscombe Berks 22 SU7976
Rush Green Essex 25 TM1515
Rush Green Gt Lon 23 TQ5187
Rushall H & W 27 SO6435
Rushall Norfk 33 TM1982
Rushall Wilts 20 SU1255
Rushbrooke Suffk 32 TL8961
Rushbury Shrops 37 SO5191
Rushden Herts 31 TL3031
Rushden Nhants 30 SP9566
Rushford Norfk 32 TL9281
Rushlake Green E Susx 13 TQ6218
Rushmere Suffk 33 TM4986
Rushmoor Surrey 11 SU8740
Rushock H & W 27 SO3058
Rushock H & W 38 SO8871
Rusholme Gt Man 47 SJ8594
Rushton Ches 47 SJ5863
Rushton Nhants 40 SP8482
Rushton Spencer Staffs 48 SJ9362
Rushwick H & W 28 SO8254
Rushyford Dur 61 NZ2828
Ruskie Cent 81 NN6200
Ruskington Lincs 50 TF0851
Rusland Cumb 59 SD3488
Rusper W Susx 12 TQ2037
Ruspidge Gloucs 28 SO6611
Russ Hill Surrey 12 TQ2240
Russell's Water Oxon 22 SU7089
Rusthall Kent 13 TQ5639
Rustington W Susx 12 TQ0402
Ruston N York 63 SE9583
Ruston Parva Humb 57 TA0661
Ruswarp N York 63 NZ8809
Rutherford Border 76 NT6430
Rutherglen Strath 74 NS6161
Ruthernbridge Cnwll 3 SX0166
Ruthin Clwyd 46 SJ1258
Ruthrieston Gramp 89 NJ9204
Ruthven Gramp 94 NJ5046
Ruthven Highld 93 NH8132
Ruthven Highld 87 NN7699
Ruthven Tays 88 NO2848
Ruthven House Tays 88 NO3047
Ruthvoes Cnwll 3 SW9260
Ruthwell D & G 67 NY0967
Ruyton-XI-Towns Shrops 36 SJ3922
Ryal Nthumb 68 NZ0174
Ryall Dorset 8 SY4095
Ryall H & W 28 SO8640
Ryarsh Kent 14 TQ6660
Rydal Cumb 59 NY3606
Ryde IOW 11 SZ5992
Rye E Susx 14 TQ9220
Rye Foreign E Susx 14 TQ8922
Rye Street H & W 28 SO7835
Ryhall Leics 40 TF0310
Ryhope T & W 69 NZ4152
Ryland Lincs 50 TF0179
Rylands Notts 39 SK5335
Rylstone N York 54 SD9658
Ryme Intrinseca Dorset 9 ST5810
Ryther N York 56 SE5539
Ryton Shrops 37 SJ7602
Ryton T & W 69 NZ1564
Ryton-on-Dunsmore Warwks 39 SP3874

S

Sabden Lancs 54 SD7837
Sacombe Herts 31 TL3319
Sacombe Green Herts 31 TL3419
Sacriston T & W 69 NZ2447
Sadberge Dur 62 NZ3416
Saddell Strath 72 NR7832
Saddington Leics 39 SP6691
Saddle Bow Norfk 41 TF6015
Saddlescombe W Susx 12 TQ2711
Saffron Walden Essex 24 TL5438
Sageston Dyfed 16 SN0503
Saham Hills Norfk 42 TF9003
Saham Toney Norfk 42 TF8901
Saighton Ches 46 SJ4462
Saintbury Gloucs 28 SP1139
St Abbs Border 77 NT9167
St Agnes Cnwll 2 SW7150
St Agnes Loth 76 NT6763
St Albans Herts 22 TL1407
St Allen Cnwll 2 SW8250
St Andrew Guern 101 GN5007
St Andrew's Major S Glam 18 ST1371
St Andrews Fife 83 NO5116
St Andrews Well Dorset 8 SY4793
St Ann's D & G 66 NY0793
St Ann's Chapel Devon 5 SX6647
St Anne's Lancs 53 SD3228
St Anthony Cnwll 2 SW7825
St Anthony's Hill E Susx 13 TQ6201
St Arvans Gwent 19 ST5296
St Asaph Clwyd 45 SJ0374
St Athan S Glam 18 ST0167
St Aubin Jersey 101 JS1008
St Austell Cnwll 3 SX0152
St Bees Cumb 58 NX9711
St Blazey Cnwll 3 SX0654
St Boswells Border 76 NT5930
St Brelade Jersey 101 JS0809
St Brelades Bay Jersey 101 JS0808
St Breock Cnwll 3 SW9771
St Breward Cnwll 3 SX0977
St Briavels Gloucs 27 SO5604
St Bride's Major M Glam 18 SS8974
St Brides super-Ely S Glam 18 ST0977
St Brides Wentlooge Gwent 19 ST2982
St Budeaux Devon 4 SX4558
St Buryan Cnwll 2 SW4025
St Catherines Strath 80 NN1207
St Chloe Gloucs 20 SO8401
St Clears Dyfed 17 SN2816
St Cleer Cnwll 4 SX2468
St Clement Cnwll 3 SW8543
St Clement Jersey 101 JS1807
St Clether Cnwll 4 SX2084
St Colmac Strath 72 NS0467
St Columb Major Cnwll 3 SW9163
St Columb Minor Cnwll 3 SW8362
St Columb Road Cnwll 3 SW9159
St Combs Gramp 95 NK0563
St Cross South Elmham Suffk 33 TM2984
St Cyrus Gramp 89 NO7464
St David's Tays 82 NN9420
St Davids Dyfed 16 SM7525
St Day Cnwll 2 SW7242
St Decumans Somset 7 ST0642
St Dennis Cnwll 3 SW9557
St Dogmaels Dyfed 17 SN1645
St Donats S Glam 18 SS9368
St Endellion Cnwll 3 SW9978
St Enoder Cnwll 3 SW8956
St Erme Cnwll 3 SW8449
St Erney Cnwll 4 SX3759
St Erth Cnwll 2 SW5535
St Erth Praze Cnwll 2 SW5735
St Ervan Cnwll 3 SW8970
St Ewe Cnwll 3 SW9746
St Fagans S Glam 18 ST1277
St Fergus Gramp 95 NK0952
St Fillans Tays 81 NN6924
St Florence Dyfed 16 SN0801
St Gennys Cnwll 6 SX1497
St George Clwyd 45 SH9775
St George's S Glam 18 ST1076
St Georges Avon 19 ST3762
St Germans Cnwll 4 SX3657
St Giles in the Wood Devon 6 SS5319
St Giles-on-the-Heath Cnwll 4 SX3690
St Harmon Powys 35 SN9872
St Helen Auckland Dur 61 NZ1826
St Helena Norfk 43 TG1816
St Helens IOW 11 SZ6289
St Helens Mersyd 46 SJ5195
St Helier Gt Lon 23 TQ2567
St Helier Jersey 101 JS1508
St Hilary Cnwll 2 SW5431
St Hilary S Glam 18 ST0173
St Ibbs Herts 31 TL1926
St Illtyd Gwent 19 SO2202
St Ishmaels Dyfed 16 SM8307
St Issey Cnwll 3 SW9271
St Ive Cnwll 4 SX3167
St Ives Cambs 31 TL3171
St Ives Cnwll 2 SW5140
St Jame's End Nhants 30 SP7460
St James South Elmham Suffk 33 TM3281
St John Cnwll 4 SX4053
St John Jersey 101 JS1215
St John's IOM 52 SC2781
St John's Chapel Devon 6 SS5329
St John's Chapel Dur 60 NY8837
St John's Fen End Norfk 41 TF5312
St John's Kirk Strath 75 NS9836
St John's Town of Dalry D & G 65 NX6281
St John's Wood Gt Lon 23 TQ2683
St Johns H & W 28 SO8454
St Johns Kent 23 TQ5356
St Johns Surrey 22 SU9857
St Jude's IOM 52 SC3996
St Just Cnwll 2 SW3731
St Just Cnwll 3 SW8435
St Katherines Gramp 95 NJ7834
St Keverne Cnwll 2 SW7921
St Kew Cnwll 3 SX0276
St Kew Highway Cnwll 3 SX0375
St Keyne Cnwll 4 SX2461
St Laurence Kent 15 TR3665
St Lawrence Essex 25 TL9604
St Lawrence IOW 11 SZ5376
St Lawrence Jersey 101 JS1211
St Leonards Bucks 22 SP9007
St Leonards Dorset 10 SU1103
St Leonards E Susx 14 TQ8009
St Leonards Street Kent 14 TQ6756
St Levan Cnwll 2 SW3822
St Lythans S Glam 18 ST1072
St Mabyn Cnwll 3 SX0473
St Madoes Tays 82 NO1921
St Margaret South Elmham Suffk 33 TM3183
St Margaret's at Cliffe Kent 15 TR3544
St Margarets H & W 27 SO3533
St Margarets Herts 23 TL3811
St Margarets Hope Ork 103 ND4493
St Marks IOM 52 SC2974
St Martin Cnwll 4 SX2555
St Martin Guern 101 GN5206
St Martin Jersey 101 JS1912
St Martin's Tays 82 NO1530
St Martins Shrops 36 SJ3236
St Mary Jersey 101 JS1014
St Mary Bourne Hants 21 SU4250
St Mary Church S Glam 18 ST0071
St Mary Cray Gt Lon 23 TQ4768
St Mary in the Marsh Kent 15 TR0627
St Mary's Ork 103 HY4701
St Mary's Bay Kent 15 TR0827
St Mary's Hoo Kent 14 TQ8076
St Marychurch Devon 5 SX9166
St Marylebone Gt Lon 23 TQ2782
St Maughans Green Gwent 27 SO4717
St Mawes Cnwll 3 SW8433
St Mawgan Cnwll 3 SW8765
St Mellion Cnwll 4 SX3965
St Mellons S Glam 19 ST2281
St Merryn Cnwll 3 SW8874
St Mewan Cnwll 3 SW9951
St Michael Caerhays Cnwll 3 SW9642
St Michael Church Somset 8 ST3030
St Michael Penkevil Cnwll 3 SW8541
St Michael South Elmham Suffk 33 TM3483
St Michael's on Wyre Lancs 53 SD4641
St Michaels H & W 27 SO5865
St Michaels Kent 14 TQ8835
St Minver Cnwll 3 SW9677
St Monans Fife 83 NO5201
St Neot Cnwll 3 SX1868
St Neots Cambs 31 TL1860
St Newlyn East Cnwll 2 SW8256
St Nicholas Dyfed 16 SM9035
St Nicholas S Glam 18 ST0974
St Nicholas at Wade Kent 15 TR2666
St Ninians Cent 81 NS7991
St Olaves Norfk 43 TM4599
St Osyth Essex 25 TM1215
St Ouen Jersey 101 JS0713
St Owens Cross H & W 27 SO5324
St Paul's Walden Herts 31 TL1922
St Pauls Cray Gt Lon 23 TQ4768
St Peter Jersey 101 JS0911
St Peter Port Guern 101 GN5308
St Peter's Guern 101 GN4706
St Peter's Kent 15 TR3868
St Pinnock Cnwll 4 SX2063
St Quivox Strath 73 NS3723
St Sampson Guern 101 GN5411
St Saviour Guern 101 GN4807
St Saviour Jersey 101 JS0000
St Stephen Cnwll 3 SW9453
St Stephen's Coombe Cnwll 3 SW9451
St Stephens Cnwll 4 SX3285
St Stephens Cnwll 4 SX4158
St Teath Cnwll 3 SX0680
St Tudy Cnwll 3 SX0676
St Twynnells Dyfed 16 SR9597
St Veep Cnwll 3 SX1455
St Vigeans Tays 89 NO6443
St Wenn Cnwll 3 SW9664
St Weonards H & W 27 SO4924
Salachail Strath 86 NN0551
Salcombe Devon 5 SX7439
Salcombe Regis Devon 8 SY1588
Salcott Essex 25 TL9413
Sale Gt Man 47 SJ7991
Sale Green H & W 28 SO9358
Saleby Lincs 51 TF4578
Salehurst E Susx 14 TQ7524
Salem Dyfed 35 SN6684
Salem Gwynd 44 SH5456
Salen Highld 79 NM6864
Salen Strath 79 NM5743
Salford Beds 30 SP9339
Salford Gt Man 47 SJ8197
Salford Oxon 29 SP2828
Salford Priors Warwks 28 SP0751
Salfords Surrey 12 TQ2846
Salhouse Norfk 43 TG3114
Saline Fife 82 NT0292
Salisbury Wilts 10 SU1429
Salkeld Dykes Cumb 59 NY5437
Sallachy Highld 96 NC5408
Salle Norfk 43 TG1024
Salmonby Lincs 51 TF3273
Salperton Gloucs 28 SP0720
Salsburgh Strath 74 NS8262
Salt Staffs 38 SJ9527
Saltaire W York 55 SE1438
Saltash Cnwll 4 SX4258
Saltburn Highld 93 NH7270
Saltburn-by-the-Sea Cleve 62 NZ6621
Saltby Leics 40 SK8526
Saltcoats Strath 73 NS2441
Saltdean E Susx 13 TQ3802
Salterbeck Cumb 58 NX9926
Salterforth Lancs 54 SD8845
Salterton Wilts 10 SU1236
Saltfleet Lincs 51 TF4593
Saltfleetby All Saints Lincs 51 TF4590
Saltfleetby St. Clements Lincs 51 TF4691
Saltfleetby St. Peter Lincs 51 TF4489
Saltford Avon 20 ST6867
Salthouse Norfk 42 TG0743
Saltmarshe Humb 56 SE7824
Saltney Ches 46 SJ3865
Salton N York 63 SE7179
Saltrens Devon 6 SS4522
Saltwood Kent 15 TR1535
Salvington W Susx 12 TQ1205
Salwarpe H & W 28 SO8762
Salwayash Dorset 8 SY4596
Sambourne Warwks 28 SP0662
Sambrook Shrops 37 SJ7124
Samlesbury Lancs 54 SD5930
Sampford Arundel Somset 8 ST1118
Sampford Brett Somset 18 ST0741
Sampford Courtenay Devon 7 SS6301
Sampford Moor Somset 8 ST1118
Sampford Peverell Devon 7 ST0314
Sampford Spiney Devon 4 SX5372
Samsonlane Ork 103 HY6526
Samuelston Loth 76 NT4870
Sanaigmore Strath 70 NR2370
Sancreed Cnwll 2 SW4129
Sancton Humb 56 SE8939
Sand Hills W York 55 SE3739
Sand Hole Humb 56 SE8137
Sand Hutton N York 56 SE6958
Sandaig Highld 85 NG7102
Sandal Magna W York 55 SE3417
Sandavore Highld 84 NM4785
Sandbach Ches 47 SJ7560
Sandbank Strath 80 NS1680
Sandbanks Dorset 10 SZ0487
Sandend Gramp 94 NJ5566
Sanderstead Gt Lon 23 TQ3461
Sandford Avon 19 ST4259
Sandford Cumb 60 NY7316
Sandford Devon 7 SS8202
Sandford Hants 10 SU1601
Sandford IOW 11 SZ5381
Sandford Strath 74 NS7143
Sandford Orcas Dorset 9 ST6220
Sandford St. Martin Oxon 29 SP4226
Sandford-on-Thames Oxon 21 SP5301
Sandgate Kent 15 TR2035
Sandhaven Gramp 95 NJ9667
Sandhead D & G 64 NX0949
Sandhills Surrey 12 SU9337
Sandhoe Nthumb 68 NY9666
Sandhole Strath 80 NS0098
Sandholme Humb 56 SE8230
Sandhurst Berks 22 SU8361
Sandhurst Gloucs 28 SO8223
Sandhurst Kent 14 TQ8028
Sandhutton N York 62 SE3881
Sandilands Lincs 51 TF5280
Sandleheath Hants 10 SU1215
Sandley Dorset 9 ST7724
Sandness Shet 103 HU1957
Sandon Essex 24 TL7404
Sandon Herts 31 TL3234
Sandon Staffs 38 SJ9429
Sandon Bank Staffs 38 SJ9428
Sandown IOW 11 SZ5984
Sandplace Cnwll 4 SX2557
Sandridge Herts 23 TL1710
Sandringham Norfk 42 TF6928
Sandsend N York 63 NZ8612
Sandtoft Humb 56 SE7408
Sandwich Kent 15 TR3358
Sandwick Shet 103 HU4323
Sandwith Cumb 58 NX9614
Sandy Beds 31 TL1649
Sandy Lane Wilts 20 ST9668
Sandy Park Devon 5 SX7189
Sandyford D & G 67 NY2093
Sandygate Devon 5 SX8674
Sandygate IOM 52 SC3797
Sandyhills D & G 66 NX8855
Sandylands Lancs 53 SD4263
Sangobeg Highld 98 NC4266
Sangomore Highld 98 NC4067
Sankyn's Green H & W 28 SO7965
Sanna Bay Highld 79 NM4469
Sanquhar D & G 66 NS7809
Santon Bridge Cumb 58 NY1101
Santon Downham Suffk 32 TL8187
Sapcote Leics 39 SP4893
Sapey Common H & W 28 SO7064
Sapiston Suffk 32 TL9175
Sapperton Gloucs 20 SO9403
Sapperton Lincs 40 TF0133
Saracen's Head Lincs 41 TF3427
Sarclet Highld 100 ND3443
Sarisbury Hants 11 SU5008
Sarn Gwynd 44 SH2432
Sarn Powys 35 SN9597
Sarn Powys 36 SO2090
Sarnau Dyfed 17 SN3150
Sarnau Powys 36 SJ2315
Sarnesfield H & W 27 SO3750
Saron Dyfed 17 SN6012
Saron Gwynd 44 SH5365
Sarratt Herts 22 TQ0499
Sarre Kent 15 TR2565
Sarsden Oxon 29 SP2822
Satley Dur 69 NZ1143
Satterleigh Devon 7 SS6622
Satterthwaite Cumb 59 SD3392
Sauchen Gramp 95 NJ7011
Saucher Tays 82 NO1933
Sauchieburn Gramp 89 NO6669
Saul Gloucs 28 SO7409
Saundby Notts 50 SK7888
Saundersfoot Dyfed 16 SN1304
Saunderton Bucks 22 SP7901
Saunton Devon 6 SS4637
Sausthorpe Lincs 51 TF3868
Savile Town W York 55 SE2420
Sawbridge Warwks 29 SP5065
Sawbridgeworth Herts 31 TL4814
Sawdon N York 63 SE9485
Sawley Lancs 54 SD7746
Sawley N York 55 SE2467
Sawston Cambs 31 TL4849
Sawtry Cambs 40 TL1683
Saxby Leics 40 SK8219
Saxby Lincs 50 TF0086
Saxby All Saints Humb 56 SE9816
Saxelbye Leics 40 SK6921
Saxham Street Suffk 32 TM0861
Saxilby Lincs 50 SK8975
Saxlingham Norfk 42 TG0239
Saxlingham Green Norfk 43 TM2396
Saxlingham Nethergate Norfk 43 TM2297
Saxlingham Thorpe Norfk 43 TM2197
Saxmundham Suffk 33 TM3863
Saxon Street Cambs 32 TL6759
Saxondale Notts 49 SK6839
Saxtead Suffk 33 TM2665
Saxtead Green Suffk 33 TM2564
Saxtead Little Green Suffk 33 TM2466
Saxthorpe Norfk 43 TG1130
Saxton N York 55 SE4736
Sayers Common W Susx 12 TQ2618
Scackleton N York 56 SE6472
Scaftworth Notts 49 SK6691
Scagglethorpe N York 56 SE8372
Scalasaig Strath 70 NR3993
Scalby Humb 56 SE8429
Scalby N York 63 TA0090
Scaldwell Nhants 30 SP7672
Scaleby Cumb 67 NY4463
Scalebyhill Cumb 67 NY4463
Scales Cumb 59 NY3426
Scales Cumb 53 SD2772
Scalford Leics 40 SK7624
Scaling N York 63 NZ7413
Scalloway Shet 103 HU4039
Scamblesby Lincs 51 TF2778
Scamodale Highld 85 NM8373
Scampston N York 63 SE8575
Scampton Lincs 50 SK9579
Scaniport Highld 92 NH6239
Scapegoat Hill W York 55 SE0916
Scarborough N York 63 TA0488
Scarcewater Cnwll 3 SW9154
Scarcliffe Derbys 49 SK4968
Scarcroft Hill W York 55 SE3741
Scarfskerry Highld 100 ND2674
Scargill Dur 61 NZ0510
Scarinish Strath 78 NM0444
Scarisbrick Lancs 53 SD3713
Scarning Norfk 42 TF9512
Scarrington Notts 50 SK7341
Scartho Humb 57 TA2606
Scawby Humb 56 SE9605
Scawthorpe S York 56 SE5506
Scawton N York 62 SE5483
Scayne's Hill W Susx 12 TQ3623
Scethrog Powys 26 SO1025
Scholes Gt Man 47 SD5905
Scholes S York 49 SK3895
Scholes W York 55 SE1507
Scissett W York 55 SE2410
Scleddau Dyfed 16 SM9434
Scofton Notts 49 SK6280

Scole Skigersta

Scole *Norfk* **33** TM1579
Sconser *Highld* **84** NG5132
Scoonie *Fife* **83** NO3801
Scopwick *Lincs* **50** TF0757
Scoraig *Highld* **91** NH0096
Scorborough *Humb* **56** TA0145
Scorrier *Cnwll* **2** SW7244
Scorton *Lancs* **53** SD5048
Scorton *N York* **61** NZ2500
Scot's Gap *Nthumb* **68** NZ0386
Scotby *Cumb* **67** NY4455
Scotch Corner *N York* **61** NZ2105
Scotforth *Lancs* **53** SD4859
Scothern *Lincs* **50** TF0377
Scotlandwell *Tays* **82** NO1801
Scotscalder Station *Highld* **100** ND0956
Scotscraig *Fife* **83** NO4428
Scotsmill *Gramp* **94** NJ5618
Scotstoun *Strath* **74** NS5267
Scotswood *T & W* **69** NZ2063
Scotter *Lincs* **50** SE8800
Scotterthorpe *Lincs* **50** SE8701
Scotton *Lincs* **50** SK8899
Scotton *N York* **61** SE1895
Scotton *N York* **55** SE3259
Scoulton *Norfk* **42** TF9800
Scourie *Highld* **98** NC1544
Scouriemore *Highld* **98** NC1443
Scousburgh *Shet* **103** HU3717
Scrabster *Highld* **100** ND1070
Scraesburgh *Border* **76** NT6718
Scrane End *Lincs* **51** TF3841
Scraptoft *Leics* **39** SK6405
Scratby *Norfk* **43** TG5015
Scrayingham *N York* **56** SE7359
Scredington *Lincs* **50** TF0940
Screel *D & G* **66** NX8053
Scremby *Lincs* **51** TF4467
Scremerston *Nthumb* **77** NU0148
Screveton *Notts* **50** SK7343
Scriven *N York* **55** SE3458
Scrooby *Notts* **49** SK6590
Scropton *Derbys* **39** SK1930
Scrub Hill *Lincs* **51** TF2355
Scruschloch *Tays* **88** NO2357
Scruton *N York* **61** SE2992
Sculthorpe *Norfk* **42** TF8930
Scunthorpe *Humb* **56** SE8910
Sea Palling *Norfk* **43** TG4226
Seaborough *Dorset* **8** ST4206
Seabrook *Kent* **15** TR1835
Seaburn *T & W* **69** NZ4059
Seacroft *W York* **55** SE3635
Seafield *Highld* **90** NG4743
Seafield *Loth* **75** NT0066
Seaford *E Susx* **13** TV4899
Seaforth *Mersyd* **46** SJ3297
Seagrave *Leics* **39** SK6117
Seaham *Dur* **69** NZ4149
Seahouses *Nthumb* **77** NU2231
Seal *Kent* **23** TQ5556
Seale *Surrey* **22** SU8947
Seamer *N York* **62** NZ4910
Seamer *N York* **63** TA0183
Seamill *Strath* **73** NS2047
Searby *Lincs* **57** TA0705
Seasalter *Kent* **15** TR0864
Seascale *Cumb* **58** NY0301
Seathwaite *Cumb* **58** SD2295
Seatoller *Cumb* **58** NY2413
Seaton *Cnwll* **4** SX3054
Seaton *Cumb* **58** NY0130
Seaton *Devon* **8** SY2490
Seaton *Humb* **57** TA1646
Seaton *Kent* **15** TR2258
Seaton *Leics* **40** SP9098
Seaton *Nthumb* **69** NZ3276
Seaton Delaval *Nthumb* **69** NZ3075
Seaton Ross *Humb* **56** SE7040
Seaton Sluice *Nthumb* **69** NZ3376
Seatown *Dorset* **8** SY4291
Seave Green *N York* **62** NZ5500
Seaview *IOW* **11** SZ6291
Seaville *Cumb* **67** NY1553
Seavington St. Mary *Somset* **8** ST4014
Seavington St. Michael *Somset* **8** ST4015
Sebergham *Cumb* **59** NY3641
Seckington *Warwks* **39** SK2507
Sedbergh *Cumb* **60** SD6591
Sedbury *Gloucs* **19** ST5493
Sedbusk *N York* **60** SD8891
Sedgeberrow *H & W* **28** SP0238
Sedgebrook *Lincs* **40** SK8537
Sedgefield *Dur* **62** NZ3528
Sedgeford *Norfk* **42** TF7036
Sedgehill *Wilts* **9** ST8627
Sedgley *W Mids* **38** SO9193
Sedgwick *Cumb* **59** SD5186
Sedlescombe *E Susx* **14** TQ7818
Sedrup *Bucks* **22** SP8011
Seend *Wilts* **20** ST9460
Seend Cleeve *Wilts* **20** ST9360
Seer Green *Bucks* **22** SU9692
Seething *Norfk* **43** TM3197
Sefton *Mersyd* **46** SD3501
Seighford *Staffs* **38** SJ8825
Seion *Gwynd* **44** SH5466
Seisdon *Staffs* **38** SO8495
Selattyn *Shrops* **36** SJ2633
Selborne *Hants* **11** SU7433
Selby *N York* **56** SE6132
Selham *W Susx* **12** SU9320
Selhurst *Gt Lon* **23** TQ3267
Selkirk *Border* **76** NT4728
Sellack *H & W* **27** SO5627
Sellafirth *Shet* **103** HU5198
Sellick's Green *Somset* **8** ST2119
Sellindge *Kent* **15** TR0938
Selling *Kent* **15** TR0456
Sells Green *Wilts* **20** ST9462
Selly Oak *W Mids* **38** SP0482
Selmeston *E Susx* **13** TQ5007
Selsdon *Gt Lon* **23** TQ3562
Selsey *W Susx* **11** SZ8593
Selside *N York* **60** SD7875
Selstead *Kent* **15** TR2144
Selston *Notts* **49** SK4553
Selworthy *Somset* **7** SS9246
Semer *Suffk* **32** TL9946
Semington *Wilts* **20** ST8960
Semley *Wilts* **9** ST8926
Send *Surrey* **22** TQ0155
Senghenydd *M Glam* **18** ST1190
Sennen *Cnwll* **2** SW3525
Sennen Cove *Cnwll* **2** SW3526
Sennybridge *Powys* **26** SN9228
Sessay *N York* **62** SE4575
Setchey *Norfk* **41** TF6313
Seton Mains *Loth* **76** NT4275
Settle *N York* **54** SD8163
Settrington *N York* **56** SE8370
Seven Ash *Somset* **8** ST1533
Seven Kings *Gt Lon* **23** TQ4587
Seven Sisters *W Glam* **26** SN8208
Seven Wells *Gloucs* **28** SP1134
Sevenhampton *Gloucs* **28** SP0321
Sevenhampton *Wilts* **21** SU2090
Sevenoaks *Kent* **23** TQ5255
Sevenoaks Weald *Kent* **13** TQ5250
Severn Beach *Avon* **19** ST5484
Severn Stoke *H & W* **28** SO8644
Sevicks End *Beds* **30** TL0954
Sevington *Kent* **15** TR0340
Sewards End *Essex* **24** TL5738
Sewell *Beds* **30** SP9922
Sewerby *Humb* **57** TA1968
Seworgan *Cnwll* **2** SW7030
Sewstern *Leics* **40** SK8821
Shabbington *Bucks* **22** SP6606
Shackerstone *Leics* **39** SK3706
Shackleford *Surrey* **12** SU9345
Shader *W Isls* **102** NB3854
Shadforth *Dur* **62** NZ3440
Shadingfield *Suffk* **33** TM4384
Shadoxhurst *Kent* **15** TQ9737
Shadwell *Norfk* **32** TL9383
Shaftenhoe End *Herts* **31** TL4037
Shaftesbury *Dorset* **9** ST8623
Shafton *S York* **55** SE3911
Shalbourne *Wilts* **21** SU3163
Shalden *Hants* **11** SU6941
Shaldon *Devon* **5** SX9372
Shalfleet *IOW* **10** SZ4189
Shalford *Essex* **24** TL7229
Shalford *Surrey* **12** TQ0047
Shalford Green *Essex* **24** TL7127
Shalmsford Street *Kent* **15** TR0954
Shalstone *Bucks* **29** SP6436
Shamley Green *Surrey* **12** TQ0343
Shandford *Tays* **89** NO4962
Shandon *Strath* **80** NS2586
Shandwick *Highld* **97** NH8575
Shangton *Leics* **40** SP7196
Shanklin *IOW* **11** SZ5881
Shap *Cumb* **59** NY5615
Shapwick *Dorset* **9** ST9301
Shapwick *Somset* **19** ST4138
Shardlow *Derbys* **39** SK4330
Shareshill *Staffs* **38** SJ9406
Sharlston *W York* **55** SE3918
Sharnbrook *Beds* **30** SP9959
Sharnford *Leics* **39** SP4891
Sharoe Green *Lancs* **53** SD5333
Sharow *N York* **55** SE3371
Sharpenhoe *Beds* **30** TL0630
Sharperton *Nthumb* **68** NT9503
Sharpness *Gloucs* **20** SO6702
Sharrington *Norfk* **42** TG0337
Shatterford *H & W* **37** SO7981
Shaugh Prior *Devon* **4** SX5463
Shavington *Ches* **47** SJ6951
Shaw *Berks* **21** SU4768
Shaw *Gt Man* **54** SD9308
Shaw *Wilts* **20** ST8965
Shaw Mills *N York* **55** SE2562
Shawbost *W Isls* **102** NB2646
Shawbury *Shrops* **37** SJ5521
Shawell *Leics* **39** SP5480
Shawford *Hants* **10** SU4625
Shawhead *D & G* **66** NX8675
Shearington *D & G* **66** NY0266
Shearsby *Leics* **39** SP6290
Shearston *Somset* **8** ST2830
Shebbear *Devon* **6** SS4409
Shebdon *Staffs* **37** SJ7625
Shebster *Highld* **100** ND0164
Shedfield *Hants* **11** SU5613
Sheen *Derbys* **48** SK1161
Sheepscar *W York* **55** SE3134
Sheepscombe *Gloucs* **28** SO8910
Sheepstor *Devon* **5** SX5667
Sheepwash *Devon* **6** SS4806
Sheepy Magna *Leics* **39** SK3201
Sheepy Parva *Leics* **39** SK3301
Sheering *Essex* **31** TL5014
Sheerness *Kent* **14** TQ9174
Sheerwater *Surrey* **22** TQ0461
Sheet *Hants* **11** SU7524
Sheffield *S York* **49** SK3587
Shefford *Beds* **30** TL1439
Shegra *Highld* **98** NC1860
Sheinton *Shrops* **37** SJ6003
Shelderton *Shrops* **36** SO4077
Sheldon *Derbys* **48** SK1768
Sheldon *Devon* **8** ST1208
Sheldon *W Mids* **38** SP1584
Sheldwich *Kent* **15** TR0156
Shelfanger *Norfk* **33** TM1083
Shelford *Notts* **49** SK6642
Shellacres *Border* **77** NT8943
Shelley *Suffk* **25** TM0238
Shelley *W York* **55** SE2011
Shellingford *Oxon* **21** SU3193
Shellow Bowells *Essex* **24** TL6007
Shelsley Beauchamp *H & W* **28** SO7363
Shelsley Walsh *H & W* **28** SO7263
Shelton *Beds* **30** TL0368
Shelton *Norfk* **33** TM2291
Shelton *Notts* **50** SK7844
Shelton Under Harley *Staffs* **37** SJ8139
Shelve *Shrops* **36** SO3399
Shelwick *H & W* **27** SO5242
Shenfield *Essex* **24** TQ6095
Shenington *Oxon* **29** SP3742
Shenley *Herts* **23** TL1800
Shenley Brook End *Bucks* **30** SP8335
Shenley Church End *Bucks* **30** SP8336
Shenmore *H & W* **27** SO3937
Shennanton *D & G* **64** NX3363
Shenstone *H & W* **38** SO8673
Shenstone *Staffs* **38** SK1004
Shenton *Leics* **39** SK3800
Shephall *Herts* **31** TL2623
Shepherd's Bush *Gt Lon* **23** TQ2380
Shepherd's Green *Oxon* **22** SU7183
Shepherdswell *Kent* **15** TR2647
Shepley *W York* **55** SE1909
Shepperton *Surrey* **22** TQ0766
Shepreth *Cambs* **31** TL3947
Shepshed *Leics* **39** SK4819
Shepton Beauchamp *Somset* **8** ST4017
Shepton Mallet *Somset* **19** ST6143
Shepton Montague *Somset* **9** ST6831
Shepway *Kent* **14** TQ7753
Sheraton *Dur* **62** NZ4435
Sherborne *Dorset* **9** ST6316
Sherborne *Gloucs* **28** SP1614
Sherborne *Somset* **19** ST5855
Sherborne St. John *Hants* **21** SU6255
Sherbourne *Warwks* **29** SP2661
Sherburn *Dur* **62** NZ3142
Sherburn *N York* **63** SE9576
Sherburn Hill *Dur* **62** NZ3342
Sherburn in Elmet *N York* **55** SE4933
Shere *Surrey* **12** TQ0747
Shereford *Norfk* **42** TF8829
Sherfield English *Hants* **10** SU2922
Sherfield on Loddon *Hants* **22** SU6858
Sherford *Devon* **5** SX7844
Sherford *Dorset* **9** SY9193
Sheriff Hutton *N York* **56** SE6566
Sheriffhales *Shrops* **37** SJ7512
Sheringham *Norfk* **43** TG1543
Sherington *Bucks* **30** SP8846
Shernborne *Norfk* **42** TF7132
Sherrington *Wilts* **20** ST9639
Sherston *Wilts* **20** ST8586
Sherwood *Notts* **49** SK5643
Shettleston *Strath* **74** NS6464
Shevington *Gt Man* **47** SD5408
Sheviock *Cnwll* **4** SX3755
Shibden Head *W York* **55** SE0928
Shide *IOW* **11** SZ5088
Shidlaw *Nthumb* **76** NT8037
Shiel Bridge *Highld* **85** NG9318
Shieldaig *Highld* **91** NG8154
Shieldhill *Cent* **74** NS8976
Shieldhill *D & G* **66** NY0385
Shieldhill House Hotel *Strath* **75** NT0040
Shields *Strath* **74** NS7755
Shielhill *Strath* **80** NS2472
Shielhill *Tays* **88** NO4257
Shifnal *Shrops* **37** SJ7407
Shilbottle *Nthumb* **69** NU1908
Shildon *Dur* **61** NZ2226
Shillingford *Devon* **7** SS9824
Shillingford *Oxon* **21** SU5992
Shillingford Abbot *Devon* **5** SX9088
Shillingford St. George *Devon* **5** SX9087
Shillingstone *Dorset* **9** ST8211
Shillington *Beds* **30** TL1234
Shilton *Oxon* **29** SP2608
Shilton *Warwks* **39** SP4084
Shimpling *Norfk* **33** TM1583
Shimpling *Suffk* **32** TL8651
Shimpling Street *Suffk* **32** TL8753
Shincliffe *Dur* **61** NZ2940
Shinfield *Berks* **22** SU7368
Shinness *Highld* **96** NC5215
Shipbourne *Kent* **13** TQ5952
Shipdham *Norfk* **42** TF9507
Shipham *Somset* **19** ST4457
Shiphay *Devon* **5** SX8965
Shiplake *Oxon* **22** SU7678
Shiplake Row *Oxon* **22** SU7478
Shipley *W Susx* **12** TQ1421
Shipley *W York* **55** SE1537
Shipley Bridge *Surrey* **12** TQ3040
Shipmeadow *Suffk* **33** TM3790
Shippon *Oxon* **21** SU4898
Shipston on Stour *Warwks* **29** SP2540
Shipton *Gloucs* **28** SP0318
Shipton *N York* **56** SE5558
Shipton *Shrops* **37** SO5692
Shipton Bellinger *Hants* **21** SU2345
Shipton Gorge *Dorset* **8** SY4991
Shipton Green *W Susx* **11** SZ8099
Shipton Moyne *Gloucs* **20** ST8989
Shipton-on-Cherwell *Oxon* **29** SP4716
Shipton-under-Wychwood *Oxon* **29** SP2817
Shiptonthorpe *Humb* **56** SE8543
Shirburn *Oxon* **22** SU6995
Shirdley Hill *Lancs* **53** SD3612
Shirebrook *Notts* **49** SK5267
Shiregreen *S York* **49** SK3691
Shirehampton *Avon* **19** ST5376
Shiremoor *T & W* **69** NZ3171
Shirenewton *Gwent* **19** ST4793
Shireoaks *Notts* **49** SK5580
Shirland *Derbys* **49** SK4058
Shirley *Derbys* **48** SK2141
Shirley *Gt Lon* **23** TQ3565
Shirley *Hants* **10** SU4014
Shirley *W Mids* **38** SP1278
Shirrell Heath *Hants* **11** SU5714
Shirven *Strath* **71** NR8784
Shirwell *Devon* **6** SS6037
Shirwell Cross *Devon* **6** SS5936
Shobdon *H & W* **27** SO4062
Shobrooke *Devon* **7** SS8601
Shoby *Leics* **39** SK6820
Shoeburyness *Essex* **25** TQ9385
Sholden *Kent* **15** TR3552
Sholing *Hants* **10** SU4511
Shop *Cnwll* **6** SS2214
Shop *Cnwll* **3** SW8773
Shop Street *Suffk* **33** TM2268
Shoreditch *Gt Lon* **23** TQ3382
Shoreditch *Somset* **8** ST2422
Shoreham *Kent* **23** TQ5161
Shoreham-by-Sea *W Susx* **12** TQ2105
Shorley *Hants* **11** SU5726
Shorne *Kent* **14** TQ6971
Shortgate *E Susx* **13** TQ4915
Shortlanesend *Cnwll* **2** SW8047
Shorwell *IOW* **10** SZ4583
Shoscombe *Avon* **20** ST7156
Shotesham *Norfk* **43** TM2499
Shotgate *Essex* **24** TQ7592
Shotley *Suffk* **25** TM2335
Shotley Gate *Suffk* **25** TM2433
Shotley Street *Suffk* **25** TM2335
Shottenden *Kent* **15** TR0454
Shottery *Warwks* **29** SP1854
Shotteswell *Warwks* **29** SP4245
Shottisham *Suffk* **33** TM3244
Shottle *Derbys* **49** SK3149
Shottlegate *Derbys* **49** SK3147
Shotton *Clwyd* **46** SJ3168
Shotton *Dur* **62** NZ4139
Shotwick *Ches* **46** SJ3371
Shougle *Gramp* **94** NJ2155
Shouldham *Norfk* **42** TF6709
Shouldham Thorpe *Norfk* **42** TF6607
Shoulton *H & W* **28** SO8159
Shrawardine *Shrops* **36** SJ3915
Shrawley *H & W* **28** SO8065
Shrewley *Warwks* **29** SP2167
Shrewsbury *Shrops* **37** SJ4912
Shrewton *Wilts* **20** SU0743
Shripney *W Susx* **12** SU9302
Shrivenham *Oxon* **21** SU2389
Shropham *Norfk* **42** TL9893
Shucknall *H & W* **27** SO5842
Shudy Camps *Cambs* **32** TL6244
Shurdington *Gloucs* **28** SO9218
Shurlock Row *Berks* **22** SU8374
Shurrery *Highld* **100** ND0458
Shurrery Lodge *Highld* **100** ND0456
Shurton *Somset* **19** ST2044
Shustoke *Warwks* **39** SP2290
Shut Heath *Staffs* **38** SJ8621
Shute *Devon* **8** SY2597
Shutford *Oxon* **29** SP3840
Shuthonger *Gloucs* **28** SO8935
Shutlanger *Nhants* **30** SP7249
Shuttington *Warwks* **39** SK2505
Shuttlewood *Derbys* **49** SK4673
Shuttleworth *Lancs* **54** SD8017
Sibbertoft *Nhants* **39** SP6882
Sibdon Carwood *Shrops* **36** SO4183
Sibford Ferris *Oxon* **29** SP3537
Sibford Gower *Oxon* **29** SP3537
Sible Hedingham *Essex* **24** TL7734
Sibley's Green *Essex* **24** TL6128
Sibsey *Lincs* **51** TF3550
Sibson *Cambs* **40** TL0997
Sibson *Leics* **39** SK3500
Sibster *Highld* **100** ND3253
Sibthorpe *Notts* **49** SK7273
Sibthorpe *Notts* **50** SK7645
Sicklesmere *Suffk* **32** TL8760
Sicklinghall *N York* **55** SE3648
Sidbury *Devon* **8** SY1391
Sidbury *Shrops* **37** SO6885
Sidcot *Somset* **19** ST4257
Sidcup *Gt Lon* **23** TQ4672
Siddington *Ches* **47** SJ8470
Siddington *Gloucs* **20** SU0399
Sidestrand *Norfk* **43** TG2539
Sidford *Devon* **8** SY1390
Sidlesham *W Susx* **11** SZ8599
Sidley *E Susx* **14** TQ7408
Sidmouth *Devon* **8** SY1287
Sigglesthorne *Humb* **57** TA1545
Sigingstone *S Glam* **18** SS9771
Silchester *Hants* **21** SU6261
Sileby *Leics* **39** SK6015
Silecroft *Cumb* **58** SD1381
Silfield *Norfk* **43** TM1299
Silk Willoughby *Lincs* **50** TF0542
Silkstone *S York* **55** SE2805
Silkstone Common *S York* **55** SE2904
Silksworth *T & W* **69** NZ3752
Silloth *Cumb* **67** NY1153
Silpho *N York* **63** SE9692
Silsden *W York* **55** SE0446
Silsoe *Beds* **30** TL0835
Silver End *Beds* **30** TL1042
Silver End *Essex* **24** TL8119
Silver Street *H & W* **38** SP0776
Silverburn *Loth* **75** NT2060
Silverdale *Lancs* **59** SD4674
Silverdale *Staffs* **47** SJ8146
Silverford *Gramp* **95** NJ7763
Silverstone *Nhants* **30** SP6743
Silverton *Devon* **7** SS9502
Silvington *Shrops* **37** SO6279
Simonburn *Nthumb* **68** NY8773
Simons Burrow *Devon* **8** ST1416
Simonsbath *Somset* **7** SS7739
Simonstone *Lancs* **54** SD7734
Simpson *Bucks* **30** SP8836
Simpson Cross *Dyfed* **16** SM8919
Sinclair's Hill *Border* **76** NT8150
Sinclairston *Strath* **73** NS4716
Sinderby *N York* **62** SE3482
Sinderland Green *Gt Man* **47** SJ7389
Sindlesham *Berks* **22** SU7769
Singleton *Lancs* **53** SD3838
Singleton *W Susx* **11** SU8713
Singlewell *Kent* **14** TQ6570
Sinnarhard *Gramp* **94** NJ4713
Sinnington *N York* **63** SE7485
Sinton *H & W* **28** SO8160
Sinton Green *H & W* **28** SO8160
Sissinghurst *Kent* **14** TQ7937
Siston *Avon* **20** ST6875
Sithney *Cnwll* **2** SW6328
Sittingbourne *Kent* **14** TQ9063
Six Ashes *Staffs* **37** SO7988
Six Mile Bottom *Cambs* **31** TL5756
Six Rues *Jersey* **101** JS1113
Sixhills *Lincs* **50** TF1787
Sixpenny Handley *Dorset* **9** ST9917
Skaill *Ork* **103** HY5806
Skares *Strath* **74** NS5317
Skateraw *Loth* **76** NT7375
Skeabost *Highld* **90** NG4148
Skeeby *N York* **61** NZ1902
Skeffington *Leics* **40** SK7402
Skeffling *Humb* **57** TA3719
Skegby *Notts* **49** SK4961
Skegby *Notts* **50** SK7869
Skegness *Lincs* **51** TF5663
Skelbo *Highld* **97** NH7895
Skelbo Street *Highld* **97** NH7994
Skelbrooke *S York* **55** SE5012
Skeldyke *Lincs* **41** TF3337
Skellingthorpe *Lincs* **50** SK9272
Skelmanthorpe *W York* **55** SE2310
Skelmersdale *Lancs* **46** SD4606
Skelmorlie *Strath* **73** NS1967
Skelpick *Highld* **99** NC7256
Skelston *D & G* **66** NX8825
Skelton *Cleve* **62** NZ6618
Skelton *Cumb* **59** NY4335
Skelton *Humb* **56** SE7625
Skelton *N York* **55** SE3668
Skelton *N York* **56** SE5756
Skelwith Bridge *Cumb* **59** NY3403
Skendleby *Lincs* **51** TF4369
Skene House *Gramp* **95** NJ7610
Skenfrith *Gwent* **27** SO4520
Skerne *Humb* **57** TA0455
Skerray *Highld* **99** NC6563
Skerricha *Highld* **98** NC2350
Skerton *Lancs* **53** SD4763
Sketchley *Leics* **39** SP4292
Sketty *W Glam* **17** SS6292
Skewsby *N York* **56** SE6270
Skiall *Highld* **100** ND0267
Skidby *Humb* **56** TA0133
Skigersta *W Isls* **102** NB5461

Skilgate Stanmore

Skilgate *Somset*	7	SS9827
Skillington *Lincs*	40	SK8925
Skinburness *Cumb*	67	NY1256
Skinflats *Cent*	82	NS9082
Skinidin *Highld*	90	NG2247
Skipness *Strath*	71	NR9057
Skipsea *Humb*	57	TA1654
Skipton *N York*	54	SD9851
Skipton-on-Swale *N York*	62	SE3679
Skipwith *N York*	56	SE6638
Skirling *Border*	75	NT0739
Skirmett *Bucks*	22	SU7790
Skirpenbeck *Humb*	56	SE7456
Skirwith *Cumb*	59	NY6132
Skirza *Highld*	100	ND3868
Skulamus *Highld*	85	NG6622
Skullomie *Highld*	99	NC6161
Skye Green *Essex*	24	TL8722
Skye of Curr *Highld*	93	NH9924
Slack *W York*	54	SD9728
Slacks of Cairnbanno *Gramp*	95	NJ8445
Slad *Gloucs*	28	SO8707
Slade *Devon*	6	SS5046
Slade *Somset*	7	SS8327
Slade Green *Kent*	23	TQ5276
Slade Hooton *S York*	49	SK5288
Slaggan *Highld*	91	NG8494
Slaggyford *Nthumb*	68	NY6752
Slagnaw *D & G*	65	NX7458
Slaidburn *Lancs*	54	SD7152
Slaithwaite *W York*	55	SE0813
Slaley *Nthumb*	68	NY9657
Slamannan *Cent*	74	NS8572
Slapton *Bucks*	30	SP9320
Slapton *Devon*	5	SX8245
Slapton *Nhants*	29	SP6446
Slaugham *W Susx*	12	TQ2528
Slaughterford *Wilts*	20	ST8473
Slawston *Leics*	40	SP7894
Sleaford *Hants*	11	SU8038
Sleaford *Lincs*	50	TF0645
Sleagill *Cumb*	59	NY5919
Sleapford *Shrops*	37	SJ6315
Sleasdairidh *Highld*	97	NH6496
Sledmere *Humb*	56	SE9364
Sleightholme *Dur*	61	NY9510
Sleights *N York*	63	NZ8607
Slickly *Highld*	100	ND2966
Sliddery *Strath*	72	NR9323
Sligachan *Highld*	84	NG4829
Sligrachan *Strath*	80	NS1791
Slimbridge *Gloucs*	20	SO7303
Slindon *Staffs*	38	SJ8232
Slindon *W Susx*	12	SU9608
Slinfold *W Susx*	12	TQ1131
Slingsby *N York*	62	SE6974
Slip End *Beds*	30	TL0718
Slip End *Herts*	31	TL2837
Slipton *Nhants*	40	SP9579
Slitting Mill *Staffs*	38	SK0217
Slockavullin *Strath*	71	NR8297
Slogarie *D & G*	65	NX6568
Sloncombe *Devon*	5	SX7386
Sloothby *Lincs*	51	TF4970
Slough *Berks*	22	SU9879
Slough Green *Somset*	8	ST2719
Slumbay *Highld*	85	NG8938
Slyne *Lancs*	53	SD4765
Smailholm *Border*	76	NT6436
Small Dole *W Susx*	12	TQ2112
Small Heath *W Mids*	38	SP1085
Small Hythe *Kent*	14	TQ8930
Smallburgh *Norfk*	43	TG3324
Smalley *Derbys*	49	SK4044
Smallfield *Surrey*	12	TQ3143
Smallridge *Devon*	8	ST3001
Smallworth *Norfk*	32	TM0080
Smannell *Hants*	21	SU3749
Smarden *Kent*	14	TQ8742
Smarden Bell *Kent*	14	TQ8742
Smart's Hill *Kent*	13	TQ5242
Smearisary *Highld*	85	NM6476
Smeatharpe *Devon*	8	ST1910
Smeeth *Kent*	15	TR0739
Smeeton Westerby *Leics*	39	SP6892
Smerral *Highld*	100	ND1733
Smestow *Staffs*	38	SO8591
Smethwick *W Mids*	38	SP0287
Smisby *Derbys*	39	SK3418
Smith's Green *Essex*	32	TL6640
Smithfield *Cumb*	67	NY4465
Smithstown *Highld*	91	NG7977
Smithton *Highld*	93	NH7145
Smoo *Highld*	98	NC4167
Smythe's Green *Essex*	24	TL9218
Snade *D & G*	66	NX8485
Snailwell *Cambs*	32	TL6467
Snainton *N York*	63	SE9282
Snaith *Humb*	56	SE6422
Snape *N York*	61	SE2684
Snape *Suffk*	33	TM3959
Snape Street *Suffk*	33	TM3958
Snarestone *Leics*	39	SK3409
Snarford *Lincs*	50	TF0482
Snargate *Kent*	15	TQ9928
Snave *Kent*	15	TR0129
Sneaton *N York*	63	NZ8907
Snelland *Lincs*	50	TF0780
Snelston *Derbys*	48	SK1543
Snetterton *Norfk*	32	TL9991
Snettisham *Norfk*	42	TF6834
Snig's End *Gloucs*	28	SO7828
Snitter *Nthumb*	68	NU0203
Snitterby *Lincs*	50	SK9894
Snitterfield *Warwks*	29	SP2159
Snitton *Shrops*	37	SO5575
Snodland *Kent*	14	TQ7061
Snow End *Herts*	31	TL4032
Snowshill *Gloucs*	28	SP0933
Soake *Hants*	11	SU6611
Soberton *Hants*	11	SU6116
Soberton Heath *Hants*	11	SU6014
Sockburn *Nthumb*	62	NZ3406
Soham *Cambs*	31	TL5973
Soldridge *Hants*	11	SU6535
Sole Street *Kent*	15	TR0949
Solihull *W Mids*	38	SP1679
Sollas *W Isls*	102	NF8074
Sollers Dilwyn *H & W*	27	SO4255
Sollers Hope *H & W*	27	SO6132
Solva *Dyfed*	16	SM8024
Solwaybank *D & G*	67	NY3077
Somerby *Leics*	40	SK7710
Somerby *Lincs*	57	TA0606
Somercotes *Derbys*	49	SK4253
Somerford Keynes *Gloucs*	20	SU0195
Somerley *W Susx*	11	SZ8198
Somerleyton *Suffk*	43	TM4897
Somersal Herbert *Derbys*	38	SK1335
Somersby *Lincs*	51	TF3472
Somersham *Cambs*	31	TL3678
Somersham *Suffk*	32	TM0848
Somerton *Oxon*	29	SP4928
Somerton *Somset*	8	ST4928
Somerton *Suffk*	32	TL8153
Sompting *W Susx*	12	TQ1505
Sonning *Berks*	22	SU7575
Sonning Common *Oxon*	22	SU7180
Sonning Eye *Oxon*	22	SU7476
Sopley *Hants*	10	SZ1596
Sopworth *Wilts*	20	ST8286
Sorbie *D & G*	64	NX4346
Sordale *Highld*	100	ND1462
Sorisdale *Strath*	78	NM2763
Sorn *Strath*	74	NS5526
Sortat *Highld*	100	ND2863
Sosgill *Cumb*	58	NY1024
Sotby *Lincs*	51	TF2078
Sots Hole *Lincs*	50	TF1264
Sotterly *Suffk*	33	TM4484
Sotwell *Oxon*	21	SU5890
Soughton *Clwyd*	46	SJ2466
Soulbury *Bucks*	30	SP8826
Soulby *Cumb*	60	NY7411
Souldern *Oxon*	29	SP5231
Souldrop *Beds*	30	SP9861
Sound Muir *Gramp*	94	NJ3652
Soundwell *Avon*	19	ST6575
Sourton *Devon*	4	SX5390
Soutergate *Cumb*	58	SD2281
South Acre *Norfk*	42	TF8114
South Alkham *Kent*	15	TR2441
South Allington *Devon*	5	SX7938
South Alloa *Cent*	82	NS8791
South Ambersham *W Susx*	11	SU9120
South Anston *S York*	49	SK5183
South Ashford *Kent*	15	TR0041
South Baddesley *Hants*	10	SZ3596
South Bank *N York*	56	SE5950
South Barrow *Somset*	9	ST6028
South Beddington *Gt Lon*	23	TQ2863
South Benfleet *Essex*	24	TQ7787
South Bersted *W Susx*	12	SU9300
South Bramwith *S York*	56	SE6211
South Brent *Devon*	5	SX6960
South Brewham *Somset*	20	ST7236
South Broomhill *Nthumb*	69	NZ2499
South Burlingham *Norfk*	43	TG3807
South Cadbury *Somset*	9	ST6325
South Cairn *D & G*	64	NW9769
South Carlton *Lincs*	50	SK9476
South Carlton *Notts*	49	SK5883
South Cave *Humb*	56	SE9230
South Cerney *Gloucs*	20	SU0497
South Charlton *Nthumb*	77	NU1620
South Cheriton *Somset*	9	ST6924
South Church *Dur*	61	NZ2128
South Cliffe *Humb*	56	SE8735
South Clifton *Notts*	50	SK8270
South Collingham *Notts*	50	SK8261
South Cornelly *M Glam*	18	SS8280
South Cove *Suffk*	33	TM4981
South Creake *Norfk*	42	TF8536
South Croxton *Leics*	39	SK6810
South Dalton *Humb*	56	SE9645
South Duffield *N York*	56	SE6833
South Elkington *Lincs*	51	TF2988
South Elmsall *W York*	55	SE4711
South Erradale *Highld*	91	NG7471
South Fambridge *Essex*	24	TQ8694
South Fawley *Berks*	21	SU3880
South Feorline *Strath*	72	NR9028
South Ferriby *Humb*	56	SE9820
South Field *Humb*	56	TA0225
South Gorley *Hants*	10	SU1610
South Gosworth *T & W*	69	NZ2467
South Green *Essex*	24	TQ6893
South Green *Kent*	14	TQ8560
South Green *Norfk*	42	TG0510
South Hanningfield *Essex*	24	TQ7497
South Harting *W Susx*	11	SU7819
South Hayling *Hants*	11	SZ7299
South Heath *Bucks*	22	SP9101
South Hetton *Cleve*	69	NZ3845
South Hiendley *W York*	55	SE3912
South Hill *Cnwll*	4	SX3272
South Hinksey *Oxon*	29	SP5104
South Holmwood *Surrey*	12	TQ1744
South Hornchurch *Gt Lon*	23	TQ5183
South Huish *Devon*	5	SX6941
South Hykeham *Lincs*	50	SK9364
South Hylton *T & W*	69	NZ3556
South Kelsey *Lincs*	50	TF0498
South Kessock *Highld*	93	NH6547
South Killingholme *Humb*	57	TA1416
South Kilvington *N York*	62	SE4284
South Kilworth *Nhants*	39	SP6081
South Kirkby *W York*	55	SE4410
South Kyme *Lincs*	50	TF1749
South Lambeth *Gt Lon*	23	TQ3077
South Lawn *Oxon*	29	SP2814
South Leigh *Oxon*	29	SP3909
South Leverton *Notts*	50	SK7881
South Lopham *Norfk*	32	TM0481
South Luffenham *Leics*	40	SK9301
South Mains *D & G*	66	NS7807
South Malling *E Susx*	13	TQ4210
South Marston *Wilts*	21	SU1987
South Milford *N York*	55	SE4931
South Milton *Devon*	5	SX7042
South Mimms *Herts*	23	TL2201
South Molton *Devon*	7	SS7125
South Moor *Dur*	69	NZ1951
South Moreton *Oxon*	21	SU5688
South Mundham *W Susx*	11	SU8700
South Newbald *Humb*	56	SE9035
South Newington *Oxon*	29	SP4033
South Newton *Wilts*	10	SU0834
South Normanton *Derbys*	49	SK4456
South Norwood *Gt Lon*	23	TQ3368
South Ockendon *Essex*	24	TQ5983
South Ormsby *Lincs*	51	TF3675
South Otterington *N York*	62	SE3787
South Owersby *Lincs*	50	TF0693
South Park *Surrey*	12	TQ2448
South Perrott *Dorset*	8	ST4706
South Petherton *Somset*	8	ST4316
South Petherwin *Cnwll*	4	SX3181
South Pickenham *Norfk*	42	TF8504
South Pill *Cnwll*	4	SX4259
South Pool *Devon*	5	SX7740
South Poorton *Dorset*	8	SY5297
South Queensferry *Loth*	82	NT1378
South Radworthy *Devon*	7	SS7432
South Rauceby *Lincs*	50	TF0245
South Raynham *Norfk*	42	TF8723
South Reston *Lincs*	51	TF4083
South Runcton *Norfk*	41	TF6308
South Scarle *Notts*	50	SK8463
South Shian *Strath*	79	NM9042
South Shields *T & W*	69	NZ3666
South Shore *Lancs*	53	SD3033
South Skirlaugh *Humb*	57	TA1438
South Stainley *N York*	55	SE3063
South Stoke *Avon*	20	ST7461
South Stoke *Oxon*	21	SU5983
South Stoke *W Susx*	12	TQ0209
South Street *E Susx*	13	TQ3918
South Street *Kent*	15	TR0557
South Street *Kent*	15	TR1265
South Tarbrax *Strath*	75	NT0353
South Tawton *Devon*	7	SX6594
South Thoresby *Lincs*	51	TF4076
South Tidworth *Hants*	21	SU2347
South Walsham *Norfk*	43	TG3613
South Warnborough *Hants*	22	SU7247
South Weald *Essex*	24	TQ5694
South Weston *Oxon*	22	SU7098
South Wheatley *Cnwll*	4	SX2492
South Widcombe *Somset*	19	ST5856
South Wigston *Leics*	39	SP5897
South Willesborough *Kent*	15	TR0240
South Willingham *Lincs*	50	TF1983
South Wingate *Dur*	62	NZ4134
South Wingfield *Derbys*	49	SK3755
South Witham *Lincs*	40	SK9219
South Woodham Ferrers *Essex*	24	TQ8097
South Wootton *Norfk*	42	TF6422
South Wraxall *Wilts*	20	ST8364
South Zeal *Devon*	5	SX6593
Southall *Gt Lon*	22	TQ1279
Southam *Gloucs*	28	SO9725
Southam *Warwks*	29	SP4161
Southampton *Hants*	10	SU4112
Southborough *Gt Lon*	23	TQ4267
Southborough *Kent*	13	TQ5842
Southbourne *Dorset*	10	SZ1491
Southbourne *W Susx*	11	SU7705
Southburgh *Norfk*	42	TG0005
Southburn *Humb*	56	SE9854
Southchurch *Essex*	24	TQ9086
Southcott *Cnwll*	6	SX1995
Southcott *Devon*	6	SX5495
Southcott *Devon*	5	SX7580
Southcourt *Bucks*	30	SP8112
Southease *E Susx*	13	TQ4205
Southend *Strath*	72	NR6908
Southend-on-Sea *Essex*	24	TQ8885
Southerndown *M Glam*	18	SS8873
Southerness *D & G*	66	NX9754
Southery *Norfk*	41	TL6194
Southfield *Cent*	74	NS8472
Southfleet *Kent*	14	TQ6171
Southgate *Gt Lon*	23	TQ2994
Southgate *W Glam*	17	SS5587
Southill *Beds*	30	TL1542
Southington *Hants*	21	SU5049
Southleigh *Devon*	8	SY2093
Southminster *Essex*	25	TQ9599
Southmoor *Oxon*	21	SU3998
Southmuir *Tays*	88	NO3852
Southoe *Cambs*	31	TL1864
Southolt *Suffk*	33	TM1968
Southorpe *Cambs*	40	TF0803
Southover *Dorset*	9	SY6294
Southowram *W York*	55	SE1123
Southport *Mersyd*	53	SD3317
Southrepps *Norfk*	43	TG2536
Southrey *Lincs*	50	TF1366
Southrop *Gloucs*	21	SP1903
Southrope *Hants*	22	SU6644
Southsea *Hants*	11	SZ6599
Southside *Dur*	61	NZ1026
Southtown *Norfk*	43	TG5106
Southwaite *Cumb*	67	NY4445
Southwark *Gt Lon*	23	TQ3279
Southwater *W Susx*	12	TQ1526
Southwell *Notts*	49	SK6953
Southwick *Hants*	11	SU6208
Southwick *Nhants*	40	TL0292
Southwick *T & W*	69	NZ3758
Southwick *W Susx*	12	TQ2405
Southwick *Wilts*	20	ST8355
Southwold *Suffk*	33	TM5076
Sowerby *N York*	62	SE4380
Sowerby Bridge *W York*	55	SE0523
Sowood *W York*	55	SE0818
Sowton *Devon*	4	SX5065
Sowton *Devon*	5	SX9792
Soyland Town *W York*	55	SE0320
Spain's End *Essex*	24	TL6637
Spalding *Lincs*	41	TF2422
Spaldington *Humb*	56	SE7633
Spaldwick *Cambs*	30	TL1372
Spalford *Notts*	50	SK8369
Sparham *Norfk*	42	TG0719
Spark Bridge *Cumb*	58	SD3084
Sparkford *Somset*	9	ST6025
Sparkhill *W Mids*	38	SP1083
Sparkwell *Devon*	5	SX5857
Sparrowpit *Derbys*	48	SK0880
Sparrows Green *E Susx*	13	TQ6332
Sparsholt *Hants*	10	SU4331
Sparsholt *Oxon*	21	SU3487
Spaunton *N York*	63	SE7289
Spaxton *Somset*	19	ST2237
Spean Bridge *Highld*	86	NN2281
Spearywell *Hants*	10	SU3127
Speen *Berks*	21	SU4567
Speen *Bucks*	22	SU8499
Speeton *N York*	63	TA1574
Speke *Mersyd*	46	SJ4383
Speldhurst *Kent*	13	TQ5541
Spellbrook *Herts*	31	TL4817
Spen Green *Ches*	47	SJ8160
Spencers Wood *Berks*	22	SU7166
Spennithorne *N York*	61	SE1388
Spennymoor *Dur*	61	NZ2533
Spetchley *H & W*	28	SO8953
Spettisbury *Dorset*	9	ST9102
Spexhall *Suffk*	33	TM3780
Spey Bay *Gramp*	94	NJ3565
Speybridge *Highld*	93	NJ0326
Speyview *Gramp*	94	NJ2541
Spilsby *Lincs*	51	TF4066
Spinkhill *Derbys*	49	SK4578
Spinningdale *Highld*	97	NH6789
Spital *Berks*	22	SU9675
Spital Hill *Notts*	49	SK6193
Spittal *Dyfed*	16	SM9723
Spittal *Highld*	100	ND1654
Spittal *Loth*	76	NT4677
Spittal *Nthumb*	77	NU0051
Spittal of Glenmuick *Gramp*	88	NO3085
Spittal of Glenshee *Tays*	88	NO1070
Spittal-on-Rule *Border*	76	NT5819
Spittalfield *Tays*	82	NO1040
Spixworth *Norfk*	43	TG2415
Splatt *Devon*	6	SS6005
Splayne's Green *E Susx*	13	TQ4224
Splottlands *S Glam*	19	ST2077
Spofforth *N York*	55	SE3651
Spooner Row *Norfk*	43	TM0997
Sporle *Norfk*	42	TF8411
Spott *Loth*	76	NT6775
Spottiswoode *Border*	76	NT6049
Spratton *Nhants*	30	SP7169
Spreakley *Surrey*	11	SU8341
Spreyton *Devon*	7	SX6996
Spriddlestone *Devon*	4	SX5351
Spridlington *Lincs*	50	TF0084
Springburn *Strath*	74	NS6068
Springfield *D & G*	67	NY3268
Springfield *Essex*	24	TL7208
Springfield *Fife*	83	NO3411
Springholm *D & G*	66	NX8070
Springkell *D & G*	67	NY2575
Springside *Strath*	73	NS3738
Springthorpe *Lincs*	50	SK8789
Springwell *T & W*	69	NZ2858
Sproatley *Humb*	57	TA1934
Sproston Green *Ches*	47	SJ7366
Sprotbrough *S York*	49	SE5301
Sproughton *Suffk*	33	TM1244
Sprouston *Border*	76	NT7535
Sprowston *Norfk*	43	TG2512
Sproxton *Leics*	40	SK8524
Sproxton *N York*	62	SE6181
Spurstow *Ches*	47	SJ5657
Spyway *Dorset*	8	SY5293
Squirrel's Heath *Gt Lon*	23	TQ5389
Stableford *Shrops*	37	SO7598
Stacey Bank *Derbys*	49	SK2890
Stackhouse *N York*	54	SD8165
Stackpole *Dyfed*	16	SR9896
Staddiscombe *Devon*	4	SX5151
Stadhampton *Oxon*	21	SU6098
Staffield *Cumb*	59	NY5442
Staffin *Highld*	90	NG4967
Stafford *Staffs*	38	SJ9223
Stagsden *Beds*	30	SP9848
Stainburn *Cumb*	58	NY0129
Stainburn *N York*	55	SE2548
Stainby *Lincs*	40	SK9022
Staincross *S York*	55	SE3210
Staindrop *Dur*	61	NZ1220
Staines *Surrey*	22	TQ0371
Stainforth *N York*	54	SD8267
Stainforth *S York*	56	SE6411
Staining *Lancs*	53	SD3436
Stainland *W York*	55	SE0719
Stainsacre *N York*	63	NZ9108
Stainton *Cleve*	62	NZ4714
Stainton *Cumb*	59	NY4828
Stainton *Cumb*	59	SD5285
Stainton *Dur*	61	NZ0718
Stainton *S York*	49	SK5593
Stainton by Langworth *Lincs*	50	TF0677
Stainton le Vale *Lincs*	50	TF1794
Stainton with Adgarley *Cumb*	53	SD2472
Staintondale *N York*	63	SE9998
Stair *Strath*	73	NS4423
Stair Haven *D & G*	64	NX2153
Staithes *N York*	63	NZ7818
Stakeford *Nthumb*	69	NZ2685
Stakes *Hants*	11	SU6808
Stalbridge *Dorset*	9	ST7317
Stalbridge Weston *Dorset*	9	ST7116
Stalham *Norfk*	43	TG3725
Stalisfield Green *Kent*	14	TQ9552
Stallen *Dorset*	9	ST6016
Stallingborough *Humb*	57	TA1911
Stalmine *Lancs*	53	SD3745
Stalybridge *Gt Man*	48	SJ9698
Stambourne *Essex*	24	TL7238
Stambourne Green *Essex*	24	TL6938
Stamford *Lincs*	40	TF0307
Stamford *Nthumb*	77	NU2219
Stamford Bridge *Ches*	46	SJ4667
Stamford Bridge *Humb*	56	SE7155
Stamford Hill *Gt Lon*	23	TQ3387
Stamfordham *Nthumb*	68	NZ0771
Stamton Lees *Derbys*	48	SK2562
Stanbridge *Beds*	30	SP9624
Stanbury *W York*	54	SE0137
Stand *Strath*	74	NS7668
Standburn *Cent*	75	NS9274
Standeford *Staffs*	38	SJ9107
Standen *Kent*	14	TQ8540
Standerwick *Somset*	20	ST8150
Standford *Hants*	11	SU8134
Standingstone *Cumb*	58	NY0533
Standish *Gt Man*	53	SD5610
Standlake *Oxon*	21	SP3903
Standon *Hants*	10	SU4226
Standon *Herts*	31	TL3922
Standon *Staffs*	37	SJ8135
Stane *Strath*	74	NS8859
Stanfield *Norfk*	42	TF9320
Stanford *Beds*	31	TL1640
Stanford *Kent*	15	TR1238
Stanford Bishop *H & W*	28	SO6851
Stanford Bridge *H & W*	28	SO7265
Stanford Dingley *Berks*	21	SU5771
Stanford in the Vale *Oxon*	21	SU3493
Stanford le Hope *Essex*	24	TQ6882
Stanford on Avon *Nhants*	39	SP5978
Stanford on Soar *Notts*	39	SK5421
Stanford on Teme *H & W*	28	SO7065
Stanfree *Derbys*	49	SK4773
Stanghow *Cleve*	62	NZ6715
Stanground *Cambs*	41	TL2097
Stanhoe *Norfk*	42	TF8036
Stanhope *Border*	75	NT1229
Stanhope *Dur*	61	NY9939
Stanion *Nhants*	40	SP9186
Stanley *Derbys*	49	SK4140
Stanley *Dur*	69	NZ1953
Stanley *Staffs*	48	SJ9352
Stanley *Tays*	82	NO1033
Stanley Crook *Dur*	61	NZ1637
Stanley Pontlarge *Gloucs*	28	SP0030
Stanmer *E Susx*	12	TQ3309
Stanmore *Gt Lon*	23	TQ1692

Thornton Steward Trevalyn

Thornton Steward *N York* 61 SE1787
Thornton Watlass *N York* 61 SE2385
Thornton-in-Craven *N York* 54 SD9048
Thornton-le-Beans *N York* 62 SE3990
Thornton-le-Clay *N York* 56 SE6865
Thornton-le-Moor *N York* 62 SE3988
Thornton-le-Moors *Ches* 46 SJ4474
Thornton-le-Street *N York* 62 SE4186
Thorntonhall *Strath* 74 NS5955
Thorntonloch *Loth* 76 NT7574
Thornydykes *Border* 76 NT6148
Thornythwaite *Cumb* 59 NY3922
Thoroton *Notts* 50 SK7642
Thorp Arch *W York* 55 SE4345
Thorpe *Derbys* 48 SK1550
Thorpe *Humb* 56 SE9946
Thorpe *N York* 54 SE0161
Thorpe *Notts* 50 SK7649
Thorpe *Surrey* 22 TQ0168
Thorpe Abbotts *Norfk* 33 TM1979
Thorpe Arnold *Leics* 40 SK7720
Thorpe Audlin *W York* 55 SE4715
Thorpe Bassett *N York* 63 SE8673
Thorpe Bay *Essex* 24 TQ9185
Thorpe by Water *Leics* 40 SP8996
Thorpe Constantine *Staffs* 39 SK2508
Thorpe End *Norfk* 43 TG2810
Thorpe Green *Essex* 25 TM1623
Thorpe Green *Suffk* 32 TL9354
Thorpe Hesley *S York* 49 SK3796
Thorpe in Balne *S York* 56 SE5910
Thorpe in the Fallows *Lincs* 50 SK9180
Thorpe Langton *Leics* 40 SP7492
Thorpe Lea *Surrey* 22 TQ0170
Thorpe le Street *Humb* 56 SE8343
Thorpe Malsor *Nhants* 30 SP8378
Thorpe Mandeville *Nhants* 29 SP5244
Thorpe Market *Norfk* 43 TG2436
Thorpe Morieux *Suffk* 32 TL9453
Thorpe on the Hill *Lincs* 50 SK9065
Thorpe Salvin *S York* 49 SK5281
Thorpe Satchville *Leics* 40 SK7311
Thorpe St. Andrew *Norfk* 43 TG2508
Thorpe St. Peter *Lincs* 51 TF4860
Thorpe Thewles *Cleve* 62 NZ3923
Thorpe Tilney *Lincs* 50 TF1257
Thorpe Underwood *N York* 55 SE4659
Thorpe Waterville *Nhants* 40 TL0281
Thorpe Willoughby *N York* 56 SE5731
Thorpe-le-Soken *Essex* 25 TM1722
Thorpeness *Suffk* 33 TM4759
Thorrington *Essex* 25 TM0919
Thorverton *Devon* 7 SS9202
Thrandeston *Suffk* 33 TM1176
Thrapston *Nhants* 30 SP9978
Threapwood *Ches* 46 SJ4344
Threapwood *Staffs* 48 SK0342
Threave *Strath* 73 NS3306
Three Bridges *W Susx* 12 TQ2837
Three Chimneys *Kent* 14 TQ8238
Three Cocks *Powys* 27 SO1737
Three Crosses *W Glam* 17 SS5794
Three Cups Corner *E Susx* 13 TQ6320
Three Leg Cross *E Susx* 14 TQ6831
Three Legged Cross *Dorset* 10 SU0805
Three Mile Cross *Berks* 22 SU7167
Three Miletown *Loth* 75 NT0675
Three Oaks *E Susx* 14 TQ8314
Threekingham *Lincs* 40 TF0836
Threepwood *Border* 76 NT5143
Threlkeld *Cumb* 58 NY3125
Threshfield *N York* 54 SD9863
Thrigby *Norfk* 43 TG4612
Thringstone *Leics* 39 SK4217
Thrintoft *N York* 62 SE3192
Thriplow *Cambs* 31 TL4346
Throcking *Herts* 31 TL3330
Throckley *T & W* 69 NZ1566
Throckmorton *H & W* 28 SO9850
Throop *Dorset* 9 SY8292
Throop *Dorset* 10 SZ1195
Thropton *Nthumb* 68 NU0202
Throughgate *D & G* 66 NX8784
Throwleigh *Devon* 5 SX6690
Throwley Forstal *Kent* 15 TQ9854
Thrumpton *Notts* 39 SK5031
Thrumster *Highld* 100 ND3345
Thrunscoe *Humb* 57 TA3107
Thrupp *Gloucs* 20 SO8603
Thrushesbush *Essex* 23 TL4909
Thrussington *Leics* 39 SK6515
Thruxton *H & W* 27 SO4334
Thruxton *Hants* 21 SU2945
Thulston *Derbys* 39 SK4031
Thundersley *Essex* 24 TQ7988
Thurcaston *Leics* 39 SK5610
Thurcroft *S York* 49 SK4988
Thurdistoft *Highld* 100 ND2167
Thurgarton *Norfk* 43 TG1834
Thurgarton *Notts* 49 SK6949
Thurgoland *S York* 49 SE2901
Thurlaston *Leics* 39 SP5099
Thurlaston *Warwks* 29 SP4670
Thurlbear *Somset* 8 ST2621
Thurlby *Lincs* 50 SK9061
Thurlby *Lincs* 40 TF0916
Thurlby *Lincs* 51 TF4776
Thurleigh *Beds* 30 TL0558
Thurlestone *Devon* 5 SX6742
Thurlow *Suffk* 32 TL6750
Thurloxton *Somset* 8 ST2730
Thurlstone *S York* 55 SE2303
Thurlton *Norfk* 43 TM4198
Thurmaston *Leics* 39 SK6109
Thurnby *Leics* 39 SK6403
Thurne *Norfk* 43 TG4015
Thurnham *Kent* 14 TQ8057
Thurning *Nhants* 40 TL0882
Thurning *Norfk* 42 TG0729
Thurnscoe *S York* 55 SE4505
Thursby *Cumb* 67 NY3250
Thursford *Norfk* 42 TF9833
Thursley *Surrey* 11 SU9039
Thurso *Highld* 100 ND1168
Thurstaston *Mersyd* 46 SJ2484
Thurston *Suffk* 32 TL9265
Thurstonfield *Cumb* 67 NY3156
Thurstonland *W York* 55 SE1610
Thurton *Norfk* 43 TG3200
Thurvaston *Derbys* 48 SK2437
Thuxton *Norfk* 42 TG0307
Thwaite *N York* 60 SD8998
Thwaite *Suffk* 33 TM1168
Thwaite Head *Cumb* 59 SD3490
Thwaite St. Mary *Norfk* 43 TM3395
Thwing *Humb* 57 TA0470
Tibbermore *Tays* 82 NO0423
Tibbers *D & G* 66 NX8696
Tibberton *Gloucs* 28 SO7521
Tibberton *H & W* 28 SO9057
Tibberton *Shrops* 37 SJ6820
Tibbie Shiels Inn *Border* 75 NT2420
Tibenham *Norfk* 33 TM1389
Tibshelf *Derbys* 49 SK4461
Tibthorpe *Humb* 56 SE9555
Ticehurst *E Susx* 14 TQ6830
Tichborne *Hants* 11 SU5730
Tickencote *Leics* 40 SK9809
Tickenham *Avon* 19 ST4571
Tickhill *S York* 49 SK5993
Ticklerton *Shrops* 37 SO4890
Ticknall *Derbys* 39 SK3523
Tickton *Humb* 57 TA0541
Tidcombe *Wilts* 21 SU2858
Tiddington *Oxon* 29 SP6404
Tiddington *Warwks* 29 SP2255
Tidebrook *E Susx* 13 TQ6130
Tideford *Cnwll* 4 SX3559
Tidenham *Gloucs* 19 ST5595
Tideswell *Derbys* 48 SK1575
Tidmarsh *Berks* 21 SU6374
Tidmington *Warwks* 29 SP2538
Tiers Cross *Dyfed* 16 SM9010
Tiffield *Nhants* 30 SP7051
Tifty *Gramp* 95 NJ7740
Tigerton *Tays* 89 NO5364
Tigharry *W Isls* 102 NF7172
Tighnabruaich *Strath* 71 NR9873
Tigley *Devon* 5 SX7660
Tilbrook *Cambs* 30 TL0869
Tilbury *Essex* 14 TQ6476
Tilbury Green *Essex* 32 TL7441
Tile Hill *W Mids* 39 SP2777
Tilehurst *Berks* 22 SU6673
Tilford *Surrey* 11 SU8743
Tilgate *W Susx* 12 TQ2734
Tilham Street *Somset* 9 ST5535
Tillicoultry *Cent* 82 NS9197
Tillingham *Essex* 25 TL9904
Tillington *H & W* 27 SO4644
Tillington *W Susx* 12 SU9621
Tillington Common *H & W* 27 SO4545
Tillybirloch *Gramp* 95 NJ6807
Tillycairn *Gramp* 89 NO4697
Tillyfourie *Gramp* 94 NJ6412
Tillygreig *Gramp* 95 NJ8822
Tillyrie *Tays* 82 NO1006
Tilmanstone *Kent* 15 TR3051
Tilney All Saints *Norfk* 41 TF5618
Tilney High End *Norfk* 41 TF5617
Tilney St. Lawrence *Norfk* 41 TF5414
Tilshead *Wilts* 20 SU0347
Tilstock *Shrops* 37 SJ5437
Tilston *Ches* 46 SJ4650
Tilstone Fearnall *Ches* 47 SJ5660
Tilsworth *Beds* 30 SP9824
Tilton on the Hill *Leics* 40 SK7405
Tiltups End *Gloucs* 20 ST8497
Timberland *Lincs* 50 TF1258
Timbersbrook *Ches* 48 SJ8962
Timberscombe *Somset* 7 SS9542
Timble *N York* 55 SE1853
Timpanheck *D & G* 67 NY3274
Timperley *Gt Man* 47 SJ7888
Timsbury *Avon* 20 ST6758
Timsbury *Hants* 10 SU3424
Timsgarry *W Isls* 102 NB0534
Timworth *Suffk* 32 TL8669
Timworth Green *Suffk* 32 TL8669
Tincleton *Dorset* 9 SY7692
Tindale *Cumb* 68 NY6159
Tindale Crescent *Dur* 61 NZ1927
Tingewick *Bucks* 29 SP6532
Tingley *W York* 55 SE2826
Tingrith *Beds* 30 TL0032
Tinhay *Devon* 4 SX3985
Tinsley *S York* 49 SK4090
Tinsley Green *W Susx* 12 TQ2839
Tintagel *Cnwll* 4 SX0588
Tintern Parva *Gwent* 19 SO5200
Tintinhull *Somset* 8 ST4919
Tintwistle *Derbys* 48 SK0197
Tinwald *D & G* 66 NY0081
Tinwell *Leics* 40 TF0006
Tipp's End *Norfk* 41 TL5095
Tippacott *Devon* 18 SS7647
Tipton *W Mids* 38 SO9492
Tipton St. John *Devon* 8 SY0991
Tiptree *Essex* 24 TL8916
Tiptree Heath *Essex* 24 TL8815
Tirabad *Powys* 26 SN8741
Tiretigan *Strath* 71 NR7162
Tirley *Gloucs* 28 SO8328
Tirphil *M Glam* 18 SO1303
Tirril *Cumb* 59 NY5026
Tisbury *Wilts* 9 ST9429
Tissington *Derbys* 48 SK1752
Titchberry *Devon* 6 SS2427
Titchfield *Hants* 11 SU5405
Titchmarsh *Nhants* 40 TL0279
Titchwell *Norfk* 42 TF7643
Tithby *Notts* 49 SK6937
Titley *H & W* 27 SO3360
Titmore Green *Herts* 31 TL2126
Titsey *Surrey* 23 TQ4054
Tittensor *Staffs* 38 SJ8738
Tittleshall *Norfk* 42 TF8921
Titton *H & W* 28 SO8370
Tiverton *Ches* 47 SJ5560
Tiverton *Devon* 7 SS9512
Tivetshall St. Margaret *Norfk* 33 TM1787
Tivetshall St. Mary *Norfk* 33 TM1686
Tivington *Somset* 7 SS9345
Tixall *Staffs* 38 SJ9722
Tixover *Leics* 40 SK9700
Toab *Shet* 103 HU3811
Toadmoor *Derbys* 49 SK3451
Tobermory *Strath* 79 NM5055
Toberonochy *Strath* 79 NM7408
Tocher *Gramp* 95 NJ6932
Tochieneal *Gramp* 94 NJ5165
Tockenham *Wilts* 20 SU0379
Tockington *Avon* 19 ST6086
Tockwith *N York* 55 SE4652
Todber *Dorset* 9 ST7919
Todburn *Nthumb* 69 NZ1295
Toddington *Beds* 30 TL0128
Toddington *Gloucs* 28 SP0333
Todds Green *Herts* 31 TL2226
Todenham *Gloucs* 29 SP2335
Todhills *Cumb* 67 NY3762
Todhills *Tays* 83 NO4239
Todmorden *W York* 54 SD9324
Todwick *S York* 49 SK4984
Toft *Cambs* 31 TL3656
Toft *Lincs* 40 TF0717
Toft *Shet* 103 HU4376
Toft Hill *Dur* 61 NZ1528
Toft Monks *Norfk* 43 TM4294
Toft next Newton *Lincs* 50 TF0388
Toftrees *Norfk* 42 TF8927
Tofts *Highld* 100 ND3668
Togston *Nthumb* 69 NU2402
Tokavaig *Highld* 84 NG6011
Tokers Green *Oxon* 22 SU7077
Toll Bar *S York* 56 SE5507
Tolland *Somset* 8 ST1032
Tollard Royal *Wilts* 9 ST9417
Toller Fratrum *Dorset* 9 SY5797
Toller Porcorum *Dorset* 9 SY5698
Toller Whelme *Dorset* 8 ST5101
Tollerton *N York* 55 SE5164
Tollerton *Notts* 39 SK6134
Tollesbury *Essex* 25 TL9510
Tolleshunt D'Arcy *Essex* 24 TL9211
Tolleshunt Knights *Essex* 24 TL9114
Tolleshunt Major *Essex* 24 TL9011
Tolpuddle *Dorset* 9 SY7994
Tolsta *W Isls* 102 NB5347
Tolworth *Gt Lon* 23 TQ1966
Tomaknock *Tays* 82 NN8721
Tomatin *Highld* 93 NH8028
Tomchrasky *Highld* 92 NH2512
Tomdoun *Highld* 86 NH1500
Tomich *Highld* 97 NC6005
Tomich *Highld* 92 NH3027
Tomich *Highld* 92 NH5348
Tomich *Highld* 93 NH6971
Tomintoul *Gramp* 94 NJ1619
Tomintoul *Gramp* 88 NO1490
Tomnacross *Highld* 92 NH5141
Tomnavoulin *Gramp* 94 NJ2126
Tonbridge *Kent* 13 TQ5846
Tondu *M Glam* 18 SS8984
Tonedale *Somset* 8 ST1321
Tong *Kent* 14 TQ9556
Tong *Shrops* 37 SJ7907
Tong *W York* 55 SE2230
Tong Norton *Shrops* 37 SJ7908
Tong Street *W York* 55 SE1930
Tonge *Leics* 39 SK4223
Tongham *Surrey* 22 SU8848
Tongland *D & G* 65 NX6954
Tongue *Highld* 99 NC5956
Tongwynlais *S Glam* 18 ST1382
Tonna *W Glam* 18 SS7798
Tonwell *Herts* 31 TL3316
Tonypandy *M Glam* 18 SS9991
Tonyrefail *M Glam* 18 ST0188
Toot Baldon *Oxon* 21 SP5600
Toot Hill *Essex* 23 TL5102
Toothill *Wilts* 20 SU1183
Tooting *Gt Lon* 23 TQ2771
Tooting Bec *Gt Lon* 23 TQ2872
Topcliffe *N York* 62 SE3976
Topcroft *Norfk* 43 TM2693
Topcroft Street *Norfk* 33 TM2691
Toppesfield *Essex* 24 TL7437
Toprow *Norfk* 43 TM1698
Topsham *Devon* 5 SX9688
Torbeg *Strath* 72 NR8929
Torboll *Highld* 97 NH7599
Torbreck *Highld* 92 NH6441
Torbryan *Devon* 5 SX8266
Torcastle *Highld* 86 NN1378
Torcross *Devon* 5 SX8241
Tore *Highld* 92 NH6052
Torksey *Lincs* 50 SK8378
Tormarton *Avon* 20 ST7678
Tormitchell *Strath* 64 NX2304
Tormore *Strath* 72 NR8932
Tornagrain *Highld* 93 NH7650
Tornaveen *Gramp* 89 NJ6106
Torness *Highld* 92 NH5826
Toronto *Nthumb* 61 NZ1930
Torosay Castle *Strath* 79 NM7335
Torpenhow *Cumb* 58 NY2039
Torphichen *Loth* 75 NS9672
Torphins *Gramp* 89 NJ6202
Torpoint *Cnwll* 4 SX4355
Torquay *Devon* 5 SX9164
Torquhan *Border* 76 NT4448
Torran *Highld* 90 NG5949
Torrance *Strath* 74 NS6173
Torranyard *Strath* 73 NS3544
Torridon *Highld* 91 NG9055
Torridon House *Highld* 91 NG8657
Torrin *Highld* 84 NG5721
Torrisdale *Highld* 99 NC6761
Torrisdale Square *Strath* 72 NR7936
Torrish *Highld* 97 NC9718
Torrisholme *Lancs* 53 SD4563
Torrobull *Highld* 97 NC5904
Torry *Gramp* 89 NJ9405
Torryburn *Fife* 82 NT0286
Torrylin *Strath* 72 NR9521
Tortan *H & W* 38 SO8472
Torteval *Guern* 101 GN4505
Torthorwald *D & G* 66 NY0378
Tortington *W Susx* 12 TQ0004
Tortworth *Avon* 20 ST7093
Torvaig *Highld* 90 NG4944
Torver *Cumb* 58 SD2894
Torwood *Cent* 82 NS8385
Torwoodlee *Border* 76 NT4738
Torworth *Notts* 49 SK6586
Toscaig *Highld* 85 NG7138
Toseland *Cambs* 31 TL2462
Tosside *Lancs* 54 SD7656
Tostock *Suffk* 32 TL9563
Totaig *Highld* 90 NG2050
Tote *Highld* 90 NG4149
Tote Hill *W Susx* 11 SU8624
Totland *IOW* 10 SZ3287
Totley *S York* 49 SK3079
Totnes *Devon* 5 SX8060
Totronald *Strath* 78 NM1656
Totscore *Highld* 90 NG3866
Tottenham *Gt Lon* 23 TQ3390
Tottenhill *Norfk* 42 TF6411
Totteridge *Gt Lon* 23 TQ2494
Totternhoe *Beds* 30 SP9821
Tottington *Gt Man* 54 SD7712
Totton *Hants* 10 SU3613
Toulton *Somset* 8 ST1931
Toulvaddie *Highld* 97 NH8880
Toux *Gramp* 94 NJ5459
Tovil *Kent* 14 TQ7554
Tow Law *Dur* 61 NZ1138
Toward *Strath* 73 NS1368
Toward Quay *Strath* 73 NS1167
Towcester *Nhants* 30 SP6948
Towednack *Cnwll* 2 SW4838
Towersey *Oxon* 22 SP7305
Towie *Gramp* 94 NJ4312
Town End *Cambs* 41 TL4195
Town Littleworth *E Susx* 13 TQ4117
Town Street *Suffk* 32 TL7785
Town Yetholm *Border* 76 NT8128
Townhead *D & G* 66 NY0088
Townhead *S York* 55 SE1602
Townhead of Greenlaw *D & G* 65 NX7464
Townhill *Loth* 82 NT1089
Towns End *Hants* 21 SU5659
Townshend *Cnwll* 2 SW5932
Towthorpe *N York* 56 SE6258
Towton *N York* 55 SE4839
Toxteth *Mersyd* 46 SJ3588
Toy's Hill *Kent* 13 TQ4651
Toynton All Saints *Lincs* 51 TF3963
Trabboch *Strath* 73 NS4421
Trabbochburn *Strath* 73 NS4621
Tradespark *Highld* 93 NH8656
Traethsaith *Dyfed* 17 SN2851
Trafford Park *Gt Man* 47 SJ7896
Trallong *Powys* 26 SN9629
Tranent *Loth* 76 NT4072
Tranmere *Mersyd* 46 SJ3187
Trantelbeg *Highld* 99 NC8952
Trantlemore *Highld* 99 NC8953
Trap *Dyfed* 26 SN6518
Traquair *Border* 75 NT3334
Traveller's Rest *Devon* 7 SS6127
Trawden *Lancs* 54 SD9138
Trawsfynydd *Gwynd* 45 SH7035
Tre-groes *Dyfed* 17 SN4044
Trealaw *M Glam* 18 ST0092
Treales *Lancs* 53 SD4332
Trearddur Bay *Gwynd* 44 SH2579
Treaslane *Highld* 90 NG3953
Trebarwith *Cnwll* 4 SX0586
Trebetherick *Cnwll* 3 SW9378
Trebullett *Cnwll* 4 SX3278
Treburley *Cnwll* 4 SX3577
Trecastle *Powys* 26 SN8829
Trecwn *Dyfed* 16 SM9632
Trecynon *M Glam* 18 SN9903
Tredaule *Cnwll* 4 SX2381
Tredegar *Gwent* 26 SO1408
Tredington *Gloucs* 28 SO9029
Tredington *Warwks* 29 SP2543
Tredunhock *Gwent* 19 ST3794
Treen *Cnwll* 2 SW3923
Treeton *S York* 49 SK4387
Trefacca *Powys* 26 SO1431
Trefasser *Dyfed* 16 SM8938
Trefeglwys *Powys* 35 SN9690
Treffgarne *Dyfed* 16 SM9523
Treffgarne Owen *Dyfed* 16 SM8625
Trefforest *M Glam* 18 ST0888
Trefilan *Dyfed* 34 SN5456
Trefnant *Clwyd* 45 SJ0570
Trefonen *Shrops* 36 SJ2526
Trefrew *Cnwll* 4 SX1084
Trefriw *Gwynd* 45 SH7863
Tregadillett *Cnwll* 4 SX2983
Tregare *Gwent* 27 SO4110
Tregaron *Dyfed* 26 SN6759
Tregarth *Gwynd* 44 SH6067
Tregeare *Cnwll* 4 SX2486
Tregeiriog *Clwyd* 36 SJ1733
Tregele *Gwynd* 44 SH3592
Tregidden *Cnwll* 2 SW7523
Treglemais *Dyfed* 16 SM8229
Tregole *Cnwll* 6 SX1998
Tregonce *Cnwll* 3 SW9373
Tregonetha *Cnwll* 3 SW9563
Tregony *Cnwll* 3 SW9244
Tregoyd *Powys* 27 SO1937
Tregynon *Powys* 36 SO0998
Trehafod *M Glam* 18 ST0490
Trehan *Cnwll* 4 SX4058
Treharris *M Glam* 18 ST0996
Treherbert *M Glam* 18 SS9498
Trekenner *Cnwll* 4 SX3478
Treknow *Cnwll* 4 SX0586
Trelawnyd *Clwyd* 46 SJ0979
Trelech *Dyfed* 17 SN2830
Treleddyd-fawr *Dyfed* 16 SM7528
Trelewis *M Glam* 18 ST1096
Trelights *Cnwll* 3 SW9979
Trelill *Cnwll* 3 SX0478
Trelleck *Gwent* 27 SO5005
Trelogan *Clwyd* 46 SJ1180
Trelow *Cnwll* 3 SW9269
Tremadog *Gwynd* 44 SH5640
Tremail *Cnwll* 4 SX1686
Tremain *Dyfed* 17 SN2047
Tremaine *Cnwll* 4 SX2389
Tremar *Cnwll* 4 SX2568
Trematon *Cnwll* 4 SX3959
Tremeirchion *Clwyd* 46 SJ0873
Trenance *Cnwll* 3 SW8568
Trenance *Cnwll* 3 SW9270
Trencreek *Cnwll* 6 SX1896
Trenear *Cnwll* 2 SW6731
Treneglos *Cnwll* 4 SX2088
Trent *Dorset* 9 ST5918
Trentishoe *Devon* 18 SS6448
Treoes *S Glam* 18 SS9478
Treorchy *M Glam* 18 SS9597
Trequite *Cnwll* 3 SX0377
Trerhyngyll *S Glam* 18 ST0077
Trerulefoot *Cnwll* 4 SX3358
Trescowe *Cnwll* 2 SW5731
Tresean *Cnwll* 2 SW7858
Tresham *Avon* 20 ST7991
Tresillian *Cnwll* 3 SW8646
Treskinnick Cross *Cnwll* 6 SX2098
Tresmeer *Cnwll* 4 SX2387
Tresparrett *Cnwll* 4 SX1491
Tressait *Tays* 87 NN8160
Tresta *Shet* 103 HU3650
Tresta *Shet* 103 HU6090
Treswell *Notts* 50 SK7879
Trethevey *Cnwll* 4 SX0789
Trethewey *Cnwll* 2 SW3823
Trethurgy *Cnwll* 3 SX0355
Tretire *H & W* 27 SO5123
Tretower *Powys* 27 SO1821
Treuddyn *Clwyd* 46 SJ2557
Trevague *Cnwll* 4 SX2379
Trevalga *Cnwll* 4 SX0890
Trevalyn *Clwyd* 46 SJ3856

Trevanson Wainscott

Trevanson Cnwll 3 SW9773
Trevarrian Cnwll 3 SW8566
Treveal Cnwll 2 SW7858
Treveighan Cnwll 3 SX0779
Trevellas Downs Cnwll 2 SW7452
Trevelmond Cnwll 4 SX2063
Treverva Cnwll 2 SW7531
Trevescan Cnwll 2 SW3524
Trevine Dyfed 16 SM8432
Treviscoe Cnwll 3 SW9455
Trevone Cnwll 3 SW8975
Trevor Clwyd 36 SJ2742
Trevor Gwynd 44 SH3746
Trewalder Cnwll 3 SX0782
Trewarlett Cnwll 4 SX3380
Trewarmett Cnwll 4 SX0686
Treween Cnwll 4 SX2182
Trewen Cnwll 3 SX0577
Trewint Cnwll 4 SX2180
Trewithian Cnwll 3 SW8737
Trewoon Cnwll 3 SW9952
Treyford W Susx 11 SU8218
Triangle W York 55 SE0422
Trimdon Dur 62 NZ3634
Trimdon Colliery Dur 62 NZ3735
Trimdon Grange Dur 62 NZ3635
Trimingham Norfk 43 TG2838
Trimley Suffk 25 TM2737
Trimley Heath Suffk 25 TM2738
Trimsaran Dyfed 17 SN4504
Trimstone Devon 6 SS5043
Trinafour Tays 87 NN7264
Tring Herts 22 SP9211
Trinity Jersey 101 JS1614
Trinity Tays 89 NO6061
Trinity Gask Tays 82 NN9718
Triscombe Somset 7 SS9237
Triscombe Somset 8 ST1535
Trislaig Highld 86 NN0874
Trispen Cnwll 3 SW8450
Tritlington Nthumb 69 NZ2092
Trochry Tays 82 NN9740
Troedrhiwfuwch M Glam 26 SO1204
Troedyraur Dyfed 17 SN3245
Troedyrhiw M Glam 18 SO0702
Trois Bois Jersey 101 JS1212
Troon Cnwll 2 SW6638
Troon Strath 73 NS3230
Trossachs Hotel Cent 81 NN5107
Troston Suffk 32 TL8972
Trots Hill H & W 28 SO8855
Trottiscliffe Kent 14 TQ6460
Trotton W Susx 11 SU8322
Troughend Nthumb 68 NY8692
Troutbeck Cumb 59 NY4002
Troutbeck Bridge Cumb 59 NY4000
Troway Derbys 49 SK3879
Trowbridge Wilts 20 ST8558
Trowse Newton Norfk 43 TG2406
Trudoxhill Somset 20 ST7443
Trull Somset 8 ST2122
Trumpan Highld 90 NG2261
Trumpet H & W 27 SO6539
Trumpington Cambs 31 TL4454
Trunch Norfk 43 TG2834
Truro Cnwll 2 SW8244
Trusham Devon 5 SX8582
Trusley Derbys 39 SK2535
Trysull Staffs 38 SO8594
Tubney Oxon 21 SU4399
Tuckenhay Devon 5 SX8156
Tuckhill Shrops 37 SO7888
Tuckingmill Cnwll 2 SW6540
Tuckingmill Wilts 9 ST9329
Tuckton Dorset 10 SZ1492
Tuddenham Suffk 32 TL7371
Tuddenham Suffk 33 TM1948
Tudeley Kent 13 TQ6245
Tudhoe Dur 61 NZ2535
Tudweiloig Gwynd 44 SH2436
Tuffley Gloucs 28 SO8314
Tufton Dyfed 16 SN0428
Tufton Hants 21 SU4546
Tugby Leics 40 SK7601
Tugford Shrops 37 SO5587
Tughall Nthumb 77 NU2126
Tullibody Cent 82 NS8595
Tullich Highld 92 NH6328
Tullich Highld 97 NH8576
Tullich Strath 80 NN0815
Tulliemet Tays 88 NO0052
Tulloch Cent 81 NN5120
Tulloch Gramp 95 NJ8031
Tulloch Station Highld 86 NN3580
Tullochgorm Strath 71 NR9695
Tullybeagles Lodge Tays 82 NO0136
Tullynessle Gramp 94 NJ5519
Tumble Dyfed 17 SN5411
Tumby Lincs 51 TF2359
Tumby Woodside Lincs 51 TF2757
Tummel Bridge Tays 87 NN7659
Tunbridge Wells Kent 13 TQ5839
Tundergarth D & G 67 NY1780
Tunstall Humb 57 TA3031
Tunstall Kent 14 TQ8961
Tunstall Lancs 59 SD6073
Tunstall N York 61 SE2196
Tunstall Norfk 43 TG4107
Tunstall Staffs 37 SJ7727
Tunstall Staffs 47 SJ8651
Tunstall Suffk 33 TM3655
Tunstall T & W 69 NZ3953
Tunstead Derbys 48 SK1074
Tunstead Norfk 43 TG3022
Tunstead Milton Derbys 48 SK0180
Tunworth Hants 22 SU6748
Tur Langton Leics 40 SP7194
Turgis Green Hants 22 SU6959
Turkdean Gloucs 28 SP1017
Turleigh Wilts 20 ST8060
Turnastone H & W 27 SO3536
Turnberry Strath 73 NS2005
Turnditch Derbys 49 SK2946
Turner's Hill W Susx 12 TQ3435
Turners Puddle Dorset 9 SY8393
Turnworth Dorset 9 ST8207
Turriff Gramp 95 NJ7250
Turton Bottoms Gt Man 54 SD7315
Turvey Beds 30 SP9452
Turville Bucks 22 SU7691
Turweston Bucks 29 SP6037
Tushielaw Inn Border 75 NT3017
Tushingham cum Grindley Ches 46 SJ5246
Tutbury Staffs 39 SK2128
Tutshill Gloucs 19 ST5494
Tuttington Norfk 43 TG2227
Tuxford Notts 50 SK7471
Twatt Ork 103 HY2724
Twatt Shet 103 HU3253
Twechar Strath 74 NS6975
Tweedmouth Nthumb 77 NT9952
Tweedsmuir Border 75 NT1024
Twelve Oaks E Susx 14 TQ6820
Twelveheads Cnwll 2 SW7542
Twemlow Green Ches 47 SJ7868
Twenty Lincs 40 TF1520
Twerton Avon 20 ST7264
Twickenham Gt Lon 23 TQ1673
Twigworth Gloucs 28 SO8422
Twineham W Susx 12 TQ2519
Twinstead Essex 24 TL8636
Twitchen Devon 7 SS7930
Two Dales Derbys 49 SK2763
Twycross Leics 39 SK3304
Twyford Berks 22 SU7976
Twyford Bucks 30 SP6626
Twyford Derbys 39 SK3228
Twyford Hants 11 SU4824
Twyford Leics 40 SK7210
Twyford Norfk 42 TG0123
Twynholm D & G 65 NX6654
Twyning Gloucs 28 SO8936
Twyning Green Gloucs 28 SO9036
Twynllanan Dyfed 26 SN7524
Twywell Nhants 30 SP9578
Ty'n-dwr Clwyd 36 SJ2341
Ty'n-y-groes Gwynd 45 SH7771
Ty-croes Dyfed 17 SN6010
Ty-nant Clwyd 45 SH9944
Tyberton H & W 27 SO3839
Tycrwyn Powys 36 SJ1018
Tydd Gote Lincs 41 TF4518
Tydd St. Giles Cambs 41 TF4216
Tydd St. Mary Lincs 41 TF4418
Tye Green Essex 24 TL5424
Tye Green Essex 24 TL5935
Tyldesley Gt Man 47 SD6802
Tyler Hill Kent 15 TR1461
Tylorstown M Glam 18 ST0095
Tyn-y-nant M Glam 18 ST0685
Tyndrum Cent 80 NN3230
Tynemouth T & W 69 NZ3669
Tyninghame Loth 83 NT6179
Tynron D & G 66 NX8093
Tynygraig Dyfed 35 SN6969
Tyringham Bucks 30 SP8547
Tythegston M Glam 18 SS8578
Tytherington Avon 20 ST6688
Tytherington Ches 48 SJ9175
Tytherington Wilts 20 ST9141
Tytherleigh Devon 8 ST3103
Tywardreath Cnwll 3 SX0854
Tywyn Gwynd 34 SH5800

U

Ubbeston Green Suffk 33 TM3271
Ubley Avon 19 ST5258
Uckerby N York 61 NZ2402
Uckfield E Susx 13 TQ4721
Uckinghall H & W 28 SO8637
Uckington Gloucs 28 SO9124
Uckington Shrops 37 SJ5709
Uddingston Strath 74 NS6960
Uddington Strath 74 NS8633
Udimore E Susx 14 TQ8719
Udny Green Gramp 95 NJ8726
Uffculme Devon 7 ST0612
Uffington Oxon 21 SU3089
Ufford Cambs 40 TF0903
Ufford Suffk 33 TM2952
Ufton Warwks 29 SP3762
Ufton Nervet Berks 21 SU6367
Ugadale Strath 72 NR7828
Ugborough Devon 5 SX6755
Uggeshall Suffk 33 TM4480
Ugglebarnby N York 63 NZ8707
Ughill Derbys 48 SK2590
Ugley Essex 31 TL5228
Ugley Green Essex 31 TL5227
Ugthorpe N York 63 NZ7911
Uig Highld 90 NG1952
Uig Highld 90 NG3963
Uig Strath 78 NM1654
Uig W Isls 102 NB0533
Uigshader Highld 90 NG4346
Uisken Strath 78 NM3919
Ulbster Highld 100 ND3241
Ulcat Row Cumb 59 NY4022
Ulceby Humb 57 TA1014
Ulceby Lincs 51 TF4272
Ulceby Skitter Humb 57 TA1215
Ulcombe Kent 14 TQ8448
Uldale Cumb 58 NY2437
Uley Gloucs 20 ST7898
Ulgham Nthumb 69 NZ2392
Ullapool Highld 96 NH1294
Ullenhall Warwks 28 SP1267
Ulleskelf N York 55 SE5239
Ullesthorpe Leics 39 SP5087
Ulley S York 49 SK4687
Ullingswick H & W 27 SO5949
Ullinish Lodge Hotel Highld 84 NG3237
Ullock Cumb 58 NY0724
Ulpha Cumb 58 SD1993
Ulrome Humb 57 TA1656
Ulsta Shet 103 HU4680
Ulverston Cumb 58 SD2878
Ulwell Dorset 10 SZ0280
Umachan Highld 90 NG6050
Umberleigh Devon 6 SS6023
Unapool Highld 98 NC2333
Under Burnmouth D & G 67 NY4783
Under River Kent 13 TQ5552
Underbarrow Cumb 59 SD4692
Undercliffe W York 55 SE1834
Underdale Shrops 37 SJ5013
Underwood Notts 49 SK4750
Undy Gwent 19 ST4386
Union Mills IOM 52 SC3577
Unstone Derbys 49 SK3777
Up Cerne Dorset 9 ST6502
Up Exe Devon 7 SS9402
Up Holland Lancs 46 SD5205
Up Marden W Susx 11 SU7913
Up Mudford Somset 9 ST5718
Up Nately Hants 22 SU6951
Up Somborne Hants 10 SU3932
Up Sydling Dorset 9 ST6201
Upavon Wilts 20 SU1354
Upchurch Kent 14 TQ8467
Upcott Devon 7 SS7529
Upcott Somset 7 SS9025
Upgate Norfk 43 TG1318
Uphall Dorset 9 ST5502
Uphall Loth 75 NT0671
Upham Devon 7 SS8808
Upham Hants 11 SU5320
Uphampton H & W 27 SO3963
Uphampton H & W 28 SO8364
Uphill Avon 19 ST3158
Uplawmoor Strath 73 NS4355
Upleadon Gloucs 28 SO7527
Upleatham Cleve 62 NZ6319
Uploders Dorset 8 SY5093
Uplowman Devon 7 ST0115
Uplyme Devon 8 SY3293
Upminster Gt Lon 24 TQ5686
Upottery Devon 8 ST2007
Upper Affcot Shrops 36 SO4486
Upper Ardchronie Highld 97 NH6188
Upper Arley H & W 37 SO7680
Upper Basildon Berks 21 SU5976
Upper Beeding W Susx 12 TQ1910
Upper Benefield Nhants 40 SP9789
Upper Bentley H & W 28 SO9966
Upper Bighouse Highld 99 NC8856
Upper Boddington Nhants 29 SP4852
Upper Brailes Warwks 29 SP3039
Upper Breakish Highld 85 NG6823
Upper Broadheath H & W 28 SO8056
Upper Broughton Notts 39 SK6826
Upper Bucklebury Berks 21 SU5468
Upper Burgate Hants 10 SU1516
Upper Cairn D & G 66 NS6912
Upper Caldecote Beds 31 TL1645
Upper Catesby Nhants 29 SP5259
Upper Chapel Powys 26 SO0040
Upper Chicksgrove Wilts 9 ST9529
Upper Chute Wilts 21 SU2953
Upper Clapton Gt Lon 23 TQ3487
Upper Clatford Hants 21 SU3543
Upper Coberley Gloucs 28 SO9816
Upper Cound Shrops 37 SJ5505
Upper Cumberworth W York 55 SE2008
Upper Dallachy Gramp 94 NJ3662
Upper Deal Kent 15 TR3651
Upper Dean Beds 30 TL0467
Upper Denby W York 55 SE2207
Upper Dicker E Susx 13 TQ5509
Upper Dovercourt Essex 25 TM2330
Upper Drumbane Cent 81 NN6606
Upper Dunsforth N York 55 SE4463
Upper Eashing Surrey 12 SU9543
Upper Egleton H & W 27 SO6344
Upper Elkstone Staffs 48 SK0558
Upper Ellastone Staffs 48 SK1043
Upper Ethrie Highld 93 NH7662
Upper Farringdon Hants 11 SU7135
Upper Framilode Gloucs 28 SO7510
Upper Froyle Hants 11 SU7543
Upper Godney Somset 19 ST4842
Upper Gravenhurst Beds 30 TL1136
Upper Green Berks 21 SU3763
Upper Green Essex 24 TL5935
Upper Hale Surrey 22 SU8349
Upper Halliford Surrey 22 TQ0968
Upper Hambleton Leics 40 SK9007
Upper Harbledown Kent 15 TR1158
Upper Hartfield E Susx 13 TQ4634
Upper Hatherley Gloucs 28 SO9220
Upper Heaton W York 55 SE1719
Upper Helmsley N York 56 SE6956
Upper Hergest H & W 27 SO2654
Upper Heyford Nhants 30 SP6659
Upper Heyford Oxon 29 SP4925
Upper Hill H & W 27 SO4753
Upper Hopton W York 55 SE1918
Upper Hulme Staffs 48 SK0160
Upper Inglesham Wilts 21 SU2096
Upper Keith Loth 76 NT4562
Upper Killay W Glam 17 SS5892
Upper Kinchrackine Strath 80 NN1627
Upper Lambourn Berks 21 SU3080
Upper Landywood Staffs 38 SJ9805
Upper Langford Avon 19 ST4659
Upper Langwith Derbys 49 SK5169
Upper Largo Fife 83 NO4203
Upper Leigh Staffs 38 SK0136
Upper Lochton Gramp 89 NO6997
Upper Longdon Staffs 38 SK0614
Upper Lybster Highld 100 ND2537
Upper Lydbrook Gloucs 27 SO6015
Upper Lye H & W 27 SO3965
Upper Milton H & W 37 SO8172
Upper Minety Wilts 20 SU0091
Upper Moor H & W 28 SO9747
Upper Mulben Gramp 94 NJ3551
Upper Nesbet Border 76 NT6727
Upper Netchwood Shrops 37 SO6092
Upper Nobut Staffs 38 SK0335
Upper Norwood W Susx 12 SU9317
Upper Pond Street Essex 31 TL4636
Upper Poppleton N York 56 SE5553
Upper Quinton Warwks 29 SP1846
Upper Ratley Hants 10 SU3223
Upper Rochford H & W 27 SO6367
Upper Ruscoe D & G 65 NX5661
Upper Sapey H & W 28 SO6863
Upper Seagry Wilts 20 ST9480
Upper Shelton Beds 30 SP9843
Upper Sheringham Norfk 43 TG1441
Upper Slaughter Gloucs 28 SP1523
Upper Soudley Gloucs 27 SO6510
Upper Standen Kent 15 TR2139
Upper Stepford D & G 66 NX8681
Upper Stoke Norfk 43 TG2502
Upper Stondon Beds 30 TL1435
Upper Stowe Nhants 29 SP6456
Upper Street Hants 10 SU1518
Upper Street Norfk 43 TG3217
Upper Street Norfk 43 TG3616
Upper Street Suffk 32 TL7851
Upper Street Suffk 33 TM1050
Upper Sundon Beds 30 TL0428
Upper Swell Gloucs 29 SP1726
Upper Tasburgh Norfk 43 TM2095
Upper Tean Staffs 48 SK0139
Upper Town Avon 19 ST5265
Upper Town Derbys 48 SK2361
Upper Town H & W 27 SO5848
Upper Town Suffk 32 TL9267
Upper Tysoe Warwks 29 SP3343
Upper Victoria Tays 83 NO5336
Upper Wardington Oxon 29 SP4945
Upper Weedon Nhants 29 SP6258
Upper Wellingham E Susx 13 TQ4313
Upper Weybread Suffk 33 TM2379
Upper Wield Hants 11 SU6238
Upper Winchendon Bucks 30 SP7414
Upper Woodford Wilts 10 SU1237
Upper Wraxall Wilts 20 ST8074
Upperby Cumb 67 NY4153
Upperglen Highld 90 NG3151
Uppermill Gt Man 54 SD9905
Upperthong W York 55 SE1208
Upperton W Susx 12 SU9522
Uppertown Highld 100 ND3576
Uppingham Leics 40 SP8699
Uppington Shrops 37 SJ5909
Upsall N York 62 SE4586
Upsettlington Border 77 NT8846
Upshire Essex 23 TL4101
Upstreet Kent 15 TR2263
Upton Berks 22 SU9779
Upton Bucks 22 SP7711
Upton Cambs 40 TF1000
Upton Cambs 31 TL1778
Upton Ches 46 SJ4069
Upton Cnwll 4 SX2772
Upton Devon 8 ST0902
Upton Devon 5 SX7043
Upton Dorset 9 SY7483
Upton Dorset 9 SY9893
Upton Hants 21 SU3555
Upton Hants 10 SU3716
Upton Leics 39 SP3699
Upton Lincs 50 SK8686
Upton Mersyd 46 SJ2788
Upton Norfk 43 TG3912
Upton Notts 50 SK7354
Upton Notts 50 SK7476
Upton Oxon 21 SU5187
Upton Somset 7 SS9928
Upton Somset 8 ST4526
Upton W York 55 SE4713
Upton Cheyney Avon 20 ST6970
Upton Cressett Shrops 37 SO6592
Upton Crews H & W 27 SO6527
Upton Cross Cnwll 4 SX2872
Upton Grey Hants 22 SU6948
Upton Hellions Devon 7 SS8403
Upton Lovell Wilts 20 ST9440
Upton Magna Shrops 37 SJ5512
Upton Noble Somset 20 ST7139
Upton Pyne Devon 7 SX9198
Upton Scudamore Wilts 20 ST8647
Upton Snodsbury H & W 28 SO9454
Upton St. Leonards Gloucs 28 SO8615
Upton upon Severn H & W 28 SO8540
Upton Warren H & W 28 SO9267
Upwaltham W Susx 12 SU9413
Upwell Norfk 41 TF4902
Upwick Green Herts 31 TL4524
Upwood Cambs 41 TL2582
Urchfont Wilts 20 SU0357
Urmston Gt Man 47 SJ7694
Urquhart Gramp 94 NJ2862
Urra N York 62 NZ5601
Urray Highld 92 NH5052
Usan Tays 89 NO7254
Ushaw Moor Dur 61 NZ2242
Usk Gwent 19 SO3700
Usselby Lincs 50 TF0993
Usworth T & W 69 NZ3057
Utley W York 55 SE0542
Uton Devon 7 SX8298
Utterby Lincs 51 TF3093
Uttoxeter Staffs 38 SK0933
Uxbridge Gt Lon 22 TQ0584
Uyeasound Shet 103 HP5901
Uzmaston Dyfed 16 SM9714

V

Vale Guern 101 GN5312
Valley End Surrey 22 SU9564
Valtos Highld 90 NG5163
Valtos W Isls 102 NB0936
Vange Essex 24 TQ7186
Vatsetter Shet 103 HU5389
Vatten Highld 90 NG2843
Vaynor M Glam 26 SO0410
Velindre Powys 27 SO1836
Venn Ottery Devon 8 SY0891
Venngreen Devon 6 SS3711
Ventnor IOW 11 SZ5677
Venton Devon 5 SX5956
Vernham Dean Hants 21 SU3356
Vernham Street Hants 21 SU3457
Verwood Dorset 10 SU0809
Veryan Cnwll 3 SW9139
Vickerstown Cumb 53 SD1868
Victoria Cnwll 3 SW9861
Vidlin Shet 103 HU4765
Viewfield Gramp 94 NJ2864
Viewpark Strath 74 NS7061
Vigo Kent 14 TQ6361
Ville la Bas Jersey 101 JS0515
Villiaze Guern 101 GN4906
Vine's Cross E Susx 13 TQ5917
Virginia Water Surrey 22 TQ0067
Virginstow Devon 4 SX3792
Vobster Somset 20 ST7048
Voe Shet 103 HU4062
Vowchurch H & W 27 SO3636

W

Wackerfield Dur 61 NZ1522
Wacton Norfk 33 TM1791
Wadborough H & W 28 SO9047
Waddesdon Bucks 30 SP7416
Waddeton Devon 5 SX8756
Waddingham Lincs 50 SK9896
Waddington Lancs 54 SD7343
Waddington Lincs 50 SK9764
Waddon Dorset 9 SY6285
Wadebridge Cnwll 3 SW9972
Wadeford Somset 8 ST3110
Wadenhoe Nhants 40 TL0183
Wadesmill Herts 31 TL3617
Wadhurst E Susx 13 TQ6431
Wadshelf Derbys 49 SK3170
Wadworth S York 49 SK5696
Wainfleet All Saints Lincs 51 TF4959
Wainhouse Corner Cnwll 6 SX1895
Wainscott Kent 14 TQ7470

Wainstalls West Lexham

Wainstalls W York 55 SE0428
Waitby Cumb 60 NY7508
Waithe Lincs 51 TA2800
Wakefield W York 55 SE3320
Wakerley Nhants 40 SP9599
Wakes Colne Essex 24 TL8928
Walberswick Suffk 33 TM4974
Walberton W Susx 12 SU9705
Walbutt D & G 65 NX7468
Walcombe Somset 19 ST5546
Walcot Lincs 40 TF0635
Walcot Lincs 50 TF1356
Walcot Shrops 37 SJ5912
Walcot Wilts 20 SU1684
Walcot Green Norfk 33 TM1280
Walcote Leics 39 SP5683
Walcott Norfk 43 TG3532
Walden Stubbs N York 56 SE5516
Walderslade Kent 14 TQ7663
Walderton W Susx 11 SU7910
Walditch Dorset 8 SY4892
Waldridge Dur 69 NZ2549
Waldringfield Suffk 33 TM2845
Waldron E Susx 13 TQ5419
Wales S York 49 SK4882
Wales Somset 9 ST5824
Walesby Lincs 50 TF1392
Walesby Notts 49 SK6870
Walford H & W 36 SO3872
Walford H & W 27 SO5820
Walford Heath Shrops 36 SJ4419
Walgherton Ches 47 SJ6948
Walgrave Nhants 30 SP8071
Walk Mill Lancs 54 SD8729
Walkden Gt Man 47 SD7302
Walker T & W 69 NZ2864
Walker's Green H & W 27 SO5247
Walkerburn Border 76 NT3637
Walkeringham Notts 50 SK7792
Walkerith Notts 50 SK7892
Walkern Herts 31 TL2826
Walkerton Fife 83 NO2301
Walkhampton Devon 4 SX5369
Walkington Humb 56 SE9936
Walkley S York 49 SK3388
Walkwood H & W 28 SP0364
Wall Border 76 NT4622
Wall Nthumb 68 NY9168
Wall Staffs 38 SK1006
Wallacetown Strath 73 NS2703
Wallacetown Strath 73 NS3422
Wallands Park E Susx 13 TQ4010
Wallasey Mersyd 46 SJ2992
Wallfield Fife 82 NO1909
Wallingford Oxon 21 SU6089
Wallington Gt Lon 23 TQ2864
Wallington Hants 11 SU5806
Wallington Herts 31 TL2933
Wallisdown Dorset 10 SZ0694
Walls Shet 103 HU2449
Wallsend T & W 69 NZ2966
Wallyford Loth 76 NT3671
Walmer Kent 15 TR3750
Walmer Bridge Lancs 53 SD4724
Walpole Suffk 33 TM3674
Walpole Cross Keys Norfk 41 TF5119
Walpole Highway Norfk 41 TF5114
Walpole St. Andrew Norfk 41 TF5017
Walpole St. Peter Norfk 41 TF5016
Walsall W Mids 38 SP0198
Walsden W York 54 SD9321
Walsham le Willows Suffk 32 TM0071
Walshaw W York 54 SD9731
Walshford N York 55 SE4153
Walsoken Norfk 41 TF4710
Walston Strath 75 NT0545
Walsworth Herts 31 TL1930
Waltham Humb 57 TA2603
Waltham Kent 15 TR1048
Waltham Abbey Essex 23 TL3800
Waltham Chase Hants 11 SU5614
Waltham Cross Herts 23 TL3600
Waltham on the Wolds Leics 40 SK8024
Waltham St. Lawrence Berks 22 SU8276
Walthamstow Gt Lon 23 TQ3689
Walton Bucks 30 SP8936
Walton Cumb 67 NY5264
Walton Derbys 49 SK3568
Walton Leics 39 SP5987
Walton Powys 27 SO2559
Walton Shrops 37 SJ5818
Walton Somset 19 ST4636
Walton Suffk 25 TM2935
Walton W Susx 11 SU8104
Walton W York 55 SE3516
Walton W York 55 SE4447
Walton Cardiff Gloucs 28 SO9032
Walton East Dyfed 16 SN0223
Walton Elm Dorset 9 ST7717
Walton Lower Street Suffk 25 TM2834
Walton on the Hill Surrey 23 TQ2255
Walton on the Naze Essex 25 TM2522
Walton on the Wolds Leics 39 SK5919
Walton Park Avon 19 ST4172
Walton West Dyfed 16 SM8612
Walton-in-Gordano Avon 19 ST4273
Walton-le-Dale Lancs 53 SD5628
Walton-on-Thames Surrey 22 TQ1066
Walton-on-Trent Derbys 39 SK2118
Walton-on-the-Hill Staffs 38 SJ9520
Walworth Dur 61 NZ2318
Walwyn's Castle Dyfed 16 SM8711
Wambrook Somset 8 ST2907
Wamphray D & G 67 NY1295
Wanborough Surrey 12 SU9348
Wanborough Wilts 21 SU2082
Wandel Strath 75 NS9427
Wandsworth Gt Lon 23 TQ2574
Wangford Suffk 33 TM4679
Wanlip Leics 39 SK5910
Wanlockhead D & G 66 NS8712
Wannock E Susx 13 TQ5703
Wansford Cambs 40 TL0799
Wansford Humb 57 TA0656
Wanshurst Green Kent 14 TQ7645
Wanstead Gt Lon 23 TQ4088
Wanstrow Somset 20 ST7141
Wanswell Gloucs 20 SO6801
Wantage Oxon 21 SU3988
Wapley Avon 20 ST7179
Wappenbury Warwks 29 SP3769
Wappenham Nhants 29 SP6245
Warbister Ork 103 HY3932
Warbleton E Susx 13 TQ6018
Warborough Oxon 21 SU5993
Warboys Cambs 41 TL3080
Warbreck Lancs 53 SD3238
Warbstow Cnwll 4 SX2090
Warburton Gt Man 47 SJ7089
Warcop Cumb 60 NY7415
Warden Nthumb 68 NY9166
Wardington Oxon 29 SP4846
Wardle Ches 47 SJ6156
Wardle Gt Man 54 SD9116
Wardley Leics 40 SK8300
Wardlow Derbys 48 SK1874
Wardy Hill Cambs 41 TL4782
Ware Herts 31 TL3514
Wareham Dorset 9 SY9287
Warehorne Kent 15 TQ9832
Warenford Nthumb 77 NU1328
Wareside Herts 31 TL3915
Waresley Cambs 31 TL2554
Warfield Berks 22 SU8872
Warfleet Devon 5 SX8750
Wargrave Berks 22 SU7978
Warham All Saints Norfk 42 TF9541
Warham St. Mary Norfk 42 TF9441
Wark Nthumb 77 NT8238
Wark Nthumb 68 NY8577
Warkleigh Devon 7 SS6422
Warkton Nhants 40 SP8979
Warkworth Nhants 29 SP4840
Warkworth Nthumb 69 NU2406
Warlaby N York 62 SE3491
Warleggan Cnwll 3 SX1569
Warley Town W York 55 SE0524
Warlingham Surrey 23 TQ3658
Warmanbie D & G 67 NY1969
Warmfield W York 55 SE3720
Warmingham Ches 47 SJ7061
Warmington Nhants 40 TL0790
Warmington Warwks 29 SP4147
Warminster Wilts 20 ST8745
Warmley Avon 20 ST6673
Warmsworth S York 49 SE5400
Warmwell Dorset 9 SY7585
Warnford Hants 11 SU6223
Warnham W Susx 12 TQ1533
Warningcamp W Susx 12 TQ0307
Warninglid W Susx 12 TQ2426
Warren Ches 47 SJ8870
Warren Dyfed 16 SR9397
Warren Row Berks 22 SU8180
Warren Street Kent 14 TQ9252
Warrenhill Strath 75 NS9438
Warrington Bucks 30 SP8953
Warrington Ches 47 SJ6088
Warriston Loth 75 NT2575
Warsash Hants 11 SU4906
Warslow Staffs 48 SK0858
Warsop Notts 49 SK5667
Warter Humb 56 SE8750
Warthermaske N York 61 SE2078
Warthill N York 56 SE6755
Wartling E Susx 13 TQ6509
Wartnaby Leics 40 SK7123
Warton Lancs 53 SD4128
Warton Lancs 53 SD4972
Warton Warwks 39 SK2803
Warwick Cumb 67 NY4656
Warwick Warwks 29 SP2865
Wasdale Head Cumb 58 NY1808
Washaway Cnwll 3 SX0369
Washbourne Devon 5 SX7954
Washbrook Suffk 33 TM1142
Washfield Devon 7 SS9315
Washfold N York 61 NZ0502
Washford Somset 7 ST0541
Washford Pyne Devon 7 SS8111
Washingborough Lincs 50 TF0170
Washington T & W 69 NZ3155
Washington W Susx 12 TQ1112
Wasperton Warwks 29 SP2658
Wass N York 62 SE5579
Watchet Somset 18 ST0743
Watchfield Oxon 21 SU2490
Watchgate Cumb 59 SD5398
Water Devon 5 SX7580
Water Eaton Oxon 29 SP5112
Water End Essex 31 TL5840
Water End Herts 22 TL0310
Water End Humb 56 SE7938
Water Newton Cambs 40 TL1097
Water Orton Warwks 38 SP1790
Water Stratford Bucks 29 SP6534
Waterbeach Cambs 31 TL4965
Waterbeach W Susx 11 SU8908
Waterbeck D & G 67 NY2477
Watercombe Dorset 9 SY7585
Waterfall Staffs 48 SK0851
Waterfoot Strath 74 NS5655
Waterford Herts 31 TL3114
Watergate Cnwll 3 SX1181
Waterhead Strath 73 NS5411
Waterheads Border 75 NT2451
Waterhouses Staffs 48 SK0850
Wateringbury Kent 14 TQ6853
Waterloo Dyfed 16 SM9803
Waterloo Highld 85 NG6623
Waterloo Mersyd 46 SJ3298
Waterloo Strath 74 NS8154
Waterloo Tays 82 NO0537
Waterlooville Hants 11 SU6809
Watermillock Cumb 59 NY4422
Waterperry Oxon 29 SP6206
Waterrow Somset 7 ST0525
Waters Upton Shrops 37 SJ6319
Watersfield W Susx 12 TQ0115
Waterside Lancs 54 SD7123
Waterside Strath 73 NS4308
Waterside Strath 73 NS4843
Waterside Strath 74 NS6773
Waterstock Oxon 29 SP6305
Waterston Dyfed 16 SM9305
Watford Herts 22 TQ1196
Watford Nhants 29 SP6069
Wath N York 55 SE1467
Wath N York 62 SE3277
Wath upon Dearne S York 49 SE4300
Watlington Norfk 41 TF6111
Watlington Oxon 22 SU6894
Watten Highld 100 ND2454
Wattisfield Suffk 32 TM0074
Wattisham Suffk 32 TM0151
Watton Dorset 8 SY4591
Watton Humb 56 TA0150
Watton Norfk 42 TF9100
Watton-at-Stone Herts 31 TL3019
Wattsville Gwent 19 ST2091
Wauldby Humb 56 SE9629
Waulkmill Gramp 89 NO6492
Waunarlwydd W Glam 17 SS6095
Waunfawr Dyfed 34 SN6081
Waunfawr Gwynd 44 SH5259
Wavendon Bucks 30 SP9137
Waverbridge Cumb 67 NY2249
Waverton Ches 46 SJ4663
Waverton Cumb 67 NY2247
Wawne Humb 57 TA0936
Waxham Norfk 43 TG4426
Way Village Devon 7 SS8810
Wayford Somset 8 ST4006
Waytown Dorset 8 SY4797
Weacombe Somset 18 ST1140
Weald Oxon 21 SP3002
Wealdstone Gt Lon 22 TQ1589
Wear Head Dur 60 NY8539
Weardley W York 55 SE2944
Weare Somset 19 ST4152
Weare Giffard Devon 6 SS4721
Wearne Somset 8 ST4228
Weasenham All Saints Norfk 42 TF8421
Weasenham St. Peter Norfk 42 TF8522
Weasle Gt Man 47 SJ8098
Weaverham Ches 47 SJ6174
Weaverthorpe N York 56 SE9670
Webheath H & W 28 SP0266
Wedderlairs Gramp 95 NJ8532
Weddington Warwks 39 SP3693
Wedhampton Wilts 20 SU0557
Wedmore Somset 19 ST4347
Wednesbury W Mids 38 SO9895
Wednesfield W Mids 38 SJ9400
Weedon Bucks 30 SP8118
Weedon Lois Nhants 29 SP6046
Weeford Staffs 38 SK1403
Week Somset 7 SS9133
Week St. Mary Cnwll 6 SX2397
Weeke Hants 10 SU4630
Weekley Nhants 40 SP8881
Weel Humb 57 TA0639
Weeley Essex 25 TM1422
Weeley Heath Essex 25 TM1520
Weem Tays 87 NN8449
Weethley Hamlet Warwks 28 SP0555
Weeting Norfk 32 TL7788
Weeton Humb 57 TA3520
Weeton Lancs 53 SD3834
Weeton W York 55 SE2847
Weetwood W York 55 SE2737
Weir Lancs 54 SD8625
Weir Quay Devon 4 SX4365
Welborne Norfk 42 TG0610
Welbourn Lincs 50 SK9654
Welburn N York 56 SE7267
Welbury N York 62 NZ3902
Welby Lincs 40 SK9738
Welches Dam Cambs 41 TL4686
Welcombe Devon 6 SS2318
Welford Berks 21 SU4073
Welford Nhants 39 SP6480
Welford-on-Avon Warwks 28 SP1452
Welham Leics 40 SP7692
Welham Notts 49 SK7281
Welham Green Herts 23 TL2305
Well Hants 22 SU7646
Well Lincs 51 TF4473
Well N York 61 SE2681
Well Head Herts 31 TL1727
Welland H & W 28 SO7940
Wellbank Tays 83 NO4737
Wellbury Herts 30 TL1329
Wellesbourne Warwks 29 SP2855
Welling Gt Lon 23 TQ4675
Wellingborough Nhants 30 SP8967
Wellingham Norfk 42 TF8722
Wellingore Lincs 50 SK9856
Wellington Cumb 58 NY0704
Wellington H & W 27 SO4948
Wellington Shrops 37 SJ6511
Wellington Somset 8 ST1320
Wellington Heath H & W 28 SO7140
Wellow Avon 20 ST7458
Wellow IOW 10 SZ3888
Wellow Notts 49 SK6766
Wells Somset 19 ST5445
Wells-Next-The-Sea Norfk 42 TF9143
Wellstye Green Essex 24 TL6318
Welltree Tays 82 NN9622
Wellwood Fife 82 NT0988
Welney Norfk 41 TL5293
Welsh Frankton Shrops 36 SJ3533
Welsh Newton H & W 27 SO5017
Welsh St. Donats S Glam 18 ST0276
Welshampton Shrops 36 SJ4335
Welshpool Powys 36 SJ2207
Welton Cumb 67 NY3544
Welton Humb 56 SE9627
Welton Lincs 50 TF0179
Welton Nhants 29 SP5865
Welton le Marsh Lincs 51 TF4768
Welton le Wold Lincs 51 TF2787
Welwick Humb 57 TA3421
Welwyn Herts 31 TL2316
Welwyn Garden City Herts 31 TL2312
Wem Shrops 37 SJ5128
Wembdon Somset 19 ST2837
Wembley Gt Lon 23 TQ1885
Wembury Devon 4 SX5248
Wembworthy Devon 7 SS6609
Wemyss Bay Strath 73 NS1969
Wendens Ambo Essex 31 TL5136
Wendlebury Oxon 29 SP5619
Wendling Norfk 42 TF9312
Wendover Bucks 22 SP8607
Wendron Cnwll 2 SW6731
Wendy Cambs 31 TL3247
Wenhaston Suffk 33 TM4275
Wennington Cambs 41 TL2379
Wennington Lancs 54 SD6170
Wensley Derbys 49 SK2661
Wensley N York 61 SE0989
Wentbridge W York 55 SE4817
Wentnor Shrops 36 SO3892
Wentworth Cambs 31 TL4878
Wentworth S York 49 SK3898
Wenvoe S Glam 18 ST1272
Weobley H & W 27 SO4051
Weobley Marsh H & W 27 SO4151
Wepham W Susx 12 TQ0408
Wereham Norfk 42 TF6801
Werrington Cambs 40 TF1603
Werrington Cnwll 4 SX3287
Wervin Ches 46 SJ4271
Wesham Lancs 53 SD4133
Wessington Derbys 49 SK3757
West Acre Norfk 42 TF7815
West Alvington Devon 5 SX7243
West Anstey Devon 7 SS8527
West Appleton N York 61 SE2294
West Ashby Lincs 51 TF2672
West Ashling W Susx 11 SU8107
West Ashton Wilts 20 ST8755
West Auckland Dur 61 NZ1826
West Ayton N York 63 SE9884
West Bagborough Somset 8 ST1733
West Bank Ches 46 SJ5183
West Barkwith Lincs 50 TF1580
West Barnby N York 63 NZ8212
West Barns Loth 83 NT6578
West Barsham Norfk 42 TF9033
West Bay Dorset 8 SY4690
West Beckham Norfk 43 TG1439
West Bedfont Surrey 22 TQ0674
West Bergholt Essex 25 TL9527
West Bexington Dorset 8 SY5386
West Bilney Norfk 42 TF7115
West Blatchington E Susx 12 TQ2707
West Boldon T & W 69 NZ3561
West Bourton Dorset 9 ST7629
West Bowling W York 55 SE1630
West Brabourne Kent 15 TR0842
West Bradenham Norfk 42 TF9108
West Bradford Lancs 54 SD7444
West Bradley Somset 19 ST5536
West Bretton W York 55 SE2813
West Bridgford Notts 39 SK5836
West Bromwich W Mids 38 SP0091
West Buccleigh Hotel Border 67 NT3214
West Buckland Devon 7 SS6531
West Burton N York 61 SE0186
West Butterwick Humb 56 SE8305
West Byfleet Surrey 22 TQ0461
West Cairngaan D & G 64 NX1231
West Caister Norfk 43 TG5011
West Calder Loth 75 NT0163
West Camel Somset 9 ST5724
West Chaldon Dorset 9 SY7782
West Challow Oxon 21 SU3688
West Charleton Devon 5 SX7542
West Chelborough Dorset 8 ST5405
West Chevington Nthumb 69 NZ2297
West Chiltington W Susx 12 TQ0818
West Chinnock Somset 8 ST4613
West Cliffe Kent 15 TR3444
West Coker Somset 8 ST5113
West Compton Dorset 9 SY5694
West Compton Somset 19 ST5942
West Cottingwith N York 56 SE6942
West Cowick Humb 56 SE6421
West Cross W Glam 17 SS6189
West Curthwaite Cumb 67 NY3249
West Dean W Susx 11 SU8612
West Dean Wilts 10 SU2526
West Deeping Lincs 40 TF1008
West Derby Mersyd 46 SJ3993
West Dereham Norfk 42 TF6500
West Down Devon 6 SS5142
West Drayton Gt Lon 22 TQ0579
West Drayton Notts 49 SK7074
West Dunnet Highld 100 ND2171
West Ella Humb 56 TA0029
West End Avon 19 ST4569
West End Beds 30 SP9853
West End Berks 22 SU8275
West End Hants 10 SU4614
West End Herts 23 TL2608
West End Herts 23 TL3306
West End Norfk 43 TG5011
West End Surrey 22 SU9461
West End Surrey 22 TQ1263
West End Wilts 9 ST9824
West End Green Hants 22 SU6661
West Farleigh Kent 14 TQ7152
West Farndon Nhants 29 SP5251
West Felton Shrops 36 SJ3425
West Firle E Susx 13 TQ4707
West Grafton Wilts 21 SU2460
West Green Hants 22 SU7456
West Grimstead Wilts 10 SU2026
West Grinstead W Susx 12 TQ1720
West Haddlesey N York 56 SE5626
West Haddon Nhants 39 SP6371
West Hagbourne Oxon 21 SU5187
West Hagley H & W 38 SO9080
West Hallam Derbys 49 SK4341
West Halton Humb 56 SE9020
West Ham Gt Lon 23 TQ3983
West Handley Derbys 49 SK3977
West Hanney Oxon 21 SU4092
West Hanningfield Essex 24 TQ7399
West Harnham Wilts 10 SU1329
West Harptree Avon 19 ST5556
West Harting W Susx 11 SU7820
West Hatch Somset 8 ST2821
West Hatch Wilts 9 ST9227
West Haven Tays 83 NO5735
West Heath W Mids 38 SP0277
West Helmsdale Highld 97 ND0115
West Hendred Oxon 21 SU4488
West Heslerton N York 63 SE9176
West Hewish Avon 19 ST3963
West Hill Devon 8 SY0794
West Hoathly W Susx 12 TQ3632
West Holme Dorset 9 SY8885
West Horrington Somset 19 ST5747
West Horsley Surrey 12 TQ0752
West Hougham Kent 15 TR2640
West Howe Dorset 10 SZ0595
West Huntingtower Tays 82 NO0724
West Huntspill Somset 19 ST3044
West Hythe Kent 15 TR1234
West Ilsley Berks 21 SU4782
West Itchenor W Susx 11 SU7901
West Kennet Wilts 20 SU1168
West Kilbride Strath 73 NS2048
West Kingsdown Kent 14 TQ5763
West Kington Wilts 20 ST8077
West Kirby Mersyd 46 SJ2186
West Knapton N York 63 SE8775
West Knighton Dorset 9 SY7387
West Knoyle Wilts 9 ST8632
West Lambrook Somset 8 ST4118
West Langdon Kent 15 TR3247
West Laroch Highld 86 NN0758
West Lavington W Susx 11 SU8920
West Lavington Wilts 20 SU0052
West Layton N York 61 NZ1410
West Leake Notts 39 SK5226
West Leigh Devon 7 SS6805
West Leigh Devon 5 SX7557
West Leigh Somset 8 ST1230
West Lexham Norfk 42 TF8417

West Lilling Wilby

West Lilling *N York* 56 SE6465
West Linton *Border* 75 NT1551
West Littleton *Avon* 20 ST7675
West Lockinge *Oxon* 21 SU4187
West Lulworth *Dorset* 9 SY8280
West Lutton *N York* 56 SE9369
West Lydford *Somset* 9 ST5631
West Lyng *Somset* 8 ST3128
West Lynn *Norfk* 41 TF6120
West Malling *Kent* 14 TQ6757
West Malvern *H & W* 28 SO7646
West Marden *W Susx* 11 SU7713
West Markham *Notts* 49 SK7272
West Marsh *Humb* 57 TA2509
West Marton *N York* 54 SD8950
West Melbury *Dorset* 9 ST8720
West Meon *Hants* 11 SU6423
West Mersea *Essex* 25 TM0112
West Milton *Dorset* 8 SY5096
West Minster *Kent* 14 TQ9073
West Monkton *Somset* 8 ST2628
West Moors *Dorset* 10 SU0802
West Morden *Dorset* 9 SY9095
West Mudford *Somset* 9 ST5620
West Ness *N York* 62 SE6879
West Newton *Humb* 57 TA2037
West Newton *Norfk* 42 TF6928
West Newton *Somset* 8 ST2829
West Norwood *Gt Lon* 23 TQ3171
West Ogwell *Devon* 5 SX8270
West Orchard *Dorset* 9 ST8216
West Overton *Wilts* 20 SU1267
West Parley *Dorset* 10 SZ0896
West Peckham *Kent* 13 TQ6452
West Pelton *Dur* 69 NZ2353
West Pennard *Somset* 19 ST5438
West Pentire *Cnwll* 2 SW7760
West Perry *Cambs* 30 TL1466
West Preston *W Susx* 12 TQ0602
West Pulham *Dorset* 9 ST7008
West Putford *Devon* 6 SS3616
West Quantoxhead *Somset* 18 ST1141
West Raddon *Devon* 7 SS8902
West Rainton *T & W* 69 NZ3246
West Rasen *Lincs* 50 TF0689
West Raynham *Norfk* 42 TF8725
West Rounton *N York* 62 NZ4103
West Row *Suffk* 32 TL6775
West Rudham *Norfk* 42 TF8127
West Runton *Norfk* 43 TG1842
West Saltoun *Loth* 76 NT4667
West Sandford *Devon* 7 SS8102
West Sandwick *Shet* 103 HU4588
West Scrafton *N York* 61 SE0783
West Stafford *Dorset* 9 SY7289
West Stockwith *Notts* 50 SK7895
West Stoke *W Susx* 11 SU8208
West Stour *Dorset* 9 ST7822
West Stourmouth *Kent* 15 TR2562
West Stow *Suffk* 32 TL8171
West Stowell *Wilts* 20 SU1361
West Street *Suffk* 32 TL9871
West Tanfield *N York* 61 SE2678
West Taphouse *Cnwll* 3 SX1463
West Tarbert *Strath* 71 NR8467
West Tarring *W Susx* 12 TQ1103
West Thorney *W Susx* 11 SU7602
West Thorpe *Notts* 39 SK6225
West Thurrock *Essex* 24 TQ5877
West Tilbury *Essex* 24 TQ6678
West Tisted *Hants* 11 SU6529
West Torrington *Lincs* 50 TF1381
West Town *Avon* 19 ST4868
West Town *Hants* 11 SZ7199
West Tytherley *Hants* 10 SU2729
West Tytherton *Wilts* 20 ST9474
West Walton *Norfk* 41 TF4613
West Walton Highway *Norfk* 41 TF4913
West Wellow *Hants* 10 SU2819
West Wembury *Devon* 4 SX5249
West Wemyss *Fife* 83 NT3294
West Wick *Avon* 19 ST3761
West Wickham *Cambs* 31 TL6149
West Wickham *Gt Lon* 23 TQ3766
West Williamston *Dyfed* 16 SN0305
West Winch *Norfk* 41 TF6316
West Winterslow *Wilts* 10 SU2331
West Wittering *W Susx* 11 SZ7898
West Witton *N York* 61 SE0588
West Woodburn *Nthumb* 68 NY8987
West Woodhay *Berks* 21 SU3963
West Worldham *Hants* 11 SU7436
West Worthing *W Susx* 12 TQ1302
West Wratting *Essex* 31 TL6052
West Youlstone *Cnwll* 6 SS2615
Westbere *Kent* 15 TR1961
Westborough *Lincs* 50 SK8544
Westbourne *W Susx* 11 SU7507
Westbrook *Berks* 21 SU4272
Westbrook *Kent* 15 TR3470
Westbury *Bucks* 29 SP6235
Westbury *Shrops* 36 SJ3509
Westbury *Wilts* 20 ST8751
Westbury Leigh *Wilts* 20 ST8649
Westbury on Severn *Gloucs* 28 SO7114
Westbury-on-Trym *Avon* 19 ST5777
Westbury-sub-Mendip *Somset* 19 ST5049
Westby *Lancs* 53 SD3831
Westcliff-on-Sea *Essex* 24 TQ8685
Westcombe *Somset* 20 ST6739
Westcote *Gloucs* 29 SP2120
Westcott *Bucks* 30 SP7116
Westcott *Devon* 7 ST0204
Westcott *Surrey* 12 TQ1448
Westcourt *Wilts* 21 SU2261
Westdean *E Susx* 13 TV5299
Westdowns *Cnwll* 3 SX0582
Wester Drumashie *Highld* 92 NH6032
Wester Essenside *Border* 76 NT4320
Wester Ochiltree *Loth* 75 NT0374
Wester Pitkierie *Fife* 83 NO5505
Westerdale *Highld* 100 ND1251
Westerdale *N York* 62 NZ6605
Westerfield *Suffk* 33 TM1747
Westergate *W Susx* 12 SU9305
Westerham *Kent* 23 TQ4454
Westerhope *T & W* 69 NZ1966
Westerland *Devon* 5 SX8662
Westerleigh *Avon* 20 ST6979
Westerton *Tays* 89 NO6754
Westfield *Avon* 20 ST6753
Westfield *D & G* 58 NX9926
Westfield *E Susx* 14 TQ8115
Westfield *Loth* 75 NS9472
Westfield *Norfk* 42 TF9909
Westfields of Rattray *Tays* 88 NO1746
Westgate *Dur* 60 NY9038
Westgate *Humb* 56 SE7707
Westgate *Norfk* 42 TF9740
Westgate on Sea *Kent* 15 TR3270
Westhall *Suffk* 33 TM4280
Westham *Dorset* 9 SY6679
Westham *E Susx* 13 TQ6404
Westham *Somset* 19 ST4046
Westhampnett *W Susx* 11 SU8806
Westhay *Somset* 19 ST4342
Westhide *H & W* 27 SO5843
Westhill *Gramp* 95 NJ8307
Westhope *H & W* 27 SO4651
Westhope *Shrops* 37 SO4786
Westhorpe *Lincs* 41 TF2231
Westhorpe *Suffk* 32 TM0468
Westhoughton *Gt Man* 47 SD6506
Westhouse *N York* 60 SD6773
Westhouses *Derbys* 49 SK4157
Westhumble *Surrey* 12 TQ1651
Westlake *Devon* 5 SX6253
Westleigh *Devon* 6 SS4728
Westleigh *Devon* 7 ST0617
Westleton *Suffk* 33 TM4369
Westley *Suffk* 32 TL8264
Westley Waterless *Cambs* 31 TL6156
Westlington *Bucks* 22 SP7610
Westlinton *Cumb* 67 NY3964
Westmarsh *Kent* 15 TR2761
Westmeston *E Susx* 12 TQ3313
Westmill *Herts* 31 TL3627
Westmuir *Tays* 88 NO3652
Westnewton *Cumb* 67 NY1344
Westoe *T & W* 69 NZ3765
Weston *Avon* 20 ST7366
Weston *Berks* 21 SU3973
Weston *Ches* 47 SJ7352
Weston *Devon* 8 ST1400
Weston *Devon* 8 SY1688
Weston *Hants* 11 SU7221
Weston *Herts* 31 TL2530
Weston *Lincs* 41 TF2924
Weston *Nhants* 29 SP5846
Weston *Notts* 50 SK7767
Weston *Shrops* 36 SJ2927
Weston *Shrops* 37 SJ5629
Weston *Staffs* 38 SJ9726
Weston *W York* 55 SE1747
Weston Beggard *H & W* 27 SO5841
Weston by Welland *Nhants* 40 SP7791
Weston Colley *Hants* 11 SU5039
Weston Colville *Cambs* 31 TL6153
Weston Corbett *Hants* 22 SU6846
Weston Coyney *Staffs* 48 SJ9343
Weston Favell *Nhants* 30 SP7962
Weston Green *Cambs* 32 TL6252
Weston Heath *Shrops* 37 SJ7713
Weston Jones *Staffs* 37 SJ7624
Weston Longville *Norfk* 43 TG1115
Weston Lullingfields *Shrops* 36 SJ4224
Weston Patrick *Hants* 22 SU6946
Weston Rhyn *Shrops* 36 SJ2835
Weston Subedge *Gloucs* 28 SP1241
Weston Turville *Bucks* 22 SP8510
Weston Underwood *Bucks* 30 SP8650
Weston Underwood *Derbys* 49 SK2942
Weston under Penyard *H & W* 27 SO6322
Weston under Wetherley *Warwks* 29 SP3669
Weston-in-Gordano *Avon* 19 ST4474
Weston-on-Trent *Derbys* 39 SK4027
Weston-on-the-Green *Oxon* 29 SP5318
Weston-Super-Mare *Avon* 19 ST3260
Weston-under-Lizard *Staffs* 37 SJ8010
Westonbirt *Gloucs* 20 ST8589
Westoning *Beds* 30 TL0332
Westonzoyland *Somset* 8 ST3534
Westow *N York* 56 SE7565
Westport *Somset* 8 ST3820
Westport *Strath* 72 NR6526
Westquarter *Cent* 82 NS9178
Westridge Green *Berks* 21 SU5679
Westrigg *Loth* 74 NS9067
Westrop *Wilts* 21 SU2093
Westruther *Border* 76 NT6349
Westry *Cambs* 41 TL4098
Westward *Cumb* 67 NY2744
Westward Ho *Devon* 6 SS4329
Westwell *Kent* 15 TQ9947
Westwell *Oxon* 29 SP2209
Westwell Leacon *Kent* 15 TQ9647
Westwick *Cambs* 31 TL4265
Westwood *Devon* 7 SY0199
Westwood *Kent* 15 TR3667
Westwood *Wilts* 20 ST8059
Westwoodside *Humb* 50 SE7400
Wetheral *Cumb* 67 NY4654
Wetherby *W York* 55 SE4048
Wetherden *Suffk* 32 TM0062
Wetheringsett *Suffk* 33 TM1266
Wethersfield *Essex* 24 TL7131
Wetherup Street *Suffk* 33 TM1464
Wetley Rocks *Staffs* 48 SJ9649
Wettenhall *Ches* 47 SJ6261
Wetton *Staffs* 48 SK1055
Wetwang *Humb* 56 SE9359
Wetwood *Staffs* 37 SJ7733
Wexcombe *Wilts* 21 SU2758
Weybourne *Norfk* 43 TG1142
Weybread *Suffk* 33 TM2480
Weybread Street *Suffk* 33 TM2479
Weybridge *Surrey* 22 TQ0764
Weydale *Highld* 100 ND1564
Weyhill *Hants* 21 SU3146
Weymouth *Dorset* 9 SY6779
Whaddon *Bucks* 30 SP8034
Whaddon *Cambs* 31 TL3546
Whaddon *Gloucs* 28 SO8313
Whaddon *Wilts* 20 ST8861
Whaddon *Wilts* 10 SU1926
Whaley *Derbys* 49 SK5171
Whaley Bridge *Derbys* 48 SK0180
Whaligoe *Highld* 100 ND3140
Whalley *Lancs* 54 SD7336
Whalton *Nthumb* 61 NZ1318
Whaplode *Lincs* 41 TF3224
Whaplode Drove *Lincs* 41 TF3213
Wharf *Warwks* 29 SP4352
Wharfe *N York* 54 SD7869
Wharles *Lancs* 53 SD4435
Wharncliffe Side *S York* 49 SK2994
Wharram-le-Street *N York* 56 SE8665
Wharton *H & W* 27 SO5055
Whasset *Cumb* 59 SD5080
Whaston *N York* 61 NZ1506
Whatcote *Warwks* 29 SP2944
Whateley *Warwks* 39 SP2299
Whatfield *Suffk* 32 TM0246
Whatley *Somset* 8 ST3607
Whatley *Somset* 20 ST7347
Whatlington *E Susx* 14 TQ7618
Whatsole Street *Kent* 15 TR1144
Whatstandwell *Derbys* 49 SK3354
Whatton *Notts* 40 SK7439
Whauphill *D & G* 64 NX4049
Wheatacre *Norfk* 43 TM4694
Wheathampstead *Herts* 31 TL1714
Wheathill *Shrops* 37 SO6282
Wheatley *Hants* 11 SU7840
Wheatley *Oxon* 29 SP5905
Wheatley Hill *Dur* 62 NZ3738
Wheatley Hills *S York* 56 SE5904
Wheaton Aston *Staffs* 38 SJ8512
Wheddon Cross *Somset* 7 SS9238
Wheelock *Ches* 47 SJ7559
Wheelton *Lancs* 54 SD6021
Wheldrake *N York* 56 SE6844
Whelpley Hill *Bucks* 22 SP9904
Whempstead *Herts* 31 TL3221
Whenby *N York* 56 SE6369
Whepstead *Suffk* 32 TL8358
Wherstead *Suffk* 33 TM1540
Wherwell *Hants* 21 SU3841
Wheston *Derbys* 48 SK1376
Whetsted *Kent* 14 TQ6646
Whetstone *Leics* 39 SP5597
Whicham *Cumb* 58 SD1382
Whichford *Warwks* 29 SP3134
Whickham *T & W* 69 NZ2061
Whiddon Down *Devon* 5 SX6992
Whigstreet *Tays* 89 NO4844
Whiligh *E Susx* 13 TQ6431
Whilton *Nhants* 29 SP6364
Whimple *Devon* 7 SY0497
Whimpwell Green *Norfk* 43 TG3829
Whinburgh *Norfk* 42 TG0009
Whinnie Liggate *D & G* 65 NX7252
Whinnyfold *Gramp* 95 NK0733
Whippingham *IOW* 11 SZ5193
Whipsnade *Beds* 30 TL0117
Whipton *Devon* 5 SX9493
Whisby *Lincs* 50 SK9067
Whissendine *Leics* 40 SK8214
Whissonsett *Norfk* 42 TF9123
Whistlefield Inn *Strath* 80 NS1492
Whistley Green *Berks* 22 SU7974
Whiston *Mersyd* 46 SJ4791
Whiston *Nhants* 30 SP8460
Whiston *S York* 49 SK4489
Whiston *Staffs* 38 SJ8914
Whiston *Staffs* 48 SK0347
Whitbeck *Cumb* 58 SD1184
Whitbourne *H & W* 28 SO7257
Whitburn *Loth* 75 NS9464
Whitburn *T & W* 69 NZ4062
Whitby *N York* 63 NZ8910
Whitchurch *Avon* 19 ST6167
Whitchurch *Bucks* 30 SP8020
Whitchurch *Devon* 4 SX4972
Whitchurch *Dyfed* 16 SM8025
Whitchurch *H & W* 27 SO5517
Whitchurch *Hants* 21 SU4648
Whitchurch *Oxon* 21 SU6377
Whitchurch *S Glam* 19 ST1579
Whitchurch *Shrops* 37 SJ5341
Whitchurch Canonicorum *Dorset* 8 SY3995
Whitchurch Hill *Oxon* 21 SU6378
Whitcombe *Dorset* 9 SY7188
Whitcot *Shrops* 36 SO3791
Whitcott Keysett *Shrops* 36 SO2782
White Ball *Somset* 8 ST1019
White Chapel *Lancs* 53 SD5541
White Colne *Essex* 24 TL8729
White Cross *Cnwll* 2 SW6821
White End *H & W* 28 SO7834
White Lackington *Dorset* 9 SY7198
White Ladies Aston *H & W* 28 SO9252
White Notley *Essex* 24 TL7818
White Pit *Lincs* 51 TF3777
White Roding *Essex* 24 TL5613
White Stone *H & W* 27 SO5642
White Waltham *Berks* 22 SU8577
Whiteacre Heath *Warwks* 39 SP2292
Whitebridge *Highld* 92 NH4815
Whitebrook *Gwent* 27 SO5306
Whitecairns *Gramp* 95 NJ9218
Whitechapel *Gt Lon* 23 TQ3381
Whitecliffe *Gloucs* 27 SO5609
Whitecraig *Loth* 75 NT3470
Whitecrook *D & G* 64 NX1656
Whiteface *Highld* 97 NH7088
Whitefarland *Strath* 72 NR8642
Whitefield *Gt Man* 47 SD8006
Whiteford *Gramp* 95 NJ7126
Whitegate *Ches* 47 SJ6269
Whitehall *Ork* 103 HY6528
Whitehaven *Cumb* 58 NX9718
Whitehill *Hants* 11 SU7934
Whitehills *Gramp* 94 NJ6565
Whitehouse *Gramp* 94 NJ6114
Whitehouse *Strath* 71 NR8161
Whitekirk *Loth* 83 NT5981
Whitelackington *Somset* 8 ST3815
Whiteley Bank *IOW* 11 SZ5581
Whitemire *Gramp* 93 NH9854
Whitemoor *Cnwll* 3 SW9757
Whitemoor *Notts* 49 SK5441
Whiteness *Shet* 103 HU3844
Whiteparish *Wilts* 10 SU2423
Whiterashes *Gramp* 95 NJ8523
Whiterow *Gramp* 93 NJ0257
Whiterow *Highld* 100 ND3648
Whiteshill *Gloucs* 28 SO8406
Whitesmith *E Susx* 13 TQ5213
Whitestaunton *Somset* 8 ST2810
Whitestone Cross *Devon* 5 SX8993
Whitewell *Lancs* 54 SD6646
Whitfield *Avon* 20 ST6791
Whitfield *Kent* 15 TR3045
Whitfield *Nhants* 29 SP6039
Whitfield *Nthumb* 68 NY7758
Whitford *Clwyd* 46 SJ1478
Whitford *Devon* 8 SY2595
Whitgift *Humb* 56 SE8122
Whitgreave *Staffs* 38 SJ9028
Whithorn *D & G* 64 NX4440
Whiting Bay *Strath* 72 NS0425
Whitington *Norfk* 42 TL7199
Whitkirk *W York* 55 SE3633
Whitland *Dyfed* 17 SN1916
Whitlaw *Border* 67 NT5012
Whitletts *Strath* 73 NS3623
Whitley *Berks* 22 SU7270
Whitley *N York* 56 SE5620
Whitley *S York* 49 SK3494
Whitley *Wilts* 20 ST8866
Whitley Bay *T & W* 69 NZ3571
Whitley Chapel *Nthumb* 68 NY9257
Whitley Lower *W York* 55 SE2217
Whitminster *Gloucs* 28 SO7708
Whitmore *Staffs* 37 SJ8140
Whitnage *Devon* 7 ST0215
Whitnash *Warwks* 29 SP3263
Whitney *H & W* 27 SO2747
Whitrigglees *Cumb* 67 NY2457
Whitsbury *Hants* 10 SU1219
Whitsome *Border* 77 NT8650
Whitson *Gwent* 19 ST3883
Whitstable *Kent* 15 TR1066
Whitstone *Cnwll* 6 SX2698
Whittingehame *Loth* 76 NT6073
Whittingham *Nthumb* 68 NU0611
Whittingslow *Shrops* 36 SO4388
Whittington *Derbys* 49 SK3875
Whittington *Gloucs* 28 SP0120
Whittington *H & W* 28 SO8753
Whittington *Lancs* 59 SD6075
Whittington *Shrops* 36 SJ3231
Whittington *Staffs* 38 SK1508
Whittington *Staffs* 38 SO8682
Whittington *Warwks* 39 SP2999
Whittle-le-Woods *Lancs* 54 SD5821
Whittlebury *Nhants* 30 SP6943
Whittlesey *Cambs* 41 TL2697
Whittlesford *Cambs* 31 TL4748
Whitton *Cleve* 62 NZ3822
Whitton *Humb* 56 SE9024
Whitton *Powys* 27 SO2767
Whitton *Shrops* 37 SO5772
Whittonstall *Nthumb* 68 NZ0757
Whitway *Hants* 21 SU4559
Whitwell *Derbys* 49 SK5276
Whitwell *Herts* 31 TL1820
Whitwell *IOW* 11 SZ5277
Whitwell *Leics* 40 SK9208
Whitwell *N York* 61 SE2899
Whitwell Street *Norfk* 43 TG1022
Whitwell-on-the-Hill *N York* 56 SE7265
Whitwick *Leics* 39 SK4315
Whitworth *Lancs* 54 SD8818
Whixall *Shrops* 37 SJ5134
Whixley *N York* 55 SE4458
Whorlton *Dur* 61 NZ1014
Whorlton *N York* 62 NZ4802
Whyle *H & W* 27 SO5561
Whyteleafe *Surrey* 23 TQ3358
Wibdon *Gloucs* 19 ST5797
Wibsey *W York* 55 SE1430
Wibtoft *Warwks* 39 SP4887
Wichenford *H & W* 28 SO7860
Wichling *Kent* 14 TQ9256
Wick *Avon* 20 ST7072
Wick *Dorset* 10 SZ1591
Wick *H & W* 28 SO9645
Wick *Highld* 100 ND3650
Wick *M Glam* 18 SS9271
Wick *W Susx* 12 TQ0203
Wick Rissington *Gloucs* 29 SP1821
Wick St. Lawrence *Avon* 19 ST3665
Wicken *Cambs* 31 TL5770
Wicken *Nhants* 30 SP7439
Wicken Bonhunt *Essex* 31 TL4933
Wickenby *Lincs* 50 TF0982
Wicker Street Green *Suffk* 32 TL9742
Wickersley *S York* 49 SK4791
Wickford *Essex* 24 TQ7493
Wickham *Berks* 21 SU3971
Wickham *Hants* 11 SU5711
Wickham Bishops *Essex* 24 TL8412
Wickham Green *Suffk* 33 TM0969
Wickham Market *Suffk* 33 TM3055
Wickham Skeith *Suffk* 33 TM0969
Wickham St. Paul *Essex* 24 TL8336
Wickham Street *Suffk* 32 TM0869
Wickhambreaux *Kent* 15 TR2158
Wickhambrook *Suffk* 32 TL7554
Wickhamford *H & W* 28 SP0641
Wickhampton *Norfk* 43 TG4205
Wicklewood *Norfk* 42 TG0702
Wickmere *Norfk* 43 TG1733
Wickwar *Avon* 20 ST7288
Widdington *Essex* 31 TL5331
Widdrington *T & W* 69 NZ2595
Widecombe in the Moor *Devon* 5 SX7176
Widegates *Cnwll* 4 SX2858
Widemouth Bay *Cnwll* 6 SS2002
Widford *Essex* 24 TL6904
Widford *Herts* 31 TL4216
Widmer End *Bucks* 22 SU8896
Widmerpool *Notts* 39 SK6327
Widmore *Gt Lon* 23 TQ4268
Widnes *Ches* 46 SJ5184
Wigan *Gt Man* 47 SD5805
Wigborough *Somset* 8 ST4415
Wiggaton *Devon* 8 SY1093
Wiggenhall St. Germans *Norfk* 41 TF5914
Wiggenhall St. Mary Magdalen *Norfk* 41 TF5911
Wiggenhall St. Mary the Virgin *Norfk* 41 TF5813
Wiggens Green *Essex* 32 TL6642
Wigginton *Herts* 22 SP9310
Wigginton *N York* 56 SE6058
Wigginton *Oxon* 29 SP3833
Wigginton *Staffs* 39 SK2006
Wigglesworth *N York* 54 SD8156
Wiggold *Gloucs* 28 SP0404
Wiggonby *Cumb* 67 NY2952
Wighill *N York* 55 SE4746
Wighton *Norfk* 42 TF9439
Wigley *Hants* 10 SU3217
Wigmore *H & W* 27 SO4169
Wigmore *Kent* 14 TQ7964
Wigsley *Notts* 50 SK8570
Wigsthorpe *Nhants* 40 TL0482
Wigston *Leics* 39 SP6198
Wigston Parva *Leics* 39 SP4689
Wigthorpe *Notts* 49 SK5983
Wigtoft *Lincs* 41 TF2636
Wigton *Cumb* 67 NY2548
Wigtown *D & G* 64 NX4355
Wike *W York* 55 SE3342
Wilbarston *Nhants* 40 SP8188
Wilberfoss *Humb* 56 SE7350
Wilburton *Cambs* 31 TL4775
Wilby *Nhants* 30 SP8666
Wilby *Norfk* 32 TM0389
Wilby *Suffk* 33 TM2472

Wraxall *Somset*	19	ST6036
Wray *Lancs*	54	SD6067
Wraysbury *Berks*	22	TQ0074
Wrayton *Lancs*	54	SD6172
Wrea Green *Lancs*	53	SD3931
Wreay *Cumb*	67	NY4348
Wrecclesham *Surrey*	22	SU8244
Wrekenton *T & W*	69	NZ2759
Wrelton *N York*	63	SE7686
Wrenbury *Ches*	47	SJ5947
Wreningham *Norfk*	43	TM1698
Wrentham *Suffk*	33	TM4982
Wrentnall *Shrops*	36	SJ4203
Wressle *Humb*	56	SE7131
Wressle *Humb*	56	SE9709
Wrestlingworth *Beds*	31	TL2547
Wretton *Norfk*	42	TF6900
Wrexham *Clwyd*	46	SJ3350
Wribbenhall *H & W*	37	SO7975
Wrinehill *Staffs*	47	SJ7547
Wrington *Avon*	19	ST4762
Writhlington *Somset*	20	ST6954
Wrockwardine *Shrops*	37	SJ6212
Wroot *Humb*	56	SE7103
Wrose *W York*	55	SE1636
Wrotham *Kent*	14	TQ6158
Wroughton *Wilts*	20	SU1480
Wroxall *IOW*	11	SZ5579
Wroxall *Warwks*	39	SP2271
Wroxeter *Shrops*	37	SJ5608
Wroxham *Norfk*	43	TG3017
Wroxton *Oxon*	29	SP4141
Wyaston *Derbys*	48	SK1842
Wyberton *Lincs*	51	TF3240
Wyboston *Beds*	31	TL1656
Wybunbury *Ches*	47	SJ6949
Wychbold *H & W*	28	SO9266
Wychnor *Staffs*	38	SK1715
Wyck *Hants*	11	SU7539
Wycliffe *Dur*	61	NZ1114
Wycoller *Lancs*	54	SD9339
Wycomb *Leics*	40	SK7724
Wycombe Marsh *Bucks*	22	SU8892
Wyddial *Herts*	31	TL3731
Wye *Kent*	15	TR0546
Wyke *Dorset*	9	ST7926
Wyke *W York*	55	SE1526
Wyke Champflower *Somset*	9	ST6634

Wyke Regis *Dorset*	9	SY6677
Wykeham *N York*	63	SE9683
Wyken *Shrops*	37	SO7695
Wyken *W Mids*	39	SP3780
Wykey *Shrops*	36	SJ3824
Wylam *Nthumb*	69	NZ1164
Wylde Green *W Mids*	38	SP1294
Wylye *Wilts*	10	SU0037
Wymeswold *Leics*	39	SK6023
Wymington *Beds*	30	SP9564
Wymondham *Leics*	40	SK8418
Wymondham *Norfk*	43	TG1001
Wynford Eagle *Dorset*	9	SY5896
Wyre Piddle *H & W*	28	SO9647
Wysall *Notts*	39	SK6027
Wythall *H & W*	38	SP0774
Wytham *Oxon*	29	SP4708
Wythenshawe *Gt Man*	47	SJ8386
Wyton *Cambs*	31	TL2772
Wyton *Humb*	57	TA1733
Wyverstone *Suffk*	32	TM0468
Wyverstone Street *Suffk*	32	TM0367

Y

Y Ferwig *Dyfed*	17	SN1849
Y Gyffylliog *Clwyd*	45	SJ0557
Y Maerdy *Clwyd*	45	SJ0144
Y Rhiw *Gwynd*	44	SH2227
Yaddlethorpe *Humb*	56	SE8806
Yafforth *N York*	62	SE3494
Yalberton *Devon*	5	SX8658
Yalding *Kent*	14	TQ6950
Yalverton *Devon*	4	SX5267
Yanwath *Cumb*	59	NY5127
Yanworth *Gloucs*	28	SP0713
Yapham *Humb*	56	SE7851
Yapton *W Susx*	12	SU9703
Yarborough *Avon*	19	ST3857
Yarburgh *Lincs*	51	TF3592
Yarcombe *Devon*	8	ST2408
Yard *Devon*	7	SS7721
Yardley *W Mids*	38	SP1386
Yardley Gobion *Nhants*	30	SP7644
Yardley Hastings *Nhants*	30	SP8657
Yardley Wood *W Mids*	38	SP1079

Yarkhill *H & W*	27	SO6042
Yarlet *Staffs*	38	SJ9129
Yarley *Somset*	19	ST5044
Yarlington *Somset*	9	ST6529
Yarm *Cleve*	62	NZ4112
Yarmouth *IOW*	10	SZ3589
Yarnbrook *Wilts*	20	ST8654
Yarnfield *Staffs*	38	SJ8632
Yarnscombe *Devon*	6	SS5623
Yarnton *Oxon*	29	SP4711
Yarpole *H & W*	27	SO4764
Yarrow *Border*	75	NT3528
Yarrow Feus *Border*	75	NT3325
Yarrowford *Border*	76	NT4030
Yarwell *Nhants*	40	TL0697
Yate *Avon*	20	ST7081
Yateley *Hants*	22	SU8161
Yatesbury *Wilts*	20	SU0671
Yattendon *Berks*	21	SU5574
Yatton *Avon*	19	ST4365
Yatton *H & W*	27	SO4366
Yatton *H & W*	27	SO6330
Yatton Keynell *Wilts*	20	ST8676
Yaverland *IOW*	11	SZ6185
Yaxham *Norfk*	42	TG0010
Yaxley *Cambs*	40	TL1891
Yaxley *Suffk*	33	TM1273
Yazor *H & W*	27	SO4046
Yeading *Gt Lon*	22	TQ1182
Yeadon *W York*	55	SE2041
Yealand Conyers *Lancs*	59	SD5074
Yealand Redmayne *Lancs*	59	SD4975
Yealmpton *Devon*	5	SX5851
Yearsley *N York*	62	SE5874
Yeaton *Shrops*	36	SJ4319
Yeaveley *Derbys*	48	SK1840
Yeavering *Nthumb*	77	NT9330
Yedingham *N York*	63	SE8979
Yelford *Oxon*	29	SP3604
Yelling *Cambs*	31	TL2662
Yelvertoft *Nhants*	39	SP5975
Yelverton *Norfk*	43	TG2902
Yenston *Somset*	9	ST7121
Yeoford *Devon*	7	SX7899
Yeolmbridge *Cnwll*	4	SX3187
Yeovil *Somset*	9	ST5515
Yeovil Marsh *Somset*	8	ST5418
Yeovilton *Somset*	8	ST5423

Yesnaby *Ork*	103	HY2215
Yetminster *Dorset*	9	ST5910
Yettington *Devon*	8	SY0585
Yetts o'Muckhart *Cent*	82	NO0001
Yielden *Beds*	30	TL0167
Yieldshields *Strath*	74	NS8750
Yiewsley *Gt Lon*	22	TQ0680
Ynysboeth *M Glam*	18	ST0695
Ynysddu *Gwent*	19	ST1792
Ynyshir *M Glam*	18	ST0292
Ynysybwl *M Glam*	18	ST0594
Yockleton *Shrops*	36	SJ3910
Yokefleet *Humb*	56	SE8124
Yoker *Strath*	74	NS5069
Yonder Bognie *Gramp*	94	NJ6046
York *N York*	56	SE6051
York Town *Hants*	22	SU8660
Yorkletts *Kent*	15	TR0963
Yorkley *Gloucs*	27	SO6307
Youlgreave *Derbys*	48	SK2064
Youlthorpe *Humb*	56	SE7655
Youlton *N York*	55	SE4963
Young's End *Essex*	24	TL7319
Yoxall *Staffs*	38	SK1418
Yoxford *Suffk*	33	TM3969
Ysbyty Ifan *Gwynd*	45	SH8448
Ysbyty Ystwyth *Dyfed*	35	SN7371
Ysceifiog *Clwyd*	46	SJ1571
Ystalyfera *W Glam*	26	SN7608
Ystrad *M Glam*	18	SS9895
Ystrad Aeron *Dyfed*	34	SN5256
Ystrad Meurig *Dyfed*	35	SN7067
Ystrad Mynach *M Glam*	18	ST1494
Ystradfellte *Powys*	26	SN9313
Ystradgynlais *Powys*	26	SN7910
Ystradowen *S Glam*	18	ST0077
Ythanwells *Gramp*	94	NJ6338
Ythsie *Gramp*	95	NJ8830

Z

Zeal Monachorum *Devon*	7	SS7204
Zeals *Wilts*	9	ST7831
Zelah *Cnwll*	2	SW8151
Zennor *Cnwll*	2	SW4538
Zouch *Notts*	39	SK5023